# Means Residential Repair & Remodeling Costs

Contractor's Pricing Guide 2008

The 2008 Contractor's Pricing Guide: Residential Repair & Remodeling Costs, and all of RSMeans Annual Cost Data Books for 2008, are dedicated to the memory of our respected colleague and friend, Senior Engineering Operations Manager, John Ferguson.

*Senior Editor*
Robert W. Mewis, CCC

*Contributing Editors*
Christopher Babbit
Ted Baker
Barbara Balboni
Robert A. Bastoni
John H. Chiang, PE
Gary W. Christensen
David G. Drain, PE
Cheryl Elsmore
Robert J. Kuchta
Robert C. McNichols
Melville J. Mossman, PE
Jeannene D. Murphy
Stephen C. Plotner
Eugene R. Spencer
Marshall J. Stetson
Phillip R. Waier, PE

*Senior Engineering
Operations Manager*
John H. Ferguson, PE

*Senior Vice President
& General Manager*
John Ware

*Vice President
of Direct Response*
John M. Shea

*Director of Sales*
Brian Hare

*Director of
Product Development*
Thomas J. Dion

*Production Manager*
Michael Kokernak

*Production Coordinator*
Wayne D. Anderson

*Technical Support*
Jonathan Forgit
Mary Lou Geary
Jill Goodman
Roger Hancock
Gary L. Hoitt
Genevieve Medeiros
Paula Reale-Camelio
Kathryn S. Rodriguez
Sheryl A. Rose

*Book & Cover Design*
Norman R. Forgit

**RSMeans**

# Means Residential Repair & Remodeling Costs

## Contractor's Pricing Guide 2008

- Quick Costs to Help You Estimate
- New, Easy-to-Use Format . . . Organized the Way You Build
- Hundreds of Work Items with Material, Labor & Equipment

$39.95 per copy (in United States)
Price subject to change without prior notice.

Copyright © 2007
Reed Construction Data, Inc.
Construction Publishers & Consultants
63 Smiths Lane
Kingston, MA 02364-0800
781-422-5000
www.rsmeans.com
RSMeans is a product line of Reed Construction Data.

Printed in the United States of America


ISSN 1074-0481

ISBN 978-0-87629-057-6

# Foreword

## Our Mission

Since 1942, RSMeans has been actively engaged in construction cost publishing and consulting throughout North America.

Today, over 60 years after RSMeans began, our primary objective remains the same: to provide you, the construction and facilities professional, with the most current and comprehensive construction cost data possible.

Whether you are a contractor, an owner, an architect, an engineer, a facilities manager, or anyone else who needs a reliable construction cost estimate, you'll find this publication to be a highly useful and necessary tool.

With the constant flow of new construction methods and materials today, it's difficult to find the time to look at and evaluate all the different construction cost possibilities. In addition, because labor and material costs keep changing, last year's cost information is not a reliable basis for today's estimate or budget.

That's why so many construction professionals turn to RSMeans. We keep track of the costs for you, along with a wide range of other key information, from city cost indexes . . . to productivity rates . . . to crew composition . . . to contractor's overhead and profit rates.

RSMeans performs these functions by collecting data from all facets of the industry and organizing it in a format that is instantly accessible to you. From the preliminary budget to the detailed unit price estimate, you'll find the data in this book useful for all phases of construction cost determination.

## The Staff, the Organization, and Our Services

When you purchase one of RSMeans' publications, you are, in effect, hiring the services of a full-time staff of construction and engineering professionals.

Our thoroughly experienced and highly qualified staff works daily at collecting, analyzing, and disseminating comprehensive cost information for your needs. These staff members have years of practical construction experience and engineering training prior to joining the firm. As a result, you can count on them not only for the cost figures, but also for additional background reference information that will help you create a realistic estimate.

The RSMeans organization is always prepared to help you solve construction problems through its four major divisions: Construction and Cost Data Publishing, Electronic Products and Services, Consulting and Business Solutions, and Professional Development Services.

Besides a full array of construction cost estimating books, RSMeans also publishes a number of other reference works for the construction industry. Subjects include construction estimating and project and business management; special topics such as HVAC, roofing, plumbing, and hazardous waste remediation; and a library of facility management references.

In addition, you can access all of our construction cost data electronically using *Means CostWorks*® CD or on the Web.

What's more, you can increase your knowledge and improve your construction estimating and management performance with an RSMeans Construction Seminar or In-House Training Program. These two-day seminar programs offer unparalleled opportunities for everyone in your organization to get updated on a wide variety of construction-related issues.

RSMeans is also a worldwide provider of construction cost management and analysis services for commercial and government owners.

In short, RSMeans can provide you with the tools and expertise for constructing accurate and dependable construction estimates and budgets in a variety of ways.

## Part of a Family of Companies Dedicated to the Construction Industry

RSMeans is owned by Reed Construction Data, a leader in providing information solutions to the construction industry. Headquartered near Atlanta, Georgia, Reed Construction Data is a subsidiary of Reed Business Information, North America's largest business-to-business information provider. With more than 80 market-leading publications and 55 websites, Reed Business Information's wide range of services also includes research, business development, direct marketing lists, training and development programs, and technology solutions. Reed Business Information is a member of the Reed Elsevier PLC group (NYSE: RUK and ENL), a leading provider of global information-driven services and solutions in the science and medical, legal, education, and business-to-business industry sectors.

## Robert Snow Means Established a Tradition of Quality That Continues Today

Robert Snow Means spent years building RSMeans, making certain he always delivered a quality product.

Today, at RSMeans, we do more than talk about the quality of our data and the usefulness of our books. We stand behind all of our data, from historical cost indexes to construction materials and techniques to current costs.

If you have any questions about our products or services, please call us toll-free at 1-800-334-3509. Our customer service representatives will be happy to assist you. You can also visit our Web site at www.rsmeans.com.

# Table of Contents

# How the Book is Built: An Overview

## A Powerful Construction Tool

You have in your hands one of the most powerful construction tools available today. A successful project is built on the foundation of an accurate and dependable estimate. This book will enable you to construct just such an estimate.

For the casual user the book is designed to be:

- quickly and easily understood so you can get right to your estimate.
- filled with valuable information so you can understand the necessary factors that go into the cost estimate.

For the regular user, the book is designed to be:

- a handy desk reference that can be quickly referred to for key costs.
- a comprehensive, fully reliable source of current construction costs, so you'll be prepared to estimate any project.
- a source book for project cost, product selections, and alternate materials and methods.

To meet all of these requirements we have organized the book into the following clearly defined sections.

## Unit Price Section

The cost data has been divided into 23 sections representing the order of construction. Within each section is a listing of components and variations to those components applicable to that section. Costs are shown for the various actions that must be done to that component.

## Reference Section

This section includes information on Location Factors and a listing of Abbreviations.

**Location Factors:** You can adjust total project costs to over 900 locations throughout the U.S. and Canada by using the data in this section.

**Abbreviations:** A listing of the abbreviations used throughout this book, along with the terms they represent, is included.

## Index

A comprehensive listing of all terms and subjects in this book will help you quickly find what you need when you are not sure where it falls in the order of construction.

## The Scope of This Book

This book is designed to be as comprehensive and as easy to use as possible. To that end we have made certain assumptions and limited its scope in two key ways:

1. We have established material prices based on a national average.
2. We have computed labor costs based on a seven major-region average of open shop wage rates.

## Project Size

This book is intended for use by those involved primarily in Residential Repair and Remodeling construction costing between $10,000-$100,000.

With reasonable exercise of judgment the figures can be used for any building work. For other types of projects, such as new home construction or commercial buildings, consult the appropriate RSMeans publication for more information.

# How to Use the Book: The Details

## What's Behind the Numbers? The Development of Cost Data

The staff at RSMeans continuously monitors developments in the construction industry in order to ensure reliable, thorough, and up-to-date cost information.

While *overall* construction costs may vary relative to general economic conditions, price fluctuations within the industry are dependent upon many factors. Individual price variations may, in fact, be opposite to overall economic trends. Therefore, costs are continually monitored and complete updates are published yearly. Also, new items are frequently added in response to changes in materials and methods.

## Costs–$ (U.S.)

All costs represent U.S. national averages and are given in U.S. dollars. The RSMeans Location Factors can be used to adjust costs to a particular location. The Location Factors for Canada can be used to adjust U.S. national averages to local costs in Canadian dollars. No exchange rate conversion is necessary.

## Material Costs

The RSMeans staff contacts manufacturers, dealers, distributors, and contractors all across the U.S. and Canada to determine national average material costs. If you have access to current material costs for your specific location, you may wish to make adjustments to reflect differences from the national average.

Included within material costs are fasteners for a normal installation. RSMeans engineers use manufacturers' recommendations, written specifications, and/or standard construction practice for size and spacing of fasteners. Adjustments to material costs may be required for your specific application or location. Material costs do not include sales tax.

## Labor Costs

Labor costs are based on the average of residential wages from across the U.S. for the current year. Rates, along with overhead and profit markups, are listed on the inside back cover of this book.

- If wage rates in your area vary from those used in this book, or if rate increases are expected within a given year, labor costs should be adjusted accordingly.

Labor costs reflect productivity based on actual working conditions. These figures include time spent during a normal workday on tasks other than actual installation, such as material receiving and handling, mobilization at site, site movement, breaks, and cleanup.

Productivity data is developed over an extended period so as not to be influenced by abnormal variations and reflects a typical average.

## Equipment Costs

Equipment costs include not only rental costs, but also operating costs for equipment under normal use. Equipment and rental rates are obtained from industry sources throughout North America—contractors, suppliers, dealers, manufacturers, and distributors.

## Factors Affecting Costs

Costs can vary depending upon a number of variables. Here's how we have handled the main factors affecting costs.

**Quality**—The prices for materials and the workmanship upon which productivity is based represent sound construction work. They are also in line with U.S. government specifications.

**Overtime**—We have made no allowance for overtime. If you anticipate premium time or work beyond normal working hours, be sure to make an appropriate adjustment to your labor costs.

**Productivity**—The labor costs for each line item are based on working an eight-hour day in daylight hours in moderate temperatures. For work that extends beyond normal work hours or is performed under adverse conditions, productivity may decrease.

**Size of Project**—The size, scope of work, and type of construction project will have a significant impact on cost. Economies of scale can reduce costs for large projects. Unit costs can often run higher for small projects. Costs in this book are intended for the size and type of project as previously described in "How the Book Is Built: An Overview." Costs for projects of a significantly different size or type should be adjusted accordingly.

**Location**—Material prices in this book are for metropolitan areas. However, in dense urban areas, traffic and site storage limitations may increase costs. Beyond a 20-mile radius of large cities, extra trucking or transportation charges may also increase the material costs slightly. On the other hand, lower wage rates may be in effect. Be sure to consider both of these factors when preparing an estimate, particularly if the job site is located in a central city or remote rural location.

In addition, highly specialized subcontract items may require travel and per diem expenses for mechanics.

### Other Factors–

- season of year
- contractor management
- weather conditions
- building code requirements
- availability of:
  - adequate energy
  - skilled labor
  - building materials
- owner's special requirements/ restrictions
- safety requirements
- environmental considerations

**Overhead & Profit**—The extreme right-hand column of each chart gives the "Totals." These figures contain the installing contractor's O&P. Therefore, it is necessary for a general contractor to add a percentage of all subcontracted items. For a detailed breakdown of O&P see the inside back cover of this book.

**Unpredictable Factors**—General business conditions influence "in-place" costs of all items. Substitute materials and construction methods may have to be employed. These may affect the installed cost and/or life cycle costs. Such factors may be difficult to evaluate and cannot necessarily be predicted on the basis of the job's location in a particular section of the country. Thus, where these factors apply, you may find significant but unavoidable cost variations for which you will have to apply a measure of judgment to your estimate.

## Final Checklist

Estimating can be a straightforward process provided you remember the basics. Here's a checklist of some of the steps you should remember to complete before finalizing your estimate.

Did you remember to . . .

- factor in the Location Factor for your locale?
- take into consideration which items have been marked up and by how much?
- mark up the entire estimate sufficiently for your purposes?
- include all components of your project in the final estimate?
- double check your figures to be sure of your accuracy?
- call RSMeans if you have any questions about your estimate or the data you've found in our publications?

Remember, RSMeans stands behind its publications. If you have any questions about your estimate . . . about the costs you've used from our books . . . or even about the technical aspects of the job that may affect your estimate, feel free to call the RSMeans editors at 1-800-334-3509.

# Unit Price Section

## Table of Contents

# Unit Price Section

## Table of Contents (cont.)

# How to Use the Unit Price Pages

The prices in this publication include all overhead and profit mark-ups for the installing contractor. If a general contractor is involved, an additional 10% should be added to the cost shown in the "Total" column.

The book is arranged into 23 categories that follow the order of construction for residential projects. The category is shown as white letters on a black background at the top of each page.

Graphics representing some of the cost items are found at the beginning of each category.

The cost data is arranged in a tree structure format. Major cost sections are left justified and are shown as bold headings within a grey background. Cost items and sub-cost items are found under the bold headings. The complete description should read as "bold heading, cost item, sub-cost item."
For example, the identified item's description is "Beam/Girder, Solid Wood Beam, 2" x 8"."

Each action performed to the cost item is conveniently listed to the right of the description. See the explanation below for the scope of work included as part of the action.

The unit of measure upon which all the costs are based is shown here. An abbreviations list is included within the reference section found at the back of this book.

The costs for material, labor and any equipment are shown here. Material costs include delivery and a 10% mark-up. No sales taxes are included. Labor costs include all mark-ups as shown on the inside back cover of this book. Equipment costs also include a 10% mark-up.

The cost in the total column should be multiplied by the quantity of each item to determine the total cost for that item. The sum of all item's total costs becomes the project's total cost.

A brief specification of the cost item is shown here.

## Rough Frame / Structure

Rough Framing

| Beam / Girder | | Unit | Material | Labor | Equip. | Total | Specification |
|---|---|---|---|---|---|---|---|
| Solid Wood Beam | | | | | | | |
| 2" x 8" | | | | | | | |
| | Demolish | L.F. | | .72 | | .72 | Cost includes material and labor to install 2" x 8" beam. |
| | Install | L.F. | .84 | 1.11 | | 1.95 | |
| | Demolish and Install | L.F. | .84 | 1.83 | | 2.67 | |
| | Clean | L.F. | .12 | .24 | | .36 | |
| | Paint | L.F. | .12 | 1.70 | | 1.82 | |
| | Minimum Charge | Job | | 181 | | 181 | |
| 2" x 10" | | | | | | | |
| | Demolish | L.F. | | .89 | | .89 | Cost includes material and labor to install 2" x 10" beam. |
| | Install | L.F. | 1.13 | 1.21 | | 2.34 | |
| | Demolish and Install | L.F. | 1.13 | 2.10 | | 3.23 | |
| | Clean | L.F. | .14 | .29 | | .43 | |
| | Paint | L.F. | .18 | 1.05 | | 1.23 | |
| | Minimum Charge | Job | | 181 | | 181 | |
| 2" x 12" | | | | | | | |
| | Demolish | L.F. | | 1.08 | | 1.08 | Cost includes material and labor to install 2" x 12" beam. |
| | Install | L.F. | 1.36 | 1.31 | | 2.67 | |
| | Demolish and Install | L.F. | 1.36 | 2.39 | | 3.75 | |
| | Clean | L.F. | .17 | .33 | | .50 | |
| | Paint | L.F. | .19 | 2.52 | | 2.71 | |
| | Minimum Charge | Job | | 181 | | 181 | |
| 4" x 8" | | | | | | | |
| | Demolish | L.F. | | 2.23 | | 2.23 | Cost includes material and labor to install 4" x 8" beam. |
| | Install | L.F. | 4.71 | 1.64 | .84 | 7.19 | |
| | Demolish and Install | L.F. | 4.71 | 3.87 | .84 | 9.42 | |
| | Clean | L.F. | .14 | .29 | | .43 | |
| | Paint | L.F. | .18 | 1.05 | | 1.23 | |
| | Minimum Charge | Job | | 181 | | 181 | |
| 4" x 10" | | | | | | | |
| | Demolish | L.F. | | 2.79 | | 2.79 | Cost includes material and labor to install 4" x 10" beam. |
| | Install | L.F. | 6.10 | 1.73 | .89 | 8.72 | |
| | Demolish and Install | L.F. | 6.10 | 4.52 | .89 | 11.51 | |
| | Clean | L.F. | .17 | .33 | | .50 | |
| | Paint | L.F. | .20 | 1.23 | | 1.43 | |
| | Minimum Charge | Job | | 181 | | 181 | |
| 4" x 12" | | | | | | | |
| | Demolish | L.F. | | 3.34 | | 3.34 | Cost includes material and labor to install 4" x 12" beam. |
| | Install | L.F. | 7.25 | 1.82 | .94 | 10.01 | |
| | Demolish and Install | L.F. | 7.25 | 5.16 | .94 | 13.35 | |
| | Clean | L.F. | .19 | .38 | | .57 | |
| | Paint | L.F. | .19 | 2.52 | | 2.71 | |
| | Minimum Charge | Job | | 181 | | 181 | |

| Action | Scope |
|---|---|
| Demolish | Includes removal of the item and hauling the debris to a truck, dumpster, or storage area. |
| Install | Includes the installation of the item with normal placement and spacing of fasteners. |
| Demolish and Install | Includes the demolish action and the install action. |
| Reinstall | Includes the reinstallation of a removed item. |
| Clean | Includes cleaning of the item. |
| Paint | Includes up to two coats of finish on the item (unless otherwise indicated). |
| Minimum Charge | Includes the minimum labor or the minimum labor and equipment cost. Use this charge for small quantities of material. |

| Scaffolding | Temporary Electrical Service | Air Compressor |
|---|---|---|

| **Construction Fees** | | Unit | Material | Labor | Equip. | Total | Specification |
|---|---|---|---|---|---|---|---|
| **Asbestos Test** | Minimum Charge | Job | | 217 | | 217 | Minimum charge for testing. |
| **Architectural** | Minimum Charge | Day | 730 | | | 730 | Minimum labor charge for architect. |
| **Engineering** | Minimum Charge | Day | 266 | | | 266 | Minimum labor charge for field engineer. |

| **Construction Permits** | | Unit | Material | Labor | Equip. | Total | Specification |
|---|---|---|---|---|---|---|---|
| **Job (less than 5K)** | Minimum Charge | Job | 110 | | | 110 | Permit fees, job less than 5K. |
| **Job (5K to 10K)** | Minimum Charge | Job | 220 | | | 220 | Permit fees, job more than 5K, but less than 10K. |
| **Job (10K to 25K)** | Minimum Charge | Job | 550 | | | 550 | Permit fees, job more than 10K, but less than 25K. |
| **Job (25K to 50K)** | Minimum Charge | Job | 1100 | | | 1100 | Permit fees, job more than 25K, but less than 50K. |
| **Job (50K to 100K)** | Minimum Charge | Job | 2200 | | | 2200 | Permit fees, job more than 50K, but less than 100K. |
| **Job (100K to 250K)** | Minimum Charge | Job | 5500 | | | 5500 | Permit fees, job more than 100K, but less than 250K. |
| **Job (250K to 500K)** | Minimum Charge | Job | 11000 | | | 11000 | Permit fees, job more than 250K, but less than 500K. |
| **Job (500K to 1M)** | Minimum Charge | Job | 22000 | | | 22000 | Permit fees, job more than 500K, but less than 1 million. |

| Trade Labor | | Unit | Material | Labor | Equip. | Total | Specification |
|---|---|---|---|---|---|---|---|
| **Carpenter** | | | | | | | |
| Daily (8 hours) | | | | | | | |
| | Install | Day | | 360 | | 360 | Daily labor rate for one carpenter. |
| | Minimum Charge | Job | | 181 | | 181 | |
| Weekly (40 hours) | | | | | | | |
| | Install | Week | | 1800 | | 1800 | Weekly labor rate for one carpenter. |
| | Minimum Charge | Job | | 181 | | 181 | |
| **Drywaller** | | | | | | | |
| Daily (8 hours) | | | | | | | |
| | Install | Day | | 360 | | 360 | Daily labor rate for one carpenter. |
| | Minimum Charge | Job | | 181 | | 181 | |
| Weekly (40 hours) | | | | | | | |
| | Install | Week | | 1800 | | 1800 | Weekly labor rate for one carpenter. |
| | Minimum Charge | Job | | 181 | | 181 | |
| **Roofer** | | | | | | | |
| Daily (8 hours) | | | | | | | |
| | Install | Day | | 335 | | 335 | Daily labor rate for one skilled roofer. |
| | Minimum Charge | Job | | 168 | | 168 | |
| Weekly (40 hours) | | | | | | | |
| | Install | Week | | 1675 | | 1675 | Weekly labor rate for one skilled |
| | Minimum Charge | Job | | 168 | | 168 | roofer. |
| **Painter** | | | | | | | |
| Daily (8 hours) | | | | | | | |
| | Install | Day | | 315 | | 315 | Daily labor rate for one painter. |
| | Minimum Charge | Job | | 157 | | 157 | |
| Weekly (40 hours) | | | | | | | |
| | Install | Week | | 1575 | | 1575 | Weekly labor rate for one painter. |
| | Minimum Charge | Job | | 157 | | 157 | |
| **Mason** | | | | | | | |
| Daily (8 hours) | | | | | | | |
| | Install | Day | | 365 | | 365 | Daily labor rate for one skilled mason. |
| | Minimum Charge | Job | | 182 | | 182 | |
| Weekly (40 hours) | | | | | | | |
| | Install | Week | | 1825 | | 1825 | Weekly labor rate for one skilled |
| | Minimum Charge | Job | | 182 | | 182 | mason. |
| **Electrician** | | | | | | | |
| Daily (8 hours) | | | | | | | |
| | Install | Day | | 400 | | 400 | Daily labor rate for an electrician. |
| | Minimum Charge | Job | | 199 | | 199 | |
| Weekly (40 hours) | | | | | | | |
| | Install | Week | | 2000 | | 2000 | Weekly labor rate for an electrician. |
| | Minimum Charge | Job | | 199 | | 199 | |
| **Plumber** | | | | | | | |
| Daily (8 hours) | | | | | | | |
| | Install | Day | | 405 | | 405 | Daily labor rate for a plumber. |
| | Minimum Charge | Job | | 203 | | 203 | |
| Weekly (40 hours) | | | | | | | |
| | Install | Week | | 2025 | | 2025 | Weekly labor rate for a plumber. |
| | Minimum Charge | Job | | 203 | | 203 | |
| **Common Laborer** | | | | | | | |
| Daily (8 hours) | | | | | | | |
| | Install | Day | | 267 | | 267 | Daily labor rate for a common |
| | Minimum Charge | Job | | 133 | | 133 | laborer. |

# Job Costs

## Trade Labor

| Trade Labor | | Unit | Material | Labor | Equip. | Total | Specification |
|---|---|---|---|---|---|---|---|
| Weekly (40 hours) | | Week | | | | | |
| | Install | Week | | 1325 | | 1325 | Weekly labor rate for a common |
| | Minimum Charge | Job | | 133 | | 133 | laborer. |

## Temporary Utilities

| Temporary Utilities | | Unit | Material | Labor | Equip. | Total | Specification |
|---|---|---|---|---|---|---|---|
| **Power Pole** | | | | | | | |
| Job Site Electricity | | | | | | | |
| | Install | Month | 40.50 | | | 40.50 | Includes average cost of electricity per |
| | Minimum Charge | Job | | 199 | | 199 | month. |
| **Water Service** | | | | | | | |
| Job Site Water | | | | | | | |
| | Install | Month | 68 | | | 68 | Includes average costs for water for |
| | Minimum Charge | Month | 68 | | | 68 | one month. |
| **Telephone** | | | | | | | |
| | Install | Month | 231 | | | 231 | Includes average cost for local and |
| | Minimum Charge | Month | 231 | | | 231 | long distance telephone service for |
| | | | | | | | one month. |
| **Chemical Toilet** | | | | | | | |
| | Install | Month | | | 262 | 262 | Monthly rental of portable toilet. |
| | Minimum Charge | Day | | | 13.10 | 13.10 | |
| **Office Trailer** | | | | | | | |
| Place and Remove | | | | | | | |
| | Install | Job | 345 | | | 345 | Includes cost to a contractor to deliver, |
| | Minimum Charge | Job | | 147 | | 147 | place and level an office trailer and |
| | | | | | | | remove at end of job. |
| **Storage Container** | | | | | | | |
| | Install | Job | 193 | | | 193 | Includes cost to a contractor to deliver |
| | Minimum Charge | Job | | 147 | | 147 | and place a storage container and |
| | | | | | | | remove at end of job. |
| **Fencing** | | | | | | | |
| | Install | L.F. | 2.17 | | | 2.17 | Includes material costs for temporary |
| | Minimum Charge | L.F. | 275 | | | 275 | fencing. |
| **Railing** | | | | | | | |
| | Install | L.F. | 14.05 | 10.35 | .83 | 25.23 | Includes material and labor to install |
| | Minimum Charge | L.F. | 275 | | | 275 | primed steel pipe. |

## Equipment Rental

| Equipment Rental | | Unit | Material | Labor | Equip. | Total | Specification |
|---|---|---|---|---|---|---|---|
| **Flatbed Truck** | | | | | | | |
| Daily Rental | | | | | | | |
| | Install | Day | | | 156 | 156 | Daily rental of flatbed truck. |
| | Minimum Charge | Job | | | 156 | 156 | |
| Weekly Rental | | | | | | | |
| | Install | Week | | | 780 | 780 | Weekly rental of flatbed truck. |
| | Minimum Charge | Job | | | 156 | 156 | |
| Monthly Rental | | | | | | | |
| | Install | Month | | | 3100 | 3100 | Monthly rental of flatbed truck. |
| | Minimum Charge | Job | | | 156 | 156 | |

# Job Costs

| Equipment Rental | | Unit | Material | Labor | Equip. | Total | Specification |
|---|---|---|---|---|---|---|---|
| **Dump Truck** | | | | | | | |
| Daily Rental | | | | | | | |
| | Install | Day | | | 405 | 405 | Daily rental of dump truck. |
| | Minimum Charge | Day | | | 405 | 405 | |
| Weekly Rental | | | | | | | |
| | Install | Week | | | 2025 | 2025 | Weekly rental of dump truck. |
| | Minimum Charge | Day | | | 405 | 405 | |
| Monthly Rental | | | | | | | |
| | Install | Month | | | 8100 | 8100 | Monthly rental of dump truck. |
| | Minimum Charge | Day | | | 405 | 405 | |
| **Forklift** | | | | | | | |
| Daily Rental | | | | | | | |
| | Install | Day | | | 295 | 295 | Daily rental of forklift. |
| | Minimum Charge | Day | | | 295 | 295 | |
| Weekly Rental | | | | | | | |
| | Install | Week | | | 1475 | 1475 | Weekly rental of forklift. |
| | Minimum Charge | Day | | | 295 | 295 | |
| Monthly Rental | | | | | | | |
| | Install | Month | | | 5900 | 5900 | Monthly rental of forklift. |
| | Minimum Charge | Day | | | 295 | 295 | |
| **Bobcat** | | | | | | | |
| Daily Rental | | | | | | | |
| | Install | Day | | | 134 | 134 | Daily rental of wheeled, skid steer |
| | Minimum Charge | Day | | | 134 | 134 | loader. |
| Weekly Rental | | | | | | | |
| | Install | Week | | | 670 | 670 | Weekly rental of wheeled, skid steer |
| | Minimum Charge | Day | | | 134 | 134 | loader. |
| Monthly Rental | | | | | | | |
| | Install | Month | | | 2675 | 2675 | Monthly rental of wheeled, skid steer |
| | Minimum Charge | Day | | | 134 | 134 | loader. |
| **Air Compressor** | | | | | | | |
| Daily Rental | | | | | | | |
| | Install | Day | | | 120 | 120 | Daily rental of air compressor. |
| | Minimum Charge | Day | | | 120 | 120 | |
| Weekly Rental | | | | | | | |
| | Install | Week | | | 600 | 600 | Weekly rental of air compressor. |
| | Minimum Charge | Day | | | 120 | 120 | |
| Monthly Rental | | | | | | | |
| | Install | Month | | | 2400 | 2400 | Monthly rental of air compressor. |
| | Minimum Charge | Day | | | 120 | 120 | |
| **Jackhammer** | | | | | | | |
| Daily Rental | | | | | | | |
| | Install | Day | | | 9.30 | 9.30 | Daily rental of air tool, jackhammer. |
| | Minimum Charge | Day | | | 9.30 | 9.30 | |
| Weekly Rental | | | | | | | |
| | Install | Week | | | 46.50 | 46.50 | Weekly rental of air tool, jackhammer. |
| | Minimum Charge | Day | | | 9.30 | 9.30 | |
| Monthly Rental | | | | | | | |
| | Install | Month | | | 186 | 186 | Monthly rental of air tool, |
| | Minimum Charge | Day | | | 9.30 | 9.30 | jackhammer. |
| **Concrete Mixer** | | | | | | | |
| Daily Rental | | | | | | | |
| | Install | Day | | | 125 | 125 | Daily rental of concrete mixer. |
| | Minimum Charge | Day | | | 125 | 125 | |

# Job Costs

| Equipment Rental | | Unit | Material | Labor | Equip. | Total | Specification |
|---|---|---|---|---|---|---|---|
| **Weekly Rental** | | | | | | | |
| | Install | Week | | | 625 | 625 | Weekly rental of concrete mixer. |
| | Minimum Charge | Day | | | 125 | 125 | |
| **Monthly Rental** | | | | | | | |
| | Install | Month | | | 2500 | 2500 | Monthly rental of concrete mixer. |
| | Minimum Charge | Day | | | 125 | 125 | |
| **Concrete Bucket** | | | | | | | |
| **Daily Rental** | | | | | | | |
| | Install | Day | | | 16.70 | 16.70 | Daily rental of concrete bucket. |
| | Minimum Charge | Day | | | 16.70 | 16.70 | |
| **Weekly Rental** | | | | | | | |
| | Install | Week | | | 83.50 | 83.50 | Weekly rental of concrete bucket. |
| | Minimum Charge | Day | | | 16.70 | 16.70 | |
| **Monthly Rental** | | | | | | | |
| | Install | Month | | | 335 | 335 | Monthly rental of concrete bucket. |
| | Minimum Charge | Day | | | 16.70 | 16.70 | |
| **Concrete Pump** | | | | | | | |
| **Daily Rental** | | | | | | | |
| | Install | Day | | | 780 | 780 | Daily rental of concrete pump. |
| | Minimum Charge | Day | | | 780 | 780 | |
| **Weekly Rental** | | | | | | | |
| | Install | Week | | | 3900 | 3900 | Weekly rental of concrete pump. |
| | Minimum Charge | Day | | | 780 | 780 | |
| **Monthly Rental** | | | | | | | |
| | Install | Month | | | 15600 | 15600 | Monthly rental of concrete pump. |
| | Minimum Charge | Day | | | 780 | 780 | |
| **Generator** | | | | | | | |
| **Daily Rental** | | | | | | | |
| | Install | Day | | | 29.50 | 29.50 | Daily rental of generator. |
| | Minimum Charge | Day | | | 29.50 | 29.50 | |
| **Weekly Rental** | | | | | | | |
| | Install | Week | | | 148 | 148 | Weekly rental of generator. |
| | Minimum Charge | Day | | | 29.50 | 29.50 | |
| **Monthly Rental** | | | | | | | |
| | Install | Month | | | 590 | 590 | Monthly rental of generator. |
| | Minimum Charge | Day | | | 29.50 | 29.50 | |
| **Welder** | | | | | | | |
| **Daily Rental** | | | | | | | |
| | Install | Day | | | 50.50 | 50.50 | Daily rental of welder. |
| | Minimum Charge | Day | | | 50.50 | 50.50 | |
| **Weekly Rental** | | | | | | | |
| | Install | Week | | | 253 | 253 | Weekly rental of welder. |
| | Minimum Charge | Day | | | 50.50 | 50.50 | |
| **Monthly Rental** | | | | | | | |
| | Install | Month | | | 1000 | 1000 | Monthly rental of welder. |
| | Minimum Charge | Day | | | 50.50 | 50.50 | |
| **Sandblaster** | | | | | | | |
| **Daily Rental** | | | | | | | |
| | Install | Day | | | 17.20 | 17.20 | Daily rental of sandblaster. |
| | Minimum Charge | Day | | | 17.20 | 17.20 | |
| **Weekly Rental** | | | | | | | |
| | Install | Week | | | 86 | 86 | Weekly rental of sandblaster. |
| | Minimum Charge | Day | | | 17.20 | 17.20 | |

# Job Costs

## Equipment Rental

| Equipment Rental | | Unit | Material | Labor | Equip. | Total | Specification |
|---|---|---|---|---|---|---|---|
| **Monthly Rental** | | | | | | | |
| | Install | Month | | | 345 | 345 | Monthly rental of sandblaster. |
| | Minimum Charge | Day | | | 17.20 | 17.20 | |
| **Space Heater** | | | | | | | |
| **Daily Rental** | | | | | | | |
| | Install | Day | | | 19.45 | 19.45 | Daily rental of space heater. |
| | Minimum Charge | Day | | | 18.55 | 18.55 | |
| **Weekly Rental** | | | | | | | |
| | Install | Day | | | 97 | 97 | Weekly rental of space heater. |
| | Minimum Charge | Day | | | 18.55 | 18.55 | |
| **Monthly Rental** | | | | | | | |
| | Install | Day | | | 390 | 390 | Monthly rental of space heater. |
| | Minimum Charge | Day | | | 18.55 | 18.55 | |

## Move / Reset Contents

| Move / Reset Contents | | Unit | Material | Labor | Equip. | Total | Specification |
|---|---|---|---|---|---|---|---|
| **Small Room** | | | | | | | |
| | Install | Room | | 32.50 | | 32.50 | Includes cost to remove and reset the |
| | Minimum Charge | Job | | 133 | | 133 | contents of a small room. |
| **Average Room** | | | | | | | |
| | Install | Room | | 39 | | 39 | Includes cost to remove and reset the |
| | Minimum Charge | Job | | 133 | | 133 | contents of an average room. |
| **Large Room** | | | | | | | |
| | Install | Room | | 54 | | 54 | Includes cost to remove and reset the |
| | Minimum Charge | Job | | 133 | | 133 | contents of a large room. |
| **Extra Large Room** | | | | | | | |
| | Install | Room | | 85.50 | | 85.50 | Includes cost to remove and reset the |
| | Minimum Charge | Job | | 133 | | 133 | contents of a extra large room. |
| **Store Contents** | | | | | | | |
| **Weekly** | | | | | | | |
| | Install | Week | 171 | | | 171 | Storage fee, per week. |
| **Monthly** | | | | | | | |
| | Install | Month | 510 | | | 510 | Storage fee, per month. |

## Cover and Protect

| Cover and Protect | | Unit | Material | Labor | Equip. | Total | Specification |
|---|---|---|---|---|---|---|---|
| **Cover / Protect Walls** | | | | | | | |
| | Install | SF Wall | | .10 | | .10 | Includes labor costs to cover and |
| | Minimum Charge | Job | | 133 | | 133 | protect walls. |
| **Cover / Protect Floors** | | | | | | | |
| | Install | SF Flr. | | .10 | | .10 | Includes labor costs to cover and |
| | Minimum Charge | Job | | 133 | | 133 | protect floors. |

## Temporary Bracing

| Temporary Bracing | | Unit | Material | Labor | Equip. | Total | Specification |
|---|---|---|---|---|---|---|---|
| **Shim Support Piers** | | | | | | | |
| | Install | Ea. | 3.76 | 106 | | 109.76 | Includes labor and material to install |
| | Minimum Charge | Job | | 315 | | 315 | shims support for piers. |

# Job Costs

## Jack and Relevel

| | Unit | Material | Labor | Equip. | Total | Specification |
|---|---|---|---|---|---|---|
| **Single Story** | | | | | | |
| Install | S.F. | 1.46 | 1.27 | | 2.73 | Includes labor and equipment to jack |
| Minimum Charge | Job | | 315 | | 315 | and relevel single-story building. |
| **Two-story** | | | | | | |
| Install | S.F. | 1.46 | 2.11 | | 3.57 | Includes labor and equipment to jack |
| Minimum Charge | Job | | 315 | | 315 | and relevel two-story building. |

## Dumpster Rental

| | Unit | Material | Labor | Equip. | Total | Specification |
|---|---|---|---|---|---|---|
| **Small Load** | | | | | | |
| Install | Week | | | 475 | 475 | Dumpster, weekly rental, 2 dumps, 5 |
| Minimum Charge | Week | | | 475 | 475 | yard container. |
| **Medium Load** | | | | | | |
| Install | Week | | | 570 | 570 | Dumpster, weekly rental, 2 dumps, 10 |
| Minimum Charge | Week | | | 570 | 570 | yard container. |
| **Large Load** | | | | | | |
| Install | Week | | | 985 | 985 | Dumpster, weekly rental, 2 dumps, 30 |
| Minimum Charge | Week | | | 985 | 985 | yard container. |

## Debris Hauling

| | Unit | Material | Labor | Equip. | Total | Specification |
|---|---|---|---|---|---|---|
| **Per Ton** | | | | | | |
| Install | Ton | | 83 | 41 | 124 | Includes hauling of debris by trailer or |
| Minimum Charge | Ton | | 625 | 305 | 930 | dump truck. |
| **Per Cubic Yard** | | | | | | |
| Install | C.Y. | | 27.50 | 13.65 | 41.15 | Includes hauling of debris by trailer or |
| Minimum Charge | Job | | 625 | 305 | 930 | dump truck. |
| **Per Pick-up Truck Load** | | | | | | |
| Install | Ea. | | 148 | | 148 | Includes hauling of debris by pick-up |
| Minimum Charge | Ea. | | 148 | | 148 | truck. |

## Dump Fees

| | Unit | Material | Labor | Equip. | Total | Specification |
|---|---|---|---|---|---|---|
| **Per Cubic Yard** | | | | | | |
| Install | C.Y. | 7.45 | | | 7.45 | Dump charges, building materials. |
| Minimum Charge | C.Y. | 7.45 | | | 7.45 | |
| **Per Ton** | | | | | | |
| Install | Ton | 121 | | | 121 | Dump charges, building materials. |
| Minimum Charge | Ton | 121 | | | 121 | |

## Scaffolding

| | Unit | Material | Labor | Equip. | Total | Specification |
|---|---|---|---|---|---|---|
| **4' to 6' High** | | | | | | |
| Install | Month | 67 | | | 67 | Includes monthly rental of scaffolding, |
| Minimum Charge | Month | 67 | | | 67 | steel tubular, 30" wide, 7' long, 5' high. |
| **7' to 11' High** | | | | | | |
| Install | Month | 80.50 | | | 80.50 | Includes monthly rental of scaffolding, |
| Minimum Charge | Month | 80.50 | | | 80.50 | steel tubular, 30" wide, 7' long, 10' high. |

# Job Costs

| Scaffolding | | Unit | Material | Labor | Equip. | Total | Specification |
|---|---|---|---|---|---|---|---|
| **12' to 16' High** | | | | | | | |
| | Install | Month | 93.50 | | | 93.50 | Includes monthly rental of scaffolding, |
| | Minimum Charge | Month | 93.50 | | | 93.50 | steel tubular, 30" wide, 7' long, 15' high. |
| **17' to 21' High** | | | | | | | |
| | Install | Month | 122 | | | 122 | Includes monthly rental of scaffolding, |
| | Minimum Charge | Month | 122 | | | 122 | steel tubular, 30" wide, 7' long, 20' high. |
| **22' to 26' High** | | | | | | | |
| | Install | Month | 135 | | | 135 | Includes monthly rental of scaffolding, |
| | Minimum Charge | Month | 135 | | | 135 | steel tubular, 30" wide, 7' long, 25' high. |
| **27' to 30' High** | | | | | | | |
| | Install | Month | 149 | | | 149 | Includes monthly rental of scaffolding, |
| | Minimum Charge | Month | 149 | | | 149 | steel tubular, 30" wide, 7' long, 30' high. |

| Construction Clean-up | | Unit | Material | Labor | Equip. | Total | Specification |
|---|---|---|---|---|---|---|---|
| **Initial** | | | | | | | |
| | Clean | S.F. | | .33 | | .33 | Includes labor for general clean-up. |
| | Minimum Charge | Job | | 133 | | 133 | |
| **Progressive** | | | | | | | |
| | Clean | S.F. | | .17 | | .17 | Includes labor for progressive site/job |
| | Minimum Charge | Job | | 133 | | 133 | clean-up on a weekly basis. |

| Building Demolition | | Unit | Material | Labor | Equip. | Total | Specification |
|---|---|---|---|---|---|---|---|
| **Wood-framed Building** | | | | | | | |
| 1 Story Demolition | Demolish | S.F. | | 1.25 | 1.47 | 2.72 | Includes demolition of 1 floor only light wood-framed building, including hauling of debris. Dump fees not included. |
| | Minimum Charge | Job | | 1975 | 2325 | 4300 | |
| 2nd Story Demolition | Demolish | S.F. | | 1.27 | 1.49 | 2.76 | Includes demolition of 2nd floor only light wood-framed building, including hauling of debris. Dump fees not included. |
| | Minimum Charge | Job | | 1975 | 2325 | 4300 | |
| 3rd Story Demolition | Demolish | S.F. | | 1.65 | 1.94 | 3.59 | Includes demolition of 3rd floor only light wood-framed building, including hauling of debris. Dump fees not included. |
| | Minimum Charge | Job | | 1975 | 2325 | 4300 | |
| **Masonry Building** | Demolish | S.F. | | 1.78 | 2.09 | 3.87 | Includes demolition of one story masonry building, including hauling of debris. Dump fees not included. |
| | Minimum Charge | Job | | 1975 | 2325 | 4300 | |
| **Concrete Building** | | | | | | | |
| Unreinforced | Demolish | S.F. | | 3.64 | .99 | 4.63 | Includes demolition of a one story non-reinforced concrete building, including hauling of debris. Dump fees not included. |
| | Minimum Charge | Job | | 1975 | 2325 | 4300 | |
| Reinforced | Demolish | S.F. | | 4.18 | 1.14 | 5.32 | Includes demolition of a one story reinforced concrete building, including hauling of debris. Dump fees not included. |
| | Minimum Charge | Job | | 1975 | 2325 | 4300 | |
| **Steel Building** | Demolish | S.F. | | 2.37 | 2.79 | 5.16 | Includes demolition of a metal building, including hauling of debris. Dump fees not included. No salvage value assumed for scrap metal. |
| | Minimum Charge | Job | | 1975 | 2325 | 4300 | |

# Job Preparation

## General Clean-up

| General Clean-up | | Unit | Material | Labor | Equip. | Total | Specification |
|---|---|---|---|---|---|---|---|
| **Remove Debris** | | | | | | | Includes removal of debris caused by the loss including contents items and loose debris. |
| | Clean | S.F. | | .82 | .20 | 1.02 | |
| | Minimum Charge | Job | | 410 | 98.50 | 508.50 | |
| **Muck-out** | | | | | | | Includes labor to remove 2" of muck and mud after a flood loss. |
| | Clean | S.F. | | .52 | | .52 | |
| | Minimum Charge | Job | | 133 | | 133 | |
| **Deodorize / Disinfect** | | | | | | | Includes deodorizing building with application of mildicide and disinfectant to floors and walls - will vary depending on the extent of deodorization required. |
| | Clean | SF Flr. | | .18 | | .18 | |
| | Minimum Charge | Job | | 133 | | 133 | |
| **Clean Walls** | | | | | | | |
| Heavy | | | | | | | Includes labor and material for heavy cleaning (multiple applications) with detergent and solvent. |
| | Clean | S.F. | | .13 | | .13 | |
| | Minimum Charge | Job | | 133 | | 133 | |
| **Clean Ceiling** | | | | | | | |
| Light | | | | | | | Includes labor and material to clean light to moderate smoke and soot. |
| | Clean | S.F. | | .21 | | .21 | |
| | Minimum Charge | Job | | 133 | | 133 | |
| Heavy | | | | | | | Includes labor and material to clean heavy smoke and soot. |
| | Clean | S.F. | | .31 | | .31 | |
| | Minimum Charge | Job | | 133 | | 133 | |

## Flood Clean-up

| Flood Clean-up | | Unit | Material | Labor | Equip. | Total | Specification |
|---|---|---|---|---|---|---|---|
| **Emergency Service Call** | | | | | | | |
| After Hours / Weekend | | | | | | | Includes minimum charges for deflooding clean-up after hours or on weekends. |
| | Minimum Charge | Job | | 178 | | 178 | |
| Grey Water / Sewage | | | | | | | Includes minimum charges for deflooding clean-up. |
| | Minimum Charge | Job | | 133 | | 133 | |
| **Water Extraction** | | | | | | | |
| Clean (non-grey) | | | | | | | Includes labor to remove clean uncontaminated water from the loss. |
| | Clean | SF Flr. | .03 | .53 | | .56 | |
| | Minimum Charge | Job | | 133 | | 133 | |
| Grey (non-solids) | | | | | | | Includes labor to remove non-solid grey water from the loss. |
| | Clean | SF Flr. | .03 | 1.07 | | 1.10 | |
| | Minimum Charge | Job | | 133 | | 133 | |
| Sewage / Solids | | | | | | | Includes labor to remove water from the loss that may contain sewage or solids. |
| | Clean | SF Flr. | .04 | 1.33 | | 1.37 | |
| | Minimum Charge | Job | | 133 | | 133 | |

| Flood Clean-up | | Unit | Material | Labor | Equip. | Total | Specification |
|---|---|---|---|---|---|---|---|
| **Mildicide Walls** | | | | | | | |
| Topographical | | | | | | | |
| | Clean | SF Wall | | .24 | | .24 | Clean-up of deflooding including |
| | Minimum Charge | Job | | 133 | | 133 | topographical mildicide application. |
| Injection Treatments | | | | | | | |
| | Clean | SF Flr. | 22.50 | 4.10 | | 26.60 | Clean-up of deflooding including |
| | Minimum Charge | Job | | 133 | | 133 | mildicide injection. |
| **Carpet Cleaning** | | | | | | | |
| Uncontaminated | | | | | | | |
| | Clean | SF Flr. | | .17 | | .17 | Includes labor to clean carpet. |
| | Minimum Charge | Job | | 133 | | 133 | |
| Contaminated | | | | | | | |
| | Clean | SF Flr. | | .27 | | .27 | Includes labor to clean contaminated |
| | Minimum Charge | Job | | 133 | | 133 | carpet. |
| Stairway | | | | | | | |
| | Clean | Ea. | .10 | 3.14 | | 3.24 | Includes labor to clean contaminated |
| | Minimum Charge | Job | | 133 | | 133 | carpet on a stairway. |
| **Carpet Treatment** | | | | | | | |
| Disinfect / Deodorize | | | | | | | |
| | Clean | SF Flr. | | .17 | | .17 | Includes disinfecting and deodorizing |
| | Minimum Charge | Job | | 133 | | 133 | of carpet. |
| Disinfect For Sewage | | | | | | | |
| | Clean | SF Flr. | | .43 | | .43 | Includes labor to disinfect and |
| | Minimum Charge | Job | | 133 | | 133 | deodorize carpet exposed to sewage. |
| Mildicide | | | | | | | |
| | Clean | SF Flr. | .01 | .17 | | .18 | Includes labor and materials to apply |
| | Minimum Charge | Job | | 133 | | 133 | mildicide to carpet. |
| **Thermal Fog Area** | | | | | | | |
| | Clean | SF Flr. | .03 | .41 | | .44 | Includes labor and materials to |
| | Minimum Charge | Job | | 133 | | 133 | perform thermal fogging during |
| | | | | | | | deflooding clean-up. |
| **Wet Fog / ULV Area** | | | | | | | |
| | Clean | SF Flr. | .02 | .23 | | .25 | Includes labor and materials to |
| | Minimum Charge | Job | | 133 | | 133 | perform wet fogging / ULV during |
| | | | | | | | deflooding clean-up. |
| **Steam Clean Fixtures** | | | | | | | |
| | Clean | Ea. | .01 | 26.50 | | 26.51 | Includes labor and materials to steam |
| | Minimum Charge | Job | | 133 | | 133 | clean fixtures during deflooding |
| | | | | | | | clean-up. |
| **Pressure Wash Sewage** | | | | | | | |
| | Clean | SF Flr. | | 2.43 | | 2.43 | Includes labor to pressure wash |
| | Minimum Charge | Job | | 133 | | 133 | sewage contamination. |
| **Air Mover** | | | | | | | |
| | Minimum Charge | Day | | | 18.55 | 18.55 | Daily rental of air mover. |

# Job Preparation

## Flood Clean-up

| Flood Clean-up | Unit | Material | Labor | Equip. | Total | Specification |
|---|---|---|---|---|---|---|
| **Dehumidifier** | | | | | | |
|   **Medium Size** | | | | | | |
|     Minimum Charge | Day | | | 38.50 | 38.50 | Daily rental of dehumidifier, medium. |
|   **Large Size** | | | | | | |
|     Minimum Charge | Day | | | 76.50 | 76.50 | Daily rental of dehumidifier, large. |
| **Air Purifier** | | | | | | |
|   **HEPA Filter-Bacteria** | | | | | | |
|     Minimum Charge | Ea. | 238 | | | 238 | HEPA filter for air purifier. |

## Asbestos Removal

| Asbestos Removal | Unit | Material | Labor | Equip. | Total | Specification |
|---|---|---|---|---|---|---|
| **Asbestos Analysis** | | | | | | |
|   Minimum Charge | Job | | 217 | | 217 | Minimum charge for testing. |
| **Asbestos Pipe Insulation** | | | | | | |
|   **1/2″ to 3/4″ Diameter** | | | | | | |
|     Demolish | L.F. | .36 | 5.60 | | 5.96 | Minimum charge to remove asbestos. Includes full Tyvek suits for workers changed four times per eight-hour shift with respirators, air monitoring and supervision by qualified professionals. |
|     Minimum Charge | Job | | 3475 | | 3475 | |
|   **1″ to 3″ Diameter** | | | | | | |
|     Demolish | L.F. | 1.13 | 17.35 | | 18.48 | Minimum charge to remove asbestos. Includes full Tyvek suits for workers changed four times per eight-hour shift with respirators, air monitoring and supervision by qualified professionals. |
|     Minimum Charge | Job | | 3475 | | 3475 | |
| **Asbestos-based Siding** | | | | | | |
|     Demolish | S.F. | 2.53 | 38.50 | | 41.03 | Minimum charge to remove asbestos. Includes full Tyvek suits for workers changed four times per eight-hour shift with respirators, air monitoring and supervision by qualified professionals. |
|     Minimum Charge | Job | | 3475 | | 3475 | |
| **Asbestos-based Plaster** | | | | | | |
|     Demolish | S.F. | 1.95 | 29.50 | | 31.45 | Minimum charge to remove asbestos. Includes full Tyvek suits for workers changed four times per eight-hour shift with respirators, air monitoring and supervision by qualified professionals. |
|     Minimum Charge | Job | | 3475 | | 3475 | |
| **Encapsulate Asbestos Ceiling** | | | | | | |
|     Install | S.F. | .30 | .17 | | .47 | Includes encapsulation with penetrating sealant sprayed onto ceiling and walls with airless sprayer. |
|     Minimum Charge | Job | | 3475 | | 3475 | |
| **Scrape Acoustical Ceiling** | | | | | | |
|     Demolish | S.F. | .07 | .98 | | 1.05 | Minimum charge to remove asbestos. Includes full Tyvek suits for workers changed four times per eight-hour shift with respirators, air monitoring and supervision by qualified professionals. |
|     Minimum Charge | Job | | 3475 | | 3475 | |

| Asbestos Removal | | Unit | Material | Labor | Equip. | Total | Specification |
|---|---|---|---|---|---|---|---|
| **Seal Ceiling Asbestos** | | | | | | | Includes attaching plastic cover to ceiling area and sealing where asbestos exists, taping all seams, caulk or foam insulation in cracks and negative air system. |
| | Install | S.F. | 1.28 | 3.27 | | 4.55 | |
| | Minimum Charge | Job | | 3475 | | 3475 | |
| **Seal Wall Asbestos** | | | | | | | Includes attaching plastic cover to wall area and sealing where asbestos exists, taping all seams, caulk or foam insulation in cracks and negative air system. |
| | Install | S.F. | 1.28 | 2.91 | | 4.19 | |
| | Minimum Charge | Job | | 3475 | | 3475 | |
| **Seal Floor Asbestos** | | | | | | | Includes attaching plastic cover to floor area and sealing where asbestos exists, taping all seams, caulk or foam insulation in cracks and negative air system. |
| | Install | S.F. | 2.05 | 5.80 | | 7.85 | |
| | Minimum Charge | Job | | 3475 | | 3475 | |
| **Negative Air Vent System** | | | | | | | Daily rental of negative air vent system. |
| | Install | Day | | | 44 | 44 | |
| | Minimum Charge | Week | | | 219 | 219 | |
| **HEPA Vacuum Cleaner** | | | | | | | Daily rental of HEPA vacuum, 16 gallon. |
| | Install | Day | | | 22.50 | 22.50 | |
| | Minimum Charge | Week | | | 113 | 113 | |
| **Airless Sprayer** | | | | | | | Daily rental of airless sprayer. |
| | Install | Day | | | 49.50 | 49.50 | |
| | Minimum Charge | Week | | | 248 | 248 | |
| **Decontamination Unit** | | | | | | | Daily rental of decontamination unit. |
| | Install | Day | | | 133 | 133 | |
| | Minimum Charge | Week | | | 665 | 665 | |
| **Light Stand** | | | | | | | Daily rental of floodlight w/tripod. |
| | Install | Day | | | 10.65 | 10.65 | |
| | Minimum Charge | Week | | | 53 | 53 | |

| Room Demolition | | Unit | Material | Labor | Equip. | Total | Specification |
|---|---|---|---|---|---|---|---|
| **Strip Typical Room** | | | | | | | Includes 4 labor hours for general demolition. |
| | Demolish | S.F. | | 2.67 | | 2.67 | |
| | Minimum Charge | Job | | 148 | | 148 | |
| **Strip Typical Bathroom** | | | | | | | Includes 4 labor hours for general demolition. |
| | Demolish | S.F. | | 3.56 | | 3.56 | |
| | Minimum Charge | Job | | 148 | | 148 | |
| **Strip Typical Kitchen** | | | | | | | Includes 4 labor hours for general demolition. |
| | Demolish | S.F. | | 3.42 | | 3.42 | |
| | Minimum Charge | Job | | 148 | | 148 | |
| **Strip Typical Laundry** | | | | | | | Includes 4 labor hours for general demolition. |
| | Demolish | S.F. | | 3.05 | | 3.05 | |
| | Minimum Charge | Job | | 148 | | 148 | |

| Selective Demolition | | Unit | Material | Labor | Equip. | Total | Specification |
|---|---|---|---|---|---|---|---|
| **Concrete Slab** | | | | | | | |
| 4" Unreinforced | | | | | | | |
| | Demolish | S.F. | | 1.78 | .28 | 2.06 | Includes labor and equipment to |
| | Minimum Charge | Job | | 755 | 117 | 872 | remove unreinforced concrete slab and haul debris to truck or dumpster. |
| 6" Unreinforced | | | | | | | |
| | Demolish | S.F. | | 2.52 | .39 | 2.91 | Includes labor and equipment to |
| | Minimum Charge | Job | | 755 | 117 | 872 | remove unreinforced concrete slab and haul debris to truck or dumpster. |
| 8" Unreinforced | | | | | | | |
| | Demolish | S.F. | | 4.14 | .64 | 4.78 | Includes labor and equipment to |
| | Minimum Charge | Job | | 755 | 117 | 872 | remove unreinforced concrete slab and haul debris to truck or dumpster. |
| 4" Reinforced | | | | | | | |
| | Demolish | S.F. | | 2.24 | .35 | 2.59 | Includes labor and equipment to |
| | Minimum Charge | Job | | 755 | 117 | 872 | remove reinforced concrete slab and haul debris to truck or dumpster. |
| 6" Reinforced | | | | | | | |
| | Demolish | S.F. | | 3.36 | .52 | 3.88 | Includes labor and equipment to |
| | Minimum Charge | Job | | 755 | 117 | 872 | remove reinforced concrete slab and haul debris to truck or dumpster. |
| 8" Reinforced | | | | | | | |
| | Demolish | S.F. | | 5.50 | .85 | 6.35 | Includes labor and equipment to |
| | Minimum Charge | Job | | 755 | 117 | 872 | remove reinforced concrete slab and haul debris to truck or dumpster. |
| **Brick Wall** | | | | | | | |
| 4" Thick | | | | | | | |
| | Demolish | S.F. | | 2.47 | .38 | 2.85 | Includes labor and equipment to |
| | Minimum Charge | Job | | 755 | 117 | 872 | remove brick wall and haul debris to a central location for disposal. |
| 8" Thick | | | | | | | |
| | Demolish | S.F. | | 3.40 | .53 | 3.93 | Includes labor and equipment to |
| | Minimum Charge | Job | | 755 | 117 | 872 | remove brick wall and haul debris to a central location for disposal. |
| 12" Thick | | | | | | | |
| | Demolish | S.F. | | 4.54 | .70 | 5.24 | Includes labor and equipment to |
| | Minimum Charge | Job | | 755 | 117 | 872 | remove brick wall and haul debris to a central location for disposal. |
| **Concrete Masonry Wall** | | | | | | | |
| 4" Thick | | | | | | | |
| | Demolish | S.F. | | 2.75 | .43 | 3.18 | Includes minimum labor and |
| | Minimum Charge | Job | | 755 | 117 | 872 | equipment to remove 4" block wall and haul debris to a central location for disposal. |
| 6" Thick | | | | | | | |
| | Demolish | S.F. | | 3.40 | .53 | 3.93 | Includes minimum labor and |
| | Minimum Charge | Job | | 755 | 117 | 872 | equipment to remove 6" block wall and haul debris to a central location for disposal. |

# Job Preparation

| Selective Demolition | | Unit | Material | Labor | Equip. | Total | Specification |
|---|---|---|---|---|---|---|---|
| **8" Thick** | | | | | | | |
| | Demolish | S.F. | | 4.19 | .65 | 4.84 | Includes minimum labor and |
| | Minimum Charge | Job | | 755 | 117 | 872 | equipment to remove 8" block wall and haul debris to a central location for disposal. |
| **12" Thick** | | | | | | | |
| | Demolish | S.F. | | 6.05 | .94 | 6.99 | Includes minimum labor and |
| | Minimum Charge | Job | | 755 | 117 | 872 | equipment to remove 12" block wall and haul debris to a central location for disposal. |
| **Tree Removal** | | | | | | | |
| **Small, 4" - 8"** | | | | | | | |
| | Demolish | Ea. | | 95.50 | 72.50 | 168 | Minimum charge, tree removal. |
| | Minimum Charge | Job | | 133 | | 133 | |
| **Medium, 9" - 12"** | | | | | | | |
| | Demolish | Ea. | | 144 | 108 | 252 | Minimum charge, tree removal. |
| | Minimum Charge | Job | | 133 | | 133 | |
| **Large, 13" - 18"** | | | | | | | |
| | Demolish | Ea. | | 172 | 130 | 302 | Minimum charge, tree removal. |
| | Minimum Charge | Job | | 440 | 149 | 589 | |
| **Very Large, 19" - 24"** | | | | | | | |
| | Demolish | Ea. | | 215 | 163 | 378 | Minimum charge, tree removal. |
| | Minimum Charge | Job | | 440 | 149 | 589 | |
| **Stump Removal** | | | | | | | |
| | Demolish | Ea. | | 59.50 | 126 | 185.50 | Includes minimum charges for a site |
| | Minimum Charge | Job | | 244 | 87 | 331 | demolition crew and backhoe / loader. |

# Excavation

| Backhoe/Loader - Wheel Type | Tractor Loader - Wheel Type | Backhoe - Crawler Type |
|---|---|---|

| Excavation | | Unit | Material | Labor | Equip. | Total | Specification |
|---|---|---|---|---|---|---|---|
| **Footings** | | | | | | | |
| Hand Trenching | | | | | | | |
| | Install | L.F. | | 1.67 | | 1.67 | Includes hand excavation for footing or trench up to 10" deep and 12" wide. |
| | Minimum Charge | Job | | 66.50 | | 66.50 | |
| Machine Trenching | | | | | | | |
| | Install | L.F. | | .63 | .31 | .94 | Includes machine excavation for footing or trench up to 10" deep and 12" wide. |
| | Minimum Charge | Job | | 315 | 157 | 472 | |
| **Trenching w / Backfill** | | | | | | | |
| Hand | | | | | | | |
| | Install | L.F. | | 2.67 | | 2.67 | Includes hand excavation, backfill and compaction. |
| | Minimum Charge | Job | | 66.50 | | 66.50 | |
| Machine | | | | | | | |
| | Install | L.F. | | 3.15 | 9.55 | 12.70 | Includes machine excavation, backfill and compaction. |
| | Minimum Charge | Job | | 133 | 31 | 164 | |

| Backfill | | Unit | Material | Labor | Equip. | Total | Specification |
|---|---|---|---|---|---|---|---|
| **Hand (no compaction)** | | | | | | | |
| | Install | L.C.Y. | | 22 | | 22 | Includes backfill by hand in average soil without compaction. |
| | Minimum Charge | Job | | 133 | | 133 | |
| **Hand (w / compaction)** | | | | | | | |
| | Install | E.C.Y. | | 31.50 | | 31.50 | Includes backfill by hand in average soil with compaction. |
| | Minimum Charge | Job | | 133 | | 133 | |
| **Machine (no compaction)** | | | | | | | |
| | Install | L.C.Y. | | 3.15 | 1.57 | 4.72 | Includes backfill, by 55 HP wheel loader, of trenches from loose material piled adjacent without compaction. |
| | Minimum Charge | Job | | 315 | 157 | 472 | |
| **Machine (w / compaction)** | | | | | | | |
| | Install | L.C.Y. | | 8.40 | 4.19 | 12.59 | Includes backfill, by 55 HP wheel loader, of trenches from loose material piled adjacent with compaction by vibrating tampers. |
| | Minimum Charge | Job | | 315 | 157 | 472 | |

**Concrete Footing and Formwork**

**Wood Pile**

| Piles | Unit | Material | Labor | Equip. | Total | Specification |
|---|---|---|---|---|---|---|
| **Treated Wood, 12" Butt** | | | | | | |
| **To 30'** | | | | | | |
| Demolish | L.F. | | 4.24 | 1.52 | 5.76 | Includes material, labor and |
| Install | V.L.F. | 11.15 | 4.03 | 3.07 | 18.25 | equipment to install up to 30' long |
| Demolish and Install | V.L.F. | 11.15 | 8.27 | 4.59 | 24.01 | treated wood piling. |
| Paint | L.F. | .41 | 1.80 | | 2.21 | |
| Minimum Charge | Job | | 2525 | 1925 | 4450 | |
| **30' to 40'** | | | | | | |
| Demolish | L.F. | | 4.24 | 1.52 | 5.76 | Includes material, labor and |
| Install | V.L.F. | 10.95 | 3.60 | 2.74 | 17.29 | equipment to install 30' to 40' long |
| Demolish and Install | V.L.F. | 10.95 | 7.84 | 4.26 | 23.05 | treated wood piling. |
| Paint | L.F. | .41 | 1.80 | | 2.21 | |
| Minimum Charge | Job | | 2525 | 1925 | 4450 | |
| **40' to 50'** | | | | | | |
| Demolish | L.F. | | 4.24 | 1.52 | 5.76 | Includes material, labor and |
| Install | V.L.F. | 11.70 | 3.50 | 2.66 | 17.86 | equipment to install 40' to 50' long |
| Demolish and Install | V.L.F. | 11.70 | 7.74 | 4.18 | 23.62 | treated wood piling. |
| Paint | L.F. | .41 | 1.80 | | 2.21 | |
| Minimum Charge | Job | | 2525 | 1925 | 4450 | |
| **50' to 60'** | | | | | | |
| Demolish | L.F. | | 4.24 | 1.52 | 5.76 | Includes material, labor and |
| Install | V.L.F. | 12.95 | 3.15 | 2.40 | 18.50 | equipment to install 50' to 60' long |
| Demolish and Install | V.L.F. | 12.95 | 7.39 | 3.92 | 24.26 | treated wood piling. |
| Paint | L.F. | .41 | 1.80 | | 2.21 | |
| Minimum Charge | Job | | 2525 | 1925 | 4450 | |
| **60' to 80'** | | | | | | |
| Demolish | L.F. | | 4.24 | 1.52 | 5.76 | Includes material, labor and |
| Install | V.L.F. | 22 | 3.50 | 2.95 | 28.45 | equipment to install 60' to 80' long |
| Demolish and Install | V.L.F. | 22 | 7.74 | 4.47 | 34.21 | treated wood piling. |
| Paint | L.F. | .41 | 1.80 | | 2.21 | |
| Minimum Charge | Job | | 2525 | 1925 | 4450 | |
| **Untreated Wood, 12" Butt** | | | | | | |
| **To 30'** | | | | | | |
| Demolish | L.F. | | 4.24 | 1.52 | 5.76 | Includes material, labor and |
| Install | V.L.F. | 7.60 | 4.03 | 3.07 | 14.70 | equipment to install up to 30' long |
| Demolish and Install | V.L.F. | 7.60 | 8.27 | 4.59 | 20.46 | untreated wood piling. |
| Paint | L.F. | .41 | 1.80 | | 2.21 | |
| Minimum Charge | Job | | 2525 | 1925 | 4450 | |

| Piles | | Unit | Material | Labor | Equip. | Total | Specification |
|---|---|---|---|---|---|---|---|
| **30' to 40'** | | | | | | | |
| | Demolish | L.F. | | 4.24 | 1.52 | 5.76 | Includes material, labor and |
| | Install | V.L.F. | 7.60 | 3.60 | 2.74 | 13.94 | equipment to install 30' to 40' long |
| | Demolish and Install | V.L.F. | 7.60 | 7.84 | 4.26 | 19.70 | untreated wood piling. |
| | Paint | L.F. | .41 | 1.80 | | 2.21 | |
| | Minimum Charge | Job | | 2525 | 1925 | 4450 | |
| **40' to 50'** | | | | | | | |
| | Demolish | L.F. | | 4.24 | 1.52 | 5.76 | Includes material, labor and |
| | Install | V.L.F. | 7.60 | 3.50 | 2.66 | 13.76 | equipment to install 40' to 50' long |
| | Demolish and Install | V.L.F. | 7.60 | 7.74 | 4.18 | 19.52 | untreated wood piling. |
| | Paint | L.F. | .41 | 1.80 | | 2.21 | |
| | Minimum Charge | Job | | 2525 | 1925 | 4450 | |
| **50' to 60'** | | | | | | | |
| | Demolish | L.F. | | 4.24 | 1.52 | 5.76 | Includes material, labor and |
| | Install | V.L.F. | 7.65 | 3.15 | 2.40 | 13.20 | equipment to install 50' to 60' long |
| | Demolish and Install | V.L.F. | 7.65 | 7.39 | 3.92 | 18.96 | untreated wood piling. |
| | Paint | L.F. | .41 | 1.80 | | 2.21 | |
| | Minimum Charge | Job | | 2525 | 1925 | 4450 | |
| **60' to 80'** | | | | | | | |
| | Demolish | L.F. | | 4.24 | 1.52 | 5.76 | Includes material, labor and |
| | Install | V.L.F. | 9.55 | 3 | 2.28 | 14.83 | equipment to install 60' to 80' long |
| | Demolish and Install | V.L.F. | 9.55 | 7.24 | 3.80 | 20.59 | untreated wood piling. |
| | Paint | L.F. | .41 | 1.80 | | 2.21 | |
| | Minimum Charge | Job | | 2525 | 1925 | 4450 | |
| **Precast Concrete** | | | | | | | |
| **10" Square** | | | | | | | |
| | Demolish | L.F. | | 4.33 | 1.55 | 5.88 | Includes material, labor and |
| | Install | V.L.F. | 12.20 | 3.60 | 2.74 | 18.54 | equipment to install a precast, |
| | Demolish and Install | V.L.F. | 12.20 | 7.93 | 4.29 | 24.42 | prestressed, 40' long, 10" square |
| | Paint | L.F. | .41 | 1.80 | | 2.21 | concrete pile. |
| | Minimum Charge | Job | | 2525 | 1925 | 4450 | |
| **12" Square** | | | | | | | |
| | Demolish | L.F. | | 4.64 | 1.66 | 6.30 | Includes material, labor and |
| | Install | V.L.F. | 15.35 | 3.70 | 2.82 | 21.87 | equipment to install a precast, |
| | Demolish and Install | V.L.F. | 15.35 | 8.34 | 4.48 | 28.17 | prestressed, 40' long, 12" square |
| | Paint | L.F. | .41 | 1.80 | | 2.21 | concrete pile. |
| | Minimum Charge | Job | | 2525 | 1925 | 4450 | |
| **14" Square** | | | | | | | |
| | Demolish | L.F. | | 4.75 | 1.70 | 6.45 | Includes material, labor and |
| | Install | V.L.F. | 18.10 | 4.20 | 3.19 | 25.49 | equipment to install a precast, |
| | Demolish and Install | V.L.F. | 18.10 | 8.95 | 4.89 | 31.94 | prestressed, 40' long, 14" square |
| | Paint | L.F. | .41 | 1.80 | | 2.21 | concrete pile. |
| | Minimum Charge | Job | | 2525 | 1925 | 4450 | |
| **16" Square** | | | | | | | |
| | Demolish | L.F. | | 5 | 1.79 | 6.79 | Includes material, labor and |
| | Install | V.L.F. | 28.50 | 4.50 | 3.42 | 36.42 | equipment to install a precast, |
| | Demolish and Install | V.L.F. | 28.50 | 9.50 | 5.21 | 43.21 | prestressed, 40' long, 16" square |
| | Paint | L.F. | .41 | 1.80 | | 2.21 | concrete pile. |
| | Minimum Charge | Job | | 2525 | 1925 | 4450 | |
| **18" Square** | | | | | | | |
| | Demolish | L.F. | | 5.40 | 1.94 | 7.34 | Includes material, labor and |
| | Install | V.L.F. | 34.50 | 5.65 | 4.77 | 44.92 | equipment to install a precast, |
| | Demolish and Install | V.L.F. | 34.50 | 11.05 | 6.71 | 52.26 | prestressed, 40' long, 18" square |
| | Paint | L.F. | .41 | 1.80 | | 2.21 | concrete pile. |
| | Minimum Charge | Job | | 2525 | 1925 | 4450 | |

| Piles | | Unit | Material | Labor | Equip. | Total | Specification |
|---|---|---|---|---|---|---|---|
| **Cross Bracing** | | | | | | | |
| **Treated 2″ x 6″** | | | | | | | |
| | Demolish | L.F. | | .87 | | .87 | Cost includes material and labor to |
| | Install | L.F. | .88 | 5.10 | | 5.98 | install 2″ x 6″ lumber for cross-bracing |
| | Demolish and Install | L.F. | .88 | 5.97 | | 6.85 | of foundation piling or posts. |
| | Reinstall | L.F. | | 4.09 | | 4.09 | |
| | Clean | S.F. | | .33 | | .33 | |
| | Paint | L.F. | .17 | 1.21 | | 1.38 | |
| | Minimum Charge | Job | | 635 | | 635 | |
| **Treated 2″ x 8″** | | | | | | | |
| | Demolish | L.F. | | .87 | | .87 | Cost includes material and labor to |
| | Install | L.F. | 1.16 | 5.30 | | 6.46 | install 2″ x 8″ lumber for cross-bracing |
| | Demolish and Install | L.F. | 1.16 | 6.17 | | 7.33 | of foundation piling or posts. |
| | Reinstall | L.F. | | 4.22 | | 4.22 | |
| | Clean | S.F. | | .33 | | .33 | |
| | Paint | L.F. | .22 | 1.26 | | 1.48 | |
| | Minimum Charge | Job | | 635 | | 635 | |
| **Treated 2″ x 10″** | | | | | | | |
| | Demolish | L.F. | | .90 | | .90 | Cost includes material and labor to |
| | Install | L.F. | 1.43 | 5.45 | | 6.88 | install 2″ x 10″ lumber for |
| | Demolish and Install | L.F. | 1.43 | 6.35 | | 7.78 | cross-bracing of foundation piling or |
| | Reinstall | L.F. | | 4.37 | | 4.37 | posts. |
| | Clean | S.F. | | .33 | | .33 | |
| | Paint | L.F. | .28 | 1.28 | | 1.56 | |
| | Minimum Charge | Job | | 635 | | 635 | |
| **Treated 2″ x 12″** | | | | | | | |
| | Demolish | L.F. | | 1.08 | | 1.08 | Cost includes material and labor to |
| | Install | L.F. | 2.29 | 5.65 | | 7.94 | install 2″ x 12″ lumber for |
| | Demolish and Install | L.F. | 2.29 | 6.73 | | 9.02 | cross-bracing of foundation piling or |
| | Reinstall | L.F. | | 4.52 | | 4.52 | posts. |
| | Clean | S.F. | | .33 | | .33 | |
| | Paint | L.F. | .32 | 1.31 | | 1.63 | |
| | Minimum Charge | Job | | 635 | | 635 | |
| **Metal Pipe** | | | | | | | |
| **6″ Concrete Filled** | | | | | | | |
| | Demolish | L.F. | | 6 | 2.15 | 8.15 | Includes material, labor and |
| | Install | V.L.F. | 20 | 5.25 | 3.99 | 29.24 | equipment to install concrete filled |
| | Demolish and Install | V.L.F. | 20 | 11.25 | 6.14 | 37.39 | steel pipe pile. |
| | Paint | L.F. | .31 | 1.80 | | 2.11 | |
| | Minimum Charge | Job | | 2525 | 1925 | 4450 | |
| **6″ Unfilled** | | | | | | | |
| | Demolish | L.F. | | 6 | 2.15 | 8.15 | Includes material, labor and |
| | Install | V.L.F. | 17.10 | 4.80 | 3.65 | 25.55 | equipment to install unfilled steel pipe |
| | Demolish and Install | V.L.F. | 17.10 | 10.80 | 5.80 | 33.70 | pile. |
| | Paint | L.F. | .31 | 1.80 | | 2.11 | |
| | Minimum Charge | Job | | 2525 | 1925 | 4450 | |
| **8″ Concrete Filled** | | | | | | | |
| | Demolish | L.F. | | 6 | 2.15 | 8.15 | Includes material, labor and |
| | Install | V.L.F. | 18.35 | 5.45 | 4.17 | 27.97 | equipment to install concrete filled |
| | Demolish and Install | V.L.F. | 18.35 | 11.45 | 6.32 | 36.12 | steel pipe pile. |
| | Paint | L.F. | .31 | 1.80 | | 2.11 | |
| | Minimum Charge | Job | | 2525 | 1925 | 4450 | |
| **8″ Unfilled** | | | | | | | |
| | Demolish | L.F. | | 6 | 2.15 | 8.15 | Includes material, labor and |
| | Install | V.L.F. | 17.25 | 5.05 | 3.83 | 26.13 | equipment to install unfilled steel pipe |
| | Demolish and Install | V.L.F. | 17.25 | 11.05 | 5.98 | 34.28 | pile. |
| | Paint | L.F. | .31 | 1.80 | | 2.11 | |
| | Minimum Charge | Job | | 2525 | 1925 | 4450 | |

# Foundation

| Piles | Unit | Material | Labor | Equip. | Total | Specification |
|---|---|---|---|---|---|---|
| **10" Concrete Filled** | | | | | | |
| Demolish | L.F. | | 6.20 | 2.22 | 8.42 | Includes material, labor and |
| Install | V.L.F. | 23.50 | 5.60 | 4.26 | 33.36 | equipment to install concrete filled |
| Demolish and Install | V.L.F. | 23.50 | 11.80 | 6.48 | 41.78 | steel pipe pile. |
| Paint | L.F. | .31 | 1.80 | | 2.11 | |
| Minimum Charge | Job | | 2525 | 1925 | 4450 | |
| **10" Unfilled** | | | | | | |
| Demolish | L.F. | | 6.20 | 2.22 | 8.42 | Includes material, labor and |
| Install | V.L.F. | 21.50 | 5.05 | 3.83 | 30.38 | equipment to install unfilled steel pipe |
| Demolish and Install | V.L.F. | 21.50 | 11.25 | 6.05 | 38.80 | pile. |
| Paint | L.F. | .31 | 1.80 | | 2.11 | |
| Minimum Charge | Job | | 2525 | 1925 | 4450 | |
| **12" Concrete Filled** | | | | | | |
| Demolish | L.F. | | 6.20 | 2.22 | 8.42 | Includes material, labor and |
| Install | V.L.F. | 27.50 | 6.05 | 4.62 | 38.17 | equipment to install concrete filled |
| Demolish and Install | V.L.F. | 27.50 | 12.25 | 6.84 | 46.59 | steel pipe pile. |
| Paint | L.F. | .31 | 1.80 | | 2.11 | |
| Minimum Charge | Job | | 2525 | 1925 | 4450 | |
| **12" Unfilled** | | | | | | |
| Demolish | L.F. | | 6.20 | 2.22 | 8.42 | Includes material, labor and |
| Install | V.L.F. | 26.50 | 5.30 | 4.04 | 35.84 | equipment to install unfilled steel pipe |
| Demolish and Install | V.L.F. | 26.50 | 11.50 | 6.26 | 44.26 | pile. |
| Paint | L.F. | .31 | 1.80 | | 2.11 | |
| Minimum Charge | Job | | 2525 | 1925 | 4450 | |
| **Steel H Section** | | | | | | |
| **H Section 8 x 8 x 36#** | | | | | | |
| Demolish | L.F. | | 4.20 | 1.50 | 5.70 | Includes material, labor and |
| Install | V.L.F. | 15.95 | 3.93 | 3 | 22.88 | equipment to install steel H section |
| Demolish and Install | V.L.F. | 15.95 | 8.13 | 4.50 | 28.58 | pile. |
| Paint | L.F. | .31 | 1.80 | | 2.11 | |
| Minimum Charge | Job | | 2525 | 1925 | 4450 | |
| **H Section 10 x 10 x 57#** | | | | | | |
| Demolish | L.F. | | 4.60 | 1.65 | 6.25 | Includes material, labor and |
| Install | V.L.F. | 25.50 | 4.13 | 3.14 | 32.77 | equipment to install steel H section |
| Demolish and Install | V.L.F. | 25.50 | 8.73 | 4.79 | 39.02 | pile. |
| Paint | L.F. | .31 | 1.80 | | 2.11 | |
| Minimum Charge | Job | | 2525 | 1925 | 4450 | |
| **H Section 12 x 12 x 74#** | | | | | | |
| Demolish | L.F. | | 4.75 | 1.70 | 6.45 | Includes material, labor and |
| Install | V.L.F. | 33.50 | 4.99 | 4.20 | 42.69 | equipment to install steel H section |
| Demolish and Install | V.L.F. | 33.50 | 9.74 | 5.90 | 49.14 | pile. |
| Paint | L.F. | .31 | 1.80 | | 2.11 | |
| Minimum Charge | Job | | 2525 | 1925 | 4450 | |
| **H Section 14 x 14 x 89#** | | | | | | |
| Demolish | L.F. | | 5 | 1.79 | 6.79 | Includes material, labor and |
| Install | V.L.F. | 40 | 5.45 | 4.59 | 50.04 | equipment to install steel H section |
| Demolish and Install | V.L.F. | 40 | 10.45 | 6.38 | 56.83 | pile. |
| Paint | L.F. | .31 | 1.80 | | 2.11 | |
| Minimum Charge | Job | | 2525 | 1925 | 4450 | |

# Foundation

| Foundation Post | | Unit | Material | Labor | Equip. | Total | Specification |
|---|---|---|---|---|---|---|---|
| **Wood Foundation Post** | | | | | | | |
| 4" x 4" | | | | | | | |
| | Demolish | L.F. | | .68 | .24 | .92 | Cost includes material and labor to |
| | Install | L.F. | 1.05 | 4.45 | | 5.50 | install 4" x 4" treated wood post by |
| | Demolish and Install | L.F. | 1.05 | 5.13 | .24 | 6.42 | hand in normal soil conditions. |
| | Reinstall | L.F. | | 3.56 | | 3.56 | |
| | Minimum Charge | Job | | 635 | | 635 | |
| 4" x 6" | | | | | | | |
| | Demolish | L.F. | | .68 | .24 | .92 | Cost includes material and labor to |
| | Install | L.F. | 1.56 | 4.45 | | 6.01 | install 4" x 6" treated wood post by |
| | Demolish and Install | L.F. | 1.56 | 5.13 | .24 | 6.93 | hand in normal soil conditions. |
| | Reinstall | L.F. | | 3.56 | | 3.56 | |
| | Minimum Charge | Job | | 635 | | 635 | |
| 6" x 6" | | | | | | | |
| | Demolish | L.F. | | .68 | .24 | .92 | Cost includes material and labor to |
| | Install | L.F. | 2.32 | 4.45 | | 6.77 | install 6" x 6" treated wood post by |
| | Demolish and Install | L.F. | 2.32 | 5.13 | .24 | 7.69 | hand in normal soil conditions. |
| | Reinstall | L.F. | | 3.56 | | 3.56 | |
| | Minimum Charge | Job | | 635 | | 635 | |
| **Water Jet** | | | | | | | |
| | Demolish | Ea. | | 79 | | 79 | Includes material, labor and |
| | Install | Ea. | 61.50 | 610 | | 671.50 | equipment to water jet a 6" x 6" wood |
| | Demolish and Install | Ea. | 61.50 | 689 | | 750.50 | post under an existing building. Cost |
| | Reinstall | Ea. | | 609.83 | | 609.83 | may vary depending upon location |
| | Minimum Charge | Job | | 535 | | 535 | and access. |
| **Shim** | | | | | | | |
| | Install | Ea. | 3.41 | 63.50 | | 66.91 | Includes labor and material to trim or |
| | Minimum Charge | Job | | 635 | | 635 | readjust existing foundation posts |
| | | | | | | | under an existing building. Access of |
| | | | | | | | 2 - 4 foot assumed. |
| **Cross-bracing** | | | | | | | |
| Treated 2" x 6" | | | | | | | |
| | Demolish | L.F. | | .87 | | .87 | Cost includes material and labor to |
| | Install | L.F. | .88 | 5.10 | | 5.98 | install 2" x 6" lumber for cross-bracing |
| | Demolish and Install | L.F. | .88 | 5.97 | | 6.85 | of foundation piling or posts. |
| | Reinstall | L.F. | | 4.09 | | 4.09 | |
| | Clean | S.F. | | .33 | | .33 | |
| | Paint | L.F. | .17 | 1.21 | | 1.38 | |
| | Minimum Charge | Job | | 635 | | 635 | |
| Treated 2" x 8" | | | | | | | |
| | Demolish | L.F. | | .87 | | .87 | Cost includes material and labor to |
| | Install | L.F. | 1.16 | 5.30 | | 6.46 | install 2" x 8" lumber for cross-bracing |
| | Demolish and Install | L.F. | 1.16 | 6.17 | | 7.33 | of foundation piling or posts. |
| | Reinstall | L.F. | | 4.22 | | 4.22 | |
| | Clean | S.F. | | .33 | | .33 | |
| | Paint | L.F. | .22 | 1.26 | | 1.48 | |
| | Minimum Charge | Job | | 635 | | 635 | |
| Treated 2" x 10" | | | | | | | |
| | Demolish | L.F. | | .90 | | .90 | Cost includes material and labor to |
| | Install | L.F. | 1.43 | 5.45 | | 6.88 | install 2" x 10" lumber for |
| | Demolish and Install | L.F. | 1.43 | 6.35 | | 7.78 | cross-bracing of foundation piling or |
| | Reinstall | L.F. | | 4.37 | | 4.37 | posts. |
| | Clean | S.F. | | .33 | | .33 | |
| | Paint | L.F. | .28 | 1.28 | | 1.56 | |
| | Minimum Charge | Job | | 635 | | 635 | |

| Foundation Post | | Unit | Material | Labor | Equip. | Total | Specification |
|---|---|---|---|---|---|---|---|
| **Treated 2″ x 12″** | | | | | | | Cost includes material and labor to install 2″ x 12″ lumber for cross-bracing of foundation piling or posts. |
| | Demolish | L.F. | | 1.08 | | 1.08 | |
| | Install | L.F. | 2.29 | 5.65 | | 7.94 | |
| | Demolish and Install | L.F. | 2.29 | 6.73 | | 9.02 | |
| | Reinstall | L.F. | | 4.52 | | 4.52 | |
| | Clean | S.F. | | .33 | | .33 | |
| | Paint | L.F. | .32 | 1.31 | | 1.63 | |
| | Minimum Charge | Job | | 635 | | 635 | |

| Concrete Footing | | Unit | Material | Labor | Equip. | Total | Specification |
|---|---|---|---|---|---|---|---|
| **Continuous** | | | | | | | |
| **12″ w x 6″ d** | | | | | | | Includes material and labor to install continuous reinforced concrete footing poured by chute cast against earth including reinforcing, forming and finishing. |
| | Demolish | L.F. | | 1.29 | 1.06 | 2.35 | |
| | Install | L.F. | 4.18 | 2.99 | .02 | 7.19 | |
| | Demolish and Install | L.F. | 4.18 | 4.28 | 1.08 | 9.54 | |
| | Minimum Charge | Job | | 725 | | 725 | |
| **12″ w x 12″ d** | | | | | | | Includes material and labor to install continuous reinforced concrete footing poured by chute cast against earth including reinforcing, forming and finishing. |
| | Demolish | L.F. | | 2.49 | 2.04 | 4.53 | |
| | Install | L.F. | 8.55 | 5.95 | .03 | 14.53 | |
| | Demolish and Install | L.F. | 8.55 | 8.44 | 2.07 | 19.06 | |
| | Minimum Charge | Job | | 725 | | 725 | |
| **18″ w x 10″ d** | | | | | | | Includes material and labor to install continuous reinforced concrete footing poured by chute cast against earth including reinforcing, forming and finishing. |
| | Demolish | L.F. | | 3.24 | 2.65 | 5.89 | |
| | Install | L.F. | 8.05 | 7.35 | .04 | 15.44 | |
| | Demolish and Install | L.F. | 8.05 | 10.59 | 2.69 | 21.33 | |
| | Minimum Charge | Job | | 725 | | 725 | |
| **24″ w x 24″ d** | | | | | | | Includes material and labor to install continuous reinforced concrete footing poured by chute cast against earth including reinforcing, forming and finishing. |
| | Demolish | L.F. | | 5.40 | 4.42 | 9.82 | |
| | Install | L.F. | 24 | 24 | .13 | 48.13 | |
| | Demolish and Install | L.F. | 24 | 29.40 | 4.55 | 57.95 | |
| | Minimum Charge | Job | | 725 | | 725 | |
| **Stem Wall** | | | | | | | |
| **Single Story** | | | | | | | Includes material and labor to install stem wall 24″ above and 18″ below grade for a single story structure. Includes 12″ wide and 8″ deep footing. |
| | Demolish | L.F. | | 12 | 9.80 | 21.80 | |
| | Install | L.F. | 23 | 63.50 | 52 | 138.50 | |
| | Demolish and Install | L.F. | 23 | 75.50 | 61.80 | 160.30 | |
| | Minimum Charge | Job | | 725 | | 725 | |
| **Two Story** | | | | | | | Includes material and labor to install stem wall 24″ above and 18″ below grade typical for a two story structure, includes 18″ wide and 10″ deep footing. |
| | Demolish | L.F. | | 12 | 9.80 | 21.80 | |
| | Install | L.F. | 28 | 91 | 74.50 | 193.50 | |
| | Demolish and Install | L.F. | 28 | 103 | 84.30 | 215.30 | |
| | Minimum Charge | Job | | 725 | | 725 | |

# Foundation

| Concrete Slab | | Unit | Material | Labor | Equip. | Total | Specification |
|---|---|---|---|---|---|---|---|
| **Reinforced** | | | | | | | |
| 4" | | | | | | | |
| | Demolish | S.F. | | 2.24 | .35 | 2.59 | Cost includes material and labor to |
| | Install | S.F. | 2.13 | .34 | | 2.47 | install 4" reinforced concrete |
| | Demolish and Install | S.F. | 2.13 | 2.58 | .35 | 5.06 | slab-on-grade poured by chute |
| | Clean | S.F. | .07 | .30 | | .37 | including forms, vapor barrier, wire |
| | Paint | S.F. | .11 | .68 | | .79 | mesh, 3000 PSI concrete, float finish, |
| | Minimum Charge | Job | | 166 | | 166 | and curing. |
| 6" | | | | | | | |
| | Demolish | S.F. | | 3.36 | .52 | 3.88 | Cost includes material and labor to |
| | Install | S.F. | 2.93 | .51 | .01 | 3.45 | install 6" reinforced concrete |
| | Demolish and Install | S.F. | 2.93 | 3.87 | .53 | 7.33 | slab-on-grade poured by chute |
| | Clean | S.F. | .07 | .30 | | .37 | including forms, vapor barrier, wire |
| | Paint | S.F. | .11 | .68 | | .79 | mesh, 3000 PSI concrete, float finish, |
| | Minimum Charge | Job | | 166 | | 166 | and curing. |
| 8" | | | | | | | |
| | Demolish | S.F. | | 5.50 | .85 | 6.35 | Cost includes material and labor to |
| | Install | S.F. | 3.74 | .67 | .01 | 4.42 | install 8" reinforced concrete |
| | Demolish and Install | S.F. | 3.74 | 6.17 | .86 | 10.77 | slab-on-grade poured by chute |
| | Clean | S.F. | .07 | .30 | | .37 | including forms, vapor barrier, wire |
| | Paint | S.F. | .11 | .68 | | .79 | mesh, 3000 PSI concrete, float finish, |
| | Minimum Charge | Job | | 166 | | 166 | and curing. |
| **Unreinforced** | | | | | | | |
| 4" | | | | | | | |
| | Demolish | S.F. | | 1.78 | .28 | 2.06 | Cost includes material and labor to |
| | Install | S.F. | 1.47 | .82 | .01 | 2.30 | install 4" concrete slab-on-grade |
| | Demolish and Install | S.F. | 1.47 | 2.60 | .29 | 4.36 | poured by chute, including forms, |
| | Clean | S.F. | .07 | .30 | | .37 | vapor barrier, 3000 PSI concrete, float |
| | Paint | S.F. | .11 | .68 | | .79 | finish, and curing. |
| | Minimum Charge | Job | | 166 | | 166 | |
| 6" | | | | | | | |
| | Demolish | S.F. | | 2.52 | .39 | 2.91 | Cost includes material and labor to |
| | Install | S.F. | 2.15 | .84 | .01 | 3 | install 6" concrete slab-on-grade |
| | Demolish and Install | S.F. | 2.15 | 3.36 | .40 | 5.91 | poured by chute, including forms, |
| | Clean | S.F. | .07 | .30 | | .37 | vapor barrier, 3000 PSI concrete, float |
| | Paint | S.F. | .11 | .68 | | .79 | finish, and curing. |
| | Minimum Charge | Job | | 166 | | 166 | |
| 8" | | | | | | | |
| | Demolish | S.F. | | 4.14 | .64 | 4.78 | Cost includes material and labor to |
| | Install | S.F. | 2.94 | .89 | .01 | 3.84 | install 8" concrete slab-on-grade |
| | Demolish and Install | S.F. | 2.94 | 5.03 | .65 | 8.62 | poured by chute, including forms, |
| | Clean | S.F. | .07 | .30 | | .37 | vapor barrier, 3000 PSI concrete, float |
| | Paint | S.F. | .11 | .68 | | .79 | finish, and curing. |
| | Minimum Charge | Job | | 166 | | 166 | |
| **Lightweight** | | | | | | | |
| | Demolish | S.F. | | .79 | .20 | .99 | Includes material and labor to install |
| | Install | S.F. | 2 | 2.49 | | 4.49 | lightweight concrete, 3" - 4" thick. |
| | Demolish and Install | S.F. | 2 | 3.28 | .20 | 5.48 | |
| | Clean | S.F. | .07 | .30 | | .37 | |
| | Paint | S.F. | .11 | .68 | | .79 | |
| | Minimum Charge | Job | | 166 | | 166 | |

| Concrete Slab | | Unit | Material | Labor | Equip. | Total | Specification |
|---|---|---|---|---|---|---|---|
| **Gunite** | | | | | | | |
| | Demolish | S.F. | | .97 | .35 | 1.32 | Includes material and labor to install |
| | Install | S.F. | .35 | 1.06 | .40 | 1.81 | gunite on flat plane per inch of |
| | Demolish and Install | S.F. | .35 | 2.03 | .75 | 3.13 | thickness using 1" as base price. No |
| | Clean | S.F. | .07 | .30 | | .37 | forms or reinforcing are included. |
| | Paint | S.F. | .11 | .68 | | .79 | |
| | Minimum Charge | Job | | 930 | | 930 | |
| **Epoxy Inject** | | | | | | | |
| | Install | L.F. | 6.75 | 3.33 | | 10.08 | Includes labor and material to inject |
| | Minimum Charge | Job | | 166 | | 166 | epoxy into cracks. |
| **Pressure Grout** | | | | | | | |
| | Install | S.F. | 2.43 | 2.47 | | 4.90 | Includes labor, material and |
| | Minimum Charge | Job | | 166 | | 166 | equipment to install pressure grout |
| | | | | | | | under an existing building. |
| **Scrape and Paint** | | | | | | | |
| | Paint | S.F. | .20 | .79 | | .99 | Includes labor and materials to scrape |
| | Minimum Charge | Job | | 157 | | 157 | and paint a concrete floor. |
| **Vapor Barrier** | | | | | | | |
| | Install | S.F. | .03 | .10 | | .13 | Cost includes material and labor to |
| | Minimum Charge | Job | | 181 | | 181 | install 4 mil polyethylene vapor barrier |
| | | | | | | | 10' wide sheets with 6" overlaps. |

**Rough Framing**

| Beam / Girder | Unit | Material | Labor | Equip. | Total | Specification |
|---|---|---|---|---|---|---|
| **Solid Wood Beam** | | | | | | |
| **2″ x 8″** | | | | | | |
| Demolish | L.F. | | .72 | | .72 | Cost includes material and labor to |
| Install | L.F. | .84 | 1.11 | | 1.95 | install 2″ x 8″ beam. |
| Demolish and Install | L.F. | .84 | 1.83 | | 2.67 | |
| Clean | L.F. | .12 | .24 | | .36 | |
| Paint | L.F. | .12 | 1.70 | | 1.82 | |
| Minimum Charge | Job | | 181 | | 181 | |
| **2″ x 10″** | | | | | | |
| Demolish | L.F. | | .89 | | .89 | Cost includes material and labor to |
| Install | L.F. | 1.13 | 1.21 | | 2.34 | install 2″ x 10″ beam. |
| Demolish and Install | L.F. | 1.13 | 2.10 | | 3.23 | |
| Clean | L.F. | .14 | .29 | | .43 | |
| Paint | L.F. | .18 | 1.05 | | 1.23 | |
| Minimum Charge | Job | | 181 | | 181 | |
| **2″ x 12″** | | | | | | |
| Demolish | L.F. | | 1.08 | | 1.08 | Cost includes material and labor to |
| Install | L.F. | 1.36 | 1.31 | | 2.67 | install 2″ x 12″ beam. |
| Demolish and Install | L.F. | 1.36 | 2.39 | | 3.75 | |
| Clean | L.F. | .17 | .33 | | .50 | |
| Paint | L.F. | .19 | 2.52 | | 2.71 | |
| Minimum Charge | Job | | 181 | | 181 | |
| **4″ x 8″** | | | | | | |
| Demolish | L.F. | | 2.23 | | 2.23 | Cost includes material and labor to |
| Install | L.F. | 4.71 | 1.64 | .84 | 7.19 | install 4″ x 8″ beam. |
| Demolish and Install | L.F. | 4.71 | 3.87 | .84 | 9.42 | |
| Clean | L.F. | .14 | .29 | | .43 | |
| Paint | L.F. | .18 | 1.05 | | 1.23 | |
| Minimum Charge | Job | | 181 | | 181 | |
| **4″ x 10″** | | | | | | |
| Demolish | L.F. | | 2.79 | | 2.79 | Cost includes material and labor to |
| Install | L.F. | 6.10 | 1.73 | .89 | 8.72 | install 4″ x 10″ beam. |
| Demolish and Install | L.F. | 6.10 | 4.52 | .89 | 11.51 | |
| Clean | L.F. | .17 | .33 | | .50 | |
| Paint | L.F. | .20 | 1.23 | | 1.43 | |
| Minimum Charge | Job | | 181 | | 181 | |
| **4″ x 12″** | | | | | | |
| Demolish | L.F. | | 3.34 | | 3.34 | Cost includes material and labor to |
| Install | L.F. | 7.25 | 1.82 | .94 | 10.01 | install 4″ x 12″ beam. |
| Demolish and Install | L.F. | 7.25 | 5.16 | .94 | 13.35 | |
| Clean | L.F. | .19 | .38 | | .57 | |
| Paint | L.F. | .19 | 2.52 | | 2.71 | |
| Minimum Charge | Job | | 181 | | 181 | |

| Beam / Girder | | Unit | Material | Labor | Equip. | Total | Specification |
|---|---|---|---|---|---|---|---|
| **6" x 8"** | | | | | | | |
| | Demolish | L.F. | | 3.34 | | 3.34 | Cost includes material and labor to |
| | Install | L.F. | 8.35 | 3.12 | 1.61 | 13.08 | install 6" x 8" beam. |
| | Demolish and Install | L.F. | 8.35 | 6.46 | 1.61 | 16.42 | |
| | Clean | L.F. | .17 | .33 | | .50 | |
| | Paint | L.F. | .20 | 1.22 | | 1.42 | |
| | Minimum Charge | Job | | 181 | | 181 | |
| **6" x 10"** | | | | | | | |
| | Demolish | L.F. | | 4.18 | | 4.18 | Cost includes material and labor to |
| | Install | L.F. | 3.41 | 1.45 | | 4.86 | install 6" x 10" triple beam. |
| | Demolish and Install | L.F. | 3.41 | 5.63 | | 9.04 | |
| | Clean | L.F. | .19 | .38 | | .57 | |
| | Paint | L.F. | .23 | 1.40 | | 1.63 | |
| | Minimum Charge | Job | | 181 | | 181 | |
| **6" x 12"** | | | | | | | |
| | Demolish | L.F. | | 4.97 | | 4.97 | Cost includes material and labor to |
| | Install | L.F. | 4.10 | 1.52 | | 5.62 | install 6" x 12" triple beam. |
| | Demolish and Install | L.F. | 4.10 | 6.49 | | 10.59 | |
| | Clean | L.F. | .21 | .43 | | .64 | |
| | Paint | L.F. | .25 | 1.57 | | 1.82 | |
| | Minimum Charge | Job | | 181 | | 181 | |
| **Steel I-type** | | | | | | | |
| **W8 x 31** | | | | | | | |
| | Demolish | L.F. | | 7.70 | 3.84 | 11.54 | Includes material and labor to install |
| | Install | L.F. | 41.50 | 2.45 | 1.60 | 45.55 | W shaped steel beam / girder. |
| | Demolish and Install | L.F. | 41.50 | 10.15 | 5.44 | 57.09 | |
| | Minimum Charge | Job | | 450 | | 450 | |
| **W8 x 48** | | | | | | | |
| | Demolish | L.F. | | 7.70 | 3.84 | 11.54 | Includes material and labor to install |
| | Install | L.F. | 64 | 2.56 | 1.67 | 68.23 | W shaped steel beam / girder. |
| | Demolish and Install | L.F. | 64 | 10.26 | 5.51 | 79.77 | |
| | Minimum Charge | Job | | 450 | | 450 | |
| **W8 x 67** | | | | | | | |
| | Demolish | L.F. | | 7.70 | 3.84 | 11.54 | Includes material and labor to install |
| | Install | L.F. | 89 | 2.69 | 1.75 | 93.44 | W shaped steel beam / girder. |
| | Demolish and Install | L.F. | 89 | 10.39 | 5.59 | 104.98 | |
| | Minimum Charge | Job | | 450 | | 450 | |
| **W10 x 45** | | | | | | | |
| | Demolish | L.F. | | 7.70 | 3.84 | 11.54 | Includes material and labor to install |
| | Install | L.F. | 60 | 2.56 | 1.67 | 64.23 | W shaped steel beam / girder. |
| | Demolish and Install | L.F. | 60 | 10.26 | 5.51 | 75.77 | |
| | Minimum Charge | Job | | 450 | | 450 | |
| **W10 x 68** | | | | | | | |
| | Demolish | L.F. | | 7.70 | 3.84 | 11.54 | Includes material and labor to install |
| | Install | L.F. | 91 | 2.69 | 1.75 | 95.44 | W shaped steel beam / girder. |
| | Demolish and Install | L.F. | 91 | 10.39 | 5.59 | 106.98 | |
| | Minimum Charge | Job | | 450 | | 450 | |
| **W12 x 50** | | | | | | | |
| | Demolish | L.F. | | 7.70 | 3.84 | 11.54 | Includes material and labor to install |
| | Install | L.F. | 66.50 | 2.56 | 1.67 | 70.73 | W shaped steel beam / girder. |
| | Demolish and Install | L.F. | 66.50 | 10.26 | 5.51 | 82.27 | |
| | Minimum Charge | Job | | 450 | | 450 | |
| **W12 x 87** | | | | | | | |
| | Demolish | L.F. | | 11.35 | 5.65 | 17 | Includes material and labor to install |
| | Install | L.F. | 116 | 2.69 | 1.75 | 120.44 | W shaped steel beam / girder. |
| | Demolish and Install | L.F. | 116 | 14.04 | 7.40 | 137.44 | |
| | Minimum Charge | Job | | 450 | | 450 | |

# Rough Frame / Structure

## Beam / Girder

| | Unit | Material | Labor | Equip. | Total | Specification |
|---|---|---|---|---|---|---|
| **W12 x 120** | | | | | | |
| Demolish | L.F. | | 11.35 | 5.65 | 17 | Includes material and labor to install |
| Install | L.F. | 160 | 2.75 | 1.80 | 164.55 | W shaped steel beam / girder. |
| Demolish and Install | L.F. | 160 | 14.10 | 7.45 | 181.55 | |
| Minimum Charge | Job | | 450 | | 450 | |
| **W14 x 74** | | | | | | |
| Demolish | L.F. | | 11.35 | 5.65 | 17 | Includes material and labor to install |
| Install | L.F. | 98.50 | 2.69 | 1.75 | 102.94 | W shaped steel beam / girder. |
| Demolish and Install | L.F. | 98.50 | 14.04 | 7.40 | 119.94 | |
| Minimum Charge | Job | | 450 | | 450 | |
| **W14 x 120** | | | | | | |
| Demolish | L.F. | | 11.35 | 5.65 | 17 | Includes material and labor to install |
| Install | L.F. | 160 | 2.75 | 1.80 | 164.55 | W shaped steel beam / girder. |
| Demolish and Install | L.F. | 160 | 14.10 | 7.45 | 181.55 | |
| Minimum Charge | Job | | 450 | | 450 | |

## Column

| | Unit | Material | Labor | Equip. | Total | Specification |
|---|---|---|---|---|---|---|
| **Concrete** | | | | | | |
| **Small Diameter** | | | | | | |
| Demolish | L.F. | | 12.60 | 1.95 | 14.55 | Includes material and labor to install |
| Install | L.F. | 71.50 | 11.45 | 2.47 | 85.42 | small diameter concrete column. |
| Demolish and Install | L.F. | 71.50 | 24.05 | 4.42 | 99.97 | |
| Minimum Charge | Job | | 570 | 124 | 694 | |
| **Large Diameter** | | | | | | |
| Demolish | L.F. | | 38 | 5.85 | 43.85 | Includes material and labor to install |
| Install | L.F. | 93 | 13.45 | 2.91 | 109.36 | large diameter concrete column. |
| Demolish and Install | L.F. | 93 | 51.45 | 8.76 | 153.21 | |
| Minimum Charge | Job | | 570 | 124 | 694 | |

## Floor Framing System

| | Unit | Material | Labor | Equip. | Total | Specification |
|---|---|---|---|---|---|---|
| **12" O.C.** | | | | | | |
| **2" x 6" Joists** | | | | | | |
| Demolish | S.F. | | .61 | | .61 | Cost includes material and labor to |
| Install | S.F. | .70 | .29 | | .99 | install 2" x 6" joists, 12" O.C. |
| Demolish and Install | S.F. | .70 | .90 | | 1.60 | including box or band joist. Blocking |
| Reinstall | S.F. | | .23 | | .23 | or bridging not included. |
| Minimum Charge | Job | | 181 | | 181 | |
| **2" x 8" Joists** | | | | | | |
| Demolish | S.F. | | .63 | | .63 | Cost includes material and labor to |
| Install | S.F. | .98 | .33 | | 1.31 | install 2" x 8" joists, 12" O.C. |
| Demolish and Install | S.F. | .98 | .96 | | 1.94 | including box or band joist. Blocking |
| Reinstall | S.F. | | .26 | | .26 | or bridging not included. |
| Minimum Charge | Job | | 181 | | 181 | |
| **2" x 10" Joists** | | | | | | |
| Demolish | S.F. | | .65 | | .65 | Cost includes material and labor to |
| Install | S.F. | 1.33 | .40 | | 1.73 | install 2" x 10" joists, 12" O.C. |
| Demolish and Install | S.F. | 1.33 | 1.05 | | 2.38 | including box or band joist. Blocking |
| Reinstall | S.F. | | .32 | | .32 | or bridging not included. |
| Minimum Charge | Job | | 181 | | 181 | |

| Floor Framing System | | Unit | Material | Labor | Equip. | Total | Specification |
|---|---|---|---|---|---|---|---|
| **2" x 12" Joists** | | | | | | | |
| | Demolish | S.F. | | .67 | | .67 | Cost includes material and labor to |
| | Install | S.F. | 1.61 | .41 | | 2.02 | install 2" x 12" joists, 12" O.C. |
| | Demolish and Install | S.F. | 1.61 | 1.08 | | 2.69 | including box or band joist. Blocking |
| | Reinstall | S.F. | | .33 | | .33 | or bridging not included. |
| | Minimum Charge | Job | | 181 | | 181 | |
| **Block / Bridge** | | | | | | | |
| | Demolish | Ea. | | .93 | | .93 | Includes material and labor to install |
| | Install | Ea. | 1.52 | 2.03 | | 3.55 | set of cross bridging or per block of |
| | Demolish and Install | Ea. | 1.52 | 2.96 | | 4.48 | solid bridging for 2" x 10" joists cut to |
| | Minimum Charge | Job | | 181 | | 181 | size on site. |
| **16" O.C.** | | | | | | | |
| **2" x 6" Joists** | | | | | | | |
| | Demolish | S.F. | | .46 | | .46 | Cost includes material and labor to |
| | Install | S.F. | .54 | .43 | | .97 | install 2" x 6" joists including box or |
| | Demolish and Install | S.F. | .54 | .89 | | 1.43 | band joist installed 16" O.C. Does not |
| | Reinstall | S.F. | | .35 | | .35 | include beams, blocking or bridging. |
| | Minimum Charge | Job | | 181 | | 181 | |
| **2" x 8" Joists** | | | | | | | |
| | Demolish | S.F. | | .47 | | .47 | Cost includes material and labor to |
| | Install | S.F. | .75 | .49 | | 1.24 | install 2" x 8" joists including box or |
| | Demolish and Install | S.F. | .75 | .96 | | 1.71 | band joist installed 16" O.C. Does not |
| | Reinstall | S.F. | | .39 | | .39 | include beams, blocking or bridging. |
| | Minimum Charge | Job | | 181 | | 181 | |
| **2" x 10" Joists** | | | | | | | |
| | Demolish | S.F. | | .49 | | .49 | Cost includes material and labor to |
| | Install | S.F. | 1.02 | .60 | | 1.62 | install 2" x 10" joists including box or |
| | Demolish and Install | S.F. | 1.02 | 1.09 | | 2.11 | band joist 16" O.C. Does not include |
| | Reinstall | S.F. | | .48 | | .48 | beams, blocking or bridging. |
| | Minimum Charge | Job | | 181 | | 181 | |
| **2" x 12" Joists** | | | | | | | |
| | Demolish | S.F. | | .50 | | .50 | Cost includes material and labor to |
| | Install | S.F. | 1.23 | .62 | | 1.85 | install 2" x 12" joists including box or |
| | Demolish and Install | S.F. | 1.23 | 1.12 | | 2.35 | band joist installed 16" O.C. Does not |
| | Reinstall | S.F. | | .50 | | .50 | include beams, blocking or bridging. |
| | Minimum Charge | Job | | 181 | | 181 | |
| **Block / Bridge** | | | | | | | |
| | Demolish | Ea. | | .93 | | .93 | Includes material and labor to install |
| | Install | Ea. | 1.52 | 2.03 | | 3.55 | set of cross bridging or per block of |
| | Demolish and Install | Ea. | 1.52 | 2.96 | | 4.48 | solid bridging for 2" x 10" joists cut to |
| | Minimum Charge | Job | | 181 | | 181 | size on site. |
| **24" O.C.** | | | | | | | |
| **2" x 6" Joists** | | | | | | | |
| | Demolish | S.F. | | .31 | | .31 | Cost includes material and labor to |
| | Install | S.F. | .39 | .14 | | .53 | install 2" x 6" joists including box or |
| | Demolish and Install | S.F. | .39 | .45 | | .84 | band joist installed 24" O.C. Does not |
| | Reinstall | S.F. | | .12 | | .12 | include beams, blocking or bridging. |
| | Minimum Charge | Job | | 181 | | 181 | |
| **2" x 8" Joists** | | | | | | | |
| | Demolish | S.F. | | .32 | | .32 | Cost includes material and labor to |
| | Install | S.F. | .53 | .16 | | .69 | install 2" x 8" joists including box or |
| | Demolish and Install | S.F. | .53 | .48 | | 1.01 | band joist installed 24" O.C. Does not |
| | Reinstall | S.F. | | .13 | | .13 | include beams, blocking or bridging. |
| | Minimum Charge | Job | | 181 | | 181 | |

| Floor Framing System | | Unit | Material | Labor | Equip. | Total | Specification |
|---|---|---|---|---|---|---|---|
| **2" x 10" Joists** | | | | | | | |
| | Demolish | S.F. | | .33 | | .33 | Cost includes material and labor to |
| | Install | S.F. | .73 | .20 | | .93 | install 2" x 10" joists including box or |
| | Demolish and Install | S.F. | .73 | .53 | | 1.26 | band joist installed 24" O.C. Does not |
| | Reinstall | S.F. | | .16 | | .16 | include beams, blocking or bridging. |
| | Minimum Charge | Job | | 181 | | 181 | |
| **2" x 12" Joists** | | | | | | | |
| | Demolish | S.F. | | .34 | | .34 | Cost includes material and labor to |
| | Install | S.F. | .88 | .21 | | 1.09 | install 2" x 12" joists including box or |
| | Demolish and Install | S.F. | .88 | .55 | | 1.43 | band joist installed 24" O.C. Does not |
| | Reinstall | S.F. | | .17 | | .17 | include beams, blocking or bridging. |
| | Minimum Charge | Job | | 181 | | 181 | |
| **Block / Bridge** | | | | | | | |
| | Demolish | Ea. | | .93 | | .93 | Includes material and labor to install |
| | Install | Ea. | 1.52 | 2.03 | | 3.55 | set of cross bridging or per block of |
| | Demolish and Install | Ea. | 1.52 | 2.96 | | 4.48 | solid bridging for 2" x 10" joists cut to |
| | Minimum Charge | Job | | 181 | | 181 | size on site. |
| **Engineered Lumber, Joist** | | | | | | | |
| **9-1/2"** | | | | | | | |
| | Demolish | S.F. | | .49 | | .49 | Includes material and labor to install |
| | Install | S.F. | 2 | .36 | | 2.36 | engineered lumber truss / joists per |
| | Demolish and Install | S.F. | 2 | .85 | | 2.85 | S.F. of floor area based on joists 16" |
| | Reinstall | S.F. | | .29 | | .29 | O.C. Beams, supports and bridging |
| | Minimum Charge | Job | | 181 | | 181 | are not included. |
| **11-7/8"** | | | | | | | |
| | Demolish | S.F. | | .50 | | .50 | Includes material and labor to install |
| | Install | S.F. | 2.15 | .37 | | 2.52 | engineered lumber truss / joists per |
| | Demolish and Install | S.F. | 2.15 | .87 | | 3.02 | S.F. of floor area based on joists 16" |
| | Reinstall | S.F. | | .30 | | .30 | O.C. Beams, supports and bridging |
| | Minimum Charge | Job | | 181 | | 181 | are not included. |
| **14"** | | | | | | | |
| | Demolish | S.F. | | .52 | | .52 | Includes material and labor to install |
| | Install | S.F. | 2.54 | .40 | | 2.94 | engineered lumber truss / joists per |
| | Demolish and Install | S.F. | 2.54 | .92 | | 3.46 | S.F. of floor area based on joists 16" |
| | Reinstall | S.F. | | .32 | | .32 | O.C. Beams, supports and bridging |
| | Minimum Charge | Job | | 181 | | 181 | are not included. |
| **16"** | | | | | | | |
| | Demolish | S.F. | | .54 | | .54 | Includes material and labor to install |
| | Install | S.F. | 2.81 | .42 | | 3.23 | engineered lumber truss / joists per |
| | Demolish and Install | S.F. | 2.81 | .96 | | 3.77 | S.F. of floor area based on joists 16" |
| | Reinstall | S.F. | | .33 | | .33 | O.C. Beams, supports and bridging |
| | Minimum Charge | Job | | 181 | | 181 | are not included. |
| **Block / Bridge** | | | | | | | |
| | Demolish | Pr. | | .93 | | .93 | Includes material and labor to install |
| | Install | Pr. | 1.41 | 2.68 | | 4.09 | set of steel, one-nail type cross |
| | Demolish and Install | Pr. | 1.41 | 3.61 | | 5.02 | bridging for trusses placed 16" O.C. |
| | Minimum Charge | Job | | 181 | | 181 | |
| **Block / Bridge** | | | | | | | |
| **2" x 6"** | | | | | | | |
| | Demolish | Ea. | | .93 | | .93 | Includes material and labor to install |
| | Install | Ea. | .81 | 1.63 | | 2.44 | set of cross bridging or per block of |
| | Demolish and Install | Ea. | .81 | 2.56 | | 3.37 | solid bridging for 2" x 6" joists cut to |
| | Minimum Charge | Job | | 181 | | 181 | size on site. |

| Floor Framing System | Unit | Material | Labor | Equip. | Total | Specification |
|---|---|---|---|---|---|---|
| **2" x 8"** | | | | | | |
| Demolish | Ea. | | .93 | | .93 | Includes material and labor to install |
| Install | Ea. | 1.11 | 1.81 | | 2.92 | set of cross bridging or per block of |
| Demolish and Install | Ea. | 1.11 | 2.74 | | 3.85 | solid bridging for 2" x 8" joists cut to |
| Minimum Charge | Job | | 181 | | 181 | size on site. |
| **2" x 10"** | | | | | | |
| Demolish | Ea. | | .93 | | .93 | Includes material and labor to install |
| Install | Ea. | 1.52 | 2.03 | | 3.55 | set of cross bridging or per block of |
| Demolish and Install | Ea. | 1.52 | 2.96 | | 4.48 | solid bridging for 2" x 10" joists cut to |
| Minimum Charge | Job | | 181 | | 181 | size on site. |
| **2" x 12"** | | | | | | |
| Demolish | Ea. | | .93 | | .93 | Includes material and labor to install |
| Install | Ea. | 1.84 | 2.39 | | 4.23 | set of cross bridging or per block of |
| Demolish and Install | Ea. | 1.84 | 3.32 | | 5.16 | solid bridging for 2" x 12" joists cut to |
| Minimum Charge | Job | | 181 | | 181 | size on site. |
| **Ledger Strips** | | | | | | |
| **1" x 2"** | | | | | | |
| Demolish | L.F. | | .25 | | .25 | Cost includes material and labor to |
| Install | L.F. | .13 | 1.05 | | 1.18 | install 1" x 2" ledger strip nailed to the |
| Demolish and Install | L.F. | .13 | 1.30 | | 1.43 | face of studs, beams or joist. |
| Minimum Charge | Job | | 181 | | 181 | |
| **1" x 3"** | | | | | | |
| Demolish | L.F. | | .25 | | .25 | Includes material and labor to install |
| Install | L.F. | .43 | 1.21 | | 1.64 | up to 1" x 4" ledger strip nailed to the |
| Demolish and Install | L.F. | .43 | 1.46 | | 1.89 | face of studs, beams or joist. |
| Minimum Charge | Job | | 181 | | 181 | |
| **1" x 4"** | | | | | | |
| Demolish | L.F. | | .25 | | .25 | Includes material and labor to install |
| Install | L.F. | .43 | 1.21 | | 1.64 | up to 1" x 4" ledger strip nailed to the |
| Demolish and Install | L.F. | .43 | 1.46 | | 1.89 | face of studs, beams or joist. |
| Minimum Charge | Job | | 181 | | 181 | |
| **2" x 2"** | | | | | | |
| Demolish | L.F. | | .27 | | .27 | Cost includes material and labor to |
| Install | L.F. | .36 | 1.10 | | 1.46 | install 2" x 2" ledger strip nailed to the |
| Demolish and Install | L.F. | .36 | 1.37 | | 1.73 | face of studs, beams or joist. |
| Minimum Charge | Job | | 181 | | 181 | |
| **2" x 4"** | | | | | | |
| Demolish | L.F. | | .30 | | .30 | Cost includes material and labor to |
| Install | L.F. | .39 | 1.45 | | 1.84 | install 2" x 4" ledger strip nailed to the |
| Demolish and Install | L.F. | .39 | 1.75 | | 2.14 | face of studs, beams or joist. |
| Reinstall | L.F. | | 1.16 | | 1.16 | |
| Minimum Charge | Job | | 181 | | 181 | |
| **Ledger Boards** | | | | | | |
| **2" x 6"** | | | | | | |
| Demolish | L.F. | | .30 | | .30 | Cost includes material and labor to |
| Install | L.F. | 1.94 | 2.26 | | 4.20 | install 2" x 6" ledger board fastened to |
| Demolish and Install | L.F. | 1.94 | 2.56 | | 4.50 | a wall, joists or studs. |
| Reinstall | L.F. | | 1.81 | | 1.81 | |
| Minimum Charge | Job | | 181 | | 181 | |
| **4" x 6"** | | | | | | |
| Demolish | L.F. | | .49 | | .49 | Cost includes material and labor to |
| Install | L.F. | 4.27 | 2.26 | | 6.53 | install 4" x 6" ledger board fastened to |
| Demolish and Install | L.F. | 4.27 | 2.75 | | 7.02 | a wall, joists or studs. |
| Reinstall | L.F. | | 1.81 | | 1.81 | |
| Minimum Charge | Job | | 181 | | 181 | |

# Rough Frame / Structure

| Floor Framing System | | Unit | Material | Labor | Equip. | Total | Specification |
|---|---|---|---|---|---|---|---|
| **4" x 8"** | | | | | | | Cost includes material and labor to |
| | Demolish | L.F. | | .66 | | .66 | install 4" x 8" ledger board fastened to |
| | Install | L.F. | 6.40 | 2.26 | | 8.66 | a wall, joists or studs. |
| | Demolish and Install | L.F. | 6.40 | 2.92 | | 9.32 | |
| | Reinstall | L.F. | | 1.81 | | 1.81 | |
| | Minimum Charge | Job | | 181 | | 181 | |
| **Sill Plate Per L.F.** | | | | | | | |
| **2" x 4"** | | | | | | | Cost includes material and labor to |
| | Demolish | L.F. | | .25 | | .25 | install 2" x 4" pressure treated lumber, |
| | Install | L.F. | .65 | 1.31 | | 1.96 | drilled and installed on foundation |
| | Demolish and Install | L.F. | .65 | 1.56 | | 2.21 | bolts 48" O.C. Bolts, nuts and washers |
| | Reinstall | L.F. | | 1.05 | | 1.05 | are not included. |
| | Minimum Charge | Job | | 181 | | 181 | |
| **2" x 6"** | | | | | | | Cost includes material and labor to |
| | Demolish | L.F. | | .38 | | .38 | install 2" x 6" pressure treated lumber, |
| | Install | L.F. | .88 | 1.45 | | 2.33 | drilled and installed on foundation |
| | Demolish and Install | L.F. | .88 | 1.83 | | 2.71 | bolts 48" O.C. Bolts, nuts and washers |
| | Reinstall | L.F. | | 1.16 | | 1.16 | not included. |
| | Minimum Charge | Job | | 181 | | 181 | |
| **2" x 8"** | | | | | | | Cost includes material and labor to |
| | Demolish | L.F. | | .51 | | .51 | install 2" x 8" pressure treated lumber, |
| | Install | L.F. | 1.16 | 1.61 | | 2.77 | drilled and installed on foundation |
| | Demolish and Install | L.F. | 1.16 | 2.12 | | 3.28 | bolts 48" O.C. Bolts, nuts and washers |
| | Reinstall | L.F. | | 1.29 | | 1.29 | not included. |
| | Minimum Charge | Job | | 181 | | 181 | |
| **Earthquake Strapping** | | | | | | | |
| | Install | Ea. | 2.56 | 2.26 | | 4.82 | Includes labor and material to replace |
| | Minimum Charge | Job | | 181 | | 181 | an earthquake strap. |

| Subflooring | | Unit | Material | Labor | Equip. | Total | Specification |
|---|---|---|---|---|---|---|---|
| **Plywood** | | | | | | | |
| **1/2"** | | | | | | | Cost includes material and labor to |
| | Demolish | S.F. | | .77 | | .77 | install 1/2" plywood subfloor, CD |
| | Install | SF Flr. | .43 | .39 | | .82 | standard interior grade, plugged and |
| | Demolish and Install | SF Flr. | .43 | 1.16 | | 1.59 | touch sanded. |
| | Minimum Charge | Job | | 181 | | 181 | |
| **5/8"** | | | | | | | Cost includes material and labor to |
| | Demolish | S.F. | | .78 | | .78 | install 5/8" plywood subfloor, CD |
| | Install | SF Flr. | .57 | .43 | | 1 | standard interior grade, plugged and |
| | Demolish and Install | SF Flr. | .57 | 1.21 | | 1.78 | touch sanded. |
| | Reinstall | SF Flr. | | .35 | | .35 | |
| | Minimum Charge | Job | | 181 | | 181 | |
| **3/4"** | | | | | | | Cost includes material and labor to |
| | Demolish | S.F. | | .79 | | .79 | install 3/4" plywood subfloor, CD |
| | Install | SF Flr. | .73 | .47 | | 1.20 | standard interior grade, plugged and |
| | Demolish and Install | SF Flr. | .73 | 1.26 | | 1.99 | touch sanded. |
| | Reinstall | SF Flr. | | .37 | | .37 | |
| | Minimum Charge | Job | | 181 | | 181 | |

# Rough Frame / Structure

| Subflooring | Unit | Material | Labor | Equip. | Total | Specification |
|---|---|---|---|---|---|---|
| **Particle Board** | | | | | | |
| **1/2"** | | | | | | |
| Demolish | S.F. | | .39 | | .39 | Cost includes material and labor to |
| Install | SF Flr. | .41 | .48 | | .89 | install 1/2" particle board subfloor. |
| Demolish and Install | SF Flr. | .41 | .87 | | 1.28 | |
| Minimum Charge | Job | | 181 | | 181 | |
| **5/8"** | | | | | | |
| Demolish | S.F. | | .39 | | .39 | Cost includes material and labor to |
| Install | S.F. | .45 | .53 | | .98 | install 5/8" particle board subfloor. |
| Demolish and Install | S.F. | .45 | .92 | | 1.37 | |
| Minimum Charge | Job | | 181 | | 181 | |
| **3/4"** | | | | | | |
| Demolish | S.F. | | .40 | | .40 | Cost includes material and labor to |
| Install | SF Flr. | .76 | .58 | | 1.34 | install 3/4" particle board subfloor. |
| Demolish and Install | SF Flr. | .76 | .98 | | 1.74 | |
| Minimum Charge | Job | | 181 | | 181 | |
| **Plank Board** | | | | | | |
| Demolish | S.F. | | 1.24 | | 1.24 | Cost includes material and labor to |
| Install | S.F. | 1.50 | .40 | | 1.90 | install 1" x 6" standard grade plank |
| Demolish and Install | S.F. | 1.50 | 1.64 | | 3.14 | flooring. |
| Reinstall | S.F. | | .40 | | .40 | |
| Minimum Charge | Job | | 181 | | 181 | |
| **Felt Underlay** | | | | | | |
| Demolish | S.F. | | .07 | | .07 | Includes material and labor to install |
| Install | S.F. | .04 | .10 | | .14 | #15 felt building paper. |
| Demolish and Install | S.F. | .04 | .17 | | .21 | |
| Minimum Charge | Job | | 181 | | 181 | |
| **Prep (for flooring)** | | | | | | |
| Install | S.F. | | .32 | | .32 | Preparation of subflooring for |
| Minimum Charge | Job | | 167 | | 167 | installation of new finished flooring. Cost reflects average time to prep area. |

| Wall Framing System | Unit | Material | Labor | Equip. | Total | Specification |
|---|---|---|---|---|---|---|
| **2" x 4"** | | | | | | |
| **8' High** | | | | | | |
| Demolish | L.F. | | 3.95 | | 3.95 | Cost includes material and labor to |
| Install | L.F. | 4.14 | 4.25 | | 8.39 | install 2" x 4" x 8' high wall system, |
| Demolish and Install | L.F. | 4.14 | 8.20 | | 12.34 | including studs, treated bottom plate, |
| Reinstall | L.F. | | 3.40 | | 3.40 | double top plate and one row of fire |
| Minimum Charge | Job | | 181 | | 181 | blocking. |
| **9' High** | | | | | | |
| Demolish | L.F. | | 4.42 | | 4.42 | Cost includes material and labor to |
| Install | L.F. | 4.42 | 4.25 | | 8.67 | install 2" x 4" x 9' wall system |
| Demolish and Install | L.F. | 4.42 | 8.67 | | 13.09 | including studs, treated bottom plate, |
| Reinstall | L.F. | | 3.40 | | 3.40 | double top plate and one row of fire |
| Minimum Charge | Job | | 181 | | 181 | blocking. |
| **10' High** | | | | | | |
| Demolish | L.F. | | 4.94 | | 4.94 | Cost includes material and labor to |
| Install | L.F. | 4.72 | 4.25 | | 8.97 | install 2" x 4" x 10' wall system |
| Demolish and Install | L.F. | 4.72 | 9.19 | | 13.91 | including studs, treated bottom plate, |
| Reinstall | L.F. | | 3.40 | | 3.40 | double top plate and one row of fire |
| Minimum Charge | Job | | 181 | | 181 | blocking. |

| Wall Framing System | Unit | Material | Labor | Equip. | Total | Specification |
|---|---|---|---|---|---|---|
| **12' High** | | | | | | |
| Demolish | L.F. | | 5.95 | | 5.95 | Cost includes material and labor to |
| Install | L.F. | 5.30 | 5.15 | | 10.45 | install 2" x 4" x 12' wall system |
| Demolish and Install | L.F. | 5.30 | 11.10 | | 16.40 | including studs, treated bottom plate, |
| Reinstall | L.F. | | 4.13 | | 4.13 | double top plate and one row of fire |
| Minimum Charge | Job | | 181 | | 181 | blocking. |
| **2" x 6"** | | | | | | |
| **8' High** | | | | | | |
| Demolish | L.F. | | 3.71 | | 3.71 | Cost includes material and labor to |
| Install | L.F. | 6.35 | 7.90 | | 14.25 | install 2" x 6" x 8' wall system |
| Demolish and Install | L.F. | 6.35 | 11.61 | | 17.96 | including studs, treated bottom plate, |
| Reinstall | L.F. | | 6.33 | | 6.33 | double top plate and one row of fire |
| Minimum Charge | Job | | 181 | | 181 | blocking. |
| **9' High** | | | | | | |
| Demolish | L.F. | | 4.18 | | 4.18 | Cost includes material and labor to |
| Install | L.F. | 6.75 | 7.90 | | 14.65 | install 2" x 6" x 9' wall system |
| Demolish and Install | L.F. | 6.75 | 12.08 | | 18.83 | including studs, treated bottom plate, |
| Reinstall | L.F. | | 6.33 | | 6.33 | double top plate and one row of fire |
| Minimum Charge | Job | | 181 | | 181 | blocking. |
| **10' High** | | | | | | |
| Demolish | L.F. | | 4.56 | | 4.56 | Cost includes material and labor to |
| Install | L.F. | 7.20 | 7.90 | | 15.10 | install 2" x 6" x 10' wall system |
| Demolish and Install | L.F. | 7.20 | 12.46 | | 19.66 | including studs, treated bottom plate, |
| Reinstall | L.F. | | 6.33 | | 6.33 | double top plate and one row of fire |
| Minimum Charge | Job | | 181 | | 181 | blocking. |
| **12' High** | | | | | | |
| Demolish | L.F. | | 5.40 | | 5.40 | Cost includes material and labor to |
| Install | L.F. | 8.15 | 9.75 | | 17.90 | install 2" x 6" x 12' wall system |
| Demolish and Install | L.F. | 8.15 | 15.15 | | 23.30 | including studs, treated bottom plate, |
| Reinstall | L.F. | | 7.79 | | 7.79 | double top plate and one row of fire |
| Minimum Charge | Job | | 181 | | 181 | blocking. |
| **Fireblock** | | | | | | |
| **2" x 4", 16" O.C. System** | | | | | | |
| Demolish | L.F. | | .49 | | .49 | Cost includes material and labor to |
| Install | L.F. | .39 | 1.21 | | 1.60 | install 2" x 4" fireblocks in wood frame |
| Demolish and Install | L.F. | .39 | 1.70 | | 2.09 | walls per L.F. of wall to be blocked. |
| Reinstall | L.F. | | .96 | | .96 | |
| Minimum Charge | Job | | 181 | | 181 | |
| **2" x 4", 24" O.C. System** | | | | | | |
| Demolish | L.F. | | .49 | | .49 | Cost includes material and labor to |
| Install | L.F. | .39 | 1.21 | | 1.60 | install 2" x 4" fireblocks in wood frame |
| Demolish and Install | L.F. | .39 | 1.70 | | 2.09 | walls per L.F. of wall to be blocked. |
| Reinstall | L.F. | | .96 | | .96 | |
| Minimum Charge | Job | | 181 | | 181 | |
| **2" x 6", 16" O.C. System** | | | | | | |
| Demolish | L.F. | | .74 | | .74 | Cost includes material and labor to |
| Install | L.F. | .61 | 1.21 | | 1.82 | install 2" x 6" fireblocks in wood frame |
| Demolish and Install | L.F. | .61 | 1.95 | | 2.56 | walls per L.F. of wall to be blocked. |
| Reinstall | L.F. | | .96 | | .96 | |
| Minimum Charge | Job | | 181 | | 181 | |
| **2" x 6", 24" O.C. System** | | | | | | |
| Demolish | L.F. | | .74 | | .74 | Cost includes material and labor to |
| Install | L.F. | .61 | 1.21 | | 1.82 | install 2" x 6" fireblocks in wood frame |
| Demolish and Install | L.F. | .61 | 1.95 | | 2.56 | walls per L.F. of wall to be blocked. |
| Reinstall | L.F. | | .96 | | .96 | |
| Minimum Charge | Job | | 181 | | 181 | |

| Wall Framing System | | Unit | Material | Labor | Equip. | Total | Specification |
|---|---|---|---|---|---|---|---|
| **Bracing** | | | | | | | |
| **1" x 3"** | | | | | | | |
| | Demolish | L.F. | | .28 | | .28 | Cost includes material and labor to |
| | Install | L.F. | .19 | 2.26 | | 2.45 | install 1" x 3" let-in bracing. |
| | Demolish and Install | L.F. | .19 | 2.54 | | 2.73 | |
| | Minimum Charge | Job | | 181 | | 181 | |
| **1" x 4"** | | | | | | | |
| | Demolish | L.F. | | .28 | | .28 | Cost includes material and labor to |
| | Install | L.F. | .43 | 2.26 | | 2.69 | install 1" x 4" let-in bracing. |
| | Demolish and Install | L.F. | .43 | 2.54 | | 2.97 | |
| | Minimum Charge | Job | | 181 | | 181 | |
| **1" x 6"** | | | | | | | |
| | Demolish | L.F. | | .28 | | .28 | Cost includes material and labor to |
| | Install | L.F. | .69 | 2.41 | | 3.10 | install 1" x 6" let-in bracing. |
| | Demolish and Install | L.F. | .69 | 2.69 | | 3.38 | |
| | Minimum Charge | Job | | 181 | | 181 | |
| **2" x 3"** | | | | | | | |
| | Demolish | L.F. | | .37 | | .37 | Cost includes material and labor to |
| | Install | L.F. | .36 | 2.41 | | 2.77 | install 2" x 3" let-in bracing. |
| | Demolish and Install | L.F. | .36 | 2.78 | | 3.14 | |
| | Reinstall | L.F. | | 1.93 | | 1.93 | |
| | Minimum Charge | Job | | 181 | | 181 | |
| **2" x 4"** | | | | | | | |
| | Demolish | L.F. | | .37 | | .37 | Cost includes material and labor to |
| | Install | L.F. | .39 | 2.41 | | 2.80 | install 2" x 4" let-in bracing. |
| | Demolish and Install | L.F. | .39 | 2.78 | | 3.17 | |
| | Reinstall | L.F. | | 1.93 | | 1.93 | |
| | Minimum Charge | Job | | 181 | | 181 | |
| **2" x 6"** | | | | | | | |
| | Demolish | L.F. | | .37 | | .37 | Cost includes material and labor to |
| | Install | L.F. | .61 | 2.58 | | 3.19 | install 2" x 6" let-in bracing. |
| | Demolish and Install | L.F. | .61 | 2.95 | | 3.56 | |
| | Reinstall | L.F. | | 2.07 | | 2.07 | |
| | Minimum Charge | Job | | 181 | | 181 | |
| **2" x 8"** | | | | | | | |
| | Demolish | L.F. | | .37 | | .37 | Cost includes material and labor to |
| | Install | L.F. | .84 | 2.58 | | 3.42 | install 2" x 8" let-in bracing. |
| | Demolish and Install | L.F. | .84 | 2.95 | | 3.79 | |
| | Reinstall | L.F. | | 2.07 | | 2.07 | |
| | Minimum Charge | Job | | 181 | | 181 | |
| **Earthquake Strapping** | | | | | | | |
| | Install | Ea. | 2.56 | 2.26 | | 4.82 | Includes labor and material to replace |
| | Minimum Charge | Job | | 181 | | 181 | an earthquake strap. |
| **Hurricane Clips** | | | | | | | |
| | Install | Ea. | .96 | 2.49 | | 3.45 | Includes labor and material to install a |
| | Minimum Charge | Job | | 181 | | 181 | hurricane clip. |
| **Stud** | | | | | | | |
| **2" x 4"** | | | | | | | |
| | Demolish | L.F. | | .30 | | .30 | Cost includes material and labor to |
| | Install | L.F. | .39 | .66 | | 1.05 | install 2" x 4" wall stud per L.F. of stud. |
| | Demolish and Install | L.F. | .39 | .96 | | 1.35 | |
| | Reinstall | L.F. | | .53 | | .53 | |
| | Minimum Charge | Job | | 181 | | 181 | |

# Rough Frame / Structure

| Wall Framing System | | Unit | Material | Labor | Equip. | Total | Specification |
|---|---|---|---|---|---|---|---|
| **2" x 6"** | | | | | | | |
| | Demolish | L.F. | | .37 | | .37 | Cost includes material and labor to |
| | Install | L.F. | .61 | .72 | | 1.33 | install 2" x 6" stud per L.F. of stud. |
| | Demolish and Install | L.F. | .61 | 1.09 | | 1.70 | |
| | Reinstall | L.F. | | .58 | | .58 | |
| | Minimum Charge | Job | | 181 | | 181 | |
| **Plates** | | | | | | | |
| **2" x 4"** | | | | | | | |
| | Demolish | L.F. | | .27 | | .27 | Cost includes material and labor to |
| | Install | L.F. | .39 | .90 | | 1.29 | install 2" x 4" plate per L.F. of plate. |
| | Demolish and Install | L.F. | .39 | 1.17 | | 1.56 | |
| | Reinstall | L.F. | | .72 | | .72 | |
| | Minimum Charge | Job | | 181 | | 181 | |
| **2" x 6"** | | | | | | | |
| | Demolish | L.F. | | .28 | | .28 | Cost includes material and labor to |
| | Install | L.F. | .61 | .96 | | 1.57 | install 2" x 6" plate per L.F. of plate. |
| | Demolish and Install | L.F. | .61 | 1.24 | | 1.85 | |
| | Reinstall | L.F. | | .77 | | .77 | |
| | Minimum Charge | Job | | 181 | | 181 | |
| **Headers** | | | | | | | |
| | Demolish | L.F. | | .26 | | .26 | Includes material and labor to install |
| | Install | L.F. | .61 | 2.01 | | 2.62 | header over wall openings and |
| | Demolish and Install | L.F. | .61 | 2.27 | | 2.88 | around floor, ceiling and roof |
| | Clean | L.F. | .02 | .34 | | .36 | openings or flush beam. |
| | Paint | L.F. | .09 | 1.26 | | 1.35 | |
| | Minimum Charge | Job | | 181 | | 181 | |
| **2" x 8"** | | | | | | | |
| | Demolish | L.F. | | .28 | | .28 | Includes material and labor to install |
| | Install | L.F. | .84 | 2.13 | | 2.97 | header over wall openings and |
| | Demolish and Install | L.F. | .84 | 2.41 | | 3.25 | around floor, ceiling and roof |
| | Clean | L.F. | .02 | .34 | | .36 | openings or flush beam. |
| | Paint | L.F. | .12 | 1.70 | | 1.82 | |
| | Minimum Charge | Job | | 181 | | 181 | |
| **2" x 10"** | | | | | | | |
| | Demolish | L.F. | | .28 | | .28 | Includes material and labor to install |
| | Install | L.F. | 1.13 | 2.26 | | 3.39 | header over wall openings and |
| | Demolish and Install | L.F. | 1.13 | 2.54 | | 3.67 | around floor, ceiling and roof |
| | Clean | L.F. | .03 | .34 | | .37 | openings or flush beam. |
| | Paint | L.F. | .15 | 2.10 | | 2.25 | |
| | Minimum Charge | Job | | 181 | | 181 | |
| **2" x 12"** | | | | | | | |
| | Demolish | L.F. | | .30 | | .30 | Includes material and labor to install |
| | Install | L.F. | 1.36 | 2.41 | | 3.77 | header over wall openings and |
| | Demolish and Install | L.F. | 1.36 | 2.71 | | 4.07 | around floor, ceiling and roof |
| | Clean | L.F. | .03 | .34 | | .37 | openings or flush beam. |
| | Paint | L.F. | .19 | 2.52 | | 2.71 | |
| | Minimum Charge | Job | | 181 | | 181 | |
| **4" x 8"** | | | | | | | |
| | Demolish | L.F. | | .53 | | .53 | Includes material and labor to install |
| | Install | L.F. | 4.71 | 2.78 | | 7.49 | header over wall openings and |
| | Demolish and Install | L.F. | 4.71 | 3.31 | | 8.02 | around floor, ceiling and roof |
| | Clean | L.F. | .02 | .34 | | .36 | openings or flush beam. |
| | Paint | L.F. | .12 | 1.70 | | 1.82 | |
| | Minimum Charge | Job | | 181 | | 181 | |

# Rough Frame / Structure

## Wall Framing System

| Wall Framing System | | Unit | Material | Labor | Equip. | Total | Specification |
|---|---|---|---|---|---|---|---|
| **4" x 10"** | | | | | | | |
| | Demolish | L.F. | | .56 | | .56 | Includes material and labor to install |
| | Install | L.F. | 6.10 | 3.01 | | 9.11 | header over wall openings and |
| | Demolish and Install | L.F. | 6.10 | 3.57 | | 9.67 | around floor, ceiling and roof |
| | Clean | L.F. | .03 | .34 | | .37 | openings or flush beam. |
| | Paint | L.F. | .15 | 2.10 | | 2.25 | |
| | Minimum Charge | Job | | 181 | | 181 | |
| **4" x 12"** | | | | | | | |
| | Demolish | L.F. | | .59 | | .59 | Includes material and labor to install |
| | Install | L.F. | 7.25 | 3.81 | | 11.06 | header over wall openings and |
| | Demolish and Install | L.F. | 7.25 | 4.40 | | 11.65 | around floor, ceiling and roof |
| | Clean | L.F. | .03 | .34 | | .37 | openings or flush beam. |
| | Paint | L.F. | .19 | 2.52 | | 2.71 | |
| | Minimum Charge | Job | | 181 | | 181 | |
| **6" x 8"** | | | | | | | |
| | Demolish | L.F. | | .53 | | .53 | Includes material and labor to install |
| | Install | L.F. | 8.35 | 2.01 | | 10.36 | header over wall openings and |
| | Demolish and Install | L.F. | 8.35 | 2.54 | | 10.89 | around floor, ceiling and roof |
| | Clean | L.F. | .02 | .34 | | .36 | openings or flush beam. |
| | Paint | L.F. | .12 | 1.70 | | 1.82 | |
| | Minimum Charge | Job | | 181 | | 181 | |
| **6" x 10"** | | | | | | | |
| | Demolish | L.F. | | .56 | | .56 | Includes material and labor to install |
| | Install | L.F. | 12 | 4.38 | | 16.38 | header over wall openings and |
| | Demolish and Install | L.F. | 12 | 4.94 | | 16.94 | around floor, ceiling and roof |
| | Clean | L.F. | .03 | .34 | | .37 | openings or flush beam. |
| | Paint | L.F. | .15 | 2.10 | | 2.25 | |
| | Minimum Charge | Job | | 181 | | 181 | |
| **6" x 12"** | | | | | | | |
| | Demolish | L.F. | | .59 | | .59 | Includes material and labor to install |
| | Install | L.F. | 10.05 | 5.15 | | 15.20 | header over wall openings and |
| | Demolish and Install | L.F. | 10.05 | 5.74 | | 15.79 | around floor, ceiling and roof |
| | Clean | L.F. | .03 | .34 | | .37 | openings or flush beam. |
| | Paint | L.F. | .19 | .87 | | 1.06 | |
| | Minimum Charge | Job | | 181 | | 181 | |

## Rough-in Opening

| Rough-in Opening | | Unit | Material | Labor | Equip. | Total | Specification |
|---|---|---|---|---|---|---|---|
| **Door w / 2" x 4" Lumber** | | | | | | | |
| **3' Wide** | | | | | | | |
| | Demolish | Ea. | | 9.25 | | 9.25 | Includes material and labor to install |
| | Install | Ea. | 16.35 | 11.30 | | 27.65 | header, double studs each side, |
| | Demolish and Install | Ea. | 16.35 | 20.55 | | 36.90 | cripples, blocking and nails, up to 3' |
| | Reinstall | Ea. | | 9.04 | | 9.04 | opening in 2" x 4" stud wall 8' high. |
| | Minimum Charge | Job | | 181 | | 181 | |
| **4' Wide** | | | | | | | |
| | Demolish | Ea. | | 9.25 | | 9.25 | Includes material and labor to install |
| | Install | Ea. | 17.55 | 11.30 | | 28.85 | header, double studs each side, |
| | Demolish and Install | Ea. | 17.55 | 20.55 | | 38.10 | cripples, blocking and nails, up to 4' |
| | Reinstall | Ea. | | 9.04 | | 9.04 | opening in 2" x 4" stud wall 8' high. |
| | Minimum Charge | Job | | 181 | | 181 | |
| **5' Wide** | | | | | | | |
| | Demolish | Ea. | | 9.25 | | 9.25 | Includes material and labor to install |
| | Install | Ea. | 21 | 11.30 | | 32.30 | header, double studs each side, |
| | Demolish and Install | Ea. | 21 | 20.55 | | 41.55 | cripples, blocking and nails, up to 5' |
| | Reinstall | Ea. | | 9.04 | | 9.04 | opening in 2" x 4" stud wall 8' high. |
| | Minimum Charge | Job | | 181 | | 181 | |

| Rough-in Opening | | Unit | Material | Labor | Equip. | Total | Specification |
|---|---|---|---|---|---|---|---|
| **6' Wide** | | | | | | | |
| | Demolish | Ea. | | 9.25 | | 9.25 | Includes material and labor to install |
| | Install | Ea. | 22.50 | 11.30 | | 33.80 | header, double studs each side, |
| | Demolish and Install | Ea. | 22.50 | 20.55 | | 43.05 | cripples, blocking and nails, up to 6' |
| | Reinstall | Ea. | | 9.04 | | 9.04 | opening in 2" x 4" stud wall 8' high. |
| | Minimum Charge | Job | | 181 | | 181 | |
| **8' Wide** | | | | | | | |
| | Demolish | Ea. | | 9.90 | | 9.90 | Includes material and labor to install |
| | Install | Ea. | 31.50 | 12.05 | | 43.55 | header, double studs each side, |
| | Demolish and Install | Ea. | 31.50 | 21.95 | | 53.45 | cripples, blocking and nails, up to 8' |
| | Reinstall | Ea. | | 9.64 | | 9.64 | opening in 2" x 4" stud wall 8' high. |
| | Minimum Charge | Job | | 181 | | 181 | |
| **10' Wide** | | | | | | | |
| | Demolish | Ea. | | 9.90 | | 9.90 | Includes material and labor to install |
| | Install | Ea. | 40.50 | 12.05 | | 52.55 | header, double studs each side, |
| | Demolish and Install | Ea. | 40.50 | 21.95 | | 62.45 | cripples, blocking and nails, up to 10' |
| | Reinstall | Ea. | | 9.64 | | 9.64 | opening in 2" x 4" stud wall 8' high. |
| | Minimum Charge | Job | | 181 | | 181 | |
| **12' Wide** | | | | | | | |
| | Demolish | Ea. | | 9.90 | | 9.90 | Includes material and labor to install |
| | Install | Ea. | 71 | 12.05 | | 83.05 | header, double studs each side, |
| | Demolish and Install | Ea. | 71 | 21.95 | | 92.95 | cripples, blocking and nails, up to 12' |
| | Reinstall | Ea. | | 9.64 | | 9.64 | opening in 2" x 4" stud wall 8' high. |
| | Minimum Charge | Job | | 181 | | 181 | |
| **Door w / 2" x 6" Lumber** | | | | | | | |
| **3' Wide** | | | | | | | |
| | Demolish | Ea. | | 9.25 | | 9.25 | Includes material and labor to install |
| | Install | Ea. | 23 | 11.30 | | 34.30 | header, double studs each side, |
| | Demolish and Install | Ea. | 23 | 20.55 | | 43.55 | cripples, blocking and nails, up to 3' |
| | Reinstall | Ea. | | 9.04 | | 9.04 | opening in 2" x 6" stud wall 8' high. |
| | Minimum Charge | Job | | 181 | | 181 | |
| **4' Wide** | | | | | | | |
| | Demolish | Ea. | | 9.25 | | 9.25 | Includes material and labor to install |
| | Install | Ea. | 24 | 11.30 | | 35.30 | header, double studs each side, |
| | Demolish and Install | Ea. | 24 | 20.55 | | 44.55 | cripples, blocking and nails, up to 4' |
| | Reinstall | Ea. | | 9.04 | | 9.04 | opening in 2" x 6" stud wall 8' high. |
| | Minimum Charge | Job | | 181 | | 181 | |
| **5' Wide** | | | | | | | |
| | Demolish | Ea. | | 9.25 | | 9.25 | Includes material and labor to install |
| | Install | Ea. | 28 | 11.30 | | 39.30 | header, double studs each side, |
| | Demolish and Install | Ea. | 28 | 20.55 | | 48.55 | cripples, blocking and nails up to 5' |
| | Reinstall | Ea. | | 9.04 | | 9.04 | opening in 2" x 6" stud wall 8' high. |
| | Minimum Charge | Job | | 181 | | 181 | |
| **6' Wide** | | | | | | | |
| | Demolish | Ea. | | 9.25 | | 9.25 | Includes material and labor to install |
| | Install | Ea. | 29.50 | 11.30 | | 40.80 | header, double studs each side, |
| | Demolish and Install | Ea. | 29.50 | 20.55 | | 50.05 | cripples, blocking and nails up to 6' |
| | Reinstall | Ea. | | 9.04 | | 9.04 | opening in 2" x 6" stud wall 8' high. |
| | Minimum Charge | Job | | 181 | | 181 | |
| **8' Wide** | | | | | | | |
| | Demolish | Ea. | | 9.90 | | 9.90 | Includes material and labor to install |
| | Install | Ea. | 38 | 12.05 | | 50.05 | header, double studs each side, |
| | Demolish and Install | Ea. | 38 | 21.95 | | 59.95 | cripples, blocking and nails up to 8' |
| | Reinstall | Ea. | | 9.64 | | 9.64 | opening in 2" x 6" stud wall 8' high. |
| | Minimum Charge | Job | | 181 | | 181 | |
| **10' Wide** | | | | | | | |
| | Demolish | Ea. | | 9.90 | | 9.90 | Includes material and labor to install |
| | Install | Ea. | 47.50 | 12.05 | | 59.55 | header, double studs each side, |
| | Demolish and Install | Ea. | 47.50 | 21.95 | | 69.45 | cripples, blocking and nails up to 10' |
| | Reinstall | Ea. | | 9.64 | | 9.64 | opening in 2" x 6" stud wall 8' high. |
| | Minimum Charge | Job | | 181 | | 181 | |

# Rough Frame / Structure

| Rough-in Opening | Unit | Material | Labor | Equip. | Total | Specification |
|---|---|---|---|---|---|---|
| **12' Wide** | | | | | | |
| Demolish | Ea. | | 9.90 | | 9.90 | Includes material and labor to install |
| Install | Ea. | 78 | 12.05 | | 90.05 | header, double studs each side, |
| Demolish and Install | Ea. | 78 | 21.95 | | 99.95 | cripples, blocking and nails, up to 12' |
| Reinstall | Ea. | | 9.64 | | 9.64 | opening in 2" x 6" stud wall 8' high. |
| Minimum Charge | Job | | 181 | | 181 | |

| Rough-in Opening | Unit | Material | Labor | Equip. | Total | Specification |
|---|---|---|---|---|---|---|
| **Window w / 2" x 4" Lumber** | | | | | | |
| **2' Wide** | | | | | | |
| Demolish | Ea. | | 12.35 | | 12.35 | Includes material and labor to install |
| Install | Ea. | 17.20 | 15.05 | | 32.25 | header, double studs each side of |
| Demolish and Install | Ea. | 17.20 | 27.40 | | 44.60 | opening, cripples, blocking, nails and |
| Reinstall | Ea. | | 12.05 | | 12.05 | sub-sills for opening up to 2' in a 2" x |
| Minimum Charge | Job | | 181 | | 181 | 4" stud wall 8' high. |
| **3' Wide** | | | | | | |
| Demolish | Ea. | | 12.35 | | 12.35 | Includes material and labor to install |
| Install | Ea. | 20 | 15.05 | | 35.05 | header, double studs each side of |
| Demolish and Install | Ea. | 20 | 27.40 | | 47.40 | opening, cripples, blocking, nails and |
| Reinstall | Ea. | | 12.05 | | 12.05 | sub-sills for opening up to 3' in a 2" x |
| Minimum Charge | Job | | 181 | | 181 | 4" stud wall 8' high. |
| **4' Wide** | | | | | | |
| Demolish | Ea. | | 12.35 | | 12.35 | Includes material and labor to install |
| Install | Ea. | 22 | 15.05 | | 37.05 | header, double studs each side of |
| Demolish and Install | Ea. | 22 | 27.40 | | 49.40 | opening, cripples, blocking, nails and |
| Reinstall | Ea. | | 12.05 | | 12.05 | sub-sills for opening up to 4' in a 2" x |
| Minimum Charge | Job | | 181 | | 181 | 4" stud wall 8' high. |
| **5' Wide** | | | | | | |
| Demolish | Ea. | | 12.35 | | 12.35 | Includes material and labor to install |
| Install | Ea. | 26 | 15.05 | | 41.05 | header, double studs each side of |
| Demolish and Install | Ea. | 26 | 27.40 | | 53.40 | opening, cripples, blocking, nails and |
| Reinstall | Ea. | | 12.05 | | 12.05 | sub-sills for opening up to 5' in a 2" x |
| Minimum Charge | Job | | 181 | | 181 | 4" stud wall 8' high. |
| **6' Wide** | | | | | | |
| Demolish | Ea. | | 12.35 | | 12.35 | Includes material and labor to install |
| Install | Ea. | 28.50 | 15.05 | | 43.55 | header, double studs each side of |
| Demolish and Install | Ea. | 28.50 | 27.40 | | 55.90 | opening, cripples, blocking, nails and |
| Reinstall | Ea. | | 12.05 | | 12.05 | sub-sills for opening up to 6' in a 2" x |
| Minimum Charge | Job | | 181 | | 181 | 4" stud wall 8' high. |
| **7' Wide** | | | | | | |
| Demolish | Ea. | | 12.35 | | 12.35 | Includes material and labor to install |
| Install | Ea. | 36 | 15.05 | | 51.05 | header, double studs each side of |
| Demolish and Install | Ea. | 36 | 27.40 | | 63.40 | opening, cripples, blocking, nails and |
| Reinstall | Ea. | | 12.05 | | 12.05 | sub-sills for opening up to 7' in a 2" x |
| Minimum Charge | Job | | 181 | | 181 | 4" stud wall 8' high. |
| **8' Wide** | | | | | | |
| Demolish | Ea. | | 13.45 | | 13.45 | Includes material and labor to install |
| Install | Ea. | 39 | 16.45 | | 55.45 | header, double studs each side of |
| Demolish and Install | Ea. | 39 | 29.90 | | 68.90 | opening, cripples, blocking, nails and |
| Reinstall | Ea. | | 13.15 | | 13.15 | sub-sills for opening up to 8' in a 2" x |
| Minimum Charge | Job | | 181 | | 181 | 4" stud wall 8' high. |

# Rough Frame / Structure

| Rough-in Opening | | Unit | Material | Labor | Equip. | Total | Specification |
|---|---|---|---|---|---|---|---|
| **10' Wide** | | | | | | | |
| | Demolish | Ea. | | 13.45 | | 13.45 | Includes material and labor to install |
| | Install | Ea. | 49.50 | 16.45 | | 65.95 | header, double studs each side of |
| | Demolish and Install | Ea. | 49.50 | 29.90 | | 79.40 | opening, cripples, blocking, nails and |
| | Reinstall | Ea. | | 13.15 | | 13.15 | sub-sills for opening up to 10' in a 2" |
| | Minimum Charge | Job | | 181 | | 181 | x 4" stud wall 8' high. |
| **12' Wide** | | | | | | | |
| | Demolish | Ea. | | 13.45 | | 13.45 | Includes material and labor to install |
| | Install | Ea. | 82.50 | 16.45 | | 98.95 | header, double studs each side of |
| | Demolish and Install | Ea. | 82.50 | 29.90 | | 112.40 | opening, cripples, blocking, nails and |
| | Reinstall | Ea. | | 13.15 | | 13.15 | sub-sills for opening up to 12' in a 2" |
| | Minimum Charge | Job | | 181 | | 181 | x 4" stud wall 8' high. |

## Window w / 2" x 6" Lumber

| Rough-in Opening | | Unit | Material | Labor | Equip. | Total | Specification |
|---|---|---|---|---|---|---|---|
| **2' Wide** | | | | | | | |
| | Demolish | Ea. | | 12.35 | | 12.35 | Includes material and labor to install |
| | Install | Ea. | 26 | 15.05 | | 41.05 | header, double studs each side of |
| | Demolish and Install | Ea. | 26 | 27.40 | | 53.40 | opening, cripples, blocking, nails and |
| | Reinstall | Ea. | | 12.05 | | 12.05 | sub-sills for opening up to 2' in a 2" x |
| | Minimum Charge | Job | | 181 | | 181 | 6" stud wall 8' high. |
| **3' Wide** | | | | | | | |
| | Demolish | Ea. | | 12.35 | | 12.35 | Includes material and labor to install |
| | Install | Ea. | 29 | 15.05 | | 44.05 | header, double studs each side of |
| | Demolish and Install | Ea. | 29 | 27.40 | | 56.40 | opening, cripples, blocking, nails and |
| | Reinstall | Ea. | | 12.05 | | 12.05 | sub-sills for opening up to 3' in a 2" x |
| | Minimum Charge | Job | | 181 | | 181 | 6" stud wall 8' high. |
| **4' Wide** | | | | | | | |
| | Demolish | Ea. | | 12.35 | | 12.35 | Includes material and labor to install |
| | Install | Ea. | 31.50 | 15.05 | | 46.55 | header, double studs each side of |
| | Demolish and Install | Ea. | 31.50 | 27.40 | | 58.90 | opening, cripples, blocking, nails and |
| | Reinstall | Ea. | | 12.05 | | 12.05 | sub-sills for opening up to 4' in a 2" x |
| | Minimum Charge | Job | | 181 | | 181 | 6" stud wall 8' high. |
| **5' Wide** | | | | | | | |
| | Demolish | Ea. | | 12.35 | | 12.35 | Includes material and labor to install |
| | Install | Ea. | 35 | 15.05 | | 50.05 | header, double studs each side of |
| | Demolish and Install | Ea. | 35 | 27.40 | | 62.40 | opening, cripples, blocking, nails and |
| | Reinstall | Ea. | | 12.05 | | 12.05 | sub-sills for opening up to 5' in a 2" x |
| | Minimum Charge | Job | | 181 | | 181 | 6" stud wall 8' high. |
| **6' Wide** | | | | | | | |
| | Demolish | Ea. | | 12.35 | | 12.35 | Includes material and labor to install |
| | Install | Ea. | 39 | 15.05 | | 54.05 | header, double studs each side of |
| | Demolish and Install | Ea. | 39 | 27.40 | | 66.40 | opening, cripples, blocking, nails and |
| | Reinstall | Ea. | | 12.05 | | 12.05 | sub-sills for opening up to 6' in a 2" x |
| | Minimum Charge | Job | | 181 | | 181 | 6" stud wall 8' high. |
| **7' Wide** | | | | | | | |
| | Demolish | Ea. | | 12.35 | | 12.35 | Includes material and labor to install |
| | Install | Ea. | 47 | 15.05 | | 62.05 | header, double studs each side of |
| | Demolish and Install | Ea. | 47 | 27.40 | | 74.40 | opening, cripples, blocking, nails and |
| | Reinstall | Ea. | | 12.05 | | 12.05 | sub-sills for opening up to 7' in a 2" x |
| | Minimum Charge | Job | | 181 | | 181 | 6" stud wall 8' high. |

# Rough Frame / Structure

## Rough-in Opening

| | Unit | Material | Labor | Equip. | Total | Specification |
|---|---|---|---|---|---|---|
| **8' Wide** | | | | | | |
| Demolish | Ea. | | 13.45 | | 13.45 | Includes material and labor to install |
| Install | Ea. | 50.50 | 16.45 | | 66.95 | header, double studs each side of |
| Demolish and Install | Ea. | 50.50 | 29.90 | | 80.40 | opening, cripples, blocking, nails and |
| Reinstall | Ea. | | 13.15 | | 13.15 | sub-sills for opening up to 8' in a 2" x |
| Minimum Charge | Job | | 181 | | 181 | 6" stud wall 8' high. |
| **10' Wide** | | | | | | |
| Demolish | Ea. | | 13.45 | | 13.45 | Includes material and labor to install |
| Install | Ea. | 62 | 16.45 | | 78.45 | header, double studs each side of |
| Demolish and Install | Ea. | 62 | 29.90 | | 91.90 | opening, cripples, blocking, nails and |
| Reinstall | Ea. | | 13.15 | | 13.15 | sub-sills for opening up to 10' in a 2" |
| Minimum Charge | Job | | 181 | | 181 | x 6" stud wall 8' high. |
| **12' Wide** | | | | | | |
| Demolish | Ea. | | 13.45 | | 13.45 | Includes material and labor to install |
| Install | Ea. | 96.50 | 16.45 | | 112.95 | header, double studs each side of |
| Demolish and Install | Ea. | 96.50 | 29.90 | | 126.40 | opening, cripples, blocking, nails and |
| Reinstall | Ea. | | 13.15 | | 13.15 | sub-sills for opening up to 12' in a 2" |
| Minimum Charge | Job | | 181 | | 181 | x 6" stud wall 8' high. |

## Glue-Laminated Beams

| | Unit | Material | Labor | Equip. | Total | Specification |
|---|---|---|---|---|---|---|
| **3-1/2" x 6"** | | | | | | |
| Demolish | L.F. | | 2.23 | | 2.23 | Includes material and labor to install |
| Install | L.F. | 5.65 | 2.73 | 1.41 | 9.79 | glue-laminated wood beam. |
| Demolish and Install | L.F. | 5.65 | 4.96 | 1.41 | 12.02 | |
| Reinstall | L.F. | | 2.19 | 1.12 | 3.31 | |
| Clean | L.F. | .12 | .33 | | .45 | |
| Paint | L.F. | .32 | .93 | | 1.25 | |
| Minimum Charge | Job | | 181 | | 181 | |
| **3-1/2" x 9"** | | | | | | |
| Demolish | L.F. | | 2.23 | | 2.23 | Includes material and labor to install |
| Install | L.F. | 7.60 | 2.73 | 1.41 | 11.74 | glue-laminated wood beam. |
| Demolish and Install | L.F. | 7.60 | 4.96 | 1.41 | 13.97 | |
| Reinstall | L.F. | | 2.19 | 1.12 | 3.31 | |
| Clean | L.F. | .15 | .34 | | .49 | |
| Paint | L.F. | .41 | 1.20 | | 1.61 | |
| Minimum Charge | Job | | 181 | | 181 | |
| **3-1/2" x 12"** | | | | | | |
| Demolish | L.F. | | 3.34 | | 3.34 | Includes material and labor to install |
| Install | L.F. | 10.05 | 2.73 | 1.41 | 14.19 | glue-laminated wood beam. |
| Demolish and Install | L.F. | 10.05 | 6.07 | 1.41 | 17.53 | |
| Reinstall | L.F. | | 2.19 | 1.12 | 3.31 | |
| Clean | L.F. | .20 | .36 | | .56 | |
| Paint | L.F. | .51 | 1.50 | | 2.01 | |
| Minimum Charge | Job | | 181 | | 181 | |
| **3-1/2" x 15"** | | | | | | |
| Demolish | L.F. | | 3.34 | | 3.34 | Includes material and labor to install |
| Install | L.F. | 12.60 | 2.83 | 1.45 | 16.88 | glue-laminated wood beam. |
| Demolish and Install | L.F. | 12.60 | 6.17 | 1.45 | 20.22 | |
| Reinstall | L.F. | | 2.26 | 1.16 | 3.42 | |
| Clean | L.F. | .23 | .37 | | .60 | |
| Paint | L.F. | .59 | 1.75 | | 2.34 | |
| Minimum Charge | Job | | 181 | | 181 | |

| Glue-Laminated Beams | | Unit | Material | Labor | Equip. | Total | Specification |
|---|---|---|---|---|---|---|---|
| **3-1/2" x 18"** | | | | | | | |
| | Demolish | L.F. | | 4.18 | | 4.18 | Includes material and labor to install |
| | Install | L.F. | 16.95 | 2.83 | 1.45 | 21.23 | glue-laminated wood beam. |
| | Demolish and Install | L.F. | 16.95 | 7.01 | 1.45 | 25.41 | |
| | Reinstall | L.F. | | 2.26 | 1.16 | 3.42 | |
| | Clean | L.F. | .26 | .38 | | .64 | |
| | Paint | L.F. | .70 | 2.03 | | 2.73 | |
| | Minimum Charge | Job | | 181 | | 181 | |
| **5-1/8" x 6"** | | | | | | | |
| | Demolish | L.F. | | 3.34 | | 3.34 | Includes material and labor to install |
| | Install | L.F. | 8.25 | 2.73 | 1.41 | 12.39 | glue-laminated wood beam. |
| | Demolish and Install | L.F. | 8.25 | 6.07 | 1.41 | 15.73 | |
| | Reinstall | L.F. | | 2.19 | 1.12 | 3.31 | |
| | Clean | L.F. | .13 | .33 | | .46 | |
| | Paint | L.F. | .34 | 1.02 | | 1.36 | |
| | Minimum Charge | Job | | 181 | | 181 | |
| **5-1/8" x 9"** | | | | | | | |
| | Demolish | L.F. | | 4.18 | | 4.18 | Includes material and labor to install |
| | Install | L.F. | 12.45 | 2.73 | 1.41 | 16.59 | glue-laminated wood beam. |
| | Demolish and Install | L.F. | 12.45 | 6.91 | 1.41 | 20.77 | |
| | Reinstall | L.F. | | 2.19 | 1.12 | 3.31 | |
| | Clean | L.F. | .17 | .34 | | .51 | |
| | Paint | L.F. | .44 | 1.30 | | 1.74 | |
| | Minimum Charge | Job | | 181 | | 181 | |
| **5-1/8" x 12"** | | | | | | | |
| | Demolish | L.F. | | 4.97 | | 4.97 | Includes material and labor to install |
| | Install | L.F. | 16.55 | 2.73 | 1.41 | 20.69 | glue-laminated wood beam. |
| | Demolish and Install | L.F. | 16.55 | 7.70 | 1.41 | 25.66 | |
| | Reinstall | L.F. | | 2.19 | 1.12 | 3.31 | |
| | Clean | L.F. | .21 | .36 | | .57 | |
| | Paint | L.F. | .54 | 1.57 | | 2.11 | |
| | Minimum Charge | Job | | 181 | | 181 | |
| **5-1/8" x 18"** | | | | | | | |
| | Demolish | L.F. | | 8.35 | | 8.35 | Includes material and labor to install |
| | Install | L.F. | 25 | 2.83 | 1.45 | 29.28 | glue-laminated wood beam. |
| | Demolish and Install | L.F. | 25 | 11.18 | 1.45 | 37.63 | |
| | Reinstall | L.F. | | 2.26 | 1.16 | 3.42 | |
| | Clean | L.F. | .28 | .38 | | .66 | |
| | Paint | L.F. | .63 | 2.13 | | 2.76 | |
| | Minimum Charge | Job | | 181 | | 181 | |
| **6-3/4" x 12"** | | | | | | | |
| | Demolish | L.F. | | 4.97 | | 4.97 | Includes material and labor to install |
| | Install | L.F. | 22 | 2.83 | 1.45 | 26.28 | glue-laminated wood beam. |
| | Demolish and Install | L.F. | 22 | 7.80 | 1.45 | 31.25 | |
| | Reinstall | L.F. | | 2.26 | 1.16 | 3.42 | |
| | Clean | L.F. | .23 | .37 | | .60 | |
| | Paint | L.F. | .59 | 1.75 | | 2.34 | |
| | Minimum Charge | Job | | 181 | | 181 | |
| **6-3/4" x 15"** | | | | | | | |
| | Demolish | L.F. | | 8.35 | | 8.35 | Includes material and labor to install |
| | Install | L.F. | 27.50 | 2.83 | 1.45 | 31.78 | glue-laminated wood beam. |
| | Demolish and Install | L.F. | 27.50 | 11.18 | 1.45 | 40.13 | |
| | Reinstall | L.F. | | 2.26 | 1.16 | 3.42 | |
| | Clean | L.F. | .26 | .38 | | .64 | |
| | Paint | L.F. | .70 | 2.03 | | 2.73 | |
| | Minimum Charge | Job | | 181 | | 181 | |

# Rough Frame / Structure

| Glue-Laminated Beams | | Unit | Material | Labor | Equip. | Total | Specification |
|---|---|---|---|---|---|---|---|
| **6-3/4" x 18"** | | | | | | | |
| | Demolish | L.F. | | 8.35 | | 8.35 | Includes material and labor to install |
| | Install | L.F. | 32.50 | 2.93 | 1.51 | 36.94 | glue-laminated wood beam. |
| | Demolish and Install | L.F. | 32.50 | 11.28 | 1.51 | 45.29 | |
| | Reinstall | L.F. | | 2.34 | 1.20 | 3.54 | |
| | Clean | L.F. | .31 | .40 | | .71 | |
| | Paint | L.F. | .79 | 2.31 | | 3.10 | |
| | Minimum Charge | Job | | 181 | | 181 | |
| **Hardware** | | | | | | | |
| **5-1/4" Glue-Lam Seat** | | | | | | | |
| | Install | Ea. | 179 | 2.01 | | 181.01 | Includes labor and material to install |
| | Minimum Charge | Job | | 181 | | 181 | beam hangers. |
| **6-3/4" Glue-Lam Seat** | | | | | | | |
| | Install | Ea. | 184 | 2.01 | | 186.01 | Includes labor and material to install |
| | Minimum Charge | Job | | 181 | | 181 | beam hangers. |
| **Earthquake Strapping** | | | | | | | |
| | Install | Ea. | 2.56 | 2.26 | | 4.82 | Includes labor and material to replace |
| | Minimum Charge | Job | | 181 | | 181 | an earthquake strap. |
| **Hurricane Clips** | | | | | | | |
| | Install | Ea. | .96 | 2.49 | | 3.45 | Includes labor and material to install a |
| | Minimum Charge | Job | | 181 | | 181 | hurricane clip. |

| Metal Stud Framing | | Unit | Material | Labor | Equip. | Total | Specification |
|---|---|---|---|---|---|---|---|
| **16" O.C. System** | | | | | | | |
| **4", 16 Ga.** | | | | | | | |
| | Demolish | S.F. | | 1.09 | | 1.09 | Includes material and labor to install |
| | Install | S.F. | 1.45 | 1.11 | | 2.56 | load bearing cold rolled metal stud |
| | Demolish and Install | S.F. | 1.45 | 2.20 | | 3.65 | walls, to 10' high, including studs, top |
| | Reinstall | S.F. | | .89 | | .89 | and bottom track and screws. |
| | Minimum Charge | Job | | 181 | | 181 | |
| **6", 16 Ga.** | | | | | | | |
| | Demolish | S.F. | | 1.09 | | 1.09 | Includes material and labor to install |
| | Install | S.F. | 1.83 | 1.13 | | 2.96 | load bearing cold rolled metal stud |
| | Demolish and Install | S.F. | 1.83 | 2.22 | | 4.05 | walls, to 10' high, including studs, top |
| | Reinstall | S.F. | | .90 | | .90 | and bottom track and screws. |
| | Minimum Charge | Job | | 181 | | 181 | |
| **4", 25 Ga.** | | | | | | | |
| | Demolish | S.F. | | .76 | | .76 | Includes material and labor to install |
| | Install | S.F. | .43 | .76 | | 1.19 | cold rolled metal stud walls, to 10' |
| | Demolish and Install | S.F. | .43 | 1.52 | | 1.95 | high, including studs, top and bottom |
| | Reinstall | S.F. | | .61 | | .61 | track and screws. |
| | Minimum Charge | Job | | 181 | | 181 | |
| **6", 25 Ga.** | | | | | | | |
| | Demolish | S.F. | | .76 | | .76 | Includes material and labor to install |
| | Install | S.F. | .59 | .77 | | 1.36 | cold rolled metal stud walls, to 10' |
| | Demolish and Install | S.F. | .59 | 1.53 | | 2.12 | high, including studs, top and bottom |
| | Reinstall | S.F. | | .62 | | .62 | track and screws. |
| | Minimum Charge | Job | | 181 | | 181 | |
| **24" O.C. System** | | | | | | | |
| **4", 25 Ga.** | | | | | | | |
| | Demolish | S.F. | | .64 | | .64 | Includes material and labor to install |
| | Install | S.F. | .32 | .49 | | .81 | cold rolled metal stud walls, to 10' |
| | Demolish and Install | S.F. | .32 | 1.13 | | 1.45 | high, including studs, top and bottom |
| | Reinstall | S.F. | | .39 | | .39 | track and screws. |
| | Minimum Charge | Job | | 181 | | 181 | |

## Metal Stud Framing

| | Unit | Material | Labor | Equip. | Total | Specification |
|---|---|---|---|---|---|---|
| **6", 25 Ga.** | | | | | | |
| Demolish | S.F. | | .64 | | .64 | Includes material and labor to install |
| Install | S.F. | .44 | .50 | | .94 | cold rolled metal stud walls, to 10' |
| Demolish and Install | S.F. | .44 | 1.14 | | 1.58 | high, including studs, top and bottom |
| Reinstall | S.F. | | .40 | | .40 | track and screws. |
| Minimum Charge | Job | | 181 | | 181 | |
| **4", 16 Ga.** | | | | | | |
| Demolish | L.F. | | 7.35 | | 7.35 | Includes material and labor to install |
| Install | S.F. | 1.06 | .80 | | 1.86 | load bearing cold rolled metal stud |
| Demolish and Install | S.F. | 1.06 | 8.15 | | 9.21 | walls, to 10' high, including studs, top |
| Reinstall | S.F. | | .64 | | .64 | and bottom track and screws. |
| Minimum Charge | Job | | 181 | | 181 | |
| **6", 16 Ga.** | | | | | | |
| Demolish | L.F. | | 7.35 | | 7.35 | Includes material and labor to install |
| Install | S.F. | 1.33 | .82 | | 2.15 | load bearing cold rolled metal stud |
| Demolish and Install | S.F. | 1.33 | 8.17 | | 9.50 | walls, to 10' high, including studs, top |
| Reinstall | S.F. | | .66 | | .66 | and bottom track and screws. |
| Minimum Charge | Job | | 181 | | 181 | |

## Metal Joist

| | Unit | Material | Labor | Equip. | Total | Specification |
|---|---|---|---|---|---|---|
| **Bar Joist** | | | | | | |
| **18K9** | | | | | | |
| Demolish | L.F. | | .88 | .44 | 1.32 | Includes material, labor and |
| Install | L.F. | 8.45 | 1.99 | 1.01 | 11.45 | equipment to install open web joist. |
| Demolish and Install | L.F. | 8.45 | 2.87 | 1.45 | 12.77 | |
| Reinstall | L.F. | | 1.59 | .81 | 2.40 | |
| Minimum Charge | Job | | 1625 | 845 | 2470 | |
| **16K6** | | | | | | |
| Demolish | L.F. | | .88 | .44 | 1.32 | Includes material, labor and |
| Install | L.F. | 5.65 | 1.35 | .11 | 7.11 | equipment to install open web joist. |
| Demolish and Install | L.F. | 5.65 | 2.23 | .55 | 8.43 | |
| Reinstall | L.F. | | 1.08 | .09 | 1.17 | |
| Minimum Charge | Job | | 1625 | 845 | 2470 | |

## Exterior Sheathing

| | Unit | Material | Labor | Equip. | Total | Specification |
|---|---|---|---|---|---|---|
| **CDX Plywood** | | | | | | |
| **5/16"** | | | | | | |
| Demolish | S.F. | | .50 | | .50 | Cost includes material and labor to |
| Install | S.F. | .68 | .45 | | 1.13 | install 5/16" CDX plywood sheathing. |
| Demolish and Install | S.F. | .68 | .95 | | 1.63 | |
| Minimum Charge | Job | | 181 | | 181 | |
| **3/8"** | | | | | | |
| Demolish | S.F. | | .52 | | .52 | Cost includes material and labor to |
| Install | S.F. | .51 | .60 | | 1.11 | install 3/8" CDX plywood sheathing. |
| Demolish and Install | S.F. | .51 | 1.12 | | 1.63 | |
| Minimum Charge | Job | | 181 | | 181 | |
| **1/2"** | | | | | | |
| Demolish | S.F. | | .53 | | .53 | Cost includes material and labor to |
| Install | S.F. | .57 | .64 | | 1.21 | install 1/2" CDX plywood sheathing. |
| Demolish and Install | S.F. | .57 | 1.17 | | 1.74 | |
| Minimum Charge | Job | | 181 | | 181 | |

# Rough Frame / Structure

| Exterior Sheathing | | Unit | Material | Labor | Equip. | Total | Specification |
|---|---|---|---|---|---|---|---|
| **5/8″** | | | | | | | |
| | Demolish | S.F. | | .54 | | .54 | Cost includes material and labor to |
| | Install | S.F. | .75 | .69 | | 1.44 | install 5/8″ CDX plywood sheathing. |
| | Demolish and Install | S.F. | .75 | 1.23 | | 1.98 | |
| | Minimum Charge | Job | | 181 | | 181 | |
| **3/4″** | | | | | | | |
| | Demolish | S.F. | | .55 | | .55 | Cost includes material and labor to |
| | Install | S.F. | .96 | .74 | | 1.70 | install 3/4″ CDX plywood sheathing. |
| | Demolish and Install | S.F. | .96 | 1.29 | | 2.25 | |
| | Minimum Charge | Job | | 181 | | 181 | |
| **OSB** | | | | | | | |
| **1/2″** | | | | | | | |
| | Demolish | S.F. | | .53 | | .53 | Cost includes material and labor to |
| | Install | S.F. | .28 | .27 | | .55 | install 4′ x 8′ x 1/2″ OSB sheathing. |
| | Demolish and Install | S.F. | .28 | .80 | | 1.08 | |
| | Minimum Charge | Job | | 181 | | 181 | |
| **5/8″** | | | | | | | |
| | Demolish | S.F. | | .54 | | .54 | Cost includes material and labor to |
| | Install | S.F. | .43 | .29 | | .72 | install 4′ x 8′ x 5/8″ OSB sheathing. |
| | Demolish and Install | S.F. | .43 | .83 | | 1.26 | |
| | Minimum Charge | Job | | 181 | | 181 | |
| **Vapor Barrier** | | | | | | | |
| **Black Paper** | | | | | | | |
| | Install | S.F. | .04 | .10 | | .14 | Includes material and labor to install |
| | Minimum Charge | Job | | 181 | | 181 | #15 felt building paper. |

| Plywood Sheathing | | Unit | Material | Labor | Equip. | Total | Specification |
|---|---|---|---|---|---|---|---|
| **Finish Plywood** | | | | | | | |
| **5/16″** | | | | | | | |
| | Demolish | S.F. | | .50 | | .50 | Includes material and labor to install |
| | Install | S.F. | .89 | .23 | | 1.12 | exterior 5/16″ AC plywood on walls. |
| | Demolish and Install | S.F. | .89 | .73 | | 1.62 | |
| | Minimum Charge | Job | | 181 | | 181 | |
| **3/8″** | | | | | | | |
| | Demolish | S.F. | | .52 | | .52 | Includes material and labor to install |
| | Install | S.F. | .89 | .30 | | 1.19 | exterior 3/8″ AC plywood on walls. |
| | Demolish and Install | S.F. | .89 | .82 | | 1.71 | |
| | Minimum Charge | Job | | 181 | | 181 | |
| **1/2″** | | | | | | | |
| | Demolish | S.F. | | .53 | | .53 | Includes material and labor to install |
| | Install | S.F. | .99 | .32 | | 1.31 | exterior 1/2″ AC plywood on walls. |
| | Demolish and Install | S.F. | .99 | .85 | | 1.84 | |
| | Minimum Charge | Job | | 181 | | 181 | |
| **5/8″** | | | | | | | |
| | Demolish | S.F. | | .54 | | .54 | Includes material and labor to install |
| | Install | S.F. | 1.20 | .32 | | 1.52 | exterior 5/8″ AC plywood on walls. |
| | Demolish and Install | S.F. | 1.20 | .86 | | 2.06 | |
| | Reinstall | S.F. | | .32 | | .32 | |
| | Minimum Charge | Job | | 181 | | 181 | |
| **3/4″** | | | | | | | |
| | Demolish | S.F. | | .55 | | .55 | Includes material and labor to install |
| | Install | S.F. | 1.22 | .32 | | 1.54 | exterior 3/4″ AC plywood on walls. |
| | Demolish and Install | S.F. | 1.22 | .87 | | 2.09 | |
| | Reinstall | S.F. | | .32 | | .32 | |
| | Minimum Charge | Job | | 181 | | 181 | |

## Stairs

| | Unit | Material | Labor | Equip. | Total | Specification |
|---|---|---|---|---|---|---|
| **Job-built** | | | | | | |
| **Treads and Risers** | | | | | | Includes material and labor to install |
| Demolish | Ea. | | 37 | | 37 | three 2" x 12" stringers, treads and |
| Install | Ea. | 505 | 360 | | 865 | risers of 3/4" CDX plywood, installed |
| Demolish and Install | Ea. | 505 | 397 | | 902 | in a straight or "L" shaped run |
| Clean | Flight | 3.63 | 23 | | 26.63 | including carpet. |
| Paint | Ea. | .09 | 63 | | 63.09 | |
| Minimum Charge | Job | | 181 | | 181 | |
| **Landing** | | | | | | |
| Demolish | S.F. | | .30 | | .30 | Includes material and labor to install |
| Install | S.F. | 60.50 | 2.51 | | 63.01 | landing framing, 3/4" CDX plywood |
| Demolish and Install | S.F. | 60.50 | 2.81 | | 63.31 | surface and carpet. |
| Clean | S.F. | | .33 | | .33 | |
| Paint | S.F. | .31 | .78 | | 1.09 | |
| Minimum Charge | Job | | 181 | | 181 | |

## Ceiling Framing

| | Unit | Material | Labor | Equip. | Total | Specification |
|---|---|---|---|---|---|---|
| **16" O.C. System** | | | | | | |
| **2" x 6" Joists** | | | | | | Cost includes material and labor to |
| Demolish | S.F. | | .46 | | .46 | install 2" x 6" joists including end and |
| Install | S.F. | .46 | .59 | | 1.05 | header joist installed 16" O.C. Does |
| Demolish and Install | S.F. | .46 | 1.05 | | 1.51 | not include beams, ledger strips, |
| Reinstall | S.F. | | .48 | | .48 | blocking or bridging. |
| Minimum Charge | Job | | 181 | | 181 | |
| **2" x 8" Joists** | | | | | | Cost includes material and labor to |
| Demolish | S.F. | | .47 | | .47 | install 2" x 8" joists including end and |
| Install | S.F. | .64 | .73 | | 1.37 | header joist installed 16" O.C. Does |
| Demolish and Install | S.F. | .64 | 1.20 | | 1.84 | not include beams, ledger strips, |
| Reinstall | S.F. | | .59 | | .59 | blocking or bridging. |
| Minimum Charge | Job | | 181 | | 181 | |
| **2" x 10" Joists** | | | | | | Cost includes material and labor to |
| Demolish | S.F. | | .49 | | .49 | install 2" x 10" joists including end |
| Install | S.F. | .86 | .87 | | 1.73 | and header joist installed 16" O.C. |
| Demolish and Install | S.F. | .86 | 1.36 | | 2.22 | Does not include beams, ledger strips, |
| Reinstall | S.F. | | .69 | | .69 | blocking or bridging. |
| Minimum Charge | Job | | 181 | | 181 | |
| **2" x 12" Joists** | | | | | | Cost includes material and labor to |
| Demolish | S.F. | | .50 | | .50 | install 2" x 12" joists including end |
| Install | S.F. | 1.05 | 1.06 | | 2.11 | and header joist installed 16" O.C. |
| Demolish and Install | S.F. | 1.05 | 1.56 | | 2.61 | Does not include beams, ledger strips, |
| Reinstall | S.F. | | .85 | | .85 | blocking or bridging. |
| Minimum Charge | Job | | 181 | | 181 | |
| **Block / Bridge** | | | | | | Includes material and labor to install |
| Demolish | Ea. | | .93 | | .93 | set of cross bridging or per block of |
| Install | Ea. | 1.52 | 2.03 | | 3.55 | solid bridging for 2" x 10" joists cut to |
| Demolish and Install | Ea. | 1.52 | 2.96 | | 4.48 | size on site. |
| Minimum Charge | Job | | 181 | | 181 | |

# Rough Frame / Structure

| Ceiling Framing | Unit | Material | Labor | Equip. | Total | Specification |
|---|---|---|---|---|---|---|
| **24" O.C. System** | | | | | | |
| **2" x 6" Joists** | | | | | | |
| Demolish | S.F. | | .31 | | .31 | Cost includes material and labor to |
| Install | S.F. | .31 | .40 | | .71 | install 2" x 6" joists including end and |
| Demolish and Install | S.F. | .31 | .71 | | 1.02 | header joist installed 24" O.C. Does |
| Reinstall | S.F. | | .32 | | .32 | not include beams, ledger strips, |
| Minimum Charge | Job | | 181 | | 181 | blocking or bridging. |
| **2" x 8" Joists** | | | | | | |
| Demolish | S.F. | | .32 | | .32 | Cost includes material and labor to |
| Install | S.F. | .43 | .49 | | .92 | install 2" x 8" joists including end and |
| Demolish and Install | S.F. | .43 | .81 | | 1.24 | header joist installed 24" O.C. Does |
| Reinstall | S.F. | | .39 | | .39 | not include beams, ledger strips, |
| Minimum Charge | Job | | 181 | | 181 | blocking or bridging. |
| **2" x 10" Joists** | | | | | | |
| Demolish | S.F. | | .33 | | .33 | Cost includes material and labor to |
| Install | S.F. | .58 | .58 | | 1.16 | install 2" x 10" joists including end |
| Demolish and Install | S.F. | .58 | .91 | | 1.49 | and header joist installed 24" O.C. |
| Reinstall | S.F. | | .46 | | .46 | Does not include beams, ledger strips, |
| Minimum Charge | Job | | 181 | | 181 | blocking or bridging. |
| **2" x 12" Joists** | | | | | | |
| Demolish | S.F. | | .34 | | .34 | Cost includes material and labor to |
| Install | S.F. | .69 | .70 | | 1.39 | install 2" x 12" joists including end |
| Demolish and Install | S.F. | .69 | 1.04 | | 1.73 | and header joist installed 24" O.C. |
| Reinstall | S.F. | | .56 | | .56 | Does not include beams, ledger strips, |
| Minimum Charge | Job | | 181 | | 181 | blocking or bridging. |
| **Block / Bridge** | | | | | | |
| Demolish | Ea. | | .93 | | .93 | Includes material and labor to install |
| Install | Ea. | 1.52 | 2.03 | | 3.55 | set of cross bridging or per block of |
| Demolish and Install | Ea. | 1.52 | 2.96 | | 4.48 | solid bridging for 2" x 10" joists cut to |
| Minimum Charge | Job | | 181 | | 181 | size on site. |
| **Ledger Strips** | | | | | | |
| **1" x 2"** | | | | | | |
| Demolish | L.F. | | .25 | | .25 | Cost includes material and labor to |
| Install | L.F. | .13 | 1.05 | | 1.18 | install 1" x 2" ledger strip nailed to the |
| Demolish and Install | L.F. | .13 | 1.30 | | 1.43 | face of studs, beams or joist. |
| Minimum Charge | Job | | 181 | | 181 | |
| **1" x 3"** | | | | | | |
| Demolish | L.F. | | .25 | | .25 | Includes material and labor to install |
| Install | L.F. | .43 | 1.21 | | 1.64 | up to 1" x 4" ledger strip nailed to the |
| Demolish and Install | L.F. | .43 | 1.46 | | 1.89 | face of studs, beams or joist. |
| Minimum Charge | Job | | 181 | | 181 | |
| **1" x 4"** | | | | | | |
| Demolish | L.F. | | .25 | | .25 | Includes material and labor to install |
| Install | L.F. | .43 | 1.21 | | 1.64 | up to 1" x 4" ledger strip nailed to the |
| Demolish and Install | L.F. | .43 | 1.46 | | 1.89 | face of studs, beams or joist. |
| Minimum Charge | Job | | 181 | | 181 | |
| **2" x 2"** | | | | | | |
| Demolish | L.F. | | .27 | | .27 | Cost includes material and labor to |
| Install | L.F. | .36 | 1.10 | | 1.46 | install 2" x 2" ledger strip nailed to the |
| Demolish and Install | L.F. | .36 | 1.37 | | 1.73 | face of studs, beams or joist. |
| Minimum Charge | Job | | 181 | | 181 | |
| **2" x 4"** | | | | | | |
| Demolish | L.F. | | .30 | | .30 | Cost includes material and labor to |
| Install | L.F. | .39 | 1.45 | | 1.84 | install 2" x 4" ledger strip nailed to the |
| Demolish and Install | L.F. | .39 | 1.75 | | 2.14 | face of studs, beams or joist. |
| Reinstall | L.F. | | 1.16 | | 1.16 | |
| Minimum Charge | Job | | 181 | | 181 | |

# Rough Frame / Structure

## Ceiling Framing

| | Unit | Material | Labor | Equip. | Total | Specification |
|---|---|---|---|---|---|---|
| **Ledger Boards** | | | | | | |
| Demolish | L.F. | | .30 | | .30 | Cost includes material and labor to |
| Install | L.F. | 1.91 | 2.01 | | 3.92 | install 2" x 4" ledger board fastened to |
| Demolish and Install | L.F. | 1.91 | 2.31 | | 4.22 | a wall, joists or studs. |
| Reinstall | L.F. | | 1.61 | | 1.61 | |
| Minimum Charge | Job | | 181 | | 181 | |
| **4" x 6"** | | | | | | |
| Demolish | L.F. | | .49 | | .49 | Cost includes material and labor to |
| Install | L.F. | 4.27 | 2.26 | | 6.53 | install 4" x 6" ledger board fastened to |
| Demolish and Install | L.F. | 4.27 | 2.75 | | 7.02 | a wall, joists or studs. |
| Reinstall | L.F. | | 1.81 | | 1.81 | |
| Minimum Charge | Job | | 181 | | 181 | |
| **4" x 8"** | | | | | | |
| Demolish | L.F. | | .66 | | .66 | Cost includes material and labor to |
| Install | L.F. | 6.40 | 2.26 | | 8.66 | install 4" x 8" ledger board fastened to |
| Demolish and Install | L.F. | 6.40 | 2.92 | | 9.32 | a wall, joists or studs. |
| Reinstall | L.F. | | 1.81 | | 1.81 | |
| Minimum Charge | Job | | 181 | | 181 | |
| **Earthquake Strapping** | | | | | | |
| Install | Ea. | 2.56 | 2.26 | | 4.82 | Includes labor and material to replace |
| Minimum Charge | Job | | 181 | | 181 | an earthquake strap. |
| **Hurricane Clips** | | | | | | |
| Install | Ea. | .96 | 2.49 | | 3.45 | Includes labor and material to install a |
| Minimum Charge | Job | | 181 | | 181 | hurricane clip. |

## Roof Framing

| | Unit | Material | Labor | Equip. | Total | Specification |
|---|---|---|---|---|---|---|
| **16" O.C. System** | | | | | | |
| **2" x 4" Rafters** | | | | | | |
| Demolish | S.F. | | .67 | | .67 | Cost includes material and labor to |
| Install | S.F. | .29 | .32 | | .61 | install 2" x 4", 16" O.C. rafter framing |
| Demolish and Install | S.F. | .29 | .99 | | 1.28 | for flat, shed or gable roofs, 25' span, |
| Reinstall | S.F. | | .26 | | .26 | up to 5/12 slope, per S.F. of roof. |
| Minimum Charge | Job | | 181 | | 181 | |
| **2" x 6" Rafters** | | | | | | |
| Demolish | S.F. | | .71 | | .71 | Cost includes material and labor to |
| Install | S.F. | .45 | .34 | | .79 | install 2" x 6", 16" O.C. rafter framing |
| Demolish and Install | S.F. | .45 | 1.05 | | 1.50 | for flat, shed or gable roofs, 25' span, |
| Reinstall | S.F. | | .27 | | .27 | up to 5/12 slope, per S.F. of roof. |
| Minimum Charge | Job | | 181 | | 181 | |
| **2" x 8" Rafters** | | | | | | |
| Demolish | S.F. | | .72 | | .72 | Cost includes material and labor to |
| Install | S.F. | .63 | .36 | | .99 | install 2" x 8", 16" O.C. rafter framing |
| Demolish and Install | S.F. | .63 | 1.08 | | 1.71 | for flat, shed or gable roofs, 25' span, |
| Reinstall | S.F. | | .29 | | .29 | up to 5/12 slope, per S.F. of roof. |
| Minimum Charge | Job | | 181 | | 181 | |
| **2" x 10" Rafters** | | | | | | |
| Demolish | S.F. | | .72 | | .72 | Cost includes material and labor to |
| Install | S.F. | .85 | .55 | | 1.40 | install 2" x 10", 16" O.C. rafter |
| Demolish and Install | S.F. | .85 | 1.27 | | 2.12 | framing for flat, shed or gable roofs, |
| Reinstall | S.F. | | .44 | | .44 | 25' span, up to 5/12 slope, per S.F. |
| Minimum Charge | Job | | 181 | | 181 | of roof. |

# Rough Frame / Structure

| Roof Framing | | Unit | Material | Labor | Equip. | Total | Specification |
|---|---|---|---|---|---|---|---|
| **2" x 12" Rafters** | | | | | | | |
| | Demolish | S.F. | | .73 | | .73 | Cost includes material and labor to |
| | Install | S.F. | 1.02 | .60 | | 1.62 | install 2" x 12", 16" O.C. rafter |
| | Demolish and Install | S.F. | 1.02 | 1.33 | | 2.35 | framing for flat, shed or gable roofs, |
| | Reinstall | S.F. | | .48 | | .48 | 25' span, up to 5/12 slope, per S.F. |
| | Minimum Charge | Job | | 181 | | 181 | of roof. |
| **24" O.C. System** | | | | | | | |
| **2" x 4" Rafters** | | | | | | | |
| | Demolish | S.F. | | .51 | | .51 | Cost includes material and labor to |
| | Install | S.F. | .20 | .24 | | .44 | install 2" x 4", 24" O.C. rafter framing |
| | Demolish and Install | S.F. | .20 | .75 | | .95 | for flat, shed or gable roofs, 25' span, |
| | Reinstall | S.F. | | .19 | | .19 | up to 5/12 slope, per S.F. of roof. |
| | Minimum Charge | Job | | 181 | | 181 | |
| **2" x 6" Rafters** | | | | | | | |
| | Demolish | S.F. | | .53 | | .53 | Cost includes material and labor to |
| | Install | S.F. | .30 | .25 | | .55 | install 2" x 6", 24" O.C. rafter framing |
| | Demolish and Install | S.F. | .30 | .78 | | 1.08 | for flat, shed or gable roofs, 25' span, |
| | Reinstall | S.F. | | .20 | | .20 | up to 5/12 slope, per S.F. of roof. |
| | Minimum Charge | Job | | 181 | | 181 | |
| **2" x 8" Rafters** | | | | | | | |
| | Demolish | S.F. | | .54 | | .54 | Cost includes material and labor to |
| | Install | S.F. | .42 | .27 | | .69 | install 2" x 8", 24" O.C. rafter framing |
| | Demolish and Install | S.F. | .42 | .81 | | 1.23 | for flat, shed or gable roofs, 25' span, |
| | Reinstall | S.F. | | .22 | | .22 | up to 5/12 slope, per S.F. of roof. |
| | Minimum Charge | Job | | 181 | | 181 | |
| **2" x 10" Rafters** | | | | | | | |
| | Demolish | S.F. | | .54 | | .54 | Cost includes material and labor to |
| | Install | S.F. | .57 | .41 | | .98 | install 2" x 10", 24" O.C. rafter |
| | Demolish and Install | S.F. | .57 | .95 | | 1.52 | framing for flat, shed or gable roofs, |
| | Reinstall | S.F. | | .33 | | .33 | 25' span, up to 5/12 slope, per S.F. |
| | Minimum Charge | Job | | 181 | | 181 | of roof. |
| **2" x 12" Rafters** | | | | | | | |
| | Demolish | S.F. | | .55 | | .55 | Cost includes material and labor to |
| | Install | S.F. | .68 | .45 | | 1.13 | install 2" x 12", 24" O.C. rafter |
| | Demolish and Install | S.F. | .68 | 1 | | 1.68 | framing for flat, shed or gable roofs, |
| | Reinstall | S.F. | | .36 | | .36 | 25' span, up to 5/12 slope, per S.F. |
| | Minimum Charge | Job | | 181 | | 181 | of roof. |
| **Rafter** | | | | | | | |
| **2" x 4"** | | | | | | | |
| | Demolish | L.F. | | .69 | | .69 | Cost includes material and labor to |
| | Install | L.F. | .39 | 1.05 | | 1.44 | install 2" x 4" rafters for flat, shed or |
| | Demolish and Install | L.F. | .39 | 1.74 | | 2.13 | gable roofs, up to 5/12 slope, 25' |
| | Reinstall | L.F. | | .84 | | .84 | span, per L.F. |
| | Minimum Charge | Job | | 181 | | 181 | |
| **2" x 6"** | | | | | | | |
| | Demolish | L.F. | | .70 | | .70 | Cost includes material and labor to |
| | Install | L.F. | .61 | .90 | | 1.51 | install 2" x 6" rafters for flat, shed or |
| | Demolish and Install | L.F. | .61 | 1.60 | | 2.21 | gable roofs, up to 5/12 slope, 25' |
| | Reinstall | L.F. | | .72 | | .72 | span, per L.F. |
| | Minimum Charge | Job | | 181 | | 181 | |
| **2" x 8"** | | | | | | | |
| | Demolish | L.F. | | .71 | | .71 | Cost includes material and labor to |
| | Install | L.F. | .84 | .96 | | 1.80 | install 2" x 8" rafters for flat, shed or |
| | Demolish and Install | L.F. | .84 | 1.67 | | 2.51 | gable roofs, up to 5/12 slope, 25' |
| | Reinstall | L.F. | | .77 | | .77 | span, per L.F. |
| | Minimum Charge | Job | | 181 | | 181 | |

| Roof Framing | Unit | Material | Labor | Equip. | Total | Specification |
|---|---|---|---|---|---|---|
| **2″ x 10″** | | | | | | |
| Demolish | L.F. | | .72 | | .72 | Cost includes material and labor to |
| Install | L.F. | 1.13 | 1.46 | | 2.59 | install 2″ x 10″ rafters for flat, shed or |
| Demolish and Install | L.F. | 1.13 | 2.18 | | 3.31 | gable roofs, up to 5/12 slope, 25′ |
| Reinstall | L.F. | | 1.17 | | 1.17 | span, per L.F. |
| Minimum Charge | Job | | 181 | | 181 | |
| **2″ x 12″** | | | | | | |
| Demolish | L.F. | | .73 | | .73 | Cost includes material and labor to |
| Install | L.F. | 1.36 | 1.59 | | 2.95 | install 2″ x 12″ rafters for flat, shed or |
| Demolish and Install | L.F. | 1.36 | 2.32 | | 3.68 | gable roofs, up to 5/12 slope, 25′ |
| Reinstall | L.F. | | 1.27 | | 1.27 | span, per L.F. |
| Minimum Charge | Job | | 181 | | 181 | |
| **2″ x 4″ Valley / Jack** | | | | | | |
| Demolish | L.F. | | .69 | | .69 | Includes material and labor to install |
| Install | L.F. | .61 | 1.52 | | 2.13 | up to 2″ x 6″ valley/jack rafters for |
| Demolish and Install | L.F. | .61 | 2.21 | | 2.82 | flat, shed or gable roofs, up to 5/12 |
| Reinstall | L.F. | | 1.22 | | 1.22 | slope, 25′ span, per L.F. |
| Minimum Charge | Job | | 181 | | 181 | |
| **2″ x 6″ Valley / Jack** | | | | | | |
| Demolish | L.F. | | .70 | | .70 | Includes material and labor to install |
| Install | L.F. | .61 | 1.52 | | 2.13 | up to 2″ x 6″ valley/jack rafters for |
| Demolish and Install | L.F. | .61 | 2.22 | | 2.83 | flat, shed or gable roofs, up to 5/12 |
| Reinstall | L.F. | | 1.22 | | 1.22 | slope, 25′ span, per L.F. |
| Minimum Charge | Job | | 181 | | 181 | |
| **Ridgeboard** | | | | | | |
| **2″ x 4″** | | | | | | |
| Demolish | L.F. | | .66 | | .66 | Cost includes material and labor to |
| Install | L.F. | .39 | .66 | | 1.05 | install 2″ x 4″ ridgeboard for flat, shed |
| Demolish and Install | L.F. | .39 | 1.32 | | 1.71 | or gable roofs, up to 5/12 slope, 25′ |
| Reinstall | L.F. | | .53 | | .53 | span, per L.F. |
| Minimum Charge | Job | | 181 | | 181 | |
| **2″ x 6″** | | | | | | |
| Demolish | L.F. | | .68 | | .68 | Cost includes material and labor to |
| Install | L.F. | .61 | 1.45 | | 2.06 | install 2″ x 6″ ridgeboard for flat, shed |
| Demolish and Install | L.F. | .61 | 2.13 | | 2.74 | or gable roofs, up to 5/12 slope, 25′ |
| Reinstall | L.F. | | 1.16 | | 1.16 | span, per L.F. |
| Minimum Charge | Job | | 181 | | 181 | |
| **2″ x 8″** | | | | | | |
| Demolish | L.F. | | .70 | | .70 | Cost includes material and labor to |
| Install | L.F. | .84 | 1.61 | | 2.45 | install 2″ x 8″ ridgeboard for flat, shed |
| Demolish and Install | L.F. | .84 | 2.31 | | 3.15 | or gable roofs, up to 5/12 slope, 25′ |
| Reinstall | L.F. | | 1.29 | | 1.29 | span, per L.F. |
| Minimum Charge | Job | | 181 | | 181 | |
| **2″ x 10″** | | | | | | |
| Demolish | L.F. | | .72 | | .72 | Cost includes material and labor to |
| Install | L.F. | 1.13 | 1.81 | | 2.94 | install 2″ x 10″ ridgeboard for flat, |
| Demolish and Install | L.F. | 1.13 | 2.53 | | 3.66 | shed or gable roofs, up to 5/12 |
| Reinstall | L.F. | | 1.45 | | 1.45 | slope, 25′ span, per L.F. |
| Minimum Charge | Job | | 181 | | 181 | |
| **2″ x 12″** | | | | | | |
| Demolish | L.F. | | .74 | | .74 | Cost includes material and labor to |
| Install | L.F. | 1.36 | 1.03 | | 2.39 | install 2″ x 12″ ridgeboard for flat, |
| Demolish and Install | L.F. | 1.36 | 1.77 | | 3.13 | shed or gable roofs, up to 5/12 |
| Reinstall | L.F. | | .83 | | .83 | slope, 25′ span, per L.F. |
| Minimum Charge | Job | | 181 | | 181 | |

# Rough Frame / Structure

| Roof Framing | | Unit | Material | Labor | Equip. | Total | Specification |
|---|---|---|---|---|---|---|---|
| **Collar Beam** | | | | | | | |
| **1" x 6"** | | | | | | | |
| | Demolish | L.F. | | .52 | | .52 | Cost includes material and labor to |
| | Install | L.F. | .69 | .45 | | 1.14 | install 1" x 6" collar beam or tie for |
| | Demolish and Install | L.F. | .69 | .97 | | 1.66 | roof framing. |
| | Reinstall | L.F. | | .36 | | .36 | |
| | Minimum Charge | Job | | 181 | | 181 | |
| **2" x 6"** | | | | | | | |
| | Demolish | L.F. | | .61 | | .61 | Cost includes material and labor to |
| | Install | L.F. | .61 | .45 | | 1.06 | install 2" x 6" collar beam or tie for |
| | Demolish and Install | L.F. | .61 | 1.06 | | 1.67 | roof framing. |
| | Reinstall | L.F. | | .36 | | .36 | |
| | Minimum Charge | Job | | 181 | | 181 | |
| **Purlins** | | | | | | | |
| | Demolish | L.F. | | .59 | | .59 | Cost includes material and labor to |
| | Install | L.F. | .61 | .40 | | 1.01 | install 2" x 6" purlins below roof |
| | Demolish and Install | L.F. | .61 | .99 | | 1.60 | rafters. |
| | Reinstall | L.F. | | .32 | | .32 | |
| | Minimum Charge | Job | | 181 | | 181 | |
| **2" x 8"** | | | | | | | |
| | Demolish | L.F. | | .60 | | .60 | Cost includes material and labor to |
| | Install | L.F. | .84 | .41 | | 1.25 | install 2" x 8" purlins below roof |
| | Demolish and Install | L.F. | .84 | 1.01 | | 1.85 | rafters. |
| | Reinstall | L.F. | | .33 | | .33 | |
| | Minimum Charge | Job | | 181 | | 181 | |
| **2" x 10"** | | | | | | | |
| | Demolish | L.F. | | .60 | | .60 | Cost includes material and labor to |
| | Install | L.F. | 1.13 | .41 | | 1.54 | install 2" x 10" purlins below roof |
| | Demolish and Install | L.F. | 1.13 | 1.01 | | 2.14 | rafters. |
| | Reinstall | L.F. | | .33 | | .33 | |
| | Minimum Charge | Job | | 181 | | 181 | |
| **2" x 12"** | | | | | | | |
| | Demolish | L.F. | | .61 | | .61 | Cost includes material and labor to |
| | Install | L.F. | 1.36 | .42 | | 1.78 | install 2" x 12" purlins below roof |
| | Demolish and Install | L.F. | 1.36 | 1.03 | | 2.39 | rafters. |
| | Reinstall | L.F. | | .33 | | .33 | |
| | Minimum Charge | Job | | 181 | | 181 | |
| **4" x 6"** | | | | | | | |
| | Demolish | L.F. | | .61 | | .61 | Cost includes material and labor to |
| | Install | L.F. | 2.61 | .42 | | 3.03 | install 4" x 6" purlins below roof |
| | Demolish and Install | L.F. | 2.61 | 1.03 | | 3.64 | rafters. |
| | Reinstall | L.F. | | .33 | | .33 | |
| | Minimum Charge | Job | | 181 | | 181 | |
| **4" x 8"** | | | | | | | |
| | Demolish | L.F. | | .62 | | .62 | Cost includes material and labor to |
| | Install | L.F. | 4.71 | .43 | | 5.14 | install 4" x 8" purlins below roof |
| | Demolish and Install | L.F. | 4.71 | 1.05 | | 5.76 | rafters. |
| | Reinstall | L.F. | | .34 | | .34 | |
| | Minimum Charge | Job | | 181 | | 181 | |
| **Ledger Board** | | | | | | | |
| **2" x 6"** | | | | | | | |
| | Demolish | L.F. | | .30 | | .30 | Cost includes material and labor to |
| | Install | L.F. | .61 | 1.63 | | 2.24 | install 2" x 6" ledger board nailed to |
| | Demolish and Install | L.F. | .61 | 1.93 | | 2.54 | the face of a rafter. |
| | Reinstall | L.F. | | 1.30 | | 1.30 | |
| | Minimum Charge | Job | | 181 | | 181 | |

| Roof Framing | | Unit | Material | Labor | Equip. | Total | Specification |
|---|---|---|---|---|---|---|---|
| **4" x 6"** | | | | | | | |
| | Demolish | L.F. | | .49 | | .49 | Cost includes material and labor to |
| | Install | L.F. | 2.61 | 2.39 | | 5 | install 4" x 6" ledger board nailed to |
| | Demolish and Install | L.F. | 2.61 | 2.88 | | 5.49 | the face of a rafter. |
| | Reinstall | L.F. | | 1.92 | | 1.92 | |
| | Minimum Charge | Job | | 181 | | 181 | |
| **4" x 8"** | | | | | | | |
| | Demolish | L.F. | | .66 | | .66 | Cost includes material and labor to |
| | Install | L.F. | 4.71 | 2.76 | | 7.47 | install 4" x 8" ledger board nailed to |
| | Demolish and Install | L.F. | 4.71 | 3.42 | | 8.13 | the face of a rafter. |
| | Reinstall | L.F. | | 2.21 | | 2.21 | |
| | Minimum Charge | Job | | 181 | | 181 | |
| **Outriggers** | | | | | | | |
| **2" x 4"** | | | | | | | |
| | Demolish | L.F. | | .20 | | .20 | Cost includes material and labor to |
| | Install | L.F. | .39 | 1.45 | | 1.84 | install 2" x 4" outrigger rafters for flat, |
| | Demolish and Install | L.F. | .39 | 1.65 | | 2.04 | shed or gabled roofs, up to 5/12 |
| | Reinstall | L.F. | | 1.16 | | 1.16 | slope, per L.F. |
| | Minimum Charge | Job | | 181 | | 181 | |
| **2" x 6"** | | | | | | | |
| | Demolish | L.F. | | .31 | | .31 | Cost includes material and labor to |
| | Install | L.F. | .61 | 1.45 | | 2.06 | install 2" x 6" outrigger rafters for flat, |
| | Demolish and Install | L.F. | .61 | 1.76 | | 2.37 | shed or gabled roofs, up to 5/12 |
| | Reinstall | L.F. | | 1.16 | | 1.16 | slope, per L.F. |
| | Minimum Charge | Job | | 181 | | 181 | |
| **Lookout Rafter** | | | | | | | |
| **2" x 4"** | | | | | | | |
| | Demolish | L.F. | | .69 | | .69 | Cost includes material and labor to |
| | Install | L.F. | .39 | .60 | | .99 | install 2" x 4" lookout rafters for flat, |
| | Demolish and Install | L.F. | .39 | 1.29 | | 1.68 | shed or gabled roofs, up to 5/12 |
| | Reinstall | L.F. | | .48 | | .48 | slope, per L.F. |
| | Minimum Charge | Job | | 181 | | 181 | |
| **2" x 6"** | | | | | | | |
| | Demolish | L.F. | | .70 | | .70 | Cost includes material and labor to |
| | Install | L.F. | .61 | .61 | | 1.22 | install 2" x 6" lookout rafters for flat, |
| | Demolish and Install | L.F. | .61 | 1.31 | | 1.92 | shed or gabled roofs, up to 5/12 |
| | Reinstall | L.F. | | .49 | | .49 | slope, per L.F. |
| | Minimum Charge | Job | | 181 | | 181 | |
| **Fly Rafter** | | | | | | | |
| **2" x 4"** | | | | | | | |
| | Demolish | L.F. | | .69 | | .69 | Cost includes material and labor to |
| | Install | L.F. | .39 | .60 | | .99 | install 2" x 4" fly rafters for flat, shed |
| | Demolish and Install | L.F. | .39 | 1.29 | | 1.68 | or gabled roofs, up to 5/12 slope, |
| | Reinstall | L.F. | | .48 | | .48 | per L.F. |
| | Minimum Charge | Job | | 181 | | 181 | |
| **2" x 6"** | | | | | | | |
| | Demolish | L.F. | | .70 | | .70 | Cost includes material and labor to |
| | Install | L.F. | .61 | .61 | | 1.22 | install 2" x 6" fly rafters for flat, shed |
| | Demolish and Install | L.F. | .61 | 1.31 | | 1.92 | or gabled roofs, up to 5/12 slope, |
| | Reinstall | L.F. | | .49 | | .49 | per L.F. |
| | Minimum Charge | Job | | 181 | | 181 | |

| Residential Trusses | Unit | Material | Labor | Equip. | Total | Specification |
|---|---|---|---|---|---|---|
| **W or Fink Truss** | | | | | | |
| **24' Span** | | | | | | |
| Demolish | Ea. | | 27.50 | 14.20 | 41.70 | Includes material, labor and |
| Install | Ea. | 92.50 | 27 | 14.05 | 133.55 | equipment to install wood gang-nailed |
| Demolish and Install | Ea. | 92.50 | 54.50 | 28.25 | 175.25 | residential truss, up to 24' span. |
| Reinstall | Ea. | | 27.15 | 14.05 | 41.20 | |
| Minimum Charge | Job | | 181 | | 181 | |
| **28' Span** | | | | | | |
| Demolish | Ea. | | 29.50 | 15.10 | 44.60 | Includes material, labor and |
| Install | Ea. | 85.50 | 30.50 | 15.90 | 131.90 | equipment to install wood gang-nailed |
| Demolish and Install | Ea. | 85.50 | 60 | 31 | 176.50 | residential truss, up to 28' span. |
| Reinstall | Ea. | | 30.74 | 15.91 | 46.65 | |
| Minimum Charge | Job | | 181 | | 181 | |
| **32' Span** | | | | | | |
| Demolish | Ea. | | 32.50 | 16.75 | 49.25 | Includes material, labor and |
| Install | Ea. | 123 | 32.50 | 16.85 | 172.35 | equipment to install wood gang-nailed |
| Demolish and Install | Ea. | 123 | 65 | 33.60 | 221.60 | residential truss, up to 32' span. |
| Reinstall | Ea. | | 32.58 | 16.86 | 49.44 | |
| Minimum Charge | Job | | 181 | | 181 | |
| **36' Span** | | | | | | |
| Demolish | Ea. | | 35 | 18 | 53 | Includes material, labor and |
| Install | Ea. | 163 | 35.50 | 18.35 | 216.85 | equipment to install wood gang-nailed |
| Demolish and Install | Ea. | 163 | 70.50 | 36.35 | 269.85 | residential truss, up to 36' span. |
| Reinstall | Ea. | | 35.42 | 18.33 | 53.75 | |
| Minimum Charge | Job | | 181 | | 181 | |
| **Gable End** | | | | | | |
| **24' Span** | | | | | | |
| Demolish | Ea. | | 27.50 | 14.20 | 41.70 | Includes material, labor and |
| Install | Ea. | 129 | 29 | 15.05 | 173.05 | equipment to install wood gang-nailed |
| Demolish and Install | Ea. | 129 | 56.50 | 29.25 | 214.75 | residential gable end truss, up to 24' |
| Reinstall | Ea. | | 29.09 | 15.06 | 44.15 | span. |
| Clean | Ea. | 1.52 | 35.50 | | 37.02 | |
| Paint | Ea. | 3.98 | 42 | | 45.98 | |
| Minimum Charge | Job | | 181 | | 181 | |
| **28' Span** | | | | | | |
| Demolish | Ea. | | 29.50 | 15.10 | 44.60 | Includes material, labor and |
| Install | Ea. | 124 | 34.50 | 17.95 | 176.45 | equipment to install wood gang-nailed |
| Demolish and Install | Ea. | 124 | 64 | 33.05 | 221.05 | residential gable end truss, up to 30' |
| Reinstall | Ea. | | 34.66 | 17.94 | 52.60 | span. |
| Clean | Ea. | 1.58 | 48.50 | | 50.08 | |
| Paint | Ea. | 4.16 | 57 | | 61.16 | |
| Minimum Charge | Job | | 181 | | 181 | |
| **32' Span** | | | | | | |
| Demolish | Ea. | | 32.50 | 16.75 | 49.25 | Includes material, labor and |
| Install | Ea. | 139 | 35.50 | 18.35 | 192.85 | equipment to install wood gang-nailed |
| Demolish and Install | Ea. | 139 | 68 | 35.10 | 242.10 | residential gable end truss, up to 32' |
| Reinstall | Ea. | | 35.42 | 18.33 | 53.75 | span. |
| Clean | Ea. | 1.65 | 63.50 | | 65.15 | |
| Paint | Ea. | 4.35 | 75 | | 79.35 | |
| Minimum Charge | Job | | 181 | | 181 | |
| **36' Span** | | | | | | |
| Demolish | Ea. | | 35 | 18 | 53 | Includes material, labor and |
| Install | Ea. | 164 | 40.50 | 21 | 225.50 | equipment to install wood gang-nailed |
| Demolish and Install | Ea. | 164 | 75.50 | 39 | 278.50 | residential gable end truss, up to 36' |
| Reinstall | Ea. | | 40.73 | 21.08 | 61.81 | span. |
| Clean | Ea. | 1.73 | 80 | | 81.73 | |
| Paint | Ea. | 4.55 | 94.50 | | 99.05 | |
| Minimum Charge | Job | | 181 | | 181 | |

# Rough Frame / Structure

## Residential Trusses

| Residential Trusses | Unit | Material | Labor | Equip. | Total | Specification |
|---|---|---|---|---|---|---|
| **Truss Hardware** | | | | | | |
| **5-1/4" Glue-Lam Seat** | | | | | | |
| Install | Ea. | 179 | 2.01 | | 181.01 | Includes labor and material to install |
| Minimum Charge | Job | | 181 | | 181 | beam hangers. |
| **6-3/4" Glue-Lam Seat** | | | | | | |
| Install | Ea. | 184 | 2.01 | | 186.01 | Includes labor and material to install |
| Minimum Charge | Job | | 181 | | 181 | beam hangers. |
| **2" x 4" Joist Hanger** | | | | | | |
| Install | Ea. | .63 | 2.07 | | 2.70 | Includes labor and material to install |
| Minimum Charge | Job | | 181 | | 181 | joist and beam hangers. |
| **2" x 12" Joist Hanger** | | | | | | |
| Install | Ea. | 1.08 | 2.19 | | 3.27 | Cost includes labor and material to |
| Minimum Charge | Job | | 181 | | 181 | install 2" x 12" joist hanger. |

## Commercial Trusses

| Commercial Trusses | Unit | Material | Labor | Equip. | Total | Specification |
|---|---|---|---|---|---|---|
| **Engineered Lumber, Truss / Joist** | | | | | | |
| **9-1/2"** | | | | | | |
| Demolish | S.F. | | .49 | | .49 | Includes material and labor to install |
| Install | S.F. | 2 | .36 | | 2.36 | engineered lumber truss / joists per |
| Demolish and Install | S.F. | 2 | .85 | | 2.85 | S.F. of floor area based on joists 16" |
| Reinstall | S.F. | | .29 | | .29 | O.C. Beams, supports and bridging |
| Minimum Charge | Job | | 181 | | 181 | are not included. |
| **11-7/8"** | | | | | | |
| Demolish | S.F. | | .50 | | .50 | Includes material and labor to install |
| Install | S.F. | 2.15 | .37 | | 2.52 | engineered lumber truss / joists per |
| Demolish and Install | S.F. | 2.15 | .87 | | 3.02 | S.F. of floor area based on joists 16" |
| Reinstall | S.F. | | .30 | | .30 | O.C. Beams, supports and bridging |
| Minimum Charge | Job | | 181 | | 181 | are not included. |
| **14"** | | | | | | |
| Demolish | S.F. | | .52 | | .52 | Includes material and labor to install |
| Install | S.F. | 2.54 | .40 | | 2.94 | engineered lumber truss / joists per |
| Demolish and Install | S.F. | 2.54 | .92 | | 3.46 | S.F. of floor area based on joists 16" |
| Reinstall | S.F. | | .32 | | .32 | O.C. Beams, supports and bridging |
| Minimum Charge | Job | | 181 | | 181 | are not included. |
| **16"** | | | | | | |
| Demolish | S.F. | | .54 | | .54 | Includes material and labor to install |
| Install | S.F. | 2.81 | .42 | | 3.23 | engineered lumber truss / joists per |
| Demolish and Install | S.F. | 2.81 | .96 | | 3.77 | S.F. of floor area based on joists 16" |
| Reinstall | S.F. | | .33 | | .33 | O.C. Beams, supports and bridging |
| Minimum Charge | Job | | 181 | | 181 | are not included. |
| **Bowstring Truss** | | | | | | |
| **100' Clear Span** | | | | | | |
| Demolish | SF Flr. | | .50 | .39 | .89 | Includes material, labor and |
| Install | SF Flr. | 7.45 | .41 | .31 | 8.17 | equipment to install bow string truss |
| Demolish and Install | SF Flr. | 7.45 | .91 | .70 | 9.06 | system up to 100' clear span per S.F. |
| Minimum Charge | Job | | 181 | | 181 | of floor area. |
| **120' Clear Span** | | | | | | |
| Demolish | SF Flr. | | .55 | .44 | .99 | Includes material, labor and |
| Install | SF Flr. | 8 | .46 | .34 | 8.80 | equipment to install bow string truss |
| Demolish and Install | SF Flr. | 8 | 1.01 | .78 | 9.79 | system up to 120' clear span per S.F. |
| Minimum Charge | Job | | 181 | | 181 | of floor area. |

| Roof Sheathing | | Unit | Material | Labor | Equip. | Total | Specification |
|---|---|---|---|---|---|---|---|
| **Plywood** | | | | | | | |
| 3/8" | | | | | | | |
| | Demolish | S.F. | | .39 | | .39 | Cost includes material and labor to |
| | Install | S.F. | .51 | .47 | | .98 | install 3/8" CDX plywood roof |
| | Demolish and Install | S.F. | .51 | .86 | | 1.37 | sheathing. |
| | Reinstall | S.F. | | .47 | | .47 | |
| | Minimum Charge | Job | | 181 | | 181 | |
| 1/2" | | | | | | | |
| | Demolish | S.F. | | .39 | | .39 | Cost includes material and labor to |
| | Install | S.F. | .57 | .52 | | 1.09 | install 1/2" CDX plywood roof |
| | Demolish and Install | S.F. | .57 | .91 | | 1.48 | sheathing. |
| | Minimum Charge | Job | | 181 | | 181 | |
| 5/8" | | | | | | | |
| | Demolish | S.F. | | .39 | | .39 | Cost includes material and labor to |
| | Install | S.F. | .75 | .56 | | 1.31 | install 5/8" CDX plywood roof |
| | Demolish and Install | S.F. | .75 | .95 | | 1.70 | sheathing. |
| | Minimum Charge | Job | | 181 | | 181 | |
| 3/4" | | | | | | | |
| | Demolish | S.F. | | .39 | | .39 | Cost includes material and labor to |
| | Install | S.F. | .96 | .60 | | 1.56 | install 3/4" CDX plywood roof |
| | Demolish and Install | S.F. | .96 | .99 | | 1.95 | sheathing. |
| | Minimum Charge | Job | | 181 | | 181 | |
| **OSB** | | | | | | | |
| 1/2" | | | | | | | |
| | Demolish | S.F. | | .39 | | .39 | Cost includes material and labor to |
| | Install | S.F. | .28 | .27 | | .55 | install 4' x 8' x 1/2" OSB sheathing. |
| | Demolish and Install | S.F. | .28 | .66 | | .94 | |
| | Minimum Charge | Job | | 181 | | 181 | |
| 5/8" | | | | | | | |
| | Demolish | S.F. | | .39 | | .39 | Cost includes material and labor to |
| | Install | S.F. | .43 | .29 | | .72 | install 4' x 8' x 5/8" OSB sheathing. |
| | Demolish and Install | S.F. | .43 | .68 | | 1.11 | |
| | Minimum Charge | Job | | 181 | | 181 | |
| **Plank** | | | | | | | |
| | Demolish | S.F. | | .39 | | .39 | Cost includes material and labor to |
| | Install | S.F. | 1.50 | 1 | | 2.50 | install 1" x 6" or 1" x 8" utility T&G |
| | Demolish and Install | S.F. | 1.50 | 1.39 | | 2.89 | board sheathing laid diagonal. |
| | Reinstall | S.F. | | 1 | | 1 | |
| | Minimum Charge | Job | | 181 | | 181 | |
| **Skip-type** | | | | | | | |
| 1" x 4" | | | | | | | |
| | Demolish | S.F. | | .59 | | .59 | Includes material and labor to install |
| | Install | S.F. | .53 | .30 | | .83 | sheathing board material 1" x 4", 7" |
| | Demolish and Install | S.F. | .53 | .89 | | 1.42 | O.C. |
| | Minimum Charge | Job | | 181 | | 181 | |
| 1" x 6" | | | | | | | |
| | Demolish | S.F. | | .59 | | .59 | Includes material and labor to install |
| | Install | S.F. | .69 | .25 | | .94 | sheathing board material 1" x 6", 7" |
| | Demolish and Install | S.F. | .69 | .84 | | 1.53 | or 9" O.C. |
| | Minimum Charge | Job | | 181 | | 181 | |

| Wood Deck | | Unit | Material | Labor | Equip. | Total | Specification |
|---|---|---|---|---|---|---|---|
| **Treated** | | | | | | | |
| | Demolish | S.F. | | 1.24 | | 1.24 | Includes material and labor to install |
| | Install | S.F. | 5.15 | 9.05 | | 14.20 | unfinished deck using 2" x 4" treated |
| | Demolish and Install | S.F. | 5.15 | 10.29 | | 15.44 | decking, with 2" x 6" double beams |
| | Reinstall | S.F. | | 7.23 | | 7.23 | 24" O.C., 4" x 4" posts 5' O.C. set in |
| | Clean | S.F. | .08 | .27 | | .35 | concrete. |
| | Paint | S.F. | .06 | .24 | | .30 | |
| | Minimum Charge | Job | | 181 | | 181 | |
| **Redwood** | | | | | | | |
| | Demolish | S.F. | | 1.24 | | 1.24 | Includes material and labor to install |
| | Install | S.F. | 14.65 | 9.05 | | 23.70 | unfinished deck using 2" x 4" select |
| | Demolish and Install | S.F. | 14.65 | 10.29 | | 24.94 | redwood decking, with 2" x 6" double |
| | Reinstall | S.F. | | 7.23 | | 7.23 | beams 24" O.C., 4" x 4" posts 5' |
| | Clean | S.F. | .08 | .27 | | .35 | O.C. set in concrete. |
| | Paint | S.F. | .06 | .24 | | .30 | |
| | Minimum Charge | Job | | 181 | | 181 | |
| **Cedar** | | | | | | | |
| | Demolish | S.F. | | 1.24 | | 1.24 | Includes material and labor to install |
| | Install | S.F. | 7.75 | 9.05 | | 16.80 | unfinished deck using 2" x 4" select |
| | Demolish and Install | S.F. | 7.75 | 10.29 | | 18.04 | cedar decking, with 2" x 6" double |
| | Reinstall | S.F. | | 7.23 | | 7.23 | beams 24" O.C., 4" x 4" posts 5' |
| | Clean | S.F. | .08 | .27 | | .35 | O.C. set in concrete. |
| | Paint | S.F. | .06 | .24 | | .30 | |
| | Minimum Charge | Job | | 181 | | 181 | |
| **Stairs** | | | | | | | |
| | Demolish | Ea. | | 350 | | 350 | Includes material and labor to install |
| | Install | Ea. | 128 | 630 | | 758 | wood steps. 5 - 7 risers included. |
| | Demolish and Install | Ea. | 128 | 980 | | 1108 | |
| | Reinstall | Ea. | | 504.70 | | 504.70 | |
| | Clean | Flight | 3.63 | 23 | | 26.63 | |
| | Paint | Flight | 11.45 | 42 | | 53.45 | |
| | Minimum Charge | Job | | 181 | | 181 | |
| **Railing** | | | | | | | |
| | Demolish | L.F. | | 4.56 | | 4.56 | Includes material and labor to install |
| | Install | L.F. | 42.50 | 16.45 | | 58.95 | porch rail with balusters. |
| | Demolish and Install | L.F. | 42.50 | 21.01 | | 63.51 | |
| | Clean | L.F. | .73 | 1.67 | | 2.40 | |
| | Paint | L.F. | .63 | 2.62 | | 3.25 | |
| | Minimum Charge | Job | | 181 | | 181 | |
| **Bench Seating** | | | | | | | |
| | Demolish | L.F. | | 4.94 | | 4.94 | Includes material and labor to install |
| | Install | L.F. | 2.42 | 18.10 | | 20.52 | pressure treated bench seating. |
| | Demolish and Install | L.F. | 2.42 | 23.04 | | 25.46 | |
| | Reinstall | L.F. | | 14.46 | | 14.46 | |
| | Clean | L.F. | .14 | 1.33 | | 1.47 | |
| | Paint | L.F. | .57 | 2.52 | | 3.09 | |
| | Minimum Charge | Job | | 181 | | 181 | |
| **Privacy Wall** | | | | | | | |
| | Demolish | SF Flr. | | 1.19 | | 1.19 | Includes material, labor and |
| | Install | SF Flr. | .50 | .61 | .15 | 1.26 | equipment to install privacy wall. |
| | Demolish and Install | SF Flr. | .50 | 1.80 | .15 | 2.45 | |
| | Reinstall | SF Flr. | | .49 | .12 | .61 | |
| | Clean | SF Flr. | .08 | .27 | | .35 | |
| | Paint | S.F. | .06 | .24 | | .30 | |
| | Minimum Charge | Job | | 181 | | 181 | |

| Porch | Unit | Material | Labor | Equip. | Total | Specification |
|---|---|---|---|---|---|---|
| **Treated** | | | | | | |
| Demolish | S.F. | | 2.47 | | 2.47 | Includes material and labor to install |
| Install | S.F. | 6 | 18.10 | | 24.10 | floor and roof frame and decking |
| Demolish and Install | S.F. | 6 | 20.57 | | 26.57 | using 2" x 4" treated decking, with 2" |
| Reinstall | S.F. | | 14.46 | | 14.46 | x 6" double beams 24" O.C., 4" x 4" |
| Clean | S.F. | .14 | .55 | | .69 | posts 5' O.C. set in concrete. |
| Paint | S.F. | .19 | .63 | | .82 | |
| Minimum Charge | Job | | 181 | | 181 | |
| **Redwood** | | | | | | |
| Demolish | S.F. | | 2.47 | | 2.47 | Includes material and labor to install |
| Install | S.F. | 15.70 | 18.10 | | 33.80 | floor and roof frame and decking |
| Demolish and Install | S.F. | 15.70 | 20.57 | | 36.27 | using 2" x 4" redwood decking, with |
| Reinstall | S.F. | | 14.46 | | 14.46 | 2" x 6" double beams 24" O.C., 4" x |
| Clean | S.F. | .14 | .55 | | .69 | 4" posts 5' O.C. set in concrete. |
| Paint | S.F. | .19 | .63 | | .82 | |
| Minimum Charge | Job | | 181 | | 181 | |
| **Cedar** | | | | | | |
| Demolish | S.F. | | 2.47 | | 2.47 | Includes material and labor to install |
| Install | S.F. | 8.80 | 18.10 | | 26.90 | floor and roof frame and cedar |
| Demolish and Install | S.F. | 8.80 | 20.57 | | 29.37 | decking using 2" x 4" select cedar, |
| Reinstall | S.F. | | 14.46 | | 14.46 | with 2" x 6" double beams 24" O.C., |
| Clean | S.F. | .14 | .55 | | .69 | 4" x 4" posts 5' O.C. set in concrete. |
| Paint | S.F. | .19 | .63 | | .82 | |
| Minimum Charge | Job | | 181 | | 181 | |
| **Stairs** | | | | | | |
| Demolish | Ea. | | 350 | | 350 | Includes material and labor to install |
| Install | Ea. | 128 | 630 | | 758 | wood steps. 5 - 7 risers included. |
| Demolish and Install | Ea. | 128 | 980 | | 1108 | |
| Reinstall | Ea. | | 504.70 | | 504.70 | |
| Clean | Flight | 3.63 | 23 | | 26.63 | |
| Paint | Flight | 11.45 | 42 | | 53.45 | |
| Minimum Charge | Job | | 181 | | 181 | |
| **Railing** | | | | | | |
| Demolish | L.F. | | 4.56 | | 4.56 | Includes material and labor to install |
| Install | L.F. | 42.50 | 16.45 | | 58.95 | porch rail with balusters. |
| Demolish and Install | L.F. | 42.50 | 21.01 | | 63.51 | |
| Clean | L.F. | .73 | 2.08 | | 2.81 | |
| Paint | L.F. | .63 | 2.62 | | 3.25 | |
| Minimum Charge | Job | | 181 | | 181 | |
| **Bench Seating** | | | | | | |
| Demolish | L.F. | | 4.94 | | 4.94 | Includes material and labor to install |
| Install | L.F. | 2.42 | 18.10 | | 20.52 | pressure treated bench seating. |
| Demolish and Install | L.F. | 2.42 | 23.04 | | 25.46 | |
| Reinstall | L.F. | | 14.46 | | 14.46 | |
| Clean | L.F. | .14 | 1.33 | | 1.47 | |
| Paint | L.F. | .57 | 2.52 | | 3.09 | |
| Minimum Charge | Job | | 181 | | 181 | |
| **Privacy Wall** | | | | | | |
| Demolish | SF Flr. | | 1.19 | | 1.19 | Includes material, labor and |
| Install | SF Flr. | .50 | .61 | .15 | 1.26 | equipment to install privacy wall. |
| Demolish and Install | SF Flr. | .50 | 1.80 | .15 | 2.45 | |
| Reinstall | SF Flr. | | .49 | .12 | .61 | |
| Clean | SF Flr. | .08 | .27 | | .35 | |
| Paint | S.F. | .06 | .24 | | .30 | |
| Minimum Charge | Job | | 181 | | 181 | |

# Rough Frame / Structure

| Porch | | Unit | Material | Labor | Equip. | Total | Specification |
|---|---|---|---|---|---|---|---|
| **Wood Board Ceiling** | | | | | | | |
| | Demolish | S.F. | | .49 | | .49 | Includes material and labor to install |
| | Install | S.F. | 1.99 | 1.61 | | 3.60 | wood board on ceiling. |
| | Demolish and Install | S.F. | 1.99 | 2.10 | | 4.09 | |
| | Clean | S.F. | .03 | .16 | | .19 | |
| | Paint | S.F. | .17 | .39 | | .56 | |
| | Minimum Charge | Job | | 181 | | 181 | |
| **Re-screen** | | | | | | | |
| | Install | S.F. | 1.17 | 1.45 | | 2.62 | Includes labor and material to |
| | Minimum Charge | Job | | 181 | | 181 | re-screen wood frame. |

# Exterior Trim

**Exterior Trim**

| Exterior Trim | Unit | Material | Labor | Equip. | Total | Specification |
|---|---|---|---|---|---|---|
| **Stock Lumber** | | | | | | |
| **1″ x 2″** | | | | | | |
| Demolish | L.F. | | .25 | | .25 | Cost includes material and labor to |
| Install | L.F. | .35 | 1.10 | | 1.45 | install 1″ x 2″ pine trim. |
| Demolish and Install | L.F. | .35 | 1.35 | | 1.70 | |
| Clean | L.F. | .01 | .18 | | .19 | |
| Paint | L.F. | .02 | .49 | | .51 | |
| Minimum Charge | Job | | 181 | | 181 | |
| **1″ x 3″** | | | | | | |
| Demolish | L.F. | | .25 | | .25 | Cost includes material and labor to |
| Install | L.F. | .19 | 1.21 | | 1.40 | install 1″ x 3″ pine trim. |
| Demolish and Install | L.F. | .19 | 1.46 | | 1.65 | |
| Clean | L.F. | .01 | .18 | | .19 | |
| Paint | L.F. | .02 | .49 | | .51 | |
| Minimum Charge | Job | | 181 | | 181 | |
| **1″ x 4″** | | | | | | |
| Demolish | L.F. | | .25 | | .25 | Cost includes material and labor to |
| Install | L.F. | .73 | 1.45 | | 2.18 | install 1″ x 4″ pine trim. |
| Demolish and Install | L.F. | .73 | 1.70 | | 2.43 | |
| Clean | L.F. | .01 | .18 | | .19 | |
| Paint | L.F. | .02 | .49 | | .51 | |
| Minimum Charge | Job | | 181 | | 181 | |
| **1″ x 6″** | | | | | | |
| Demolish | L.F. | | .25 | | .25 | Cost includes material and labor to |
| Install | L.F. | 1.13 | 1.45 | | 2.58 | install 1″ x 6″ pine trim. |
| Demolish and Install | L.F. | 1.13 | 1.70 | | 2.83 | |
| Clean | L.F. | .02 | .18 | | .20 | |
| Paint | L.F. | .08 | .49 | | .57 | |
| Minimum Charge | Job | | 181 | | 181 | |
| **1″ x 8″** | | | | | | |
| Demolish | L.F. | | .27 | | .27 | Cost includes material and labor to |
| Install | L.F. | 1.51 | 1.81 | | 3.32 | install 1″ x 8″ pine trim. |
| Demolish and Install | L.F. | 1.51 | 2.08 | | 3.59 | |
| Reinstall | L.F. | | 1.45 | | 1.45 | |
| Clean | L.F. | .02 | .19 | | .21 | |
| Paint | L.F. | .08 | .49 | | .57 | |
| Minimum Charge | Job | | 181 | | 181 | |

61

| Exterior Trim | Unit | Material | Labor | Equip. | Total | Specification |
|---|---|---|---|---|---|---|
| **1" x 10"** | | | | | | |
| Demolish | L.F. | | .41 | | .41 | Cost includes material and labor to |
| Install | L.F. | 1.96 | 2.01 | | 3.97 | install 1" x 10" pine trim. |
| Demolish and Install | L.F. | 1.96 | 2.42 | | 4.38 | |
| Minimum Charge | Job | | 181 | | 181 | |
| **1" x 12"** | | | | | | |
| Demolish | L.F. | | .41 | | .41 | Cost includes material and labor to |
| Install | L.F. | 2.54 | 2.01 | | 4.55 | install 1" x 12" pine trim. |
| Demolish and Install | L.F. | 2.54 | 2.42 | | 4.96 | |
| Minimum Charge | Job | | 181 | | 181 | |

| Fascia | Unit | Material | Labor | Equip. | Total | Specification |
|---|---|---|---|---|---|---|
| **Aluminum** | | | | | | |
| Demolish | L.F. | | .52 | | .52 | Includes material and labor to install |
| Install | S.F. | 1.55 | 1.72 | | 3.27 | aluminum fascia. |
| Demolish and Install | S.F. | 1.55 | 2.24 | | 3.79 | |
| Reinstall | S.F. | | 1.38 | | 1.38 | |
| Clean | L.F. | | .33 | | .33 | |
| Minimum Charge | Job | | 181 | | 181 | |
| **Vinyl** | | | | | | |
| Demolish | L.F. | | .52 | | .52 | Cost includes material and labor to |
| Install | L.F. | 3.33 | 2.07 | | 5.40 | install 6" vinyl fascia with 12" vinyl |
| Demolish and Install | L.F. | 3.33 | 2.59 | | 5.92 | soffit and J-channel. |
| Reinstall | L.F. | | 1.65 | | 1.65 | |
| Clean | L.F. | | .33 | | .33 | |
| Minimum Charge | Job | | 181 | | 181 | |
| **Plywood** | | | | | | |
| Demolish | L.F. | | .51 | | .51 | Cost includes material and labor to |
| Install | L.F. | 1.21 | .80 | | 2.01 | install 12" wide plywood fascia. |
| Demolish and Install | L.F. | 1.21 | 1.31 | | 2.52 | |
| Reinstall | L.F. | | .64 | | .64 | |
| Clean | L.F. | .04 | .22 | | .26 | |
| Paint | L.F. | .15 | .79 | | .94 | |
| Minimum Charge | Job | | 181 | | 181 | |
| **Cedar** | | | | | | |
| Demolish | L.F. | | .51 | | .51 | Cost includes material and labor to |
| Install | L.F. | 2.35 | .80 | | 3.15 | install 12" wide cedar fascia. |
| Demolish and Install | L.F. | 2.35 | 1.31 | | 3.66 | |
| Reinstall | L.F. | | .64 | | .64 | |
| Clean | L.F. | .04 | .22 | | .26 | |
| Paint | L.F. | .15 | .79 | | .94 | |
| Minimum Charge | Job | | 181 | | 181 | |
| **Redwood** | | | | | | |
| **1" x 6"** | | | | | | |
| Demolish | L.F. | | .40 | | .40 | Cost includes material and labor to |
| Install | L.F. | 2.71 | 1.45 | | 4.16 | install 1" x 6" redwood fascia board. |
| Demolish and Install | L.F. | 2.71 | 1.85 | | 4.56 | |
| Reinstall | L.F. | | 1.16 | | 1.16 | |
| Minimum Charge | Job | | 181 | | 181 | |
| **1" x 8"** | | | | | | |
| Demolish | L.F. | | .45 | | .45 | Cost includes material and labor to |
| Install | L.F. | 3.61 | 1.61 | | 5.22 | install 1" x 8" redwood fascia board. |
| Demolish and Install | L.F. | 3.61 | 2.06 | | 5.67 | |
| Reinstall | L.F. | | 1.29 | | 1.29 | |
| Minimum Charge | Job | | 181 | | 181 | |

# Exterior Trim

| Fascia | | Unit | Material | Labor | Equip. | Total | Specification |
|---|---|---|---|---|---|---|---|
| **2″ x 6″** | | | | | | | |
| | Demolish | L.F. | | .40 | | .40 | Cost includes material and labor to |
| | Install | L.F. | 2.18 | 1.61 | | 3.79 | install 2″ x 6″ redwood fascia board. |
| | Demolish and Install | L.F. | 2.18 | 2.01 | | 4.19 | |
| | Reinstall | L.F. | | 1.29 | | 1.29 | |
| | Minimum Charge | Job | | 181 | | 181 | |
| **2″ x 8″** | | | | | | | |
| | Demolish | L.F. | | .45 | | .45 | Cost includes material and labor to |
| | Install | L.F. | 2.89 | 1.81 | | 4.70 | install 2″ x 8″ redwood fascia board. |
| | Demolish and Install | L.F. | 2.89 | 2.26 | | 5.15 | |
| | Reinstall | L.F. | | 1.45 | | 1.45 | |
| | Minimum Charge | Job | | 181 | | 181 | |

## Hem-fir Std & Better

| | | Unit | Material | Labor | Equip. | Total | Specification |
|---|---|---|---|---|---|---|---|
| **2″ x 6″** | | | | | | | |
| | Demolish | L.F. | | .40 | | .40 | Cost includes material and labor to |
| | Install | L.F. | .61 | 2.89 | | 3.50 | install 2″ x 6″ hem-fir exterior trim |
| | Demolish and Install | L.F. | .61 | 3.29 | | 3.90 | board. |
| | Reinstall | L.F. | | 2.31 | | 2.31 | |
| | Clean | L.F. | .02 | .22 | | .24 | |
| | Paint | L.F. | .15 | .79 | | .94 | |
| | Minimum Charge | Job | | 181 | | 181 | |
| **2″ x 8″** | | | | | | | |
| | Demolish | L.F. | | .45 | | .45 | Cost includes material and labor to |
| | Install | L.F. | .84 | 3.21 | | 4.05 | install 2″ x 8″ hem-fir exterior trim |
| | Demolish and Install | L.F. | .84 | 3.66 | | 4.50 | board. |
| | Reinstall | L.F. | | 2.57 | | 2.57 | |
| | Clean | L.F. | .03 | .22 | | .25 | |
| | Paint | L.F. | .15 | .79 | | .94 | |
| | Minimum Charge | Job | | 181 | | 181 | |
| **2″ x 10″** | | | | | | | |
| | Demolish | L.F. | | .51 | | .51 | Cost includes material and labor to |
| | Install | L.F. | 1.13 | 4.02 | | 5.15 | install 2″ x 10″ hem-fir exterior trim |
| | Demolish and Install | L.F. | 1.13 | 4.53 | | 5.66 | board. |
| | Reinstall | L.F. | | 3.21 | | 3.21 | |
| | Clean | L.F. | .04 | .24 | | .28 | |
| | Paint | L.F. | .15 | .79 | | .94 | |
| | Minimum Charge | Job | | 181 | | 181 | |

## Barge Rafter

| | | Unit | Material | Labor | Equip. | Total | Specification |
|---|---|---|---|---|---|---|---|
| **2″ x 6″** | | | | | | | |
| | Demolish | L.F. | | .79 | | .79 | Cost includes material and labor to |
| | Install | L.F. | .61 | .40 | | 1.01 | install 2″ x 6″ barge rafters. |
| | Demolish and Install | L.F. | .61 | 1.19 | | 1.80 | |
| | Reinstall | L.F. | | .32 | | .32 | |
| | Clean | L.F. | .02 | .22 | | .24 | |
| | Paint | L.F. | .15 | .79 | | .94 | |
| | Minimum Charge | Job | | 181 | | 181 | |
| **2″ x 8″** | | | | | | | |
| | Demolish | L.F. | | .80 | | .80 | Cost includes material and labor to |
| | Install | L.F. | .84 | .43 | | 1.27 | install 2″ x 8″ barge rafters. |
| | Demolish and Install | L.F. | .84 | 1.23 | | 2.07 | |
| | Reinstall | L.F. | | .34 | | .34 | |
| | Clean | L.F. | .03 | .22 | | .25 | |
| | Paint | L.F. | .15 | .79 | | .94 | |
| | Minimum Charge | Job | | 181 | | 181 | |

# Exterior Trim

## Fascia

| Fascia | | Unit | Material | Labor | Equip. | Total | Specification |
|---|---|---|---|---|---|---|---|
| **2" x 10"** | | | | | | | |
| | Demolish | L.F. | | .82 | | .82 | Cost includes material and labor to |
| | Install | L.F. | 1.13 | .44 | | 1.57 | install 2" x 10" barge rafters. |
| | Demolish and Install | L.F. | 1.13 | 1.26 | | 2.39 | |
| | Reinstall | L.F. | | .35 | | .35 | |
| | Clean | L.F. | .04 | .24 | | .28 | |
| | Paint | L.F. | .15 | .79 | | .94 | |
| | Minimum Charge | Job | | 181 | | 181 | |

## Soffit

| Soffit | | Unit | Material | Labor | Equip. | Total | Specification |
|---|---|---|---|---|---|---|---|
| **Aluminum** | | | | | | | |
| **12" w / Fascia** | | | | | | | |
| | Demolish | L.F. | | .52 | | .52 | Cost includes material and labor to |
| | Install | L.F. | 4.19 | 2.07 | | 6.26 | install 12" aluminum soffit with 6" |
| | Demolish and Install | L.F. | 4.19 | 2.59 | | 6.78 | fascia and J-channel. |
| | Reinstall | L.F. | | 1.65 | | 1.65 | |
| | Clean | L.F. | | .33 | | .33 | |
| | Paint | L.F. | .19 | .79 | | .98 | |
| | Minimum Charge | Job | | 181 | | 181 | |
| **18" w / Fascia** | | | | | | | |
| | Demolish | L.F. | | .52 | | .52 | Cost includes material and labor to |
| | Install | L.F. | 4.96 | 2.41 | | 7.37 | install 18" aluminum soffit with 6" |
| | Demolish and Install | L.F. | 4.96 | 2.93 | | 7.89 | fascia and J-channel. |
| | Reinstall | L.F. | | 1.93 | | 1.93 | |
| | Clean | L.F. | | .33 | | .33 | |
| | Paint | L.F. | .19 | .79 | | .98 | |
| | Minimum Charge | Job | | 181 | | 181 | |
| **24" w / Fascia** | | | | | | | |
| | Demolish | L.F. | | .52 | | .52 | Cost includes material and labor to |
| | Install | L.F. | 5.70 | 2.68 | | 8.38 | install 24" aluminum soffit with 6" |
| | Demolish and Install | L.F. | 5.70 | 3.20 | | 8.90 | fascia and J-channel. |
| | Reinstall | L.F. | | 2.14 | | 2.14 | |
| | Clean | L.F. | | .49 | | .49 | |
| | Paint | L.F. | .19 | .79 | | .98 | |
| | Minimum Charge | Job | | 181 | | 181 | |
| **Vinyl** | | | | | | | |
| | Demolish | L.F. | | .52 | | .52 | Cost includes material and labor to |
| | Install | L.F. | 3.33 | 2.07 | | 5.40 | install 6" vinyl fascia with 12" vinyl |
| | Demolish and Install | L.F. | 3.33 | 2.59 | | 5.92 | soffit and J-channel. |
| | Reinstall | L.F. | | 1.65 | | 1.65 | |
| | Clean | L.F. | | .33 | | .33 | |
| | Paint | L.F. | .19 | .79 | | .98 | |
| | Minimum Charge | Job | | 181 | | 181 | |
| **Plywood** | | | | | | | |
| | Demolish | L.F. | | .57 | | .57 | Cost includes material and labor to |
| | Install | L.F. | 1.21 | 1.03 | | 2.24 | install 12" wide plywood soffit. |
| | Demolish and Install | L.F. | 1.21 | 1.60 | | 2.81 | |
| | Reinstall | L.F. | | .83 | | .83 | |
| | Clean | L.F. | .04 | .22 | | .26 | |
| | Paint | L.F. | .15 | .79 | | .94 | |
| | Minimum Charge | Job | | 181 | | 181 | |

# Exterior Trim

| Soffit | | Unit | Material | Labor | Equip. | Total | Specification |
|---|---|---|---|---|---|---|---|
| **Redwood** | | | | | | | |
| | Demolish | L.F. | | .57 | | .57 | Cost includes material and labor to |
| | Install | L.F. | 5.40 | 1.03 | | 6.43 | install 12" wide redwood soffit. |
| | Demolish and Install | L.F. | 5.40 | 1.60 | | 7 | |
| | Reinstall | L.F. | | .83 | | .83 | |
| | Clean | L.F. | .04 | .22 | | .26 | |
| | Paint | L.F. | .15 | .79 | | .94 | |
| | Minimum Charge | Job | | 181 | | 181 | |
| **Cedar** | | | | | | | |
| | Demolish | L.F. | | .57 | | .57 | Cost includes material and labor to |
| | Install | L.F. | 2.35 | 1.03 | | 3.38 | install 12" wide cedar soffit. |
| | Demolish and Install | L.F. | 2.35 | 1.60 | | 3.95 | |
| | Reinstall | L.F. | | .83 | | .83 | |
| | Clean | L.F. | .04 | .22 | | .26 | |
| | Paint | L.F. | .15 | .79 | | .94 | |
| | Minimum Charge | Job | | 181 | | 181 | |
| **Douglas Fir** | | | | | | | |
| | Demolish | L.F. | | .57 | | .57 | Cost includes material and labor to |
| | Install | L.F. | 2.54 | 1.03 | | 3.57 | install 12" wide Douglas fir soffit. |
| | Demolish and Install | L.F. | 2.54 | 1.60 | | 4.14 | |
| | Reinstall | L.F. | | .83 | | .83 | |
| | Clean | L.F. | .04 | .22 | | .26 | |
| | Paint | L.F. | .15 | .79 | | .94 | |
| | Minimum Charge | Job | | 181 | | 181 | |

# Roofing

Roofing and Flashing

Tile Roofing

| Metal Flashing | Unit | Material | Labor | Equip. | Total | Specification |
|---|---|---|---|---|---|---|
| **Galvanized** | | | | | | |
| **6″** | | | | | | |
| Demolish | L.F. | | .20 | | .20 | Includes material and labor to install |
| Install | L.F. | .59 | .84 | | 1.43 | flat galvanized steel flashing, 6″ wide. |
| Demolish and Install | L.F. | .59 | 1.04 | | 1.63 | |
| Paint | L.F. | .11 | .39 | | .50 | |
| Minimum Charge | Job | | 168 | | 168 | |
| **14″** | | | | | | |
| Demolish | L.F. | | .20 | | .20 | Includes material and labor to install |
| Install | L.F. | 1.39 | .84 | | 2.23 | flat galvanized steel flashing, 14″ |
| Demolish and Install | L.F. | 1.39 | 1.04 | | 2.43 | wide. |
| Paint | L.F. | .11 | .39 | | .50 | |
| Minimum Charge | Job | | 168 | | 168 | |
| **20″** | | | | | | |
| Demolish | L.F. | | .20 | | .20 | Includes material and labor to install |
| Install | L.F. | 1.96 | .84 | | 2.80 | flat galvanized steel flashing, 20″ |
| Demolish and Install | L.F. | 1.96 | 1.04 | | 3 | wide. |
| Paint | L.F. | .11 | .39 | | .50 | |
| Minimum Charge | Job | | 168 | | 168 | |
| **Aluminum** | | | | | | |
| **6″** | | | | | | |
| Demolish | L.F. | | .20 | | .20 | Includes material and labor to install |
| Install | L.F. | .34 | .84 | | 1.18 | flat aluminum flashing, 6″ wide. |
| Demolish and Install | L.F. | .34 | 1.04 | | 1.38 | |
| Paint | L.F. | .11 | .39 | | .50 | |
| Minimum Charge | Job | | 168 | | 168 | |
| **14″** | | | | | | |
| Demolish | L.F. | | .20 | | .20 | Includes material and labor to install |
| Install | L.F. | .58 | .84 | | 1.42 | flat aluminum flashing, 14″ wide. |
| Demolish and Install | L.F. | .58 | 1.04 | | 1.62 | |
| Paint | L.F. | .11 | .39 | | .50 | |
| Minimum Charge | Job | | 168 | | 168 | |
| **20″** | | | | | | |
| Demolish | L.F. | | .20 | | .20 | Includes material and labor to install |
| Install | L.F. | .85 | .84 | | 1.69 | flat aluminum flashing, 20″ wide. |
| Demolish and Install | L.F. | .85 | 1.04 | | 1.89 | |
| Paint | L.F. | .11 | .39 | | .50 | |
| Minimum Charge | Job | | 168 | | 168 | |

| Metal Flashing | Unit | Material | Labor | Equip. | Total | Specification |
|---|---|---|---|---|---|---|
| **Copper** | | | | | | |
| **6"** | | | | | | |
| Demolish | L.F. | | .20 | | .20 | Includes material and labor to install |
| Install | L.F. | 3.37 | 1.12 | | 4.49 | flat copper flashing, 6" wide. |
| Demolish and Install | L.F. | 3.37 | 1.32 | | 4.69 | |
| Minimum Charge | Job | | 201 | | 201 | |
| **14"** | | | | | | |
| Demolish | L.F. | | .20 | | .20 | Includes material and labor to install |
| Install | L.F. | 7.85 | 1.12 | | 8.97 | flat copper flashing, 14" wide. |
| Demolish and Install | L.F. | 7.85 | 1.32 | | 9.17 | |
| Minimum Charge | Job | | 201 | | 201 | |
| **18"** | | | | | | |
| Demolish | L.F. | | .20 | | .20 | Includes material and labor to install |
| Install | L.F. | 11.20 | 1.12 | | 12.32 | flat copper flashing, 18" wide. |
| Demolish and Install | L.F. | 11.20 | 1.32 | | 12.52 | |
| Minimum Charge | Job | | 201 | | 201 | |
| **Aluminum Valley** | | | | | | |
| Demolish | L.F. | | .20 | | .20 | Includes material and labor to install |
| Install | L.F. | 3.21 | 2.13 | | 5.34 | aluminum valley flashing, .024" thick. |
| Demolish and Install | L.F. | 3.21 | 2.33 | | 5.54 | |
| Paint | L.F. | .11 | .39 | | .50 | |
| Minimum Charge | Job | | 181 | | 181 | |
| **Gravel Stop** | | | | | | |
| Demolish | L.F. | | .18 | | .18 | Includes material and labor to install |
| Install | L.F. | 5.55 | 2.78 | | 8.33 | aluminum gravel stop, .050" thick, 4" |
| Demolish and Install | L.F. | 5.55 | 2.96 | | 8.51 | high, mill finish. |
| Reinstall | L.F. | | 2.22 | | 2.22 | |
| Paint | L.F. | .17 | .39 | | .56 | |
| Minimum Charge | Job | | 181 | | 181 | |
| **Drip Edge** | | | | | | |
| Demolish | L.F. | | .18 | | .18 | Includes material and labor to install |
| Install | L.F. | .46 | .90 | | 1.36 | aluminum drip edge, .016" thick, 5" |
| Demolish and Install | L.F. | .46 | 1.08 | | 1.54 | wide, mill finish. |
| Reinstall | L.F. | | .72 | | .72 | |
| Paint | L.F. | .17 | .39 | | .56 | |
| Minimum Charge | Job | | 181 | | 181 | |
| **End Wall** | | | | | | |
| Demolish | L.F. | | .91 | | .91 | Includes material and labor to install |
| Install | L.F. | 2.06 | 2.13 | | 4.19 | aluminum end wall flashing, .024" |
| Demolish and Install | L.F. | 2.06 | 3.04 | | 5.10 | thick. |
| Minimum Charge | Job | | 181 | | 181 | |
| **Side Wall** | | | | | | |
| Demolish | L.F. | | .18 | | .18 | Includes material and labor to install |
| Install | L.F. | 2.06 | 2.13 | | 4.19 | aluminum side wall flashing, .024" |
| Demolish and Install | L.F. | 2.06 | 2.31 | | 4.37 | thick. |
| Minimum Charge | Job | | 181 | | 181 | |
| **Coping and Wall Cap** | | | | | | |
| Demolish | L.F. | | 1.24 | | 1.24 | Includes material and labor to install |
| Install | L.F. | 2.12 | 2.31 | | 4.43 | aluminum flashing, mill finish, 0.40 |
| Demolish and Install | L.F. | 2.12 | 3.55 | | 5.67 | thick, 12" wide. |
| Clean | L.F. | .09 | .83 | | .92 | |
| Minimum Charge | Job | | 168 | | 168 | |

# Roofing

## Roof Shingles

| Roof Shingles | | Unit | Material | Labor | Equip. | Total | Specification |
|---|---|---|---|---|---|---|---|
| **Underlayment** | | | | | | | |
| 15# | | | | | | | |
| | Demolish | Sq. | | 9.90 | | 9.90 | Includes material and labor to install |
| | Install | Sq. | 4.51 | 5.25 | | 9.76 | #15 felt underlayment. |
| | Demolish and Install | Sq. | 4.51 | 15.15 | | 19.66 | |
| | Minimum Charge | Job | | 168 | | 168 | |
| 30# | | | | | | | |
| | Demolish | Sq. | | 9.90 | | 9.90 | Includes material and labor to install |
| | Install | Sq. | 4.50 | 5.80 | | 10.30 | #30 felt underlayment. |
| | Demolish and Install | Sq. | 4.50 | 15.70 | | 20.20 | |
| | Minimum Charge | Job | | 168 | | 168 | |
| **Self Adhering** | | | | | | | |
| | Demolish | Sq. | | 24.50 | | 24.50 | Includes material and labor to install |
| | Install | Sq. | 56 | 15.25 | | 71.25 | self adhering ice barrier roofing |
| | Demolish and Install | Sq. | 56 | 39.75 | | 95.75 | underlayment. |
| | Minimum Charge | Job | | 168 | | 168 | |

## Rolled Roofing

| Rolled Roofing | | Unit | Material | Labor | Equip. | Total | Specification |
|---|---|---|---|---|---|---|---|
| **90 lb** | | | | | | | |
| | Demolish | Sq. | | 24.50 | | 24.50 | Cost includes material and labor to |
| | Install | Sq. | 19.85 | 22.50 | | 42.35 | install 90 lb mineral surface rolled |
| | Demolish and Install | Sq. | 19.85 | 47 | | 66.85 | roofing. |
| | Minimum Charge | Job | | 168 | | 168 | |

## Composition Shingles

| Composition Shingles | | Unit | Material | Labor | Equip. | Total | Specification |
|---|---|---|---|---|---|---|---|
| **Fiberglass (3-tab)** | | | | | | | |
| 225 lb, 20 Year | | | | | | | |
| | Demolish | Sq. | | 27 | | 27 | Cost includes material and labor to |
| | Install | Sq. | 40 | 65.50 | | 105.50 | install 225 lb, 20 year fiberglass |
| | Demolish and Install | Sq. | 40 | 92.50 | | 132.50 | shingles. |
| | Minimum Charge | Job | | 168 | | 168 | |
| 300 lb, 25 Year | | | | | | | |
| | Demolish | Sq. | | 27 | | 27 | Cost includes material and labor to |
| | Install | Sq. | 39.50 | 65.50 | | 105 | install 300 lb, 25 year fiberglass |
| | Demolish and Install | Sq. | 39.50 | 92.50 | | 132 | shingles. |
| | Minimum Charge | Job | | 168 | | 168 | |
| **Emergency Repairs** | | | | | | | |
| | Install | Ea. | 81.50 | 168 | | 249.50 | Includes labor and material for |
| | Minimum Charge | Job | | 168 | | 168 | emergency repairs. |
| **Architectural** | | | | | | | |
| Laminated, 25 Year | | | | | | | |
| | Demolish | Sq. | | 27 | | 27 | Cost includes material and labor to |
| | Install | Sq. | 54 | 65.50 | | 119.50 | install 25 year fiberglass roof shingles. |
| | Demolish and Install | Sq. | 54 | 92.50 | | 146.50 | |
| | Minimum Charge | Job | | 168 | | 168 | |
| Laminated, 30 Year | | | | | | | |
| | Demolish | Sq. | | 27 | | 27 | Cost includes material and labor to |
| | Install | Sq. | 55 | 65.50 | | 120.50 | install 30 year fiberglass roof shingles. |
| | Demolish and Install | Sq. | 55 | 92.50 | | 147.50 | |
| | Minimum Charge | Job | | 168 | | 168 | |

# Roofing

| Composition Shingles | | Unit | Material | Labor | Equip. | Total | Specification |
|---|---|---|---|---|---|---|---|
| **Laminated, 40 Year** | | | | | | | |
| | Demolish | Sq. | | 27 | | 27 | Cost includes material and labor to |
| | Install | Sq. | 73.50 | 65.50 | | 139 | install 40 year fiberglass roof shingles. |
| | Demolish and Install | Sq. | 73.50 | 92.50 | | 166 | |
| | Minimum Charge | Job | | 168 | | 168 | |
| **Laminated Shake, 40 Year** | | | | | | | |
| | Demolish | Sq. | | 27 | | 27 | Cost includes material and labor to |
| | Install | Sq. | 90.50 | 87 | | 177.50 | install 40 year fiberglass roof shakes. |
| | Demolish and Install | Sq. | 90.50 | 114 | | 204.50 | |
| | Minimum Charge | Job | | 168 | | 168 | |
| **Emergency Repairs** | | | | | | | |
| | Install | Ea. | 81.50 | 168 | | 249.50 | Includes labor and material for |
| | Minimum Charge | Job | | 168 | | 168 | emergency repairs. |
| **Roof Jack** | | | | | | | |
| | Demolish | Ea. | | 5.40 | | 5.40 | Includes material and labor to install |
| | Install | Ea. | 16.55 | 36.50 | | 53.05 | residential roof jack, w/bird screen, |
| | Demolish and Install | Ea. | 16.55 | 41.90 | | 58.45 | backdraft damper, 3" & 4" dia. round |
| | Paint | Ea. | .06 | 3.94 | | 4 | duct. |
| | Minimum Charge | Job | | 199 | | 199 | |
| **Ridge Vent** | | | | | | | |
| | Demolish | L.F. | | .96 | | .96 | Includes material and labor to install a |
| | Install | L.F. | 2.95 | 2.60 | | 5.55 | mill finish aluminum ridge vent strip. |
| | Demolish and Install | L.F. | 2.95 | 3.56 | | 6.51 | |
| | Minimum Charge | Job | | 181 | | 181 | |
| **Shingle Molding** | | | | | | | |
| **1" x 2"** | | | | | | | |
| | Demolish | L.F. | | .19 | | .19 | Cost includes material and labor to |
| | Install | L.F. | .35 | 1.10 | | 1.45 | install 1" x 2" pine trim. |
| | Demolish and Install | L.F. | .35 | 1.29 | | 1.64 | |
| | Paint | L.F. | .02 | .49 | | .51 | |
| | Minimum Charge | Job | | 181 | | 181 | |
| **1" x 3"** | | | | | | | |
| | Demolish | L.F. | | .19 | | .19 | Cost includes material and labor to |
| | Install | L.F. | .35 | 1.25 | | 1.60 | install 1" x 3" pine trim. |
| | Demolish and Install | L.F. | .35 | 1.44 | | 1.79 | |
| | Paint | L.F. | .02 | .49 | | .51 | |
| | Minimum Charge | Job | | 181 | | 181 | |
| **1" x 4"** | | | | | | | |
| | Demolish | L.F. | | .19 | | .19 | Cost includes material and labor to |
| | Install | L.F. | .73 | 1.45 | | 2.18 | install 1" x 4" pine trim. |
| | Demolish and Install | L.F. | .73 | 1.64 | | 2.37 | |
| | Paint | L.F. | .02 | .49 | | .51 | |
| | Minimum Charge | Job | | 181 | | 181 | |
| **Add for Steep Pitch** | | | | | | | |
| | Install | Sq. | | 21 | | 21 | Includes labor and material added for 2nd story or steep roofs. |
| **Add for Additional Story** | | | | | | | |
| | Install | Sq. | | 21 | | 21 | Includes labor and material added for 2nd story or steep roofs. |

| Wood Shingles | Unit | Material | Labor | Equip. | Total | Specification |
|---|---|---|---|---|---|---|
| **Cedar Wood Shingles** | | | | | | |
| **16″ Red Label (#2)** | | | | | | |
| Demolish | Sq. | | 66 | | 66 | Includes material and labor to install |
| Install | Sq. | 171 | 145 | | 316 | wood shingles/shakes. |
| Demolish and Install | Sq. | 171 | 211 | | 382 | |
| Minimum Charge | Job | | 181 | | 181 | |
| **16″ Blue Label (#1)** | | | | | | |
| Demolish | Sq. | | 66 | | 66 | Includes material and labor to install |
| Install | Sq. | 254 | 111 | | 365 | wood shingles/shakes. |
| Demolish and Install | Sq. | 254 | 177 | | 431 | |
| Minimum Charge | Job | | 181 | | 181 | |
| **18″ Red Label (#2)** | | | | | | |
| Demolish | Sq. | | 66 | | 66 | Includes material and labor to install |
| Install | Sq. | 350 | 92.50 | | 442.50 | wood shingles/shakes. |
| Demolish and Install | Sq. | 350 | 158.50 | | 508.50 | |
| Minimum Charge | Job | | 181 | | 181 | |
| **18″ Blue Label (#1)** | | | | | | |
| Demolish | Sq. | | 66 | | 66 | Includes material and labor to install |
| Install | Sq. | 293 | 101 | | 394 | wood shingles/shakes. |
| Demolish and Install | Sq. | 293 | 167 | | 460 | |
| Minimum Charge | Job | | 181 | | 181 | |
| **Replace Shingle** | | | | | | |
| Install | Ea. | 16.50 | 9.05 | | 25.55 | Includes labor and material to replace |
| Minimum Charge | Job | | 181 | | 181 | individual wood shingle/shake. Cost is per shingle. |
| **Cedar Shake** | | | | | | |
| **18″ Medium Handsplit** | | | | | | |
| Demolish | Sq. | | 66 | | 66 | Includes material and labor to install |
| Install | Sq. | 211 | 139 | | 350 | wood shingles/shakes. |
| Demolish and Install | Sq. | 211 | 205 | | 416 | |
| Minimum Charge | Job | | 181 | | 181 | |
| **18″ Heavy Handsplit** | | | | | | |
| Demolish | Sq. | | 66 | | 66 | Includes material and labor to install |
| Install | Sq. | 211 | 155 | | 366 | wood shingles/shakes. |
| Demolish and Install | Sq. | 211 | 221 | | 432 | |
| Minimum Charge | Job | | 181 | | 181 | |
| **24″ Heavy Handsplit** | | | | | | |
| Demolish | Sq. | | 66 | | 66 | Includes material and labor to install |
| Install | Sq. | 251 | 124 | | 375 | wood shingles/shakes. |
| Demolish and Install | Sq. | 251 | 190 | | 441 | |
| Minimum Charge | Job | | 181 | | 181 | |
| **24″ Medium Handsplit** | | | | | | |
| Demolish | Sq. | | 66 | | 66 | Includes material and labor to install |
| Install | Sq. | 251 | 111 | | 362 | wood shingles/shakes. |
| Demolish and Install | Sq. | 251 | 177 | | 428 | |
| Minimum Charge | Job | | 181 | | 181 | |
| **24″ Straight Split** | | | | | | |
| Demolish | Sq. | | 66 | | 66 | Includes material and labor to install |
| Install | Sq. | 218 | 164 | | 382 | wood shingles/shakes. |
| Demolish and Install | Sq. | 218 | 230 | | 448 | |
| Minimum Charge | Job | | 181 | | 181 | |
| **24″ Tapersplit** | | | | | | |
| Demolish | Sq. | | 66 | | 66 | Includes material and labor to install |
| Install | Sq. | 218 | 164 | | 382 | wood shingles/shakes. |
| Demolish and Install | Sq. | 218 | 230 | | 448 | |
| Minimum Charge | Job | | 181 | | 181 | |

# Roofing

## Wood Shingles

| Wood Shingles | | Unit | Material | Labor | Equip. | Total | Specification |
|---|---|---|---|---|---|---|---|
| **18″ Straight Split** | | | | | | | |
| | Demolish | Sq. | | 66 | | 66 | Includes material and labor to install |
| | Install | Sq. | 285 | 164 | | 449 | wood shingles/shakes. |
| | Demolish and Install | Sq. | 285 | 230 | | 515 | |
| | Minimum Charge | Job | | 181 | | 181 | |
| **Replace Shingle** | | | | | | | |
| | Install | Ea. | 16.50 | 9.05 | | 25.55 | Includes labor and material to replace |
| | Minimum Charge | Job | | 181 | | 181 | individual wood shingle/shake. Cost is per shingle. |

## Slate Tile Roofing

| Slate Tile Roofing | | Unit | Material | Labor | Equip. | Total | Specification |
|---|---|---|---|---|---|---|---|
| **Unfading Green** | | | | | | | |
| | Demolish | Sq. | | 59.50 | | 59.50 | Includes material and labor to install |
| | Install | Sq. | 495 | 192 | | 687 | clear Vermont slate tile. |
| | Demolish and Install | Sq. | 495 | 251.50 | | 746.50 | |
| | Reinstall | Sq. | | 153.23 | | 153.23 | |
| | Minimum Charge | Job | | 168 | | 168 | |
| **Unfading Purple** | | | | | | | |
| | Demolish | Sq. | | 59.50 | | 59.50 | Includes material and labor to install |
| | Install | Sq. | 445 | 192 | | 637 | clear Vermont slate tile. |
| | Demolish and Install | Sq. | 445 | 251.50 | | 696.50 | |
| | Reinstall | Sq. | | 153.23 | | 153.23 | |
| | Minimum Charge | Job | | 168 | | 168 | |
| **Replace Slate Tiles** | | | | | | | |
| | Install | Ea. | 6.50 | 17.65 | | 24.15 | Includes labor and material to replace |
| | Minimum Charge | Job | | 168 | | 168 | individual slate tiles. Cost is per tile. |
| **Variegated Purple** | | | | | | | |
| | Demolish | Sq. | | 59.50 | | 59.50 | Includes material and labor to install |
| | Install | Sq. | 460 | 192 | | 652 | clear Vermont slate tile. |
| | Demolish and Install | Sq. | 460 | 251.50 | | 711.50 | |
| | Reinstall | Sq. | | 153.23 | | 153.23 | |
| | Minimum Charge | Job | | 168 | | 168 | |
| **Unfading Grey / Black** | | | | | | | |
| | Demolish | Sq. | | 59.50 | | 59.50 | Includes material and labor to install |
| | Install | Sq. | 505 | 192 | | 697 | clear Vermont slate tile. |
| | Demolish and Install | Sq. | 505 | 251.50 | | 756.50 | |
| | Reinstall | Sq. | | 153.23 | | 153.23 | |
| | Minimum Charge | Job | | 168 | | 168 | |
| **Unfading Red** | | | | | | | |
| | Demolish | Sq. | | 59.50 | | 59.50 | Includes material and labor to install |
| | Install | Sq. | 1275 | 192 | | 1467 | clear Vermont slate tile. |
| | Demolish and Install | Sq. | 1275 | 251.50 | | 1526.50 | |
| | Reinstall | Sq. | | 153.23 | | 153.23 | |
| | Minimum Charge | Job | | 168 | | 168 | |
| **Weathering Black** | | | | | | | |
| | Demolish | Sq. | | 59.50 | | 59.50 | Includes material and labor to install |
| | Install | Sq. | 540 | 192 | | 732 | clear Pennsylvania slate tile. |
| | Demolish and Install | Sq. | 540 | 251.50 | | 791.50 | |
| | Reinstall | Sq. | | 153.23 | | 153.23 | |
| | Minimum Charge | Job | | 168 | | 168 | |

# Roofing

## Slate Tile Roofing

| Slate Tile Roofing | Unit | Material | Labor | Equip. | Total | Specification |
|---|---|---|---|---|---|---|
| **Weathering Green** | | | | | | |
| Demolish | Sq. | | 59.50 | | 59.50 | Includes material and labor to install |
| Install | Sq. | 390 | 192 | | 582 | clear Vermont slate tile. |
| Demolish and Install | Sq. | 390 | 251.50 | | 641.50 | |
| Reinstall | Sq. | | 153.23 | | 153.23 | |
| Minimum Charge | Job | | 168 | | 168 | |

## Flat Clay Tile Roofing

| Flat Clay Tile Roofing | Unit | Material | Labor | Equip. | Total | Specification |
|---|---|---|---|---|---|---|
| **Glazed** | | | | | | |
| Demolish | Sq. | | 66 | | 66 | Includes material and labor to install |
| Install | Sq. | 625 | 134 | | 759 | tile roofing. Cost based on terra cotta |
| Demolish and Install | Sq. | 625 | 200 | | 825 | red flat clay tile and includes ridge |
| Reinstall | Sq. | | 107.26 | | 107.26 | and rake tiles. |
| Minimum Charge | Job | | 168 | | 168 | |
| **Terra Cotta Red** | | | | | | |
| Demolish | Sq. | | 66 | | 66 | Includes material and labor to install |
| Install | Sq. | 625 | 134 | | 759 | tile roofing. Cost based on terra cotta |
| Demolish and Install | Sq. | 625 | 200 | | 825 | red flat clay tile and includes ridge |
| Reinstall | Sq. | | 107.26 | | 107.26 | and rake tiles. |
| Minimum Charge | Job | | 168 | | 168 | |

## Mission Tile Roofing

| Mission Tile Roofing | Unit | Material | Labor | Equip. | Total | Specification |
|---|---|---|---|---|---|---|
| **Glazed Red** | | | | | | |
| Demolish | Sq. | | 66 | | 66 | Includes material and labor to install |
| Install | Sq. | 835 | 223 | | 1058 | tile roofing. Cost based on glazed red |
| Demolish and Install | Sq. | 835 | 289 | | 1124 | tile and includes birdstop, ridge and |
| Reinstall | Sq. | | 178.77 | | 178.77 | rake tiles. |
| Minimum Charge | Job | | 168 | | 168 | |
| **Unglazed Red** | | | | | | |
| Demolish | Sq. | | 66 | | 66 | Includes material and labor to install |
| Install | Sq. | 835 | 223 | | 1058 | tile roofing. Cost based on unglazed |
| Demolish and Install | Sq. | 835 | 289 | | 1124 | red tile and includes birdstop, ridge |
| Reinstall | Sq. | | 178.77 | | 178.77 | and rake tiles. |
| Minimum Charge | Job | | 168 | | 168 | |
| **Glazed Blue** | | | | | | |
| Demolish | Sq. | | 66 | | 66 | Includes material and labor to install |
| Install | Sq. | 835 | 223 | | 1058 | tile roofing. Cost based on glazed |
| Demolish and Install | Sq. | 835 | 289 | | 1124 | blue tile and includes birdstop, ridge |
| Reinstall | Sq. | | 178.77 | | 178.77 | and rake tiles. |
| Minimum Charge | Job | | 168 | | 168 | |
| **Glazed White** | | | | | | |
| Demolish | Sq. | | 66 | | 66 | Includes material and labor to install |
| Install | Sq. | 835 | 223 | | 1058 | tile roofing. Cost based on glazed |
| Demolish and Install | Sq. | 835 | 289 | | 1124 | white tile and includes birdstop, ridge |
| Reinstall | Sq. | | 178.77 | | 178.77 | and rake tiles. |
| Minimum Charge | Job | | 168 | | 168 | |
| **Unglazed White** | | | | | | |
| Demolish | Sq. | | 66 | | 66 | Includes material and labor to install |
| Install | Sq. | 835 | 223 | | 1058 | tile roofing. Cost based on unglazed |
| Demolish and Install | Sq. | 835 | 289 | | 1124 | white tile and includes birdstop, ridge |
| Reinstall | Sq. | | 178.77 | | 178.77 | and rake tiles. |
| Minimum Charge | Job | | 168 | | 168 | |

| Mission Tile Roofing | Unit | Material | Labor | Equip. | Total | Specification |
|---|---|---|---|---|---|---|
| **Color Blend** | | | | | | Includes material and labor to install tile roofing. Cost based on color blend tile and includes birdstop, ridge and rake tiles. |
| Demolish | Sq. | | 66 | | 66 | |
| Install | Sq. | 835 | 223 | | 1058 | |
| Demolish and Install | Sq. | 835 | 289 | | 1124 | |
| Reinstall | Sq. | | 178.77 | | 178.77 | |
| Minimum Charge | Job | | 168 | | 168 | |
| **Accessories / Extras** | | | | | | |
| **Add for Cap Furring Strips** | | | | | | Includes labor and material to install vertically placed wood furring strips under cap tiles. |
| Install | Sq. | 98 | 210 | | 308 | |
| **Add for Tile Adhesive** | | | | | | Includes material and labor for adhesive material placed between tiles. |
| Install | Sq. | 16.80 | 12.25 | | 29.05 | |
| **Add for Wire Attachment** | | | | | | Includes labor and material to install single wire anchors for attaching tile. |
| Install | Sq. | 16.55 | 146 | | 162.55 | |
| **Add for Braided Runners** | | | | | | Includes labor and material to install braided wire runners for secure attachment in high wind areas. |
| Install | Sq. | 29.50 | 140 | | 169.50 | |
| **Add for Stainless Steel Nails** | | | | | | Includes material only for stainless steel nails. |
| Install | Sq. | 23 | | | 23 | |
| **Add for Brass Nails** | | | | | | Includes material only for brass nails. |
| Install | Sq. | 31 | | | 31 | |
| **Add for Hurricane Clips** | | | | | | Includes material and labor for Hurricane or wind clips for high wind areas. |
| Install | Sq. | 20 | 197 | | 217 | |
| **Add for Copper Nails** | | | | | | Includes material only for copper nails. |
| Install | Sq. | 31 | | | 31 | |
| **Add for Vertical Furring Strips** | | | | | | Includes labor and material to install vertically placed wood furring strips under tiles. |
| Install | Sq. | 19.30 | 39 | | 58.30 | |
| **Add for Horizontal Furring Strips** | | | | | | Includes labor and material to install horizontally placed wood furring strips under tiles. |
| Install | Sq. | 12.45 | 17.45 | | 29.90 | |

| Spanish Tile Roofing | Unit | Material | Labor | Equip. | Total | Specification |
|---|---|---|---|---|---|---|
| **Glazed Red** | | | | | | Includes material and labor to install tile roofing. Cost based on glazed red tile and includes birdstop, ridge and rake tiles. |
| Demolish | Sq. | | 66 | | 66 | |
| Install | Sq. | 655 | 140 | | 795 | |
| Demolish and Install | Sq. | 655 | 206 | | 861 | |
| Reinstall | Sq. | | 111.73 | | 111.73 | |
| Minimum Charge | Job | | 168 | | 168 | |

# Roofing

| Spanish Tile Roofing | | Unit | Material | Labor | Equip. | Total | Specification |
|---|---|---|---|---|---|---|---|
| **Glazed White** | | | | | | | Includes material and labor to install |
| | Demolish | Sq. | | 66 | | 66 | tile roofing. Cost based on glazed |
| | Install | Sq. | 665 | 140 | | 805 | white tile and includes birdstop, ridge |
| | Demolish and Install | Sq. | 665 | 206 | | 871 | and rake tiles. |
| | Reinstall | Sq. | | 111.73 | | 111.73 | |
| | Minimum Charge | Job | | 168 | | 168 | |
| **Glazed Blue** | | | | | | | Includes material and labor to install |
| | Demolish | Sq. | | 66 | | 66 | tile roofing. Cost based on glazed |
| | Install | Sq. | 665 | 140 | | 805 | blue tile and includes birdstop, ridge |
| | Demolish and Install | Sq. | 665 | 206 | | 871 | and rake tiles. |
| | Reinstall | Sq. | | 111.73 | | 111.73 | |
| | Minimum Charge | Job | | 168 | | 168 | |
| **Unglazed Red** | | | | | | | Includes material and labor to install |
| | Demolish | Sq. | | 66 | | 66 | tile roofing. Cost based on unglazed |
| | Install | Sq. | 665 | 140 | | 805 | red tile and includes birdstop, ridge |
| | Demolish and Install | Sq. | 665 | 206 | | 871 | and rake tiles. |
| | Reinstall | Sq. | | 111.73 | | 111.73 | |
| | Minimum Charge | Job | | 168 | | 168 | |
| **Unglazed White** | | | | | | | Includes material and labor to install |
| | Demolish | Sq. | | 66 | | 66 | tile roofing. Cost based on unglazed |
| | Install | Sq. | 665 | 140 | | 805 | white tile and includes birdstop, ridge |
| | Demolish and Install | Sq. | 665 | 206 | | 871 | and rake tiles. |
| | Reinstall | Sq. | | 111.73 | | 111.73 | |
| | Minimum Charge | Job | | 168 | | 168 | |
| **Color Blend** | | | | | | | Includes material and labor to install |
| | Demolish | Sq. | | 66 | | 66 | tile roofing. Cost based on color blend |
| | Install | Sq. | 665 | 140 | | 805 | tile and includes birdstop, ridge and |
| | Demolish and Install | Sq. | 665 | 206 | | 871 | rake tiles. |
| | Reinstall | Sq. | | 111.73 | | 111.73 | |
| | Minimum Charge | Job | | 168 | | 168 | |
| **Accessories / Extras** | | | | | | | |
| **Add for Vertical Furring Strips** | | | | | | | Includes labor and material to install |
| | Install | Sq. | 19.30 | 39 | | 58.30 | vertically placed wood furring strips under tiles. |
| **Add for Wire Attachment** | | | | | | | Includes labor and material to install |
| | Install | Sq. | 13.80 | 112 | | 125.80 | single wire ties. |
| **Add for Braided Runners** | | | | | | | Includes labor and material to install |
| | Install | Sq. | 24 | 96 | | 120 | braided wire runners for secure attachment in high wind areas. |
| **Add for Stainless Steel Nails** | | | | | | | Includes material only for stainless |
| | Install | Sq. | 19.30 | | | 19.30 | steel nails. |
| **Add for Copper Nails** | | | | | | | |
| | Install | Sq. | 26 | | | 26 | Includes material only for copper nails. |
| **Add for Brass Nails** | | | | | | | |
| | Install | Sq. | 26 | | | 26 | Includes material only for brass nails. |
| **Add for Hurricane Clips** | | | | | | | Includes material and labor to install |
| | Install | Sq. | 15.35 | 116 | | 131.35 | hurricane or wind clips for high wind areas. |

# Roofing

| Spanish Tile Roofing | | Unit | Material | Labor | Equip. | Total | Specification |
|---|---|---|---|---|---|---|---|
| **Add for Mortar Set Tiles** | | | | | | | Includes material and labor to install setting tiles by using mortar material placed between tiles. |
| | Install | Sq. | 48 | 168 | | 216 | |
| **Add for Tile Adhesive** | | | | | | | Includes material and labor for adhesive placed between tiles. |
| | Install | Sq. | 15.55 | 10.90 | | 26.45 | |
| **Add for Cap Furring Strips** | | | | | | | Includes labor and material to install vertically placed wood furring strips under cap tiles. |
| | Install | Sq. | 98 | 210 | | 308 | |
| **Add for Horizontal Furring Strips** | | | | | | | Includes labor and material to install horizontally placed wood furring strips under tiles. |
| | Install | Sq. | 12.45 | 17.45 | | 29.90 | |

| Concrete Tile Roofing | | Unit | Material | Labor | Equip. | Total | Specification |
|---|---|---|---|---|---|---|---|
| **Corrugated Red / Brown** | | | | | | | Includes material and labor to install tile roofing. Cost includes birdstop, booster, ridge and rake tiles. |
| | Demolish | Sq. | | 66 | | 66 | |
| | Install | Sq. | 235 | 248 | | 483 | |
| | Demolish and Install | Sq. | 235 | 314 | | 549 | |
| | Reinstall | Sq. | | 198.64 | | 198.64 | |
| | Minimum Charge | Job | | 168 | | 168 | |
| **Corrugated Gray** | | | | | | | Includes material and labor to install tile roofing. Cost includes birdstop, booster, ridge and rake tiles. |
| | Demolish | Sq. | | 66 | | 66 | |
| | Install | Sq. | 235 | 248 | | 483 | |
| | Demolish and Install | Sq. | 235 | 314 | | 549 | |
| | Reinstall | Sq. | | 198.64 | | 198.64 | |
| | Minimum Charge | Job | | 168 | | 168 | |
| **Corrugated Bright Red** | | | | | | | Includes material and labor to install tile roofing. Cost includes birdstop, booster, ridge and rake tiles. |
| | Demolish | Sq. | | 66 | | 66 | |
| | Install | Sq. | 235 | 248 | | 483 | |
| | Demolish and Install | Sq. | 235 | 314 | | 549 | |
| | Reinstall | Sq. | | 198.64 | | 198.64 | |
| | Minimum Charge | Job | | 168 | | 168 | |
| **Corrugated Black** | | | | | | | Includes material and labor to install tile roofing. Cost includes birdstop, booster, ridge and rake tiles. |
| | Demolish | Sq. | | 66 | | 66 | |
| | Install | Sq. | 235 | 248 | | 483 | |
| | Demolish and Install | Sq. | 235 | 314 | | 549 | |
| | Reinstall | Sq. | | 198.64 | | 198.64 | |
| | Minimum Charge | Job | | 168 | | 168 | |
| **Corrugated Green** | | | | | | | Includes material and labor to install tile roofing. Cost includes birdstop, booster, ridge and rake tiles. |
| | Demolish | Sq. | | 66 | | 66 | |
| | Install | Sq. | 235 | 248 | | 483 | |
| | Demolish and Install | Sq. | 235 | 314 | | 549 | |
| | Reinstall | Sq. | | 198.64 | | 198.64 | |
| | Minimum Charge | Job | | 168 | | 168 | |
| **Corrugated Blue** | | | | | | | Includes material and labor to install tile roofing. Cost includes birdstop, booster, ridge and rake tiles. |
| | Demolish | Sq. | | 66 | | 66 | |
| | Install | Sq. | 235 | 248 | | 483 | |
| | Demolish and Install | Sq. | 235 | 314 | | 549 | |
| | Reinstall | Sq. | | 198.64 | | 198.64 | |
| | Minimum Charge | Job | | 168 | | 168 | |

| Concrete Tile Roofing | | Unit | Material | Labor | Equip. | Total | Specification |
|---|---|---|---|---|---|---|---|
| **Flat Natural Gray** | | | | | | | |
| | Demolish | Sq. | | 66 | | 66 | Includes material and labor to install |
| | Install | Sq. | 228 | 248 | | 476 | tile roofing. Cost includes birdstop, |
| | Demolish and Install | Sq. | 228 | 314 | | 542 | booster, ridge and rake tiles. |
| | Reinstall | Sq. | | 198.64 | | 198.64 | |
| | Minimum Charge | Job | | 168 | | 168 | |
| **Flat Red / Brown** | | | | | | | |
| | Demolish | Sq. | | 66 | | 66 | Includes material and labor to install |
| | Install | Sq. | 228 | 248 | | 476 | tile roofing. Cost includes birdstop, |
| | Demolish and Install | Sq. | 228 | 314 | | 542 | booster, ridge and rake tiles. |
| | Reinstall | Sq. | | 198.64 | | 198.64 | |
| | Minimum Charge | Job | | 168 | | 168 | |
| **Flat Bright Red** | | | | | | | |
| | Demolish | Sq. | | 66 | | 66 | Includes material and labor to install |
| | Install | Sq. | 228 | 248 | | 476 | tile roofing. Cost includes birdstop, |
| | Demolish and Install | Sq. | 228 | 314 | | 542 | booster, ridge and rake tiles. |
| | Reinstall | Sq. | | 198.64 | | 198.64 | |
| | Minimum Charge | Job | | 168 | | 168 | |
| **Flat Green** | | | | | | | |
| | Demolish | Sq. | | 66 | | 66 | Includes material and labor to install |
| | Install | Sq. | 228 | 248 | | 476 | tile roofing. Cost includes birdstop, |
| | Demolish and Install | Sq. | 228 | 314 | | 542 | booster, ridge and rake tiles. |
| | Minimum Charge | Job | | 168 | | 168 | |
| **Flat Blue** | | | | | | | |
| | Demolish | Sq. | | 66 | | 66 | Includes material and labor to install |
| | Install | Sq. | 228 | 248 | | 476 | tile roofing. Cost includes birdstop, |
| | Demolish and Install | Sq. | 228 | 314 | | 542 | booster, ridge and rake tiles. |
| | Reinstall | Sq. | | 198.64 | | 198.64 | |
| | Minimum Charge | Job | | 168 | | 168 | |
| **Flat Black** | | | | | | | |
| | Demolish | Sq. | | 66 | | 66 | Includes material and labor to install |
| | Install | Sq. | 228 | 248 | | 476 | tile roofing. Cost includes birdstop, |
| | Demolish and Install | Sq. | 228 | 314 | | 542 | booster, ridge and rake tiles. |
| | Reinstall | Sq. | | 198.64 | | 198.64 | |
| | Minimum Charge | Job | | 168 | | 168 | |

| Aluminum Sheet | | Unit | Material | Labor | Equip. | Total | Specification |
|---|---|---|---|---|---|---|---|
| **Corrugated** | | | | | | | |
| **.019" Thick Natural** | | | | | | | |
| | Demolish | S.F. | | .70 | | .70 | Includes material and labor to install |
| | Install | S.F. | 1.10 | 1.68 | | 2.78 | aluminum sheet metal roofing. |
| | Demolish and Install | S.F. | 1.10 | 2.38 | | 3.48 | |
| | Reinstall | S.F. | | 1.34 | | 1.34 | |
| | Minimum Charge | Job | | 400 | | 400 | |
| **.016" Thick Natural** | | | | | | | |
| | Demolish | S.F. | | .70 | | .70 | Includes material and labor to install |
| | Install | S.F. | .84 | 1.68 | | 2.52 | aluminum sheet metal roofing. |
| | Demolish and Install | S.F. | .84 | 2.38 | | 3.22 | |
| | Reinstall | S.F. | | 1.34 | | 1.34 | |
| | Minimum Charge | Job | | 400 | | 400 | |
| **.016" Colored Finish** | | | | | | | |
| | Demolish | S.F. | | .70 | | .70 | Includes material and labor to install |
| | Install | S.F. | 1.21 | 1.68 | | 2.89 | aluminum sheet metal roofing. |
| | Demolish and Install | S.F. | 1.21 | 2.38 | | 3.59 | |
| | Reinstall | S.F. | | 1.34 | | 1.34 | |
| | Minimum Charge | Job | | 400 | | 400 | |

# Roofing

| Aluminum Sheet | | Unit | Material | Labor | Equip. | Total | Specification |
|---|---|---|---|---|---|---|---|
| **.019" Colored Finish** | | | | | | | |
| | Demolish | S.F. | | .70 | | .70 | Includes material and labor to install |
| | Install | S.F. | 1.35 | 1.68 | | 3.03 | aluminum sheet metal roofing. |
| | Demolish and Install | S.F. | 1.35 | 2.38 | | 3.73 | |
| | Reinstall | S.F. | | 1.34 | | 1.34 | |
| | Minimum Charge | Job | | 400 | | 400 | |
| **Ribbed** | | | | | | | |
| **.019" Thick Natural** | | | | | | | |
| | Demolish | S.F. | | .70 | | .70 | Includes material and labor to install |
| | Install | S.F. | 1.10 | 1.68 | | 2.78 | aluminum sheet metal roofing. |
| | Demolish and Install | S.F. | 1.10 | 2.38 | | 3.48 | |
| | Reinstall | S.F. | | 1.34 | | 1.34 | |
| | Minimum Charge | Job | | 400 | | 400 | |
| **.016" Thick Natural** | | | | | | | |
| | Demolish | S.F. | | .70 | | .70 | Includes material and labor to install |
| | Install | S.F. | .84 | 1.68 | | 2.52 | aluminum sheet metal roofing. |
| | Demolish and Install | S.F. | .84 | 2.38 | | 3.22 | |
| | Reinstall | S.F. | | 1.34 | | 1.34 | |
| | Minimum Charge | Job | | 400 | | 400 | |
| **.050" Colored Finish** | | | | | | | |
| | Demolish | S.F. | | .70 | | .70 | Includes material and labor to install |
| | Install | S.F. | 3.76 | 1.68 | | 5.44 | aluminum sheet metal roofing. |
| | Demolish and Install | S.F. | 3.76 | 2.38 | | 6.14 | |
| | Reinstall | S.F. | | 1.34 | | 1.34 | |
| | Minimum Charge | Job | | 400 | | 400 | |
| **.032" Thick Natural** | | | | | | | |
| | Demolish | S.F. | | .70 | | .70 | Includes material and labor to install |
| | Install | S.F. | 2.13 | 1.68 | | 3.81 | aluminum sheet metal roofing. |
| | Demolish and Install | S.F. | 2.13 | 2.38 | | 4.51 | |
| | Reinstall | S.F. | | 1.34 | | 1.34 | |
| | Minimum Charge | Job | | 400 | | 400 | |
| **.040" Thick Natural** | | | | | | | |
| | Demolish | S.F. | | .70 | | .70 | Includes material and labor to install |
| | Install | S.F. | 2.60 | 1.68 | | 4.28 | aluminum sheet metal roofing. |
| | Demolish and Install | S.F. | 2.60 | 2.38 | | 4.98 | |
| | Reinstall | S.F. | | 1.34 | | 1.34 | |
| | Minimum Charge | Job | | 400 | | 400 | |
| **.050" Thick Natural** | | | | | | | |
| | Demolish | S.F. | | .70 | | .70 | Includes material and labor to install |
| | Install | S.F. | 3.11 | 1.68 | | 4.79 | aluminum sheet metal roofing. |
| | Demolish and Install | S.F. | 3.11 | 2.38 | | 5.49 | |
| | Reinstall | S.F. | | 1.34 | | 1.34 | |
| | Minimum Charge | Job | | 400 | | 400 | |
| **.016" Colored Finish** | | | | | | | |
| | Demolish | S.F. | | .70 | | .70 | Includes material and labor to install |
| | Install | S.F. | 1.21 | 1.68 | | 2.89 | aluminum sheet metal roofing. |
| | Demolish and Install | S.F. | 1.21 | 2.38 | | 3.59 | |
| | Reinstall | S.F. | | 1.34 | | 1.34 | |
| | Minimum Charge | Job | | 400 | | 400 | |
| **.019" Colored Finish** | | | | | | | |
| | Demolish | S.F. | | .70 | | .70 | Includes material and labor to install |
| | Install | S.F. | 1.35 | 1.68 | | 3.03 | aluminum sheet metal roofing. |
| | Demolish and Install | S.F. | 1.35 | 2.38 | | 3.73 | |
| | Reinstall | S.F. | | 1.34 | | 1.34 | |
| | Minimum Charge | Job | | 400 | | 400 | |

# Roofing

## Aluminum Sheet

| Aluminum Sheet | Unit | Material | Labor | Equip. | Total | Specification |
|---|---|---|---|---|---|---|
| **.032" Colored Finish** | | | | | | |
| Demolish | S.F. | | .70 | | .70 | Includes material and labor to install |
| Install | S.F. | 2.62 | 1.68 | | 4.30 | aluminum sheet metal roofing. |
| Demolish and Install | S.F. | 2.62 | 2.38 | | 5 | |
| Reinstall | S.F. | | 1.34 | | 1.34 | |
| Minimum Charge | Job | | 400 | | 400 | |
| **.040" Colored Finish** | | | | | | |
| Demolish | S.F. | | .70 | | .70 | Includes material and labor to install |
| Install | S.F. | 3.12 | 1.68 | | 4.80 | aluminum sheet metal roofing. |
| Demolish and Install | S.F. | 3.12 | 2.38 | | 5.50 | |
| Reinstall | S.F. | | 1.34 | | 1.34 | |
| Minimum Charge | Job | | 400 | | 400 | |

## Fiberglass Sheet

| Fiberglass Sheet | Unit | Material | Labor | Equip. | Total | Specification |
|---|---|---|---|---|---|---|
| **12 Ounce Corrugated** | | | | | | |
| Demolish | S.F. | | 1.26 | | 1.26 | Cost includes material and labor to |
| Install | S.F. | 3.77 | 1.34 | | 5.11 | install 12 ounce corrugated fiberglass |
| Demolish and Install | S.F. | 3.77 | 2.60 | | 6.37 | sheet roofing. |
| Reinstall | S.F. | | 1.07 | | 1.07 | |
| Minimum Charge | Job | | 168 | | 168 | |
| **8 Ounce Corrugated** | | | | | | |
| Demolish | S.F. | | 1.26 | | 1.26 | Cost includes material and labor to |
| Install | S.F. | 1.74 | 1.34 | | 3.08 | install 8 ounce corrugated fiberglass |
| Demolish and Install | S.F. | 1.74 | 2.60 | | 4.34 | roofing. |
| Reinstall | S.F. | | 1.07 | | 1.07 | |
| Minimum Charge | Job | | 168 | | 168 | |

## Galvanized Steel

| Galvanized Steel | Unit | Material | Labor | Equip. | Total | Specification |
|---|---|---|---|---|---|---|
| **Corrugated** | | | | | | |
| **24 Gauge** | | | | | | |
| Demolish | S.F. | | .70 | | .70 | Includes material and labor to install |
| Install | S.F. | 2.86 | 1.41 | | 4.27 | galvanized steel sheet metal roofing. |
| Demolish and Install | S.F. | 2.86 | 2.11 | | 4.97 | Cost based on 24 gauge corrugated |
| Reinstall | S.F. | | 1.13 | | 1.13 | or ribbed steel roofing. |
| Minimum Charge | Job | | 168 | | 168 | |
| **26 Gauge** | | | | | | |
| Demolish | S.F. | | .70 | | .70 | Includes material and labor to install |
| Install | S.F. | 1.23 | 1.34 | | 2.57 | galvanized steel sheet metal roofing. |
| Demolish and Install | S.F. | 1.23 | 2.04 | | 3.27 | Cost based on 26 gauge corrugated |
| Reinstall | S.F. | | 1.07 | | 1.07 | or ribbed steel roofing. |
| Minimum Charge | Job | | 168 | | 168 | |
| **28 Gauge** | | | | | | |
| Demolish | S.F. | | .70 | | .70 | Includes material and labor to install |
| Install | S.F. | 1.76 | 1.28 | | 3.04 | galvanized steel sheet metal roofing. |
| Demolish and Install | S.F. | 1.76 | 1.98 | | 3.74 | Cost based on 28 gauge corrugated |
| Reinstall | S.F. | | 1.02 | | 1.02 | or ribbed steel roofing. |
| Minimum Charge | Job | | 168 | | 168 | |
| **30 Gauge** | | | | | | |
| Demolish | S.F. | | .70 | | .70 | Includes material and labor to install |
| Install | S.F. | 1.65 | 1.22 | | 2.87 | galvanized steel sheet metal roofing. |
| Demolish and Install | S.F. | 1.65 | 1.92 | | 3.57 | Cost based on 30 gauge corrugated |
| Reinstall | S.F. | | .97 | | .97 | or ribbed steel roofing. |
| Minimum Charge | Job | | 168 | | 168 | |

| Galvanized Steel | Unit | Material | Labor | Equip. | Total | Specification |
|---|---|---|---|---|---|---|
| **Ribbed** | | | | | | |
| **24 Gauge** | | | | | | |
| Demolish | S.F. | | .70 | | .70 | Includes material and labor to install |
| Install | S.F. | 2.86 | 1.41 | | 4.27 | galvanized steel sheet metal roofing. |
| Demolish and Install | S.F. | 2.86 | 2.11 | | 4.97 | Cost based on 24 gauge corrugated |
| Reinstall | S.F. | | 1.13 | | 1.13 | or ribbed steel roofing. |
| Minimum Charge | Job | | 168 | | 168 | |
| **26 Gauge** | | | | | | |
| Demolish | S.F. | | .70 | | .70 | Includes material and labor to install |
| Install | S.F. | 1.23 | 1.34 | | 2.57 | galvanized steel sheet metal roofing. |
| Demolish and Install | S.F. | 1.23 | 2.04 | | 3.27 | Cost based on 26 gauge corrugated |
| Reinstall | S.F. | | 1.07 | | 1.07 | or ribbed steel roofing. |
| Minimum Charge | Job | | 168 | | 168 | |
| **28 Gauge** | | | | | | |
| Demolish | S.F. | | .70 | | .70 | Includes material and labor to install |
| Install | S.F. | 1.76 | 1.28 | | 3.04 | galvanized steel sheet metal roofing. |
| Demolish and Install | S.F. | 1.76 | 1.98 | | 3.74 | Cost based on 28 gauge corrugated |
| Reinstall | S.F. | | 1.02 | | 1.02 | or ribbed steel roofing. |
| Minimum Charge | Job | | 168 | | 168 | |
| **30 Gauge** | | | | | | |
| Demolish | S.F. | | .70 | | .70 | Includes material and labor to install |
| Install | S.F. | 1.65 | 1.22 | | 2.87 | galvanized steel sheet metal roofing. |
| Demolish and Install | S.F. | 1.65 | 1.92 | | 3.57 | Cost based on 30 gauge corrugated |
| Reinstall | S.F. | | .97 | | .97 | or ribbed steel roofing. |
| Minimum Charge | Job | | 168 | | 168 | |

| Standing Seam | Unit | Material | Labor | Equip. | Total | Specification |
|---|---|---|---|---|---|---|
| **Copper** | | | | | | |
| **16 Ounce** | | | | | | |
| Demolish | Sq. | | 70.50 | | 70.50 | Includes material and labor to install |
| Install | Sq. | 1000 | 310 | | 1310 | copper standing seam metal roofing. |
| Demolish and Install | Sq. | 1000 | 380.50 | | 1380.50 | Cost based on 16 ounce copper |
| Reinstall | Sq. | | 247.63 | | 247.63 | roofing. |
| Minimum Charge | Job | | 201 | | 201 | |
| **18 Ounce** | | | | | | |
| Demolish | Sq. | | 70.50 | | 70.50 | Includes material and labor to install |
| Install | Sq. | 1125 | 335 | | 1460 | copper standing seam metal roofing. |
| Demolish and Install | Sq. | 1125 | 405.50 | | 1530.50 | Cost based on 18 ounce copper |
| Reinstall | Sq. | | 268.27 | | 268.27 | roofing. |
| Minimum Charge | Job | | 201 | | 201 | |
| **20 Ounce** | | | | | | |
| Demolish | Sq. | | 70.50 | | 70.50 | Includes material and labor to install |
| Install | Sq. | 1200 | 365 | | 1565 | copper standing seam metal roofing. |
| Demolish and Install | Sq. | 1200 | 435.50 | | 1635.50 | Cost based on 20 ounce copper |
| Reinstall | Sq. | | 292.65 | | 292.65 | roofing. |
| **Stainless Steel** | | | | | | |
| **26 Gauge** | | | | | | |
| Demolish | Sq. | | 70.50 | | 70.50 | Cost includes material and labor to |
| Install | Sq. | 820 | 350 | | 1170 | install 26 gauge stainless steel |
| Demolish and Install | Sq. | 820 | 420.50 | | 1240.50 | standing seam metal roofing. |
| Reinstall | Sq. | | 279.93 | | 279.93 | |
| Minimum Charge | Job | | 201 | | 201 | |

# Reed Construction Data®

Reed Construction Data is your all-inclusive source of information encompassing all phases of the construction process. Our products and services are designed specifically to help industry professionals advance their businesses with timely, accurate and actionable project, product and cost data.

Reed Bulletin and Reed Connect™ deliver the most comprehensive, timely and reliable project information to support contractors, distributors and building product manufacturers in identifying, bidding, and tracking projects — private and public, general building and civil. Reed Construction Data also offers in-depth construction activity statistics and forecasts covering major project categories, many at the county and metropolitan level.

For more information about Reed Construction Data, please call **877-REED411** or visit our website at **www.reedconstructiondata.com**.

## Reed Connect

- Customized web-based project lead delivery service featuring advanced search capabilities.

- Manage and track actionable leads from planning to quote through winning the job.

- Competitive analysis tool to analyze lost sales opportunities.

- Potential integration with your CRM application.

## Reed Bulletin

- Project leads targeted by geographic region and formatted by construction stage — available online or in print.

- Locate those hard-to-find jobs that are more profitable to your business.

- Optional automatic e-mail updates sent whenever project details change.

- Download plans and specs online or order print copies.

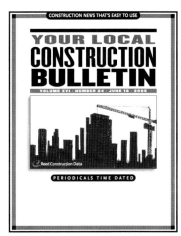

CONSTRUCTION NEWS THAT'S EASY TO USE

**YOUR LOCAL CONSTRUCTION BULLETIN**

VOLUME XVI · NUMBER 24 · JUNE 16 · 2008

Reed Construction Data

PERIODICALS TIME DATED

## Reed Research & Analytics

### Reed Construction Forecast
- Delivers timely construction industry activity combining historical data, current year projections and forecasts.

- Modeled at the individual MSA-level to capture changing local market conditions.

- Covers 21 major project categories.

### Reed Construction Starts
- Available in a monthly report or as an interactive database.

- Data provided in square footage and dollar value.

- Highly effective and efficient business planning tool.

### Market Fundamentals
- Metropolitan area-specific reporting.

- Five-year forecast of industry performance including major projects in development and underway.

- Property types include office, retail, hotel, warehouse and apartment.

# Roofing

| Elastomeric Roofing | Unit | Material | Labor | Equip. | Total | Specification |
|---|---|---|---|---|---|---|
| **48 mil (attached)** | | | | | | |
| Demolish | Sq. | | 36 | | 36 | Cost includes material and labor to |
| Install | Sq. | 171 | 59 | 7 | 237 | install 48 mil PVC elastomeric roofing |
| Demolish and Install | Sq. | 171 | 95 | 7 | 273 | fully attached to roof deck. |
| Minimum Charge | Job | | 765 | 91 | 856 | |
| **60 mil (attached)** | | | | | | |
| Demolish | Sq. | | 36 | | 36 | Cost includes material and labor to |
| Install | Sq. | 173 | 59 | 7 | 239 | install 60 mil PVC elastomeric roofing |
| Demolish and Install | Sq. | 173 | 95 | 7 | 275 | fully attached to roof deck. |
| Minimum Charge | Job | | 765 | 91 | 856 | |
| **CSPE Type** | | | | | | |
| **45 mil (loose laid w / stone)** | | | | | | |
| Demolish | Sq. | | 24.50 | | 24.50 | Cost includes material and labor to |
| Install | Sq. | 164 | 30 | 3.57 | 197.57 | install 45 mil CSPE (chlorosulfonated |
| Demolish and Install | Sq. | 164 | 54.50 | 3.57 | 222.07 | polyethylene-hypalon) roofing material |
| Minimum Charge | Job | | 765 | 91 | 856 | loose laid on deck and ballasted with stone. |
| **45 mil (attached at seams)** | | | | | | |
| Demolish | Sq. | | 58 | | 58 | Cost includes material and labor to |
| Install | Sq. | 157 | 44 | 5.20 | 206.20 | install 45 mil CSPE (chlorosulfonated |
| Demolish and Install | Sq. | 157 | 102 | 5.20 | 264.20 | polyethylene-hypalon) roofing material |
| Minimum Charge | Job | | 765 | 91 | 856 | attached to deck at seams with batten strips. |
| **45 mil (fully attached)** | | | | | | |
| Demolish | Sq. | | 36 | | 36 | Cost includes material and labor to |
| Install | Sq. | 155 | 59 | 7 | 221 | install 45 mil CSPE (chlorosulfonated |
| Demolish and Install | Sq. | 155 | 95 | 7 | 257 | polyethylene-hypalon) roofing material |
| Minimum Charge | Job | | 765 | 91 | 856 | fully attached to deck. |
| **EPDM Type** | | | | | | |
| **45 mil (attached at seams)** | | | | | | |
| Demolish | Sq. | | 58 | | 58 | Cost includes material and labor to |
| Install | Sq. | 65 | 44 | 5.20 | 114.20 | install 45 mil EPDM (ethylene |
| Demolish and Install | Sq. | 65 | 102 | 5.20 | 172.20 | propylene diene monomer) roofing |
| Minimum Charge | Job | | 765 | 91 | 856 | material attached to deck at seams. |
| **45 mil (fully attached)** | | | | | | |
| Demolish | Sq. | | 36 | | 36 | Cost includes material and labor to |
| Install | Sq. | 94.50 | 59 | 7 | 160.50 | install 45 mil EPDM (ethylene |
| Demolish and Install | Sq. | 94.50 | 95 | 7 | 196.50 | propylene diene monomer) roofing |
| Minimum Charge | Job | | 765 | 91 | 856 | material fully attached to deck. |
| **45 mil (loose laid w / stone)** | | | | | | |
| Demolish | Sq. | | 24.50 | | 24.50 | Cost includes material and labor to |
| Install | Sq. | 75.50 | 30 | 3.57 | 109.07 | install 45 mil EPDM (ethylene |
| Demolish and Install | Sq. | 75.50 | 54.50 | 3.57 | 133.57 | propylene diene monomer) roofing |
| Minimum Charge | Job | | 765 | 91 | 856 | material loose laid on deck and ballasted with stones (approx. 1/2 ton of stone per square). |
| **60 mil (attached at seams)** | | | | | | |
| Demolish | Sq. | | 58 | | 58 | Cost includes material and labor to |
| Install | Sq. | 83.50 | 44 | 5.20 | 132.70 | install 60 mil EPDM (ethylene |
| Demolish and Install | Sq. | 83.50 | 102 | 5.20 | 190.70 | propylene diene monomer) roofing |
| Minimum Charge | Job | | 765 | 91 | 856 | material attached to deck at seams. |
| **60 mil (fully attached)** | | | | | | |
| Demolish | Sq. | | 36 | | 36 | Cost includes material and labor to |
| Install | Sq. | 112 | 59 | 7 | 178 | install 60 mil EPDM (ethylene |
| Demolish and Install | Sq. | 112 | 95 | 7 | 214 | propylene diene monomer) roofing |
| Minimum Charge | Job | | 765 | 91 | 856 | material fully attached to deck. |

| Standing Seam | | Unit | Material | Labor | Equip. | Total | Specification |
|---|---|---|---|---|---|---|---|
| **28 Gauge** | | | | | | | Includes material and labor to install |
| | Demolish | Sq. | | 70.50 | | 70.50 | standing seam metal roofing. Cost |
| | Install | Sq. | 655 | 335 | | 990 | based on 28 gauge stainless steel |
| | Demolish and Install | Sq. | 655 | 405.50 | | 1060.50 | roofing. |
| | Reinstall | Sq. | | 268.27 | | 268.27 | |
| | Minimum Charge | Job | | 201 | | 201 | |

| Elastomeric Roofing | | Unit | Material | Labor | Equip. | Total | Specification |
|---|---|---|---|---|---|---|---|
| **Neoprene** | | | | | | | |
| **1/16"** | | | | | | | Includes material and labor to install |
| | Demolish | Sq. | | 24.50 | | 24.50 | neoprene membrane, fully adhered, |
| | Install | Sq. | 281 | 160 | 33 | 474 | 1/16" thick. |
| | Demolish and Install | Sq. | 281 | 184.50 | 33 | 498.50 | |
| | Minimum Charge | Job | | 765 | 91 | 856 | |
| **GRM Membrane** | | | | | | | |
| | Demolish | Sq. | | 24.50 | | 24.50 | Includes material and labor to install |
| | Install | Sq. | 279 | 256 | 30.50 | 565.50 | coal tar based elastomeric roofing |
| | Demolish and Install | Sq. | 279 | 280.50 | 30.50 | 590 | membrane, polyester fiber reinforced. |
| | Minimum Charge | Job | | 765 | 91 | 856 | |
| **Cant Strips** | | | | | | | |
| **3"** | | | | | | | Includes material and labor to install |
| | Demolish | L.F. | | .76 | | .76 | cants 3" x 3", treated timber, cut |
| | Install | L.F. | .59 | 1.03 | | 1.62 | diagonally. |
| | Demolish and Install | L.F. | .59 | 1.79 | | 2.38 | |
| | Minimum Charge | Job | | 168 | | 168 | |
| **4"** | | | | | | | Includes material and labor to install |
| | Demolish | L.F. | | .76 | | .76 | cants 4" x 4", treated timber, cut |
| | Install | L.F. | 1.54 | 1.03 | | 2.57 | diagonally. |
| | Demolish and Install | L.F. | 1.54 | 1.79 | | 3.33 | |
| | Minimum Charge | Job | | 168 | | 168 | |
| **Polyvinyl Chloride (PVC)** | | | | | | | |
| **45 mil (loose laid)** | | | | | | | Cost includes material and labor to |
| | Demolish | Sq. | | 24.50 | | 24.50 | install 45 mil PVC elastomeric roofing, |
| | Install | Sq. | 110 | 30 | 3.57 | 143.57 | loose-laid with stone. |
| | Demolish and Install | Sq. | 110 | 54.50 | 3.57 | 168.07 | |
| | Minimum Charge | Job | | 765 | 91 | 856 | |
| **48 mil (loose laid)** | | | | | | | Cost includes material and labor to |
| | Demolish | Sq. | | 24.50 | | 24.50 | install 48 mil PVC elastomeric roofing, |
| | Install | Sq. | 128 | 30 | 3.57 | 161.57 | loose-laid with stone. |
| | Demolish and Install | Sq. | 128 | 54.50 | 3.57 | 186.07 | |
| | Minimum Charge | Job | | 765 | 91 | 856 | |
| **60 mil (loose laid)** | | | | | | | Cost includes material and labor to |
| | Demolish | Sq. | | 24.50 | | 24.50 | install 60 mil PVC elastomeric roofing, |
| | Install | Sq. | 130 | 30 | 3.57 | 163.57 | loose-laid with stone. |
| | Demolish and Install | Sq. | 130 | 54.50 | 3.57 | 188.07 | |
| | Minimum Charge | Job | | 765 | 91 | 856 | |
| **45 mil (attached)** | | | | | | | Cost includes material and labor to |
| | Demolish | Sq. | | 36 | | 36 | install 45 mil PVC elastomeric roofing |
| | Install | Sq. | 96.50 | 59 | 7 | 162.50 | fully attached to roof deck. |
| | Demolish and Install | Sq. | 96.50 | 95 | 7 | 198.50 | |
| | Minimum Charge | Job | | 765 | 91 | 856 | |

| Elastomeric Roofing | | Unit | Material | Labor | Equip. | Total | Specification |
|---|---|---|---|---|---|---|---|
| **48 mil (attached)** | | | | | | | Cost includes material and labor to |
| | Demolish | Sq. | | 36 | | 36 | install 48 mil PVC elastomeric roofing |
| | Install | Sq. | 171 | 59 | 7 | 237 | fully attached to roof deck. |
| | Demolish and Install | Sq. | 171 | 95 | 7 | 273 | |
| | Minimum Charge | Job | | 765 | 91 | 856 | |
| **60 mil (attached)** | | | | | | | Cost includes material and labor to |
| | Demolish | Sq. | | 36 | | 36 | install 60 mil PVC elastomeric roofing |
| | Install | Sq. | 173 | 59 | 7 | 239 | fully attached to roof deck. |
| | Demolish and Install | Sq. | 173 | 95 | 7 | 275 | |
| | Minimum Charge | Job | | 765 | 91 | 856 | |
| **CSPE Type** | | | | | | | |
| **45 mil (loose laid w / stone)** | | | | | | | Cost includes material and labor to |
| | Demolish | Sq. | | 24.50 | | 24.50 | install 45 mil CSPE (chlorosulfonated |
| | Install | Sq. | 164 | 30 | 3.57 | 197.57 | polyethylene-hypalon) roofing material |
| | Demolish and Install | Sq. | 164 | 54.50 | 3.57 | 222.07 | loose laid on deck and ballasted with |
| | Minimum Charge | Job | | 765 | 91 | 856 | stone. |
| **45 mil (attached at seams)** | | | | | | | Cost includes material and labor to |
| | Demolish | Sq. | | 58 | | 58 | install 45 mil CSPE (chlorosulfonated |
| | Install | Sq. | 157 | 44 | 5.20 | 206.20 | polyethylene-hypalon) roofing material |
| | Demolish and Install | Sq. | 157 | 102 | 5.20 | 264.20 | attached to deck at seams with batten |
| | Minimum Charge | Job | | 765 | 91 | 856 | strips. |
| **45 mil (fully attached)** | | | | | | | Cost includes material and labor to |
| | Demolish | Sq. | | 36 | | 36 | install 45 mil CSPE (chlorosulfonated |
| | Install | Sq. | 155 | 59 | 7 | 221 | polyethylene-hypalon) roofing material |
| | Demolish and Install | Sq. | 155 | 95 | 7 | 257 | fully attached to deck. |
| | Minimum Charge | Job | | 765 | 91 | 856 | |
| **EPDM Type** | | | | | | | |
| **45 mil (attached at seams)** | | | | | | | Cost includes material and labor to |
| | Demolish | Sq. | | 58 | | 58 | install 45 mil EPDM (ethylene |
| | Install | Sq. | 65 | 44 | 5.20 | 114.20 | propylene diene monomer) roofing |
| | Demolish and Install | Sq. | 65 | 102 | 5.20 | 172.20 | material attached to deck at seams. |
| | Minimum Charge | Job | | 765 | 91 | 856 | |
| **45 mil (fully attached)** | | | | | | | Cost includes material and labor to |
| | Demolish | Sq. | | 36 | | 36 | install 45 mil EPDM (ethylene |
| | Install | Sq. | 94.50 | 59 | 7 | 160.50 | propylene diene monomer) roofing |
| | Demolish and Install | Sq. | 94.50 | 95 | 7 | 196.50 | material fully attached to deck. |
| | Minimum Charge | Job | | 765 | 91 | 856 | |
| **45 mil (loose laid w / stone)** | | | | | | | Cost includes material and labor to |
| | Demolish | Sq. | | 24.50 | | 24.50 | install 45 mil EPDM (ethylene |
| | Install | Sq. | 75.50 | 30 | 3.57 | 109.07 | propylene diene monomer) roofing |
| | Demolish and Install | Sq. | 75.50 | 54.50 | 3.57 | 133.57 | material loose laid on deck and |
| | Minimum Charge | Job | | 765 | 91 | 856 | ballasted with stones (approx. 1/2 ton |
| | | | | | | | of stone per square). |
| **60 mil (attached at seams)** | | | | | | | Cost includes material and labor to |
| | Demolish | Sq. | | 58 | | 58 | install 60 mil EPDM (ethylene |
| | Install | Sq. | 83.50 | 44 | 5.20 | 132.70 | propylene diene monomer) roofing |
| | Demolish and Install | Sq. | 83.50 | 102 | 5.20 | 190.70 | material attached to deck at seams. |
| | Minimum Charge | Job | | 765 | 91 | 856 | |
| **60 mil (fully attached)** | | | | | | | Cost includes material and labor to |
| | Demolish | Sq. | | 36 | | 36 | install 60 mil EPDM (ethylene |
| | Install | Sq. | 112 | 59 | 7 | 178 | propylene diene monomer) roofing |
| | Demolish and Install | Sq. | 112 | 95 | 7 | 214 | material fully attached to deck. |
| | Minimum Charge | Job | | 765 | 91 | 856 | |

# Reed Construction Data®

Reed Construction Data is your all-inclusive source of information encompassing all phases of the construction process. Our products and services are designed specifically to help industry professionals advance their businesses with timely, accurate and actionable project, product and cost data.

Reed Bulletin and Reed Connect™ deliver the most comprehensive, timely and reliable project information to support contractors, distributors and building product manufacturers in identifying, bidding, and tracking projects — private and public, general building and civil. Reed Construction Data also offers in-depth construction activity statistics and forecasts covering major project categories, many at the county and metropolitan level.

For more information about Reed Construction Data, please call **877-REED411** or visit our website at **www.reedconstructiondata.com**.

## Reed Connect

- Customized web-based project lead delivery service featuring advanced search capabilities.

- Manage and track actionable leads from planning to quote through winning the job.

- Competitive analysis tool to analyze lost sales opportunities.

- Potential integration with your CRM application.

## Reed Bulletin

- Project leads targeted by geographic region and formatted by construction stage — available online or in print.

- Locate those hard-to-find jobs that are more profitable to your business.

- Optional automatic e-mail updates sent whenever project details change.

- Download plans and specs online or order print copies.

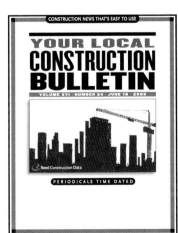

## Reed Research & Analytics

**Reed Construction Forecast**
- Delivers timely construction industry activity combining historical data, current year projections and forecasts.

- Modeled at the individual MSA-level to capture changing local market conditions.

- Covers 21 major project categories.

**Reed Construction Starts**
- Available in a monthly report or as an interactive database.

- Data provided in square footage and dollar value.

- Highly effective and efficient business planning tool.

**Market Fundamentals**
- Metropolitan area-specific reporting.

- Five-year forecast of industry performance including major projects in development and underway.

- Property types include office, retail, hotel, warehouse and apartment.

# Reed Construction Data®

Reed Construction Data is a leading provider of information resources to the design community. Through our products and services we offer many ways for architects, engineers, designers, and contractors to better serve their clients and build their businesses.

For more information about Reed Construction Data, please call **877-REED411** or visit our website at **www.reedconstructiondata.com**.

## Reed Registry
### The Premier Source of Architectural Firms
The Reed Registry contains over 30,000 architecture firms and is used by industry professionals to find architects throughout the U.S. and Canada.

Architecture firms can add or update their listing, or enhance their listing to include logos, projects, and web links by visiting **www.reedregistry.com**.

## Reed First Source and Buildcore
### Leading Product Information Solutions for Design Professionals
Reed First Source and Buildcore are leading information solutions that allow design professionals to search, select, and specify building products throughout the design and construction cycle.

Covering both U.S. and Canadian markets, FirstSource and BuildCore provide access to over 11,000 commercial building manufacturers, all classified by MasterFormat™ 2004 categories. In addition, our specialists can create and publish SPEC-DATA 10-part format and MANU-SPEC three-part specifications for building product manufacturers.

Learn more at **www.reedfirstsource.com.**

# Roofing

## Elastomeric Roofing

| | Unit | Material | Labor | Equip. | Total | Specification |
|---|---|---|---|---|---|---|
| **60 mil (loose laid w / stone)** | | | | | | Cost includes material and labor to |
| Demolish | Sq. | | 24.50 | | 24.50 | install 60 mil EPDM (ethylene |
| Install | Sq. | 95 | 30 | 3.57 | 128.57 | propylene diene monomer) roofing |
| Demolish and Install | Sq. | 95 | 54.50 | 3.57 | 153.07 | material loose laid on deck and |
| Minimum Charge | Job | | 765 | 91 | 856 | ballasted with stones (approx. 1/2 ton of stone per square). |
| **Silicone-urethane Foam** | | | | | | |
| **Prep Roof for Foam System** | | | | | | Includes labor and material to removal |
| Install | Sq. | 6 | 134 | | 140 | of any gravel and prepare existing |
| Minimum Charge | Job | | 765 | 91 | 856 | built-up roof for application of silicone-urethane foam system. |

## Modified Bitumen Roofing

| | Unit | Material | Labor | Equip. | Total | Specification |
|---|---|---|---|---|---|---|
| **Fully Attached** | | | | | | |
| **120 mil** | | | | | | Cost includes material and labor to |
| Demolish | Sq. | | 58 | | 58 | install 120 mil modified bitumen |
| Install | Sq. | 90 | 7.45 | 1.54 | 98.99 | roofing, fully attached to deck by |
| Demolish and Install | Sq. | 90 | 65.45 | 1.54 | 156.99 | torch. |
| Minimum Charge | Job | | 168 | | 168 | |
| **150 mil** | | | | | | Cost includes material and labor to |
| Demolish | Sq. | | 58 | | 58 | install 150 mil modified bitumen |
| Install | Sq. | 130 | 18.35 | 3.78 | 152.13 | roofing, fully attached to deck by |
| Demolish and Install | Sq. | 130 | 76.35 | 3.78 | 210.13 | torch. |
| Minimum Charge | Job | | 1100 | 227 | 1327 | |
| **160 mil** | | | | | | Cost includes material and labor to |
| Demolish | Sq. | | 58 | | 58 | install 160 mil modified bitumen |
| Install | Sq. | 104 | 19.15 | 3.94 | 127.09 | roofing, fully attached to deck by |
| Demolish and Install | Sq. | 104 | 77.15 | 3.94 | 185.09 | torch. |
| Minimum Charge | Job | | 1100 | 227 | 1327 | |

## Built-up Roofing

| | Unit | Material | Labor | Equip. | Total | Specification |
|---|---|---|---|---|---|---|
| **Emergency Repairs** | | | | | | Minimum charge for work requiring |
| Install | Ea. | 174 | 1575 | 325 | 2074 | hot asphalt. |
| Minimum Charge | Job | | 1100 | 227 | 1327 | |
| **Asphalt** | | | | | | |
| **3-ply Asphalt** | | | | | | Cost includes material and labor to |
| Demolish | Sq. | | 60.50 | | 60.50 | install 3-ply asphalt built-up roof |
| Install | Sq. | 49 | 92 | 18.90 | 159.90 | including one 30 lb and two 15 lb |
| Demolish and Install | Sq. | 49 | 152.50 | 18.90 | 220.40 | layers of felt. |
| Minimum Charge | Job | | 1100 | 227 | 1327 | |
| **4-ply Asphalt** | | | | | | Cost includes material and labor to |
| Demolish | Sq. | | 72 | | 72 | install 4-ply asphalt built-up roof |
| Install | Sq. | 73 | 100 | 20.50 | 193.50 | including one 30 lb and three 15 lb |
| Demolish and Install | Sq. | 73 | 172 | 20.50 | 265.50 | layers of felt. |
| Minimum Charge | Job | | 1100 | 227 | 1327 | |

| Built-up Roofing | | Unit | Material | Labor | Equip. | Total | Specification |
|---|---|---|---|---|---|---|---|
| **5-ply Asphalt** | | | | | | | Cost includes material and labor to install 5-ply asphalt built-up roof including one 30 lb and four 15 lb layers of felt. |
| | Demolish | Sq. | | 94.50 | | 94.50 | |
| | Install | Sq. | 102 | 110 | 22.50 | 234.50 | |
| | Demolish and Install | Sq. | 102 | 204.50 | 22.50 | 329 | |
| | Minimum Charge | Job | | 1100 | 227 | 1327 | |
| **Components / Accessories** | | | | | | | |
| **Flood Coat** | | | | | | | Includes labor and material to install flood coat. |
| | Install | Sq. | 19 | 51.50 | | 70.50 | |
| **R / R Gravel and Flood Coat** | | | | | | | Includes labor and material to install flood coat and gravel. |
| | Install | Sq. | 25 | 168 | | 193 | |
| **Aluminum UV Coat** | | | | | | | Includes labor and material to install aluminum-based UV coating. |
| | Install | Sq. | 17.60 | 192 | 23 | 232.60 | |
| **Gravel Coat** | | | | | | | Includes labor and material to install gravel coat. |
| | Demolish | Sq. | | 30 | | 30 | |
| | Install | Sq. | 5.70 | 28 | | 33.70 | |
| | Demolish and Install | Sq. | 5.70 | 58 | | 63.70 | |
| **Mineral Surface Cap Sheet** | | | | | | | Cost includes labor and material to install 50 # mineral surfaced cap sheet. |
| | Install | Sq. | 24 | 5.80 | | 29.80 | |
| **Fibrated Aluminum UV Coating** | | | | | | | Includes labor and material to install fibered aluminum-based UV coating. |
| | Install | Sq. | 20 | 51.50 | | 71.50 | |
| **Impregnated Walk** | | | | | | | |
| **1"** | | | | | | | Cost includes labor and material to install 1" layer of asphalt coating. |
| | Install | S.F. | 2.53 | 1.79 | | 4.32 | |
| **1/2"** | | | | | | | Cost includes labor and material to install 1/2" layer of asphalt coating. |
| | Install | S.F. | 1.76 | 1.41 | | 3.17 | |
| **3/4"** | | | | | | | Cost includes labor and material to install 3/4" layer of asphalt coating. |
| | Install | S.F. | 2.20 | 1.49 | | 3.69 | |

# Exterior Doors and Windows

| Doors | Roof Window | Double Hung Window |
|---|---|---|

| Exterior Type Door | Unit | Material | Labor | Equip. | Total | Specification |
|---|---|---|---|---|---|---|
| **Entry** | | | | | | |
| **Flush (1-3/4")** | | | | | | |
| Demolish | Ea. | | 33.50 | | 33.50 | Cost includes material and labor to |
| Install | Ea. | 227 | 19.05 | | 246.05 | install 3' x 6' 8" pre-hung 1-3/4" |
| Demolish and Install | Ea. | 227 | 52.55 | | 279.55 | door, including casing and stop, |
| Reinstall | Ea. | | 19.03 | | 19.03 | hinges, jamb, aluminum sill, |
| Clean | Ea. | 3.63 | 11.10 | | 14.73 | weatherstripped. |
| Paint | Ea. | 9.30 | 45 | | 54.30 | |
| Minimum Charge | Job | | 181 | | 181 | |
| **Raised Panel** | | | | | | |
| Demolish | Ea. | | 33.50 | | 33.50 | Cost includes material and labor to |
| Install | Ea. | 445 | 20 | | 465 | install 3' x 6' 8" pre-hung 1-3/4" |
| Demolish and Install | Ea. | 445 | 53.50 | | 498.50 | door, jamb, including casing and |
| Reinstall | Ea. | | 20.09 | | 20.09 | stop, hinges, aluminum sill, |
| Clean | Ea. | 3.63 | 11.10 | | 14.73 | weatherstripping. |
| Paint | Ea. | 9.30 | 45 | | 54.30 | |
| Minimum Charge | Job | | 181 | | 181 | |
| **Entry w / Lights** | | | | | | |
| **Good Quality** | | | | | | |
| Demolish | Ea. | | 33.50 | | 33.50 | Cost includes material and labor to |
| Install | Ea. | 300 | 45 | | 345 | install 3' x 6' 8" pre-hung 1-3/4" |
| Demolish and Install | Ea. | 300 | 78.50 | | 378.50 | door, solid wood lower panelm with |
| Reinstall | Ea. | | 45.20 | | 45.20 | up to 9-light glass panels, casing, sill, |
| Clean | Ea. | 3.63 | 11.10 | | 14.73 | weatherstripped. |
| Paint | Ea. | 6.05 | 21 | | 27.05 | |
| Minimum Charge | Job | | 181 | | 181 | |
| **Better Quality** | | | | | | |
| Demolish | Ea. | | 33.50 | | 33.50 | Cost includes material and labor to |
| Install | Ea. | 315 | 45 | | 360 | install 3' x 6' 8" pre-hung 1-3/4" Ash |
| Demolish and Install | Ea. | 315 | 78.50 | | 393.50 | door, solid wood, raised panel door |
| Reinstall | Ea. | | 45.20 | | 45.20 | without glass panels. |
| Clean | Ea. | 3.63 | 11.10 | | 14.73 | |
| Paint | Ea. | 9.30 | 45 | | 54.30 | |
| Minimum Charge | Job | | 181 | | 181 | |
| **Premium Quality** | | | | | | |
| Demolish | Ea. | | 33.50 | | 33.50 | Cost includes material and labor to |
| Install | Ea. | 705 | 21.50 | | 726.50 | install 3' x 6' 8" pre-hung 1-3/4" Oak |
| Demolish and Install | Ea. | 705 | 55 | | 760 | door, solid wood, raised panel door |
| Reinstall | Ea. | | 21.27 | | 21.27 | without glass panels. |
| Clean | Ea. | 3.63 | 11.10 | | 14.73 | |
| Paint | Ea. | 9.30 | 45 | | 54.30 | |
| Minimum Charge | Job | | 181 | | 181 | |

| Exterior Type Door | | Unit | Material | Labor | Equip. | Total | Specification |
|---|---|---|---|---|---|---|---|
| **Custom Quality** | | | | | | | |
| | Demolish | Ea. | | 33.50 | | 33.50 | Cost includes material and labor to |
| | Install | Ea. | 500 | 48 | | 548 | install 3' x 6' 8" pre-hung 1-3/4", |
| | Demolish and Install | Ea. | 500 | 81.50 | | 581.50 | hand-made, solid wood, raised panel |
| | Reinstall | Ea. | | 48.21 | | 48.21 | door with custom stained glass. |
| | Clean | Ea. | .25 | 11.10 | | 11.35 | |
| | Paint | Ea. | 2.17 | 105 | | 107.17 | |
| | Minimum Charge | Job | | 181 | | 181 | |
| **Miami Style** | | | | | | | |
| | Demolish | Ea. | | 33.50 | | 33.50 | Cost includes material and labor to |
| | Install | Ea. | 215 | 18.10 | | 233.10 | install 3' x 6' 8" pre-hung 1-3/4" |
| | Demolish and Install | Ea. | 215 | 51.60 | | 266.60 | lauan door of solid wood. |
| | Reinstall | Ea. | | 18.08 | | 18.08 | |
| | Clean | Ea. | .25 | 11.10 | | 11.35 | |
| | Paint | Ea. | 9.30 | 45 | | 54.30 | |
| | Minimum Charge | Job | | 181 | | 181 | |
| **French Style** | | | | | | | |
| **1-Light** | | | | | | | |
| | Demolish | Ea. | | 33.50 | | 33.50 | Cost includes material and labor to |
| | Install | Ea. | 385 | 26 | | 411 | install 3' x 6' 8" pre-hung 1-3/4" |
| | Demolish and Install | Ea. | 385 | 59.50 | | 444.50 | french style door with 1 light. |
| | Reinstall | Ea. | | 25.83 | | 25.83 | |
| | Clean | Ea. | 2.27 | 16.70 | | 18.97 | |
| | Paint | Ea. | 9.45 | 78.50 | | 87.95 | |
| | Minimum Charge | Job | | 181 | | 181 | |
| **9-Light** | | | | | | | |
| | Demolish | Ea. | | 33.50 | | 33.50 | Cost includes material and labor to |
| | Install | Ea. | 365 | 26 | | 391 | install 3' x 6' 8" pre-hung 1-3/4" |
| | Demolish and Install | Ea. | 365 | 59.50 | | 424.50 | french style door with 9 lights. |
| | Reinstall | Ea. | | 25.83 | | 25.83 | |
| | Clean | Ea. | .50 | 22 | | 22.50 | |
| | Paint | Ea. | 9.45 | 78.50 | | 87.95 | |
| | Minimum Charge | Job | | 181 | | 181 | |
| **10-Light** | | | | | | | |
| | Demolish | Ea. | | 37 | | 37 | Cost includes material and labor to |
| | Install | Ea. | 595 | 45 | | 640 | install 3' x 6' 8" pre-hung 1-3/4" |
| | Demolish and Install | Ea. | 595 | 82 | | 677 | french style door with 10 lights. |
| | Reinstall | Ea. | | 45.20 | | 45.20 | |
| | Clean | Ea. | .50 | 22 | | 22.50 | |
| | Paint | Ea. | 9.45 | 78.50 | | 87.95 | |
| | Minimum Charge | Job | | 181 | | 181 | |
| **15-Light** | | | | | | | |
| | Demolish | Ea. | | 37 | | 37 | Cost includes material and labor to |
| | Install | Ea. | 665 | 51.50 | | 716.50 | install 3' x 6' 8" pre-hung 1-3/4" |
| | Demolish and Install | Ea. | 665 | 88.50 | | 753.50 | french style door with 15 lights. |
| | Reinstall | Ea. | | 51.66 | | 51.66 | |
| | Clean | Ea. | .50 | 22 | | 22.50 | |
| | Paint | Ea. | 9.45 | 78.50 | | 87.95 | |
| | Minimum Charge | Job | | 181 | | 181 | |
| **Jamb** | | | | | | | |
| **Wood** | | | | | | | |
| | Demolish | Ea. | | 20 | | 20 | Includes material and labor to install |
| | Install | Ea. | 100 | 9.75 | | 109.75 | flat pine jamb with square cut heads |
| | Demolish and Install | Ea. | 100 | 29.75 | | 129.75 | and rabbeted sides for 6' 8" high and |
| | Clean | Ea. | .12 | 6.65 | | 6.77 | 3-9/16" door including trim sets for |
| | Paint | Ea. | 6.05 | 21 | | 27.05 | both sides. |
| | Minimum Charge | Job | | 181 | | 181 | |

| Exterior Type Door | | Unit | Material | Labor | Equip. | Total | Specification |
|---|---|---|---|---|---|---|---|
| **Metal 6' 8" High** | | | | | | | |
| | Demolish | Ea. | | 20 | | 20 | Cost includes material and labor to |
| | Install | Ea. | 138 | 22.50 | | 160.50 | install 18 gauge hollow metal door |
| | Demolish and Install | Ea. | 138 | 42.50 | | 180.50 | frame to fit a 4-1/2" jamb 6' 8" high |
| | Reinstall | Ea. | | 22.60 | | 22.60 | and up to 3' 6" opening. |
| | Clean | Ea. | .76 | 5.55 | | 6.31 | |
| | Paint | Ea. | 1.24 | 6.30 | | 7.54 | |
| | Minimum Charge | Job | | 181 | | 181 | |
| **Metal 7' High** | | | | | | | |
| | Demolish | Ea. | | 20 | | 20 | Cost includes material and labor to |
| | Install | Ea. | 143 | 24 | | 167 | install 18 gauge hollow metal door |
| | Demolish and Install | Ea. | 143 | 44 | | 187 | frame to fit a 4-1/2" jamb 7' high and |
| | Reinstall | Ea. | | 24.11 | | 24.11 | up to 3' 6" opening. |
| | Clean | Ea. | .76 | 5.55 | | 6.31 | |
| | Paint | Ea. | 1.24 | 6.30 | | 7.54 | |
| | Minimum Charge | Job | | 181 | | 181 | |
| **Metal 8' High** | | | | | | | |
| | Demolish | Ea. | | 20 | | 20 | Cost includes material and labor to |
| | Install | Ea. | 175 | 30 | | 205 | install 18 gauge hollow metal door |
| | Demolish and Install | Ea. | 175 | 50 | | 225 | frame to fit a 4-1/2" jamb 8' high and |
| | Reinstall | Ea. | | 30.13 | | 30.13 | up to 3' 6" opening. |
| | Clean | Ea. | 1.07 | 6.65 | | 7.72 | |
| | Paint | Ea. | 1.39 | 7 | | 8.39 | |
| | Minimum Charge | Job | | 181 | | 181 | |
| **Metal 9' High** | | | | | | | |
| | Demolish | Ea. | | 20 | | 20 | Cost includes material and labor to |
| | Install | Ea. | 194 | 36 | | 230 | install 18 gauge hollow metal door |
| | Demolish and Install | Ea. | 194 | 56 | | 250 | frame to fit a 4-1/2" jamb 9' high and |
| | Reinstall | Ea. | | 36.16 | | 36.16 | up to 3' 6" opening. |
| | Clean | Ea. | 1.07 | 6.65 | | 7.72 | |
| | Paint | Ea. | 1.39 | 7 | | 8.39 | |
| | Minimum Charge | Job | | 181 | | 181 | |
| **Casing Trim** | | | | | | | |
| **Single Width** | | | | | | | |
| | Demolish | Ea. | | 6.40 | | 6.40 | Cost includes material and labor to |
| | Install | Opng. | 23.50 | 61.50 | | 85 | install 11/16" x 2-1/2" pine ranch |
| | Demolish and Install | Opng. | 23.50 | 67.90 | | 91.40 | style casing for one side of a standard |
| | Reinstall | Opng. | | 49.03 | | 49.03 | door opening. |
| | Clean | Opng. | .52 | 2.67 | | 3.19 | |
| | Paint | Ea. | 3.65 | 6.30 | | 9.95 | |
| | Minimum Charge | Job | | 181 | | 181 | |
| **Double Width** | | | | | | | |
| | Demolish | Ea. | | 7.60 | | 7.60 | Cost includes material and labor to |
| | Install | Opng. | 27.50 | 72.50 | | 100 | install 11/16" x 2-1/2" pine ranch |
| | Demolish and Install | Opng. | 27.50 | 80.10 | | 107.60 | style door casing for one side of a |
| | Reinstall | Opng. | | 57.86 | | 57.86 | double door opening. |
| | Clean | Opng. | .61 | 5.35 | | 5.96 | |
| | Paint | Ea. | 3.65 | 7.15 | | 10.80 | |
| | Minimum Charge | Job | | 181 | | 181 | |

# Exterior Doors and Windows

| Residential Metal Door | | Unit | Material | Labor | Equip. | Total | Specification |
|---|---|---|---|---|---|---|---|
| **Pre-hung, Steel-clad** | | | | | | | |
| **2' 8" x 6' 8"** | | | | | | | |
| | Demolish | Ea. | | 33.50 | | 33.50 | Cost includes material and labor to |
| | Install | Ea. | 248 | 45 | | 293 | install 2' 6" x 6' 8" pre-hung 1-3/4" |
| | Demolish and Install | Ea. | 248 | 78.50 | | 326.50 | 24 gauge steel clad door with 4-1/2" |
| | Reinstall | Ea. | | 45.20 | | 45.20 | wood frame, trims, hinges, aluminum |
| | Clean | Ea. | 3.63 | 11.10 | | 14.73 | sill, weatherstripped. |
| | Paint | Ea. | 9.45 | 45 | | 54.45 | |
| | Minimum Charge | Job | | 181 | | 181 | |
| **3' x 6' 8"** | | | | | | | |
| | Demolish | Ea. | | 33.50 | | 33.50 | Cost includes material and labor to |
| | Install | Ea. | 248 | 48 | | 296 | install 3' x 6' 8" pre-hung 1-3/4" 24 |
| | Demolish and Install | Ea. | 248 | 81.50 | | 329.50 | gauge steel clad door with 4-1/2" |
| | Reinstall | Ea. | | 48.21 | | 48.21 | wood frame, trims, hinges, aluminum |
| | Clean | Ea. | 3.63 | 11.10 | | 14.73 | sill, weatherstripped. |
| | Paint | Ea. | 9.45 | 45 | | 54.45 | |
| | Minimum Charge | Job | | 181 | | 181 | |

| Metal Door | | Unit | Material | Labor | Equip. | Total | Specification |
|---|---|---|---|---|---|---|---|
| **2' 8" x 6' 8", 18 Gauge** | | | | | | | |
| | Demolish | Ea. | | 7.15 | | 7.15 | Cost includes material and labor to |
| | Install | Ea. | 335 | 22.50 | | 357.50 | install 18 gauge 2' 8" x 6' 8" steel |
| | Demolish and Install | Ea. | 335 | 29.65 | | 364.65 | door only, 1-3/4" thick, hinges. |
| | Reinstall | Ea. | | 22.60 | | 22.60 | |
| | Clean | Ea. | 1.52 | 8.35 | | 9.87 | |
| | Paint | Ea. | 4.50 | 26 | | 30.50 | |
| | Minimum Charge | Job | | 181 | | 181 | |
| **3' x 6' 8", 18 Gauge** | | | | | | | |
| | Demolish | Ea. | | 7.15 | | 7.15 | Cost includes material and labor to |
| | Install | Ea. | 325 | 24 | | 349 | install 18 gauge 3' x 6' 8" steel door |
| | Demolish and Install | Ea. | 325 | 31.15 | | 356.15 | only, 1-3/4" thick, hinges. |
| | Reinstall | Ea. | | 24.11 | | 24.11 | |
| | Clean | Ea. | 1.52 | 8.35 | | 9.87 | |
| | Paint | Ea. | 4.50 | 26 | | 30.50 | |
| | Minimum Charge | Job | | 181 | | 181 | |
| **2' 8" x 7', 18 Gauge** | | | | | | | |
| | Demolish | Ea. | | 7.15 | | 7.15 | Cost includes material and labor to |
| | Install | Ea. | 425 | 24 | | 449 | install 18 gauge 2' 8" x 7' steel door |
| | Demolish and Install | Ea. | 425 | 31.15 | | 456.15 | only, 1-3/4" thick, hinges. |
| | Reinstall | Ea. | | 24.11 | | 24.11 | |
| | Clean | Ea. | 1.52 | 8.35 | | 9.87 | |
| | Paint | Ea. | 4.50 | 26 | | 30.50 | |
| | Minimum Charge | Job | | 181 | | 181 | |
| **3' x 7', 18 Gauge** | | | | | | | |
| | Demolish | Ea. | | 7.15 | | 7.15 | Cost includes material and labor to |
| | Install | Ea. | 400 | 26 | | 426 | install 18 gauge 3' x 7' steel door |
| | Demolish and Install | Ea. | 400 | 33.15 | | 433.15 | only, 1-3/4" thick, hinges. |
| | Reinstall | Ea. | | 25.83 | | 25.83 | |
| | Clean | Ea. | 1.52 | 8.35 | | 9.87 | |
| | Paint | Ea. | 4.50 | 26 | | 30.50 | |
| | Minimum Charge | Job | | 181 | | 181 | |

# Exterior Doors and Windows

| Metal Door | | Unit | Material | Labor | Equip. | Total | Specification |
|---|---|---|---|---|---|---|---|
| **3' 6" x 7', 18 Gauge** | | | | | | | |
| | Demolish | Ea. | | 7.15 | | 7.15 | Cost includes material and labor to |
| | Install | Ea. | 435 | 28 | | 463 | install 18 gauge 3' 6" x 7' steel door |
| | Demolish and Install | Ea. | 435 | 35.15 | | 470.15 | only, 1-3/4" thick, hinges. |
| | Reinstall | Ea. | | 27.82 | | 27.82 | |
| | Clean | Ea. | 1.52 | 8.35 | | 9.87 | |
| | Paint | Ea. | 4.50 | 26 | | 30.50 | |
| | Minimum Charge | Job | | 181 | | 181 | |
| **Casing Trim** | | | | | | | |
| **Single Width** | | | | | | | |
| | Demolish | Ea. | | 6.40 | | 6.40 | Cost includes material and labor to |
| | Install | Opng. | 23.50 | 61.50 | | 85 | install 11/16" x 2-1/2" pine ranch |
| | Demolish and Install | Opng. | 23.50 | 67.90 | | 91.40 | style casing for one side of a standard |
| | Reinstall | Opng. | | 49.03 | | 49.03 | door opening. |
| | Clean | Opng. | .52 | 2.67 | | 3.19 | |
| | Paint | Ea. | 3.65 | 6.30 | | 9.95 | |
| | Minimum Charge | Job | | 181 | | 181 | |
| **Double Width** | | | | | | | |
| | Demolish | Ea. | | 7.60 | | 7.60 | Cost includes material and labor to |
| | Install | Opng. | 27.50 | 72.50 | | 100 | install 11/16" x 2-1/2" pine ranch |
| | Demolish and Install | Opng. | 27.50 | 80.10 | | 107.60 | style door casing for one side of a |
| | Reinstall | Opng. | | 57.86 | | 57.86 | double door opening. |
| | Clean | Opng. | .61 | 5.35 | | 5.96 | |
| | Paint | Ea. | 3.65 | 7.15 | | 10.80 | |
| | Minimum Charge | Job | | 181 | | 181 | |

| Solid Core Door | | Unit | Material | Labor | Equip. | Total | Specification |
|---|---|---|---|---|---|---|---|
| **Exterior Type** | | | | | | | |
| **Flush (1-3/4")** | | | | | | | |
| | Demolish | Ea. | | 33.50 | | 33.50 | Cost includes material and labor to |
| | Install | Ea. | 390 | 45 | | 435 | install 3' x 6' 8" pre-hung 1-3/4" |
| | Demolish and Install | Ea. | 390 | 78.50 | | 468.50 | door, including casing and stop, |
| | Reinstall | Ea. | | 45.20 | | 45.20 | hinges, jamb, aluminum sill, |
| | Clean | Ea. | 3.63 | 11.10 | | 14.73 | weatherstripped. |
| | Paint | Ea. | 9.45 | 45 | | 54.45 | |
| | Minimum Charge | Job | | 181 | | 181 | |
| **Raised Panel** | | | | | | | |
| | Demolish | Ea. | | 33.50 | | 33.50 | Cost includes material and labor to |
| | Install | Ea. | 445 | 20 | | 465 | install 3' x 6' 8" pre-hung 1-3/4" |
| | Demolish and Install | Ea. | 445 | 53.50 | | 498.50 | door, jamb, including casing and |
| | Reinstall | Ea. | | 20.09 | | 20.09 | stop, hinges, aluminum sill, |
| | Clean | Ea. | 3.63 | 11.10 | | 14.73 | weatherstripping. |
| | Paint | Ea. | 9.45 | 105 | | 114.45 | |
| | Minimum Charge | Job | | 181 | | 181 | |
| **Entry w / Lights** | | | | | | | |
| | Demolish | Ea. | | 33.50 | | 33.50 | Cost includes material and labor to |
| | Install | Ea. | 300 | 45 | | 345 | install 3' x 6' 8" pre-hung 1-3/4" |
| | Demolish and Install | Ea. | 300 | 78.50 | | 378.50 | door, solid wood lower panel, with up |
| | Reinstall | Ea. | | 45.20 | | 45.20 | to 9-light glass panels, casing, sill, |
| | Clean | Ea. | 3.63 | 11.10 | | 14.73 | weatherstripped. |
| | Paint | Ea. | 2.17 | 105 | | 107.17 | |
| | Minimum Charge | Job | | 181 | | 181 | |

## Solid Core Door

| Solid Core Door | Unit | Material | Labor | Equip. | Total | Specification |
|---|---|---|---|---|---|---|
| **Custom Entry** | | | | | | |
| Demolish | Ea. | | 33.50 | | 33.50 | Cost includes material and labor to |
| Install | Ea. | 1475 | 72.50 | | 1547.50 | install pre-hung fir, single glazed with |
| Demolish and Install | Ea. | 1475 | 106 | | 1581 | lead caming, 1-3/4" x 6'8" x 3'. |
| Reinstall | Ea. | | 72.32 | | 72.32 | |
| Clean | Ea. | 3.63 | 11.10 | | 14.73 | |
| Paint | Ea. | 4.50 | 26 | | 30.50 | |
| Minimum Charge | Job | | 181 | | 181 | |
| **Dutch Style** | | | | | | |
| Demolish | Ea. | | 33.50 | | 33.50 | Includes material and labor to install |
| Install | Ea. | 755 | 60.50 | | 815.50 | dutch door, pine, 1-3/4" x 6' 8" x 2' |
| Demolish and Install | Ea. | 755 | 94 | | 849 | 8" wide. |
| Reinstall | Ea. | | 60.27 | | 60.27 | |
| Clean | Ea. | 3.63 | 11.10 | | 14.73 | |
| Paint | Ea. | 2.17 | 105 | | 107.17 | |
| Minimum Charge | Job | | 181 | | 181 | |
| **Miami Style** | | | | | | |
| Demolish | Ea. | | 33.50 | | 33.50 | Cost includes material and labor to |
| Install | Ea. | 215 | 18.10 | | 233.10 | install 3' x 6' 8" pre-hung 1-3/4" |
| Demolish and Install | Ea. | 215 | 51.60 | | 266.60 | lauan door of solid wood. |
| Reinstall | Ea. | | 18.08 | | 18.08 | |
| Clean | Ea. | 3.63 | 11.10 | | 14.73 | |
| Paint | Ea. | 9.30 | 45 | | 54.30 | |
| Minimum Charge | Job | | 181 | | 181 | |
| **French Style** | | | | | | |
| Demolish | Ea. | | 37 | | 37 | Cost includes material and labor to |
| Install | Ea. | 665 | 51.50 | | 716.50 | install 3' x 6' 8" pre-hung 1-3/4" |
| Demolish and Install | Ea. | 665 | 88.50 | | 753.50 | french style door with 15 lights. |
| Reinstall | Ea. | | 51.66 | | 51.66 | |
| Clean | Ea. | .25 | 11.10 | | 11.35 | |
| Paint | Ea. | 7.10 | 157 | | 164.10 | |
| Minimum Charge | Job | | 181 | | 181 | |
| **Double** | | | | | | |
| Demolish | Ea. | | 24.50 | | 24.50 | Includes material and labor to install a |
| Install | Ea. | 1150 | 90.50 | | 1240.50 | pre-hung double entry door including |
| Demolish and Install | Ea. | 1150 | 115 | | 1265 | frame and exterior trim. |
| Clean | Ea. | .13 | 38.50 | | 38.63 | |
| Paint | Ea. | 19 | 157 | | 176 | |
| Minimum Charge | Job | | 90.50 | | 90.50 | |
| **Commercial Grade** | | | | | | |
| **3' x 6' 8"** | | | | | | |
| Demolish | Ea. | | 33.50 | | 33.50 | Includes material and labor to install |
| Install | Ea. | 300 | 21.50 | | 321.50 | flush solid core 1-3/4" hardwood |
| Demolish and Install | Ea. | 300 | 55 | | 355 | veneer 3' x 6' 8' door only. |
| Reinstall | Ea. | | 21.27 | | 21.27 | |
| Clean | Ea. | 3.63 | 11.10 | | 14.73 | |
| Paint | Ea. | 7.50 | 26 | | 33.50 | |
| Minimum Charge | Job | | 181 | | 181 | |
| **3' 6" x 6' 8"** | | | | | | |
| Demolish | Ea. | | 33.50 | | 33.50 | Includes material and labor to install |
| Install | Ea. | 405 | 21.50 | | 426.50 | flush solid core 1-3/4" hardwood |
| Demolish and Install | Ea. | 405 | 55 | | 460 | veneer 3' 6" x 6' 8' door only. |
| Reinstall | Ea. | | 21.27 | | 21.27 | |
| Clean | Ea. | 3.63 | 11.10 | | 14.73 | |
| Paint | Ea. | 7.50 | 26 | | 33.50 | |
| Minimum Charge | Job | | 181 | | 181 | |

# Exterior Doors and Windows

| Solid Core Door | | Unit | Material | Labor | Equip. | Total | Specification |
|---|---|---|---|---|---|---|---|
| **3' x 7'** | | | | | | | |
| | Demolish | Ea. | | 33.50 | | 33.50 | Includes material and labor to install |
| | Install | Ea. | 315 | 51.50 | | 366.50 | flush solid core 1-3/4" hardwood |
| | Demolish and Install | Ea. | 315 | 85 | | 400 | veneer 3' x 7' door only. |
| | Reinstall | Ea. | | 51.66 | | 51.66 | |
| | Clean | Ea. | 3.63 | 11.10 | | 14.73 | |
| | Paint | Ea. | 7.50 | 26 | | 33.50 | |
| | Minimum Charge | Job | | 181 | | 181 | |
| **3' 6" x 7'** | | | | | | | |
| | Demolish | Ea. | | 33.50 | | 33.50 | Includes material and labor to install |
| | Install | Ea. | 435 | 26 | | 461 | flush solid core 1-3/4" hardwood |
| | Demolish and Install | Ea. | 435 | 59.50 | | 494.50 | veneer 3' 6" x 7' door only. |
| | Reinstall | Ea. | | 25.83 | | 25.83 | |
| | Clean | Ea. | 3.63 | 11.10 | | 14.73 | |
| | Paint | Ea. | 7.50 | 26 | | 33.50 | |
| | Minimum Charge | Job | | 181 | | 181 | |
| **3' x 8'** | | | | | | | |
| | Demolish | Ea. | | 33.50 | | 33.50 | Includes material and labor to install |
| | Install | Ea. | 380 | 45 | | 425 | flush solid core 1-3/4" hardwood |
| | Demolish and Install | Ea. | 380 | 78.50 | | 458.50 | veneer 3' x 8' door only. |
| | Reinstall | Ea. | | 45.20 | | 45.20 | |
| | Clean | Ea. | 4.36 | 16.70 | | 21.06 | |
| | Paint | Ea. | 7.50 | 26 | | 33.50 | |
| | Minimum Charge | Job | | 181 | | 181 | |
| **3' 6" x 8'** | | | | | | | |
| | Demolish | Ea. | | 33.50 | | 33.50 | Includes material and labor to install |
| | Install | Ea. | 460 | 45 | | 505 | flush solid core 1-3/4" hardwood |
| | Demolish and Install | Ea. | 460 | 78.50 | | 538.50 | veneer 3' 6" x 8' door only. |
| | Reinstall | Ea. | | 45.20 | | 45.20 | |
| | Clean | Ea. | 4.36 | 16.70 | | 21.06 | |
| | Paint | Ea. | 7.50 | 26 | | 33.50 | |
| | Minimum Charge | Job | | 181 | | 181 | |
| **3' x 9'** | | | | | | | |
| | Demolish | Ea. | | 33.50 | | 33.50 | Includes material and labor to install |
| | Install | Ea. | 485 | 51.50 | | 536.50 | flush solid core 1-3/4" hardwood |
| | Demolish and Install | Ea. | 485 | 85 | | 570 | veneer 3' x 9' door only. |
| | Reinstall | Ea. | | 51.66 | | 51.66 | |
| | Clean | Ea. | 4.36 | 16.70 | | 21.06 | |
| | Paint | Ea. | 7.50 | 26 | | 33.50 | |
| | Minimum Charge | Job | | 181 | | 181 | |
| **Stain** | | | | | | | |
| | Install | Ea. | 7 | 35 | | 42 | Includes labor and material to stain |
| | Minimum Charge | Job | | 157 | | 157 | exterior type door and trim on both sides. |
| **Door Only (SC)** | | | | | | | |
| **2' 4" x 6' 8"** | | | | | | | |
| | Demolish | Ea. | | 7.15 | | 7.15 | Cost includes material and labor to |
| | Install | Ea. | 205 | 20 | | 225 | install 2' 4" x 6' 8" lauan solid core |
| | Demolish and Install | Ea. | 205 | 27.15 | | 232.15 | door slab. |
| | Reinstall | Ea. | | 20.09 | | 20.09 | |
| | Clean | Ea. | 1.52 | 8.35 | | 9.87 | |
| | Paint | Ea. | 2.66 | 39.50 | | 42.16 | |
| | Minimum Charge | Job | | 181 | | 181 | |

# Exterior Doors and Windows

| Solid Core Door | Unit | Material | Labor | Equip. | Total | Specification |
|---|---|---|---|---|---|---|
| **2' 8" x 6' 8"** | | | | | | |
| Demolish | Ea. | | 7.15 | | 7.15 | Cost includes material and labor to |
| Install | Ea. | 210 | 20 | | 230 | install 2' 8" x 6' 8" lauan solid core |
| Demolish and Install | Ea. | 210 | 27.15 | | 237.15 | door slab. |
| Reinstall | Ea. | | 20.09 | | 20.09 | |
| Clean | Ea. | 1.52 | 8.35 | | 9.87 | |
| Paint | Ea. | 2.66 | 39.50 | | 42.16 | |
| Minimum Charge | Job | | 181 | | 181 | |
| **3' x 6' 8"** | | | | | | |
| Demolish | Ea. | | 7.15 | | 7.15 | Cost includes material and labor to |
| Install | Ea. | 218 | 21.50 | | 239.50 | install 3' x 6' 8" lauan solid core door |
| Demolish and Install | Ea. | 218 | 28.65 | | 246.65 | slab. |
| Reinstall | Ea. | | 21.27 | | 21.27 | |
| Clean | Ea. | 1.52 | 8.35 | | 9.87 | |
| Paint | Ea. | 2.66 | 39.50 | | 42.16 | |
| Minimum Charge | Job | | 181 | | 181 | |
| **3' 6" x 6' 8"** | | | | | | |
| Demolish | Ea. | | 7.15 | | 7.15 | Cost includes material and labor to |
| Install | Ea. | 248 | 22.50 | | 270.50 | install 3' 6" x 6' 8" lauan solid core |
| Demolish and Install | Ea. | 248 | 29.65 | | 277.65 | door slab. |
| Reinstall | Ea. | | 22.60 | | 22.60 | |
| Clean | Ea. | 1.52 | 8.35 | | 9.87 | |
| Paint | Ea. | 2.66 | 39.50 | | 42.16 | |
| Minimum Charge | Job | | 181 | | 181 | |
| **Panel** | | | | | | |
| Demolish | Ea. | | 7.15 | | 7.15 | Cost includes material and labor to |
| Install | Ea. | 179 | 42.50 | | 221.50 | install 3' x 6' 8" six (6) panel interior |
| Demolish and Install | Ea. | 179 | 49.65 | | 228.65 | door. |
| Reinstall | Ea. | | 42.54 | | 42.54 | |
| Clean | Ea. | 1.82 | 8.35 | | 10.17 | |
| Paint | Ea. | 2.66 | 39.50 | | 42.16 | |
| Minimum Charge | Job | | 181 | | 181 | |
| **Casing Trim** | | | | | | |
| **Single Width** | | | | | | |
| Demolish | Ea. | | 6.40 | | 6.40 | Cost includes material and labor to |
| Install | Opng. | 23.50 | 61.50 | | 85 | install 11/16" x 2-1/2" pine ranch |
| Demolish and Install | Opng. | 23.50 | 67.90 | | 91.40 | style casing for one side of a standard |
| Reinstall | Opng. | | 49.03 | | 49.03 | door opening. |
| Clean | Opng. | .52 | 2.67 | | 3.19 | |
| Paint | Ea. | 3.65 | 6.30 | | 9.95 | |
| Minimum Charge | Job | | 181 | | 181 | |
| **Double Width** | | | | | | |
| Demolish | Ea. | | 7.60 | | 7.60 | Cost includes material and labor to |
| Install | Opng. | 27.50 | 72.50 | | 100 | install 11/16" x 2-1/2" pine ranch |
| Demolish and Install | Opng. | 27.50 | 80.10 | | 107.60 | style door casing for one side of a |
| Reinstall | Opng. | | 57.86 | | 57.86 | double door opening. |
| Clean | Opng. | .61 | 5.35 | | 5.96 | |
| Paint | Ea. | 3.65 | 7.15 | | 10.80 | |
| Minimum Charge | Job | | 181 | | 181 | |

# Exterior Doors and Windows

| Components | | Unit | Material | Labor | Equip. | Total | Specification |
|---|---|---|---|---|---|---|---|
| **Hardware** | | | | | | | |
| **Doorknob** | | | | | | | |
| | Demolish | Ea. | | 13.40 | | 13.40 | Includes material and labor to install |
| | Install | Ea. | 19.80 | 22.50 | | 42.30 | residential passage lockset, keyless |
| | Demolish and Install | Ea. | 19.80 | 35.90 | | 55.70 | bored type. |
| | Reinstall | Ea. | | 18.08 | | 18.08 | |
| | Clean | Ea. | .36 | 8.35 | | 8.71 | |
| | Minimum Charge | Job | | 181 | | 181 | |
| **Doorknob w / Lock** | | | | | | | |
| | Demolish | Ea. | | 13.40 | | 13.40 | Includes material and labor to install |
| | Install | Ea. | 26 | 22.50 | | 48.50 | privacy lockset. |
| | Demolish and Install | Ea. | 26 | 35.90 | | 61.90 | |
| | Reinstall | Ea. | | 18.08 | | 18.08 | |
| | Clean | Ea. | .36 | 8.35 | | 8.71 | |
| | Minimum Charge | Job | | 181 | | 181 | |
| **Lever Handle** | | | | | | | |
| | Demolish | Ea. | | 13.40 | | 13.40 | Includes material and labor to install |
| | Install | Ea. | 28.50 | 36 | | 64.50 | residential passage lockset, keyless |
| | Demolish and Install | Ea. | 28.50 | 49.40 | | 77.90 | bored type with lever handle. |
| | Reinstall | Ea. | | 28.93 | | 28.93 | |
| | Clean | Ea. | .36 | 8.35 | | 8.71 | |
| | Minimum Charge | Job | | 181 | | 181 | |
| **Deadbolt** | | | | | | | |
| | Demolish | Ea. | | 12.55 | | 12.55 | Includes material and labor to install a |
| | Install | Ea. | 55.50 | 26 | | 81.50 | deadbolt. |
| | Demolish and Install | Ea. | 55.50 | 38.55 | | 94.05 | |
| | Reinstall | Ea. | | 20.66 | | 20.66 | |
| | Clean | Ea. | .36 | 8.35 | | 8.71 | |
| | Minimum Charge | Job | | 181 | | 181 | |
| **Grip Handle Entry** | | | | | | | |
| | Demolish | Ea. | | 11.50 | | 11.50 | Includes material and labor to install |
| | Install | Ea. | 132 | 40 | | 172 | residential keyed entry lock set with |
| | Demolish and Install | Ea. | 132 | 51.50 | | 183.50 | grip type handle. |
| | Reinstall | Ea. | | 32.14 | | 32.14 | |
| | Clean | Ea. | .36 | 8.35 | | 8.71 | |
| | Minimum Charge | Job | | 181 | | 181 | |
| **Panic Device** | | | | | | | |
| | Demolish | Ea. | | 29.50 | | 29.50 | Includes material and labor to install |
| | Install | Ea. | 375 | 60.50 | | 435.50 | touch bar, low profile, exit only. |
| | Demolish and Install | Ea. | 375 | 90 | | 465 | |
| | Reinstall | Ea. | | 48.21 | | 48.21 | |
| | Clean | Ea. | .19 | 14.80 | | 14.99 | |
| | Minimum Charge | Job | | 181 | | 181 | |
| **Closer** | | | | | | | |
| | Demolish | Ea. | | 7.55 | | 7.55 | Includes material and labor to install |
| | Install | Ea. | 182 | 60.50 | | 242.50 | pneumatic heavy duty closer for |
| | Demolish and Install | Ea. | 182 | 68.05 | | 250.05 | exterior type doors. |
| | Reinstall | Ea. | | 48.21 | | 48.21 | |
| | Clean | Ea. | .19 | 11.10 | | 11.29 | |
| | Minimum Charge | Job | | 181 | | 181 | |
| **Peep-hole** | | | | | | | |
| | Demolish | Ea. | | 6.60 | | 6.60 | Includes material and labor to install |
| | Install | Ea. | 16.25 | 11.30 | | 27.55 | peep-hole for door. |
| | Demolish and Install | Ea. | 16.25 | 17.90 | | 34.15 | |
| | Reinstall | Ea. | | 9.04 | | 9.04 | |
| | Clean | Ea. | .02 | 2.95 | | 2.97 | |
| | Minimum Charge | Job | | 181 | | 181 | |

| Components | | Unit | Material | Labor | Equip. | Total | Specification |
|---|---|---|---|---|---|---|---|
| **Exit Sign** | | | | | | | |
| | Demolish | Ea. | | 20 | | 20 | Includes material and labor to install a |
| | Install | Ea. | 93.50 | 49.50 | | 143 | wall mounted interior electric exit sign. |
| | Demolish and Install | Ea. | 93.50 | 69.50 | | 163 | |
| | Reinstall | Ea. | | 39.76 | | 39.76 | |
| | Clean | Ea. | .02 | 6 | | 6.02 | |
| | Minimum Charge | Job | | 181 | | 181 | |
| **Kickplate** | | | | | | | |
| | Demolish | Ea. | | 11.15 | | 11.15 | Includes material and labor to install |
| | Install | Ea. | 23 | 24 | | 47 | aluminum kickplate, 10" x 28". |
| | Demolish and Install | Ea. | 23 | 35.15 | | 58.15 | |
| | Reinstall | Ea. | | 19.29 | | 19.29 | |
| | Clean | Ea. | .36 | 8.35 | | 8.71 | |
| | Minimum Charge | Job | | 181 | | 181 | |
| **Threshold** | | | | | | | |
| | Install | L.F. | 4.19 | 3.62 | | 7.81 | Includes labor and material to install |
| | Minimum Charge | Job | | 90.50 | | 90.50 | oak threshold. |
| **Weatherstripping** | | | | | | | |
| | Install | L.F. | .30 | .90 | | 1.20 | Includes labor and material to install |
| | Minimum Charge | Job | | 90.50 | | 90.50 | rubber weatherstripping for door. |
| **Metal Jamb** | | | | | | | |
| **6' 8" High** | | | | | | | |
| | Demolish | Ea. | | 20 | | 20 | Cost includes material and labor to |
| | Install | Ea. | 138 | 22.50 | | 160.50 | install 18 gauge hollow metal door |
| | Demolish and Install | Ea. | 138 | 42.50 | | 180.50 | frame to fit a 4-1/2" jamb 6' 8" high |
| | Reinstall | Ea. | | 22.60 | | 22.60 | and up to 3' 6" opening. |
| | Clean | Ea. | .76 | 5.55 | | 6.31 | |
| | Paint | Ea. | 1.24 | 6.30 | | 7.54 | |
| | Minimum Charge | Job | | 181 | | 181 | |
| **7' High** | | | | | | | |
| | Demolish | Ea. | | 20 | | 20 | Cost includes material and labor to |
| | Install | Ea. | 143 | 24 | | 167 | install 18 gauge hollow metal door |
| | Demolish and Install | Ea. | 143 | 44 | | 187 | frame to fit a 4-1/2" jamb 7' high and |
| | Reinstall | Ea. | | 24.11 | | 24.11 | up to 3' 6" opening. |
| | Clean | Ea. | .76 | 5.55 | | 6.31 | |
| | Paint | Ea. | 1.24 | 6.30 | | 7.54 | |
| | Minimum Charge | Job | | 181 | | 181 | |
| **8' High** | | | | | | | |
| | Demolish | Ea. | | 20 | | 20 | Cost includes material and labor to |
| | Install | Ea. | 175 | 30 | | 205 | install 18 gauge hollow metal door |
| | Demolish and Install | Ea. | 175 | 50 | | 225 | frame to fit a 4-1/2" jamb 8' high and |
| | Reinstall | Ea. | | 30.13 | | 30.13 | up to 3' 6" opening. |
| | Clean | Ea. | 1.07 | 6.65 | | 7.72 | |
| | Paint | Ea. | 1.39 | 7 | | 8.39 | |
| | Minimum Charge | Job | | 181 | | 181 | |
| **9' High** | | | | | | | |
| | Demolish | Ea. | | 20 | | 20 | Cost includes material and labor to |
| | Install | Ea. | 194 | 36 | | 230 | install 18 gauge hollow metal door |
| | Demolish and Install | Ea. | 194 | 56 | | 250 | frame to fit a 4-1/2" jamb 9' high and |
| | Reinstall | Ea. | | 36.16 | | 36.16 | up to 3' 6" opening. |
| | Clean | Ea. | 1.07 | 6.65 | | 7.72 | |
| | Paint | Ea. | 1.39 | 7 | | 8.39 | |
| | Minimum Charge | Job | | 181 | | 181 | |

# Exterior Doors and Windows

| Components | | Unit | Material | Labor | Equip. | Total | Specification |
|---|---|---|---|---|---|---|---|
| **Wood Jamb** | | | | | | | |
| | Demolish | Ea. | | 25 | | 25 | Includes material and labor to install |
| | Install | Ea. | 100 | 9.75 | | 109.75 | flat pine jamb with square cut heads |
| | Demolish and Install | Ea. | 100 | 34.75 | | 134.75 | and rabbeted sides for 6' 8" high and |
| | Clean | Ea. | .12 | 6.65 | | 6.77 | 3-9/16" door including trim sets for |
| | Paint | Ea. | 6.05 | 21 | | 27.05 | both sides. |
| | Minimum Charge | Job | | 90.50 | | 90.50 | |
| **Stain** | | | | | | | |
| | Install | Ea. | 4.81 | 26 | | 30.81 | Includes labor and material to stain |
| | Minimum Charge | Job | | 157 | | 157 | single door and trim on both sides. |
| **Shave & Refit** | | | | | | | |
| | Install | Ea. | | 30 | | 30 | Includes labor to shave and rework |
| | Minimum Charge | Job | | 90.50 | | 90.50 | door to fit opening at the job site. |

| Sliding Patio Door | | Unit | Material | Labor | Equip. | Total | Specification |
|---|---|---|---|---|---|---|---|
| **Aluminum** | | | | | | | |
| **6' Single Pane** | | | | | | | |
| | Demolish | Ea. | | 50 | | 50 | Cost includes material and labor to |
| | Install | Ea. | 450 | 181 | | 631 | install 6' x 6' 8" sliding anodized |
| | Demolish and Install | Ea. | 450 | 231 | | 681 | aluminum patio door with single pane |
| | Reinstall | Ea. | | 144.64 | | 144.64 | tempered safety glass, anodized |
| | Clean | Ea. | 2.27 | 16.70 | | 18.97 | frame, screen, weatherstripped. |
| | Minimum Charge | Job | | 181 | | 181 | |
| **8' Single Pane** | | | | | | | |
| | Demolish | Ea. | | 50 | | 50 | Cost includes material and labor to |
| | Install | Ea. | 515 | 241 | | 756 | install 8' x 6' 8" sliding aluminum |
| | Demolish and Install | Ea. | 515 | 291 | | 806 | patio door with single pane tempered |
| | Reinstall | Ea. | | 192.85 | | 192.85 | safety glass, anodized frame, screen, |
| | Clean | Ea. | 2.27 | 16.70 | | 18.97 | weatherstripped. |
| | Minimum Charge | Job | | 181 | | 181 | |
| **10' Single Pane** | | | | | | | |
| | Demolish | Ea. | | 50 | | 50 | Cost includes material and labor to |
| | Install | Ea. | 670 | 360 | | 1030 | install 10' x 6' 8" sliding aluminum |
| | Demolish and Install | Ea. | 670 | 410 | | 1080 | patio door with single pane tempered |
| | Reinstall | Ea. | | 289.28 | | 289.28 | safety glass, anodized frame, screen, |
| | Clean | Ea. | 2.27 | 16.70 | | 18.97 | weatherstripped. |
| | Minimum Charge | Job | | 181 | | 181 | |
| **6' Insulated** | | | | | | | |
| | Demolish | Ea. | | 50 | | 50 | Cost includes material and labor to |
| | Install | Ea. | 615 | 181 | | 796 | install 6' x 6' 8" sliding aluminum |
| | Demolish and Install | Ea. | 615 | 231 | | 846 | patio door with double insulated |
| | Reinstall | Ea. | | 144.64 | | 144.64 | tempered glass, baked-on enamel |
| | Clean | Ea. | 2.27 | 16.70 | | 18.97 | finish, screen, weatherstripped. |
| | Minimum Charge | Job | | 181 | | 181 | |
| **8' Insulated** | | | | | | | |
| | Demolish | Ea. | | 50 | | 50 | Cost includes material and labor to |
| | Install | Ea. | 720 | 241 | | 961 | install 8' x 6' 8" sliding aluminum |
| | Demolish and Install | Ea. | 720 | 291 | | 1011 | patio door with insulated tempered |
| | Reinstall | Ea. | | 192.85 | | 192.85 | glass, baked-on enamel finish, screen, |
| | Clean | Ea. | 2.27 | 16.70 | | 18.97 | weatherstripped. |
| | Minimum Charge | Job | | 181 | | 181 | |

| Sliding Patio Door | Unit | Material | Labor | Equip. | Total | Specification |
|---|---|---|---|---|---|---|
| **10' Insulated** | | | | | | |
| Demolish | Ea. | | 50 | | 50 | Cost includes material and labor to |
| Install | Ea. | 805 | 360 | | 1165 | install 10' x 6' 8" sliding aluminum |
| Demolish and Install | Ea. | 805 | 410 | | 1215 | patio door with double insulated |
| Reinstall | Ea. | | 289.28 | | 289.28 | tempered glass, baked-on enamel |
| Clean | Ea. | 2.27 | 16.70 | | 18.97 | finish, screen, weatherstripped. |
| Minimum Charge | Job | | 181 | | 181 | |
| **Vinyl** | | | | | | |
| **6' Single Pane** | | | | | | |
| Demolish | Ea. | | 50 | | 50 | Cost includes material and labor to |
| Install | Ea. | 440 | 181 | | 621 | install 6' x 6' 8" sliding vinyl patio |
| Demolish and Install | Ea. | 440 | 231 | | 671 | door with single pane tempered safety |
| Reinstall | Ea. | | 144.64 | | 144.64 | glass, anodized frame, screen, |
| Clean | Ea. | 2.27 | 16.70 | | 18.97 | weatherstripped. |
| Minimum Charge | Job | | 181 | | 181 | |
| **8' Single Pane** | | | | | | |
| Demolish | Ea. | | 50 | | 50 | Cost includes material and labor to |
| Install | Ea. | 495 | 241 | | 736 | install 8' x 6' 8" sliding vinyl patio |
| Demolish and Install | Ea. | 495 | 291 | | 786 | door with single pane tempered safety |
| Reinstall | Ea. | | 192.85 | | 192.85 | glass, anodized frame, screen, |
| Clean | Ea. | 2.27 | 16.70 | | 18.97 | weatherstripped. |
| Minimum Charge | Job | | 181 | | 181 | |
| **10' Single Pane** | | | | | | |
| Demolish | Ea. | | 50 | | 50 | Cost includes material and labor to |
| Install | Ea. | 640 | 360 | | 1000 | install 10' x 6' 8" sliding vinyl patio |
| Demolish and Install | Ea. | 640 | 410 | | 1050 | door with single pane tempered safety |
| Reinstall | Ea. | | 289.28 | | 289.28 | glass, anodized frame, screen, |
| Clean | Ea. | 2.27 | 16.70 | | 18.97 | weatherstripped. |
| Minimum Charge | Job | | 181 | | 181 | |
| **6' Insulated** | | | | | | |
| Demolish | Ea. | | 50 | | 50 | Cost includes material and labor to |
| Install | Ea. | 755 | 181 | | 936 | install 6' x 6' 8" sliding vinyl patio |
| Demolish and Install | Ea. | 755 | 231 | | 986 | door with double insulated tempered |
| Reinstall | Ea. | | 144.64 | | 144.64 | glass, anodized frame, screen, |
| Clean | Ea. | 2.27 | 16.70 | | 18.97 | weatherstripped. |
| Minimum Charge | Job | | 181 | | 181 | |
| **8' Insulated** | | | | | | |
| Demolish | Ea. | | 50 | | 50 | Cost includes material and labor to |
| Install | Ea. | 965 | 241 | | 1206 | install 8' x 6' 8" sliding vinyl patio |
| Demolish and Install | Ea. | 965 | 291 | | 1256 | door with double insulated tempered |
| Reinstall | Ea. | | 192.85 | | 192.85 | glass, anodized frame, screen, |
| Clean | Ea. | 2.27 | 16.70 | | 18.97 | weatherstripped. |
| Minimum Charge | Job | | 181 | | 181 | |
| **10' Insulated** | | | | | | |
| Demolish | Ea. | | 50 | | 50 | Cost includes material and labor to |
| Install | Ea. | 1025 | 360 | | 1385 | install 10' x 6' 8" sliding vinyl patio |
| Demolish and Install | Ea. | 1025 | 410 | | 1435 | door with double insulated tempered |
| Reinstall | Ea. | | 289.28 | | 289.28 | glass, anodized frame, screen, |
| Clean | Ea. | 2.27 | 16.70 | | 18.97 | weatherstripped. |
| Minimum Charge | Job | | 181 | | 181 | |

# Exterior Doors and Windows

| Sliding Patio Door | | Unit | Material | Labor | Equip. | Total | Specification |
|---|---|---|---|---|---|---|---|
| **Wood Framed** | | | | | | | |
| **6' Premium Insulated** | | | | | | | |
| | Demolish | Ea. | | 50 | | 50 | Cost includes material and labor to |
| | Install | Ea. | 1300 | 181 | | 1481 | install 6' x 6' 8" sliding wood patio |
| | Demolish and Install | Ea. | 1300 | 231 | | 1531 | door with pine frame, double insulated |
| | Reinstall | Ea. | | 144.64 | | 144.64 | glass, screen, lock and dead bolt, |
| | Clean | Ea. | 2.27 | 16.70 | | 18.97 | weatherstripped. Add for casing and |
| | Minimum Charge | Job | | 181 | | 181 | finishing. |
| **8' Premium Insulated** | | | | | | | |
| | Demolish | Ea. | | 50 | | 50 | Cost includes material and labor to |
| | Install | Ea. | 1525 | 241 | | 1766 | install 8' x 6' 8" sliding wood patio |
| | Demolish and Install | Ea. | 1525 | 291 | | 1816 | door with pine frame, double insulated |
| | Reinstall | Ea. | | 192.85 | | 192.85 | glass, screen, lock and dead bolt, |
| | Clean | Ea. | 2.27 | 16.70 | | 18.97 | weatherstripped. Add for casing and |
| | Minimum Charge | Job | | 181 | | 181 | finishing. |
| **9' Premium Insulated** | | | | | | | |
| | Demolish | Ea. | | 50 | | 50 | Cost includes material and labor to |
| | Install | Ea. | 1525 | 241 | | 1766 | install 9' x 6' 8" sliding wood patio |
| | Demolish and Install | Ea. | 1525 | 291 | | 1816 | door with pine frame, double insulated |
| | Reinstall | Ea. | | 192.85 | | 192.85 | glass, screen, lock and dead bolt, |
| | Clean | Ea. | 2.27 | 16.70 | | 18.97 | weatherstripped. Add for casing and |
| | Minimum Charge | Job | | 181 | | 181 | finishing. |
| **Stain** | | | | | | | |
| | Install | Ea. | 7 | 35 | | 42 | Includes labor and material to stain |
| | Minimum Charge | Job | | 157 | | 157 | exterior type door and trim on both |
| | | | | | | | sides. |
| **Casing Trim** | | | | | | | |
| | Demolish | Ea. | | 7.60 | | 7.60 | Cost includes material and labor to |
| | Install | Opng. | 27.50 | 72.50 | | 100 | install 11/16" x 2-1/2" pine ranch |
| | Demolish and Install | Opng. | 27.50 | 80.10 | | 107.60 | style door casing for one side of a |
| | Reinstall | Opng. | | 57.86 | | 57.86 | double door opening. |
| | Clean | Opng. | .61 | 5.35 | | 5.96 | |
| | Paint | Ea. | 3.65 | 7.15 | | 10.80 | |
| | Minimum Charge | Job | | 181 | | 181 | |
| **Sliding Screen** | | | | | | | |
| | Demolish | Ea. | | 7.15 | | 7.15 | Includes material and labor to install |
| | Install | Ea. | 121 | 18.10 | | 139.10 | sliding screen door, 6' 8" x 3'. |
| | Demolish and Install | Ea. | 121 | 25.25 | | 146.25 | |
| | Reinstall | Ea. | | 14.46 | | 14.46 | |
| | Clean | Ea. | .76 | 5.55 | | 6.31 | |
| | Minimum Charge | Job | | 181 | | 181 | |

| Screen Door | | Unit | Material | Labor | Equip. | Total | Specification |
|---|---|---|---|---|---|---|---|
| **Aluminum** | | | | | | | |
| | Demolish | Ea. | | 33.50 | | 33.50 | Includes material and labor to install |
| | Install | Ea. | 108 | 51.50 | | 159.50 | aluminum frame screen door with |
| | Demolish and Install | Ea. | 108 | 85 | | 193 | fiberglass screen cloth, closer, hinges, |
| | Reinstall | Ea. | | 41.33 | | 41.33 | latch. |
| | Clean | Ea. | 3.63 | 11.10 | | 14.73 | |
| | Paint | Ea. | 3.51 | 12.60 | | 16.11 | |
| | Minimum Charge | Job | | 181 | | 181 | |

# Exterior Doors and Windows

| Screen Door | | Unit | Material | Labor | Equip. | Total | Specification |
|---|---|---|---|---|---|---|---|
| **Wood** | | | | | | | Includes material and labor to install |
| | Demolish | Ea. | | 33.50 | | 33.50 | wood screen door with aluminum cloth |
| | Install | Ea. | 146 | 60.50 | | 206.50 | screen. Frame and hardware not |
| | Demolish and Install | Ea. | 146 | 94 | | 240 | included. |
| | Reinstall | Ea. | | 48.21 | | 48.21 | |
| | Clean | Ea. | 3.63 | 11.10 | | 14.73 | |
| | Paint | Ea. | 3.51 | 12.60 | | 16.11 | |
| | Minimum Charge | Job | | 181 | | 181 | |
| **Shave & Refit** | | | | | | | |
| | Install | Ea. | | 30 | | 30 | Includes labor to shave and rework |
| | Minimum Charge | Job | | 181 | | 181 | door to fit opening at the job site. |

| Storm Door | | Unit | Material | Labor | Equip. | Total | Specification |
|---|---|---|---|---|---|---|---|
| **Good Grade** | | | | | | | |
| | Demolish | Ea. | | 33.50 | | 33.50 | Includes material and labor to install |
| | Install | Ea. | 172 | 51.50 | | 223.50 | aluminum frame storm door with |
| | Demolish and Install | Ea. | 172 | 85 | | 257 | fiberglass screen cloth, upper glass |
| | Reinstall | Ea. | | 41.33 | | 41.33 | panel, closer, hinges, latch. |
| | Clean | Ea. | 3.63 | 11.10 | | 14.73 | |
| | Paint | Ea. | 3.51 | 12.60 | | 16.11 | |
| | Minimum Charge | Job | | 181 | | 181 | |
| **Better Grade** | | | | | | | |
| | Demolish | Ea. | | 33.50 | | 33.50 | Includes material and labor to install |
| | Install | Ea. | 227 | 51.50 | | 278.50 | aluminum frame storm door with |
| | Demolish and Install | Ea. | 227 | 85 | | 312 | fiberglass screen cloth, upper and |
| | Reinstall | Ea. | | 41.33 | | 41.33 | lower glass panel, closer, latch. |
| | Clean | Ea. | 3.63 | 11.10 | | 14.73 | |
| | Paint | Ea. | 3.51 | 12.60 | | 16.11 | |
| | Minimum Charge | Job | | 181 | | 181 | |
| **Premium Grade** | | | | | | | |
| | Demolish | Ea. | | 33.50 | | 33.50 | Includes material and labor to install |
| | Install | Ea. | 282 | 51.50 | | 333.50 | aluminum frame storm door with |
| | Demolish and Install | Ea. | 282 | 85 | | 367 | fiberglass screen cloth, upper and |
| | Reinstall | Ea. | | 41.33 | | 41.33 | lower glass panel, closer, latch. |
| | Clean | Ea. | 3.63 | 11.10 | | 14.73 | |
| | Paint | Ea. | 3.51 | 12.60 | | 16.11 | |
| | Minimum Charge | Job | | 181 | | 181 | |
| **Insulated** | | | | | | | |
| | Demolish | Ea. | | 33.50 | | 33.50 | Includes material and labor to install |
| | Install | Ea. | 260 | 26 | | 286 | aluminum frame storm door with |
| | Demolish and Install | Ea. | 260 | 59.50 | | 319.50 | fiberglass screen cloth, upper and |
| | Reinstall | Ea. | | 20.66 | | 20.66 | lower glass panel, closer, latch. |
| | Clean | Ea. | 3.63 | 11.10 | | 14.73 | |
| | Paint | Ea. | 3.51 | 12.60 | | 16.11 | |
| | Minimum Charge | Job | | 181 | | 181 | |

# Exterior Doors and Windows

| Garage Door | | Unit | Material | Labor | Equip. | Total | Specification |
|---|---|---|---|---|---|---|---|
| **9′ One Piece Metal** | | | | | | | |
| | Demolish | Ea. | | 84.50 | | 84.50 | Includes material and labor to install |
| | Install | Ea. | 415 | 90.50 | | 505.50 | one piece steel garage door 9′ x 7′ |
| | Demolish and Install | Ea. | 415 | 175 | | 590 | primed including hardware. |
| | Reinstall | Ea. | | 72.32 | | 72.32 | |
| | Clean | Ea. | 4.54 | 33.50 | | 38.04 | |
| | Paint | Ea. | 7.80 | 78.50 | | 86.30 | |
| | Minimum Charge | Job | | 181 | | 181 | |
| **16′ One Piece Metal** | | | | | | | |
| | Demolish | Ea. | | 100 | | 100 | Includes material and labor to install |
| | Install | Ea. | 650 | 121 | | 771 | one piece steel garage door 16′ x 7′ |
| | Demolish and Install | Ea. | 650 | 221 | | 871 | primed including hardware. |
| | Reinstall | Ea. | | 96.43 | | 96.43 | |
| | Clean | Ea. | 9.10 | 44.50 | | 53.60 | |
| | Paint | Ea. | 15.60 | 90 | | 105.60 | |
| | Minimum Charge | Job | | 181 | | 181 | |
| **9′ Metal Sectional** | | | | | | | |
| | Demolish | Ea. | | 84.50 | | 84.50 | Includes material and labor to install |
| | Install | Ea. | 555 | 137 | | 692 | sectional metal garage door 9′ x 7′ |
| | Demolish and Install | Ea. | 555 | 221.50 | | 776.50 | primed including hardware. |
| | Reinstall | Ea. | | 109.58 | | 109.58 | |
| | Clean | Ea. | 4.65 | 38 | | 42.65 | |
| | Paint | Ea. | 15.60 | 90 | | 105.60 | |
| | Minimum Charge | Job | | 181 | | 181 | |
| **16′ Metal Sectional** | | | | | | | |
| | Demolish | Ea. | | 100 | | 100 | Includes material and labor to install |
| | Install | Ea. | 710 | 241 | | 951 | sectional metal garage door 16′ x 7′ |
| | Demolish and Install | Ea. | 710 | 341 | | 1051 | primed including hardware. |
| | Reinstall | Ea. | | 192.85 | | 192.85 | |
| | Clean | Ea. | 9.10 | 44.50 | | 53.60 | |
| | Paint | Ea. | 15.60 | 90 | | 105.60 | |
| | Minimum Charge | Job | | 181 | | 181 | |
| **Metal / Steel Roll Up** | | | | | | | |
| **8′ x 8′ Steel** | | | | | | | |
| | Demolish | Ea. | | 115 | | 115 | Cost includes material and labor to |
| | Install | Ea. | 1050 | 560 | | 1610 | install 8′ x 8′ steel overhead roll-up, |
| | Demolish and Install | Ea. | 1050 | 675 | | 1725 | chain hoist operated service door. |
| | Reinstall | Ea. | | 448 | | 448 | |
| | Clean | Ea. | 4.65 | 38 | | 42.65 | |
| | Paint | Ea. | 16.65 | 105 | | 121.65 | |
| | Minimum Charge | Job | | 895 | | 895 | |
| **10′ x 10′ Steel** | | | | | | | |
| | Demolish | Ea. | | 134 | | 134 | Cost includes material and labor to |
| | Install | Ea. | 1850 | 640 | | 2490 | install 10′ x 10′ steel overhead roll-up, |
| | Demolish and Install | Ea. | 1850 | 774 | | 2624 | chain hoist operated service door. |
| | Reinstall | Ea. | | 512 | | 512 | |
| | Clean | Ea. | 7.25 | 53.50 | | 60.75 | |
| | Paint | Ea. | 26 | 105 | | 131 | |
| | Minimum Charge | Job | | 895 | | 895 | |
| **12′ x 12′ Steel** | | | | | | | |
| | Demolish | Ea. | | 161 | | 161 | Cost includes material and labor to |
| | Install | Ea. | 1900 | 745 | | 2645 | install 12′ x 12′ steel overhead roll-up, |
| | Demolish and Install | Ea. | 1900 | 906 | | 2806 | chain hoist operated service door. |
| | Reinstall | Ea. | | 597.33 | | 597.33 | |
| | Clean | Ea. | 10.45 | 59.50 | | 69.95 | |
| | Paint | Ea. | 37.50 | 126 | | 163.50 | |
| | Minimum Charge | Job | | 895 | | 895 | |

# Exterior Doors and Windows

| Garage Door | | Unit | Material | Labor | Equip. | Total | Specification |
|---|---|---|---|---|---|---|---|
| **14' x 14' Steel** | | | | | | | |
| | Demolish | Ea. | | 201 | | 201 | Cost includes material and labor to |
| | Install | Ea. | 3075 | 1125 | | 4200 | install 14' x 14' steel overhead roll-up, |
| | Demolish and Install | Ea. | 3075 | 1326 | | 4401 | chain hoist operated service door. |
| | Reinstall | Ea. | | 896 | | 896 | |
| | Clean | Ea. | 14.25 | 76 | | 90.25 | |
| | Paint | Ea. | 44 | 157 | | 201 | |
| | Minimum Charge | Job | | 895 | | 895 | |
| **18' x 18' Steel** | | | | | | | |
| | Demolish | Ea. | | 223 | | 223 | Cost includes material and labor to |
| | Install | Opng. | 2975 | 1500 | | 4475 | install 18' x 18' steel overhead roll-up, |
| | Demolish and Install | Opng. | 2975 | 1723 | | 4698 | chain hoist operated service door. |
| | Reinstall | Opng. | | 1194.67 | | 1194.67 | |
| | Clean | Ea. | 14.25 | 44.50 | | 58.75 | |
| | Paint | Ea. | 84 | 315 | | 399 | |
| | Minimum Charge | Job | | 895 | | 895 | |
| **Automatic Motor** | | | | | | | |
| | Install | Ea. | 435 | 36 | | 471 | Includes labor and material to install |
| | Minimum Charge | Job | | 181 | | 181 | electric opener motor, 1/3 HP. |
| **9' One Piece Wood** | | | | | | | |
| | Demolish | Ea. | | 84.50 | | 84.50 | Includes material and labor to install |
| | Install | Ea. | 455 | 90.50 | | 545.50 | one piece wood garage door 9' x 7' |
| | Demolish and Install | Ea. | 455 | 175 | | 630 | primed including hardware. |
| | Reinstall | Ea. | | 72.32 | | 72.32 | |
| | Clean | Ea. | 4.54 | 33.50 | | 38.04 | |
| | Paint | Ea. | 7.80 | 78.50 | | 86.30 | |
| | Minimum Charge | Job | | 181 | | 181 | |
| **9' Wood Sectional** | | | | | | | |
| | Demolish | Ea. | | 84.50 | | 84.50 | Includes material and labor to install |
| | Install | Ea. | 595 | 90.50 | | 685.50 | sectional wood garage door 9' x 7' |
| | Demolish and Install | Ea. | 595 | 175 | | 770 | unfinished including hardware. |
| | Reinstall | Ea. | | 72.32 | | 72.32 | |
| | Clean | Ea. | 4.54 | 33.50 | | 38.04 | |
| | Paint | Ea. | 7.80 | 78.50 | | 86.30 | |
| | Minimum Charge | Job | | 181 | | 181 | |
| **16' Wood Sectional** | | | | | | | |
| | Demolish | Ea. | | 100 | | 100 | Includes material and labor to install |
| | Install | Ea. | 1300 | 121 | | 1421 | sectional fiberglass garage door 16' x |
| | Demolish and Install | Ea. | 1300 | 221 | | 1521 | 7' unfinished including hardware. |
| | Reinstall | Ea. | | 96.43 | | 96.43 | |
| | Clean | Ea. | 9.10 | 44.50 | | 53.60 | |
| | Paint | Ea. | 15.60 | 90 | | 105.60 | |
| | Minimum Charge | Job | | 181 | | 181 | |
| **Electric Opener** | | | | | | | |
| | Demolish | Ea. | | 59.50 | | 59.50 | Includes material and labor to install |
| | Install | Ea. | 287 | 68 | | 355 | electric opener, 1/3 HP economy. |
| | Demolish and Install | Ea. | 287 | 127.50 | | 414.50 | |
| | Reinstall | Ea. | | 54.27 | | 54.27 | |
| | Clean | Ea. | .19 | 14.80 | | 14.99 | |
| | Minimum Charge | Job | | 181 | | 181 | |
| **Springs** | | | | | | | |
| | Install | Pr. | 43.50 | 90.50 | | 134 | Includes labor and material to replace |
| | Minimum Charge | Job | | 181 | | 181 | springs for garage door. |

# Exterior Doors and Windows

| Commercial Metal Door | | Unit | Material | Labor | Equip. | Total | Specification |
|---|---|---|---|---|---|---|---|
| **Pre-hung Steel Door** | | | | | | | |
| **2' 8" x 6' 8"** | | | | | | | |
| | Demolish | Ea. | | 50 | | 50 | Cost includes material and labor to |
| | Install | Ea. | 570 | 22.50 | | 592.50 | install 2' 8" x 6' 8" pre-hung 1-3/4" |
| | Demolish and Install | Ea. | 570 | 72.50 | | 642.50 | 18 gauge steel door with steel frame, |
| | Reinstall | Ea. | | 22.60 | | 22.60 | hinges, aluminum sill, |
| | Clean | Ea. | 3.63 | 11.10 | | 14.73 | weather-stripped. |
| | Paint | Ea. | 4.50 | 26 | | 30.50 | |
| | Minimum Charge | Job | | 181 | | 181 | |
| **3' x 6' 8"** | | | | | | | |
| | Demolish | Ea. | | 50 | | 50 | Cost includes material and labor to |
| | Install | Ea. | 540 | 24 | | 564 | install 3' x 6' 8" pre-hung 1-3/4" 18 |
| | Demolish and Install | Ea. | 540 | 74 | | 614 | gauge steel door with steel frame, |
| | Reinstall | Ea. | | 24.11 | | 24.11 | hinges, aluminum sill, |
| | Clean | Ea. | 3.63 | 11.10 | | 14.73 | weather-stripped. |
| | Paint | Ea. | 4.50 | 26 | | 30.50 | |
| | Minimum Charge | Job | | 181 | | 181 | |
| **3' 6" x 6' 8"** | | | | | | | |
| | Demolish | Ea. | | 50 | | 50 | Cost includes material and labor to |
| | Install | Ea. | 620 | 28 | | 648 | install 3' 6" x 6' 8" pre-hung 1-3/4" |
| | Demolish and Install | Ea. | 620 | 78 | | 698 | 18 gauge steel door with steel frame, |
| | Reinstall | Ea. | | 27.82 | | 27.82 | hinges, aluminum sill, |
| | Clean | Ea. | 3.63 | 11.10 | | 14.73 | weather-stripped. |
| | Paint | Ea. | 4.50 | 26 | | 30.50 | |
| | Minimum Charge | Job | | 181 | | 181 | |
| **4' x 6' 8"** | | | | | | | |
| | Demolish | Ea. | | 50 | | 50 | Cost includes material and labor to |
| | Install | Ea. | 675 | 36 | | 711 | install 4' x 6' 8" pre-hung 1-3/4" 18 |
| | Demolish and Install | Ea. | 675 | 86 | | 761 | gauge steel door with steel frame, |
| | Reinstall | Ea. | | 36.16 | | 36.16 | hinges, aluminum sill, |
| | Clean | Ea. | 3.63 | 11.10 | | 14.73 | weather-stripped. |
| | Paint | Ea. | 4.50 | 26 | | 30.50 | |
| | Minimum Charge | Job | | 181 | | 181 | |
| **Metal Jamb** | | | | | | | |
| **6' 8" High** | | | | | | | |
| | Demolish | Ea. | | 20 | | 20 | Cost includes material and labor to |
| | Install | Ea. | 138 | 22.50 | | 160.50 | install 18 gauge hollow metal door |
| | Demolish and Install | Ea. | 138 | 42.50 | | 180.50 | frame to fit a 4-1/2" jamb 6' 8" high |
| | Reinstall | Ea. | | 22.60 | | 22.60 | and up to 3' 6" opening. |
| | Clean | Ea. | .76 | 5.55 | | 6.31 | |
| | Paint | Ea. | 1.24 | 6.30 | | 7.54 | |
| | Minimum Charge | Job | | 181 | | 181 | |
| **7' High** | | | | | | | |
| | Demolish | Ea. | | 20 | | 20 | Cost includes material and labor to |
| | Install | Ea. | 143 | 24 | | 167 | install 18 gauge hollow metal door |
| | Demolish and Install | Ea. | 143 | 44 | | 187 | frame to fit a 4-1/2" jamb 7' high and |
| | Reinstall | Ea. | | 24.11 | | 24.11 | up to 3' 6" opening. |
| | Clean | Ea. | .76 | 5.55 | | 6.31 | |
| | Paint | Ea. | 1.24 | 6.30 | | 7.54 | |
| | Minimum Charge | Job | | 181 | | 181 | |
| **8' High** | | | | | | | |
| | Demolish | Ea. | | 20 | | 20 | Cost includes material and labor to |
| | Install | Ea. | 175 | 30 | | 205 | install 18 gauge hollow metal door |
| | Demolish and Install | Ea. | 175 | 50 | | 225 | frame to fit a 4-1/2" jamb 8' high and |
| | Reinstall | Ea. | | 30.13 | | 30.13 | up to 3' 6" opening. |
| | Clean | Ea. | 1.07 | 6.65 | | 7.72 | |
| | Paint | Ea. | 1.39 | 7 | | 8.39 | |
| | Minimum Charge | Job | | 181 | | 181 | |

# Exterior Doors and Windows

| Commercial Metal Door | Unit | Material | Labor | Equip. | Total | Specification |
|---|---|---|---|---|---|---|
| **9′ High** | | | | | | |
| Demolish | Ea. | | 20 | | 20 | Cost includes material and labor to |
| Install | Ea. | 194 | 36 | | 230 | install 18 gauge hollow metal door |
| Demolish and Install | Ea. | 194 | 56 | | 250 | frame to fit a 4-1/2″ jamb 9′ high and |
| Reinstall | Ea. | | 36.16 | | 36.16 | up to 3′ 6″ opening. |
| Clean | Ea. | 1.07 | 6.65 | | 7.72 | |
| Paint | Ea. | 1.39 | 7 | | 8.39 | |
| Minimum Charge | Job | | 181 | | 181 | |
| **Hardware** | | | | | | |
| **Doorknob w / Lock** | | | | | | |
| Demolish | Ea. | | 13.40 | | 13.40 | Includes material and labor to install |
| Install | Ea. | 111 | 30 | | 141 | keyed entry lock set, bored type |
| Demolish and Install | Ea. | 111 | 43.40 | | 154.40 | including knob trim, strike and strike |
| Reinstall | Ea. | | 24.11 | | 24.11 | box for standard commercial |
| Clean | Ea. | .36 | 8.35 | | 8.71 | application. |
| Minimum Charge | Job | | 181 | | 181 | |
| **Lever Handle** | | | | | | |
| Demolish | Ea. | | 13.40 | | 13.40 | Includes material and labor to install |
| Install | Ea. | 58.50 | 36 | | 94.50 | passage lockset, keyless bored type |
| Demolish and Install | Ea. | 58.50 | 49.40 | | 107.90 | with lever handle, non-locking |
| Reinstall | Ea. | | 28.93 | | 28.93 | standard commercial latchset. |
| Clean | Ea. | .36 | 8.35 | | 8.71 | |
| Minimum Charge | Job | | 181 | | 181 | |
| **Deadbolt** | | | | | | |
| Demolish | Ea. | | 12.55 | | 12.55 | Includes material and labor to install a |
| Install | Ea. | 55.50 | 26 | | 81.50 | deadbolt. |
| Demolish and Install | Ea. | 55.50 | 38.55 | | 94.05 | |
| Reinstall | Ea. | | 20.66 | | 20.66 | |
| Clean | Ea. | .36 | 8.35 | | 8.71 | |
| Minimum Charge | Job | | 181 | | 181 | |
| **Panic Device** | | | | | | |
| Demolish | Ea. | | 29.50 | | 29.50 | Includes material and labor to install |
| Install | Ea. | 375 | 60.50 | | 435.50 | touch bar, low profile, exit only. |
| Demolish and Install | Ea. | 375 | 90 | | 465 | |
| Reinstall | Ea. | | 48.21 | | 48.21 | |
| Clean | Ea. | .19 | 14.80 | | 14.99 | |
| Minimum Charge | Job | | 181 | | 181 | |
| **Closer** | | | | | | |
| Demolish | Ea. | | 7.55 | | 7.55 | Includes material and labor to install |
| Install | Ea. | 191 | 60.50 | | 251.50 | pneumatic heavy duty model for |
| Demolish and Install | Ea. | 191 | 68.05 | | 259.05 | exterior type doors. |
| Reinstall | Ea. | | 48.21 | | 48.21 | |
| Clean | Ea. | .19 | 11.10 | | 11.29 | |
| Minimum Charge | Job | | 181 | | 181 | |
| **Peep-Hole** | | | | | | |
| Demolish | Ea. | | 6.60 | | 6.60 | Includes material and labor to install |
| Install | Ea. | 16.25 | 11.30 | | 27.55 | peep-hole for door. |
| Demolish and Install | Ea. | 16.25 | 17.90 | | 34.15 | |
| Reinstall | Ea. | | 9.04 | | 9.04 | |
| Clean | Ea. | .02 | 2.95 | | 2.97 | |
| Minimum Charge | Job | | 181 | | 181 | |
| **Exit Sign** | | | | | | |
| Demolish | Ea. | | 20 | | 20 | Includes material and labor to install a |
| Install | Ea. | 93.50 | 49.50 | | 143 | wall mounted interior electric exit sign. |
| Demolish and Install | Ea. | 93.50 | 69.50 | | 163 | |
| Reinstall | Ea. | | 39.76 | | 39.76 | |
| Clean | Ea. | .02 | 6 | | 6.02 | |
| Minimum Charge | Job | | 181 | | 181 | |

# Exterior Doors and Windows

## Commercial Metal Door

| | Unit | Material | Labor | Equip. | Total | Specification |
|---|---|---|---|---|---|---|
| **Kickplate** | | | | | | |
| Demolish | Ea. | | 11.15 | | 11.15 | Includes material and labor to install |
| Install | Ea. | 50 | 24 | | 74 | stainless steel kickplate, 10" x 36". |
| Demolish and Install | Ea. | 50 | 35.15 | | 85.15 | |
| Reinstall | Ea. | | 19.29 | | 19.29 | |
| Clean | Ea. | .36 | 8.35 | | 8.71 | |
| Minimum Charge | Job | | 181 | | 181 | |

## Aluminum Window

| | Unit | Material | Labor | Equip. | Total | Specification |
|---|---|---|---|---|---|---|
| **Single Hung Two Light** | | | | | | |
| **2' x 2'** | | | | | | |
| Demolish | Ea. | | 18.55 | | 18.55 | Cost includes material and labor to |
| Install | Ea. | 69.50 | 81.50 | | 151 | install 2' x 2' single hung, two light, |
| Demolish and Install | Ea. | 69.50 | 100.05 | | 169.55 | double glazed aluminum window |
| Reinstall | Ea. | | 65.16 | | 65.16 | including screen. |
| Clean | Ea. | .04 | 6.85 | | 6.89 | |
| Minimum Charge | Job | | 224 | | 224 | |
| **2' x 2' 6"** | | | | | | |
| Demolish | Ea. | | 18.55 | | 18.55 | Cost includes material and labor to |
| Install | Ea. | 72.50 | 81.50 | | 154 | install 2' x 2' 6" single hung, two |
| Demolish and Install | Ea. | 72.50 | 100.05 | | 172.55 | light, double glazed aluminum |
| Reinstall | Ea. | | 65.16 | | 65.16 | window including screen. |
| Clean | Ea. | .04 | 6.85 | | 6.89 | |
| Minimum Charge | Job | | 224 | | 224 | |
| **3' x 1' 6"** | | | | | | |
| Demolish | Ea. | | 18.55 | | 18.55 | Cost includes material and labor to |
| Install | Ea. | 68 | 89.50 | | 157.50 | install 3' x 1' 6" single hung, two |
| Demolish and Install | Ea. | 68 | 108.05 | | 176.05 | light, double glazed aluminum |
| Reinstall | Ea. | | 71.68 | | 71.68 | window including screen. |
| Clean | Ea. | .02 | 6 | | 6.02 | |
| Minimum Charge | Job | | 224 | | 224 | |
| **3' x 2'** | | | | | | |
| Demolish | Ea. | | 18.55 | | 18.55 | Cost includes material and labor to |
| Install | Ea. | 82.50 | 89.50 | | 172 | install 3' x 2' single hung, two light, |
| Demolish and Install | Ea. | 82.50 | 108.05 | | 190.55 | double glazed aluminum window |
| Reinstall | Ea. | | 71.68 | | 71.68 | including screen. |
| Clean | Ea. | .02 | 6 | | 6.02 | |
| Minimum Charge | Job | | 224 | | 224 | |
| **3' x 2' 6"** | | | | | | |
| Demolish | Ea. | | 18.55 | | 18.55 | Cost includes material and labor to |
| Install | Ea. | 86.50 | 89.50 | | 176 | install 3' x 2' 6" single hung, two |
| Demolish and Install | Ea. | 86.50 | 108.05 | | 194.55 | light, double glazed aluminum |
| Reinstall | Ea. | | 71.68 | | 71.68 | window including screen. |
| Clean | Ea. | .04 | 6.85 | | 6.89 | |
| Minimum Charge | Job | | 224 | | 224 | |
| **3' x 3'** | | | | | | |
| Demolish | Ea. | | 18.55 | | 18.55 | Cost includes material and labor to |
| Install | Ea. | 96.50 | 89.50 | | 186 | install 3' x 3' single hung, two light, |
| Demolish and Install | Ea. | 96.50 | 108.05 | | 204.55 | double glazed aluminum window |
| Reinstall | Ea. | | 71.68 | | 71.68 | including screen. |
| Clean | Ea. | .04 | 6.85 | | 6.89 | |
| Minimum Charge | Job | | 224 | | 224 | |

| Aluminum Window | Unit | Material | Labor | Equip. | Total | Specification |
|---|---|---|---|---|---|---|
| **3' x 3' 6"** | | | | | | |
| Demolish | Ea. | | 18.55 | | 18.55 | Cost includes material and labor to |
| Install | Ea. | 105 | 89.50 | | 194.50 | install 3' x 3' 6" single hung, two |
| Demolish and Install | Ea. | 105 | 108.05 | | 213.05 | light, double glazed aluminum |
| Reinstall | Ea. | | 71.68 | | 71.68 | window including screen. |
| Clean | Ea. | .06 | 8 | | 8.06 | |
| Minimum Charge | Job | | 224 | | 224 | |
| **3' x 4'** | | | | | | |
| Demolish | Ea. | | 18.55 | | 18.55 | Cost includes material and labor to |
| Install | Ea. | 114 | 89.50 | | 203.50 | install 3' x 4' single hung, two light, |
| Demolish and Install | Ea. | 114 | 108.05 | | 222.05 | double glazed aluminum window |
| Reinstall | Ea. | | 71.68 | | 71.68 | including screen. |
| Clean | Ea. | .06 | 8 | | 8.06 | |
| Minimum Charge | Job | | 224 | | 224 | |
| **3' x 5'** | | | | | | |
| Demolish | Ea. | | 27 | | 27 | Cost includes material and labor to |
| Install | Ea. | 123 | 89.50 | | 212.50 | install 3' x 5' single hung, two light, |
| Demolish and Install | Ea. | 123 | 116.50 | | 239.50 | double glazed aluminum window |
| Reinstall | Ea. | | 71.68 | | 71.68 | including screen. |
| Clean | Ea. | .07 | 9.60 | | 9.67 | |
| Minimum Charge | Job | | 224 | | 224 | |
| **3' x 6'** | | | | | | |
| Demolish | Ea. | | 27 | | 27 | Cost includes material and labor to |
| Install | Ea. | 138 | 99.50 | | 237.50 | install 3' x 6' single hung, two light, |
| Demolish and Install | Ea. | 138 | 126.50 | | 264.50 | double glazed aluminum window |
| Reinstall | Ea. | | 79.64 | | 79.64 | including screen. |
| Clean | Ea. | .08 | 11.25 | | 11.33 | |
| Minimum Charge | Job | | 224 | | 224 | |

## Double Hung Two Light

| | Unit | Material | Labor | Equip. | Total | Specification |
|---|---|---|---|---|---|---|
| **2' x 2'** | | | | | | |
| Demolish | Ea. | | 18.55 | | 18.55 | Cost includes material and labor to |
| Install | Ea. | 116 | 81.50 | | 197.50 | install 2' x 2' double hung, two light, |
| Demolish and Install | Ea. | 116 | 100.05 | | 216.05 | double glazed aluminum window |
| Reinstall | Ea. | | 65.16 | | 65.16 | including screen. |
| Clean | Ea. | .02 | 6 | | 6.02 | |
| Minimum Charge | Job | | 224 | | 224 | |
| **2' x 2' 6"** | | | | | | |
| Demolish | Ea. | | 18.55 | | 18.55 | Cost includes material and labor to |
| Install | Ea. | 125 | 81.50 | | 206.50 | install 2' x 2' 6" double hung, two |
| Demolish and Install | Ea. | 125 | 100.05 | | 225.05 | light, double glazed aluminum |
| Reinstall | Ea. | | 65.16 | | 65.16 | window including screen. |
| Clean | Ea. | .02 | 6 | | 6.02 | |
| Minimum Charge | Job | | 224 | | 224 | |
| **3' x 1' 6"** | | | | | | |
| Demolish | Ea. | | 18.55 | | 18.55 | Cost includes material and labor to |
| Install | Ea. | 298 | 89.50 | | 387.50 | install 3' x 1' 6" double hung, two |
| Demolish and Install | Ea. | 298 | 108.05 | | 406.05 | light, double glazed aluminum |
| Reinstall | Ea. | | 71.68 | | 71.68 | window including screen. |
| Clean | Ea. | .02 | 6 | | 6.02 | |
| Minimum Charge | Job | | 224 | | 224 | |
| **3' x 2'** | | | | | | |
| Demolish | Ea. | | 18.55 | | 18.55 | Cost includes material and labor to |
| Install | Ea. | 315 | 89.50 | | 404.50 | install 3' x 2' double hung, two light, |
| Demolish and Install | Ea. | 315 | 108.05 | | 423.05 | double glazed aluminum window |
| Reinstall | Ea. | | 71.68 | | 71.68 | including screen. |
| Clean | Ea. | .02 | 6 | | 6.02 | |
| Minimum Charge | Job | | 224 | | 224 | |

# Exterior Doors and Windows

| Aluminum Window | | Unit | Material | Labor | Equip. | Total | Specification |
|---|---|---|---|---|---|---|---|
| **3' x 2' 6"** | | | | | | | |
| | Demolish | Ea. | | 18.55 | | 18.55 | Cost includes material and labor to |
| | Install | Ea. | 315 | 89.50 | | 404.50 | install 3' x 2' 6" double hung, two |
| | Demolish and Install | Ea. | 315 | 108.05 | | 423.05 | light, double glazed aluminum |
| | Reinstall | Ea. | | 71.68 | | 71.68 | window including screen. |
| | Clean | Ea. | .04 | 6.85 | | 6.89 | |
| | Minimum Charge | Job | | 224 | | 224 | |
| **3' x 3'** | | | | | | | |
| | Demolish | Ea. | | 18.55 | | 18.55 | Cost includes material and labor to |
| | Install | Ea. | 340 | 89.50 | | 429.50 | install 3' x 3' double hung, two light, |
| | Demolish and Install | Ea. | 340 | 108.05 | | 448.05 | double glazed aluminum window |
| | Reinstall | Ea. | | 71.68 | | 71.68 | including screen. |
| | Clean | Ea. | .04 | 6.85 | | 6.89 | |
| | Minimum Charge | Job | | 224 | | 224 | |
| **3' x 3' 6"** | | | | | | | |
| | Demolish | Ea. | | 18.55 | | 18.55 | Cost includes material and labor to |
| | Install | Ea. | 375 | 89.50 | | 464.50 | install 3' x 3' 6" double hung, two |
| | Demolish and Install | Ea. | 375 | 108.05 | | 483.05 | light, double glazed aluminum |
| | Reinstall | Ea. | | 71.68 | | 71.68 | window including screen. |
| | Clean | Ea. | .06 | 8 | | 8.06 | |
| | Minimum Charge | Job | | 224 | | 224 | |
| **3' x 4'** | | | | | | | |
| | Demolish | Ea. | | 18.55 | | 18.55 | Cost includes material and labor to |
| | Install | Ea. | 390 | 89.50 | | 479.50 | install 3' x 4' double hung, two light, |
| | Demolish and Install | Ea. | 390 | 108.05 | | 498.05 | double glazed aluminum window |
| | Reinstall | Ea. | | 71.68 | | 71.68 | including screen. |
| | Clean | Ea. | .06 | 8 | | 8.06 | |
| | Minimum Charge | Job | | 224 | | 224 | |
| **3' x 5'** | | | | | | | |
| | Demolish | Ea. | | 27 | | 27 | Cost includes material and labor to |
| | Install | Ea. | 435 | 89.50 | | 524.50 | install 3' x 5' double hung, two light, |
| | Demolish and Install | Ea. | 435 | 116.50 | | 551.50 | double glazed aluminum window |
| | Reinstall | Ea. | | 71.68 | | 71.68 | including screen. |
| | Clean | Ea. | .07 | 9.60 | | 9.67 | |
| | Minimum Charge | Job | | 224 | | 224 | |
| **3' x 6'** | | | | | | | |
| | Demolish | Ea. | | 27 | | 27 | Cost includes material and labor to |
| | Install | Ea. | 560 | 99.50 | | 659.50 | install 3' x 6' double hung, two light, |
| | Demolish and Install | Ea. | 560 | 126.50 | | 686.50 | double glazed aluminum window |
| | Reinstall | Ea. | | 79.64 | | 79.64 | including screen. |
| | Clean | Ea. | .08 | 11.25 | | 11.33 | |
| | Minimum Charge | Job | | 224 | | 224 | |
| **Sliding Sash** | | | | | | | |
| **1' 6" x 3'** | | | | | | | |
| | Demolish | Ea. | | 18.55 | | 18.55 | Cost includes material and labor to |
| | Install | Ea. | 66.50 | 81.50 | | 148 | install 1' 6" x 3' sliding sash, two |
| | Demolish and Install | Ea. | 66.50 | 100.05 | | 166.55 | light, double glazed aluminum |
| | Reinstall | Ea. | | 65.16 | | 65.16 | window including screen. |
| | Clean | Ea. | .02 | 6 | | 6.02 | |
| | Minimum Charge | Job | | 224 | | 224 | |
| **2' x 2'** | | | | | | | |
| | Demolish | Ea. | | 18.55 | | 18.55 | Cost includes material and labor to |
| | Install | Ea. | 59 | 89.50 | | 148.50 | install 2' x 2' sliding sash, two light, |
| | Demolish and Install | Ea. | 59 | 108.05 | | 167.05 | double glazed aluminum window |
| | Reinstall | Ea. | | 71.68 | | 71.68 | including screen. |
| | Clean | Ea. | .02 | 6 | | 6.02 | |
| | Minimum Charge | Job | | 224 | | 224 | |

| Aluminum Window | | Unit | Material | Labor | Equip. | Total | Specification |
|---|---|---|---|---|---|---|---|
| **3' x 2'** | | | | | | | |
| | Demolish | Ea. | | 18.55 | | 18.55 | Cost includes material and labor to |
| | Install | Ea. | 77 | 89.50 | | 166.50 | install 3' x 2' sliding sash, two light, |
| | Demolish and Install | Ea. | 77 | 108.05 | | 185.05 | double glazed aluminum window |
| | Reinstall | Ea. | | 71.68 | | 71.68 | including screen. |
| | Clean | Ea. | .02 | 6 | | 6.02 | |
| | Minimum Charge | Job | | 224 | | 224 | |
| **3' x 2' 6"** | | | | | | | |
| | Demolish | Ea. | | 18.55 | | 18.55 | Cost includes material and labor to |
| | Install | Ea. | 80 | 89.50 | | 169.50 | install 3' x 2' 6" sliding sash, two |
| | Demolish and Install | Ea. | 80 | 108.05 | | 188.05 | light, double glazed aluminum |
| | Reinstall | Ea. | | 71.68 | | 71.68 | window including screen. |
| | Clean | Ea. | .04 | 6.85 | | 6.89 | |
| | Minimum Charge | Job | | 224 | | 224 | |
| **3' x 3'** | | | | | | | |
| | Demolish | Ea. | | 18.55 | | 18.55 | Cost includes material and labor to |
| | Install | Ea. | 82 | 89.50 | | 171.50 | install 3' x 3' sliding sash, two light, |
| | Demolish and Install | Ea. | 82 | 108.05 | | 190.05 | double glazed aluminum window |
| | Reinstall | Ea. | | 71.68 | | 71.68 | including screen. |
| | Clean | Ea. | .04 | 6.85 | | 6.89 | |
| | Minimum Charge | Job | | 224 | | 224 | |
| **3' x 3' 6"** | | | | | | | |
| | Demolish | Ea. | | 18.55 | | 18.55 | Cost includes material and labor to |
| | Install | Ea. | 95 | 89.50 | | 184.50 | install 3' x 3' 6" sliding sash, two |
| | Demolish and Install | Ea. | 95 | 108.05 | | 203.05 | light, double glazed aluminum |
| | Reinstall | Ea. | | 71.68 | | 71.68 | window including screen. |
| | Clean | Ea. | .06 | 8 | | 8.06 | |
| | Minimum Charge | Job | | 224 | | 224 | |
| **3' x 4'** | | | | | | | |
| | Demolish | Ea. | | 18.55 | | 18.55 | Cost includes material and labor to |
| | Install | Ea. | 103 | 99.50 | | 202.50 | install 3' x 4' sliding sash, two light, |
| | Demolish and Install | Ea. | 103 | 118.05 | | 221.05 | double glazed aluminum window |
| | Reinstall | Ea. | | 79.64 | | 79.64 | including screen. |
| | Clean | Ea. | .06 | 8 | | 8.06 | |
| | Minimum Charge | Job | | 224 | | 224 | |
| **3' x 5'** | | | | | | | |
| | Demolish | Ea. | | 27 | | 27 | Cost includes material and labor to |
| | Install | Ea. | 131 | 99.50 | | 230.50 | install 3' x 5' sliding sash, two light, |
| | Demolish and Install | Ea. | 131 | 126.50 | | 257.50 | double glazed aluminum window |
| | Reinstall | Ea. | | 79.64 | | 79.64 | including screen. |
| | Clean | Ea. | .07 | 9.60 | | 9.67 | |
| | Minimum Charge | Job | | 224 | | 224 | |
| **4' x 5'** | | | | | | | |
| | Demolish | Ea. | | 27 | | 27 | Cost includes material and labor to |
| | Install | Ea. | 133 | 128 | | 261 | install 4' x 5' sliding sash, two light, |
| | Demolish and Install | Ea. | 133 | 155 | | 288 | double glazed aluminum window |
| | Reinstall | Ea. | | 102.40 | | 102.40 | including screen. |
| | Clean | Ea. | .11 | 13.70 | | 13.81 | |
| | Minimum Charge | Job | | 224 | | 224 | |
| **5' x 5'** | | | | | | | |
| | Demolish | Ea. | | 27 | | 27 | Cost includes material and labor to |
| | Install | Ea. | 187 | 128 | | 315 | install 5' x 5' sliding sash, two light, |
| | Demolish and Install | Ea. | 187 | 155 | | 342 | double glazed aluminum window |
| | Reinstall | Ea. | | 102.40 | | 102.40 | including screen. |
| | Clean | Ea. | .11 | 13.70 | | 13.81 | |
| | Minimum Charge | Job | | 224 | | 224 | |

# Exterior Doors and Windows

| Aluminum Window | | Unit | Material | Labor | Equip. | Total | Specification |
|---|---|---|---|---|---|---|---|
| **Awning Sash** | | | | | | | |
| **26″ x 26″, 2 Light** | | | | | | | |
| | Demolish | Ea. | | 18.55 | | 18.55 | Cost includes material and labor to |
| | Install | Ea. | 285 | 99.50 | | 384.50 | install 26″ x 26″ two light awning, |
| | Demolish and Install | Ea. | 285 | 118.05 | | 403.05 | double glazed aluminum window |
| | Reinstall | Ea. | | 79.64 | | 79.64 | including screen. |
| | Clean | Ea. | .04 | 6.85 | | 6.89 | |
| | Minimum Charge | Job | | 224 | | 224 | |
| **26″ x 37″, 2 Light** | | | | | | | |
| | Demolish | Ea. | | 18.55 | | 18.55 | Cost includes material and labor to |
| | Install | Ea. | 325 | 99.50 | | 424.50 | install 26″ x 37″ two light awning, |
| | Demolish and Install | Ea. | 325 | 118.05 | | 443.05 | double glazed aluminum window |
| | Reinstall | Ea. | | 79.64 | | 79.64 | including screen. |
| | Clean | Ea. | .04 | 6.85 | | 6.89 | |
| | Minimum Charge | Job | | 224 | | 224 | |
| **38″ x 26″, 3 Light** | | | | | | | |
| | Demolish | Ea. | | 18.55 | | 18.55 | Cost includes material and labor to |
| | Install | Ea. | 365 | 99.50 | | 464.50 | install 38″ x 26″ three light awning, |
| | Demolish and Install | Ea. | 365 | 118.05 | | 483.05 | double glazed aluminum window |
| | Reinstall | Ea. | | 79.64 | | 79.64 | including screen. |
| | Clean | Ea. | .06 | 8 | | 8.06 | |
| | Minimum Charge | Job | | 224 | | 224 | |
| **38″ x 37″, 3 Light** | | | | | | | |
| | Demolish | Ea. | | 18.55 | | 18.55 | Cost includes material and labor to |
| | Install | Ea. | 370 | 112 | | 482 | install 38″ x 37″ three light awning, |
| | Demolish and Install | Ea. | 370 | 130.55 | | 500.55 | double glazed aluminum window |
| | Reinstall | Ea. | | 89.60 | | 89.60 | including screen. |
| | Clean | Ea. | .06 | 8 | | 8.06 | |
| | Minimum Charge | Job | | 224 | | 224 | |
| **38″ x 53″, 3 Light** | | | | | | | |
| | Demolish | Ea. | | 27 | | 27 | Cost includes material and labor to |
| | Install | Ea. | 605 | 112 | | 717 | install 38″ x 53″ three light awning, |
| | Demolish and Install | Ea. | 605 | 139 | | 744 | double glazed aluminum window |
| | Reinstall | Ea. | | 89.60 | | 89.60 | including screen. |
| | Clean | Ea. | .07 | 9.60 | | 9.67 | |
| | Minimum Charge | Job | | 224 | | 224 | |
| **50″ x 37″, 4 Light** | | | | | | | |
| | Demolish | Ea. | | 27 | | 27 | Cost includes material and labor to |
| | Install | Ea. | 610 | 112 | | 722 | install 50″ x 37″ four light awning, |
| | Demolish and Install | Ea. | 610 | 139 | | 749 | double glazed aluminum window |
| | Reinstall | Ea. | | 89.60 | | 89.60 | including screen. |
| | Clean | Ea. | .07 | 9.60 | | 9.67 | |
| | Minimum Charge | Job | | 224 | | 224 | |
| **50″ x 53″, 4 Light** | | | | | | | |
| | Demolish | Ea. | | 27 | | 27 | Cost includes material and labor to |
| | Install | Ea. | 1000 | 128 | | 1128 | install 50″ x 53″ four light awning, |
| | Demolish and Install | Ea. | 1000 | 155 | | 1155 | double glazed aluminum window |
| | Reinstall | Ea. | | 102.40 | | 102.40 | including screen. |
| | Clean | Ea. | .08 | 11.25 | | 11.33 | |
| | Minimum Charge | Job | | 224 | | 224 | |
| **63″ x 37″, 5 Light** | | | | | | | |
| | Demolish | Ea. | | 27 | | 27 | Cost includes material and labor to |
| | Install | Ea. | 785 | 128 | | 913 | install 63″ x 37″ five light awning, |
| | Demolish and Install | Ea. | 785 | 155 | | 940 | double glazed aluminum window |
| | Reinstall | Ea. | | 102.40 | | 102.40 | including screen. |
| | Clean | Ea. | .08 | 11.25 | | 11.33 | |
| | Minimum Charge | Job | | 224 | | 224 | |

| Aluminum Window | | Unit | Material | Labor | Equip. | Total | Specification |
|---|---|---|---|---|---|---|---|
| **63" x 53", 5 Light** | | | | | | | |
| | Demolish | Ea. | | 27 | | 27 | Cost includes material and labor to |
| | Install | Ea. | 1075 | 128 | | 1203 | install 63" x 53" five light awning, |
| | Demolish and Install | Ea. | 1075 | 155 | | 1230 | double glazed aluminum window |
| | Reinstall | Ea. | | 102.40 | | 102.40 | including screen. |
| | Clean | Ea. | .11 | 13.70 | | 13.81 | |
| | Minimum Charge | Job | | 224 | | 224 | |
| **Mullion Bars** | | | | | | | |
| | Install | Ea. | 10.90 | 36 | | 46.90 | Includes labor and material to install |
| | Minimum Charge | Job | | 224 | | 224 | mullions for sliding aluminum window. |
| **Bay** | | | | | | | |
| **4' 8" x 6' 4"** | | | | | | | |
| | Demolish | Ea. | | 19.75 | | 19.75 | Cost includes material and labor to |
| | Install | Ea. | 1275 | 90.50 | | 1365.50 | install 4' 8" x 6' 4" angle bay double |
| | Demolish and Install | Ea. | 1275 | 110.25 | | 1385.25 | hung unit, pine frame with aluminum |
| | Reinstall | Ea. | | 72.32 | | 72.32 | cladding, picture center sash, |
| | Clean | Ea. | .15 | 15.95 | | 16.10 | hardware, screens. |
| | Minimum Charge | Job | | 224 | | 224 | |
| **4' 8" x 7' 2"** | | | | | | | |
| | Demolish | Ea. | | 19.75 | | 19.75 | Cost includes material and labor to |
| | Install | Ea. | 1300 | 90.50 | | 1390.50 | install 4' 8" x 7' 2" angle bay double |
| | Demolish and Install | Ea. | 1300 | 110.25 | | 1410.25 | hung unit, pine frame with aluminum |
| | Reinstall | Ea. | | 72.32 | | 72.32 | cladding, picture center sash, |
| | Clean | Ea. | .15 | 15.95 | | 16.10 | hardware, screens. |
| | Minimum Charge | Job | | 224 | | 224 | |
| **4' 8" x 7' 10"** | | | | | | | |
| | Demolish | Ea. | | 19.75 | | 19.75 | Cost includes material and labor to |
| | Install | Ea. | 1300 | 90.50 | | 1390.50 | install 4' 8" x 7' 10" angle bay |
| | Demolish and Install | Ea. | 1300 | 110.25 | | 1410.25 | double hung unit, pine frame with |
| | Reinstall | Ea. | | 72.32 | | 72.32 | aluminum cladding, picture center |
| | Clean | Ea. | .15 | 15.95 | | 16.10 | sash, hardware, screens. |
| | Minimum Charge | Job | | 224 | | 224 | |
| **4' 8" x 8' 6"** | | | | | | | |
| | Demolish | Ea. | | 23 | | 23 | Cost includes material and labor to |
| | Install | Ea. | 1400 | 103 | | 1503 | install 4' 8" x 8' 6" angle bay double |
| | Demolish and Install | Ea. | 1400 | 126 | | 1526 | hung unit, pine frame with aluminum |
| | Reinstall | Ea. | | 82.65 | | 82.65 | cladding, picture center sash, |
| | Clean | Ea. | .02 | 21.50 | | 21.52 | hardware, screens. |
| | Minimum Charge | Job | | 224 | | 224 | |
| **4' 8" x 8' 10"** | | | | | | | |
| | Demolish | Ea. | | 23 | | 23 | Cost includes material and labor to |
| | Install | Ea. | 1450 | 103 | | 1553 | install 4' 8" x 8' 10" angle bay |
| | Demolish and Install | Ea. | 1450 | 126 | | 1576 | double hung unit, pine frame with |
| | Reinstall | Ea. | | 82.65 | | 82.65 | aluminum cladding, picture center |
| | Clean | Ea. | .02 | 21.50 | | 21.52 | sash, hardware, screens. |
| | Minimum Charge | Job | | 224 | | 224 | |
| **4' 8" x 9' 2"** | | | | | | | |
| | Demolish | Ea. | | 23 | | 23 | Cost includes material and labor to |
| | Install | Ea. | 1525 | 181 | | 1706 | install 4' 8" x 9' 2" angle bay double |
| | Demolish and Install | Ea. | 1525 | 204 | | 1729 | hung unit, pine frame with aluminum |
| | Reinstall | Ea. | | 144.64 | | 144.64 | cladding, picture center sash, |
| | Clean | Ea. | .02 | 21.50 | | 21.52 | hardware, screens. |
| | Minimum Charge | Job | | 224 | | 224 | |

| Aluminum Window | | Unit | Material | Labor | Equip. | Total | Specification |
|---|---|---|---|---|---|---|---|
| **4' 8" x 9' 10"** | | | | | | | |
| | Demolish | Ea. | | 23 | | 23 | Cost includes material and labor to |
| | Install | Ea. | 1600 | 181 | | 1781 | install 4' 8" x 9' 10" angle bay |
| | Demolish and Install | Ea. | 1600 | 204 | | 1804 | double hung unit, pine frame with |
| | Reinstall | Ea. | | 144.64 | | 144.64 | aluminum cladding, picture center |
| | Clean | Ea. | .02 | 21.50 | | 21.52 | sash, hardware, screens. |
| | Minimum Charge | Job | | 224 | | 224 | |
| **Casing** | | | | | | | |
| | Demolish | Ea. | | 8.35 | | 8.35 | Cost includes material and labor to |
| | Install | Opng. | 32 | 28 | | 60 | install 11/16" x 2-1/2" pine ranch |
| | Demolish and Install | Opng. | 32 | 36.35 | | 68.35 | style window casing. |
| | Reinstall | Opng. | | 22.25 | | 22.25 | |
| | Clean | Opng. | .52 | 2.67 | | 3.19 | |
| | Paint | Ea. | 3.65 | 6.30 | | 9.95 | |
| | Minimum Charge | Job | | 224 | | 224 | |
| **Storm Window** | | | | | | | |
| **2' x 3' 6"** | | | | | | | |
| | Demolish | Ea. | | 11 | | 11 | Includes material and labor to install |
| | Install | Ea. | 79 | 24 | | 103 | residential aluminum storm window |
| | Demolish and Install | Ea. | 79 | 35 | | 114 | with mill finish, 2' x 3' 5" high. |
| | Reinstall | Ea. | | 19.29 | | 19.29 | |
| | Clean | Ea. | .02 | 6 | | 6.02 | |
| | Minimum Charge | Job | | 224 | | 224 | |
| **2' 6" x 5'** | | | | | | | |
| | Demolish | Ea. | | 11 | | 11 | Includes material and labor to install |
| | Install | Ea. | 88.50 | 26 | | 114.50 | residential aluminum storm window |
| | Demolish and Install | Ea. | 88.50 | 37 | | 125.50 | with mill finish, 2' 6" x 5' high. |
| | Reinstall | Ea. | | 20.66 | | 20.66 | |
| | Clean | Ea. | .06 | 8 | | 8.06 | |
| | Minimum Charge | Job | | 224 | | 224 | |
| **4' x 6'** | | | | | | | |
| | Demolish | Ea. | | 21 | | 21 | Includes material and labor to install |
| | Install | Ea. | 105 | 29 | | 134 | residential aluminum storm window, 4' |
| | Demolish and Install | Ea. | 105 | 50 | | 155 | x 6' high. |
| | Reinstall | Ea. | | 23.14 | | 23.14 | |
| | Clean | Ea. | .11 | 12 | | 12.11 | |
| | Minimum Charge | Job | | 224 | | 224 | |
| **Hardware** | | | | | | | |
| **Weatherstripping** | | | | | | | |
| | Install | L.F. | .30 | 3.01 | | 3.31 | Includes labor and material to install |
| | Minimum Charge | Job | | 121 | | 121 | vinyl V strip weatherstripping for |
| | | | | | | | double-hung window. |
| **Trim Set** | | | | | | | |
| | Demolish | Ea. | | 8.35 | | 8.35 | Cost includes material and labor to |
| | Install | Opng. | 32 | 28 | | 60 | install 11/16" x 2-1/2" pine ranch |
| | Demolish and Install | Opng. | 32 | 36.35 | | 68.35 | style window casing. |
| | Reinstall | Opng. | | 22.25 | | 22.25 | |
| | Clean | Opng. | .52 | 2.67 | | 3.19 | |
| | Paint | Ea. | 3.65 | 6.30 | | 9.95 | |
| | Minimum Charge | Job | | 181 | | 181 | |

| Vinyl Window | Unit | Material | Labor | Equip. | Total | Specification |
|---|---|---|---|---|---|---|
| **Double Hung** | | | | | | |
| **2' x 2' 6"** | | | | | | |
| Demolish | Ea. | | 13.45 | | 13.45 | Cost includes material and labor to |
| Install | Ea. | 188 | 48 | | 236 | install 2' x 2' 6" double hung, two |
| Demolish and Install | Ea. | 188 | 61.45 | | 249.45 | light, vinyl window with screen. |
| Reinstall | Ea. | | 38.57 | | 38.57 | |
| Clean | Ea. | .02 | 6 | | 6.02 | |
| Minimum Charge | Job | | 360 | | 360 | |
| **2' x 3' 6"** | | | | | | |
| Demolish | Ea. | | 13.45 | | 13.45 | Cost includes material and labor to |
| Install | Ea. | 193 | 51.50 | | 244.50 | install 2' x 3' 6" double hung, two |
| Demolish and Install | Ea. | 193 | 64.95 | | 257.95 | light, vinyl window with screen. |
| Reinstall | Ea. | | 41.33 | | 41.33 | |
| Clean | Ea. | .04 | 6.85 | | 6.89 | |
| Minimum Charge | Job | | 360 | | 360 | |
| **2' 6" x 4' 6"** | | | | | | |
| Demolish | Ea. | | 13.45 | | 13.45 | Cost includes material and labor to |
| Install | Ea. | 230 | 55.50 | | 285.50 | install 2' 6" x 4' 6" double hung, two |
| Demolish and Install | Ea. | 230 | 68.95 | | 298.95 | light, vinyl window with screen. |
| Reinstall | Ea. | | 44.50 | | 44.50 | |
| Clean | Ea. | .06 | 8 | | 8.06 | |
| Minimum Charge | Job | | 360 | | 360 | |
| **3' x 4'** | | | | | | |
| Demolish | Ea. | | 13.45 | | 13.45 | Includes material and labor to install |
| Install | Ea. | 241 | 72.50 | | 313.50 | medium size double hung, 3' x 4', |
| Demolish and Install | Ea. | 241 | 85.95 | | 326.95 | two light, vinyl window with screen. |
| Reinstall | Ea. | | 57.86 | | 57.86 | |
| Clean | Ea. | .06 | 8 | | 8.06 | |
| Minimum Charge | Job | | 360 | | 360 | |
| **3' x 4' 6"** | | | | | | |
| Demolish | Ea. | | 16.45 | | 16.45 | Cost includes material and labor to |
| Install | Ea. | 259 | 80.50 | | 339.50 | install 3' x 4' 6" double hung, two |
| Demolish and Install | Ea. | 259 | 96.95 | | 355.95 | light, vinyl window with screen. |
| Reinstall | Ea. | | 64.28 | | 64.28 | |
| Clean | Ea. | .07 | 9.60 | | 9.67 | |
| Minimum Charge | Job | | 360 | | 360 | |
| **4' x 4' 6"** | | | | | | |
| Demolish | Ea. | | 16.45 | | 16.45 | Cost includes material and labor to |
| Install | Ea. | 330 | 90.50 | | 420.50 | install 4' x 4' 6" double hung, two |
| Demolish and Install | Ea. | 330 | 106.95 | | 436.95 | light, vinyl window with screen. |
| Reinstall | Ea. | | 72.32 | | 72.32 | |
| Clean | Ea. | .08 | 11.25 | | 11.33 | |
| Minimum Charge | Job | | 360 | | 360 | |
| **4' x 6'** | | | | | | |
| Demolish | Ea. | | 16.45 | | 16.45 | Includes material and labor to install |
| Install | Ea. | 330 | 103 | | 433 | large double hung, 4' x 6', two light, |
| Demolish and Install | Ea. | 330 | 119.45 | | 449.45 | vinyl window with screen. |
| Reinstall | Ea. | | 82.65 | | 82.65 | |
| Clean | Ea. | .11 | 13.70 | | 13.81 | |
| Minimum Charge | Job | | 360 | | 360 | |
| **Trim Set** | | | | | | |
| Demolish | Ea. | | 8.35 | | 8.35 | Cost includes material and labor to |
| Install | Opng. | 32 | 28 | | 60 | install 11/16" x 2-1/2" pine ranch |
| Demolish and Install | Opng. | 32 | 36.35 | | 68.35 | style window casing. |
| Reinstall | Opng. | | 22.25 | | 22.25 | |
| Clean | Opng. | .52 | 2.67 | | 3.19 | |
| Paint | Ea. | 3.65 | 6.30 | | 9.95 | |
| Minimum Charge | Job | | 224 | | 224 | |

# Exterior Doors and Windows

| Wood Window | Unit | Material | Labor | Equip. | Total | Specification |
|---|---|---|---|---|---|---|
| **2' 2" x 3' 4"** | | | | | | |
| Demolish | Ea. | | 13.45 | | 13.45 | Cost includes material and labor to |
| Install | Ea. | 204 | 48 | | 252 | install 2' 2" x 3' 4" double hung, two |
| Demolish and Install | Ea. | 204 | 61.45 | | 265.45 | light, double glazed wood window |
| Reinstall | Ea. | | 38.57 | | 38.57 | with screen. |
| Clean | Ea. | .04 | 6.85 | | 6.89 | |
| Paint | Ea. | 2.29 | 13.10 | | 15.39 | |
| Minimum Charge | Job | | 181 | | 181 | |
| **2' 2" x 4' 4"** | | | | | | |
| Demolish | Ea. | | 13.45 | | 13.45 | Cost includes material and labor to |
| Install | Ea. | 228 | 51.50 | | 279.50 | install 2' 2" x 4' 4" double hung, two |
| Demolish and Install | Ea. | 228 | 64.95 | | 292.95 | light, double glazed wood window |
| Reinstall | Ea. | | 41.33 | | 41.33 | with screen. |
| Clean | Ea. | .04 | 6.85 | | 6.89 | |
| Paint | Ea. | 2.29 | 13.10 | | 15.39 | |
| Minimum Charge | Job | | 181 | | 181 | |
| **2' 6" x 3' 4"** | | | | | | |
| Demolish | Ea. | | 13.45 | | 13.45 | Cost includes material and labor to |
| Install | Ea. | 213 | 55.50 | | 268.50 | install 2' 6" x 3' 4" double hung, two |
| Demolish and Install | Ea. | 213 | 68.95 | | 281.95 | light, double glazed wood window |
| Reinstall | Ea. | | 44.50 | | 44.50 | with screen. |
| Clean | Ea. | .06 | 8 | | 8.06 | |
| Paint | Ea. | 2.93 | 15.75 | | 18.68 | |
| Minimum Charge | Job | | 181 | | 181 | |
| **2' 6" x 4'** | | | | | | |
| Demolish | Ea. | | 13.45 | | 13.45 | Cost includes material and labor to |
| Install | Ea. | 231 | 60.50 | | 291.50 | install 2' 6" x 4' double hung, two |
| Demolish and Install | Ea. | 231 | 73.95 | | 304.95 | light, double glazed wood window |
| Reinstall | Ea. | | 48.21 | | 48.21 | with screen. |
| Clean | Ea. | .06 | 8 | | 8.06 | |
| Paint | Ea. | 2.93 | 15.75 | | 18.68 | |
| Minimum Charge | Job | | 181 | | 181 | |
| **2' 6" x 4' 8"** | | | | | | |
| Demolish | Ea. | | 13.45 | | 13.45 | Cost includes material and labor to |
| Install | Ea. | 254 | 60.50 | | 314.50 | install 2' 6" x 4' 8" double hung, two |
| Demolish and Install | Ea. | 254 | 73.95 | | 327.95 | light, double glazed wood window |
| Reinstall | Ea. | | 48.21 | | 48.21 | with screen. |
| Clean | Ea. | .06 | 8 | | 8.06 | |
| Paint | Ea. | 2.93 | 15.75 | | 18.68 | |
| Minimum Charge | Job | | 181 | | 181 | |
| **2' 10" x 3' 4"** | | | | | | |
| Demolish | Ea. | | 13.45 | | 13.45 | Cost includes material and labor to |
| Install | Ea. | 226 | 72.50 | | 298.50 | install 2' 10" x 3' 4" double hung, two |
| Demolish and Install | Ea. | 226 | 85.95 | | 311.95 | light, double glazed wood window |
| Reinstall | Ea. | | 57.86 | | 57.86 | with screen. |
| Clean | Ea. | .06 | 8 | | 8.06 | |
| Paint | Ea. | 2.93 | 15.75 | | 18.68 | |
| Minimum Charge | Job | | 181 | | 181 | |
| **2' 10" x 4'** | | | | | | |
| Demolish | Ea. | | 13.45 | | 13.45 | Cost includes material and labor to |
| Install | Ea. | 248 | 72.50 | | 320.50 | install 2' 10" x 4' double hung, two |
| Demolish and Install | Ea. | 248 | 85.95 | | 333.95 | light, double glazed wood window |
| Reinstall | Ea. | | 57.86 | | 57.86 | with screen. |
| Clean | Ea. | .06 | 8 | | 8.06 | |
| Paint | Ea. | 2.93 | 15.75 | | 18.68 | |
| Minimum Charge | Job | | 181 | | 181 | |

| Wood Window | | Unit | Material | Labor | Equip. | Total | Specification |
|---|---|---|---|---|---|---|---|
| **3' 7" x 3' 4"** | | | | | | | |
| | Demolish | Ea. | | 13.45 | | 13.45 | Cost includes material and labor to |
| | Install | Ea. | 254 | 80.50 | | 334.50 | install 3' 7" x 3' 4" double hung, two |
| | Demolish and Install | Ea. | 254 | 93.95 | | 347.95 | light, double glazed wood window |
| | Reinstall | Ea. | | 64.28 | | 64.28 | with screen. |
| | Clean | Ea. | .06 | 8 | | 8.06 | |
| | Paint | Ea. | 2.93 | 15.75 | | 18.68 | |
| | Minimum Charge | Job | | 181 | | 181 | |
| **3' 7" x 5' 4"** | | | | | | | |
| | Demolish | Ea. | | 16.45 | | 16.45 | Cost includes material and labor to |
| | Install | Ea. | 325 | 80.50 | | 405.50 | install 3' 7" x 5' 4" double hung, two |
| | Demolish and Install | Ea. | 325 | 96.95 | | 421.95 | light, double glazed wood window |
| | Reinstall | Ea. | | 64.28 | | 64.28 | with screen. |
| | Clean | Ea. | .11 | 13.70 | | 13.81 | |
| | Paint | Ea. | 4.87 | 26 | | 30.87 | |
| | Minimum Charge | Job | | 181 | | 181 | |
| **4' 3" x 5' 4"** | | | | | | | |
| | Demolish | Ea. | | 16.45 | | 16.45 | Cost includes material and labor to |
| | Install | Ea. | 510 | 90.50 | | 600.50 | install 4' 3" x 5' 4" double hung, two |
| | Demolish and Install | Ea. | 510 | 106.95 | | 616.95 | light, double glazed wood window |
| | Reinstall | Ea. | | 72.32 | | 72.32 | with screen. |
| | Clean | Ea. | .11 | 13.70 | | 13.81 | |
| | Paint | Ea. | 2.60 | 31.50 | | 34.10 | |
| | Minimum Charge | Job | | 181 | | 181 | |
| **Casement** | | | | | | | |
| **2' x 3' 4"** | | | | | | | |
| | Demolish | Ea. | | 13.45 | | 13.45 | Cost includes material and labor to |
| | Install | Ea. | 244 | 36 | | 280 | install 2' x 3' 4 " casement window |
| | Demolish and Install | Ea. | 244 | 49.45 | | 293.45 | with 3/4" insulated glass, screens, |
| | Reinstall | Ea. | | 28.93 | | 28.93 | weatherstripping, hardware. |
| | Clean | Ea. | .04 | 6.85 | | 6.89 | |
| | Paint | Ea. | 2.29 | 13.10 | | 15.39 | |
| | Minimum Charge | Job | | 360 | | 360 | |
| **2' x 4'** | | | | | | | |
| | Demolish | Ea. | | 13.45 | | 13.45 | Cost includes material and labor to |
| | Install | Ea. | 267 | 40 | | 307 | install 2' x 4' casement window with |
| | Demolish and Install | Ea. | 267 | 53.45 | | 320.45 | 3/4" insulated glass, screens, |
| | Reinstall | Ea. | | 32.14 | | 32.14 | weatherstripping, hardware. |
| | Clean | Ea. | .04 | 6.85 | | 6.89 | |
| | Paint | Ea. | 2.29 | 13.10 | | 15.39 | |
| | Minimum Charge | Job | | 360 | | 360 | |
| **2' x 5'** | | | | | | | |
| | Demolish | Ea. | | 13.45 | | 13.45 | Cost includes material and labor to |
| | Install | Ea. | 305 | 42.50 | | 347.50 | install 2' x 5' casement window with |
| | Demolish and Install | Ea. | 305 | 55.95 | | 360.95 | 3/4" insulated glass, screens, |
| | Reinstall | Ea. | | 34.03 | | 34.03 | weatherstripping, hardware. |
| | Clean | Ea. | .06 | 8 | | 8.06 | |
| | Paint | Ea. | 2.93 | 15.75 | | 18.68 | |
| | Minimum Charge | Job | | 360 | | 360 | |
| **2' x 6'** | | | | | | | |
| | Demolish | Ea. | | 13.45 | | 13.45 | Cost includes material and labor to |
| | Install | Ea. | 305 | 45 | | 350 | install 2' x 6' casement window with |
| | Demolish and Install | Ea. | 305 | 58.45 | | 363.45 | 3/4" insulated glass, screens, |
| | Reinstall | Ea. | | 36.16 | | 36.16 | weatherstripping, hardware. |
| | Clean | Ea. | .06 | 8 | | 8.06 | |
| | Paint | Ea. | 2.93 | 15.75 | | 18.68 | |
| | Minimum Charge | Job | | 360 | | 360 | |

# Exterior Doors and Windows

| Wood Window | | Unit | Material | Labor | Equip. | Total | Specification |
|---|---|---|---|---|---|---|---|
| **4' x 3' 4"** | | | | | | | |
| | Demolish | Ea. | | 16.45 | | 16.45 | Cost includes material and labor to |
| | Install | Ea. | 615 | 48 | | 663 | install 4' x 3' 4 " casement windows |
| | Demolish and Install | Ea. | 615 | 64.45 | | 679.45 | with 3/4" insulated glass, screens, |
| | Reinstall | Ea. | | 38.57 | | 38.57 | weatherstripping, hardware. |
| | Clean | Ea. | .06 | 8 | | 8.06 | |
| | Paint | Ea. | 1.30 | 15.75 | | 17.05 | |
| | Minimum Charge | Job | | 360 | | 360 | |
| **4' x 4'** | | | | | | | |
| | Demolish | Ea. | | 16.45 | | 16.45 | Cost includes material and labor to |
| | Install | Ea. | 675 | 48 | | 723 | install 4' x 4' casement windows with |
| | Demolish and Install | Ea. | 675 | 64.45 | | 739.45 | 3/4" insulated glass, screens, |
| | Reinstall | Ea. | | 38.57 | | 38.57 | weatherstripping, hardware. |
| | Clean | Ea. | .08 | 11.25 | | 11.33 | |
| | Paint | Ea. | 1.53 | 19.70 | | 21.23 | |
| | Minimum Charge | Job | | 360 | | 360 | |
| **4' x 5'** | | | | | | | |
| | Demolish | Ea. | | 16.45 | | 16.45 | Cost includes material and labor to |
| | Install | Ea. | 765 | 51.50 | | 816.50 | install 4' x 5' casement windows with |
| | Demolish and Install | Ea. | 765 | 67.95 | | 832.95 | 3/4" insulated glass, screens, |
| | Reinstall | Ea. | | 41.33 | | 41.33 | weatherstripping, hardware. |
| | Clean | Ea. | .11 | 13.70 | | 13.81 | |
| | Paint | Ea. | 2 | 26 | | 28 | |
| | Minimum Charge | Job | | 360 | | 360 | |
| **4' x 6'** | | | | | | | |
| | Demolish | Ea. | | 16.45 | | 16.45 | Cost includes material and labor to |
| | Install | Ea. | 865 | 60.50 | | 925.50 | install 4' x 6' casement windows with |
| | Demolish and Install | Ea. | 865 | 76.95 | | 941.95 | 3/4" insulated glass, screens, |
| | Reinstall | Ea. | | 48.21 | | 48.21 | weatherstripping, hardware. |
| | Clean | Ea. | .11 | 13.70 | | 13.81 | |
| | Paint | Ea. | 2.35 | 31.50 | | 33.85 | |
| | Minimum Charge | Job | | 360 | | 360 | |
| **Casement Bow** | | | | | | | |
| **4' 8" x 8' 1"** | | | | | | | |
| | Demolish | Ea. | | 23 | | 23 | Includes material and labor to install |
| | Install | Ea. | 1625 | 136 | | 1761 | casement bow window unit with 4 |
| | Demolish and Install | Ea. | 1625 | 159 | | 1784 | lights, pine frame, 1/2" insulated |
| | Reinstall | Ea. | | 108.48 | | 108.48 | glass, weatherstripping, hardware, |
| | Clean | Ea. | .15 | 15.95 | | 16.10 | screens. |
| | Paint | Ea. | 4.36 | 63 | | 67.36 | |
| | Minimum Charge | Job | | 360 | | 360 | |
| **4' 8" x 10'** | | | | | | | |
| | Demolish | Ea. | | 23 | | 23 | Includes material and labor to install |
| | Install | Ea. | 1725 | 181 | | 1906 | casement bow window unit with 5 |
| | Demolish and Install | Ea. | 1725 | 204 | | 1929 | lights, pine frame, 1/2" insulated |
| | Reinstall | Ea. | | 144.64 | | 144.64 | glass, weatherstripping, hardware, |
| | Clean | Ea. | .02 | 21.50 | | 21.52 | screens. |
| | Paint | Ea. | 5.40 | 78.50 | | 83.90 | |
| | Minimum Charge | Job | | 360 | | 360 | |
| **5' 4" x 8' 1"** | | | | | | | |
| | Demolish | Ea. | | 23 | | 23 | Includes material and labor to install |
| | Install | Ea. | 1800 | 136 | | 1936 | casement bow window unit with 4 |
| | Demolish and Install | Ea. | 1800 | 159 | | 1959 | lights, pine frame, 1/2" insulated |
| | Reinstall | Ea. | | 108.48 | | 108.48 | glass, weatherstripping, hardware, |
| | Clean | Ea. | .02 | 21.50 | | 21.52 | screens. |
| | Paint | Ea. | 4.95 | 63 | | 67.95 | |
| | Minimum Charge | Job | | 360 | | 360 | |

| Wood Window | Unit | Material | Labor | Equip. | Total | Specification |
|---|---|---|---|---|---|---|
| **5' 4" x 10'** | | | | | | |
| Demolish | Ea. | | 23 | | 23 | Includes material and labor to install |
| Install | Ea. | 1975 | 181 | | 2156 | casement bow window unit with 5 |
| Demolish and Install | Ea. | 1975 | 204 | | 2179 | lights, pine frame, 1/2" insulated |
| Reinstall | Ea. | | 144.64 | | 144.64 | glass, weatherstripping, hardware, |
| Clean | Ea. | .02 | 21.50 | | 21.52 | screens. |
| Paint | Ea. | 6.25 | 78.50 | | 84.75 | |
| Minimum Charge | Job | | 360 | | 360 | |
| **6' x 8' 1"** | | | | | | |
| Demolish | Ea. | | 23 | | 23 | Includes material and labor to install |
| Install | Ea. | 1725 | 181 | | 1906 | casement bow window unit with 5 |
| Demolish and Install | Ea. | 1725 | 204 | | 1929 | lights, pine frame, 1/2" insulated |
| Reinstall | Ea. | | 144.64 | | 144.64 | glass, weatherstripping, hardware, |
| Clean | Ea. | .02 | 21.50 | | 21.52 | screens. |
| Paint | Ea. | 5.65 | 78.50 | | 84.15 | |
| Minimum Charge | Job | | 360 | | 360 | |
| **6' x 10'** | | | | | | |
| Demolish | Ea. | | 23 | | 23 | Includes material and labor to install |
| Install | Ea. | 2075 | 181 | | 2256 | casement bow window unit with 5 |
| Demolish and Install | Ea. | 2075 | 204 | | 2279 | lights, pine frame, 1/2" insulated |
| Reinstall | Ea. | | 144.64 | | 144.64 | glass, weatherstripping, hardware, |
| Clean | Ea. | .02 | 21.50 | | 21.52 | screens. |
| Paint | Ea. | 7.10 | 105 | | 112.10 | |
| Minimum Charge | Job | | 360 | | 360 | |
| **Casing** | | | | | | |
| Demolish | Ea. | | 8.35 | | 8.35 | Cost includes material and labor to |
| Install | Opng. | 32 | 28 | | 60 | install 11/16" x 2-1/2" pine ranch |
| Demolish and Install | Opng. | 32 | 36.35 | | 68.35 | style window casing. |
| Reinstall | Opng. | | 22.25 | | 22.25 | |
| Clean | Opng. | .52 | 2.67 | | 3.19 | |
| Paint | Ea. | 3.65 | 6.30 | | 9.95 | |
| Minimum Charge | Job | | 224 | | 224 | |
| **Trim Set** | | | | | | |
| Demolish | Ea. | | 6.40 | | 6.40 | Cost includes material and labor to |
| Install | Opng. | 32 | 28 | | 60 | install 11/16" x 2-1/2" pine ranch |
| Demolish and Install | Opng. | 32 | 34.40 | | 66.40 | style window casing. |
| Reinstall | Opng. | | 22.25 | | 22.25 | |
| Clean | Opng. | .52 | 2.67 | | 3.19 | |
| Paint | Ea. | 3.65 | 6.30 | | 9.95 | |
| Minimum Charge | Job | | 181 | | 181 | |
| **Wood Picture Window** | | | | | | |
| **3' 6" x 4'** | | | | | | |
| Demolish | Ea. | | 16.45 | | 16.45 | Includes material and labor to install a |
| Install | Ea. | 505 | 60.50 | | 565.50 | wood framed picture window |
| Demolish and Install | Ea. | 505 | 76.95 | | 581.95 | including exterior trim. |
| Clean | Ea. | .11 | 13.70 | | 13.81 | |
| Paint | Ea. | 1.90 | 24 | | 25.90 | |
| Minimum Charge | Job | | 360 | | 360 | |
| **4' x 4' 6"** | | | | | | |
| Demolish | Ea. | | 16.45 | | 16.45 | Includes material and labor to install a |
| Install | Ea. | 505 | 66 | | 571 | wood framed picture window |
| Demolish and Install | Ea. | 505 | 82.45 | | 587.45 | including exterior trim. |
| Clean | Ea. | .11 | 13.70 | | 13.81 | |
| Paint | Ea. | 1.90 | 24 | | 25.90 | |
| Minimum Charge | Job | | 360 | | 360 | |

# Exterior Doors and Windows

## Wood Window

| Wood Window | | Unit | Material | Labor | Equip. | Total | Specification |
|---|---|---|---|---|---|---|---|
| **5' x 4'** | | | | | | | |
| | Demolish | Ea. | | 16.45 | | 16.45 | Includes material and labor to install a |
| | Install | Ea. | 590 | 66 | | 656 | wood framed picture window |
| | Demolish and Install | Ea. | 590 | 82.45 | | 672.45 | including exterior trim. |
| | Clean | Ea. | .11 | 13.70 | | 13.81 | |
| | Paint | Ea. | 4.06 | 39.50 | | 43.56 | |
| | Minimum Charge | Job | | 360 | | 360 | |
| **6' x 4' 6"** | | | | | | | |
| | Demolish | Ea. | | 16.45 | | 16.45 | Includes material and labor to install a |
| | Install | Ea. | 635 | 72.50 | | 707.50 | wood framed picture window |
| | Demolish and Install | Ea. | 635 | 88.95 | | 723.95 | including exterior trim. |
| | Clean | Ea. | .11 | 13.70 | | 13.81 | |
| | Paint | Ea. | 4.06 | 39.50 | | 43.56 | |
| | Minimum Charge | Job | | 360 | | 360 | |

## Window Screens

| Window Screens | | Unit | Material | Labor | Equip. | Total | Specification |
|---|---|---|---|---|---|---|---|
| **Small** | | | | | | | |
| | Demolish | Ea. | | 3.09 | | 3.09 | Includes material and labor to install |
| | Install | Ea. | 17.70 | 10.95 | | 28.65 | small window screen, 4 S.F. |
| | Demolish and Install | Ea. | 17.70 | 14.04 | | 31.74 | |
| | Reinstall | Ea. | | 8.77 | | 8.77 | |
| | Clean | Ea. | .36 | 5.55 | | 5.91 | |
| | Minimum Charge | Job | | 90.50 | | 90.50 | |
| **Standard Size** | | | | | | | |
| | Demolish | Ea. | | 3.09 | | 3.09 | Includes material and labor to install |
| | Install | Ea. | 43 | 10.95 | | 53.95 | medium window screen, 12 S.F. |
| | Demolish and Install | Ea. | 43 | 14.04 | | 57.04 | |
| | Reinstall | Ea. | | 8.77 | | 8.77 | |
| | Clean | Ea. | .36 | 5.55 | | 5.91 | |
| | Minimum Charge | Job | | 90.50 | | 90.50 | |
| **Large** | | | | | | | |
| | Demolish | Ea. | | 3.09 | | 3.09 | Includes material and labor to install |
| | Install | Ea. | 57 | 10.95 | | 67.95 | large window screen, 16 S.F. |
| | Demolish and Install | Ea. | 57 | 14.04 | | 71.04 | |
| | Reinstall | Ea. | | 8.77 | | 8.77 | |
| | Clean | Ea. | .36 | 5.55 | | 5.91 | |
| | Minimum Charge | Job | | 90.50 | | 90.50 | |

## Window Glass

| Window Glass | | Unit | Material | Labor | Equip. | Total | Specification |
|---|---|---|---|---|---|---|---|
| **Plate, Clear, 1/4"** | | | | | | | |
| | Demolish | S.F. | | 1.48 | | 1.48 | Includes material and labor to install |
| | Install | S.F. | 7.10 | 5.85 | | 12.95 | clear glass. |
| | Demolish and Install | S.F. | 7.10 | 7.33 | | 14.43 | |
| | Reinstall | S.F. | | 4.68 | | 4.68 | |
| | Clean | S.F. | .03 | .16 | | .19 | |
| | Minimum Charge | Job | | 175 | | 175 | |
| **Insulated** | | | | | | | |
| | Demolish | S.F. | | 1.48 | | 1.48 | Includes material and labor to install |
| | Install | S.F. | 13.15 | 10 | | 23.15 | insulated glass. |
| | Demolish and Install | S.F. | 13.15 | 11.48 | | 24.63 | |
| | Reinstall | S.F. | | 8.02 | | 8.02 | |
| | Clean | S.F. | .03 | .16 | | .19 | |
| | Minimum Charge | Job | | 175 | | 175 | |

# Exterior Doors and Windows

| Window Glass | | Unit | Material | Labor | Equip. | Total | Specification |
|---|---|---|---|---|---|---|---|
| **Tinted** | | | | | | | |
| | Demolish | S.F. | | 1.48 | | 1.48 | Includes material and labor to install |
| | Install | S.F. | 7.30 | 5.40 | | 12.70 | tinted glass. |
| | Demolish and Install | S.F. | 7.30 | 6.88 | | 14.18 | |
| | Reinstall | S.F. | | 4.32 | | 4.32 | |
| | Clean | S.F. | .03 | .16 | | .19 | |
| | Minimum Charge | Job | | 175 | | 175 | |
| **Obscure / Florentine** | | | | | | | |
| | Demolish | S.F. | | 1.48 | | 1.48 | Includes material and labor to install |
| | Install | S.F. | 8.70 | 5 | | 13.70 | obscure glass. |
| | Demolish and Install | S.F. | 8.70 | 6.48 | | 15.18 | |
| | Reinstall | S.F. | | 4.01 | | 4.01 | |
| | Clean | S.F. | .03 | .16 | | .19 | |
| | Minimum Charge | Job | | 175 | | 175 | |
| **Laminated Safety** | | | | | | | |
| | Demolish | S.F. | | 1.48 | | 1.48 | Includes material and labor to install |
| | Install | S.F. | 11.35 | 7.80 | | 19.15 | clear laminated glass. |
| | Demolish and Install | S.F. | 11.35 | 9.28 | | 20.63 | |
| | Reinstall | S.F. | | 6.24 | | 6.24 | |
| | Clean | S.F. | .03 | .16 | | .19 | |
| | Minimum Charge | Job | | 175 | | 175 | |
| **Wired** | | | | | | | |
| | Demolish | S.F. | | 1.48 | | 1.48 | Includes material and labor to install |
| | Install | S.F. | 14.45 | 5.20 | | 19.65 | rough obscure wire glass. |
| | Demolish and Install | S.F. | 14.45 | 6.68 | | 21.13 | |
| | Reinstall | S.F. | | 4.16 | | 4.16 | |
| | Clean | S.F. | .03 | .16 | | .19 | |
| | Minimum Charge | Job | | 175 | | 175 | |
| **Tempered** | | | | | | | |
| | Demolish | S.F. | | 1.48 | | 1.48 | Includes material and labor to install |
| | Install | S.F. | 7.10 | 5.85 | | 12.95 | clear glass. |
| | Demolish and Install | S.F. | 7.10 | 7.33 | | 14.43 | |
| | Reinstall | S.F. | | 4.68 | | 4.68 | |
| | Clean | S.F. | .03 | .16 | | .19 | |
| | Minimum Charge | Job | | 175 | | 175 | |
| **Stained** | | | | | | | |
| | Demolish | S.F. | | 1.48 | | 1.48 | Includes material and labor to install |
| | Install | S.F. | 61 | 5.85 | | 66.85 | stained glass. |
| | Demolish and Install | S.F. | 61 | 7.33 | | 68.33 | |
| | Reinstall | S.F. | | 4.68 | | 4.68 | |
| | Clean | S.F. | .03 | .16 | | .19 | |
| | Minimum Charge | Job | | 175 | | 175 | |
| **Etched** | | | | | | | |
| | Demolish | S.F. | | 1.48 | | 1.48 | Includes material and labor to install |
| | Install | S.F. | 50 | 5.85 | | 55.85 | etched glass. |
| | Demolish and Install | S.F. | 50 | 7.33 | | 57.33 | |
| | Reinstall | S.F. | | 4.68 | | 4.68 | |
| | Clean | S.F. | .03 | .16 | | .19 | |
| | Minimum Charge | Job | | 175 | | 175 | |
| **Wall Mirror** | | | | | | | |
| | Demolish | S.F. | | 1.48 | | 1.48 | Includes material and labor to install |
| | Install | S.F. | 7.60 | 5.60 | | 13.20 | distortion-free float glass mirror, 1/4" |
| | Demolish and Install | S.F. | 7.60 | 7.08 | | 14.68 | thick, cut and polished edges. |
| | Reinstall | S.F. | | 4.49 | | 4.49 | |
| | Clean | S.F. | .03 | .16 | | .19 | |
| | Minimum Charge | Job | | 175 | | 175 | |

# Exterior Doors and Windows

| Window Glass | | Unit | Material | Labor | Equip. | Total | Specification |
|---|---|---|---|---|---|---|---|
| **Bullet Resistant** | | | | | | | |
| | Demolish | S.F. | | 1.48 | | 1.48 | Includes material and labor to install |
| | Install | S.F. | 106 | 70 | | 176 | bullet resistant clear laminated glass. |
| | Demolish and Install | S.F. | 106 | 71.48 | | 177.48 | |
| | Reinstall | S.F. | | 56.13 | | 56.13 | |
| | Clean | S.F. | .03 | .16 | | .19 | |
| | Minimum Charge | Job | | 175 | | 175 | |

| Storefront System | | Unit | Material | Labor | Equip. | Total | Specification |
|---|---|---|---|---|---|---|---|
| **Clear Glass** | | | | | | | |
| **Stub Wall to 8'** | | | | | | | |
| | Demolish | S.F. | | 2.32 | | 2.32 | Includes material and labor to install |
| | Install | S.F. | 18.80 | 9.70 | | 28.50 | commercial grade 4-1/2" section, |
| | Demolish and Install | S.F. | 18.80 | 12.02 | | 30.82 | anodized aluminum with clear glass in |
| | Reinstall | S.F. | | 7.75 | | 7.75 | upper section and safety glass in |
| | Clean | S.F. | | .32 | | .32 | lower section. |
| | Minimum Charge | Job | | 224 | | 224 | |
| **Floor to 10'** | | | | | | | |
| | Demolish | S.F. | | 2.32 | | 2.32 | Includes material and labor to install |
| | Install | S.F. | 20.50 | 9.70 | | 30.20 | commercial grade 4-1/2" section, |
| | Demolish and Install | S.F. | 20.50 | 12.02 | | 32.52 | anodized aluminum with clear glass in |
| | Reinstall | S.F. | | 7.75 | | 7.75 | upper section and safety glass in |
| | Clean | S.F. | | .32 | | .32 | lower section. |
| | Minimum Charge | Job | | 224 | | 224 | |
| **Polished Plate Glass** | | | | | | | |
| **Stub Wall to 9'** | | | | | | | |
| | Demolish | S.F. | | 2.32 | | 2.32 | Cost includes material and labor to |
| | Install | S.F. | 14.30 | 9.70 | | 24 | install 4' x 9' polished plate glass |
| | Demolish and Install | S.F. | 14.30 | 12.02 | | 26.32 | window built on 8" stub wall. |
| | Reinstall | S.F. | | 7.75 | | 7.75 | |
| | Clean | S.F. | | .32 | | .32 | |
| | Minimum Charge | Job | | 224 | | 224 | |
| **Stub Wall to 13'** | | | | | | | |
| | Demolish | S.F. | | 2.32 | | 2.32 | Cost includes material and labor to |
| | Install | S.F. | 14.90 | 9.70 | | 24.60 | install 4' x 13' polished plate glass |
| | Demolish and Install | S.F. | 14.90 | 12.02 | | 26.92 | window built on 8" stub wall. |
| | Reinstall | S.F. | | 7.75 | | 7.75 | |
| | Clean | S.F. | | .32 | | .32 | |
| | Minimum Charge | Job | | 224 | | 224 | |
| **Floor to 9'** | | | | | | | |
| | Demolish | S.F. | | 2.32 | | 2.32 | Cost includes material and labor to |
| | Install | S.F. | 15.45 | 9.70 | | 25.15 | install 4' x 9' polished plate glass |
| | Demolish and Install | S.F. | 15.45 | 12.02 | | 27.47 | window built on floor. |
| | Reinstall | S.F. | | 7.75 | | 7.75 | |
| | Clean | S.F. | | .32 | | .32 | |
| | Minimum Charge | Job | | 224 | | 224 | |
| **Floor to 13'** | | | | | | | |
| | Demolish | S.F. | | 2.32 | | 2.32 | Cost includes material and labor to |
| | Install | S.F. | 16.65 | 9.70 | | 26.35 | install 4' x 13' polished plate glass |
| | Demolish and Install | S.F. | 16.65 | 12.02 | | 28.67 | window built on floor. |
| | Reinstall | S.F. | | 7.75 | | 7.75 | |
| | Clean | S.F. | | .32 | | .32 | |
| | Minimum Charge | Job | | 224 | | 224 | |

# Exterior Doors and Windows

| Storefront System | Unit | Material | Labor | Equip. | Total | Specification |
|---|---|---|---|---|---|---|
| **Clear Plate Glass** | | | | | | |
| **Floor to 9'** | | | | | | |
| Demolish | S.F. | | 2.32 | | 2.32 | Cost includes material and labor to |
| Install | S.F. | 22.50 | 9.70 | | 32.20 | install 4' x 9' clear plate glass window |
| Demolish and Install | S.F. | 22.50 | 12.02 | | 34.52 | built on floor. |
| Reinstall | S.F. | | 7.75 | | 7.75 | |
| Clean | S.F. | | .32 | | .32 | |
| Minimum Charge | Job | | 224 | | 224 | |
| **Floor to 11'** | | | | | | |
| Demolish | S.F. | | 2.32 | | 2.32 | Cost includes material and labor to |
| Install | S.F. | 21.50 | 9.70 | | 31.20 | install 4' x 11' clear plate glass |
| Demolish and Install | S.F. | 21.50 | 12.02 | | 33.52 | window built on floor. |
| Reinstall | S.F. | | 7.75 | | 7.75 | |
| Clean | S.F. | | .32 | | .32 | |
| Minimum Charge | Job | | 224 | | 224 | |
| **Floor to 13'** | | | | | | |
| Demolish | S.F. | | 2.32 | | 2.32 | Cost includes material and labor to |
| Install | S.F. | 22 | 9.70 | | 31.70 | install 4' x 13' clear plate glass |
| Demolish and Install | S.F. | 22 | 12.02 | | 34.02 | window built on floor. |
| Reinstall | S.F. | | 7.75 | | 7.75 | |
| Clean | S.F. | | .32 | | .32 | |
| Minimum Charge | Job | | 224 | | 224 | |
| **Decorative Type** | | | | | | |
| Demolish | S.F. | | 2.32 | | 2.32 | Includes material and labor to install |
| Install | S.F. | 17.05 | 7 | | 24.05 | decorative storefront system. |
| Demolish and Install | S.F. | 17.05 | 9.32 | | 26.37 | |
| Reinstall | S.F. | | 5.61 | | 5.61 | |
| Clean | S.F. | | .32 | | .32 | |
| Minimum Charge | Job | | 175 | | 175 | |
| **Decorative Curved** | | | | | | |
| Demolish | S.F. | | 2.32 | | 2.32 | Includes material and labor to install |
| Install | S.F. | 32 | 14.05 | | 46.05 | decorative curved storefront system. |
| Demolish and Install | S.F. | 32 | 16.37 | | 48.37 | |
| Reinstall | S.F. | | 11.23 | | 11.23 | |
| Clean | S.F. | | .32 | | .32 | |
| Minimum Charge | Job | | 175 | | 175 | |
| **Entrance** | | | | | | |
| **Narrow Stile 3' x 7"** | | | | | | |
| Demolish | Ea. | | 20 | | 20 | Cost includes material and labor to |
| Install | Ea. | 820 | 241 | | 1061 | install 3' x 7' narrow stile door, center |
| Demolish and Install | Ea. | 820 | 261 | | 1081 | pivot concealed closer. |
| Reinstall | Ea. | | 192.85 | | 192.85 | |
| Clean | Ea. | 4.54 | 33.50 | | 38.04 | |
| Minimum Charge | Job | | 224 | | 224 | |
| **Tempered Glass** | | | | | | |
| Demolish | Ea. | | 20 | | 20 | Cost includes material and labor to |
| Install | Ea. | 2825 | 485 | | 3310 | install 3' x 7' tempered glass door, |
| Demolish and Install | Ea. | 2825 | 505 | | 3330 | center pivot concealed closer,. |
| Reinstall | Ea. | | 387.46 | | 387.46 | |
| Clean | Ea. | 4.54 | 33.50 | | 38.04 | |
| Minimum Charge | Job | | 224 | | 224 | |
| **Heavy Section** | | | | | | |
| Demolish | Ea. | | 20 | | 20 | Includes material and labor to install |
| Install | Ea. | 1050 | 450 | | 1500 | wide stile door with 3' 6" x 7' |
| Demolish and Install | Ea. | 1050 | 470 | | 1520 | opening. |
| Reinstall | Ea. | | 358.40 | | 358.40 | |
| Clean | Ea. | .91 | 11.10 | | 12.01 | |
| Minimum Charge | Job | | 700 | | 700 | |

# Exterior Doors and Windows

| Curtain Wall System | | Unit | Material | Labor | Equip. | Total | Specification |
|---|---|---|---|---|---|---|---|
| **Regular Weight** | | | | | | | |
| **Bronze Anodized** | | | | | | | |
| | Demolish | S.F. | | 2.32 | | 2.32 | Includes material and labor to install |
| | Install | S.F. | 35 | 9.70 | | 44.70 | structural curtain wall system with |
| | Demolish and Install | S.F. | 35 | 12.02 | | 47.02 | bronze anodized frame of heavy |
| | Clean | S.F. | | .32 | | .32 | weight, float glass. |
| | Minimum Charge | Job | | 181 | | 181 | |
| **Black Anodized** | | | | | | | |
| | Demolish | S.F. | | 2.32 | | 2.32 | Includes material and labor to install |
| | Install | S.F. | 37.50 | 9.70 | | 47.20 | structural curtain wall system with |
| | Demolish and Install | S.F. | 37.50 | 12.02 | | 49.52 | black anodized frame of regular |
| | Clean | S.F. | | .32 | | .32 | weight, float glass. |
| | Minimum Charge | Job | | 181 | | 181 | |
| **Heavy Weight** | | | | | | | |
| **Bronze Anodized** | | | | | | | |
| | Demolish | S.F. | | 2.32 | | 2.32 | Includes material and labor to install |
| | Install | S.F. | 35 | 9.70 | | 44.70 | structural curtain wall system with |
| | Demolish and Install | S.F. | 35 | 12.02 | | 47.02 | bronze anodized frame of heavy |
| | Clean | S.F. | | .32 | | .32 | weight, float glass. |
| | Minimum Charge | Job | | 181 | | 181 | |
| **Black Anodized** | | | | | | | |
| | Demolish | S.F. | | 2.32 | | 2.32 | Includes material and labor to install |
| | Install | S.F. | 36 | 9.70 | | 45.70 | structural curtain wall system with |
| | Demolish and Install | S.F. | 36 | 12.02 | | 48.02 | black anodized frame of heavy |
| | Clean | S.F. | | .32 | | .32 | weight, float glass. |
| | Minimum Charge | Job | | 181 | | 181 | |
| **Glass** | | | | | | | |
| **1″ Insulated** | | | | | | | |
| | Install | S.F. | 15.35 | 9.35 | | 24.70 | Cost includes labor and material to |
| | Minimum Charge | Job | | 175 | | 175 | install 1″ insulated glass. |
| **Heat Absorbing** | | | | | | | |
| | Install | S.F. | 9.30 | 9.35 | | 18.65 | Includes labor an material to install |
| | Minimum Charge | Job | | 175 | | 175 | heat absorbing glass. |
| **Low Transmission** | | | | | | | |
| | Install | S.F. | 6.10 | 9.35 | | 15.45 | Includes labor an material to install |
| | Minimum Charge | Job | | 175 | | 175 | low transmission glass. |

| Skylight | | Unit | Material | Labor | Equip. | Total | Specification |
|---|---|---|---|---|---|---|---|
| **Dome** | | | | | | | |
| **22″ x 22″** | | | | | | | |
| | Demolish | Ea. | | 70.50 | | 70.50 | Cost includes material and labor to |
| | Install | Ea. | 49 | 112 | | 161 | install 22″ x 22″ fixed dome skylight. |
| | Demolish and Install | Ea. | 49 | 182.50 | | 231.50 | |
| | Reinstall | Ea. | | 89.24 | | 89.24 | |
| | Clean | Ea. | .41 | 9.55 | | 9.96 | |
| | Minimum Charge | Job | | 670 | | 670 | |
| **22″ x 46″** | | | | | | | |
| | Demolish | Ea. | | 70.50 | | 70.50 | Cost includes material and labor to |
| | Install | Ea. | 110 | 134 | | 244 | install 22″ x 46″ fixed dome skylight. |
| | Demolish and Install | Ea. | 110 | 204.50 | | 314.50 | |
| | Reinstall | Ea. | | 107.08 | | 107.08 | |
| | Clean | Ea. | | 14.80 | | 14.80 | |
| | Minimum Charge | Job | | 670 | | 670 | |

| Skylight | | Unit | Material | Labor | Equip. | Total | Specification |
|---|---|---|---|---|---|---|---|
| **30" x 30"** | | | | | | | |
| | Demolish | Ea. | | 70.50 | | 70.50 | Cost includes material and labor to |
| | Install | Ea. | 92 | 112 | | 204 | install 30" x 30" fixed dome skylight. |
| | Demolish and Install | Ea. | 92 | 182.50 | | 274.50 | |
| | Reinstall | Ea. | | 89.24 | | 89.24 | |
| | Clean | Ea. | | 14.80 | | 14.80 | |
| | Minimum Charge | Job | | 670 | | 670 | |
| **30" x 46"** | | | | | | | |
| | Demolish | Ea. | | 70.50 | | 70.50 | Cost includes material and labor to |
| | Install | Ea. | 160 | 134 | | 294 | install 30" x 46" fixed dome skylight. |
| | Demolish and Install | Ea. | 160 | 204.50 | | 364.50 | |
| | Reinstall | Ea. | | 107.08 | | 107.08 | |
| | Clean | Ea. | | 14.80 | | 14.80 | |
| | Minimum Charge | Job | | 670 | | 670 | |
| **Fixed** | | | | | | | |
| **22" x 27"** | | | | | | | |
| | Demolish | Ea. | | 70.50 | | 70.50 | Includes material and labor to install |
| | Install | Ea. | 234 | 112 | | 346 | double glazed skylight, 22" x 27", |
| | Demolish and Install | Ea. | 234 | 182.50 | | 416.50 | fixed. |
| | Reinstall | Ea. | | 89.24 | | 89.24 | |
| | Clean | Ea. | .41 | 9.55 | | 9.96 | |
| | Minimum Charge | Job | | 670 | | 670 | |
| **22" x 46"** | | | | | | | |
| | Demolish | Ea. | | 70.50 | | 70.50 | Includes material and labor to install |
| | Install | Ea. | 295 | 134 | | 429 | double glazed skylight, 22" x 46", |
| | Demolish and Install | Ea. | 295 | 204.50 | | 499.50 | fixed. |
| | Reinstall | Ea. | | 107.08 | | 107.08 | |
| | Clean | Ea. | | 14.80 | | 14.80 | |
| | Minimum Charge | Job | | 670 | | 670 | |
| **44" x 46"** | | | | | | | |
| | Demolish | Ea. | | 70.50 | | 70.50 | Includes material and labor to install |
| | Install | Ea. | 420 | 134 | | 554 | double glazed skylight, 44" x 46", |
| | Demolish and Install | Ea. | 420 | 204.50 | | 624.50 | fixed. |
| | Reinstall | Ea. | | 107.08 | | 107.08 | |
| | Clean | Ea. | | 16.70 | | 16.70 | |
| | Minimum Charge | Job | | 670 | | 670 | |
| **Operable** | | | | | | | |
| **22" x 27"** | | | | | | | |
| | Demolish | Ea. | | 70.50 | | 70.50 | Includes material and labor to install |
| | Install | Ea. | 345 | 112 | | 457 | double glazed skylight, 22" x 27", |
| | Demolish and Install | Ea. | 345 | 182.50 | | 527.50 | operable. |
| | Reinstall | Ea. | | 89.24 | | 89.24 | |
| | Clean | Ea. | .41 | 9.55 | | 9.96 | |
| | Minimum Charge | Job | | 670 | | 670 | |
| **22" x 46"** | | | | | | | |
| | Demolish | Ea. | | 70.50 | | 70.50 | Includes material and labor to install |
| | Install | Ea. | 405 | 134 | | 539 | double glazed skylight, 22" x 46", |
| | Demolish and Install | Ea. | 405 | 204.50 | | 609.50 | operable. |
| | Reinstall | Ea. | | 107.08 | | 107.08 | |
| | Clean | Ea. | | 14.80 | | 14.80 | |
| | Minimum Charge | Job | | 670 | | 670 | |
| **44" x 46"** | | | | | | | |
| | Demolish | Ea. | | 70.50 | | 70.50 | Includes material and labor to install |
| | Install | Ea. | 675 | 134 | | 809 | double glazed skylight, 44" x 46", |
| | Demolish and Install | Ea. | 675 | 204.50 | | 879.50 | operable. |
| | Reinstall | Ea. | | 107.08 | | 107.08 | |
| | Clean | Ea. | | 16.70 | | 16.70 | |
| | Minimum Charge | Job | | 670 | | 670 | |

# Exterior Doors and Windows

| Industrial Steel Window | Unit | Material | Labor | Equip. | Total | Specification |
|---|---|---|---|---|---|---|
| **100% Fixed** | | | | | | |
| Demolish | S.F. | | 1.90 | | 1.90 | Includes material and labor to install |
| Install | S.F. | 30.50 | 4.48 | | 34.98 | commercial grade steel windows, |
| Demolish and Install | S.F. | 30.50 | 6.38 | | 36.88 | including glazing. |
| Reinstall | S.F. | | 3.58 | | 3.58 | |
| Clean | Ea. | .17 | 1 | | 1.17 | |
| Paint | S.F. | .13 | .70 | | .83 | |
| Minimum Charge | Job | | 224 | | 224 | |
| **50% Vented** | | | | | | |
| Demolish | S.F. | | 1.90 | | 1.90 | Includes material and labor to install |
| Install | S.F. | 44 | 4.48 | | 48.48 | commercial grade steel windows, |
| Demolish and Install | S.F. | 44 | 6.38 | | 50.38 | including glazing. |
| Reinstall | S.F. | | 3.58 | | 3.58 | |
| Clean | Ea. | .17 | 1 | | 1.17 | |
| Paint | S.F. | .13 | .70 | | .83 | |
| Minimum Charge | Job | | 224 | | 224 | |

121

**Brick Veneer**                    **Concrete Masonry Units**

| Masonry Wall | | Unit | Material | Labor | Equip. | Total | Specification |
|---|---|---|---|---|---|---|---|
| **Unreinforced CMU** | | | | | | | |
| **4″ x 8″ x 16″** | | | | | | | |
| | Demolish | S.F. | | 1.65 | | 1.65 | Includes material and labor to install |
| | Install | S.F. | 1.53 | 3.61 | | 5.14 | normal weight 4″ x 8″ x 16″ block. |
| | Demolish and Install | S.F. | 1.53 | 5.26 | | 6.79 | |
| | Clean | S.F. | .07 | .41 | | .48 | |
| | Paint | S.F. | .15 | .72 | | .87 | |
| | Minimum Charge | Job | | 182 | | 182 | |
| **6″ x 8″ x 16″** | | | | | | | |
| | Demolish | S.F. | | 1.74 | | 1.74 | Includes material and labor to install |
| | Install | S.F. | 2.19 | 3.77 | | 5.96 | normal weight 6″ x 8″ x 16″ block. |
| | Demolish and Install | S.F. | 2.19 | 5.51 | | 7.70 | |
| | Clean | S.F. | .07 | .41 | | .48 | |
| | Paint | S.F. | .15 | .72 | | .87 | |
| | Minimum Charge | Job | | 182 | | 182 | |
| **8″ x 8″ x 16″** | | | | | | | |
| | Demolish | S.F. | | 1.98 | | 1.98 | Includes material and labor to install |
| | Install | S.F. | 2.38 | 4.15 | | 6.53 | normal weight 8″ x 8″ x 16″ block. |
| | Demolish and Install | S.F. | 2.38 | 6.13 | | 8.51 | |
| | Clean | S.F. | .07 | .41 | | .48 | |
| | Paint | S.F. | .15 | .72 | | .87 | |
| | Minimum Charge | Job | | 182 | | 182 | |
| **12″ x 8″ x 16″** | | | | | | | |
| | Demolish | S.F. | | 1.98 | | 1.98 | Includes material and labor to install |
| | Install | S.F. | 3.49 | 6.30 | | 9.79 | normal weight 12″ x 8″ x 16″ block. |
| | Demolish and Install | S.F. | 3.49 | 8.28 | | 11.77 | |
| | Clean | S.F. | .07 | .41 | | .48 | |
| | Paint | S.F. | .15 | .72 | | .87 | |
| | Minimum Charge | Job | | 182 | | 182 | |
| **Reinforced CMU** | | | | | | | |
| **4″ x 8″ x 16″** | | | | | | | |
| | Demolish | S.F. | | 1.65 | .92 | 2.57 | Includes material and labor to install |
| | Install | S.F. | 1.65 | 3.69 | | 5.34 | normal weight 4″ x 8″ x 16″ block, |
| | Demolish and Install | S.F. | 1.65 | 5.34 | .92 | 7.91 | mortar and 1/2″ re-bar installed |
| | Clean | S.F. | .07 | .41 | | .48 | vertically every 24″ O.C. |
| | Paint | S.F. | .15 | .72 | | .87 | |
| | Minimum Charge | Job | | 325 | | 325 | |
| **6″ x 8″ x 16″** | | | | | | | |
| | Demolish | S.F. | | 1.73 | .43 | 2.16 | Includes material and labor to install |
| | Install | S.F. | 2.31 | 3.86 | | 6.17 | normal weight 6″ x 8″ x 16″ block, |
| | Demolish and Install | S.F. | 2.31 | 5.59 | .43 | 8.33 | mortar and 1/2″ re-bar installed |
| | Clean | S.F. | .07 | .41 | | .48 | vertically every 24″ O.C. |
| | Paint | S.F. | .15 | .72 | | .87 | |
| | Minimum Charge | Job | | 325 | | 325 | |

| Masonry Wall | | Unit | Material | Labor | Equip. | Total | Specification |
|---|---|---|---|---|---|---|---|
| **8″ x 8″ x 16″** | | | | | | | |
| | Demolish | S.F. | | 1.83 | .46 | 2.29 | Includes material and labor to install |
| | Install | S.F. | 2.50 | 4.20 | | 6.70 | normal weight 8″ x 8″ x 16″ block, |
| | Demolish and Install | S.F. | 2.50 | 6.03 | .46 | 8.99 | mortar and 1/2″ re-bar installed |
| | Clean | S.F. | .07 | .41 | | .48 | vertically every 24″ O.C. |
| | Paint | S.F. | .15 | .72 | | .87 | |
| | Minimum Charge | Job | | 325 | | 325 | |
| **12″ x 8″ x 16″** | | | | | | | |
| | Demolish | S.F. | | 1.89 | .47 | 2.36 | Includes material and labor to install |
| | Install | S.F. | 3.63 | 6.50 | | 10.13 | normal weight 12″ x 8″ x 16″ block, |
| | Demolish and Install | S.F. | 3.63 | 8.39 | .47 | 12.49 | mortar and 1/2″ re-bar installed |
| | Clean | S.F. | .07 | .41 | | .48 | vertically every 24″ O.C. |
| | Paint | S.F. | .15 | .72 | | .87 | |
| | Minimum Charge | Job | | 325 | | 325 | |
| **Structural Brick** | | | | | | | |
| **4″ Single Row** | | | | | | | |
| | Demolish | S.F. | | 2.37 | | 2.37 | Cost includes material and labor to |
| | Install | S.F. | 5.95 | 7.70 | | 13.65 | install 4″ red brick wall, running bond |
| | Demolish and Install | S.F. | 5.95 | 10.07 | | 16.02 | with 3/8″ concave joints, mortar and |
| | Clean | S.F. | .07 | .35 | | .42 | ties. |
| | Paint | S.F. | .15 | .72 | | .87 | |
| | Minimum Charge | Job | | 325 | | 325 | |
| **8″ Double Row** | | | | | | | |
| | Demolish | S.F. | | 2.37 | | 2.37 | Cost includes material and labor to |
| | Install | S.F. | 6.60 | 12.30 | | 18.90 | install 8″ red brick wall, running bond, |
| | Demolish and Install | S.F. | 6.60 | 14.67 | | 21.27 | with 3/8″ concave joints, mortar and |
| | Clean | S.F. | .07 | .35 | | .42 | wall ties. |
| | Paint | S.F. | .15 | .72 | | .87 | |
| | Minimum Charge | Job | | 325 | | 325 | |
| **12″ Triple Row** | | | | | | | |
| | Demolish | S.F. | | 3.29 | | 3.29 | Cost includes material and labor to |
| | Install | S.F. | 10 | 17.50 | | 27.50 | install 12″ red brick wall, running |
| | Demolish and Install | S.F. | 10 | 20.79 | | 30.79 | bond, with 3/8″ concave joints, |
| | Clean | S.F. | .07 | .35 | | .42 | mortar and wall ties. |
| | Paint | S.F. | .15 | .72 | | .87 | |
| | Minimum Charge | Job | | 325 | | 325 | |
| **Brick Veneer** | | | | | | | |
| **4″ Red Common** | | | | | | | |
| | Demolish | S.F. | | 2.37 | | 2.37 | Cost includes material and labor to |
| | Install | S.F. | 3.11 | 7.20 | | 10.31 | install 4″ common red face brick, |
| | Demolish and Install | S.F. | 3.11 | 9.57 | | 12.68 | running bond with 3/8″ concave |
| | Clean | S.F. | .07 | .35 | | .42 | joints, mortar and wall ties. |
| | Paint | S.F. | .15 | .72 | | .87 | |
| | Minimum Charge | Job | | 182 | | 182 | |
| **4″ Used** | | | | | | | |
| | Demolish | S.F. | | 2.37 | | 2.37 | Cost includes material and labor to |
| | Install | S.F. | 5.95 | 7.70 | | 13.65 | install 4″ red brick wall, running bond |
| | Demolish and Install | S.F. | 5.95 | 10.07 | | 16.02 | with 3/8″ concave joints, mortar and |
| | Clean | S.F. | .07 | .35 | | .42 | ties. |
| | Paint | S.F. | .15 | .72 | | .87 | |
| | Minimum Charge | Job | | 182 | | 182 | |

# Masonry

| Masonry Wall | | Unit | Material | Labor | Equip. | Total | Specification |
|---|---|---|---|---|---|---|---|
| **6" Jumbo** | | | | | | | |
| | Demolish | S.F. | | 2.37 | | 2.37 | Cost includes material and labor to |
| | Install | S.F. | 4.99 | 3.82 | | 8.81 | install 6" red jumbo brick veneer, |
| | Demolish and Install | S.F. | 4.99 | 6.19 | | 11.18 | running bond with 3/8" concave |
| | Clean | S.F. | .07 | .35 | | .42 | joints, mortar and ties. |
| | Paint | S.F. | .15 | .72 | | .87 | |
| | Minimum Charge | Job | | 182 | | 182 | |
| **Norman (11-1/2")** | | | | | | | |
| | Demolish | S.F. | | 2.37 | | 2.37 | Cost includes material and labor to |
| | Install | S.F. | 6.40 | 5.20 | | 11.60 | install 4" norman red brick wall, |
| | Demolish and Install | S.F. | 6.40 | 7.57 | | 13.97 | running bond with 3/8" concave |
| | Clean | S.F. | .07 | .35 | | .42 | joints, mortar and ties. |
| | Paint | S.F. | .15 | .72 | | .87 | |
| | Minimum Charge | Job | | 182 | | 182 | |
| **Glazed** | | | | | | | |
| | Demolish | S.F. | | 2.37 | | 2.37 | Includes material, labor and |
| | Install | S.F. | 9.70 | 7.90 | | 17.60 | equipment to install glazed brick. |
| | Demolish and Install | S.F. | 9.70 | 10.27 | | 19.97 | |
| | Clean | S.F. | .07 | .35 | | .42 | |
| | Paint | S.F. | .15 | .72 | | .87 | |
| | Minimum Charge | Job | | 182 | | 182 | |
| **Slumpstone** | | | | | | | |
| **6" x 4"** | | | | | | | |
| | Demolish | S.F. | | 1.65 | | 1.65 | Cost includes material and labor to |
| | Install | S.F. | 6.10 | 4.05 | | 10.15 | install 6" x 4" x 16" concrete slump |
| | Demolish and Install | S.F. | 6.10 | 5.70 | | 11.80 | block. |
| | Clean | S.F. | .07 | .41 | | .48 | |
| | Paint | S.F. | .15 | .72 | | .87 | |
| | Minimum Charge | Job | | 182 | | 182 | |
| **6" x 6"** | | | | | | | |
| | Demolish | S.F. | | 1.74 | | 1.74 | Cost includes material and labor to |
| | Install | S.F. | 5.35 | 4.18 | | 9.53 | install 6" x 6" x 16" concrete slump |
| | Demolish and Install | S.F. | 5.35 | 5.92 | | 11.27 | block. |
| | Clean | S.F. | .07 | .41 | | .48 | |
| | Paint | S.F. | .15 | .72 | | .87 | |
| | Minimum Charge | Job | | 182 | | 182 | |
| **8" x 6"** | | | | | | | |
| | Demolish | S.F. | | 1.74 | | 1.74 | Cost includes material and labor to |
| | Install | S.F. | 7.35 | 4.32 | | 11.67 | install 8" x 6" x 16" concrete slump |
| | Demolish and Install | S.F. | 7.35 | 6.06 | | 13.41 | block. |
| | Clean | S.F. | .07 | .41 | | .48 | |
| | Paint | S.F. | .15 | .72 | | .87 | |
| | Minimum Charge | Job | | 182 | | 182 | |
| **12" x 4"** | | | | | | | |
| | Demolish | S.F. | | 1.65 | | 1.65 | Cost includes material and labor to |
| | Install | S.F. | 12.85 | 4.99 | | 17.84 | install 12" x 4" x 16" concrete slump |
| | Demolish and Install | S.F. | 12.85 | 6.64 | | 19.49 | block. |
| | Clean | S.F. | .07 | .41 | | .48 | |
| | Paint | S.F. | .15 | .72 | | .87 | |
| | Minimum Charge | Job | | 182 | | 182 | |
| **12" x 6"** | | | | | | | |
| | Demolish | S.F. | | 1.74 | | 1.74 | Cost includes material and labor to |
| | Install | S.F. | 11.75 | 5.40 | | 17.15 | install 12" x 6" x 16" concrete slump |
| | Demolish and Install | S.F. | 11.75 | 7.14 | | 18.89 | block. |
| | Clean | S.F. | .07 | .41 | | .48 | |
| | Paint | S.F. | .15 | .72 | | .87 | |
| | Minimum Charge | Job | | 182 | | 182 | |

# Masonry

| Masonry Wall | | Unit | Material | Labor | Equip. | Total | Specification |
|---|---|---|---|---|---|---|---|
| **Stucco** | | | | | | | |
| **Three Coat** | | | | | | | |
| | Demolish | S.Y. | | 2.04 | | 2.04 | Includes material and labor to install |
| | Install | S.Y. | 3.85 | 7.75 | .67 | 12.27 | stucco on exterior masonry walls. |
| | Demolish and Install | S.Y. | 3.85 | 9.79 | .67 | 14.31 | |
| | Clean | S.Y. | | 3.71 | | 3.71 | |
| | Paint | S.F. | .12 | .51 | | .63 | |
| | Minimum Charge | Job | | 162 | | 162 | |
| **Three Coat w / Wire Mesh** | | | | | | | |
| | Demolish | S.Y. | | 3.71 | | 3.71 | Includes material and labor to install |
| | Install | S.Y. | 6.05 | 29.50 | 2.11 | 37.66 | stucco on wire mesh over wood |
| | Demolish and Install | S.Y. | 6.05 | 33.21 | 2.11 | 41.37 | framing. |
| | Clean | S.Y. | | 3.71 | | 3.71 | |
| | Paint | S.F. | .12 | .51 | | .63 | |
| | Minimum Charge | Job | | 162 | | 162 | |
| **Fill Cracks** | | | | | | | |
| | Install | S.F. | .43 | 2.60 | | 3.03 | Includes labor and material to fill-in |
| | Minimum Charge | Job | | 162 | | 162 | hairline cracks up to 1/8" with filler, |
| | | | | | | | including sand and fill per S.F. |
| **Furring** | | | | | | | |
| **1" x 2"** | | | | | | | |
| | Demolish | L.F. | | .12 | | .12 | Cost includes material and labor to |
| | Install | L.F. | .13 | .73 | | .86 | install 1" x 2" furring on masonry wall. |
| | Demolish and Install | L.F. | .13 | .85 | | .98 | |
| | Minimum Charge | Job | | 181 | | 181 | |
| **2" x 2"** | | | | | | | |
| | Demolish | L.F. | | .13 | | .13 | Cost includes material and labor to |
| | Install | L.F. | .22 | .80 | | 1.02 | install 2" x 2" furring on masonry wall. |
| | Demolish and Install | L.F. | .22 | .93 | | 1.15 | |
| | Minimum Charge | Job | | 181 | | 181 | |
| **2" x 4"** | | | | | | | |
| | Demolish | L.F. | | .14 | | .14 | Cost includes material and labor to |
| | Install | L.F. | .39 | .92 | | 1.31 | install 2" x 4" furring on masonry wall. |
| | Demolish and Install | L.F. | .39 | 1.06 | | 1.45 | |
| | Reinstall | L.F. | | .73 | | .73 | |
| | Minimum Charge | Job | | 181 | | 181 | |
| **Maintenance / Cleaning** | | | | | | | |
| **Repoint** | | | | | | | |
| | Install | S.F. | .56 | 4.55 | | 5.11 | Includes labor and material to cut and |
| | Minimum Charge | Hr. | | 45.50 | | 45.50 | repoint brick, hard mortar, running |
| | | | | | | | bond. |
| **Acid Etch** | | | | | | | |
| | Install | S.F. | .04 | .65 | | .69 | Includes labor and material to acid |
| | Minimum Charge | Job | | 133 | 33 | 166 | wash smooth brick. |
| **Pressure Wash** | | | | | | | |
| | Clean | S.F. | | .91 | .14 | 1.05 | Includes labor and material to high |
| | Minimum Charge | Job | | 133 | 33 | 166 | pressure water wash masonry, |
| | | | | | | | average. |
| **Waterproof** | | | | | | | |
| | Install | S.F. | .31 | .67 | | .98 | Includes labor and material to install |
| | Minimum Charge | Job | | 168 | | 168 | masory waterproofing. |

# Masonry

| Chimney | | Unit | Material | Labor | Equip. | Total | Specification |
|---|---|---|---|---|---|---|---|
| **Demo & Haul Exterior** | | | | | | | |
| | Demolish | C.F. | | 4.85 | | 4.85 | Includes minimum labor and |
| | Minimum Charge | Job | | 148 | | 148 | equipment to remove masonry and haul debris to truck or dumpster. |
| **Demo & Haul Interior** | | | | | | | |
| | Demolish | C.F. | | 6.65 | | 6.65 | Includes minimum labor and |
| | Minimum Charge | Job | | 148 | | 148 | equipment to remove masonry and haul debris to truck or dumpster. |
| **Install New (w / flue)** | | | | | | | |
| **Brick** | | | | | | | |
| | Install | V.L.F. | 33.50 | 40.50 | | 74 | Includes material and labor to install |
| | Minimum Charge | Job | | 182 | | 182 | brick chimney with flue from ground level up. Foundation not included. |
| **Natural Stone** | | | | | | | |
| | Install | L.F. | 94 | 65 | | 159 | Includes labor and material to install |
| | Minimum Charge | Job | | 182 | | 182 | natural stone chimney. |
| **Install From Roof Up** | | | | | | | |
| **Brick** | | | | | | | |
| | Install | V.L.F. | 33.50 | 40.50 | | 74 | Includes material and labor to install |
| | Minimum Charge | Job | | 182 | | 182 | brick chimney with flue from ground level up. Foundation not included. |
| **Natural Stone** | | | | | | | |
| | Install | L.F. | 94 | 54 | | 148 | Includes labor and material to install |
| | Minimum Charge | Job | | 182 | | 182 | natural stone chimney. |
| **Install Base Pad** | | | | | | | |
| | Install | Ea. | 265 | 199 | 1.12 | 465.12 | Includes labor and material to replace |
| | Minimum Charge | Job | | 845 | 27.50 | 872.50 | spread footing, 5' square x 16" deep. |
| **Metal Cap** | | | | | | | |
| | Install | Ea. | 48.50 | 23 | | 71.50 | Includes labor and materials to install |
| | Minimum Charge | Job | | 181 | | 181 | bird and squirrel screens in a chimney flue. |

| Fireplace | | Unit | Material | Labor | Equip. | Total | Specification |
|---|---|---|---|---|---|---|---|
| **Common Brick** | | | | | | | |
| **30"** | | | | | | | |
| | Demolish | Ea. | | 1050 | | 1050 | Includes material and labor to install a |
| | Install | Ea. | 1825 | 3250 | | 5075 | complete unit which includes common |
| | Demolish and Install | Ea. | 1825 | 4300 | | 6125 | brick, foundation, damper, flue lining |
| | Minimum Charge | Job | | 182 | | 182 | stack to 15' high and a 30" fire box. |
| **36"** | | | | | | | |
| | Demolish | Ea. | | 1050 | | 1050 | Includes material and labor to install a |
| | Install | Ea. | 1925 | 3600 | | 5525 | complete unit which includes common |
| | Demolish and Install | Ea. | 1925 | 4650 | | 6575 | brick, foundation, damper, flue lining |
| | Minimum Charge | Job | | 182 | | 182 | stack to 15' high and a 36" fire box. |
| **42"** | | | | | | | |
| | Demolish | Ea. | | 1050 | | 1050 | Includes material and labor to install a |
| | Install | Ea. | 2100 | 4050 | | 6150 | complete unit which includes common |
| | Demolish and Install | Ea. | 2100 | 5100 | | 7200 | brick, foundation, damper, flue lining |
| | Minimum Charge | Job | | 182 | | 182 | stack to 15' high and a 42" fire box. |

# Masonry

| Fireplace | | Unit | Material | Labor | Equip. | Total | Specification |
|---|---|---|---|---|---|---|---|
| **48"** | | | | | | | |
| | Demolish | Ea. | | 1050 | | 1050 | Includes material and labor to install a |
| | Install | Ea. | 2200 | 4625 | | 6825 | complete unit which includes common |
| | Demolish and Install | Ea. | 2200 | 5675 | | 7875 | brick, foundation, damper, flue lining |
| | Minimum Charge | Job | | 182 | | 182 | stack to 15' high and a 48" fire box. |
| **Raised Hearth** | | | | | | | |
| **Brick Hearth** | | | | | | | |
| | Demolish | S.F. | | 4.63 | | 4.63 | Includes material and labor to install a |
| | Install | S.F. | 17.20 | 27 | | 44.20 | brick fireplace hearth based on 30" x |
| | Demolish and Install | S.F. | 17.20 | 31.63 | | 48.83 | 29" opening. |
| | Clean | S.F. | .07 | .35 | | .42 | |
| | Minimum Charge | Job | | 182 | | 182 | |
| **Marble Hearth / Facing** | | | | | | | |
| | Demolish | Ea. | | 29.50 | | 29.50 | Includes material and labor to install |
| | Install | Ea. | 605 | 109 | | 714 | marble fireplace hearth. |
| | Demolish and Install | Ea. | 605 | 138.50 | | 743.50 | |
| | Reinstall | Ea. | | 87.57 | | 87.57 | |
| | Clean | Ea. | 21.50 | 5.35 | | 26.85 | |
| | Minimum Charge | Job | | 182 | | 182 | |
| **Breast (face) Brick** | | | | | | | |
| | Demolish | S.F. | | 4.63 | | 4.63 | Includes material and labor to install |
| | Install | S.F. | 6 | 7.55 | | 13.55 | standard red brick, running bond. |
| | Demolish and Install | S.F. | 6 | 12.18 | | 18.18 | |
| | Clean | S.F. | | .91 | .14 | 1.05 | |
| | Minimum Charge | Hr. | | 45.50 | | 45.50 | |
| **Fire Box** | | | | | | | |
| | Demolish | Ea. | | 237 | | 237 | Includes material and labor to install |
| | Install | Ea. | 185 | 325 | | 510 | fireplace box only (110 brick). |
| | Demolish and Install | Ea. | 185 | 562 | | 747 | |
| | Clean | Ea. | .13 | 12 | | 12.13 | |
| | Minimum Charge | Hr. | | 45.50 | | 45.50 | |
| **Natural Stone** | | | | | | | |
| | Demolish | S.F. | | 4.63 | | 4.63 | Includes material and labor to install |
| | Install | S.F. | 22.50 | 13.85 | | 36.35 | high priced stone, split or rock face. |
| | Demolish and Install | S.F. | 22.50 | 18.48 | | 40.98 | |
| | Clean | S.F. | .08 | .81 | | .89 | |
| | Minimum Charge | Job | | 325 | | 325 | |
| **Slumpstone Veneer** | | | | | | | |
| | Demolish | S.F. | | 1.74 | | 1.74 | Cost includes material and labor to |
| | Install | S.F. | 7.35 | 4.32 | | 11.67 | install 8" x 6" x 16" concrete slump |
| | Demolish and Install | S.F. | 7.35 | 6.06 | | 13.41 | block. |
| | Clean | S.F. | .07 | .41 | | .48 | |
| | Paint | S.F. | .15 | .72 | | .87 | |
| | Minimum Charge | Job | | 182 | | 182 | |
| **Prefabricated** | | | | | | | |
| **Firebox** | | | | | | | |
| | Demolish | Ea. | | 42.50 | | 42.50 | Includes material and labor to install |
| | Install | Ea. | 1825 | 330 | | 2155 | up to 43" radiant heat, zero |
| | Demolish and Install | Ea. | 1825 | 372.50 | | 2197.50 | clearance, prefabricated fireplace. |
| | Reinstall | Ea. | | 262.98 | | 262.98 | Flues, doors or blowers not included. |
| | Clean | Ea. | 1.82 | 16.70 | | 18.52 | |
| | Minimum Charge | Job | | 181 | | 181 | |

| Fireplace | | Unit | Material | Labor | Equip. | Total | Specification |
|---|---|---|---|---|---|---|---|
| **Flue** | | | | | | | |
| | Demolish | V.L.F. | | 4.94 | | 4.94 | Includes material and labor to install |
| | Install | V.L.F. | 14.50 | 13.90 | | 28.40 | prefabricated chimney vent, 8" |
| | Demolish and Install | V.L.F. | 14.50 | 18.84 | | 33.34 | exposed metal flue. |
| | Reinstall | V.L.F. | | 11.14 | | 11.14 | |
| | Clean | L.F. | .73 | 3.34 | | 4.07 | |
| | Minimum Charge | Job | | 360 | | 360 | |
| **Blower** | | | | | | | |
| | Demolish | Ea. | | 3.95 | | 3.95 | Includes material and labor to install |
| | Install | Ea. | 131 | 25 | | 156 | blower for metal fireplace flue. |
| | Demolish and Install | Ea. | 131 | 28.95 | | 159.95 | |
| | Reinstall | Ea. | | 20.12 | | 20.12 | |
| | Clean | Ea. | 3.63 | 33.50 | | 37.13 | |
| | Minimum Charge | Job | | 360 | | 360 | |
| **Accessories** | | | | | | | |
| **Wood Mantle** | | | | | | | |
| | Demolish | L.F. | | 4.94 | | 4.94 | Includes material and labor to install |
| | Install | L.F. | 7.20 | 10.35 | | 17.55 | wood fireplace mantel. |
| | Demolish and Install | L.F. | 7.20 | 15.29 | | 22.49 | |
| | Reinstall | L.F. | | 10.33 | | 10.33 | |
| | Clean | Ea. | .02 | .74 | | .76 | |
| | Paint | L.F. | .08 | 8.55 | | 8.63 | |
| | Minimum Charge | Job | | 181 | | 181 | |
| **Colonial Style** | | | | | | | |
| | Demolish | Ea. | | 44.50 | | 44.50 | Includes material and labor to install |
| | Install | Opng. | 2525 | 181 | | 2706 | wood fireplace mantel. |
| | Demolish and Install | Opng. | 2525 | 225.50 | | 2750.50 | |
| | Reinstall | Opng. | | 180.80 | | 180.80 | |
| | Clean | Ea. | | .53 | | .53 | |
| | Paint | Ea. | 13.65 | 118 | | 131.65 | |
| | Minimum Charge | Job | | 181 | | 181 | |
| **Modern Design** | | | | | | | |
| | Demolish | Ea. | | 44.50 | | 44.50 | Includes material and labor to install |
| | Install | Opng. | 201 | 72.50 | | 273.50 | wood fireplace mantel. |
| | Demolish and Install | Opng. | 201 | 117 | | 318 | |
| | Reinstall | Opng. | | 72.32 | | 72.32 | |
| | Clean | Ea. | | .53 | | .53 | |
| | Paint | Ea. | 13.65 | 118 | | 131.65 | |
| | Minimum Charge | Job | | 181 | | 181 | |
| **Glass Door Unit** | | | | | | | |
| | Demolish | Ea. | | 6.20 | | 6.20 | Includes material and labor to install a |
| | Install | Ea. | 201 | 7.60 | | 208.60 | fireplace glass door unit. |
| | Demolish and Install | Ea. | 201 | 13.80 | | 214.80 | |
| | Reinstall | Ea. | | 7.58 | | 7.58 | |
| | Clean | Ea. | .44 | 10.25 | | 10.69 | |
| | Minimum Charge | Job | | 181 | | 181 | |
| **Fire Screen** | | | | | | | |
| | Demolish | Ea. | | 3.09 | | 3.09 | Includes material and labor to install a |
| | Install | Ea. | 51 | 3.79 | | 54.79 | fireplace fire screen. |
| | Demolish and Install | Ea. | 51 | 6.88 | | 57.88 | |
| | Reinstall | Ea. | | 3.79 | | 3.79 | |
| | Clean | Ea. | .22 | 8.90 | | 9.12 | |
| | Minimum Charge | Job | | 181 | | 181 | |

# Siding

| Shingles | Board & Batten | Texture 1-11 |

| Exterior Siding | Unit | Material | Labor | Equip. | Total | Specification |
|---|---|---|---|---|---|---|
| **Trim** | | | | | | |
| **1″ x 2″** | | | | | | |
| Demolish | L.F. | | .25 | | .25 | Cost includes material and labor to |
| Install | L.F. | .35 | 1.10 | | 1.45 | install 1″ x 2″ pine trim. |
| Demolish and Install | L.F. | .35 | 1.35 | | 1.70 | |
| Clean | L.F. | .01 | .18 | | .19 | |
| Paint | L.F. | .02 | .49 | | .51 | |
| Minimum Charge | Job | | 181 | | 181 | |
| **1″ x 3″** | | | | | | |
| Demolish | L.F. | | .25 | | .25 | Cost includes material and labor to |
| Install | L.F. | .19 | 1.21 | | 1.40 | install 1″ x 3″ pine trim. |
| Demolish and Install | L.F. | .19 | 1.46 | | 1.65 | |
| Clean | L.F. | .01 | .18 | | .19 | |
| Paint | L.F. | .02 | .49 | | .51 | |
| Minimum Charge | Job | | 181 | | 181 | |
| **1″ x 4″** | | | | | | |
| Demolish | L.F. | | .25 | | .25 | Cost includes material and labor to |
| Install | L.F. | .73 | 1.45 | | 2.18 | install 1″ x 4″ pine trim. |
| Demolish and Install | L.F. | .73 | 1.70 | | 2.43 | |
| Clean | L.F. | .01 | .18 | | .19 | |
| Paint | L.F. | .02 | .49 | | .51 | |
| Minimum Charge | Job | | 181 | | 181 | |
| **1″ x 6″** | | | | | | |
| Demolish | L.F. | | .25 | | .25 | Cost includes material and labor to |
| Install | L.F. | 1.13 | 1.45 | | 2.58 | install 1″ x 6″ pine trim. |
| Demolish and Install | L.F. | 1.13 | 1.70 | | 2.83 | |
| Clean | L.F. | .02 | .18 | | .20 | |
| Paint | L.F. | .08 | .49 | | .57 | |
| Minimum Charge | Job | | 181 | | 181 | |
| **1″ x 8″** | | | | | | |
| Demolish | L.F. | | .27 | | .27 | Cost includes material and labor to |
| Install | L.F. | 1.51 | 1.81 | | 3.32 | install 1″ x 8″ pine trim. |
| Demolish and Install | L.F. | 1.51 | 2.08 | | 3.59 | |
| Clean | L.F. | .02 | .19 | | .21 | |
| Paint | L.F. | .08 | .49 | | .57 | |
| Minimum Charge | Job | | 181 | | 181 | |
| **Aluminum** | | | | | | |
| **8″ Non-Insulated** | | | | | | |
| Demolish | S.F. | | .67 | | .67 | Includes material and labor to install |
| Install | S.F. | 1.50 | 1.45 | | 2.95 | horizontal, colored clapboard, 8″ to |
| Demolish and Install | S.F. | 1.50 | 2.12 | | 3.62 | 10″ wide, plain. |
| Reinstall | S.F. | | 1.45 | | 1.45 | |
| Clean | S.F. | | .27 | | .27 | |
| Minimum Charge | Job | | 181 | | 181 | |

# Siding

| Exterior Siding | | Unit | Material | Labor | Equip. | Total | Specification |
|---|---|---|---|---|---|---|---|
| **8″ Insulated** | | | | | | | |
| | Demolish | S.F. | | .67 | | .67 | Includes material and labor to install |
| | Install | S.F. | 1.47 | 1.45 | | 2.92 | horizontal, colored insulated |
| | Demolish and Install | S.F. | 1.47 | 2.12 | | 3.59 | clapboard, 8″ wide, plain. |
| | Reinstall | S.F. | | 1.45 | | 1.45 | |
| | Clean | S.F. | | .27 | | .27 | |
| | Minimum Charge | Job | | 181 | | 181 | |
| **12″ Non-Insulated** | | | | | | | |
| | Demolish | S.F. | | .67 | | .67 | Includes material and labor to install |
| | Install | S.F. | 1.52 | 1.24 | | 2.76 | horizontal, colored clapboard, plain. |
| | Demolish and Install | S.F. | 1.52 | 1.91 | | 3.43 | |
| | Reinstall | S.F. | | 1.24 | | 1.24 | |
| | Clean | S.F. | | .27 | | .27 | |
| | Minimum Charge | Job | | 181 | | 181 | |
| **12″ Insulated** | | | | | | | |
| | Demolish | S.F. | | .67 | | .67 | Includes material and labor to install |
| | Install | S.F. | 1.76 | 1.24 | | 3 | horizontal, colored insulated |
| | Demolish and Install | S.F. | 1.76 | 1.91 | | 3.67 | clapboard, plain. |
| | Reinstall | S.F. | | 1.24 | | 1.24 | |
| | Clean | S.F. | | .27 | | .27 | |
| | Minimum Charge | Job | | 181 | | 181 | |
| **Clapboard 8″ to 10″** | | | | | | | |
| | Demolish | S.F. | | .67 | | .67 | Includes material and labor to install |
| | Install | S.F. | 1.50 | 1.45 | | 2.95 | horizontal, colored clapboard, 8″ to |
| | Demolish and Install | S.F. | 1.50 | 2.12 | | 3.62 | 10″ wide, plain. |
| | Reinstall | S.F. | | 1.45 | | 1.45 | |
| | Clean | S.F. | | .27 | | .27 | |
| | Minimum Charge | Job | | 181 | | 181 | |
| **Corner Strips** | | | | | | | |
| | Demolish | L.F. | | .35 | | .35 | Includes material and labor to install |
| | Install | V.L.F. | 2.26 | 1.45 | | 3.71 | corners for horizontal lapped |
| | Demolish and Install | V.L.F. | 2.26 | 1.80 | | 4.06 | aluminum siding. |
| | Reinstall | V.L.F. | | 1.45 | | 1.45 | |
| | Clean | L.F. | | .18 | | .18 | |
| | Minimum Charge | Job | | 181 | | 181 | |
| **Vinyl** | | | | | | | |
| **Non-Insulated** | | | | | | | |
| | Demolish | S.F. | | .52 | | .52 | Cost includes material and labor to |
| | Install | S.F. | 1.11 | 1.31 | | 2.42 | install 10″ non-insulated solid vinyl |
| | Demolish and Install | S.F. | 1.11 | 1.83 | | 2.94 | siding. |
| | Reinstall | S.F. | | 1.05 | | 1.05 | |
| | Clean | S.F. | | .27 | | .27 | |
| | Minimum Charge | Job | | 181 | | 181 | |
| **Insulated** | | | | | | | |
| | Demolish | S.F. | | .52 | | .52 | Includes material and labor to install |
| | Install | S.F. | 2.46 | 1.81 | | 4.27 | insulated solid vinyl siding panels. |
| | Demolish and Install | S.F. | 2.46 | 2.33 | | 4.79 | |
| | Reinstall | S.F. | | 1.45 | | 1.45 | |
| | Clean | S.F. | | .27 | | .27 | |
| | Minimum Charge | Job | | 181 | | 181 | |
| **Corner Strips** | | | | | | | |
| | Demolish | L.F. | | .33 | | .33 | Includes material and labor to install |
| | Install | L.F. | 1.67 | 1.03 | | 2.70 | corner posts for vinyl siding panels. |
| | Demolish and Install | S.F | 1.67 | 1.36 | | 3.03 | |
| | Reinstall | L.F. | | .83 | | .83 | |
| | Clean | L.F. | | .18 | | .18 | |
| | Minimum Charge | Job | | 181 | | 181 | |

# Siding

| Exterior Siding | Unit | Material | Labor | Equip. | Total | Specification |
|---|---|---|---|---|---|---|
| **Fiber Cement Siding** | | | | | | |
| **4' x 8' Panel** | | | | | | |
| Demolish | S.F. | | .54 | | .54 | Cost includes material and labor to |
| Install | S.F. | 1.16 | .96 | | 2.12 | install 4' x 8' masonite siding 7/16" |
| Clean | S.F. | | .27 | | .27 | thick. |
| Paint | S.F. | .26 | 1.06 | | 1.32 | |
| Minimum Charge | Job | | 181 | | 181 | |
| **Lap** | | | | | | |
| Demolish | S.F. | | .54 | | .54 | Cost includes material and labor to |
| Install | S.F. | 1.50 | 1.74 | | 3.24 | install 8" or 12" masonite lap siding |
| Clean | S.F. | | .27 | | .27 | 7/16" thick with wood grain finish. |
| Paint | S.F. | .26 | 1.06 | | 1.32 | |
| Minimum Charge | Job | | 181 | | 181 | |
| **Plywood Panel** | | | | | | |
| **Douglas Fir (T-1-11)** | | | | | | |
| Demolish | S.F. | | .41 | | .41 | Includes material and labor to install |
| Install | S.F. | 1.24 | 1.10 | | 2.34 | Douglas fir 4' x 8' plywood exterior |
| Demolish and Install | S.F. | 1.24 | 1.51 | | 2.75 | siding plain or patterns. |
| Reinstall | S.F. | | 1.10 | | 1.10 | |
| Clean | S.F. | | .27 | | .27 | |
| Paint | S.F. | .26 | 1.06 | | 1.32 | |
| Minimum Charge | Job | | 181 | | 181 | |
| **Redwood** | | | | | | |
| Demolish | S.F. | | .41 | | .41 | Includes material and labor to install |
| Install | S.F. | 2.13 | 1.10 | | 3.23 | redwood 4' x 8' plywood exterior |
| Demolish and Install | S.F. | 2.13 | 1.51 | | 3.64 | siding plain or patterns. |
| Reinstall | S.F. | | 1.10 | | 1.10 | |
| Clean | S.F. | | .27 | | .27 | |
| Paint | S.F. | .26 | 1.06 | | 1.32 | |
| Minimum Charge | Job | | 181 | | 181 | |
| **Cedar** | | | | | | |
| Demolish | S.F. | | .41 | | .41 | Cost includes material and labor to |
| Install | S.F. | 2.70 | 1.10 | | 3.80 | install 4' x 8' cedar plywood exterior |
| Demolish and Install | S.F. | 2.70 | 1.51 | | 4.21 | siding plain or patterns. |
| Reinstall | S.F. | | 1.10 | | 1.10 | |
| Clean | S.F. | | .27 | | .27 | |
| Paint | S.F. | .26 | 1.06 | | 1.32 | |
| Minimum Charge | Job | | 181 | | 181 | |
| **Tongue and Groove** | | | | | | |
| **Fir, Tongue and Groove** | | | | | | |
| Demolish | S.F. | | .74 | | .74 | Includes material and labor to install |
| Install | S.F. | 1.71 | 1.10 | | 2.81 | fir tongue and groove exterior siding |
| Demolish and Install | S.F. | 1.71 | 1.84 | | 3.55 | 1" x 8". |
| Reinstall | S.F. | | .88 | | .88 | |
| Clean | S.F. | | .27 | | .27 | |
| Paint | S.F. | .26 | 1.06 | | 1.32 | |
| Minimum Charge | Job | | 181 | | 181 | |
| **Pine, Tongue and Groove** | | | | | | |
| Demolish | S.F. | | .74 | | .74 | Includes labor and material to install |
| Install | S.F. | 1.21 | 1.10 | | 2.31 | pine tongue and groove exterior |
| Demolish and Install | S.F. | 1.21 | 1.84 | | 3.05 | siding 1" x 8". |
| Reinstall | S.F. | | 1.10 | | 1.10 | |
| Clean | S.F. | | .27 | | .27 | |
| Paint | S.F. | .26 | 1.06 | | 1.32 | |
| Minimum Charge | Job | | 181 | | 181 | |

# Siding

| Exterior Siding | Unit | Material | Labor | Equip. | Total | Specification |
|---|---|---|---|---|---|---|
| **Cedar, Tongue and Groove** | | | | | | |
| Demolish | S.F. | | .74 | | .74 | Includes labor and material to install |
| Install | S.F. | 1.97 | 1.64 | | 3.61 | cedar tongue and groove exterior |
| Demolish and Install | S.F. | 1.97 | 2.38 | | 4.35 | siding 1" x 8". |
| Reinstall | S.F. | | 1.31 | | 1.31 | |
| Clean | S.F. | | .27 | | .27 | |
| Paint | S.F. | .26 | 1.06 | | 1.32 | |
| Minimum Charge | Job | | 181 | | 181 | |
| **Redwood, Tongue and Groove** | | | | | | |
| Demolish | S.F. | | .74 | | .74 | Includes labor and material to install |
| Install | S.F. | 3.29 | 1.64 | | 4.93 | redwood tongue and groove exterior |
| Demolish and Install | S.F. | 3.29 | 2.38 | | 5.67 | siding 1" x 4". |
| Reinstall | S.F. | | 1.64 | | 1.64 | |
| Clean | S.F. | | .27 | | .27 | |
| Paint | S.F. | .26 | 1.06 | | 1.32 | |
| Minimum Charge | Job | | 181 | | 181 | |
| **Board and Batten** | | | | | | |
| **Fir** | | | | | | |
| Demolish | S.F. | | .74 | | .74 | Cost includes material and labor to |
| Install | S.F. | 1.93 | 1.10 | | 3.03 | install 1" x 8" fir boards with 1" x 3" |
| Demolish and Install | S.F. | 1.93 | 1.84 | | 3.77 | battens. |
| Reinstall | S.F. | | .88 | | .88 | |
| Clean | S.F. | | .27 | | .27 | |
| Paint | S.F. | .26 | 1.06 | | 1.32 | |
| Minimum Charge | Job | | 181 | | 181 | |
| **Pine** | | | | | | |
| Demolish | S.F. | | .74 | | .74 | Cost includes material and labor to |
| Install | S.F. | 2.08 | .96 | | 3.04 | install 1" x 10" pine boards with 1" x |
| Demolish and Install | S.F. | 2.08 | 1.70 | | 3.78 | 3" battens. |
| Reinstall | S.F. | | .77 | | .77 | |
| Clean | S.F. | | .27 | | .27 | |
| Paint | S.F. | .26 | 1.06 | | 1.32 | |
| Minimum Charge | Job | | 181 | | 181 | |
| **Cedar** | | | | | | |
| Demolish | S.F. | | .74 | | .74 | Cost includes material and labor to |
| Install | S.F. | 2.18 | .96 | | 3.14 | install 1" x 10" cedar boards with 1" x |
| Demolish and Install | S.F. | 2.18 | 1.70 | | 3.88 | 3" battens. |
| Reinstall | S.F. | | .77 | | .77 | |
| Clean | S.F. | | .27 | | .27 | |
| Paint | S.F. | .26 | 1.06 | | 1.32 | |
| Minimum Charge | Job | | 181 | | 181 | |
| **Redwood** | | | | | | |
| Demolish | S.F. | | .74 | | .74 | Cost includes material and labor to |
| Install | S.F. | 5.95 | .96 | | 6.91 | install 1" x 10" redwood boards with |
| Demolish and Install | S.F. | 5.95 | 1.70 | | 7.65 | 1" x 3" battens. |
| Reinstall | S.F. | | .77 | | .77 | |
| Clean | S.F. | | .27 | | .27 | |
| Paint | S.F. | .26 | 1.06 | | 1.32 | |
| Minimum Charge | Job | | 181 | | 181 | |
| **Wood Shingle** | | | | | | |
| Demolish | Sq. | | 68.50 | | 68.50 | Includes material and labor to install |
| Install | Sq. | 216 | 161 | | 377 | wood shingles/shakes. |
| Demolish and Install | Sq. | 216 | 229.50 | | 445.50 | |
| Clean | Sq. | | 28 | | 28 | |
| Paint | Sq. | 17.10 | 94.50 | | 111.60 | |
| Minimum Charge | Job | | 181 | | 181 | |

# Siding

| Exterior Siding | Unit | Material | Labor | Equip. | Total | Specification |
|---|---|---|---|---|---|---|
| **Synthetic Stucco System** | | | | | | |
| Demolish | S.F. | | 2.47 | | 2.47 | Cost includes material and labor to |
| Install | S.F. | 3.19 | 7.05 | .61 | 10.85 | install 2 coats of adhesive mixture, |
| Demolish and Install | S.F. | 3.19 | 9.52 | .61 | 13.32 | glass fiber mesh, 1" insulation board, |
| Clean | S.F. | | .24 | | .24 | and textured finish coat. |
| Paint | S.F. | .12 | .51 | | .63 | |
| Minimum Charge | Job | | 775 | 66.50 | 841.50 | |

**Front-end Loader**                               **Bulldozer**

## Grading

| Grading | | Unit | Material | Labor | Equip. | Total | Specification |
|---|---|---|---|---|---|---|---|
| **Hand (fine)** | | | | | | | |
| | Install | S.F. | | .53 | | .53 | Includes labor and material to install fine grade for slab on grade, hand grade. |
| | Minimum Charge | Job | | 133 | | 133 | |
| **Machine (fine)** | | | | | | | |
| | Install | S.Y. | | .46 | .43 | .89 | Includes labor and material to install fine grade for roadway, base or leveling course. |
| | Minimum Charge | Job | | 315 | 294 | 609 | |

## Asphalt Paving

| Asphalt Paving | | Unit | Material | Labor | Equip. | Total | Specification |
|---|---|---|---|---|---|---|---|
| **Seal Coat** | | | | | | | |
| | Install | S.F. | .10 | .10 | | .20 | Includes labor and material to install sealcoat for a small area. |
| | Minimum Charge | Job | | 133 | | 133 | |
| **Wearing Course** | | | | | | | |
| | Install | S.F. | .12 | .29 | .25 | .66 | Cost includes labor and material to install 1" thick wearing course. |
| | Minimum Charge | Job | | 133 | | 133 | |

## Masonry Pavers

| Masonry Pavers | | Unit | Material | Labor | Equip. | Total | Specification |
|---|---|---|---|---|---|---|---|
| **Natural Concrete** | | | | | | | |
| **Sand Base** | | | | | | | |
| | Demolish | S.F. | | 2.96 | | 2.96 | Includes material and labor to install concrete pavers on sand base. |
| | Install | S.F. | 2.48 | 6.05 | | 8.53 | |
| | Demolish and Install | S.F. | 2.48 | 9.01 | | 11.49 | |
| | Reinstall | S.F. | | 4.85 | | 4.85 | |
| | Clean | S.F. | | 1.07 | | 1.07 | |
| | Minimum Charge | Job | | 182 | | 182 | |
| **Mortar Base** | | | | | | | |
| | Demolish | S.F. | | 4.87 | 1.74 | 6.61 | Includes material and labor to install concrete pavers on mortar base. |
| | Install | S.F. | 3.19 | 5.05 | | 8.24 | |
| | Demolish and Install | S.F. | 3.19 | 9.92 | 1.74 | 14.85 | |
| | Reinstall | S.F. | | 4.04 | | 4.04 | |
| | Clean | S.F. | | .97 | | .97 | |
| | Minimum Charge | Job | | 182 | | 182 | |

## Masonry Pavers

| Masonry Pavers | Unit | Material | Labor | Equip. | Total | Specification |
|---|---|---|---|---|---|---|
| **Adobe** | | | | | | |
| **Sand Base** | | | | | | |
| Demolish | S.F. | | 2.96 | | 2.96 | Includes material and labor to install |
| Install | S.F. | 2.05 | 4.04 | | 6.09 | adobe pavers on sand base. |
| Demolish and Install | S.F. | 2.05 | 7 | | 9.05 | |
| Reinstall | S.F. | | 3.24 | | 3.24 | |
| Clean | S.F. | | 1.07 | | 1.07 | |
| Minimum Charge | Job | | 182 | | 182 | |
| **Mortar Base** | | | | | | |
| Demolish | S.F. | | 4.87 | 1.74 | 6.61 | Includes material and labor to install |
| Install | S.F. | 2.84 | 5.05 | | 7.89 | adobe pavers on mortar base. |
| Demolish and Install | S.F. | 2.84 | 9.92 | 1.74 | 14.50 | |
| Reinstall | S.F. | | 4.04 | | 4.04 | |
| Clean | S.F. | | .97 | | .97 | |
| Minimum Charge | Job | | 182 | | 182 | |
| **Standard Brick** | | | | | | |
| **Sand Base** | | | | | | |
| Demolish | S.F. | | 2.96 | | 2.96 | Includes material and labor to install |
| Install | S.F. | 3.09 | 6.50 | | 9.59 | standard brick pavers on sand base. |
| Demolish and Install | S.F. | 3.09 | 9.46 | | 12.55 | |
| Reinstall | S.F. | | 5.19 | | 5.19 | |
| Clean | S.F. | | 1.07 | | 1.07 | |
| Minimum Charge | Job | | 182 | | 182 | |
| **Mortar Base** | | | | | | |
| Demolish | S.F. | | 4.87 | 1.74 | 6.61 | Includes material and labor to install |
| Install | S.F. | 5.65 | 9.10 | | 14.75 | standard brick pavers on mortar base. |
| Demolish and Install | S.F. | 5.65 | 13.97 | 1.74 | 21.36 | |
| Reinstall | S.F. | | 7.28 | | 7.28 | |
| Clean | S.F. | | .97 | | .97 | |
| Minimum Charge | Job | | 182 | | 182 | |
| **Deluxe Brick** | | | | | | |
| **Sand Base** | | | | | | |
| Demolish | S.F. | | 2.96 | | 2.96 | Includes material and labor to install |
| Install | S.F. | 5.60 | 5.05 | | 10.65 | deluxe brick pavers on sand base. |
| Demolish and Install | S.F. | 5.60 | 8.01 | | 13.61 | |
| Reinstall | S.F. | | 4.04 | | 4.04 | |
| Clean | S.F. | | 1.07 | | 1.07 | |
| Minimum Charge | Job | | 182 | | 182 | |
| **Mortar Base** | | | | | | |
| Demolish | S.F. | | 4.87 | 1.74 | 6.61 | Includes material and labor to install |
| Install | S.F. | 6.05 | 9.10 | | 15.15 | deluxe brick pavers on mortar base. |
| Demolish and Install | S.F. | 6.05 | 13.97 | 1.74 | 21.76 | |
| Reinstall | S.F. | | 7.28 | | 7.28 | |
| Clean | S.F. | | .97 | | .97 | |
| Minimum Charge | Job | | 182 | | 182 | |

## Fencing

| Fencing | Unit | Material | Labor | Equip. | Total | Specification |
|---|---|---|---|---|---|---|
| **Block w / Footing** | | | | | | |
| **4″** | | | | | | |
| Demolish | S.F. | | 1.65 | | 1.65 | Cost includes material and labor to |
| Install | S.F. | 1.44 | 3.86 | | 5.30 | install 4″ non-reinforced concrete |
| Demolish and Install | S.F. | 1.44 | 5.51 | | 6.95 | block. |
| Clean | S.F. | .13 | 1.13 | .18 | 1.44 | |
| Paint | S.F. | .20 | .42 | | .62 | |
| Minimum Charge | Job | | 182 | | 182 | |

| Fencing | Unit | Material | Labor | Equip. | Total | Specification |
|---|---|---|---|---|---|---|
| **4" Reinforced** | | | | | | |
| Demolish | S.F. | | 1.65 | .92 | 2.57 | Cost includes material and labor to |
| Install | S.F. | 1.55 | 3.91 | | 5.46 | install 4" reinforced concrete block. |
| Demolish and Install | S.F. | 1.55 | 5.56 | .92 | 8.03 | |
| Clean | S.F. | .13 | 1.13 | .18 | 1.44 | |
| Paint | S.F. | .20 | .42 | | .62 | |
| Minimum Charge | Job | | 182 | | 182 | |
| **6"** | | | | | | |
| Demolish | S.F. | | 1.74 | | 1.74 | Cost includes material and labor to |
| Install | S.F. | 2.09 | 4.15 | | 6.24 | install 6" non-reinforced concrete |
| Demolish and Install | S.F. | 2.09 | 5.89 | | 7.98 | block. |
| Clean | S.F. | .13 | 1.13 | .18 | 1.44 | |
| Paint | S.F. | .20 | .42 | | .62 | |
| Minimum Charge | Job | | 182 | | 182 | |
| **6" Reinforced** | | | | | | |
| Demolish | S.F. | | 1.73 | .43 | 2.16 | Cost includes material and labor to |
| Install | S.F. | 2.21 | 4.20 | | 6.41 | install 6" reinforced concrete block. |
| Demolish and Install | S.F. | 2.21 | 5.93 | .43 | 8.57 | |
| Clean | S.F. | .13 | 1.13 | .18 | 1.44 | |
| Paint | S.F. | .20 | .42 | | .62 | |
| Minimum Charge | Job | | 182 | | 182 | |
| **Cap for Block Wall** | | | | | | |
| Demolish | L.F. | | 1.85 | | 1.85 | Includes labor and equipment to install |
| Install | L.F. | 19.75 | 8.65 | | 28.40 | precast concrete coping. |
| Demolish and Install | L.F. | 19.75 | 10.50 | | 30.25 | |
| Clean | L.F. | .01 | 2.78 | | 2.79 | |
| Paint | S.F. | .20 | .42 | | .62 | |
| Minimum Charge | Job | | 182 | | 182 | |
| **Block Pilaster** | | | | | | |
| Demolish | Ea. | | 127 | | 127 | Includes material and labor to install |
| Install | Ea. | 77.50 | 130 | | 207.50 | block pilaster for fence. |
| Demolish and Install | Ea. | 77.50 | 257 | | 334.50 | |
| Reinstall | Ea. | | 129.70 | | 129.70 | |
| Paint | Ea. | 4.30 | 14 | | 18.30 | |
| Minimum Charge | Job | | 182 | | 182 | |
| **Block w / o Footing** | | | | | | |
| **4"** | | | | | | |
| Demolish | S.F. | | 1.65 | | 1.65 | Cost includes material and labor to |
| Install | S.F. | 1.75 | 2.95 | | 4.70 | install 4" non-reinforced hollow |
| Demolish and Install | S.F. | 1.75 | 4.60 | | 6.35 | lightweight block. |
| Clean | S.F. | .13 | 1.13 | .18 | 1.44 | |
| Paint | S.F. | .20 | .42 | | .62 | |
| Minimum Charge | Job | | 182 | | 182 | |
| **4" Reinforced** | | | | | | |
| Demolish | S.F. | | 1.65 | .92 | 2.57 | Cost includes material and labor to |
| Install | S.F. | 2.48 | 3.82 | | 6.30 | install 4" reinforced hollow lightweight |
| Demolish and Install | S.F. | 2.48 | 5.47 | .92 | 8.87 | block. |
| Clean | S.F. | .13 | 1.13 | .18 | 1.44 | |
| Paint | S.F. | .20 | .42 | | .62 | |
| Minimum Charge | Job | | 182 | | 182 | |
| **6"** | | | | | | |
| Demolish | S.F. | | 1.74 | | 1.74 | Cost includes material and labor to |
| Install | S.F. | 2.38 | 3.24 | | 5.62 | install 6" non-reinforced hollow |
| Demolish and Install | S.F. | 2.38 | 4.98 | | 7.36 | lightweight block. |
| Clean | S.F. | .13 | 1.13 | .18 | 1.44 | |
| Paint | S.F. | .20 | .42 | | .62 | |
| Minimum Charge | Job | | 182 | | 182 | |

| Fencing | Unit | Material | Labor | Equip. | Total | Specification |
|---|---|---|---|---|---|---|
| **6" Reinforced** | | | | | | |
| Demolish | S.F. | | 1.73 | .43 | 2.16 | Cost includes material and labor to |
| Install | S.F. | 2.46 | 4.10 | | 6.56 | install 6" reinforced hollow lightweight |
| Demolish and Install | S.F. | 2.46 | 5.83 | .43 | 8.72 | block. |
| Clean | S.F. | .13 | 1.13 | .18 | 1.44 | |
| Paint | S.F. | .20 | .42 | | .62 | |
| Minimum Charge | Job | | 182 | | 182 | |
| **Cap for Block Wall** | | | | | | |
| Demolish | L.F. | | 1.85 | | 1.85 | Includes labor and equipment to install |
| Install | L.F. | 19.75 | 8.65 | | 28.40 | precast concrete coping. |
| Demolish and Install | L.F. | 19.75 | 10.50 | | 30.25 | |
| Clean | L.F. | .01 | 2.78 | | 2.79 | |
| Paint | S.F. | .20 | .42 | | .62 | |
| Minimum Charge | Job | | 182 | | 182 | |
| **Block Pilaster** | | | | | | |
| Demolish | Ea. | | 127 | | 127 | Includes material and labor to install |
| Install | Ea. | 77.50 | 130 | | 207.50 | block pilaster for fence. |
| Demolish and Install | Ea. | 77.50 | 257 | | 334.50 | |
| Reinstall | Ea. | | 129.70 | | 129.70 | |
| Paint | Ea. | 4.30 | 14 | | 18.30 | |
| Minimum Charge | Job | | 182 | | 182 | |
| **Chain Link** | | | | | | |
| **3' High w / o Top Rail** | | | | | | |
| Demolish | L.F. | | 2.29 | .82 | 3.11 | Includes material and labor to install |
| Install | L.F. | 3.95 | 1.55 | .39 | 5.89 | residential galvanized fence 3' high |
| Demolish and Install | L.F. | 3.95 | 3.84 | 1.21 | 9 | with 1-3/8" steel post 10' O.C. set |
| Reinstall | L.F. | | 1.24 | .31 | 1.55 | without concrete. |
| Clean | L.F. | .11 | .97 | | 1.08 | |
| Minimum Charge | Job | | 415 | | 415 | |
| **4' High w / o Top Rail** | | | | | | |
| Demolish | L.F. | | 2.29 | .82 | 3.11 | Includes material and labor to install |
| Install | L.F. | 4.13 | 1.92 | .48 | 6.53 | residential galvanized fence 4' high |
| Demolish and Install | L.F. | 4.13 | 4.21 | 1.30 | 9.64 | with 1-3/8" steel post 10' O.C. set |
| Reinstall | L.F. | | 1.53 | .39 | 1.92 | without concrete. |
| Clean | L.F. | .14 | 1.07 | | 1.21 | |
| Minimum Charge | Job | | 415 | | 415 | |
| **5' High w / o Top Rail** | | | | | | |
| Demolish | L.F. | | 2.29 | .82 | 3.11 | Includes material and labor to install |
| Install | L.F. | 4.84 | 2.51 | .63 | 7.98 | residential galvanized fence 5' high |
| Demolish and Install | L.F. | 4.84 | 4.80 | 1.45 | 11.09 | with 1-3/8" steel post 10' O.C. set |
| Reinstall | L.F. | | 2.01 | .50 | 2.51 | without concrete. |
| Clean | L.F. | .19 | 1.19 | | 1.38 | |
| Minimum Charge | Job | | 415 | | 415 | |
| **3' High w / Top Rail** | | | | | | |
| Demolish | L.F. | | 2.44 | .87 | 3.31 | Includes material and labor to install |
| Install | L.F. | 4.86 | 1.63 | .41 | 6.90 | residential galvanized fence 3' high |
| Demolish and Install | L.F. | 4.86 | 4.07 | 1.28 | 10.21 | with 1-3/8" steel post 10' O.C. set |
| Reinstall | L.F. | | 1.30 | .33 | 1.63 | without concrete. |
| Clean | L.F. | .11 | .99 | | 1.10 | |
| Minimum Charge | Job | | 415 | | 415 | |
| **4' High w / Top Rail** | | | | | | |
| Demolish | L.F. | | 2.44 | .87 | 3.31 | Includes material and labor to install |
| Install | L.F. | 5.50 | 2.04 | .51 | 8.05 | residential galvanized fence 4' high |
| Demolish and Install | L.F. | 5.50 | 4.48 | 1.38 | 11.36 | with 1-5/8" steel post 10' O.C. set |
| Reinstall | L.F. | | 1.63 | .41 | 2.04 | without concrete and 1-5/8" top rail |
| Clean | L.F. | .14 | 1.09 | | 1.23 | with sleeves. |
| Minimum Charge | Job | | 415 | | 415 | |

## Fencing

| | Unit | Material | Labor | Equip. | Total | Specification |
|---|---|---|---|---|---|---|
| **5' High w / Top Rail** | | | | | | |
| Demolish | L.F. | | 2.44 | .87 | 3.31 | Includes material and labor to install |
| Install | L.F. | 6.25 | 2.72 | .68 | 9.65 | residential galvanized fence 5' high |
| Demolish and Install | L.F. | 6.25 | 5.16 | 1.55 | 12.96 | with 1-5/8" steel post 10' O.C. set |
| Reinstall | L.F. | | 2.17 | .55 | 2.72 | without concrete and 1-5/8" top rail |
| Clean | L.F. | .19 | 1.21 | | 1.40 | with sleeves. |
| Minimum Charge | Job | | 415 | | 415 | |
| **6' High w / Top Rail** | | | | | | |
| Demolish | L.F. | | 2.44 | .87 | 3.31 | Includes material and labor to install |
| Install | L.F. | 6.70 | 4.08 | 1.02 | 11.80 | residential galvanized fence 6' high |
| Demolish and Install | L.F. | 6.70 | 6.52 | 1.89 | 15.11 | with 2" steel post 10' O.C. set without |
| Reinstall | L.F. | | 3.26 | .82 | 4.08 | concrete and 1-3/8" top rail with |
| Clean | L.F. | .21 | 1.37 | | 1.58 | sleeves. |
| Minimum Charge | Job | | 415 | | 415 | |
| **Barbed Wire** | | | | | | |
| Demolish | L.F. | | 1.38 | | 1.38 | Cost includes material and labor to |
| Install | L.F. | .43 | .53 | .16 | 1.12 | install 3 strand galvanized barbed |
| Demolish and Install | L.F. | .43 | 1.91 | .16 | 2.50 | wire fence. |
| Reinstall | L.F. | | .43 | .13 | .56 | |
| Minimum Charge | Job | | 415 | 345 | 760 | |
| **6' Redwood** | | | | | | |
| Demolish | L.F. | | 9.20 | | 9.20 | Cost includes material and labor to |
| Install | L.F. | 11.40 | 6.50 | 1.64 | 19.54 | install 6' high redwood fencing. |
| Demolish and Install | L.F. | 11.40 | 15.70 | 1.64 | 28.74 | |
| Reinstall | L.F. | | 5.22 | 1.31 | 6.53 | |
| Clean | L.F. | .21 | 1.24 | | 1.45 | |
| Paint | L.F. | .70 | 3.31 | | 4.01 | |
| Minimum Charge | Job | | 415 | | 415 | |
| **6' Red Cedar** | | | | | | |
| Demolish | L.F. | | 9.20 | | 9.20 | Cost includes material and labor to |
| Install | L.F. | 17.40 | 6.50 | 1.64 | 25.54 | install 6' cedar fence. |
| Demolish and Install | L.F. | 17.40 | 15.70 | 1.64 | 34.74 | |
| Reinstall | L.F. | | 5.22 | 1.31 | 6.53 | |
| Clean | L.F. | .21 | 1.24 | | 1.45 | |
| Paint | L.F. | .70 | 3.31 | | 4.01 | |
| Minimum Charge | Job | | 415 | | 415 | |
| **6' Shadowbox** | | | | | | |
| Demolish | L.F. | | 9.20 | | 9.20 | Cost includes material and labor to |
| Install | L.F. | 13.30 | 5.45 | 1.36 | 20.11 | install 6' pressure treated pine fence. |
| Demolish and Install | L.F. | 13.30 | 14.65 | 1.36 | 29.31 | |
| Reinstall | L.F. | | 4.35 | 1.09 | 5.44 | |
| Clean | L.F. | .21 | 1.24 | | 1.45 | |
| Paint | L.F. | .70 | 3.31 | | 4.01 | |
| Minimum Charge | Job | | 415 | | 415 | |
| **3' Picket** | | | | | | |
| Demolish | L.F. | | 9.20 | | 9.20 | Includes material, labor and |
| Install | L.F. | 5.05 | 5.80 | 1.46 | 12.31 | equipment to install pressure treated |
| Demolish and Install | L.F. | 5.05 | 15 | 1.46 | 21.51 | pine picket fence. |
| Reinstall | L.F. | | 4.66 | 1.17 | 5.83 | |
| Clean | L.F. | .11 | 1.07 | | 1.18 | |
| Paint | L.F. | .35 | 1.80 | | 2.15 | |
| Minimum Charge | Job | | 415 | | 415 | |

| Fencing | Unit | Material | Labor | Equip. | Total | Specification |
|---|---|---|---|---|---|---|
| **Wrought Iron** | | | | | | |
| Demolish | L.F. | | 19.75 | | 19.75 | Cost includes material and labor to |
| Install | L.F. | 27.50 | 11.05 | | 38.55 | install 5' high wrought iron fence with |
| Demolish and Install | L.F. | 27.50 | 30.80 | | 58.30 | pickets at 4-1/2" O.C. |
| Reinstall | L.F. | | 8.82 | | 8.82 | |
| Clean | L.F. | | 1.07 | | 1.07 | |
| Paint | L.F. | .59 | 3.70 | | 4.29 | |
| Minimum Charge | Job | | 415 | | 415 | |
| **Post** | | | | | | |
| **Dirt Based Wood** | | | | | | |
| Demolish | Ea. | | 23 | | 23 | Includes material and labor to install |
| Install | Ea. | 12.30 | 103 | | 115.30 | wood post set in earth. |
| Demolish and Install | Ea. | 12.30 | 126 | | 138.30 | |
| Reinstall | Ea. | | 82.73 | | 82.73 | |
| Clean | Ea. | | 3.34 | | 3.34 | |
| Paint | Ea. | .77 | 1.26 | | 2.03 | |
| Minimum Charge | Job | | 415 | | 415 | |
| **Concrete Based Wood** | | | | | | |
| Demolish | Ea. | | 32.50 | 11.65 | 44.15 | Includes material and labor to install |
| Install | Ea. | 12.30 | 138 | | 150.30 | wood post set in concrete. |
| Demolish and Install | Ea. | 12.30 | 170.50 | 11.65 | 194.45 | |
| Clean | Ea. | | 3.34 | | 3.34 | |
| Paint | Ea. | .77 | 1.26 | | 2.03 | |
| Minimum Charge | Job | | 415 | | 415 | |
| **Block Pilaster** | | | | | | |
| Demolish | Ea. | | 127 | | 127 | Includes material and labor to install |
| Install | Ea. | 77.50 | 130 | | 207.50 | block pilaster for fence. |
| Demolish and Install | Ea. | 77.50 | 257 | | 334.50 | |
| Reinstall | Ea. | | 129.70 | | 129.70 | |
| Paint | Ea. | 4.30 | 14 | | 18.30 | |
| Minimum Charge | Job | | 182 | | 182 | |
| **Gate** | | | | | | |
| **Chain Link** | | | | | | |
| Demolish | Ea. | | 30.50 | | 30.50 | Cost includes material and labor to |
| Install | Ea. | 116 | 46 | | 162 | install 3' wide chain link pass gate |
| Demolish and Install | Ea. | 116 | 76.50 | | 192.50 | and hardware. |
| Reinstall | Ea. | | 36.77 | | 36.77 | |
| Clean | Ea. | | 3.71 | | 3.71 | |
| Minimum Charge | Job | | 415 | | 415 | |
| **Redwood** | | | | | | |
| Demolish | Ea. | | 26.50 | | 26.50 | Includes material, labor and |
| Install | Ea. | 146 | 46 | | 192 | equipment to install redwood pass |
| Demolish and Install | Ea. | 146 | 72.50 | | 218.50 | gate and hardware. |
| Reinstall | Ea. | | 36.77 | | 36.77 | |
| Clean | Ea. | | 3.71 | | 3.71 | |
| Paint | Ea. | 1.16 | 6.30 | | 7.46 | |
| Minimum Charge | Job | | 415 | | 415 | |
| **Red Cedar** | | | | | | |
| Demolish | Ea. | | 26.50 | | 26.50 | Cost includes material and labor to |
| Install | Ea. | 79 | 46 | | 125 | install 3' wide red cedar pass gate |
| Demolish and Install | Ea. | 79 | 72.50 | | 151.50 | and hardware. |
| Reinstall | Ea. | | 36.77 | | 36.77 | |
| Clean | Ea. | | 3.71 | | 3.71 | |
| Paint | Ea. | 1.16 | 6.30 | | 7.46 | |
| Minimum Charge | Job | | 415 | | 415 | |

| Fencing | Unit | Material | Labor | Equip. | Total | Specification |
|---|---|---|---|---|---|---|
| **Wrought Iron** | | | | | | |
| Demolish | Ea. | | 19.75 | | 19.75 | Includes material, labor and |
| Install | Ea. | 144 | 103 | | 247 | equipment to install wrought iron gate |
| Demolish and Install | Ea. | 144 | 122.75 | | 266.75 | with hardware. |
| Reinstall | Ea. | | 82.73 | | 82.73 | |
| Clean | Ea. | | 3.71 | | 3.71 | |
| Paint | Ea. | 1.19 | 6.30 | | 7.49 | |
| Minimum Charge | Job | | 415 | | 415 | |

**Fire-extinguishing System**

**Space Heater**

**Hot-air Furnace**

| Plumbing | | Unit | Material | Labor | Equip. | Total | Specification |
|---|---|---|---|---|---|---|---|
| **Components** | | | | | | | |
| **3/4″ Supply** | | | | | | | |
| | Demolish | L.F. | | 2.25 | | 2.25 | Includes material and labor to install |
| | Install | L.F. | 3.86 | 5.35 | | 9.21 | type L copper tubing including |
| | Demolish and Install | L.F. | 3.86 | 7.60 | | 11.46 | couplings and hangers at 10′ O.C. |
| | Reinstall | L.F. | | 5.33 | | 5.33 | |
| | Minimum Charge | Job | | 203 | | 203 | |
| **1/2″ Fixture Supply** | | | | | | | |
| | Install | Ea. | 43.50 | 135 | | 178.50 | Includes labor and materials to install supply pipe only to a plumbing fixture. |
| **2″ Single Vent Stack** | | | | | | | |
| | Demolish | Ea. | | 37.50 | | 37.50 | Includes material and labor to install |
| | Install | Ea. | 25.50 | 203 | | 228.50 | PVC vent stack pipe with couplings at |
| | Demolish and Install | Ea. | 25.50 | 240.50 | | 266 | 10′ O.C. |
| | Reinstall | Ea. | | 202.60 | | 202.60 | |
| | Minimum Charge | Job | | 203 | | 203 | |
| **4″ Drain** | | | | | | | |
| | Demolish | L.F. | | 3 | | 3 | Includes material and labor to install |
| | Install | L.F. | 7.35 | 6.65 | | 14 | DVW type PVC pipe with couplings at |
| | Demolish and Install | L.F. | 7.35 | 9.65 | | 17 | 10′ O.C. and 3 strap hangers per 10′ |
| | Reinstall | L.F. | | 6.63 | | 6.63 | run. |
| | Minimum Charge | Job | | 203 | | 203 | |
| **1-1/2″ Drain** | | | | | | | |
| | Demolish | L.F. | | 2.25 | | 2.25 | Includes material and labor to install |
| | Install | L.F. | 1.40 | 4.31 | | 5.71 | DVW type PVC pipe with couplings at |
| | Demolish and Install | L.F. | 1.40 | 6.56 | | 7.96 | 10′ O.C. and 3 strap hangers per 10′ |
| | Reinstall | L.F. | | 4.31 | | 4.31 | run. |
| | Minimum Charge | Job | | 203 | | 203 | |
| **Sewer / Septic** | | | | | | | |
| | Install | L.F. | 2.48 | 3.73 | 1.34 | 7.55 | Includes labor and material to install sewerage and drainage piping, 6″ diameter. |
| **Maintenance** | | | | | | | |
| **Flush Out / Unclog** | | | | | | | |
| | Clean | Job | | 203 | | 203 | Minimum labor and equipment charge |
| | Minimum Charge | Job | | 203 | | 203 | to install water cooler. |

# Rough Mechanical

| Plumbing | | Unit | Material | Labor | Equip. | Total | Specification |
|---|---|---|---|---|---|---|---|
| **Vent Cap** | | | | | | | |
| **Large** | | | | | | | |
| | Demolish | Ea. | | 10.25 | | 10.25 | Includes labor and material to install a |
| | Install | Ea. | 35 | 18.40 | | 53.40 | PVC plumbing pipe vent cap. |
| | Demolish and Install | Ea. | 35 | 28.65 | | 63.65 | |
| | Clean | Ea. | .51 | 6.05 | | 6.56 | |
| | Paint | Ea. | .17 | 7.15 | | 7.32 | |
| | Minimum Charge | Job | | 101 | | 101 | |
| **Medium** | | | | | | | |
| | Demolish | Ea. | | 10.25 | | 10.25 | Includes labor and material to install a |
| | Install | Ea. | 30.50 | 17.60 | | 48.10 | PVC plumbing pipe vent cap. |
| | Demolish and Install | Ea. | 30.50 | 27.85 | | 58.35 | |
| | Clean | Ea. | .51 | 6.05 | | 6.56 | |
| | Paint | Ea. | .17 | 7.15 | | 7.32 | |
| | Minimum Charge | Job | | 101 | | 101 | |
| **Small** | | | | | | | |
| | Demolish | Ea. | | 10.25 | | 10.25 | Includes material and labor to install a |
| | Install | Ea. | 8.05 | 16.90 | | 24.95 | PVC plumbing pipe vent cap. |
| | Demolish and Install | Ea. | 8.05 | 27.15 | | 35.20 | |
| | Clean | Ea. | .51 | 6.05 | | 6.56 | |
| | Paint | Ea. | .17 | 7.15 | | 7.32 | |
| | Minimum Charge | Job | | 101 | | 101 | |

| Plumbing | | Unit | Material | Labor | Equip. | Total | Specification |
|---|---|---|---|---|---|---|---|
| **Sump Pump** | | | | | | | |
| **1/4 HP** | | | | | | | |
| | Demolish | Ea. | | 40.50 | | 40.50 | Includes material and labor to install a |
| | Install | Ea. | 144 | 67.50 | | 211.50 | submersible sump pump. |
| | Demolish and Install | Ea. | 144 | 108 | | 252 | |
| | Reinstall | Ea. | | 54.03 | | 54.03 | |
| | Clean | Ea. | 1.28 | 16.70 | | 17.98 | |
| | Minimum Charge | Job | | 203 | | 203 | |
| **1/3 HP** | | | | | | | |
| | Demolish | Ea. | | 40.50 | | 40.50 | Includes material and labor to install a |
| | Install | Ea. | 174 | 81 | | 255 | submersible sump pump. |
| | Demolish and Install | Ea. | 174 | 121.50 | | 295.50 | |
| | Reinstall | Ea. | | 64.83 | | 64.83 | |
| | Clean | Ea. | 1.28 | 16.70 | | 17.98 | |
| | Minimum Charge | Job | | 203 | | 203 | |
| **1/2 HP** | | | | | | | |
| | Demolish | Ea. | | 40.50 | | 40.50 | Includes material and labor to install a |
| | Install | Ea. | 213 | 81 | | 294 | submersible sump pump. |
| | Demolish and Install | Ea. | 213 | 121.50 | | 334.50 | |
| | Reinstall | Ea. | | 64.83 | | 64.83 | |
| | Clean | Ea. | 1.28 | 16.70 | | 17.98 | |
| | Minimum Charge | Job | | 203 | | 203 | |
| **Clean and Service** | | | | | | | |
| | Clean | Ea. | | 25.50 | | 25.50 | Includes labor to clean and service a |
| | Minimum Charge | Job | | 203 | | 203 | sump pump. |

# Rough Mechanical

| Water Heater | Unit | Material | Labor | Equip. | Total | Specification |
|---|---|---|---|---|---|---|
| **30 Gallon** | | | | | | |
| Demolish | Ea. | | 127 | | 127 | Includes material and labor to install a |
| Install | Ea. | 340 | 184 | | 524 | 30 gallon electric water heater. |
| Demolish and Install | Ea. | 340 | 311 | | 651 | |
| Reinstall | Ea. | | 147.35 | | 147.35 | |
| Clean | Ea. | 1.28 | 16.70 | | 17.98 | |
| Minimum Charge | Job | | 203 | | 203 | |
| **40 Gallon** | | | | | | |
| Demolish | Ea. | | 127 | | 127 | Includes material and labor to install a |
| Install | Ea. | 365 | 203 | | 568 | 40 gallon electric water heater. |
| Demolish and Install | Ea. | 365 | 330 | | 695 | |
| Reinstall | Ea. | | 162.08 | | 162.08 | |
| Clean | Ea. | 1.28 | 16.70 | | 17.98 | |
| Minimum Charge | Job | | 203 | | 203 | |
| **52 Gallon** | | | | | | |
| Demolish | Ea. | | 127 | | 127 | Includes material and labor to install a |
| Install | Ea. | 405 | 203 | | 608 | 52 gallon electric water heater. |
| Demolish and Install | Ea. | 405 | 330 | | 735 | |
| Reinstall | Ea. | | 162.08 | | 162.08 | |
| Clean | Ea. | 1.28 | 16.70 | | 17.98 | |
| Minimum Charge | Job | | 203 | | 203 | |
| **82 Gallon** | | | | | | |
| Demolish | Ea. | | 127 | | 127 | Includes material and labor to install |
| Install | Ea. | 615 | 253 | | 868 | an 82 gallon electric water heater. |
| Demolish and Install | Ea. | 615 | 380 | | 995 | |
| Reinstall | Ea. | | 202.60 | | 202.60 | |
| Clean | Ea. | 1.28 | 16.70 | | 17.98 | |
| Minimum Charge | Job | | 203 | | 203 | |
| **Gas-fired** | | | | | | |
| **30 Gallon Gas-fired** | | | | | | |
| Demolish | Ea. | | 156 | | 156 | Includes material and labor to install a |
| Install | Ea. | 660 | 203 | | 863 | 30 gallon gas water heater. |
| Demolish and Install | Ea. | 660 | 359 | | 1019 | |
| Reinstall | Ea. | | 162.08 | | 162.08 | |
| Clean | Ea. | 1.28 | 16.70 | | 17.98 | |
| Minimum Charge | Job | | 203 | | 203 | |
| **30 Gallon Gas-fired, Flue** | | | | | | |
| Install | Ea. | 39 | 58 | | 97 | Includes labor and materials to install |
| Minimum Charge | Job | | 203 | | 203 | a flue for a water heater (up to 50 gallon size). |
| **40 Gallon Gas-fired** | | | | | | |
| Demolish | Ea. | | 156 | | 156 | Includes material and labor to install a |
| Install | Ea. | 985 | 213 | | 1198 | 40 gallon gas water heater. |
| Demolish and Install | Ea. | 985 | 369 | | 1354 | |
| Reinstall | Ea. | | 170.61 | | 170.61 | |
| Clean | Ea. | 1.28 | 16.70 | | 17.98 | |
| Minimum Charge | Job | | 203 | | 203 | |
| **40 Gallon Gas-fired, Flue** | | | | | | |
| Install | Ea. | 39 | 58 | | 97 | Includes labor and materials to install |
| Minimum Charge | Job | | 203 | | 203 | a flue for a water heater (up to 50 gallon size). |
| **50 Gallon Gas-fired** | | | | | | |
| Demolish | Ea. | | 156 | | 156 | Includes material and labor to install a |
| Install | Ea. | 1025 | 225 | | 1250 | 50 gallon gas water heater. |
| Demolish and Install | Ea. | 1025 | 381 | | 1406 | |
| Reinstall | Ea. | | 180.09 | | 180.09 | |
| Clean | Ea. | 1.28 | 16.70 | | 17.98 | |
| Minimum Charge | Job | | 203 | | 203 | |

# Rough Mechanical

| Water Heater | Unit | Material | Labor | Equip. | Total | Specification |
|---|---|---|---|---|---|---|
| **50 Gallon Gas-fired, Flue** | | | | | | |
| Install | Ea. | 39 | 58 | | 97 | Includes labor and materials to install |
| Minimum Charge | Job | | 203 | | 203 | a flue for a water heater (up to 50 gallon size). |
| **Solar Hot Water System** | | | | | | |
| **Water Heater** | | | | | | |
| Demolish | Ea. | | 101 | | 101 | Includes material and labor to install a |
| Install | Ea. | 1075 | 270 | | 1345 | solar hot water heat exchanger |
| Demolish and Install | Ea. | 1075 | 371 | | 1446 | storage tank, 100 gallon. |
| Reinstall | Ea. | | 216.11 | | 216.11 | |
| Minimum Charge | Job | | 205 | | 205 | |
| **Solar Panel** | | | | | | |
| Demolish | S.F. | | 1.48 | | 1.48 | Includes material and labor to install |
| Install | S.F. | 23 | 2.67 | | 25.67 | solar panel. |
| Demolish and Install | S.F. | 23 | 4.15 | | 27.15 | |
| Reinstall | S.F. | | 2.13 | | 2.13 | |
| Minimum Charge | Job | | 205 | | 205 | |
| **Repair Plumbing** | | | | | | |
| Install | Job | | 205 | | 205 | Includes 4 hour minimum labor charge |
| Minimum Charge | Job | | 205 | | 205 | for a steamfitter or pipefitter. |
| **Insulating Wrap** | | | | | | |
| Demolish | Ea. | | 4.69 | | 4.69 | Includes material and labor to install |
| Install | Ea. | 18.30 | 12.65 | | 30.95 | insulating wrap around a 100 gallon |
| Demolish and Install | Ea. | 18.30 | 17.34 | | 35.64 | solar hot water heat exchanger |
| Reinstall | Ea. | | 10.13 | | 10.13 | storage tank. |
| Minimum Charge | Job | | 203 | | 203 | |
| **Water Softener** | | | | | | |
| Demolish | Ea. | | 75 | | 75 | Includes material and labor to install a |
| Install | Ea. | 1425 | 182 | | 1607 | 14 GPM water softener. |
| Demolish and Install | Ea. | 1425 | 257 | | 1682 | |
| Reinstall | Ea. | | 145.86 | | 145.86 | |
| Clean | Ea. | 1.28 | 16.70 | | 17.98 | |
| Minimum Charge | Ea. | | 203 | | 203 | |

| Ductwork | Unit | Material | Labor | Equip. | Total | Specification |
|---|---|---|---|---|---|---|
| **Galvanized, Square or Rectangular** | | | | | | |
| **6"** | | | | | | |
| Demolish | L.F. | | 1.86 | | 1.86 | Includes material and labor to install |
| Install | L.F. | 1.53 | 16.75 | | 18.28 | rectangular ductwork with a greatest |
| Demolish and Install | L.F. | 1.53 | 18.61 | | 20.14 | dimension of 6". |
| Reinstall | L.F. | | 13.41 | | 13.41 | |
| Clean | L.F. | | 2.15 | | 2.15 | |
| Minimum Charge | Job | | 201 | | 201 | |
| **8"** | | | | | | |
| Demolish | L.F. | | 1.86 | | 1.86 | Includes material and labor to install |
| Install | L.F. | 2.04 | 16.75 | | 18.79 | rectangular ductwork with a greatest |
| Demolish and Install | L.F. | 2.04 | 18.61 | | 20.65 | dimension of 8". |
| Reinstall | L.F. | | 13.41 | | 13.41 | |
| Clean | L.F. | | 2.86 | | 2.86 | |
| Minimum Charge | Job | | 201 | | 201 | |

| Ductwork | Unit | Material | Labor | Equip. | Total | Specification |
|---|---|---|---|---|---|---|
| **10″** | | | | | | |
| Demolish | L.F. | | 1.86 | | 1.86 | Includes material and labor to install |
| Install | L.F. | 2.54 | 16.75 | | 19.29 | rectangular ductwork with a greatest |
| Demolish and Install | L.F. | 2.54 | 18.61 | | 21.15 | dimension of 10″. |
| Reinstall | L.F. | | 13.41 | | 13.41 | |
| Clean | L.F. | | 3.58 | | 3.58 | |
| Minimum Charge | Job | | 201 | | 201 | |
| **Galvanized, Spiral** | | | | | | |
| **4″** | | | | | | |
| Demolish | L.F. | | 2.24 | | 2.24 | Cost includes material and labor to |
| Install | L.F. | 1.44 | 2.01 | | 3.45 | install 4″ diameter spiral pre-formed |
| Demolish and Install | L.F. | 1.44 | 4.25 | | 5.69 | steel galvanized ductwork. |
| Reinstall | L.F. | | 1.61 | | 1.61 | |
| Clean | L.F. | | 1.12 | | 1.12 | |
| Minimum Charge | Job | | 201 | | 201 | |
| **6″** | | | | | | |
| Demolish | L.F. | | 2.24 | | 2.24 | Cost includes material and labor to |
| Install | L.F. | 2.09 | 2.59 | | 4.68 | install 6″ diameter spiral pre-formed |
| Demolish and Install | L.F. | 2.09 | 4.83 | | 6.92 | steel galvanized ductwork. |
| Reinstall | L.F. | | 2.07 | | 2.07 | |
| Clean | L.F. | | 1.69 | | 1.69 | |
| Minimum Charge | Job | | 201 | | 201 | |
| **8″** | | | | | | |
| Demolish | L.F. | | 2.24 | | 2.24 | Cost includes material and labor to |
| Install | L.F. | 2.74 | 3.62 | | 6.36 | install 8″ diameter spiral pre-formed |
| Demolish and Install | L.F. | 2.74 | 5.86 | | 8.60 | steel galvanized ductwork. |
| Reinstall | L.F. | | 2.90 | | 2.90 | |
| Clean | L.F. | | 2.25 | | 2.25 | |
| Minimum Charge | Job | | 201 | | 201 | |
| **10″** | | | | | | |
| Demolish | L.F. | | 2.79 | | 2.79 | Cost includes material and labor to |
| Install | L.F. | 4.44 | 4.53 | | 8.97 | install 10″ diameter spiral pre-formed |
| Demolish and Install | L.F. | 4.44 | 7.32 | | 11.76 | steel galvanized ductwork. |
| Reinstall | L.F. | | 3.62 | | 3.62 | |
| Clean | L.F. | | 2.81 | | 2.81 | |
| Minimum Charge | Job | | 201 | | 201 | |
| **12″** | | | | | | |
| Demolish | L.F. | | 3.73 | | 3.73 | Cost includes material and labor to |
| Install | L.F. | 5.35 | 6.05 | | 11.40 | install 12″ diameter spiral pre-formed |
| Demolish and Install | L.F. | 5.35 | 9.78 | | 15.13 | steel galvanized ductwork. |
| Reinstall | L.F. | | 4.83 | | 4.83 | |
| Clean | L.F. | | 3.37 | | 3.37 | |
| Minimum Charge | Job | | 201 | | 201 | |
| **16″** | | | | | | |
| Demolish | L.F. | | 7.45 | | 7.45 | Cost includes material and labor to |
| Install | L.F. | 7.20 | 12.05 | | 19.25 | install 16″ diameter spiral pre-formed |
| Demolish and Install | L.F. | 7.20 | 19.50 | | 26.70 | steel galvanized ductwork. |
| Reinstall | L.F. | | 9.65 | | 9.65 | |
| Clean | L.F. | | 4.50 | | 4.50 | |
| Minimum Charge | Job | | 201 | | 201 | |
| **Flexible Fiberglass** | | | | | | |
| **6″ Non-insulated** | | | | | | |
| Demolish | L.F. | | 1.72 | | 1.72 | Cost includes material and labor to |
| Install | L.F. | 1.49 | 2.59 | | 4.08 | install 6″ diameter non-insulated |
| Demolish and Install | L.F. | 1.49 | 4.31 | | 5.80 | flexible fiberglass fabric on corrosion |
| Reinstall | L.F. | | 2.07 | | 2.07 | resistant metal ductwork. |
| Clean | L.F. | | 1.69 | | 1.69 | |
| Minimum Charge | Job | | 201 | | 201 | |

# Rough Mechanical

| Ductwork | Unit | Material | Labor | Equip. | Total | Specification |
|---|---|---|---|---|---|---|
| **8" Non-insulated** | | | | | | |
| Demolish | L.F. | | 2.48 | | 2.48 | Cost includes material and labor to |
| Install | L.F. | 2.05 | 3.62 | | 5.67 | install 8" diameter non-insulated |
| Demolish and Install | L.F. | 2.05 | 6.10 | | 8.15 | flexible fiberglass fabric on corrosion |
| Reinstall | L.F. | | 2.90 | | 2.90 | resistant metal ductwork. |
| Clean | L.F. | | 2.25 | | 2.25 | |
| Minimum Charge | Job | | 201 | | 201 | |
| **10" Non-insulated** | | | | | | |
| Demolish | L.F. | | 3.19 | | 3.19 | Cost includes material and labor to |
| Install | L.F. | 2.57 | 4.53 | | 7.10 | install 10" diameter non-insulated |
| Demolish and Install | L.F. | 2.57 | 7.72 | | 10.29 | flexible fiberglass fabric on corrosion |
| Reinstall | L.F. | | 3.62 | | 3.62 | resistant metal ductwork. |
| Clean | L.F. | | 2.81 | | 2.81 | |
| Minimum Charge | Job | | 201 | | 201 | |
| **12" Non-insulated** | | | | | | |
| Demolish | L.F. | | 4.47 | | 4.47 | Cost includes material and labor to |
| Install | L.F. | 3.11 | 6.05 | | 9.16 | install 12" diameter non-insulated |
| Demolish and Install | L.F. | 3.11 | 10.52 | | 13.63 | flexible fiberglass fabric on corrosion |
| Reinstall | L.F. | | 4.83 | | 4.83 | resistant metal ductwork. |
| Clean | L.F. | | 3.37 | | 3.37 | |
| Minimum Charge | Job | | 201 | | 201 | |
| **4" Insulated** | | | | | | |
| Demolish | L.F. | | 1.31 | | 1.31 | Cost includes material and labor to |
| Install | L.F. | 2.07 | 2.13 | | 4.20 | install 4" diameter insulated flexible |
| Demolish and Install | L.F. | 2.07 | 3.44 | | 5.51 | fiberglass fabric on corrosion resistant |
| Reinstall | L.F. | | 1.70 | | 1.70 | metal ductwork. |
| Clean | L.F. | | 1.12 | | 1.12 | |
| Minimum Charge | Job | | 201 | | 201 | |
| **6" Insulated** | | | | | | |
| Demolish | L.F. | | 1.72 | | 1.72 | Cost includes material and labor to |
| Install | L.F. | 2.37 | 2.78 | | 5.15 | install 6" diameter insulated flexible |
| Demolish and Install | L.F. | 2.37 | 4.50 | | 6.87 | fiberglass fabric on corrosion resistant |
| Reinstall | L.F. | | 2.23 | | 2.23 | metal ductwork. |
| Clean | L.F. | | 1.69 | | 1.69 | |
| Minimum Charge | Job | | 201 | | 201 | |
| **8" Insulated** | | | | | | |
| Demolish | L.F. | | 2.48 | | 2.48 | Cost includes material and labor to |
| Install | L.F. | 2.93 | 4.02 | | 6.95 | install 8" diameter insulated flexible |
| Demolish and Install | L.F. | 2.93 | 6.50 | | 9.43 | fiberglass fabric on corrosion resistant |
| Reinstall | L.F. | | 3.22 | | 3.22 | metal ductwork. |
| Clean | L.F. | | 2.25 | | 2.25 | |
| Minimum Charge | Job | | 201 | | 201 | |
| **10" Insulated** | | | | | | |
| Demolish | L.F. | | 3.19 | | 3.19 | Cost includes material and labor to |
| Install | L.F. | 3.45 | 5.15 | | 8.60 | install 10" diameter insulated flexible |
| Demolish and Install | L.F. | 3.45 | 8.34 | | 11.79 | fiberglass fabric on corrosion resistant |
| Reinstall | L.F. | | 4.14 | | 4.14 | metal ductwork. |
| Clean | L.F. | | 2.81 | | 2.81 | |
| Minimum Charge | Job | | 201 | | 201 | |
| **12" Insulated** | | | | | | |
| Demolish | L.F. | | 4.47 | | 4.47 | Cost includes material and labor to |
| Install | L.F. | 4.30 | 7.25 | | 11.55 | install 12" diameter insulated flexible |
| Demolish and Install | L.F. | 4.30 | 11.72 | | 16.02 | fiberglass fabric on corrosion resistant |
| Reinstall | L.F. | | 5.79 | | 5.79 | metal ductwork. |
| Clean | L.F. | | 3.37 | | 3.37 | |
| Minimum Charge | Job | | 201 | | 201 | |

# Rough Mechanical

| Heating | Unit | Material | Labor | Equip. | Total | Specification |
|---|---|---|---|---|---|---|
| **Hot Water Baseboard** | | | | | | |
| Demolish | L.F. | | 7 | | 7 | Includes material and labor to install |
| Install | L.F. | 7.90 | 12.30 | | 20.20 | baseboard radiation. |
| Demolish and Install | L.F. | 7.90 | 19.30 | | 27.20 | |
| Reinstall | L.F. | | 9.82 | | 9.82 | |
| Clean | L.F. | 1.28 | 4.17 | | 5.45 | |
| Minimum Charge | Job | | 203 | | 203 | |
| **3'** | | | | | | |
| Demolish | Ea. | | 22.50 | | 22.50 | Includes material and labor to install |
| Install | Ea. | 25.50 | 41 | | 66.50 | fin tube baseboard radiation in 3' |
| Demolish and Install | Ea. | 25.50 | 63.50 | | 89 | sections. |
| Reinstall | Ea. | | 32.75 | | 32.75 | |
| Clean | Ea. | .36 | 12.70 | | 13.06 | |
| Minimum Charge | Job | | 203 | | 203 | |
| **4'** | | | | | | |
| Demolish | Ea. | | 30 | | 30 | Includes material and labor to install |
| Install | Ea. | 33.50 | 46 | | 79.50 | fin tube baseboard radiation in 4' |
| Demolish and Install | Ea. | 33.50 | 76 | | 109.50 | sections. |
| Reinstall | Ea. | | 36.84 | | 36.84 | |
| Clean | Ea. | .73 | 16.70 | | 17.43 | |
| Minimum Charge | Job | | 203 | | 203 | |
| **5'** | | | | | | |
| Demolish | Ea. | | 37.50 | | 37.50 | Includes material and labor to install |
| Install | Ea. | 42 | 52.50 | | 94.50 | fin tube baseboard radiation in 5' |
| Demolish and Install | Ea. | 42 | 90 | | 132 | sections. |
| Reinstall | Ea. | | 42.10 | | 42.10 | |
| Clean | Ea. | .73 | 20.50 | | 21.23 | |
| Minimum Charge | Job | | 203 | | 203 | |
| **6'** | | | | | | |
| Demolish | Ea. | | 45 | | 45 | Includes material and labor to install |
| Install | Ea. | 50.50 | 61.50 | | 112 | fin tube baseboard radiation in 6' |
| Demolish and Install | Ea. | 50.50 | 106.50 | | 157 | sections. |
| Reinstall | Ea. | | 49.12 | | 49.12 | |
| Clean | Ea. | .73 | 24.50 | | 25.23 | |
| Minimum Charge | Job | | 203 | | 203 | |
| **7'** | | | | | | |
| Demolish | Ea. | | 50 | | 50 | Includes material and labor to install |
| Install | Ea. | 59 | 81 | | 140 | fin tube baseboard radiation in 7' |
| Demolish and Install | Ea. | 59 | 131 | | 190 | sections. |
| Reinstall | Ea. | | 64.83 | | 64.83 | |
| Clean | Ea. | .91 | 29.50 | | 30.41 | |
| Minimum Charge | Job | | 203 | | 203 | |
| **9'** | | | | | | |
| Demolish | Ea. | | 75 | | 75 | Includes material and labor to install |
| Install | Ea. | 76 | 116 | | 192 | fin tube baseboard radiation in 9' |
| Demolish and Install | Ea. | 76 | 191 | | 267 | sections. |
| Reinstall | Ea. | | 92.62 | | 92.62 | |
| Clean | Ea. | 1.45 | 38 | | 39.45 | |
| Minimum Charge | Job | | 203 | | 203 | |

| Heating | Unit | Material | Labor | Equip. | Total | Specification |
|---|---|---|---|---|---|---|
| **50 MBH** | | | | | | |
| Demolish | Ea. | | 37 | | 37 | Includes material and labor to install a |
| Install | Ea. | 665 | 105 | | 770 | cabinet space heater with an output of |
| Demolish and Install | Ea. | 665 | 142 | | 807 | 50 MBH. |
| Reinstall | Ea. | | 84.21 | | 84.21 | |
| Clean | Ea. | .91 | 33.50 | | 34.41 | |
| Minimum Charge | Job | | 205 | | 205 | |

# Rough Mechanical

| Heating | | Unit | Material | Labor | Equip. | Total | Specification |
|---|---|---|---|---|---|---|---|
| **75 MBH** | | | | | | | |
| | Demolish | Ea. | | 37 | | 37 | Includes material and labor to install a |
| | Install | Ea. | 765 | 123 | | 888 | cabinet space heater with an output of |
| | Demolish and Install | Ea. | 765 | 160 | | 925 | 75 MBH. |
| | Reinstall | Ea. | | 98.24 | | 98.24 | |
| | Clean | Ea. | .91 | 33.50 | | 34.41 | |
| | Minimum Charge | Job | | 205 | | 205 | |
| **125 MBH** | | | | | | | |
| | Demolish | Ea. | | 44 | | 44 | Includes material and labor to install a |
| | Install | Ea. | 990 | 147 | | 1137 | cabinet space heater with an output of |
| | Demolish and Install | Ea. | 990 | 191 | | 1181 | 125 MBH. |
| | Reinstall | Ea. | | 117.89 | | 117.89 | |
| | Clean | Ea. | .91 | 33.50 | | 34.41 | |
| | Minimum Charge | Job | | 205 | | 205 | |
| **175 MBH** | | | | | | | |
| | Demolish | Ea. | | 55.50 | | 55.50 | Includes material and labor to install a |
| | Install | Ea. | 1200 | 211 | | 1411 | cabinet space heater with an output of |
| | Demolish and Install | Ea. | 1200 | 266.50 | | 1466.50 | 175 MBH. |
| | Reinstall | Ea. | | 168.41 | | 168.41 | |
| | Clean | Ea. | .91 | 33.50 | | 34.41 | |
| | Minimum Charge | Job | | 205 | | 205 | |

| Furnace Unit | | Unit | Material | Labor | Equip. | Total | Specification |
|---|---|---|---|---|---|---|---|
| **Wall (gas-fired)** | | | | | | | |
| **25 MBH w / Thermostat** | | | | | | | |
| | Demolish | Ea. | | 90.50 | | 90.50 | Includes material and labor to install a |
| | Install | Ea. | 615 | 145 | | 760 | gas fired hot air furnace rated at 25 |
| | Demolish and Install | Ea. | 615 | 235.50 | | 850.50 | MBH. |
| | Reinstall | Ea. | | 115.84 | | 115.84 | |
| | Clean | Ea. | 1.82 | 74 | | 75.82 | |
| | Minimum Charge | Job | | 205 | | 205 | |
| **35 MBH w / Thermostat** | | | | | | | |
| | Demolish | Ea. | | 90.50 | | 90.50 | Includes material and labor to install a |
| | Install | Ea. | 675 | 161 | | 836 | gas fired hot air furnace rated at 35 |
| | Demolish and Install | Ea. | 675 | 251.50 | | 926.50 | MBH. |
| | Reinstall | Ea. | | 128.71 | | 128.71 | |
| | Clean | Ea. | 1.82 | 74 | | 75.82 | |
| | Minimum Charge | Job | | 205 | | 205 | |
| **50 MBH w / Thermostat** | | | | | | | |
| | Demolish | Ea. | | 90.50 | | 90.50 | Includes material and labor to install a |
| | Install | Ea. | 955 | 181 | | 1136 | gas fired hot air furnace rated at 50 |
| | Demolish and Install | Ea. | 955 | 271.50 | | 1226.50 | MBH. |
| | Reinstall | Ea. | | 144.80 | | 144.80 | |
| | Clean | Ea. | 1.82 | 74 | | 75.82 | |
| | Minimum Charge | Job | | 205 | | 205 | |
| **60 MBH w / Thermostat** | | | | | | | |
| | Demolish | Ea. | | 90.50 | | 90.50 | Includes material and labor to install a |
| | Install | Ea. | 1050 | 201 | | 1251 | gas fired hot air furnace rated at 60 |
| | Demolish and Install | Ea. | 1050 | 291.50 | | 1341.50 | MBH. |
| | Reinstall | Ea. | | 160.89 | | 160.89 | |
| | Clean | Ea. | 1.82 | 74 | | 75.82 | |
| | Minimum Charge | Job | | 205 | | 205 | |

| Furnace Unit | Unit | Material | Labor | Equip. | Total | Specification |
|---|---|---|---|---|---|---|
| **Floor (gas-fired)** | | | | | | |
| **30 MBH w / Thermostat** | | | | | | |
| Demolish | Ea. | | 90.50 | | 90.50 | Includes material and labor to install a |
| Install | Ea. | 845 | 145 | | 990 | gas fired hot air floor furnace rated at |
| Demolish and Install | Ea. | 845 | 235.50 | | 1080.50 | 30 MBH. |
| Reinstall | Ea. | | 115.84 | | 115.84 | |
| Clean | Ea. | 1.82 | 74 | | 75.82 | |
| Minimum Charge | Job | | 205 | | 205 | |
| **50 MBH w / Thermostat** | | | | | | |
| Demolish | Ea. | | 90.50 | | 90.50 | Includes material and labor to install a |
| Install | Ea. | 915 | 181 | | 1096 | gas fired hot air floor furnace rated at |
| Demolish and Install | Ea. | 915 | 271.50 | | 1186.50 | 50 MBH. |
| Reinstall | Ea. | | 144.80 | | 144.80 | |
| Clean | Ea. | 1.82 | 74 | | 75.82 | |
| Minimum Charge | Job | | 205 | | 205 | |
| **Gas Forced Air** | | | | | | |
| **50 MBH** | | | | | | |
| Demolish | Ea. | | 90.50 | | 90.50 | Includes material and labor to install |
| Install | Ea. | 675 | 181 | | 856 | an up flow gas fired hot air furnace |
| Demolish and Install | Ea. | 675 | 271.50 | | 946.50 | rated at 50 MBH. |
| Reinstall | Ea. | | 144.80 | | 144.80 | |
| Clean | Ea. | 1.82 | 74 | | 75.82 | |
| Minimum Charge | Job | | 205 | | 205 | |
| **80 MBH** | | | | | | |
| Demolish | Ea. | | 90.50 | | 90.50 | Includes material and labor to install |
| Install | Ea. | 765 | 201 | | 966 | an up flow gas fired hot air furnace |
| Demolish and Install | Ea. | 765 | 291.50 | | 1056.50 | rated at 80 MBH. |
| Reinstall | Ea. | | 160.89 | | 160.89 | |
| Clean | Ea. | 1.82 | 74 | | 75.82 | |
| Minimum Charge | Job | | 205 | | 205 | |
| **100 MBH** | | | | | | |
| Demolish | Ea. | | 90.50 | | 90.50 | Includes material and labor to install |
| Install | Ea. | 805 | 226 | | 1031 | an up flow gas fired hot air furnace |
| Demolish and Install | Ea. | 805 | 316.50 | | 1121.50 | rated at 100 MBH. |
| Reinstall | Ea. | | 181 | | 181 | |
| Clean | Ea. | 1.82 | 74 | | 75.82 | |
| Minimum Charge | Job | | 205 | | 205 | |
| **120 MBH** | | | | | | |
| Demolish | Ea. | | 90.50 | | 90.50 | Includes material and labor to install |
| Install | Ea. | 895 | 241 | | 1136 | an up flow gas fired hot air furnace |
| Demolish and Install | Ea. | 895 | 331.50 | | 1226.50 | rated at 120 MBH. |
| Reinstall | Ea. | | 193.07 | | 193.07 | |
| Clean | Ea. | 1.82 | 74 | | 75.82 | |
| Minimum Charge | Job | | 205 | | 205 | |
| **Electric Forced Air** | | | | | | |
| **31.4 MBH** | | | | | | |
| Demolish | Ea. | | 90.50 | | 90.50 | Includes material and labor to install |
| Install | Ea. | 1575 | 205 | | 1780 | an electric hot air furnace rated at |
| Demolish and Install | Ea. | 1575 | 295.50 | | 1870.50 | 31.4 MBH. |
| Reinstall | Ea. | | 164.05 | | 164.05 | |
| Clean | Ea. | 1.82 | 74 | | 75.82 | |
| Minimum Charge | Job | | 205 | | 205 | |

## Furnace Unit

| Furnace Unit | | Unit | Material | Labor | Equip. | Total | Specification |
|---|---|---|---|---|---|---|---|
| **47.1 MBH** | | | | | | | |
| | Demolish | Ea. | | 90.50 | | 90.50 | Includes material and labor to install |
| | Install | Ea. | 1675 | 215 | | 1890 | an electric hot air furnace rated at |
| | Demolish and Install | Ea. | 1675 | 305.50 | | 1980.50 | 47.1 MBH. |
| | Reinstall | Ea. | | 171.68 | | 171.68 | |
| | Clean | Ea. | 1.82 | 74 | | 75.82 | |
| | Minimum Charge | Job | | 205 | | 205 | |
| **62.9 MBH** | | | | | | | |
| | Demolish | Ea. | | 90.50 | | 90.50 | Includes material and labor to install |
| | Install | Ea. | 1900 | 231 | | 2131 | an electric hot air furnace rated at |
| | Demolish and Install | Ea. | 1900 | 321.50 | | 2221.50 | 62.9 MBH. |
| | Reinstall | Ea. | | 184.56 | | 184.56 | |
| | Clean | Ea. | 1.82 | 74 | | 75.82 | |
| | Minimum Charge | Job | | 205 | | 205 | |
| **78.5 MBH** | | | | | | | |
| | Demolish | Ea. | | 90.50 | | 90.50 | Includes material and labor to install |
| | Install | Ea. | 1950 | 237 | | 2187 | an electric hot air furnace rated at |
| | Demolish and Install | Ea. | 1950 | 327.50 | | 2277.50 | 78.5 MBH. |
| | Reinstall | Ea. | | 189.29 | | 189.29 | |
| | Clean | Ea. | 1.82 | 74 | | 75.82 | |
| | Minimum Charge | Job | | 205 | | 205 | |
| **110 MBH** | | | | | | | |
| | Demolish | Ea. | | 90.50 | | 90.50 | Includes material and labor to install |
| | Install | Ea. | 2700 | 249 | | 2949 | an electric hot air furnace rated at |
| | Demolish and Install | Ea. | 2700 | 339.50 | | 3039.50 | 110 MBH. |
| | Reinstall | Ea. | | 199.52 | | 199.52 | |
| | Clean | Ea. | 1.82 | 74 | | 75.82 | |
| | Minimum Charge | Job | | 205 | | 205 | |
| **A/C Junction Box** | | | | | | | |
| | Install | Ea. | 61 | 99.50 | | 160.50 | Includes labor and materials to install |
| | Minimum Charge | Job | | 205 | | 205 | a heating system emergency shut-off switch. Cost includes up to 40 feet of non-metallic cable. |

## Boiler

| Boiler | | Unit | Material | Labor | Equip. | Total | Specification |
|---|---|---|---|---|---|---|---|
| **Gas-Fired** | | | | | | | |
| **60 MBH** | | | | | | | |
| | Demolish | Ea. | | 745 | | 745 | Includes material and labor to install a |
| | Install | Ea. | 2175 | 1350 | | 3525 | gas fired cast iron boiler rated at 60 |
| | Demolish and Install | Ea. | 2175 | 2095 | | 4270 | MBH. |
| | Reinstall | Ea. | | 1071.71 | | 1071.71 | |
| | Clean | Ea. | 3.63 | 44.50 | | 48.13 | |
| | Minimum Charge | Job | | 205 | | 205 | |
| **Gas-Fired** | | | | | | | |
| **125 MBH** | | | | | | | |
| | Demolish | Ea. | | 2050 | | 2050 | Includes material and labor to install a |
| | Install | Ea. | 3725 | 1625 | | 5350 | gas fired cast iron boiler rated at 125 |
| | Demolish and Install | Ea. | 3725 | 3675 | | 7400 | MBH. |
| | Reinstall | Ea. | | 1309.87 | | 1309.87 | |
| | Clean | Ea. | 3.63 | 44.50 | | 48.13 | |
| | Minimum Charge | Job | | 205 | | 205 | |

| Boiler | | Unit | Material | Labor | Equip. | Total | Specification |
|---|---|---|---|---|---|---|---|
| **Gas-Fired** | | | | | | | |
| **400 MBH** | | | | | | | |
| | Demolish | Ea. | | 2050 | | 2050 | Includes material and labor to install a |
| | Install | Ea. | 4925 | 2300 | | 7225 | gas fired cast iron boiler rated at 400 |
| | Demolish and Install | Ea. | 4925 | 4350 | | 9275 | MBH. |
| | Reinstall | Ea. | | 2302.50 | | 2302.50 | |
| | Clean | Ea. | 3.63 | 44.50 | | 48.13 | |
| | Minimum Charge | Job | | 205 | | 205 | |

| Heat Pump | | Unit | Material | Labor | Equip. | Total | Specification |
|---|---|---|---|---|---|---|---|
| **2 Ton** | | | | | | | |
| | Demolish | Ea. | | 205 | | 205 | Includes material and labor to install a |
| | Install | Ea. | 1725 | 370 | | 2095 | 2 ton heat pump. |
| | Demolish and Install | Ea. | 1725 | 575 | | 2300 | |
| | Reinstall | Ea. | | 294.72 | | 294.72 | |
| | Clean | Ea. | 3.63 | 33.50 | | 37.13 | |
| | Minimum Charge | Job | | 205 | | 205 | |
| **3 Ton** | | | | | | | |
| | Demolish | Ea. | | 340 | | 340 | Includes material and labor to install a |
| | Install | Ea. | 2200 | 615 | | 2815 | 3 ton heat pump. |
| | Demolish and Install | Ea. | 2200 | 955 | | 3155 | |
| | Reinstall | Ea. | | 491.20 | | 491.20 | |
| | Clean | Ea. | 3.63 | 33.50 | | 37.13 | |
| | Minimum Charge | Job | | 205 | | 205 | |
| **4 Ton** | | | | | | | |
| | Demolish | Ea. | | 510 | | 510 | Includes material and labor to install a |
| | Install | Ea. | 2575 | 920 | | 3495 | 4 ton heat pump. |
| | Demolish and Install | Ea. | 2575 | 1430 | | 4005 | |
| | Reinstall | Ea. | | 736.80 | | 736.80 | |
| | Clean | Ea. | 3.63 | 33.50 | | 37.13 | |
| | Minimum Charge | Job | | 205 | | 205 | |
| **5 Ton** | | | | | | | |
| | Demolish | Ea. | | 820 | | 820 | Includes material and labor to install a |
| | Install | Ea. | 2800 | 1475 | | 4275 | 5 ton heat pump. |
| | Demolish and Install | Ea. | 2800 | 2295 | | 5095 | |
| | Reinstall | Ea. | | 1178.88 | | 1178.88 | |
| | Clean | Ea. | 3.63 | 33.50 | | 37.13 | |
| | Minimum Charge | Job | | 205 | | 205 | |
| **Thermostat** | | | | | | | |
| | Demolish | Ea. | | 11.35 | | 11.35 | Includes material and labor to install |
| | Install | Ea. | 230 | 50.50 | | 280.50 | an electric thermostat, 2 set back. |
| | Demolish and Install | Ea. | 230 | 61.85 | | 291.85 | |
| | Reinstall | Ea. | | 40.24 | | 40.24 | |
| | Clean | Ea. | .08 | 8.35 | | 8.43 | |
| | Minimum Charge | Job | | 205 | | 205 | |
| **A/C Junction Box** | | | | | | | |
| | Install | Ea. | 635 | 305 | | 940 | Includes labor and materials to install |
| | Minimum Charge | Job | | 199 | | 199 | a heat pump circuit including up to 40 |
| | | | | | | | feet of non-metallic cable. |

| Heating | | Unit | Material | Labor | Equip. | Total | Specification |
|---|---|---|---|---|---|---|---|
| **Electric Baseboard** | | | | | | | |
| | Demolish | L.F. | | 5.50 | | 5.50 | Includes material and labor to install |
| | Install | L.F. | 13.20 | 13.25 | | 26.45 | electric baseboard heating elements. |
| | Demolish and Install | L.F. | 13.20 | 18.75 | | 31.95 | |
| | Reinstall | L.F. | | 10.60 | | 10.60 | |
| | Clean | L.F. | 1.28 | 4.17 | | 5.45 | |
| | Minimum Charge | Job | | 199 | | 199 | |
| **2' 6"** | | | | | | | |
| | Demolish | Ea. | | 18.40 | | 18.40 | Includes material and labor to install a |
| | Install | Ea. | 39.50 | 49.50 | | 89 | 2' 6" long section of electric |
| | Demolish and Install | Ea. | 39.50 | 67.90 | | 107.40 | baseboard heating elements. |
| | Reinstall | Ea. | | 39.76 | | 39.76 | |
| | Clean | Ea. | .36 | 10.25 | | 10.61 | |
| | Minimum Charge | Job | | 199 | | 199 | |
| **3'** | | | | | | | |
| | Demolish | Ea. | | 20 | | 20 | Includes material and labor to install a |
| | Install | Ea. | 47.50 | 49.50 | | 97 | 3' long section of electric baseboard |
| | Demolish and Install | Ea. | 47.50 | 69.50 | | 117 | heating elements. |
| | Reinstall | Ea. | | 39.76 | | 39.76 | |
| | Clean | Ea. | .36 | 12.70 | | 13.06 | |
| | Minimum Charge | Job | | 199 | | 199 | |
| **4'** | | | | | | | |
| | Demolish | Ea. | | 22 | | 22 | Includes material and labor to install a |
| | Install | Ea. | 56 | 59.50 | | 115.50 | 4' long section of electric baseboard |
| | Demolish and Install | Ea. | 56 | 81.50 | | 137.50 | heating elements. |
| | Reinstall | Ea. | | 47.47 | | 47.47 | |
| | Clean | Ea. | .14 | 2.78 | | 2.92 | |
| | Minimum Charge | Job | | 199 | | 199 | |
| **5'** | | | | | | | |
| | Demolish | Ea. | | 24.50 | | 24.50 | Includes material and labor to install a |
| | Install | Ea. | 66 | 70 | | 136 | 5' long section of electric baseboard |
| | Demolish and Install | Ea. | 66 | 94.50 | | 160.50 | heating elements. |
| | Reinstall | Ea. | | 55.80 | | 55.80 | |
| | Clean | Ea. | .73 | 20.50 | | 21.23 | |
| | Minimum Charge | Job | | 199 | | 199 | |
| **6'** | | | | | | | |
| | Demolish | Ea. | | 27.50 | | 27.50 | Includes material and labor to install a |
| | Install | Ea. | 73.50 | 79.50 | | 153 | 6' long section of electric baseboard |
| | Demolish and Install | Ea. | 73.50 | 107 | | 180.50 | heating elements. |
| | Reinstall | Ea. | | 63.62 | | 63.62 | |
| | Clean | Ea. | .14 | 3.34 | | 3.48 | |
| | Minimum Charge | Job | | 199 | | 199 | |
| **8'** | | | | | | | |
| | Demolish | Ea. | | 37 | | 37 | Includes material and labor to install |
| | Install | Ea. | 92.50 | 99.50 | | 192 | an 8' long section of electric |
| | Demolish and Install | Ea. | 92.50 | 136.50 | | 229 | baseboard heating elements. |
| | Reinstall | Ea. | | 79.52 | | 79.52 | |
| | Clean | Ea. | .14 | 4.17 | | 4.31 | |
| | Minimum Charge | Job | | 199 | | 199 | |
| **10'** | | | | | | | |
| | Demolish | Ea. | | 44 | | 44 | Includes material and labor to install a |
| | Install | Ea. | 193 | 120 | | 313 | 10' long section of electric baseboard |
| | Demolish and Install | Ea. | 193 | 164 | | 357 | heating elements. |
| | Reinstall | Ea. | | 96.39 | | 96.39 | |
| | Clean | Ea. | 1.45 | 41.50 | | 42.95 | |
| | Minimum Charge | Job | | 199 | | 199 | |

## Heating

| Heating | | Unit | Material | Labor | Equip. | Total | Specification |
|---|---|---|---|---|---|---|---|
| **Electric Radiant Wall Panel** | | | | | | | |
| | Demolish | Ea. | | 29.50 | | 29.50 | Includes material and labor to install |
| | Install | Ea. | 490 | 79.50 | | 569.50 | an 18″ x 23″ electric radiant heat wall |
| | Demolish and Install | Ea. | 490 | 109 | | 599 | panel. |
| | Reinstall | Ea. | | 63.62 | | 63.62 | |
| | Clean | Ea. | .19 | 8.35 | | 8.54 | |
| | Minimum Charge | Job | | 199 | | 199 | |

| Heating Control | | Unit | Material | Labor | Equip. | Total | Specification |
|---|---|---|---|---|---|---|---|
| **Thermostat** | | | | | | | |
| | Demolish | Ea. | | 11.35 | | 11.35 | Includes material and labor to install |
| | Install | Ea. | 230 | 50.50 | | 280.50 | an electric thermostat, 2 set back. |
| | Demolish and Install | Ea. | 230 | 61.85 | | 291.85 | |
| | Reinstall | Ea. | | 40.24 | | 40.24 | |
| | Clean | Ea. | .08 | 8.35 | | 8.43 | |
| | Minimum Charge | Job | | 205 | | 205 | |

| Air Conditioning | | Unit | Material | Labor | Equip. | Total | Specification |
|---|---|---|---|---|---|---|---|
| **2 Ton** | | | | | | | |
| | Demolish | Ea. | | 375 | | 375 | Includes material and labor to install a |
| | Install | Ea. | 1900 | 635 | | 2535 | rooftop air conditioning unit, 2 ton. |
| | Demolish and Install | Ea. | 1900 | 1010 | | 2910 | No hoisting is included. |
| | Reinstall | Ea. | | 635.72 | | 635.72 | |
| | Clean | Ea. | 3.63 | 33.50 | | 37.13 | |
| | Minimum Charge | Job | | 205 | | 205 | |
| **3 Ton** | | | | | | | |
| | Demolish | Ea. | | 375 | | 375 | Includes material and labor to install a |
| | Install | Ea. | 2000 | 840 | | 2840 | rooftop air conditioning unit, 3 ton. |
| | Demolish and Install | Ea. | 2000 | 1215 | | 3215 | No hoisting is included. |
| | Reinstall | Ea. | | 838.23 | | 838.23 | |
| | Clean | Ea. | 3.63 | 33.50 | | 37.13 | |
| | Minimum Charge | Job | | 205 | | 205 | |
| **4 Ton** | | | | | | | |
| | Demolish | Ea. | | 375 | | 375 | Includes material and labor to install a |
| | Install | Ea. | 2375 | 970 | | 3345 | rooftop air conditioning unit, 4 ton. |
| | Demolish and Install | Ea. | 2375 | 1345 | | 3720 | No hoisting is included. |
| | Reinstall | Ea. | | 972.03 | | 972.03 | |
| | Clean | Ea. | 3.63 | 33.50 | | 37.13 | |
| | Minimum Charge | Job | | 205 | | 205 | |
| **5 Ton** | | | | | | | |
| | Demolish | Ea. | | 375 | | 375 | Includes material and labor to install a |
| | Install | Ea. | 2525 | 1050 | | 3575 | rooftop air conditioning unit, 5 ton. |
| | Demolish and Install | Ea. | 2525 | 1425 | | 3950 | No hoisting is included. |
| | Reinstall | Ea. | | 1049.57 | | 1049.57 | |
| | Clean | Ea. | 3.63 | 33.50 | | 37.13 | |
| | Minimum Charge | Job | | 205 | | 205 | |
| **Compressor** | | | | | | | |
| **2 Ton** | | | | | | | |
| | Demolish | Ea. | | 340 | | 340 | Includes material and labor to install a |
| | Install | Ea. | 275 | 205 | | 480 | refrigeration compressor. |
| | Demolish and Install | Ea. | 275 | 545 | | 820 | |
| | Reinstall | Ea. | | 163.68 | | 163.68 | |
| | Clean | Ea. | 3.63 | 33.50 | | 37.13 | |
| | Minimum Charge | Job | | 205 | | 205 | |

| Air Conditioning | Unit | Material | Labor | Equip. | Total | Specification |
|---|---|---|---|---|---|---|
| **2.5 Ton** | | | | | | |
| Demolish | Ea. | | 340 | | 340 | Includes material and labor to install a |
| Install | Ea. | 325 | 222 | | 547 | refrigeration compressor. |
| Demolish and Install | Ea. | 325 | 562 | | 887 | |
| Reinstall | Ea. | | 177.33 | | 177.33 | |
| Clean | Ea. | 3.63 | 33.50 | | 37.13 | |
| Minimum Charge | Job | | 205 | | 205 | |
| **3 Ton** | | | | | | |
| Demolish | Ea. | | 340 | | 340 | Includes material and labor to install a |
| Install | Ea. | 360 | 231 | | 591 | refrigeration compressor. |
| Demolish and Install | Ea. | 360 | 571 | | 931 | |
| Reinstall | Ea. | | 185.05 | | 185.05 | |
| Clean | Ea. | 3.63 | 33.50 | | 37.13 | |
| Minimum Charge | Job | | 205 | | 205 | |
| **4 Ton** | | | | | | |
| Demolish | Ea. | | 340 | | 340 | Includes material and labor to install a |
| Install | Ea. | 455 | 186 | | 641 | refrigeration compressor. |
| Demolish and Install | Ea. | 455 | 526 | | 981 | |
| Reinstall | Ea. | | 148.80 | | 148.80 | |
| Clean | Ea. | 3.63 | 33.50 | | 37.13 | |
| Minimum Charge | Job | | 205 | | 205 | |
| **5 Ton** | | | | | | |
| Demolish | Ea. | | 340 | | 340 | Includes material and labor to install a |
| Install | Ea. | 500 | 253 | | 753 | refrigeration compressor. |
| Demolish and Install | Ea. | 500 | 593 | | 1093 | |
| Reinstall | Ea. | | 202.70 | | 202.70 | |
| Clean | Ea. | 3.63 | 33.50 | | 37.13 | |
| Minimum Charge | Job | | 205 | | 205 | |

## Condensing Unit

| | Unit | Material | Labor | Equip. | Total | Specification |
|---|---|---|---|---|---|---|
| **2 Ton Air-cooled** | | | | | | |
| Demolish | Ea. | | 97.50 | | 97.50 | Includes material and labor to install a |
| Install | Ea. | 1200 | 350 | | 1550 | 2 ton condensing unit. |
| Demolish and Install | Ea. | 1200 | 447.50 | | 1647.50 | |
| Reinstall | Ea. | | 280.69 | | 280.69 | |
| Clean | Ea. | 3.63 | 33.50 | | 37.13 | |
| Minimum Charge | Job | | 205 | | 205 | |
| **2.5 Ton Air-cooled** | | | | | | |
| Demolish | Ea. | | 114 | | 114 | Includes material and labor to install a |
| Install | Ea. | 1325 | 435 | | 1760 | 2.5 ton condensing unit. |
| Demolish and Install | Ea. | 1325 | 549 | | 1874 | |
| Reinstall | Ea. | | 346.73 | | 346.73 | |
| Clean | Ea. | 3.63 | 33.50 | | 37.13 | |
| Minimum Charge | Job | | 205 | | 205 | |
| **3 Ton Air-cooled** | | | | | | |
| Demolish | Ea. | | 136 | | 136 | Includes material and labor to install a |
| Install | Ea. | 1350 | 565 | | 1915 | 3 ton condensing unit. |
| Demolish and Install | Ea. | 1350 | 701 | | 2051 | |
| Reinstall | Ea. | | 453.42 | | 453.42 | |
| Clean | Ea. | 3.63 | 33.50 | | 37.13 | |
| Minimum Charge | Job | | 205 | | 205 | |
| **4 Ton Air-cooled** | | | | | | |
| Demolish | Ea. | | 205 | | 205 | Includes material and labor to install a |
| Install | Ea. | 1750 | 820 | | 2570 | 4 ton condensing unit. |
| Demolish and Install | Ea. | 1750 | 1025 | | 2775 | |
| Reinstall | Ea. | | 654.93 | | 654.93 | |
| Clean | Ea. | 3.63 | 33.50 | | 37.13 | |
| Minimum Charge | Job | | 205 | | 205 | |

# Rough Mechanical

| Air Conditioning | Unit | Material | Labor | Equip. | Total | Specification |
|---|---|---|---|---|---|---|
| **5 Ton Air-cooled** | | | | | | |
| Demolish | Ea. | | 305 | | 305 | Includes material and labor to install a |
| Install | Ea. | 2125 | 1225 | | 3350 | 5 ton condensing unit. |
| Demolish and Install | Ea. | 2125 | 1530 | | 3655 | |
| Reinstall | Ea. | | 982.40 | | 982.40 | |
| Clean | Ea. | 3.63 | 33.50 | | 37.13 | |
| Minimum Charge | Job | | 205 | | 205 | |
| **Air Handler** | | | | | | |
| **1,200 CFM** | | | | | | |
| Demolish | Ea. | | 246 | | 246 | Includes material and labor to install a |
| Install | Ea. | 2475 | 565 | | 3040 | 1200 CFM capacity air handling unit. |
| Demolish and Install | Ea. | 2475 | 811 | | 3286 | |
| Reinstall | Ea. | | 453.42 | | 453.42 | |
| Clean | Ea. | 3.63 | 33.50 | | 37.13 | |
| Minimum Charge | Job | | 205 | | 205 | |
| **2,000 CFM** | | | | | | |
| Demolish | Ea. | | 246 | | 246 | Includes material and labor to install a |
| Install | Ea. | 4125 | 670 | | 4795 | 2000 CFM capacity air handling unit. |
| Demolish and Install | Ea. | 4125 | 916 | | 5041 | |
| Reinstall | Ea. | | 535.85 | | 535.85 | |
| Clean | Ea. | 3.63 | 33.50 | | 37.13 | |
| Minimum Charge | Job | | 205 | | 205 | |
| **3,000 CFM** | | | | | | |
| Demolish | Ea. | | 273 | | 273 | Includes material and labor to install a |
| Install | Ea. | 5175 | 735 | | 5910 | 3000 CFM capacity air handling unit. |
| Demolish and Install | Ea. | 5175 | 1008 | | 6183 | |
| Reinstall | Ea. | | 589.44 | | 589.44 | |
| Clean | Ea. | 3.63 | 33.50 | | 37.13 | |
| Minimum Charge | Job | | 205 | | 205 | |
| **Evaporative Cooler** | | | | | | |
| **4,300 CFM, 1/3 HP** | | | | | | |
| Demolish | Ea. | | 100 | | 100 | Includes material and labor to install |
| Install | Ea. | 785 | 226 | | 1011 | an evaporative cooler. |
| Demolish and Install | Ea. | 785 | 326 | | 1111 | |
| Reinstall | Ea. | | 181 | | 181 | |
| Clean | Ea. | 1.45 | 33.50 | | 34.95 | |
| Minimum Charge | Job | | 205 | | 205 | |
| **4,700 CFM, 1/2 HP** | | | | | | |
| Demolish | Ea. | | 100 | | 100 | Includes material and labor to install |
| Install | Ea. | 755 | 234 | | 989 | an evaporative cooler. |
| Demolish and Install | Ea. | 755 | 334 | | 1089 | |
| Reinstall | Ea. | | 186.84 | | 186.84 | |
| Clean | Ea. | 1.45 | 33.50 | | 34.95 | |
| Minimum Charge | Job | | 205 | | 205 | |
| **5,600 CFM, 3/4 HP** | | | | | | |
| Demolish | Ea. | | 100 | | 100 | Includes material and labor to install |
| Install | Ea. | 1300 | 241 | | 1541 | an evaporative cooler. |
| Demolish and Install | Ea. | 1300 | 341 | | 1641 | |
| Reinstall | Ea. | | 193.07 | | 193.07 | |
| Clean | Ea. | 1.45 | 33.50 | | 34.95 | |
| Minimum Charge | Job | | 205 | | 205 | |
| **Master Cool Brand** | | | | | | |
| Demolish | Ea. | | 100 | | 100 | Includes material and labor to install |
| Install | Ea. | 785 | 250 | | 1035 | an evaporative cooler. |
| Demolish and Install | Ea. | 785 | 350 | | 1135 | |
| Reinstall | Ea. | | 199.72 | | 199.72 | |
| Clean | Ea. | 1.45 | 33.50 | | 34.95 | |
| Minimum Charge | Job | | 205 | | 205 | |

| Air Conditioning | Unit | Material | Labor | Equip. | Total | Specification |
|---|---|---|---|---|---|---|
| **Motor** | | | | | | |
| Demolish | Ea. | | 56.50 | | 56.50 | Includes material and labor to install |
| Install | Ea. | 272 | 176 | | 448 | an evaporative cooler motor. |
| Demolish and Install | Ea. | 272 | 232.50 | | 504.50 | |
| Reinstall | Ea. | | 140.82 | | 140.82 | |
| Clean | Ea. | 1.45 | 33.50 | | 34.95 | |
| Minimum Charge | Job | | 205 | | 205 | |
| **Water Pump** | | | | | | |
| Demolish | Ea. | | 56.50 | | 56.50 | Includes material and labor to install |
| Install | Ea. | 47.50 | 101 | | 148.50 | an evaporative cooler water pump. |
| Demolish and Install | Ea. | 47.50 | 157.50 | | 205 | |
| Reinstall | Ea. | | 80.48 | | 80.48 | |
| Clean | Ea. | 1.45 | 33.50 | | 34.95 | |
| Minimum Charge | Job | | 205 | | 205 | |
| **Fan Belt** | | | | | | |
| Demolish | Ea. | | 11.25 | | 11.25 | Includes material and labor to install |
| Install | Ea. | 33.50 | 20 | | 53.50 | an evaporative cooler fan belt. |
| Demolish and Install | Ea. | 33.50 | 31.25 | | 64.75 | |
| Reinstall | Ea. | | 16.10 | | 16.10 | |
| Minimum Charge | Job | | 205 | | 205 | |
| **Pads (4 ea.)** | | | | | | |
| Demolish | Ea. | | 11.25 | | 11.25 | Includes material and labor to install |
| Install | Ea. | 36 | 50.50 | | 86.50 | pre-fabricated roof pads for an |
| Demolish and Install | Ea. | 36 | 61.75 | | 97.75 | evaporative cooler. |
| Reinstall | Ea. | | 40.24 | | 40.24 | |
| Clean | Ea. | 1.45 | 33.50 | | 34.95 | |
| Minimum Charge | Job | | 205 | | 205 | |
| **Service call** | | | | | | |
| Install | Job | | 201 | | 201 | Includes 4 hour minimum labor charge for an sheetmetal worker. |
| **Window Mounted** | | | | | | |
| **Low Output BTU** | | | | | | |
| Install | Ea. | 221 | 45 | | 266 | Includes material and labor to install a |
| Reinstall | Ea. | | 36.16 | | 36.16 | window air conditioning unit. |
| Clean | Ea. | .55 | 8.35 | | 8.90 | |
| Minimum Charge | Job | | 205 | | 205 | |
| **Mid-range Output BTU** | | | | | | |
| Demolish | Ea. | | 31.50 | | 31.50 | Includes material and labor to install a |
| Install | Ea. | 330 | 60.50 | | 390.50 | window air conditioning unit. |
| Demolish and Install | Ea. | 330 | 92 | | 422 | |
| Reinstall | Ea. | | 48.21 | | 48.21 | |
| Clean | Ea. | .55 | 8.35 | | 8.90 | |
| Minimum Charge | Job | | 205 | | 205 | |
| **High Output BTU** | | | | | | |
| Demolish | Ea. | | 40 | | 40 | Includes material and labor to install a |
| Install | Ea. | 435 | 60.50 | | 495.50 | window air conditioning unit. |
| Demolish and Install | Ea. | 435 | 100.50 | | 535.50 | |
| Reinstall | Ea. | | 48.21 | | 48.21 | |
| Clean | Ea. | .55 | 8.35 | | 8.90 | |
| Minimum Charge | Job | | 205 | | 205 | |
| **Hotel-type Hot / Cold** | | | | | | |
| Demolish | Ea. | | 67 | | 67 | Includes material and labor to install |
| Install | Ea. | 910 | 246 | | 1156 | packaged air conditioning unit, |
| Demolish and Install | Ea. | 910 | 313 | | 1223 | 15000 BTU cooling, 13900 BTU |
| Reinstall | Ea. | | 196.48 | | 196.48 | heating. |
| Clean | Ea. | .73 | 16.70 | | 17.43 | |
| Minimum Charge | Job | | 205 | | 205 | |

# Rough Mechanical

## Air Conditioning

| Air Conditioning | | Unit | Material | Labor | Equip. | Total | Specification |
|---|---|---|---|---|---|---|---|
| **Thermostat** | | | | | | | |
| | Demolish | Ea. | | 11.35 | | 11.35 | Includes material and labor to install |
| | Install | Ea. | 230 | 50.50 | | 280.50 | an electric thermostat, 2 set back. |
| | Demolish and Install | Ea. | 230 | 61.85 | | 291.85 | |
| | Reinstall | Ea. | | 40.24 | | 40.24 | |
| | Clean | Ea. | .08 | 8.35 | | 8.43 | |
| | Minimum Charge | Job | | 205 | | 205 | |
| **Concrete Pad** | | | | | | | |
| | Demolish | S.F. | | 1.85 | | 1.85 | Includes material and labor to install |
| | Install | S.F. | 2.53 | 4.16 | | 6.69 | air conditioner pad. |
| | Demolish and Install | S.F. | 2.53 | 6.01 | | 8.54 | |
| | Reinstall | S.F. | | 3.33 | | 3.33 | |
| | Clean | S.F. | .08 | .53 | | .61 | |
| | Paint | S.F. | .14 | .32 | | .46 | |
| | Minimum Charge | Job | | 205 | | 205 | |
| **A/C Junction Box** | | | | | | | |
| | Install | Ea. | 238 | 114 | | 352 | Includes labor and materials to install |
| | Minimum Charge | Job | | 199 | | 199 | an air conditioning circuit including up to 40 feet of non-metallic cable. |

## Sprinkler System

| Sprinkler System | | Unit | Material | Labor | Equip. | Total | Specification |
|---|---|---|---|---|---|---|---|
| **Exposed** | | | | | | | |
| **Wet Type** | | | | | | | |
| | Demolish | SF Flr. | | .18 | | .18 | Includes material and labor to install |
| | Install | SF Flr. | 1.27 | 1.78 | | 3.05 | an exposed wet pipe fire sprinkler |
| | Demolish and Install | SF Flr. | 1.27 | 1.96 | | 3.23 | system. |
| | Reinstall | SF Flr. | | 1.78 | | 1.78 | |
| | Minimum Charge | Job | | 203 | | 203 | |
| **Dry Type** | | | | | | | |
| | Demolish | SF Flr. | | .18 | | .18 | Includes material and labor to install |
| | Install | SF Flr. | 1.45 | 1.78 | | 3.23 | an exposed dry pipe fire sprinkler |
| | Demolish and Install | SF Flr. | 1.45 | 1.96 | | 3.41 | system. |
| | Reinstall | SF Flr. | | 1.78 | | 1.78 | |
| | Minimum Charge | Job | | 203 | | 203 | |
| **Concealed** | | | | | | | |
| **Wet Type** | | | | | | | |
| | Demolish | SF Flr. | | .36 | | .36 | Includes material and labor to install a |
| | Install | SF Flr. | 1.27 | 2.43 | | 3.70 | concealed wet pipe fire sprinkler |
| | Demolish and Install | SF Flr. | 1.27 | 2.79 | | 4.06 | system. |
| | Reinstall | SF Flr. | | 2.43 | | 2.43 | |
| | Minimum Charge | Job | | 203 | | 203 | |
| **Dry Type** | | | | | | | |
| | Demolish | SF Flr. | | .36 | | .36 | Includes material and labor to install a |
| | Install | SF Flr. | .01 | 2.43 | | 2.44 | concealed dry pipe fire sprinkler |
| | Demolish and Install | SF Flr. | .01 | 2.79 | | 2.80 | system. |
| | Reinstall | SF Flr. | | 2.43 | | 2.43 | |
| | Minimum Charge | Job | | 203 | | 203 | |

| Junction Boxes | Cable | Switch Box |
|---|---|---|

| Electrical Per S.F. | | Unit | Material | Labor | Equip. | Total | Specification |
|---|---|---|---|---|---|---|---|
| **Residential** | | | | | | | |
| **Wiring, Lighting and Fixtures** | | | | | | | Includes labor and material to replace house wiring, lighting fixtures, and built-in appliances. Apply S.F. cost to floor area including garages but not basements. |
| | Install | S.F. | 1.64 | 1.66 | | 3.30 | |
| | Minimum Charge | Job | | 199 | | 199 | |
| **Wiring Only** | | | | | | | Includes labor and material to replace house wiring only. Apply S.F. cost to floor area including garages but not basements. |
| | Install | S.F. | .28 | .65 | | .93 | |

| Main Service | | Unit | Material | Labor | Equip. | Total | Specification |
|---|---|---|---|---|---|---|---|
| **100 Amp.** | | | | | | | Cost includes material and labor to install 100 Amp. residential service panel including 12 breaker interior panel, 10 single pole breakers and hook-up. Wiring is not included. |
| | Demolish | Ea. | | 164 | | 164 | |
| | Install | Ea. | 585 | 335 | | 920 | |
| | Demolish and Install | Ea. | 585 | 499 | | 1084 | |
| | Reinstall | Ea. | | 267.29 | | 267.29 | |
| | Clean | Ea. | .36 | 66.50 | | 66.86 | |
| | Minimum Charge | Job | | 199 | | 199 | |
| **150 Amp.** | | | | | | | Cost includes material and labor to install 150 Amp. residential service, incl. 20 breaker exterior panel, main switch, 1 GFI and 14 single pole breakers, meter socket including hookup. Wiring is not included. |
| | Demolish | Ea. | | 164 | | 164 | |
| | Install | Ea. | 910 | 385 | | 1295 | |
| | Demolish and Install | Ea. | 910 | 549 | | 1459 | |
| | Reinstall | Ea. | | 308.82 | | 308.82 | |
| | Clean | Ea. | .36 | 66.50 | | 66.86 | |
| | Minimum Charge | Job | | 199 | | 199 | |
| **200 Amp.** | | | | | | | Cost includes material and labor to install 200 Amp. residential service, incl. 20 breaker exterior panel, main switch, 1 GFI and 18 single pole breakers, meter socket including hookup. Wiring is not included. |
| | Demolish | Ea. | | 164 | | 164 | |
| | Install | Ea. | 1175 | 440 | | 1615 | |
| | Demolish and Install | Ea. | 1175 | 604 | | 1779 | |
| | Reinstall | Ea. | | 353.42 | | 353.42 | |
| | Clean | Ea. | .36 | 66.50 | | 66.86 | |
| | Minimum Charge | Job | | 199 | | 199 | |

# Rough Electrical

| Main Service | Unit | Material | Labor | Equip. | Total | Specification |
|---|---|---|---|---|---|---|
| **Masthead** | | | | | | |
| Demolish | Ea. | | 27.50 | | 27.50 | Includes material and labor to install |
| Install | Ea. | 112 | 166 | | 278 | galvanized steel conduit including |
| Demolish and Install | Ea. | 112 | 193.50 | | 305.50 | masthead. |
| Reinstall | Ea. | | 132.53 | | 132.53 | |
| Minimum Charge | Job | | 199 | | 199 | |
| **Allowance to Repair** | | | | | | |
| Install | Job | | 199 | | 199 | Minimum labor charge for residential |
| Minimum Charge | Job | | 199 | | 199 | wiring. |

**Wall Insulation**

| Floor Insulation | | Unit | Material | Labor | Equip. | Total | Specification |
|---|---|---|---|---|---|---|---|
| **Kraft Faced Batt** | | | | | | | |
| **3-1/2″ (R-13)** | | | | | | | |
| | Demolish | S.F. | | .12 | | .12 | Cost includes material and labor to |
| | Install | S.F. | .50 | .52 | | 1.02 | install 3-1/2″ (R-13) kraft paper or foil |
| | Demolish and Install | S.F. | .50 | .64 | | 1.14 | faced roll and batt fiberglass |
| | Minimum Charge | Job | | 181 | | 181 | insulation, joists 16″ O.C. |
| **6″ (R-19)** | | | | | | | |
| | Demolish | S.F. | | .12 | | .12 | Cost includes material and labor to |
| | Install | S.F. | .56 | .60 | | 1.16 | install 6″ (R-19) kraft paper or foil |
| | Demolish and Install | S.F. | .56 | .72 | | 1.28 | faced roll and batt fiberglass |
| | Minimum Charge | Job | | 181 | | 181 | insulation, joists 16″ O.C. |
| **10″ (R-30)** | | | | | | | |
| | Demolish | S.F. | | .12 | | .12 | Cost includes material and labor to |
| | Install | S.F. | .86 | .72 | | 1.58 | install 10″ (R-30) kraft paper-faced roll |
| | Demolish and Install | S.F. | .86 | .84 | | 1.70 | and batt fiberglass insulation, joists |
| | Minimum Charge | Job | | 181 | | 181 | 16″ O.C. |
| **12″ (R-38)** | | | | | | | |
| | Demolish | S.F. | | .12 | | .12 | Cost includes material and labor to |
| | Install | S.F. | 1.66 | .76 | | 2.42 | install 12″ (R-38) kraft paper-faced roll |
| | Demolish and Install | S.F. | 1.66 | .88 | | 2.54 | and batt fiberglass insulation, joists |
| | Minimum Charge | Job | | 181 | | 181 | 16″ O.C. |
| **Foil Faced Batt** | | | | | | | |
| **3-1/2″ (R-13)** | | | | | | | |
| | Demolish | S.F. | | .12 | | .12 | Cost includes material and labor to |
| | Install | S.F. | .50 | .52 | | 1.02 | install 3-1/2″ (R-13) kraft paper or foil |
| | Demolish and Install | S.F. | .50 | .64 | | 1.14 | faced roll and batt fiberglass |
| | Minimum Charge | Job | | 181 | | 181 | insulation, joists 16″ O.C. |
| **6″ (R-19)** | | | | | | | |
| | Demolish | S.F. | | .12 | | .12 | Cost includes material and labor to |
| | Install | S.F. | .56 | .60 | | 1.16 | install 6″ (R-19) kraft paper or foil |
| | Demolish and Install | S.F. | .56 | .72 | | 1.28 | faced roll and batt fiberglass |
| | Minimum Charge | Job | | 181 | | 181 | insulation, joists 16″ O.C. |
| **Unfaced Batt** | | | | | | | |
| **3-1/2″ (R-13)** | | | | | | | |
| | Demolish | S.F. | | .12 | | .12 | Cost includes material and labor to |
| | Install | S.F. | .40 | .60 | | 1 | install 3-1/2″ (R-13) unfaced roll and |
| | Demolish and Install | S.F. | .40 | .72 | | 1.12 | batt fiberglass insulation, joists 16″ |
| | Minimum Charge | Job | | 181 | | 181 | O.C. |

# Insulation

## Floor Insulation

| | Unit | Material | Labor | Equip. | Total | Specification |
|---|---|---|---|---|---|---|
| **6″ (R-19)** | | | | | | |
| Demolish | S.F. | | .12 | | .12 | Cost includes material and labor to |
| Install | S.F. | .64 | .72 | | 1.36 | install 6″ (R-19) unfaced roll and batt |
| Demolish and Install | S.F. | .64 | .84 | | 1.48 | fiberglass insulation, joists 16″ O.C. |
| Minimum Charge | Job | | 181 | | 181 | |
| **10″ (R-30)** | | | | | | |
| Demolish | S.F. | | .12 | | .12 | Cost includes material and labor to |
| Install | S.F. | .86 | .80 | | 1.66 | install 10″ (R-30) unfaced roll and batt |
| Demolish and Install | S.F. | .86 | .92 | | 1.78 | fiberglass insulation, joists 16″ O.C. |
| Minimum Charge | Job | | 181 | | 181 | |
| **12″ (R-38)** | | | | | | |
| Demolish | S.F. | | .12 | | .12 | Cost includes material and labor to |
| Install | S.F. | .99 | .85 | | 1.84 | install 12″ (R-38) unfaced roll and batt |
| Demolish and Install | S.F. | .99 | .97 | | 1.96 | fiberglass insulation, joists 16″ O.C. |
| Minimum Charge | Job | | 181 | | 181 | |

### Rigid Board

| | Unit | Material | Labor | Equip. | Total | Specification |
|---|---|---|---|---|---|---|
| **1/2″** | | | | | | |
| Demolish | S.F. | | .12 | | .12 | Includes material and labor to install |
| Install | S.F. | .33 | .45 | | .78 | rigid foam insulation board foil faced |
| Demolish and Install | S.F. | .33 | .57 | | .90 | two sides. |
| Minimum Charge | Job | | 181 | | 181 | |
| **3/4″** | | | | | | |
| Demolish | S.F. | | .12 | | .12 | Includes material and labor to install |
| Install | S.F. | .39 | .45 | | .84 | rigid foam insulation board foil faced |
| Demolish and Install | S.F. | .39 | .57 | | .96 | two sides. |
| Minimum Charge | Job | | 181 | | 181 | |
| **1-1/2″** | | | | | | |
| Demolish | S.F. | | .12 | | .12 | Includes material and labor to install |
| Install | S.F. | .70 | .48 | | 1.18 | rigid foam insulation board foil faced |
| Demolish and Install | S.F. | .70 | .60 | | 1.30 | two sides. |
| Minimum Charge | Job | | 181 | | 181 | |

### Support Wire

| | Unit | Material | Labor | Equip. | Total | Specification |
|---|---|---|---|---|---|---|
| Demolish | S.F. | | .05 | | .05 | Includes material and labor to install |
| Install | S.F. | .02 | .10 | | .12 | friction fit support wire. |
| Demolish and Install | S.F. | .02 | .15 | | .17 | |
| Minimum Charge | Job | | 181 | | 181 | |

### Vapor Barrier

| | Unit | Material | Labor | Equip. | Total | Specification |
|---|---|---|---|---|---|---|
| Demolish | S.F. | | .07 | | .07 | Cost includes material and labor to |
| Install | S.F. | .03 | .10 | | .13 | install 4 mil polyethylene vapor barrier |
| Demolish and Install | S.F. | .03 | .17 | | .20 | 10′ wide sheets with 6″ overlaps. |
| Minimum Charge | Job | | 181 | | 181 | |

## Wall Insulation

| | Unit | Material | Labor | Equip. | Total | Specification |
|---|---|---|---|---|---|---|
| **Kraft Faced Batt** | | | | | | |
| **3-1/2″ (R-13)** | | | | | | |
| Demolish | S.F. | | .12 | | .12 | Cost includes material and labor to |
| Install | S.F. | .41 | .27 | | .68 | install 3-1/2″ (R-13) kraft paper-faced |
| Demolish and Install | S.F. | .41 | .39 | | .80 | roll and batt fiberglass insulation, joist |
| Minimum Charge | Job | | 181 | | 181 | or studs 16″ O.C. |
| **6″ (R-19)** | | | | | | |
| Demolish | S.F. | | .12 | | .12 | Cost includes material and labor to |
| Install | S.F. | .47 | .27 | | .74 | install 6″ (R-19) kraft paper-faced roll |
| Demolish and Install | S.F. | .47 | .39 | | .86 | and batt fiberglass insulation, joist or |
| Minimum Charge | Job | | 181 | | 181 | studs 16″ O.C. |

# Insulation

| Wall Insulation | | Unit | Material | Labor | Equip. | Total | Specification |
|---|---|---|---|---|---|---|---|
| **10″ (R-30)** | | | | | | | |
| | Demolish | S.F. | | .12 | | .12 | Cost includes material and labor to |
| | Install | S.F. | .88 | .31 | | 1.19 | install 10″ (R-30) kraft paper-faced roll |
| | Demolish and Install | S.F. | .88 | .43 | | 1.31 | and batt fiberglass insulation, joist or |
| | Minimum Charge | Job | | 181 | | 181 | studs 16″ O.C. |
| **12″ (R-38)** | | | | | | | |
| | Demolish | S.F. | | .12 | | .12 | Cost includes material and labor to |
| | Install | S.F. | 1.10 | .31 | | 1.41 | install 12″ (R-38) kraft paper-faced roll |
| | Demolish and Install | S.F. | 1.10 | .43 | | 1.53 | and batt fiberglass insulation, joist or |
| | Minimum Charge | Job | | 181 | | 181 | studs 16″ O.C. |
| **Foil Faced Batt** | | | | | | | |
| **3-1/2″ (R-13)** | | | | | | | |
| | Demolish | S.F. | | .12 | | .12 | Cost includes material and labor to |
| | Install | S.F. | .61 | .27 | | .88 | install 3-1/2″ (R-13) foil faced roll and |
| | Demolish and Install | S.F. | .61 | .39 | | 1 | batt fiberglass insulation, joist or studs |
| | Minimum Charge | Job | | 181 | | 181 | 16″ O.C. |
| **6″ (R-19)** | | | | | | | |
| | Demolish | S.F. | | .12 | | .12 | Cost includes material and labor to |
| | Install | S.F. | .59 | .27 | | .86 | install 6″ (R-19) foil faced roll and batt |
| | Demolish and Install | S.F. | .59 | .39 | | .98 | fiberglass insulation, joist or studs 16″ |
| | Minimum Charge | Job | | 181 | | 181 | O.C. |
| **Unfaced Batt** | | | | | | | |
| **3-1/2″ (R-13)** | | | | | | | |
| | Demolish | S.F. | | .12 | | .12 | Cost includes material and labor to |
| | Install | S.F. | .40 | .27 | | .67 | install 3-1/2″ (R-13) unfaced roll and |
| | Demolish and Install | S.F. | .40 | .39 | | .79 | batt fiberglass insulation, joist or studs |
| | Minimum Charge | Job | | 181 | | 181 | 16″ O.C. |
| **6″ (R-19)** | | | | | | | |
| | Demolish | S.F. | | .12 | | .12 | Cost includes material and labor to |
| | Install | S.F. | .64 | .31 | | .95 | install 6″ (R-19) unfaced roll and batt |
| | Demolish and Install | S.F. | .64 | .43 | | 1.07 | fiberglass insulation, joist or studs 16″ |
| | Minimum Charge | Job | | 181 | | 181 | O.C. |
| **10″ (R-30)** | | | | | | | |
| | Demolish | S.F. | | .12 | | .12 | Cost includes material and labor to |
| | Install | S.F. | .92 | .31 | | 1.23 | install 10″ (R-30) unfaced roll and batt |
| | Demolish and Install | S.F. | .92 | .43 | | 1.35 | fiberglass insulation, joist or studs 16″ |
| | Minimum Charge | Job | | 181 | | 181 | O.C. |
| **12″ (R-38)** | | | | | | | |
| | Demolish | S.F. | | .12 | | .12 | Cost includes material and labor to |
| | Install | S.F. | .99 | .36 | | 1.35 | install 12″ (R-38) unfaced roll and batt |
| | Demolish and Install | S.F. | .99 | .48 | | 1.47 | fiberglass insulation, joist or studs 16″ |
| | Minimum Charge | Job | | 181 | | 181 | O.C. |
| **Blown** | | | | | | | |
| **R-13** | | | | | | | |
| | Demolish | S.F. | | .12 | | .12 | Includes material and labor to install |
| | Install | S.F. | .30 | 1.20 | .51 | 2.01 | fiberglass blown-in insulation in wall |
| | Demolish and Install | S.F. | .30 | 1.32 | .51 | 2.13 | with wood siding. |
| | Minimum Charge | Job | | 415 | 174 | 589 | |
| **R-19** | | | | | | | |
| | Demolish | S.F. | | .12 | | .12 | Includes material and labor to install |
| | Install | S.F. | .46 | 1.38 | .58 | 2.42 | fiberglass blown-in insulation in wall |
| | Demolish and Install | S.F. | .46 | 1.50 | .58 | 2.54 | with wood siding. |
| | Minimum Charge | Job | | 415 | 174 | 589 | |

# Insulation

## Wall Insulation

| | Unit | Material | Labor | Equip. | Total | Specification |
|---|---|---|---|---|---|---|
| **Rigid Board** | | | | | | |
| **1/2"** | | | | | | |
| Demolish | S.F. | | .15 | | .15 | Includes material and labor to install |
| Install | S.F. | .33 | .45 | | .78 | rigid foam insulation board, foil faced, |
| Demolish and Install | S.F. | .33 | .60 | | .93 | two sides. |
| Minimum Charge | Job | | 181 | | 181 | |
| **3/4"** | | | | | | |
| Demolish | S.F. | | .15 | | .15 | Includes material and labor to install |
| Install | S.F. | .39 | .45 | | .84 | rigid foam insulation board, foil faced, |
| Demolish and Install | S.F. | .39 | .60 | | .99 | two sides. |
| Minimum Charge | Job | | 181 | | 181 | |
| **1-1/2"** | | | | | | |
| Demolish | S.F. | | .15 | | .15 | Includes material and labor to install |
| Install | S.F. | .70 | .50 | | 1.20 | rigid foam insulation board, foil faced, |
| Demolish and Install | S.F. | .70 | .65 | | 1.35 | two sides. |
| Minimum Charge | Job | | 181 | | 181 | |
| **Vapor Barrier** | | | | | | |
| Demolish | S.F. | | .04 | | .04 | Cost includes material and labor to |
| Install | S.F. | .03 | .10 | | .13 | install 4 mil polyethylene vapor barrier |
| Demolish and Install | S.F. | .03 | .14 | | .17 | 10' wide sheets with 6" overlaps. |
| Minimum Charge | Job | | 181 | | 181 | |

## Ceiling Insulation

| | Unit | Material | Labor | Equip. | Total | Specification |
|---|---|---|---|---|---|---|
| **Kraft Faced Batt** | | | | | | |
| **3-1/2" (R-13)** | | | | | | |
| Demolish | S.F. | | .12 | | .12 | Cost includes material and labor to |
| Install | S.F. | .41 | .27 | | .68 | install 3-1/2" (R-13) kraft paper-faced |
| Demolish and Install | S.F. | .41 | .39 | | .80 | roll and batt fiberglass insulation, joist |
| Minimum Charge | Job | | 181 | | 181 | or studs 16" O.C. |
| **6" (R-19)** | | | | | | |
| Demolish | S.F. | | .12 | | .12 | Cost includes material and labor to |
| Install | S.F. | .47 | .27 | | .74 | install 6" (R-19) kraft paper-faced roll |
| Demolish and Install | S.F. | .47 | .39 | | .86 | and batt fiberglass insulation, joist or |
| Minimum Charge | Job | | 181 | | 181 | studs 16" O.C. |
| **10" (R-30)** | | | | | | |
| Demolish | S.F. | | .12 | | .12 | Cost includes material and labor to |
| Install | S.F. | .88 | .31 | | 1.19 | install 10" (R-30) kraft paper-faced roll |
| Demolish and Install | S.F. | .88 | .43 | | 1.31 | and batt fiberglass insulation, joist or |
| Minimum Charge | Job | | 181 | | 181 | studs 16" O.C. |
| **12" (R-38)** | | | | | | |
| Demolish | S.F. | | .12 | | .12 | Cost includes material and labor to |
| Install | S.F. | 1.10 | .31 | | 1.41 | install 12" (R-38) kraft paper-faced roll |
| Demolish and Install | S.F. | 1.10 | .43 | | 1.53 | and batt fiberglass insulation, joist or |
| Minimum Charge | Job | | 181 | | 181 | studs 16" O.C. |
| **Foil Faced Batt** | | | | | | |
| **3-1/2" (R-13)** | | | | | | |
| Demolish | S.F. | | .12 | | .12 | Cost includes material and labor to |
| Install | S.F. | .61 | .27 | | .88 | install 3-1/2" (R-13) foil faced roll and |
| Demolish and Install | S.F. | .61 | .39 | | 1 | batt fiberglass insulation, joist or studs |
| Minimum Charge | Job | | 181 | | 181 | 16" O.C. |

# Insulation

| Ceiling Insulation | | Unit | Material | Labor | Equip. | Total | Specification |
|---|---|---|---|---|---|---|---|
| **6″ (R-19)** | | | | | | | |
| | Demolish | S.F. | | .12 | | .12 | Cost includes material and labor to |
| | Install | S.F. | .59 | .27 | | .86 | install 6″ (R-19) foil faced roll and batt |
| | Demolish and Install | S.F. | .59 | .39 | | .98 | fiberglass insulation, joist or studs 16″ |
| | Minimum Charge | Job | | 181 | | 181 | O.C. |
| **Unfaced Batt** | | | | | | | |
| **3-1/2″ (R-13)** | | | | | | | |
| | Demolish | S.F. | | .12 | | .12 | Cost includes material and labor to |
| | Install | S.F. | .40 | .27 | | .67 | install 3-1/2″ (R-13) unfaced roll and |
| | Demolish and Install | S.F. | .40 | .39 | | .79 | batt fiberglass insulation, joist or studs |
| | Minimum Charge | Job | | 181 | | 181 | 16″ O.C. |
| **6″ (R-19)** | | | | | | | |
| | Demolish | S.F. | | .12 | | .12 | Cost includes material and labor to |
| | Install | S.F. | .64 | .31 | | .95 | install 6″ (R-19) unfaced roll and batt |
| | Demolish and Install | S.F. | .64 | .43 | | 1.07 | fiberglass insulation, joist or studs 16″ |
| | Minimum Charge | Job | | 181 | | 181 | O.C. |
| **10″ (R-30)** | | | | | | | |
| | Demolish | S.F. | | .12 | | .12 | Cost includes material and labor to |
| | Install | S.F. | .92 | .31 | | 1.23 | install 10″ (R-30) unfaced roll and batt |
| | Demolish and Install | S.F. | .92 | .43 | | 1.35 | fiberglass insulation, joist or studs 16″ |
| | Minimum Charge | Job | | 181 | | 181 | O.C. |
| **12″ (R-38)** | | | | | | | |
| | Demolish | S.F. | | .12 | | .12 | Cost includes material and labor to |
| | Install | S.F. | .99 | .36 | | 1.35 | install 12″ (R-38) unfaced roll and batt |
| | Demolish and Install | S.F. | .99 | .48 | | 1.47 | fiberglass insulation, joist or studs 16″ |
| | Minimum Charge | Job | | 181 | | 181 | O.C. |
| **Blown** | | | | | | | |
| **5″** | | | | | | | |
| | Demolish | S.F. | | .37 | | .37 | Includes material and labor to install |
| | Install | S.F. | .23 | .22 | .09 | .54 | fiberglass blown-in insulation. |
| | Demolish and Install | S.F. | .23 | .59 | .09 | .91 | |
| | Minimum Charge | Job | | 415 | 174 | 589 | |
| **6″** | | | | | | | |
| | Demolish | S.F. | | .37 | | .37 | Includes material and labor to install |
| | Install | S.F. | .28 | .28 | .12 | .68 | fiberglass blown-in insulation. |
| | Demolish and Install | S.F. | .28 | .65 | .12 | 1.05 | |
| | Minimum Charge | Job | | 415 | 174 | 589 | |
| **9″** | | | | | | | |
| | Demolish | S.F. | | .37 | | .37 | Includes material and labor to install |
| | Install | S.F. | .40 | .38 | .16 | .94 | fiberglass blown-in insulation. |
| | Demolish and Install | S.F. | .40 | .75 | .16 | 1.31 | |
| | Minimum Charge | Job | | 415 | 174 | 589 | |
| **12″** | | | | | | | |
| | Demolish | S.F. | | .37 | | .37 | Includes material and labor to install |
| | Install | S.F. | .55 | .55 | .23 | 1.33 | fiberglass blown-in insulation. |
| | Demolish and Install | S.F. | .55 | .92 | .23 | 1.70 | |
| | Minimum Charge | Job | | 415 | 174 | 589 | |
| **Rigid Board** | | | | | | | |
| **1/2″** | | | | | | | |
| | Demolish | S.F. | | .21 | | .21 | Includes material and labor to install |
| | Install | S.F. | .33 | .45 | | .78 | rigid foam insulation board, foil faced, |
| | Demolish and Install | S.F. | .33 | .66 | | .99 | two sides. |
| | Minimum Charge | Job | | 181 | | 181 | |

# Insulation

## Ceiling Insulation

| | | Unit | Material | Labor | Equip. | Total | Specification |
|---|---|---|---|---|---|---|---|
| **3/4″** | | | | | | | |
| | Demolish | S.F. | | .21 | | .21 | Includes material and labor to install |
| | Install | S.F. | .39 | .45 | | .84 | rigid foam insulation board, foil faced, |
| | Demolish and Install | S.F. | .39 | .66 | | 1.05 | two sides. |
| | Minimum Charge | Job | | 181 | | 181 | |
| **1-1/2″** | | | | | | | |
| | Demolish | S.F. | | .21 | | .21 | Includes material and labor to install |
| | Install | S.F. | .70 | .50 | | 1.20 | rigid foam insulation board, foil faced, |
| | Demolish and Install | S.F. | .70 | .71 | | 1.41 | two sides. |
| | Minimum Charge | Job | | 181 | | 181 | |

## Exterior Insulation

| | | Unit | Material | Labor | Equip. | Total | Specification |
|---|---|---|---|---|---|---|---|
| **Rigid Board** | | | | | | | |
| **1/2″** | | | | | | | |
| | Demolish | S.F. | | .11 | | .11 | Includes material and labor to install |
| | Install | S.F. | .33 | .45 | | .78 | rigid foam insulation board foil faced |
| | Demolish and Install | S.F. | .33 | .56 | | .89 | two sides. |
| | Minimum Charge | Job | | 181 | | 181 | |
| **3/4″** | | | | | | | |
| | Demolish | S.F. | | .11 | | .11 | Includes material and labor to install |
| | Install | S.F. | .39 | .45 | | .84 | rigid foam insulation board foil faced |
| | Demolish and Install | S.F. | .39 | .56 | | .95 | two sides. |
| | Minimum Charge | Job | | 181 | | 181 | |
| **1-1/2″** | | | | | | | |
| | Demolish | S.F. | | .11 | | .11 | Includes material and labor to install |
| | Install | S.F. | .70 | .48 | | 1.18 | rigid foam insulation board foil faced |
| | Demolish and Install | S.F. | .70 | .59 | | 1.29 | two sides. |
| | Minimum Charge | Job | | 181 | | 181 | |
| **Vapor Barrier** | | | | | | | |
| | Demolish | S.F. | | .07 | | .07 | Cost includes material and labor to |
| | Install | S.F. | .03 | .10 | | .13 | install 4 mil polyethylene vapor barrier |
| | Demolish and Install | S.F. | .03 | .17 | | .20 | 10′ wide sheets with 6″ overlaps. |
| | Minimum Charge | Job | | 181 | | 181 | |

## Roof Insulation Board

| | | Unit | Material | Labor | Equip. | Total | Specification |
|---|---|---|---|---|---|---|---|
| **Fiberglass** | | | | | | | |
| **3/4″ Fiberglass** | | | | | | | |
| | Demolish | Sq. | | 39 | | 39 | Includes material and labor to install |
| | Install | Sq. | 61.50 | 27 | | 88.50 | fiberglass board insulation 3/4″ thick, |
| | Demolish and Install | Sq. | 61.50 | 66 | | 127.50 | R-2.80 and C-0.36 values. |
| | Minimum Charge | Job | | 181 | | 181 | |
| **1″ Fiberglass** | | | | | | | |
| | Demolish | Sq. | | 39 | | 39 | Includes material and labor to install |
| | Install | Sq. | 87 | 30 | | 117 | fiberglass board insulation 1″ thick, |
| | Demolish and Install | Sq. | 87 | 69 | | 156 | R-4.20 and C-0.24 values. |
| | Minimum Charge | Job | | 181 | | 181 | |
| **1-3/8″ Fiberglass** | | | | | | | |
| | Demolish | Sq. | | 39 | | 39 | Includes material and labor to install |
| | Install | Sq. | 139 | 33 | | 172 | fiberglass board insulation 1-3/8″ |
| | Demolish and Install | Sq. | 139 | 72 | | 211 | thick, R-5.30 and C-0.19 values. |
| | Minimum Charge | Job | | 181 | | 181 | |

# Insulation

| Roof Insulation Board | | Unit | Material | Labor | Equip. | Total | Specification |
|---|---|---|---|---|---|---|---|
| **1-5/8″ Fiberglass** | | | | | | | |
| | Demolish | Sq. | | 39 | | 39 | Includes material and labor to install |
| | Install | Sq. | 143 | 34.50 | | 177.50 | fiberglass board insulation 1-5/8″ |
| | Demolish and Install | Sq. | 143 | 73.50 | | 216.50 | thick, R-6.70 and C-0.15 values. |
| | Minimum Charge | Job | | 181 | | 181 | |
| **2-1/4″ Fiberglass** | | | | | | | |
| | Demolish | Sq. | | 39 | | 39 | Includes material and labor to install |
| | Install | Sq. | 171 | 38 | | 209 | fiberglass board insulation 2-1/4″ |
| | Demolish and Install | Sq. | 171 | 77 | | 248 | thick, R-8.30 and C-0.12 values. |
| | Minimum Charge | Job | | 181 | | 181 | |
| **Perlite** | | | | | | | |
| **1″ Perlite** | | | | | | | |
| | Demolish | Sq. | | 39 | | 39 | Includes material and labor to install |
| | Install | Sq. | 49.50 | 30 | | 79.50 | perlite board insulation 1″ thick, |
| | Demolish and Install | Sq. | 49.50 | 69 | | 118.50 | R-2.80 and C-0.36 values. |
| | Minimum Charge | Job | | 181 | | 181 | |
| **4″ Perlite** | | | | | | | |
| | Demolish | Sq. | | 39 | | 39 | Includes material and labor to install |
| | Install | Sq. | 198 | 58 | | 256 | perlite board insulation 4″ thick, |
| | Demolish and Install | Sq. | 198 | 97 | | 295 | R-10.0 and C-0.10 values. |
| | Minimum Charge | Job | | 181 | | 181 | |
| **1-1/2″ Perlite** | | | | | | | |
| | Demolish | Sq. | | 39 | | 39 | Includes material and labor to install |
| | Install | Sq. | 51.50 | 33 | | 84.50 | perlite board insulation 1-1/2″ thick, |
| | Demolish and Install | Sq. | 51.50 | 72 | | 123.50 | R-4.20 and C-0.24 values. |
| | Minimum Charge | Job | | 181 | | 181 | |
| **2″ Perlite** | | | | | | | |
| | Demolish | Sq. | | 39 | | 39 | Includes material and labor to install |
| | Install | Sq. | 87 | 40 | | 127 | perlite board insulation 2″ thick, |
| | Demolish and Install | Sq. | 87 | 79 | | 166 | R-5.30 and C-0.19 values. |
| | Minimum Charge | Job | | 181 | | 181 | |
| **2-1/2″ Perlite** | | | | | | | |
| | Demolish | Sq. | | 39 | | 39 | Includes material and labor to install |
| | Install | Sq. | 102 | 45 | | 147 | perlite board insulation 2-1/2″ thick, |
| | Demolish and Install | Sq. | 102 | 84 | | 186 | R-6.70 and C-0.15 values. |
| | Minimum Charge | Job | | 181 | | 181 | |
| **3″ Perlite** | | | | | | | |
| | Demolish | Sq. | | 39 | | 39 | Includes material and labor to install |
| | Install | Sq. | 149 | 48 | | 197 | perlite board insulation 3″ thick, |
| | Demolish and Install | Sq. | 149 | 87 | | 236 | R-8.30 and C-0.12 values. |
| | Minimum Charge | Job | | 181 | | 181 | |
| **Polystyrene** | | | | | | | |
| **2″ Polystyrene** | | | | | | | |
| | Demolish | Sq. | | 39 | | 39 | Includes material and labor to install |
| | Install | Sq. | 41.50 | 38 | | 79.50 | extruded polystyrene board, R5.0/ 2″ |
| | Demolish and Install | Sq. | 41.50 | 77 | | 118.50 | in thickness @25PSI compressive |
| | Minimum Charge | Job | | 181 | | 181 | strength. |
| **1″ Polystyrene** | | | | | | | |
| | Demolish | Sq. | | 39 | | 39 | Includes material and labor to install |
| | Install | Sq. | 39.50 | 26 | | 65.50 | extruded polystyrene board, R5.0/ 1″ |
| | Demolish and Install | Sq. | 39.50 | 65 | | 104.50 | in thickness @25PSI compressive |
| | Minimum Charge | Job | | 181 | | 181 | strength. |
| **1-1/2″ Polystyrene** | | | | | | | |
| | Demolish | Sq. | | 39 | | 39 | Includes material and labor to install |
| | Install | Sq. | 40 | 30 | | 70 | extruded polystyrene board, R5.0/ |
| | Demolish and Install | Sq. | 40 | 69 | | 109 | 1-1/2″ in thickness @25PSI |
| | Minimum Charge | Job | | 181 | | 181 | compressive strength. |

| Roof Insulation Board | | Unit | Material | Labor | Equip. | Total | Specification |
|---|---|---|---|---|---|---|---|
| **Urethane** | | | | | | | |
| **3/4″ Urethane** | | | | | | | |
| | Demolish | Sq. | | 39 | | 39 | Includes material and labor to install |
| | Install | Sq. | 56 | 22.50 | | 78.50 | urethane board insulation 3/4″ thick, |
| | Demolish and Install | Sq. | 56 | 61.50 | | 117.50 | R-5.30 and C-0.19 values. |
| | Minimum Charge | Job | | 181 | | 181 | |
| **1″ Urethane** | | | | | | | |
| | Demolish | Sq. | | 39 | | 39 | Includes material and labor to install |
| | Install | Sq. | 61.50 | 24 | | 85.50 | urethane board insulation 1″ thick, |
| | Demolish and Install | Sq. | 61.50 | 63 | | 124.50 | R-6.70 and C-0.15 values. |
| | Minimum Charge | Job | | 181 | | 181 | |
| **1-1/2″ Urethane** | | | | | | | |
| | Demolish | Sq. | | 39 | | 39 | Includes material and labor to install |
| | Install | Sq. | 65.50 | 28 | | 93.50 | urethane board insulation 1-1/2″ |
| | Demolish and Install | Sq. | 65.50 | 67 | | 132.50 | thick, R-10.1 and C-0.09 values. |
| | Minimum Charge | Job | | 181 | | 181 | |
| **2″ Urethane** | | | | | | | |
| | Demolish | Sq. | | 39 | | 39 | Includes material and labor to install |
| | Install | Sq. | 82.50 | 33 | | 115.50 | urethane board insulation 2″ thick, |
| | Demolish and Install | Sq. | 82.50 | 72 | | 154.50 | R-13.4 and C-0.06 values. |
| | Minimum Charge | Job | | 181 | | 181 | |

**Gypsum Wallboard**

**Tile Ceiling**

**Gypsum Wallboard Ceiling**

| Wall Plaster | Unit | Material | Labor | Equip. | Total | Specification |
|---|---|---|---|---|---|---|
| **Interior** | | | | | | |
| **Cement** | | | | | | |
| Demolish | S.Y. | | 4.94 | | 4.94 | Includes material and labor to install |
| Install | S.Y. | 14.85 | 21 | 1.80 | 37.65 | cement plaster on interior wood |
| Demolish and Install | S.Y. | 14.85 | 25.94 | 1.80 | 42.59 | framing with metal lath. |
| Clean | S.Y. | | 2.43 | | 2.43 | |
| Paint | S.Y. | 1.72 | 4.20 | | 5.92 | |
| Minimum Charge | Job | | 162 | | 162 | |
| **Acoustic** | | | | | | |
| Demolish | S.Y. | | 4.94 | | 4.94 | Includes material and labor to install |
| Install | S.Y. | 10.40 | 25 | 1.80 | 37.20 | acoustical cement plaster on interior |
| Demolish and Install | S.Y. | 10.40 | 29.94 | 1.80 | 42.14 | wood framing with metal lath. |
| Clean | S.Y. | | 2.43 | | 2.43 | |
| Paint | S.Y. | 1.72 | 4.20 | | 5.92 | |
| Minimum Charge | Job | | 162 | | 162 | |
| **Gypsum** | | | | | | |
| Demolish | S.Y. | | 4.94 | | 4.94 | Includes material and labor to install |
| Install | S.Y. | 9.35 | 21.50 | 1.53 | 32.38 | gypsum wall or ceiling plaster on |
| Demolish and Install | S.Y. | 9.35 | 26.44 | 1.53 | 37.32 | interior wood framing with metal lath. |
| Clean | S.Y. | | 2.43 | | 2.43 | |
| Paint | S.Y. | 1.72 | 4.20 | | 5.92 | |
| Minimum Charge | Job | | 162 | | 162 | |
| **Stucco** | | | | | | |
| Demolish | S.Y. | | 11.85 | | 11.85 | Includes material and labor to install |
| Install | S.Y. | 6.05 | 29.50 | 2.11 | 37.66 | stucco on wire mesh over wood |
| Demolish and Install | S.Y. | 6.05 | 41.35 | 2.11 | 49.51 | framing. |
| Clean | S.Y. | | 2.43 | | 2.43 | |
| Paint | S.Y. | 1.72 | 4.20 | | 5.92 | |
| Minimum Charge | Job | | 162 | | 162 | |
| **Thin Coat** | | | | | | |
| **Veneer** | | | | | | |
| Demolish | S.Y. | | 4.94 | | 4.94 | Includes materials and labor to install |
| Install | S.Y. | .72 | 3.87 | .33 | 4.92 | thin coat veneer plaster. |
| Demolish and Install | S.Y. | .72 | 8.81 | .33 | 9.86 | |
| Clean | S.Y. | | 2.43 | | 2.43 | |
| Paint | S.Y. | 1.72 | 4.20 | | 5.92 | |
| Minimum Charge | Job | | 162 | | 162 | |

## Wall Plaster

| Wall Plaster | Unit | Material | Labor | Equip. | Total | Specification |
|---|---|---|---|---|---|---|
| **Lath** | | | | | | |
| **Metal** | | | | | | |
| Demolish | S.Y. | | 1.16 | | 1.16 | Includes material and labor to install |
| Install | S.Y. | 4.22 | 4.21 | | 8.43 | wire lath on steel framed walls. |
| Demolish and Install | S.Y. | 4.22 | 5.37 | | 9.59 | |
| Clean | S.Y. | | 2.43 | | 2.43 | |
| Minimum Charge | Job | | 74.50 | | 74.50 | |
| **Gypsum** | | | | | | |
| Demolish | S.Y. | | 1.16 | | 1.16 | Includes material and labor to install |
| Install | S.Y. | 6.15 | 3.95 | | 10.10 | gypsum lath on walls. |
| Demolish and Install | S.Y. | 6.15 | 5.11 | | 11.26 | |
| Clean | S.Y. | | 2.43 | | 2.43 | |
| Minimum Charge | Job | | 162 | | 162 | |
| **Repairs** | | | | | | |
| **Fill in Small Cracks** | | | | | | |
| Install | L.F. | .06 | 2.60 | | 2.66 | Includes labor and material to fill-in |
| Minimum Charge | Job | | 162 | | 162 | hairline cracks up to 1/8" with filler, |
| | | | | | | sand and prep for paint. |
| **Repair up to 1" Crack** | | | | | | |
| Install | L.F. | .24 | 3.25 | | 3.49 | Includes labor and material to fill-in |
| Minimum Charge | Job | | 162 | | 162 | hairline cracks up to 1" with filler, |
| | | | | | | sand and prep for paint. |
| **Patch Small Hole (2")** | | | | | | |
| Install | Ea. | .06 | 3.42 | | 3.48 | Includes labor and material to patch |
| Minimum Charge | Job | | 162 | | 162 | up to a 2" diameter hole in plaster. |
| **Patch Large Hole** | | | | | | |
| Install | Ea. | 7.25 | 54 | | 61.25 | Includes labor and material to patch |
| Minimum Charge | Job | | 162 | | 162 | up to a 20" diameter hole in plaster. |
| **Patch Plaster Section** | | | | | | |
| Install | Ea. | 2.33 | 3.25 | | 5.58 | Includes labor and material to repair |
| Minimum Charge | Job | | 162 | | 162 | section of plaster wall, area less than |
| | | | | | | 20 S.F. |
| **Repair Inside Corner** | | | | | | |
| Install | L.F. | 2.90 | 8.10 | | 11 | Includes material and labor to patch |
| Minimum Charge | Job | | 162 | | 162 | plaster corners. |

## Ceiling Plaster

| Ceiling Plaster | Unit | Material | Labor | Equip. | Total | Specification |
|---|---|---|---|---|---|---|
| **Interior** | | | | | | |
| **Cement** | | | | | | |
| Demolish | S.Y. | | 4.94 | | 4.94 | Includes material and labor to install |
| Install | S.Y. | 14.85 | 21 | 1.80 | 37.65 | cement plaster on interior wood |
| Demolish and Install | S.Y. | 14.85 | 25.94 | 1.80 | 42.59 | framing with metal lath. |
| Clean | S.Y. | | 2.54 | | 2.54 | |
| Paint | S.Y. | 1.72 | 4.20 | | 5.92 | |
| Minimum Charge | Job | | 162 | | 162 | |
| **Acoustic** | | | | | | |
| Demolish | S.Y. | | 4.94 | | 4.94 | Includes material and labor to install |
| Install | S.Y. | 10.40 | 25 | 1.80 | 37.20 | acoustical cement plaster on interior |
| Demolish and Install | S.Y. | 10.40 | 29.94 | 1.80 | 42.14 | wood framing with metal lath. |
| Clean | S.Y. | | 2.54 | | 2.54 | |
| Paint | S.Y. | 1.72 | 4.20 | | 5.92 | |
| Minimum Charge | Job | | 162 | | 162 | |

# Walls / Ceilings

| Ceiling Plaster | | Unit | Material | Labor | Equip. | Total | Specification |
|---|---|---|---|---|---|---|---|
| **Gypsum** | | | | | | | |
| | Demolish | S.Y. | | 4.94 | | 4.94 | Includes material and labor to install |
| | Install | S.Y. | 9.35 | 21.50 | 1.53 | 32.38 | gypsum wall or ceiling plaster on |
| | Demolish and Install | S.Y. | 9.35 | 26.44 | 1.53 | 37.32 | interior wood framing with metal lath. |
| | Clean | S.Y. | | 2.54 | | 2.54 | |
| | Paint | S.Y. | 1.72 | 4.20 | | 5.92 | |
| | Minimum Charge | Job | | 162 | | 162 | |
| **Stucco** | | | | | | | |
| | Demolish | S.Y. | | 11.85 | | 11.85 | Includes material and labor to install |
| | Install | S.Y. | 6.05 | 29.50 | 2.11 | 37.66 | stucco on wire mesh over wood |
| | Demolish and Install | S.Y. | 6.05 | 41.35 | 2.11 | 49.51 | framing. |
| | Clean | S.Y. | | 2.54 | | 2.54 | |
| | Paint | S.Y. | 1.72 | 4.20 | | 5.92 | |
| | Minimum Charge | Job | | 162 | | 162 | |
| **Thin Coat** | | | | | | | |
| **Veneer** | | | | | | | |
| | Demolish | S.Y. | | 4.94 | | 4.94 | Includes materials and labor to install |
| | Install | S.Y. | .72 | 3.87 | .33 | 4.92 | thin coat veneer plaster. |
| | Demolish and Install | S.Y. | .72 | 8.81 | .33 | 9.86 | |
| | Clean | S.Y. | | 2.54 | | 2.54 | |
| | Paint | S.Y. | 1.72 | 4.20 | | 5.92 | |
| | Minimum Charge | Job | | 162 | | 162 | |
| **Lath** | | | | | | | |
| **Metal** | | | | | | | |
| | Demolish | S.Y. | | 1.16 | | 1.16 | Includes material and labor to install |
| | Install | S.Y. | 4.22 | 5.25 | | 9.47 | wire lath on steel framed ceilings. |
| | Demolish and Install | S.Y. | 4.22 | 6.41 | | 10.63 | |
| | Minimum Charge | Job | | 162 | | 162 | |
| **Gypsum** | | | | | | | |
| | Demolish | S.Y. | | 1.16 | | 1.16 | Includes material and labor to install |
| | Install | S.Y. | 6.15 | 3.29 | | 9.44 | gypsum lath on ceilings. |
| | Demolish and Install | S.Y. | 6.15 | 4.45 | | 10.60 | |
| | Minimum Charge | Job | | 162 | | 162 | |
| **Repairs** | | | | | | | |
| **Fill in Small Cracks** | | | | | | | |
| | Install | S.F. | .06 | .59 | | .65 | Includes labor and material to fill in |
| | Minimum Charge | Job | | 325 | | 325 | hairline cracks up to 1/8" with filler, sand and prep for paint. |

| Gypsum Wallboard | | Unit | Material | Labor | Equip. | Total | Specification |
|---|---|---|---|---|---|---|---|
| **Finished** | | | | | | | |
| **1/4"** | | | | | | | |
| | Demolish | S.F. | | .30 | | .30 | Cost includes material and labor to |
| | Install | S.F. | .25 | 1.10 | | 1.35 | install 1/4" drywall, including joint |
| | Demolish and Install | S.F. | .25 | 1.40 | | 1.65 | taping, premixed compound and |
| | Clean | S.F. | | .24 | | .24 | screws. |
| | Paint | S.F. | .23 | .28 | | .51 | |
| | Minimum Charge | Job | | 181 | | 181 | |
| **3/8"** | | | | | | | |
| | Demolish | S.F. | | .30 | | .30 | Cost includes material and labor to |
| | Install | S.F. | .21 | 1.11 | | 1.32 | install 3/8" drywall including joint |
| | Demolish and Install | S.F. | .21 | 1.41 | | 1.62 | tape, premixed compound and |
| | Clean | S.F. | | .24 | | .24 | screws. |
| | Paint | S.F. | .23 | .28 | | .51 | |
| | Minimum Charge | Job | | 181 | | 181 | |

# Walls / Ceilings

| Gypsum Wallboard | | Unit | Material | Labor | Equip. | Total | Specification |
|---|---|---|---|---|---|---|---|
| **1/2″** | | | | | | | |
| | Demolish | S.F. | | .30 | | .30 | Cost includes material and labor to |
| | Install | S.F. | .24 | 1.12 | | 1.36 | install 1/2″ drywall including joint |
| | Demolish and Install | S.F. | .24 | 1.42 | | 1.66 | tape, premixed compound and |
| | Clean | S.F. | | .24 | | .24 | screws. |
| | Paint | S.F. | .23 | .28 | | .51 | |
| | Minimum Charge | Job | | 181 | | 181 | |
| **1/2″ Water Resistant** | | | | | | | |
| | Demolish | S.F. | | .30 | | .30 | Cost includes material and labor to |
| | Install | S.F. | .29 | 1.12 | | 1.41 | install 1/2″ WR drywall including joint |
| | Demolish and Install | S.F. | .29 | 1.42 | | 1.71 | tape, premixed compound and |
| | Clean | S.F. | | .24 | | .24 | screws. |
| | Paint | S.F. | .23 | .28 | | .51 | |
| | Minimum Charge | Job | | 181 | | 181 | |
| **1/2″ Fire-rated** | | | | | | | |
| | Demolish | S.F. | | .30 | | .30 | Cost includes material and labor to |
| | Install | S.F. | .25 | 1.12 | | 1.37 | install 1/2″ FR drywall including |
| | Demolish and Install | S.F. | .25 | 1.42 | | 1.67 | screws. Taping and finishing not |
| | Clean | S.F. | | .24 | | .24 | included. |
| | Paint | S.F. | .23 | .28 | | .51 | |
| | Minimum Charge | Job | | 181 | | 181 | |
| **5/8″** | | | | | | | |
| | Demolish | S.F. | | .30 | | .30 | Cost includes material and labor to |
| | Install | S.F. | .29 | 1.27 | | 1.56 | install 5/8″ drywall including joint |
| | Demolish and Install | S.F. | .29 | 1.57 | | 1.86 | tape, premixed compound and |
| | Clean | S.F. | | .24 | | .24 | screws. |
| | Paint | S.F. | .23 | .28 | | .51 | |
| | Minimum Charge | Job | | 181 | | 181 | |
| **5/8″ Fire-rated** | | | | | | | |
| | Demolish | S.F. | | .30 | | .30 | Cost includes material and labor to |
| | Install | S.F. | .31 | 1.27 | | 1.58 | install 5/8″ FR drywall, including joint |
| | Demolish and Install | S.F. | .31 | 1.57 | | 1.88 | taping, premixed compound and |
| | Clean | S.F. | | .24 | | .24 | screws. |
| | Paint | S.F. | .23 | .28 | | .51 | |
| | Minimum Charge | Job | | 181 | | 181 | |
| **2-hour fire-rated** | | | | | | | |
| | Demolish | S.F. | | .74 | | .74 | Cost includes material and labor to |
| | Install | S.F. | .66 | 2.53 | | 3.19 | install 2 layers of 5/8″ type X drywall |
| | Demolish and Install | S.F. | .66 | 3.27 | | 3.93 | including joint taping, premixed |
| | Clean | S.F. | | .24 | | .24 | compound and screws. |
| | Paint | S.F. | .23 | .28 | | .51 | |
| | Minimum Charge | Job | | 181 | | 181 | |
| **Unfinished** | | | | | | | |
| **1/4″** | | | | | | | |
| | Demolish | S.F. | | .30 | | .30 | Cost includes material and labor to |
| | Install | S.F. | .21 | .38 | | .59 | install 1/4″ drywall including screws. |
| | Demolish and Install | S.F. | .21 | .68 | | .89 | Taping and finishing not included. |
| | Clean | S.F. | | .24 | | .24 | |
| | Minimum Charge | Job | | 181 | | 181 | |
| **3/8″** | | | | | | | |
| | Demolish | S.F. | | .30 | | .30 | Cost includes material and labor to |
| | Install | S.F. | .18 | .38 | | .56 | install 3/8″ drywall including screws. |
| | Demolish and Install | S.F. | .18 | .68 | | .86 | Tape, finish or texture is not included. |
| | Clean | S.F. | | .24 | | .24 | |
| | Minimum Charge | Job | | 181 | | 181 | |

# Walls / Ceilings

| Gypsum Wallboard | | Unit | Material | Labor | Equip. | Total | Specification |
|---|---|---|---|---|---|---|---|
| **1/2"** | | | | | | | |
| | Demolish | S.F. | | .30 | | .30 | Cost includes material and labor to |
| | Install | S.F. | .21 | .39 | | .60 | install 1/2" drywall including screws. |
| | Demolish and Install | S.F. | .21 | .69 | | .90 | Taping and finishing not included. |
| | Clean | S.F. | | .24 | | .24 | |
| | Minimum Charge | Job | | 181 | | 181 | |
| **1/2" Water Resistant** | | | | | | | |
| | Demolish | S.F. | | .30 | | .30 | Cost includes material and labor to |
| | Install | S.F. | .26 | .39 | | .65 | install 1/2" WR drywall including |
| | Demolish and Install | S.F. | .26 | .69 | | .95 | screws. Taping and finishing is not |
| | Clean | S.F. | | .24 | | .24 | included. |
| | Minimum Charge | Job | | 181 | | 181 | |
| **1/2" Fire-rated** | | | | | | | |
| | Demolish | S.F. | | .30 | | .30 | Cost includes labor and material to |
| | Install | S.F. | .21 | .26 | | .47 | install 1/2" FR drywall including |
| | Demolish and Install | S.F. | .21 | .56 | | .77 | screws. Tape, finish or texture is not |
| | Clean | S.F. | | .24 | | .24 | included. |
| | Minimum Charge | Job | | 181 | | 181 | |
| **5/8"** | | | | | | | |
| | Demolish | S.F. | | .30 | | .30 | Cost includes material and labor to |
| | Install | S.F. | .26 | .43 | | .69 | install 5/8" drywall including screws. |
| | Demolish and Install | S.F. | .26 | .73 | | .99 | Taping and finishing not included. |
| | Clean | S.F. | | .24 | | .24 | |
| | Minimum Charge | Job | | 181 | | 181 | |
| **5/8" Fire-rated** | | | | | | | |
| | Demolish | S.F. | | .30 | | .30 | Cost includes material and labor to |
| | Install | S.F. | .27 | .43 | | .70 | install 5/8" FR drywall including |
| | Demolish and Install | S.F. | .27 | .73 | | 1 | screws. Taping and finishing not |
| | Clean | S.F. | | .24 | | .24 | included. |
| | Minimum Charge | Job | | 181 | | 181 | |
| **2-hour Fire-rated** | | | | | | | |
| | Demolish | S.F. | | .74 | | .74 | Cost includes material and labor to |
| | Install | S.F. | .66 | 2.53 | | 3.19 | install 2 layers of 5/8" type X drywall |
| | Demolish and Install | S.F. | .66 | 3.27 | | 3.93 | including joint taping, premixed |
| | Clean | S.F. | | .24 | | .24 | compound and screws. |
| | Minimum Charge | Job | | 181 | | 181 | |
| **Accessories** | | | | | | | |
| **Tape & Finish** | | | | | | | |
| | Install | S.F. | .04 | .36 | | .40 | Includes labor and material for taping, |
| | Minimum Charge | Job | | 181 | | 181 | sanding and finish. |
| **Texture** | | | | | | | |
| **Sprayed** | | | | | | | |
| | Install | S.F. | .06 | .40 | | .46 | Includes labor and material to install |
| | Minimum Charge | Job | | 181 | | 181 | by spray, texture finish. |
| **Trowel** | | | | | | | |
| | Install | S.F. | .01 | .21 | | .22 | Includes labor and material to apply |
| | Minimum Charge | Job | | 181 | | 181 | hand troweled texture. |
| **Patch Hole in Gypsum Wallboard** | | | | | | | |
| | Install | S.F. | .43 | 48.50 | | 48.93 | Includes labor and material to patch a |
| | Minimum Charge | Job | | 181 | | 181 | one square foot area of damaged drywall. |
| **Furring Strips** | | | | | | | |
| | Demolish | S.F. | | .07 | | .07 | Cost includes material and labor to |
| | Install | S.F. | .10 | .80 | | .90 | install 1" x 2" furring strips, 16" O.C. |
| | Demolish and Install | S.F. | .10 | .87 | | .97 | per S.F. of surface area to be covered. |
| | Minimum Charge | Job | | 90.50 | | 90.50 | |

| Ceramic Wall Tile | Unit | Material | Labor | Equip. | Total | Specification |
|---|---|---|---|---|---|---|
| **Thin Set** | | | | | | |
| **2″ x 2″** | | | | | | |
| Demolish | S.F. | | .99 | | .99 | Cost includes material and labor to |
| Install | S.F. | 6.60 | 5.55 | | 12.15 | install 2″ x 2″ ceramic tile in organic |
| Demolish and Install | S.F. | 6.60 | 6.54 | | 13.14 | adhesive including cutting and grout. |
| Clean | S.F. | | .51 | | .51 | |
| Minimum Charge | Job | | 167 | | 167 | |
| **4-1/4″ x 4-1/4″** | | | | | | |
| Demolish | S.F. | | .99 | | .99 | Cost includes material and labor to |
| Install | S.F. | 2.44 | 3.14 | | 5.58 | install 4-1/4″ x 4-1/4″ ceramic tile in |
| Demolish and Install | S.F. | 2.44 | 4.13 | | 6.57 | organic adhesive including grout. |
| Clean | S.F. | | .51 | | .51 | |
| Minimum Charge | Job | | 167 | | 167 | |
| **6″ x 6″** | | | | | | |
| Demolish | S.F. | | .99 | | .99 | Cost includes material and labor to |
| Install | S.F. | 3.33 | 2.98 | | 6.31 | install 6″ x 6″ ceramic tile in organic |
| Demolish and Install | S.F. | 3.33 | 3.97 | | 7.30 | adhesive including and grout. |
| Clean | S.F. | | .51 | | .51 | |
| Minimum Charge | Job | | 167 | | 167 | |
| **8″ x 8″** | | | | | | |
| Demolish | S.F. | | .99 | | .99 | Cost includes material and labor to |
| Install | S.F. | 4.44 | 2.65 | | 7.09 | install 8″ x 8″ ceramic tile in organic |
| Demolish and Install | S.F. | 4.44 | 3.64 | | 8.08 | adhesive including cutting and grout. |
| Clean | S.F. | | .51 | | .51 | |
| Minimum Charge | Job | | 167 | | 167 | |
| **Thick Set** | | | | | | |
| **2″ x 2″** | | | | | | |
| Demolish | S.F. | | 1.19 | | 1.19 | Cost includes material and labor to |
| Install | S.F. | 5.15 | 6.65 | | 11.80 | install 2″ x 2″ ceramic tile in mortar |
| Demolish and Install | S.F. | 5.15 | 7.84 | | 12.99 | bed including cutting and grout. |
| Clean | S.F. | | .51 | | .51 | |
| Minimum Charge | Job | | 167 | | 167 | |
| **4-1/4″ x 4-1/4″** | | | | | | |
| Demolish | S.F. | | 1.19 | | 1.19 | Cost includes material and labor to |
| Install | S.F. | 7.25 | 6.65 | | 13.90 | install 4-1/4″ x 4-1/4″ ceramic tile in |
| Demolish and Install | S.F. | 7.25 | 7.84 | | 15.09 | mortar bed including cutting and |
| Clean | S.F. | | .51 | | .51 | grout. |
| Minimum Charge | Job | | 167 | | 167 | |
| **6″ x 6″** | | | | | | |
| Demolish | S.F. | | 1.19 | | 1.19 | Cost includes material and labor to |
| Install | S.F. | 7.75 | 6.05 | | 13.80 | install 6″ x 6″ ceramic tile in mortar |
| Demolish and Install | S.F. | 7.75 | 7.24 | | 14.99 | bed including cutting and grout. |
| Clean | S.F. | | .51 | | .51 | |
| Minimum Charge | Job | | 167 | | 167 | |
| **8″ x 8″** | | | | | | |
| Demolish | S.F. | | 1.19 | | 1.19 | Cost includes material and labor to |
| Install | S.F. | 10.10 | 5.55 | | 15.65 | install 8″ x 8″ ceramic tile in mortar |
| Demolish and Install | S.F. | 10.10 | 6.74 | | 16.84 | bed including cutting and grout. |
| Clean | S.F. | | .51 | | .51 | |
| Minimum Charge | Job | | 167 | | 167 | |
| **Re-grout** | | | | | | |
| Install | S.F. | .15 | 3.33 | | 3.48 | Includes material and labor to regrout |
| Minimum Charge | Job | | 167 | | 167 | ceramic tile walls. |

# Walls / Ceilings

| Wall Tile | | Unit | Material | Labor | Equip. | Total | Specification |
|---|---|---|---|---|---|---|---|
| **Mirror** | | | | | | | |
| **Custom Cut Wall** | | | | | | | |
| | Demolish | S.F. | | .56 | | .56 | Includes material and labor to install |
| | Install | S.F. | 1.83 | 3.60 | | 5.43 | distortion-free float glass mirror, 1/8" |
| | Demolish and Install | S.F. | 1.83 | 4.16 | | 5.99 | to 3/16" thick with cut and polished |
| | Clean | S.F. | .03 | .16 | | .19 | edges. |
| | Minimum Charge | Job | | 175 | | 175 | |
| **Beveled Wall** | | | | | | | |
| | Demolish | S.F. | | .56 | | .56 | Includes material and labor to install |
| | Install | S.F. | 5.15 | 6.40 | | 11.55 | distortion-free float glass mirror, 1/8" |
| | Demolish and Install | S.F. | 5.15 | 6.96 | | 12.11 | to 3/16" thick with beveled edges. |
| | Clean | S.F. | .03 | .16 | | .19 | |
| | Minimum Charge | Job | | 175 | | 175 | |
| **Smoked Wall** | | | | | | | |
| | Demolish | S.F. | | .56 | | .56 | Includes material and labor to install |
| | Install | S.F. | 7.35 | 6.40 | | 13.75 | distortion-free smoked float glass |
| | Demolish and Install | S.F. | 7.35 | 6.96 | | 14.31 | mirror, 1/8" to 3/16" thick with cut |
| | Clean | S.F. | .03 | .16 | | .19 | and polished edges. |
| | Minimum Charge | Job | | 175 | | 175 | |
| **Marble** | | | | | | | |
| **Good Grade** | | | | | | | |
| | Demolish | S.F. | | 1.85 | | 1.85 | Cost includes material and labor to |
| | Install | S.F. | 7.90 | 14.50 | | 22.40 | install 3/8" x 12" x 12" marble tile in |
| | Demolish and Install | S.F. | 7.90 | 16.35 | | 24.25 | mortar bed with grout. |
| | Clean | S.F. | | .51 | | .51 | |
| | Minimum Charge | Job | | 167 | | 167 | |
| **Better Grade** | | | | | | | |
| | Demolish | S.F. | | 1.85 | | 1.85 | Cost includes material and labor to |
| | Install | S.F. | 10.45 | 14.50 | | 24.95 | install 3/8" x 12" x 12" marble, in |
| | Demolish and Install | S.F. | 10.45 | 16.35 | | 26.80 | mortar bed with grout. |
| | Clean | S.F. | | .51 | | .51 | |
| | Minimum Charge | Job | | 167 | | 167 | |
| **Premium Grade** | | | | | | | |
| | Demolish | S.F. | | 1.85 | | 1.85 | Cost includes material and labor to |
| | Install | S.F. | 20 | 14.50 | | 34.50 | install 3/8" x 12" x 12" marble, in |
| | Demolish and Install | S.F. | 20 | 16.35 | | 36.35 | mortar bed with grout. |
| | Clean | S.F. | | .51 | | .51 | |
| | Minimum Charge | Job | | 167 | | 167 | |
| **Glass Block** | | | | | | | |
| | Demolish | S.F. | | 1.48 | | 1.48 | Cost includes material and labor to |
| | Install | S.F. | 21 | 14.45 | | 35.45 | install 3-7/8" thick, 6" x 6" smooth |
| | Demolish and Install | S.F. | 21 | 15.93 | | 36.93 | face glass block including mortar and |
| | Clean | S.F. | | .51 | | .51 | cleaning. |
| | Minimum Charge | Job | | 325 | | 325 | |
| **Plastic** | | | | | | | |
| | Demolish | S.F. | | .45 | | .45 | Cost includes material and labor to |
| | Install | S.F. | .99 | 1.90 | | 2.89 | install 4" plastic tile. |
| | Demolish and Install | S.F. | .99 | 2.35 | | 3.34 | |
| | Clean | S.F. | | .51 | | .51 | |
| | Minimum Charge | Job | | 167 | | 167 | |
| **Cork** | | | | | | | |
| | Demolish | S.F. | | .23 | | .23 | Cost includes material and labor to |
| | Install | S.F. | 4.46 | 1.31 | | 5.77 | install 3/16" thick cork tile and |
| | Demolish and Install | S.F. | 4.46 | 1.54 | | 6 | installation. |
| | Clean | S.F. | | .51 | | .51 | |
| | Minimum Charge | Job | | 157 | | 157 | |

# Walls / Ceilings

| Wall Tile | | Unit | Material | Labor | Equip. | Total | Specification |
|---|---|---|---|---|---|---|---|
| **Re-grout** | | | | | | | |
| | Install | S.F. | .15 | 3.33 | | 3.48 | Includes material and labor to regrout |
| | Minimum Charge | Job | | 167 | | 167 | ceramic tile walls. |

| Wall Paneling | | Unit | Material | Labor | Equip. | Total | Specification |
|---|---|---|---|---|---|---|---|
| **Plywood** | | | | | | | |
| **Good Grade** | | | | | | | |
| | Demolish | S.F. | | .30 | | .30 | Cost includes material and labor to |
| | Install | S.F. | .96 | 1.45 | | 2.41 | install 4' x 8' x 1/4" paneling, |
| | Demolish and Install | S.F. | .96 | 1.75 | | 2.71 | including nails and adhesive. |
| | Clean | S.F. | | .24 | | .24 | |
| | Paint | S.F. | .20 | .42 | | .62 | |
| | Minimum Charge | Job | | 181 | | 181 | |
| **Better Grade** | | | | | | | |
| | Demolish | S.F. | | .30 | | .30 | Cost includes material and labor to |
| | Install | S.F. | 1.45 | 1.72 | | 3.17 | install 4' x 8' x 1/4" plywood wall |
| | Demolish and Install | S.F. | 1.45 | 2.02 | | 3.47 | panel, including nails and adhesive. |
| | Clean | S.F. | | .24 | | .24 | |
| | Paint | S.F. | .20 | .42 | | .62 | |
| | Minimum Charge | Job | | 181 | | 181 | |
| **Premium Grade** | | | | | | | |
| | Demolish | S.F. | | .30 | | .30 | Cost includes material and labor to |
| | Install | S.F. | 2.12 | 2.07 | | 4.19 | install 4' x 8' x 1/4" plywood wall |
| | Demolish and Install | S.F. | 2.12 | 2.37 | | 4.49 | panel, including nails and adhesive. |
| | Clean | S.F. | | .24 | | .24 | |
| | Paint | S.F. | .20 | .42 | | .62 | |
| | Minimum Charge | Job | | 181 | | 181 | |
| **Hardboard** | | | | | | | |
| **Embossed Paneling** | | | | | | | |
| | Demolish | S.F. | | .30 | | .30 | Includes material and labor to install |
| | Install | S.F. | .70 | 1.45 | | 2.15 | hardboard embossed paneling |
| | Demolish and Install | S.F. | .70 | 1.75 | | 2.45 | including adhesives. |
| | Clean | S.F. | | .24 | | .24 | |
| | Minimum Charge | Job | | 181 | | 181 | |
| **Plastic Molding** | | | | | | | |
| | Demolish | L.F. | | .30 | | .30 | Includes material and labor to install |
| | Install | L.F. | .64 | .90 | | 1.54 | plastic trim for paneling. |
| | Demolish and Install | L.F. | .64 | 1.20 | | 1.84 | |
| | Clean | L.F. | .03 | .16 | | .19 | |
| | Minimum Charge | Job | | 181 | | 181 | |
| **Hardboard** | | | | | | | |
| **Embossed Brick** | | | | | | | |
| | Demolish | S.F. | | .30 | | .30 | Cost includes material and labor to |
| | Install | S.F. | 2.31 | 1.61 | | 3.92 | install 4' x 8' non-ceramic mineral |
| | Demolish and Install | S.F. | 2.31 | 1.91 | | 4.22 | brick-like veneer wall panels including |
| | Clean | S.F. | | .24 | | .24 | adhesive. |
| | Paint | S.F. | .19 | .47 | | .66 | |
| | Minimum Charge | Job | | 181 | | 181 | |
| **Embossed Ceramic Tile** | | | | | | | |
| | Demolish | S.F. | | .30 | | .30 | Includes material and labor to install |
| | Install | S.F. | .70 | 1.45 | | 2.15 | hardboard embossed paneling |
| | Demolish and Install | S.F. | .70 | 1.75 | | 2.45 | including adhesives. |
| | Clean | S.F. | | .24 | | .24 | |
| | Paint | S.F. | .19 | .47 | | .66 | |
| | Minimum Charge | Job | | 181 | | 181 | |

| Wall Paneling | | Unit | Material | Labor | Equip. | Total | Specification |
|---|---|---|---|---|---|---|---|
| **Pegboard** | | | | | | | |
| | Demolish | S.F. | | .30 | | .30 | Cost includes material and labor to |
| | Install | S.F. | .46 | 1.45 | | 1.91 | install 4' x 8' x 1/4" pegboard panel, |
| | Demolish and Install | S.F. | .46 | 1.75 | | 2.21 | including adhesive. |
| | Clean | S.F. | | .24 | | .24 | |
| | Paint | S.F. | .19 | .47 | | .66 | |
| | Minimum Charge | Job | | 181 | | 181 | |
| **Furring Strips** | | | | | | | |
| | Demolish | S.F. | | .07 | | .07 | Cost includes material and labor to |
| | Install | S.F. | .10 | .80 | | .90 | install 1" x 2" furring strips, 16" O.C. |
| | Demolish and Install | S.F. | .10 | .87 | | .97 | per S.F. of surface area to be covered. |
| | Minimum Charge | Job | | 181 | | 181 | |
| **Molding** | | | | | | | |
| **Unfinished Base** | | | | | | | |
| | Demolish | L.F. | | .49 | | .49 | Cost includes material and labor to |
| | Install | L.F. | .57 | 1.11 | | 1.68 | install 1/2" x 2-1/2" pine or birch |
| | Demolish and Install | L.F. | .57 | 1.60 | | 2.17 | base molding. |
| | Reinstall | L.F. | | .89 | | .89 | |
| | Clean | L.F. | .03 | .16 | | .19 | |
| | Paint | L.F. | .03 | .34 | | .37 | |
| | Minimum Charge | Job | | 181 | | 181 | |
| **Unfinished Corner** | | | | | | | |
| | Demolish | L.F. | | .49 | | .49 | Includes material and labor to install |
| | Install | L.F. | 1.74 | 1.51 | | 3.25 | unfinished pine corner molding. |
| | Demolish and Install | L.F. | 1.74 | 2 | | 3.74 | |
| | Reinstall | L.F. | | 1.21 | | 1.21 | |
| | Clean | Ea. | .91 | 24 | | 24.91 | |
| | Paint | L.F. | .13 | .50 | | .63 | |
| | Minimum Charge | Job | | 181 | | 181 | |
| **Unfinished Cove** | | | | | | | |
| | Demolish | L.F. | | .49 | | .49 | Cost includes material and labor to |
| | Install | L.F. | 1.56 | 1.34 | | 2.90 | install 3/4" x 3-1/2" unfinished pine |
| | Demolish and Install | L.F. | 1.56 | 1.83 | | 3.39 | cove molding. |
| | Reinstall | L.F. | | 1.07 | | 1.07 | |
| | Clean | Ea. | .91 | 24 | | 24.91 | |
| | Paint | L.F. | .13 | .50 | | .63 | |
| | Minimum Charge | Job | | 181 | | 181 | |
| **Unfinished Crown** | | | | | | | |
| | Demolish | L.F. | | .59 | | .59 | Includes material and labor to install |
| | Install | L.F. | 1.97 | 1.45 | | 3.42 | unfinished pine crown molding. |
| | Demolish and Install | L.F. | 1.97 | 2.04 | | 4.01 | |
| | Reinstall | L.F. | | 1.16 | | 1.16 | |
| | Clean | L.F. | .04 | .21 | | .25 | |
| | Paint | L.F. | .06 | .34 | | .40 | |
| | Minimum Charge | Job | | 181 | | 181 | |
| **Prefinished Base** | | | | | | | |
| | Demolish | L.F. | | .49 | | .49 | Cost includes material and labor to |
| | Install | L.F. | 1.69 | 1.16 | | 2.85 | install 9/16" x 3-5/16" prefinished |
| | Demolish and Install | L.F. | 1.69 | 1.65 | | 3.34 | base molding. |
| | Reinstall | L.F. | | .93 | | .93 | |
| | Clean | L.F. | .03 | .16 | | .19 | |
| | Paint | L.F. | .03 | .34 | | .37 | |
| | Minimum Charge | Job | | 181 | | 181 | |

# Walls / Ceilings

## Wall Paneling

| Wall Paneling | Unit | Material | Labor | Equip. | Total | Specification |
|---|---|---|---|---|---|---|
| **Prefinished Corner** | | | | | | |
| Demolish | L.F. | | .49 | | .49 | Includes material and labor to install |
| Install | L.F. | 2.09 | 1.51 | | 3.60 | inside or outside prefinished corner |
| Demolish and Install | L.F. | 2.09 | 2 | | 4.09 | molding. |
| Reinstall | L.F. | | 1.21 | | 1.21 | |
| Clean | L.F. | | .10 | | .10 | |
| Paint | L.F. | .13 | .50 | | .63 | |
| Minimum Charge | Job | | 181 | | 181 | |
| **Prefinished Crown** | | | | | | |
| Demolish | L.F. | | .59 | | .59 | Cost includes material and labor to |
| Install | L.F. | 2.24 | 1.45 | | 3.69 | install 3/4" x 3-13/16" prefinished |
| Demolish and Install | L.F. | 2.24 | 2.04 | | 4.28 | crown molding. |
| Reinstall | L.F. | | 1.16 | | 1.16 | |
| Clean | L.F. | .04 | .21 | | .25 | |
| Paint | L.F. | .06 | .34 | | .40 | |
| Minimum Charge | Job | | 181 | | 181 | |

## Wallcovering

| Wallcovering | Unit | Material | Labor | Equip. | Total | Specification |
|---|---|---|---|---|---|---|
| **Surface Prep** | | | | | | |
| **Patch Walls** | | | | | | |
| Install | S.F. | .12 | 3.25 | | 3.37 | Includes labor and material to repair |
| Minimum Charge | Job | | 157 | | 157 | section of plaster wall, area less than |
| | | | | | | 20 S.F. |
| **Sizing** | | | | | | |
| Install | S.F. | .08 | .16 | | .24 | Includes labor and materials to apply |
| Minimum Charge | Job | | 157 | | 157 | wall sizing. |
| **Good Grade** | | | | | | |
| **Walls** | | | | | | |
| Demolish | S.F. | | .58 | | .58 | Includes material and labor to install |
| Install | S.F. | .90 | .66 | | 1.56 | pre-pasted, vinyl-coated wallcovering. |
| Demolish and Install | S.F. | .90 | 1.24 | | 2.14 | |
| Clean | S.F. | .01 | .06 | | .07 | |
| Minimum Charge | Job | | 157 | | 157 | |
| **Ceiling** | | | | | | |
| Demolish | S.F. | | .58 | | .58 | Includes material and labor to install |
| Install | S.F. | .90 | .66 | | 1.56 | pre-pasted, vinyl-coated wallcovering. |
| Demolish and Install | S.F. | .90 | 1.24 | | 2.14 | |
| Clean | S.F. | .03 | .16 | | .19 | |
| Minimum Charge | Job | | 157 | | 157 | |
| **Better Grade** | | | | | | |
| **Walls** | | | | | | |
| Demolish | S.F. | | .58 | | .58 | Includes material and labor to install |
| Install | S.F. | 1 | .66 | | 1.66 | pre-pasted, vinyl-coated wallcovering. |
| Demolish and Install | S.F. | 1 | 1.24 | | 2.24 | |
| Clean | S.F. | .01 | .06 | | .07 | |
| Minimum Charge | Job | | 157 | | 157 | |
| **Ceiling** | | | | | | |
| Demolish | S.F. | | .58 | | .58 | Includes material and labor to install |
| Install | S.F. | 1 | .66 | | 1.66 | pre-pasted, vinyl-coated wallcovering. |
| Demolish and Install | S.F. | 1 | 1.24 | | 2.24 | |
| Clean | S.F. | .03 | .16 | | .19 | |
| Minimum Charge | Job | | 157 | | 157 | |

# Walls / Ceilings

| Wallcovering | | Unit | Material | Labor | Equip. | Total | Specification |
|---|---|---|---|---|---|---|---|
| **Premium Grade** | | | | | | | |
| **Walls** | | | | | | | |
| | Demolish | S.F. | | .73 | | .73 | Includes material and labor to install |
| | Install | S.F. | 1.27 | .66 | | 1.93 | pre-pasted, vinyl-coated wallcovering. |
| | Demolish and Install | S.F. | 1.27 | 1.39 | | 2.66 | |
| | Clean | S.F. | .01 | .06 | | .07 | |
| | Minimum Charge | Job | | 157 | | 157 | |
| **Ceiling** | | | | | | | |
| | Demolish | S.F. | | .73 | | .73 | Includes material and labor to install |
| | Install | S.F. | 1.27 | .66 | | 1.93 | pre-pasted, vinyl-coated wallcovering. |
| | Demolish and Install | S.F. | 1.27 | 1.39 | | 2.66 | |
| | Clean | S.F. | .03 | .16 | | .19 | |
| | Minimum Charge | Job | | 157 | | 157 | |
| **Mural** | | | | | | | |
| **Pre-printed** | | | | | | | |
| | Demolish | Ea. | | 92.50 | | 92.50 | Includes material and labor to install |
| | Install | Ea. | 238 | 237 | | 475 | wallcovering with a pre-printed mural. |
| | Demolish and Install | Ea. | 238 | 329.50 | | 567.50 | |
| | Clean | Ea. | | 6.65 | | 6.65 | |
| | Minimum Charge | Job | | 157 | | 157 | |
| **Hand-painted** | | | | | | | |
| | Demolish | Ea. | | 92.50 | | 92.50 | Includes material and labor to install |
| | Install | Ea. | 475 | 475 | | 950 | wallcovering with a hand-painted |
| | Demolish and Install | Ea. | 475 | 567.50 | | 1042.50 | mural. |
| | Clean | Ea. | | 6.65 | | 6.65 | |
| | Minimum Charge | Job | | 157 | | 157 | |
| **Vinyl-coated** | | | | | | | |
| **Good Grade** | | | | | | | |
| | Demolish | Ea. | | 16.45 | | 16.45 | Includes material and labor to install |
| | Install | Ea. | 19.80 | 22 | | 41.80 | pre-pasted, vinyl-coated wallcovering. |
| | Demolish and Install | Ea. | 19.80 | 38.45 | | 58.25 | Based upon 30 S.F. rolls. |
| | Clean | Ea. | | 6.65 | | 6.65 | |
| | Minimum Charge | Job | | 157 | | 157 | |
| **Better Grade** | | | | | | | |
| | Demolish | Ea. | | 16.45 | | 16.45 | Includes material and labor to install |
| | Install | Ea. | 26.50 | 22 | | 48.50 | pre-pasted, vinyl-coated wallcovering. |
| | Demolish and Install | Ea. | 26.50 | 38.45 | | 64.95 | Based upon 30 S.F. rolls. |
| | Clean | Ea. | | 6.65 | | 6.65 | |
| | Minimum Charge | Job | | 157 | | 157 | |
| **Premium Grade** | | | | | | | |
| | Demolish | Ea. | | 16.45 | | 16.45 | Includes material and labor to install |
| | Install | Ea. | 46 | 22 | | 68 | pre-pasted, vinyl-coated wallcovering. |
| | Demolish and Install | Ea. | 46 | 38.45 | | 84.45 | Based upon 30 S.F. rolls. |
| | Clean | Ea. | | 6.65 | | 6.65 | |
| | Minimum Charge | Job | | 157 | | 157 | |
| **Blank Underliner** | | | | | | | |
| | Demolish | Ea. | | 16.45 | | 16.45 | Includes material and labor to install |
| | Install | Ea. | 11.70 | 22.50 | | 34.20 | blank stock liner paper or bridging |
| | Demolish and Install | Ea. | 11.70 | 38.95 | | 50.65 | paper. Based upon 30 S.F. rolls. |
| | Clean | Ea. | | 6.65 | | 6.65 | |
| | Minimum Charge | Job | | 157 | | 157 | |
| **Solid Vinyl** | | | | | | | |
| **Good Grade** | | | | | | | |
| | Demolish | Roll | | 19.45 | | 19.45 | Includes material and labor to install |
| | Install | Ea. | 26.50 | 22 | | 48.50 | pre-pasted, vinyl wallcovering. Based |
| | Demolish and Install | Ea. | 26.50 | 41.45 | | 67.95 | upon 30 S.F. rolls. |
| | Clean | Ea. | | 6.65 | | 6.65 | |
| | Minimum Charge | Job | | 157 | | 157 | |

| Wallcovering | | Unit | Material | Labor | Equip. | Total | Specification |
|---|---|---|---|---|---|---|---|
| **Better Grade** | | | | | | | |
| | Demolish | Roll | | 19.45 | | 19.45 | Includes material and labor to install |
| | Install | Ea. | 37 | 22 | | 59 | pre-pasted, vinyl wallcovering. Based |
| | Demolish and Install | Ea. | 37 | 41.45 | | 78.45 | upon 30 S.F. rolls. |
| | Clean | Ea. | | 6.65 | | 6.65 | |
| | Minimum Charge | Job | | 157 | | 157 | |
| **Premium Grade** | | | | | | | |
| | Demolish | Roll | | 19.45 | | 19.45 | Includes material and labor to install |
| | Install | Ea. | 47 | 22 | | 69 | pre-pasted, vinyl wallcovering. Based |
| | Demolish and Install | Ea. | 47 | 41.45 | | 88.45 | upon 30 S.F. rolls. |
| | Clean | Ea. | | 6.65 | | 6.65 | |
| | Minimum Charge | Job | | 157 | | 157 | |
| **Blank Underliner** | | | | | | | |
| | Demolish | Ea. | | 16.45 | | 16.45 | Includes material and labor to install |
| | Install | Ea. | 11.70 | 22.50 | | 34.20 | blank stock liner paper or bridging |
| | Demolish and Install | Ea. | 11.70 | 38.95 | | 50.65 | paper. Based upon 30 S.F. rolls. |
| | Clean | Ea. | | 6.65 | | 6.65 | |
| | Minimum Charge | Job | | 157 | | 157 | |
| **Grasscloth / String** | | | | | | | |
| **Good Grade** | | | | | | | |
| | Demolish | Ea. | | 16.45 | | 16.45 | Includes material and labor to install |
| | Install | Ea. | 37.50 | 28.50 | | 66 | grasscloth or string wallcovering. |
| | Demolish and Install | Ea. | 37.50 | 44.95 | | 82.45 | Based upon 30 S.F. rolls. |
| | Clean | Ea. | | 8.90 | | 8.90 | |
| | Minimum Charge | Job | | 157 | | 157 | |
| **Better Grade** | | | | | | | |
| | Demolish | Ea. | | 16.45 | | 16.45 | Includes material and labor to install |
| | Install | Ea. | 48.50 | 28.50 | | 77 | grasscloth or string wallcovering. |
| | Demolish and Install | Ea. | 48.50 | 44.95 | | 93.45 | Based upon 30 S.F. rolls. |
| | Clean | Ea. | | 8.90 | | 8.90 | |
| | Minimum Charge | Job | | 157 | | 157 | |
| **Premium Grade** | | | | | | | |
| | Demolish | Ea. | | 16.45 | | 16.45 | Includes material and labor to install |
| | Install | Ea. | 61.50 | 28.50 | | 90 | grasscloth or string wallcovering. |
| | Demolish and Install | Ea. | 61.50 | 44.95 | | 106.45 | Based upon 30 S.F. rolls. |
| | Clean | Ea. | | 8.90 | | 8.90 | |
| | Minimum Charge | Job | | 157 | | 157 | |
| **Blank Underliner** | | | | | | | |
| | Demolish | Ea. | | 16.45 | | 16.45 | Includes material and labor to install |
| | Install | Ea. | 11.70 | 22.50 | | 34.20 | blank stock liner paper or bridging |
| | Demolish and Install | Ea. | 11.70 | 38.95 | | 50.65 | paper. Based upon 30 S.F. rolls. |
| | Clean | Ea. | | 6.65 | | 6.65 | |
| | Minimum Charge | Job | | 157 | | 157 | |
| **Designer** | | | | | | | |
| **Premium Grade** | | | | | | | |
| | Demolish | S.F. | | .73 | | .73 | Includes material and labor to install |
| | Install | Ea. | 116 | 33 | | 149 | paperback vinyl, untrimmed and |
| | Demolish and Install | Ea. | 116 | 33.73 | | 149.73 | hand-painted. Based upon 30 S.F. |
| | Clean | Ea. | | 6.65 | | 6.65 | rolls. |
| | Minimum Charge | Job | | 157 | | 157 | |
| **Blank Underliner** | | | | | | | |
| | Demolish | Ea. | | 16.45 | | 16.45 | Includes material and labor to install |
| | Install | Ea. | 11.70 | 22.50 | | 34.20 | blank stock liner paper or bridging |
| | Demolish and Install | Ea. | 11.70 | 38.95 | | 50.65 | paper. Based upon 30 S.F. rolls. |
| | Clean | Ea. | | 6.65 | | 6.65 | |
| | Minimum Charge | Job | | 157 | | 157 | |

# Walls / Ceilings

| Wallcovering | | Unit | Material | Labor | Equip. | Total | Specification |
|---|---|---|---|---|---|---|---|
| **Foil** | | | | | | | |
| | Demolish | Ea. | | 16.45 | | 16.45 | Includes material and labor to install |
| | Install | Ea. | 39.50 | 28.50 | | 68 | foil coated wallcovering. Based upon |
| | Demolish and Install | Ea. | 39.50 | 44.95 | | 84.45 | 30 S.F. rolls. |
| | Clean | Ea. | | 6.65 | | 6.65 | |
| | Minimum Charge | Job | | 157 | | 157 | |
| **Wallcovering Border** | | | | | | | |
| **Good Grade** | | | | | | | |
| | Demolish | L.F. | | 1.08 | | 1.08 | Includes material and labor install |
| | Install | L.F. | 1.97 | 1.21 | | 3.18 | vinyl-coated border 4" to 6" wide. |
| | Demolish and Install | L.F. | 1.97 | 2.29 | | 4.26 | |
| | Clean | L.F. | | .10 | | .10 | |
| | Minimum Charge | Job | | 157 | | 157 | |
| **Better Grade** | | | | | | | |
| | Demolish | L.F. | | 1.08 | | 1.08 | Includes material and labor install |
| | Install | L.F. | 2.63 | 1.21 | | 3.84 | vinyl-coated border 4" to 6" wide. |
| | Demolish and Install | L.F. | 2.63 | 2.29 | | 4.92 | |
| | Clean | L.F. | | .10 | | .10 | |
| | Minimum Charge | Job | | 157 | | 157 | |
| **Premium Grade** | | | | | | | |
| | Demolish | L.F. | | 1.08 | | 1.08 | Includes material and labor install |
| | Install | L.F. | 3.30 | 1.21 | | 4.51 | vinyl-coated border 4" to 6" wide. |
| | Demolish and Install | L.F. | 3.30 | 2.29 | | 5.59 | |
| | Clean | L.F. | | .10 | | .10 | |
| | Minimum Charge | Job | | 157 | | 157 | |

| Acoustical Ceiling | | Unit | Material | Labor | Equip. | Total | Specification |
|---|---|---|---|---|---|---|---|
| **Complete System** | | | | | | | |
| **2' x 2' Square Edge** | | | | | | | |
| | Demolish | S.F. | | .49 | | .49 | Includes material and labor to install |
| | Install | S.F. | 1.36 | 1.11 | | 2.47 | T-bar grid acoustical ceiling system, |
| | Demolish and Install | S.F. | 1.36 | 1.60 | | 2.96 | random pinhole 5/8" thick square |
| | Reinstall | S.F. | | .89 | | .89 | edge tile. |
| | Clean | S.F. | .04 | .20 | | .24 | |
| | Minimum Charge | Job | | 181 | | 181 | |
| **2' x 2' Reveal Edge** | | | | | | | |
| | Demolish | S.F. | | .49 | | .49 | Includes material and labor to install |
| | Install | S.F. | 2.29 | 1.45 | | 3.74 | T-bar grid acoustical ceiling system, |
| | Demolish and Install | S.F. | 2.29 | 1.94 | | 4.23 | random pinhole 5/8" thick reveal |
| | Reinstall | S.F. | | 1.16 | | 1.16 | edge tile. |
| | Clean | S.F. | .04 | .20 | | .24 | |
| | Minimum Charge | Job | | 181 | | 181 | |
| **2' x 2' Fire-rated** | | | | | | | |
| | Demolish | S.F. | | .49 | | .49 | Includes material and labor to install |
| | Install | S.F. | 2.62 | 1.11 | | 3.73 | T-bar grid FR acoustical ceiling system, |
| | Demolish and Install | S.F. | 2.62 | 1.60 | | 4.22 | random pinhole 5/8" thick square |
| | Reinstall | S.F. | | .89 | | .89 | edge tile. |
| | Clean | S.F. | .04 | .20 | | .24 | |
| | Minimum Charge | Job | | 181 | | 181 | |
| **2' x 4' Square Edge** | | | | | | | |
| | Demolish | S.F. | | .49 | | .49 | Cost includes material and labor to |
| | Install | S.F. | 1.16 | .95 | | 2.11 | install 2' x 4' T-bar grid acoustical |
| | Demolish and Install | S.F. | 1.16 | 1.44 | | 2.60 | ceiling system, random pinhole 5/8" |
| | Reinstall | S.F. | | .76 | | .76 | thick square edge tile. |
| | Clean | S.F. | .04 | .20 | | .24 | |
| | Minimum Charge | Job | | 181 | | 181 | |

# Walls / Ceilings

| Acoustical Ceiling | | Unit | Material | Labor | Equip. | Total | Specification |
|---|---|---|---|---|---|---|---|
| **2' x 4' Reveal Edge** | | | | | | | |
| | Demolish | S.F. | | .49 | | .49 | Includes material and labor to install |
| | Install | S.F. | 2.29 | 1.31 | | 3.60 | T-bar grid acoustical ceiling system, |
| | Demolish and Install | S.F. | 2.29 | 1.80 | | 4.09 | random pinhole 5/8" thick reveal |
| | Reinstall | S.F. | | 1.05 | | 1.05 | edge tile. |
| | Clean | S.F. | .04 | .20 | | .24 | |
| | Minimum Charge | Job | | 181 | | 181 | |
| **2' x 4' Fire-rated** | | | | | | | |
| | Demolish | S.F. | | .49 | | .49 | Includes material and labor to install |
| | Install | S.F. | 2.62 | 1.11 | | 3.73 | T-bar grid FR acoustical ceiling system, |
| | Demolish and Install | S.F. | 2.62 | 1.60 | | 4.22 | random pinhole 5/8" thick square |
| | Reinstall | S.F. | | .89 | | .89 | edge tile. |
| | Clean | S.F. | .04 | .20 | | .24 | |
| | Minimum Charge | Job | | 181 | | 181 | |
| **T-bar Grid** | | | | | | | |
| **2' x 2'** | | | | | | | |
| | Demolish | S.F. | | .58 | | .58 | Includes material and labor to install |
| | Install | S.F. | .73 | .56 | | 1.29 | T-bar grid acoustical ceiling |
| | Demolish and Install | S.F. | .73 | 1.14 | | 1.87 | suspension system. |
| | Reinstall | S.F. | | .45 | | .45 | |
| | Clean | S.F. | .04 | .20 | | .24 | |
| | Minimum Charge | Job | | 162 | | 162 | |
| **2' x 4'** | | | | | | | |
| | Demolish | S.F. | | .58 | | .58 | Includes material and labor to install |
| | Install | S.F. | .58 | .45 | | 1.03 | T-bar grid acoustical ceiling |
| | Demolish and Install | S.F. | .58 | 1.03 | | 1.61 | suspension system. |
| | Reinstall | S.F. | | .36 | | .36 | |
| | Clean | S.F. | .04 | .20 | | .24 | |
| | Minimum Charge | Job | | 162 | | 162 | |
| **Tile Panels** | | | | | | | |
| **2' x 2' Square Edge** | | | | | | | |
| | Demolish | S.F. | | .16 | | .16 | Includes material and labor to install |
| | Install | S.F. | .57 | .58 | | 1.15 | square edge panels 5/8" thick with |
| | Demolish and Install | S.F. | .57 | .74 | | 1.31 | pinhole pattern. T-bar grid not |
| | Reinstall | S.F. | | .46 | | .46 | included. |
| | Clean | S.F. | .04 | .20 | | .24 | |
| | Minimum Charge | Job | | 181 | | 181 | |
| **2' x 2' Reveal Edge** | | | | | | | |
| | Demolish | S.F. | | .16 | | .16 | Includes material and labor to install |
| | Install | S.F. | 1.39 | .77 | | 2.16 | reveal edge panels 5/8" thick with |
| | Demolish and Install | S.F. | 1.39 | .93 | | 2.32 | pinhole pattern. T-bar grid not |
| | Reinstall | S.F. | | .62 | | .62 | included. |
| | Clean | S.F. | .04 | .20 | | .24 | |
| | Minimum Charge | Job | | 181 | | 181 | |
| **2' x 2' Fire-rated** | | | | | | | |
| | Demolish | S.F. | | .16 | | .16 | Includes material and labor to install |
| | Install | S.F. | 1.12 | .54 | | 1.66 | FR square edge panels 5/8" thick with |
| | Demolish and Install | S.F. | 1.12 | .70 | | 1.82 | pinhole pattern. T-bar grid not |
| | Reinstall | S.F. | | .43 | | .43 | included. |
| | Clean | S.F. | .04 | .20 | | .24 | |
| | Minimum Charge | Job | | 181 | | 181 | |
| **2' x 4' Square Edge** | | | | | | | |
| | Demolish | S.F. | | .16 | | .16 | Includes material and labor to install |
| | Install | S.F. | .57 | .58 | | 1.15 | square edge panels 5/8" thick with |
| | Demolish and Install | S.F. | .57 | .74 | | 1.31 | pinhole pattern. T-bar grid not |
| | Reinstall | S.F. | | .46 | | .46 | included. |
| | Clean | S.F. | .04 | .20 | | .24 | |
| | Minimum Charge | Job | | 181 | | 181 | |

# Walls / Ceilings

| Acoustical Ceiling | | Unit | Material | Labor | Equip. | Total | Specification |
|---|---|---|---|---|---|---|---|
| **2' x 4' Reveal Edge** | | | | | | | |
| | Demolish | S.F. | | .16 | | .16 | Includes material and labor to install |
| | Install | S.F. | 1.39 | .77 | | 2.16 | reveal edge panels 5/8" thick with |
| | Demolish and Install | S.F. | 1.39 | .93 | | 2.32 | pinhole pattern. T-bar grid not |
| | Reinstall | S.F. | | .62 | | .62 | included. |
| | Clean | S.F. | .04 | .20 | | .24 | |
| | Minimum Charge | Job | | 181 | | 181 | |
| **2' x 4' Fire-rated** | | | | | | | |
| | Demolish | S.F. | | .16 | | .16 | Includes material and labor to install |
| | Install | S.F. | 1.12 | .54 | | 1.66 | FR square edge panels 5/8" thick with |
| | Demolish and Install | S.F. | 1.12 | .70 | | 1.82 | pinhole pattern. T-bar grid not |
| | Reinstall | S.F. | | .43 | | .43 | included. |
| | Clean | S.F. | .04 | .20 | | .24 | |
| | Minimum Charge | Job | | 181 | | 181 | |
| **Bleach Out Stains** | | | | | | | |
| | Install | S.F. | .10 | .27 | | .37 | Includes labor and material to apply |
| | Minimum Charge | Job | | 181 | | 181 | laundry type chlorine bleach to |
| | | | | | | | remove light staining of acoustic tile |
| | | | | | | | material. |
| **Adhesive Tile** | | | | | | | |
| **Good Grade** | | | | | | | |
| | Demolish | S.F. | | .66 | | .66 | Cost includes material and labor to |
| | Install | S.F. | .90 | 1.21 | | 2.11 | install 12" x 12" tile with embossed |
| | Demolish and Install | S.F. | .90 | 1.87 | | 2.77 | texture pattern. Furring strips not |
| | Clean | S.F. | .03 | .16 | | .19 | included. |
| | Minimum Charge | Job | | 181 | | 181 | |
| **Better Grade** | | | | | | | |
| | Demolish | S.F. | | .66 | | .66 | Cost includes material and labor to |
| | Install | S.F. | 1.21 | 1.21 | | 2.42 | install 12" x 12" tile with embossed |
| | Demolish and Install | S.F. | 1.21 | 1.87 | | 3.08 | texture pattern. Furring strips not |
| | Clean | S.F. | .03 | .16 | | .19 | included. |
| | Minimum Charge | Job | | 181 | | 181 | |
| **Premium Grade** | | | | | | | |
| | Demolish | S.F. | | .66 | | .66 | Cost includes material and labor to |
| | Install | S.F. | 3.44 | 1.21 | | 4.65 | install 12" x 12" tile with embossed |
| | Demolish and Install | S.F. | 3.44 | 1.87 | | 5.31 | texture pattern. Furring strips not |
| | Clean | S.F. | .03 | .16 | | .19 | included. |
| | Minimum Charge | Job | | 181 | | 181 | |
| **Bleach Out Stains** | | | | | | | |
| | Install | S.F. | .10 | .27 | | .37 | Includes labor and material to apply |
| | Minimum Charge | Job | | 181 | | 181 | laundry type chlorine bleach to |
| | | | | | | | remove light staining of acoustic tile |
| | | | | | | | material. |
| **Stapled Tile** | | | | | | | |
| **Good Grade** | | | | | | | |
| | Demolish | S.F. | | .40 | | .40 | Cost includes material and labor to |
| | Install | S.F. | .90 | 1.21 | | 2.11 | install 12" x 12" tile with embossed |
| | Demolish and Install | S.F. | .90 | 1.61 | | 2.51 | texture pattern. Furring strips not |
| | Clean | S.F. | .03 | .16 | | .19 | included. |
| | Minimum Charge | Job | | 181 | | 181 | |
| **Better Grade** | | | | | | | |
| | Demolish | S.F. | | .40 | | .40 | Cost includes material and labor to |
| | Install | S.F. | 1.21 | 1.21 | | 2.42 | install 12" x 12" tile with embossed |
| | Demolish and Install | S.F. | 1.21 | 1.61 | | 2.82 | texture pattern. Furring strips not |
| | Clean | S.F. | .03 | .16 | | .19 | included. |
| | Minimum Charge | Job | | 181 | | 181 | |

# Walls / Ceilings

| Acoustical Ceiling | | Unit | Material | Labor | Equip. | Total | Specification |
|---|---|---|---|---|---|---|---|
| **Premium Grade** | | | | | | | |
| | Demolish | S.F. | | .40 | | .40 | Cost includes material and labor to |
| | Install | S.F. | 3.44 | 1.21 | | 4.65 | install 12″ x 12″ tile with embossed |
| | Demolish and Install | S.F. | 3.44 | 1.61 | | 5.05 | texture pattern. Furring strips not |
| | Clean | S.F. | .03 | .16 | | .19 | included. |
| | Minimum Charge | Job | | 181 | | 181 | |
| **Bleach Out Stains** | | | | | | | |
| | Install | S.F. | .10 | .27 | | .37 | Includes labor and material to apply |
| | Minimum Charge | Job | | 181 | | 181 | laundry type chlorine bleach to |
| | | | | | | | remove light staining of acoustic tile |
| | | | | | | | material. |
| **Blown** | | | | | | | |
| **Scrape Off Existing** | | | | | | | |
| | Install | S.F. | | .55 | | .55 | Includes labor and material to remove |
| | Minimum Charge | Job | | 181 | | 181 | existing blown acoustical ceiling |
| | | | | | | | material. |
| **Seal Ceiling Gypsum Wallboard** | | | | | | | |
| | Install | S.F. | .06 | .27 | | .33 | Includes labor and material to seal |
| | Minimum Charge | Job | | 157 | | 157 | existing drywall with shellac-based |
| | | | | | | | material. |
| **Reblow Existing** | | | | | | | |
| | Install | S.F. | .06 | .40 | | .46 | Includes labor and material to install |
| | Minimum Charge | Job | | 440 | 69.50 | 509.50 | by spray, texture finish. |
| **Bleach Out Stains** | | | | | | | |
| | Install | S.F. | .10 | .27 | | .37 | Includes labor and material to apply |
| | Minimum Charge | Job | | 181 | | 181 | laundry type chlorine bleach to |
| | | | | | | | remove light staining of acoustic tile |
| | | | | | | | material. |
| **New Blown** | | | | | | | |
| | Install | S.F. | .06 | .40 | | .46 | Includes labor and material to install |
| | Minimum Charge | Job | | 157 | | 157 | by spray, texture finish. |
| **Apply Glitter To** | | | | | | | |
| | Install | S.F. | .09 | .14 | | .23 | Includes labor and material to apply |
| | Minimum Charge | Job | | 157 | | 157 | glitter material to existing or new |
| | | | | | | | drywall. |
| **Furring Strips** | | | | | | | |
| | Demolish | S.F. | | .07 | | .07 | Cost includes material and labor to |
| | Install | S.F. | .10 | .80 | | .90 | install 1″ x 2″ furring strips, 16″ O.C. |
| | Demolish and Install | S.F. | .10 | .87 | | .97 | per S.F. of surface area to be covered. |
| | Minimum Charge | Job | | 90.50 | | 90.50 | |

# Finish Carpentry

**Finished Stair**

**Bi-Fold Door**

**Raised Panel Door**

| Hollow Core Door | | Unit | Material | Labor | Equip. | Total | Specification |
|---|---|---|---|---|---|---|---|
| **Pre-hung Wood** | | | | | | | |
| **1′ 6″ x 6′ 8″** | | | | | | | |
| | Demolish | Ea. | | 33.50 | | 33.50 | Cost includes material and labor to |
| | Install | Ea. | 149 | 17.20 | | 166.20 | install 1′ 6″ x 6′ 8″ pre-hung 1-3/8″ |
| | Demolish and Install | Ea. | 149 | 50.70 | | 199.70 | lauan door with split pine jamb |
| | Reinstall | Ea. | | 17.22 | | 17.22 | including casing, stops, and hinges. |
| | Clean | Ea. | 3.63 | 11.10 | | 14.73 | |
| | Paint | Ea. | 9.30 | 45 | | 54.30 | |
| | Minimum Charge | Job | | 181 | | 181 | |
| **2′ x 6′ 8″** | | | | | | | |
| | Demolish | Ea. | | 33.50 | | 33.50 | Cost includes material and labor to |
| | Install | Ea. | 155 | 18.10 | | 173.10 | install 2′ x 6′ 8″ pre-hung 1-3/8″ |
| | Demolish and Install | Ea. | 155 | 51.60 | | 206.60 | lauan door with split pine jamb |
| | Reinstall | Ea. | | 18.08 | | 18.08 | including casing, stops, and hinges. |
| | Clean | Ea. | 3.63 | 11.10 | | 14.73 | |
| | Paint | Ea. | 9.30 | 45 | | 54.30 | |
| | Minimum Charge | Job | | 181 | | 181 | |
| **2′ 4″ x 6′ 8″** | | | | | | | |
| | Demolish | Ea. | | 33.50 | | 33.50 | Cost includes material and labor to |
| | Install | Ea. | 161 | 18.10 | | 179.10 | install 2′ 4″ x 6′ 8″ pre-hung 1-3/8″ |
| | Demolish and Install | Ea. | 161 | 51.60 | | 212.60 | lauan door with split pine jamb |
| | Reinstall | Ea. | | 18.08 | | 18.08 | including casing, stops, and hinges. |
| | Clean | Ea. | 3.63 | 11.10 | | 14.73 | |
| | Paint | Ea. | 9.30 | 45 | | 54.30 | |
| | Minimum Charge | Job | | 181 | | 181 | |
| **2′ 6″ x 6′ 8″** | | | | | | | |
| | Demolish | Ea. | | 33.50 | | 33.50 | Cost includes material and labor to |
| | Install | Ea. | 161 | 18.10 | | 179.10 | install 2′ 6″ x 6′ 8″ pre-hung 1-3/8″ |
| | Demolish and Install | Ea. | 161 | 51.60 | | 212.60 | lauan door with split pine jamb |
| | Reinstall | Ea. | | 18.08 | | 18.08 | including casing, stops, and hinges. |
| | Clean | Ea. | 3.63 | 11.10 | | 14.73 | |
| | Paint | Ea. | 9.30 | 45 | | 54.30 | |
| | Minimum Charge | Job | | 181 | | 181 | |
| **2′ 8″ x 6′ 8″** | | | | | | | |
| | Demolish | Ea. | | 33.50 | | 33.50 | Cost includes material and labor to |
| | Install | Ea. | 172 | 18.10 | | 190.10 | install 2′ 8″ x 6′ 8″ pre-hung 1-3/8″ |
| | Demolish and Install | Ea. | 172 | 51.60 | | 223.60 | lauan door with split pine jamb, |
| | Reinstall | Ea. | | 18.08 | | 18.08 | including casing, stop and hinges. |
| | Clean | Ea. | 3.63 | 11.10 | | 14.73 | |
| | Paint | Ea. | 9.30 | 45 | | 54.30 | |
| | Minimum Charge | Job | | 181 | | 181 | |

# Finish Carpentry

| Hollow Core Door | Unit | Material | Labor | Equip. | Total | Specification |
|---|---|---|---|---|---|---|
| **3' x 6' 8"** | | | | | | |
| Demolish | Ea. | | 33.50 | | 33.50 | Cost includes material and labor to |
| Install | Ea. | 178 | 19.05 | | 197.05 | install 3' x 6' 8" pre-hung 1-3/8" |
| Demolish and Install | Ea. | 178 | 52.55 | | 230.55 | lauan door with split pine jamb |
| Reinstall | Ea. | | 19.03 | | 19.03 | including casing, stops, and hinges. |
| Clean | Ea. | 3.63 | 11.10 | | 14.73 | |
| Paint | Ea. | 9.30 | 45 | | 54.30 | |
| Minimum Charge | Job | | 181 | | 181 | |
| **Pocket Type** | | | | | | |
| Demolish | Ea. | | 50 | | 50 | Cost includes material and labor to |
| Install | Ea. | 36 | 40 | | 76 | install 2' 8" x 6' 8" lauan door. |
| Demolish and Install | Ea. | 36 | 90 | | 126 | |
| Reinstall | Ea. | | 40.18 | | 40.18 | |
| Clean | Ea. | 3.63 | 11.10 | | 14.73 | |
| Paint | Ea. | 9.30 | 45 | | 54.30 | |
| Minimum Charge | Job | | 181 | | 181 | |
| **Stain** | | | | | | |
| Install | Ea. | 4.81 | 26 | | 30.81 | Includes labor and material to stain |
| Minimum Charge | Job | | 157 | | 157 | single door and trim on both sides. |
| **Pre-hung Masonite** | | | | | | |
| **1' 6" x 6' 8"** | | | | | | |
| Demolish | Ea. | | 33.50 | | 33.50 | Cost includes material and labor to |
| Install | Ea. | 205 | 17.20 | | 222.20 | install 1' 6" x 6' 8" pre-hung 1-3/8" |
| Demolish and Install | Ea. | 205 | 50.70 | | 255.70 | masonite door with split pine jamb |
| Reinstall | Ea. | | 17.22 | | 17.22 | including casing, stops, and hinges. |
| Clean | Ea. | 3.63 | 11.10 | | 14.73 | |
| Paint | Ea. | 9.30 | 45 | | 54.30 | |
| Minimum Charge | Job | | 181 | | 181 | |
| **2' x 6' 8"** | | | | | | |
| Demolish | Ea. | | 33.50 | | 33.50 | Cost includes material and labor to |
| Install | Ea. | 215 | 18.10 | | 233.10 | install 2' x 6' 8" pre-hung 1-3/8" |
| Demolish and Install | Ea. | 215 | 51.60 | | 266.60 | masonite door with split pine jamb |
| Reinstall | Ea. | | 18.08 | | 18.08 | including casing, stops, and hinges. |
| Clean | Ea. | 3.63 | 11.10 | | 14.73 | |
| Paint | Ea. | 9.30 | 45 | | 54.30 | |
| Minimum Charge | Job | | 181 | | 181 | |
| **2' 4" x 6' 8"** | | | | | | |
| Demolish | Ea. | | 33.50 | | 33.50 | Cost includes material and labor to |
| Install | Ea. | 217 | 18.10 | | 235.10 | install 2' 4" x 6' 8" pre-hung 1-3/8" |
| Demolish and Install | Ea. | 217 | 51.60 | | 268.60 | masonite door with split pine jamb |
| Reinstall | Ea. | | 18.08 | | 18.08 | including casing, stops, and hinges. |
| Clean | Ea. | 3.63 | 11.10 | | 14.73 | |
| Paint | Ea. | 9.30 | 45 | | 54.30 | |
| Minimum Charge | Job | | 181 | | 181 | |
| **2' 8" x 6' 8"** | | | | | | |
| Demolish | Ea. | | 33.50 | | 33.50 | Cost includes material and labor to |
| Install | Ea. | 219 | 18.10 | | 237.10 | install 2' 8" x 6' 8" pre-hung 1-3/8" |
| Demolish and Install | Ea. | 219 | 51.60 | | 270.60 | masonite door with split pine jamb |
| Reinstall | Ea. | | 18.08 | | 18.08 | including casing, stops, and hinges. |
| Clean | Ea. | 3.63 | 11.10 | | 14.73 | |
| Paint | Ea. | 9.30 | 45 | | 54.30 | |
| Minimum Charge | Job | | 181 | | 181 | |
| **3' x 6' 8"** | | | | | | |
| Demolish | Ea. | | 33.50 | | 33.50 | Cost includes material and labor to |
| Install | Ea. | 224 | 19.05 | | 243.05 | install 3' x 6' 8" pre-hung 1-3/8" |
| Demolish and Install | Ea. | 224 | 52.55 | | 276.55 | masonite door with split pine jamb |
| Reinstall | Ea. | | 19.03 | | 19.03 | including casing, stops, and hinges. |
| Clean | Ea. | 3.63 | 11.10 | | 14.73 | |
| Paint | Ea. | 9.30 | 45 | | 54.30 | |
| Minimum Charge | Job | | 181 | | 181 | |

| Hollow Core Door | Unit | Material | Labor | Equip. | Total | Specification |
|---|---|---|---|---|---|---|
| **Pocket Type** | | | | | | |
| Demolish | Ea. | | 50 | | 50 | Cost includes material and labor to |
| Install | Ea. | 36 | 40 | | 76 | install 2' 8" x 6' 8" lauan door. |
| Demolish and Install | Ea. | 36 | 90 | | 126 | |
| Reinstall | Ea. | | 40.18 | | 40.18 | |
| Clean | Ea. | 3.63 | 11.10 | | 14.73 | |
| Paint | Ea. | 9.30 | 45 | | 54.30 | |
| Minimum Charge | Job | | 181 | | 181 | |
| **Stain** | | | | | | |
| Install | Ea. | 4.81 | 26 | | 30.81 | Includes labor and material to stain |
| Minimum Charge | Job | | 157 | | 157 | single door and trim on both sides. |
| **Hollow Core Door Only** | | | | | | |
| **1' 6" x 6' 8'** | | | | | | |
| Demolish | Ea. | | 7.15 | | 7.15 | Cost includes material and labor to |
| Install | Ea. | 40 | 19.05 | | 59.05 | install 1' 6" x 6' 8" lauan hollow core |
| Demolish and Install | Ea. | 40 | 26.20 | | 66.20 | door slab. |
| Reinstall | Ea. | | 19.03 | | 19.03 | |
| Clean | Ea. | 1.52 | 8.35 | | 9.87 | |
| Paint | Ea. | 2.66 | 39.50 | | 42.16 | |
| Minimum Charge | Job | | 181 | | 181 | |
| **2' x 6' 8'** | | | | | | |
| Demolish | Ea. | | 7.15 | | 7.15 | Cost includes material and labor to |
| Install | Ea. | 38.50 | 20 | | 58.50 | install 2' x 6' 8" lauan hollow core |
| Demolish and Install | Ea. | 38.50 | 27.15 | | 65.65 | door slab. |
| Reinstall | Ea. | | 20.09 | | 20.09 | |
| Clean | Ea. | 1.52 | 8.35 | | 9.87 | |
| Paint | Ea. | 2.66 | 39.50 | | 42.16 | |
| Minimum Charge | Job | | 181 | | 181 | |
| **2' 4" x 6' 8'** | | | | | | |
| Demolish | Ea. | | 7.15 | | 7.15 | Cost includes material and labor to |
| Install | Ea. | 42 | 20 | | 62 | install 2' 4" x 6' 8" lauan hollow core |
| Demolish and Install | Ea. | 42 | 27.15 | | 69.15 | door slab. |
| Reinstall | Ea. | | 20.09 | | 20.09 | |
| Clean | Ea. | 1.52 | 8.35 | | 9.87 | |
| Paint | Ea. | 2.66 | 39.50 | | 42.16 | |
| Minimum Charge | Job | | 181 | | 181 | |
| **2' 8" x 6' 8'** | | | | | | |
| Demolish | Ea. | | 7.15 | | 7.15 | Cost includes material and labor to |
| Install | Ea. | 44 | 20 | | 64 | install 2' 8" x 6' 8" lauan hollow core |
| Demolish and Install | Ea. | 44 | 27.15 | | 71.15 | door slab. |
| Reinstall | Ea. | | 20.09 | | 20.09 | |
| Clean | Ea. | 1.52 | 8.35 | | 9.87 | |
| Paint | Ea. | 2.66 | 39.50 | | 42.16 | |
| Minimum Charge | Job | | 181 | | 181 | |
| **3' x 6' 8'** | | | | | | |
| Demolish | Ea. | | 7.15 | | 7.15 | Cost includes material and labor to |
| Install | Ea. | 45.50 | 21.50 | | 67 | install 3' x 6' 8" lauan hollow core |
| Demolish and Install | Ea. | 45.50 | 28.65 | | 74.15 | door slab. |
| Reinstall | Ea. | | 21.27 | | 21.27 | |
| Clean | Ea. | 1.52 | 8.35 | | 9.87 | |
| Paint | Ea. | 2.66 | 39.50 | | 42.16 | |
| Minimum Charge | Job | | 181 | | 181 | |
| **Pocket Type** | | | | | | |
| Demolish | Ea. | | 7.15 | | 7.15 | Cost includes material and labor to |
| Install | Ea. | 36 | 40 | | 76 | install 2' 8" x 6' 8" lauan door. |
| Demolish and Install | Ea. | 36 | 47.15 | | 83.15 | |
| Reinstall | Ea. | | 40.18 | | 40.18 | |
| Clean | Ea. | 1.52 | 8.35 | | 9.87 | |
| Paint | Ea. | 2.66 | 39.50 | | 42.16 | |
| Minimum Charge | Job | | 181 | | 181 | |

| Hollow Core Door | Unit | Material | Labor | Equip. | Total | Specification |
|---|---|---|---|---|---|---|
| **Stain** | | | | | | |
| Install | Ea. | 2.66 | 35 | | 37.66 | Includes labor and materials to stain a |
| Minimum Charge | Job | | 157 | | 157 | flush style door on both sides by brush. |
| **Casing Trim** | | | | | | |
| **Single Width** | | | | | | |
| Demolish | Ea. | | 6.40 | | 6.40 | Cost includes material and labor to |
| Install | Opng. | 23.50 | 61.50 | | 85 | install 11/16" x 2-1/2" pine ranch |
| Demolish and Install | Opng. | 23.50 | 67.90 | | 91.40 | style casing for one side of a standard |
| Reinstall | Opng. | | 49.03 | | 49.03 | door opening. |
| Clean | Opng. | .52 | 2.67 | | 3.19 | |
| Paint | Ea. | 3.65 | 6.30 | | 9.95 | |
| Minimum Charge | Job | | 181 | | 181 | |
| **Double Width** | | | | | | |
| Demolish | Ea. | | 7.60 | | 7.60 | Cost includes material and labor to |
| Install | Opng. | 27.50 | 72.50 | | 100 | install 11/16" x 2-1/2" pine ranch |
| Demolish and Install | Opng. | 27.50 | 80.10 | | 107.60 | style door casing for one side of a |
| Reinstall | Opng. | | 57.86 | | 57.86 | double door opening. |
| Clean | Opng. | .61 | 5.35 | | 5.96 | |
| Paint | Ea. | 3.65 | 7.15 | | 10.80 | |
| Minimum Charge | Job | | 181 | | 181 | |
| **Hardware** | | | | | | |
| **Doorknob w / Lock** | | | | | | |
| Demolish | Ea. | | 13.40 | | 13.40 | Includes material and labor to install |
| Install | Ea. | 26 | 22.50 | | 48.50 | privacy lockset. |
| Demolish and Install | Ea. | 26 | 35.90 | | 61.90 | |
| Reinstall | Ea. | | 18.08 | | 18.08 | |
| Clean | Ea. | .36 | 8.35 | | 8.71 | |
| Minimum Charge | Job | | 181 | | 181 | |
| **Doorknob** | | | | | | |
| Demolish | Ea. | | 13.40 | | 13.40 | Includes material and labor to install |
| Install | Ea. | 19.80 | 22.50 | | 42.30 | residential passage lockset, keyless |
| Demolish and Install | Ea. | 19.80 | 35.90 | | 55.70 | bored type. |
| Reinstall | Ea. | | 18.08 | | 18.08 | |
| Clean | Ea. | .36 | 8.35 | | 8.71 | |
| Minimum Charge | Job | | 181 | | 181 | |
| **Deadbolt** | | | | | | |
| Demolish | Ea. | | 12.55 | | 12.55 | Includes material and labor to install a |
| Install | Ea. | 55.50 | 26 | | 81.50 | deadbolt. |
| Demolish and Install | Ea. | 55.50 | 38.55 | | 94.05 | |
| Reinstall | Ea. | | 20.66 | | 20.66 | |
| Clean | Ea. | .36 | 8.35 | | 8.71 | |
| Minimum Charge | Job | | 181 | | 181 | |
| **Lever Handle** | | | | | | |
| Demolish | Ea. | | 13.40 | | 13.40 | Includes material and labor to install |
| Install | Ea. | 28.50 | 36 | | 64.50 | residential passage lockset, keyless |
| Demolish and Install | Ea. | 28.50 | 49.40 | | 77.90 | bored type with lever handle. |
| Reinstall | Ea. | | 28.93 | | 28.93 | |
| Clean | Ea. | .36 | 8.35 | | 8.71 | |
| Minimum Charge | Job | | 181 | | 181 | |
| **Closer** | | | | | | |
| Demolish | Ea. | | 7.55 | | 7.55 | Includes material and labor to install |
| Install | Ea. | 99.50 | 55.50 | | 155 | pneumatic light duty closer for interior |
| Demolish and Install | Ea. | 99.50 | 63.05 | | 162.55 | type doors. |
| Reinstall | Ea. | | 44.50 | | 44.50 | |
| Clean | Ea. | .19 | 11.10 | | 11.29 | |
| Minimum Charge | Job | | 181 | | 181 | |

# Finish Carpentry

## Hollow Core Door

| Hollow Core Door | | Unit | Material | Labor | Equip. | Total | Specification |
|---|---|---|---|---|---|---|---|
| **Push Plate** | | | | | | | |
| | Demolish | Ea. | | 11.15 | | 11.15 | Includes material and labor to install |
| | Install | Ea. | 20.50 | 30 | | 50.50 | bronze push-pull plate. |
| | Demolish and Install | Ea. | 20.50 | 41.15 | | 61.65 | |
| | Reinstall | Ea. | | 24.11 | | 24.11 | |
| | Clean | Ea. | .36 | 8.35 | | 8.71 | |
| | Minimum Charge | Job | | 181 | | 181 | |
| **Kickplate** | | | | | | | |
| | Demolish | Ea. | | 11.15 | | 11.15 | Includes material and labor to install |
| | Install | Ea. | 23 | 24 | | 47 | aluminum kickplate, 10" x 28". |
| | Demolish and Install | Ea. | 23 | 35.15 | | 58.15 | |
| | Reinstall | Ea. | | 19.29 | | 19.29 | |
| | Clean | Ea. | .36 | 8.35 | | 8.71 | |
| | Minimum Charge | Job | | 181 | | 181 | |
| **Exit Sign** | | | | | | | |
| | Demolish | Ea. | | 20 | | 20 | Includes material and labor to install a |
| | Install | Ea. | 93.50 | 49.50 | | 143 | wall mounted interior electric exit sign. |
| | Demolish and Install | Ea. | 93.50 | 69.50 | | 163 | |
| | Reinstall | Ea. | | 39.76 | | 39.76 | |
| | Clean | Ea. | .02 | 6 | | 6.02 | |
| | Minimum Charge | Job | | 181 | | 181 | |
| **Jamb** | | | | | | | |
| | Demolish | Ea. | | 25 | | 25 | Includes material and labor to install |
| | Install | Ea. | 100 | 9.75 | | 109.75 | flat pine jamb with square cut heads |
| | Demolish and Install | Ea. | 100 | 34.75 | | 134.75 | and rabbeted sides for 6' 8" high and |
| | Clean | Ea. | .12 | 6.65 | | 6.77 | 3-9/16" door including trim sets for |
| | Paint | Ea. | 6.05 | 21 | | 27.05 | both sides. |
| | Minimum Charge | Job | | 181 | | 181 | |
| **Shave & Refit** | | | | | | | |
| | Install | Ea. | | 30 | | 30 | Includes labor to shave and rework |
| | Minimum Charge | Job | | 181 | | 181 | door to fit opening at the job site. |

## Solid Core Door

| Solid Core Door | | Unit | Material | Labor | Equip. | Total | Specification |
|---|---|---|---|---|---|---|---|
| **Pre-hung Wood** | | | | | | | |
| **2' 4" x 6' 8"** | | | | | | | |
| | Demolish | Ea. | | 33.50 | | 33.50 | Cost includes material and labor to |
| | Install | Ea. | 213 | 18.10 | | 231.10 | install 2' 4" x 6' 8" pre-hung 1-3/4" |
| | Demolish and Install | Ea. | 213 | 51.60 | | 264.60 | door, 4-1/2" split jamb, including |
| | Reinstall | Ea. | | 18.08 | | 18.08 | casing and stop, hinges, aluminum sill, |
| | Clean | Ea. | 3.63 | 11.10 | | 14.73 | weatherstripping. |
| | Paint | Ea. | 9.45 | 45 | | 54.45 | |
| | Minimum Charge | Job | | 181 | | 181 | |
| **2' 6" x 6' 8"** | | | | | | | |
| | Demolish | Ea. | | 33.50 | | 33.50 | Cost includes material and labor to |
| | Install | Ea. | 207 | 18.10 | | 225.10 | install 2' 6" x 6' 8" pre-hung 1-3/4" |
| | Demolish and Install | Ea. | 207 | 51.60 | | 258.60 | door, 4-1/2" split jamb, including |
| | Reinstall | Ea. | | 18.08 | | 18.08 | casing and stop, hinges, aluminum sill, |
| | Clean | Ea. | 3.63 | 11.10 | | 14.73 | weatherstripping. |
| | Paint | Ea. | 9.45 | 45 | | 54.45 | |
| | Minimum Charge | Job | | 181 | | 181 | |

# Finish Carpentry

## Solid Core Door

| | Unit | Material | Labor | Equip. | Total | Specification |
|---|---|---|---|---|---|---|
| **2′ 8″ x 6′ 8″** | | | | | | |
| Demolish | Ea. | | 33.50 | | 33.50 | Cost includes material and labor to |
| Install | Ea. | 219 | 18.10 | | 237.10 | install 2′ 8″ x 6′ 8″ pre-hung 1-3/4″ |
| Demolish and Install | Ea. | 219 | 51.60 | | 270.60 | door, 4-1/2″ split jamb, including |
| Reinstall | Ea. | | 18.08 | | 18.08 | casing and stop, hinges, aluminum sill, |
| Clean | Ea. | 3.63 | 11.10 | | 14.73 | weatherstripping. |
| Paint | Ea. | 9.45 | 45 | | 54.45 | |
| Minimum Charge | Job | | 181 | | 181 | |
| **3′ x 6′ 8″** | | | | | | |
| Demolish | Ea. | | 33.50 | | 33.50 | Cost includes material and labor to |
| Install | Ea. | 227 | 19.05 | | 246.05 | install 3′ x 6′ 8″ pre-hung 1-3/4″ |
| Demolish and Install | Ea. | 227 | 52.55 | | 279.55 | door, including casing and stop, |
| Reinstall | Ea. | | 19.03 | | 19.03 | hinges, jamb, aluminum sill, |
| Clean | Ea. | 3.63 | 11.10 | | 14.73 | weatherstripped. |
| Paint | Ea. | 9.45 | 45 | | 54.45 | |
| Minimum Charge | Job | | 181 | | 181 | |
| **3′ 6″ x 6′ 8″** | | | | | | |
| Demolish | Ea. | | 33.50 | | 33.50 | Cost includes material and labor to |
| Install | Ea. | 385 | 20 | | 405 | install 3′ 6″ x 6′ 8″ pre-hung 1-3/4″ |
| Demolish and Install | Ea. | 385 | 53.50 | | 438.50 | door, 4-1/2″ split jamb, including |
| Reinstall | Ea. | | 20.09 | | 20.09 | casing and stop, hinges, aluminum sill, |
| Clean | Ea. | 3.63 | 11.10 | | 14.73 | weatherstripping. |
| Paint | Ea. | 9.45 | 45 | | 54.45 | |
| Minimum Charge | Job | | 181 | | 181 | |
| **Raised Panel** | | | | | | |
| Demolish | Ea. | | 33.50 | | 33.50 | Cost includes material and labor to |
| Install | Ea. | 445 | 20 | | 465 | install 3′ x 6′ 8″ pre-hung 1-3/4″ |
| Demolish and Install | Ea. | 445 | 53.50 | | 498.50 | door, jamb, including casing and |
| Reinstall | Ea. | | 20.09 | | 20.09 | stop, hinges, aluminum sill, |
| Clean | Ea. | 3.63 | 11.10 | | 14.73 | weatherstripping. |
| Paint | Ea. | 9.45 | 105 | | 114.45 | |
| Minimum Charge | Job | | 181 | | 181 | |
| **Stain** | | | | | | |
| Install | Ea. | 4.81 | 26 | | 30.81 | Includes labor and material to stain |
| Minimum Charge | Job | | 157 | | 157 | single door and trim on both sides. |

## Bifold Door

| | Unit | Material | Labor | Equip. | Total | Specification |
|---|---|---|---|---|---|---|
| **Wood, Single** | | | | | | |
| **3′** | | | | | | |
| Demolish | Ea. | | 25 | | 25 | Cost includes material and labor to |
| Install | Ea. | 59 | 55.50 | | 114.50 | install 3′ wide solid wood bi-fold door |
| Demolish and Install | Ea. | 59 | 80.50 | | 139.50 | not including jamb, trim, track, and |
| Reinstall | Ea. | | 55.63 | | 55.63 | hardware. |
| Clean | Ea. | 3.63 | 11.10 | | 14.73 | |
| Paint | Ea. | 9.30 | 45 | | 54.30 | |
| Minimum Charge | Job | | 181 | | 181 | |
| **5′** | | | | | | |
| Demolish | Ea. | | 25 | | 25 | Includes material and labor to install |
| Install | Ea. | 108 | 66 | | 174 | pair of 2′ 6″ wide solid wood bi-fold |
| Demolish and Install | Ea. | 108 | 91 | | 199 | doors not including jamb, trim, track, |
| Reinstall | Ea. | | 65.75 | | 65.75 | and hardware. |
| Clean | Ea. | 1.58 | 19.05 | | 20.63 | |
| Paint | Ea. | 18.55 | 78.50 | | 97.05 | |
| Minimum Charge | Job | | 181 | | 181 | |

# Finish Carpentry

| Bifold Door | | Unit | Material | Labor | Equip. | Total | Specification |
|---|---|---|---|---|---|---|---|
| **6'** | | | | | | | |
| | Demolish | Ea. | | 25 | | 25 | Includes material and labor to install |
| | Install | Ea. | 117 | 72.50 | | 189.50 | pair of 3' wide solid wood bi-fold |
| | Demolish and Install | Ea. | 117 | 97.50 | | 214.50 | doors not including jamb, trim, track, |
| | Reinstall | Ea. | | 72.32 | | 72.32 | and hardware. |
| | Clean | Ea. | 1.82 | 22 | | 23.82 | |
| | Paint | Ea. | 18.55 | 78.50 | | 97.05 | |
| | Minimum Charge | Job | | 181 | | 181 | |
| **8'** | | | | | | | |
| | Demolish | Ea. | | 25 | | 25 | Includes material and labor to install |
| | Install | Ea. | 215 | 80.50 | | 295.50 | pair of 4' wide solid wood bi-fold |
| | Demolish and Install | Ea. | 215 | 105.50 | | 320.50 | doors not including jamb, trim, track, |
| | Reinstall | Ea. | | 80.36 | | 80.36 | and hardware. |
| | Clean | Ea. | 2.50 | 26.50 | | 29 | |
| | Paint | Ea. | 9.65 | 78.50 | | 88.15 | |
| | Minimum Charge | Job | | 181 | | 181 | |
| **Mirrored** | | | | | | | |
| **5'** | | | | | | | |
| | Demolish | Ea. | | 25 | | 25 | Includes material and labor to install |
| | Install | Ea. | 450 | 40 | | 490 | pair of 2' 8" wide mirrored bi-fold |
| | Demolish and Install | Ea. | 450 | 65 | | 515 | doors including jamb, trim, track, and |
| | Reinstall | Ea. | | 40.18 | | 40.18 | hardware. |
| | Clean | Ea. | 1.58 | 9.55 | | 11.13 | |
| | Minimum Charge | Job | | 181 | | 181 | |
| **6'** | | | | | | | |
| | Demolish | Ea. | | 25 | | 25 | Includes material and labor to install |
| | Install | Ea. | 450 | 40 | | 490 | pair of 3' wide mirrored bi-fold doors |
| | Demolish and Install | Ea. | 450 | 65 | | 515 | including jamb, trim, track, and |
| | Reinstall | Ea. | | 40.18 | | 40.18 | hardware. |
| | Clean | Ea. | 1.82 | 11.10 | | 12.92 | |
| | Minimum Charge | Job | | 181 | | 181 | |
| **8'** | | | | | | | |
| | Demolish | Ea. | | 25 | | 25 | Includes material and labor to install |
| | Install | Ea. | 725 | 60.50 | | 785.50 | pair of 4' wide mirrored bi-fold doors |
| | Demolish and Install | Ea. | 725 | 85.50 | | 810.50 | including jamb, trim, track, and |
| | Reinstall | Ea. | | 60.27 | | 60.27 | hardware. |
| | Clean | Ea. | 2.50 | 13.35 | | 15.85 | |
| | Minimum Charge | Job | | 181 | | 181 | |
| **Louvered** | | | | | | | |
| **3'** | | | | | | | |
| | Demolish | Ea. | | 25 | | 25 | Cost includes material and labor to |
| | Install | Ea. | 180 | 55.50 | | 235.50 | install 3' wide louvered bi-fold door |
| | Demolish and Install | Ea. | 180 | 80.50 | | 260.50 | not including jamb, trim, track, and |
| | Reinstall | Ea. | | 55.63 | | 55.63 | hardware. |
| | Clean | Ea. | 3.63 | 11.10 | | 14.73 | |
| | Paint | Ea. | 9.30 | 45 | | 54.30 | |
| | Minimum Charge | Job | | 181 | | 181 | |
| **5'** | | | | | | | |
| | Demolish | Ea. | | 25 | | 25 | Includes material and labor to install |
| | Install | Ea. | 249 | 66 | | 315 | pair of 2' 6" wide louvered wood |
| | Demolish and Install | Ea. | 249 | 91 | | 340 | bi-fold doors not including jamb, trim, |
| | Reinstall | Ea. | | 65.75 | | 65.75 | track, and hardware. |
| | Clean | Ea. | 1.58 | 19.05 | | 20.63 | |
| | Paint | Ea. | 18.55 | 78.50 | | 97.05 | |
| | Minimum Charge | Job | | 181 | | 181 | |

| Bifold Door | | Unit | Material | Labor | Equip. | Total | Specification |
|---|---|---|---|---|---|---|---|
| **6'** | | | | | | | Includes material and labor to install |
| | Demolish | Ea. | | 25 | | 25 | pair of 3' wide louvered wood bi-fold |
| | Install | Ea. | 276 | 72.50 | | 348.50 | doors not including jamb, trim, track, |
| | Demolish and Install | Ea. | 276 | 97.50 | | 373.50 | and hardware. |
| | Reinstall | Ea. | | 72.32 | | 72.32 | |
| | Clean | Ea. | 1.82 | 22 | | 23.82 | |
| | Paint | Ea. | 18.55 | 78.50 | | 97.05 | |
| | Minimum Charge | Job | | 181 | | 181 | |
| **8'** | | | | | | | Includes material and labor to install |
| | Demolish | Ea. | | 25 | | 25 | pair of 4' wide solid wood bi-fold |
| | Install | Ea. | 440 | 72.50 | | 512.50 | doors not including jamb, trim, track, |
| | Demolish and Install | Ea. | 440 | 97.50 | | 537.50 | and hardware. |
| | Reinstall | Ea. | | 72.32 | | 72.32 | |
| | Clean | Ea. | 8.65 | 19.05 | | 27.70 | |
| | Paint | Ea. | 9.65 | 78.50 | | 88.15 | |
| | Minimum Charge | Job | | 181 | | 181 | |
| **Accordion Type** | | | | | | | Includes material and labor to install |
| | Demolish | S.F. | | .87 | | .87 | vinyl folding accordion closet doors, |
| | Install | Ea. | 31 | 72.50 | | 103.50 | including track and frame. |
| | Demolish and Install | Ea. | 31 | 73.37 | | 104.37 | |
| | Reinstall | Ea. | | 72.32 | | 72.32 | |
| | Clean | S.F. | | .32 | | .32 | |
| | Minimum Charge | Job | | 181 | | 181 | |
| **Casing Trim** | | | | | | | |
| **Single Width** | | | | | | | Cost includes material and labor to |
| | Demolish | Ea. | | 6.40 | | 6.40 | install 11/16" x 2-1/2" pine ranch |
| | Install | Opng. | 23.50 | 61.50 | | 85 | style casing for one side of a standard |
| | Demolish and Install | Opng. | 23.50 | 67.90 | | 91.40 | door opening. |
| | Reinstall | Opng. | | 49.03 | | 49.03 | |
| | Clean | Opng. | .52 | 2.67 | | 3.19 | |
| | Paint | Ea. | 3.65 | 6.30 | | 9.95 | |
| | Minimum Charge | Job | | 181 | | 181 | |
| **Double Width** | | | | | | | Cost includes material and labor to |
| | Demolish | Ea. | | 7.60 | | 7.60 | install 11/16" x 2-1/2" pine ranch |
| | Install | Opng. | 27.50 | 72.50 | | 100 | style door casing for one side of a |
| | Demolish and Install | Opng. | 27.50 | 80.10 | | 107.60 | double door opening. |
| | Reinstall | Opng. | | 57.86 | | 57.86 | |
| | Clean | Opng. | .61 | 5.35 | | 5.96 | |
| | Paint | Ea. | 3.65 | 7.15 | | 10.80 | |
| | Minimum Charge | Job | | 181 | | 181 | |
| **Jamb** | | | | | | | Includes material and labor to install |
| | Demolish | Ea. | | 25 | | 25 | flat pine jamb with square cut heads |
| | Install | Ea. | 100 | 9.75 | | 109.75 | and rabbeted sides for 6' 8" high and |
| | Demolish and Install | Ea. | 100 | 34.75 | | 134.75 | 3-9/16" door including trim sets for |
| | Clean | Ea. | .12 | 6.65 | | 6.77 | both sides. |
| | Paint | Ea. | 6.05 | 21 | | 27.05 | |
| | Minimum Charge | Job | | 90.50 | | 90.50 | |
| **Stain** | | | | | | | Includes labor and material to stain |
| | Install | Ea. | 4.81 | 26 | | 30.81 | single door and trim on both sides. |
| | Minimum Charge | Job | | 157 | | 157 | |
| **Shave & Refit** | | | | | | | Includes labor to shave and rework |
| | Install | Ea. | | 30 | | 30 | door to fit opening at the job site. |
| | Minimum Charge | Job | | 90.50 | | 90.50 | |

# Finish Carpentry

| Louver Door | | Unit | Material | Labor | Equip. | Total | Specification |
|---|---|---|---|---|---|---|---|
| **Full** | | | | | | | |
| **2' x 6' 8"** | | | | | | | |
| | Demolish | Ea. | | 7.15 | | 7.15 | Cost includes material and labor to |
| | Install | Ea. | 189 | 36 | | 225 | install 2' x 6' 8" pine full louver door, |
| | Demolish and Install | Ea. | 189 | 43.15 | | 232.15 | jamb, hinges. |
| | Reinstall | Ea. | | 36.16 | | 36.16 | |
| | Clean | Ea. | 6.70 | 33.50 | | 40.20 | |
| | Paint | Ea. | 9.30 | 45 | | 54.30 | |
| | Minimum Charge | Job | | 181 | | 181 | |
| **2' 8" x 6' 8"** | | | | | | | |
| | Demolish | Ea. | | 7.15 | | 7.15 | Cost includes material and labor to |
| | Install | Ea. | 210 | 36 | | 246 | install 2' 8" x 6' 8" pine full louver |
| | Demolish and Install | Ea. | 210 | 43.15 | | 253.15 | door, jamb, hinges. |
| | Reinstall | Ea. | | 36.16 | | 36.16 | |
| | Clean | Ea. | 6.70 | 33.50 | | 40.20 | |
| | Paint | Ea. | 9.30 | 45 | | 54.30 | |
| | Minimum Charge | Job | | 181 | | 181 | |
| **3' x 6' 8"** | | | | | | | |
| | Demolish | Ea. | | 7.15 | | 7.15 | Cost includes material and labor to |
| | Install | Ea. | 222 | 38 | | 260 | install 3' x 6' 8" pine full louver door, |
| | Demolish and Install | Ea. | 222 | 45.15 | | 267.15 | jamb, hinges. |
| | Reinstall | Ea. | | 38.06 | | 38.06 | |
| | Clean | Ea. | 6.70 | 33.50 | | 40.20 | |
| | Paint | Ea. | 9.30 | 45 | | 54.30 | |
| | Minimum Charge | Job | | 181 | | 181 | |
| **Half** | | | | | | | |
| **2' x 6' 8"** | | | | | | | |
| | Demolish | Ea. | | 7.15 | | 7.15 | Cost includes material and labor to |
| | Install | Ea. | 305 | 36 | | 341 | install 2' x 6' 8" pine half louver door, |
| | Demolish and Install | Ea. | 305 | 43.15 | | 348.15 | jamb, hinges. |
| | Reinstall | Ea. | | 36.16 | | 36.16 | |
| | Clean | Ea. | 6.70 | 33.50 | | 40.20 | |
| | Paint | Ea. | 9.30 | 45 | | 54.30 | |
| | Minimum Charge | Job | | 181 | | 181 | |
| **2' 8" x 6' 8"** | | | | | | | |
| | Demolish | Ea. | | 7.15 | | 7.15 | Cost includes material and labor to |
| | Install | Ea. | 310 | 36 | | 346 | install 2' 8" x 6' 8" pine half louver |
| | Demolish and Install | Ea. | 310 | 43.15 | | 353.15 | door, jamb, hinges. |
| | Reinstall | Ea. | | 36.16 | | 36.16 | |
| | Clean | Ea. | 6.70 | 33.50 | | 40.20 | |
| | Paint | Ea. | 9.30 | 45 | | 54.30 | |
| | Minimum Charge | Job | | 181 | | 181 | |
| **3' x 6' 8"** | | | | | | | |
| | Demolish | Ea. | | 7.15 | | 7.15 | Cost includes material and labor to |
| | Install | Ea. | 325 | 38 | | 363 | install 3' x 6' 8" pine half louver door, |
| | Demolish and Install | Ea. | 325 | 45.15 | | 370.15 | jamb, hinges. |
| | Reinstall | Ea. | | 38.06 | | 38.06 | |
| | Clean | Ea. | 6.70 | 33.50 | | 40.20 | |
| | Paint | Ea. | 9.30 | 45 | | 54.30 | |
| | Minimum Charge | Job | | 181 | | 181 | |
| **Jamb** | | | | | | | |
| | Demolish | Ea. | | 25 | | 25 | Includes material and labor to install |
| | Install | Ea. | 100 | 9.75 | | 109.75 | flat pine jamb with square cut heads |
| | Demolish and Install | Ea. | 100 | 34.75 | | 134.75 | and rabbeted sides for 6' 8" high and |
| | Clean | Ea. | .12 | 6.65 | | 6.77 | 3-9/16" door including trim sets for |
| | Paint | Ea. | 6.05 | 21 | | 27.05 | both sides. |
| | Minimum Charge | Job | | 90.50 | | 90.50 | |

# Finish Carpentry

## Louver Door

| Louver Door | | Unit | Material | Labor | Equip. | Total | Specification |
|---|---|---|---|---|---|---|---|
| **Stain** | | | | | | | |
| | Install | Ea. | 4.81 | 26 | | 30.81 | Includes labor and material to stain |
| | Minimum Charge | Job | | 157 | | 157 | single door and trim on both sides. |
| **Shave & Refit** | | | | | | | |
| | Install | Ea. | | 30 | | 30 | Includes labor to shave and rework |
| | Minimum Charge | Job | | 157 | | 157 | door to fit opening at the job site. |

## Bypass Sliding Door

| Bypass Sliding Door | | Unit | Material | Labor | Equip. | Total | Specification |
|---|---|---|---|---|---|---|---|
| **Wood** | | | | | | | |
| **5'** | | | | | | | |
| | Demolish | Ea. | | 33.50 | | 33.50 | Includes material and labor to install |
| | Install | Opng. | 204 | 66 | | 270 | pair of 2' 6" wide lauan hollow core |
| | Demolish and Install | Opng. | 204 | 99.50 | | 303.50 | wood bi-pass doors with jamb, track |
| | Reinstall | Opng. | | 65.75 | | 65.75 | hardware. |
| | Clean | Ea. | 1.58 | 19.05 | | 20.63 | |
| | Paint | Ea. | 18.55 | 78.50 | | 97.05 | |
| | Minimum Charge | Job | | 181 | | 181 | |
| **6'** | | | | | | | |
| | Demolish | Ea. | | 33.50 | | 33.50 | Includes material and labor to install |
| | Install | Opng. | 218 | 72.50 | | 290.50 | pair of 3' wide lauan hollow core |
| | Demolish and Install | Opng. | 218 | 106 | | 324 | wood bi-pass doors with jamb, track |
| | Reinstall | Opng. | | 72.32 | | 72.32 | and hardware. |
| | Clean | Ea. | 1.82 | 22 | | 23.82 | |
| | Paint | Ea. | 18.55 | 78.50 | | 97.05 | |
| | Minimum Charge | Job | | 181 | | 181 | |
| **8'** | | | | | | | |
| | Demolish | Ea. | | 33.50 | | 33.50 | Includes material and labor to install |
| | Install | Opng. | 345 | 90.50 | | 435.50 | pair of 4' wide lauan hollow core |
| | Demolish and Install | Opng. | 345 | 124 | | 469 | wood bi-pass doors with jamb, track |
| | Reinstall | Opng. | | 90.40 | | 90.40 | and hardware. |
| | Clean | Ea. | 2.50 | 26.50 | | 29 | |
| | Paint | Ea. | 9.65 | 78.50 | | 88.15 | |
| | Minimum Charge | Job | | 181 | | 181 | |
| **Mirrored** | | | | | | | |
| **6'** | | | | | | | |
| | Demolish | Ea. | | 33.50 | | 33.50 | Includes material and labor to install |
| | Install | Opng. | 256 | 72.50 | | 328.50 | pair of 3' wide mirrored bi-pass doors |
| | Demolish and Install | Opng. | 256 | 106 | | 362 | with jamb, trim, track hardware. |
| | Reinstall | Opng. | | 72.32 | | 72.32 | |
| | Clean | Ea. | 1.82 | 11.10 | | 12.92 | |
| | Minimum Charge | Job | | 181 | | 181 | |
| **8'** | | | | | | | |
| | Demolish | Ea. | | 33.50 | | 33.50 | Includes material and labor to install |
| | Install | Opng. | 540 | 80.50 | | 620.50 | pair of 4' wide mirrored bi-pass doors |
| | Demolish and Install | Opng. | 540 | 114 | | 654 | with jamb, trim, track hardware. |
| | Reinstall | Opng. | | 80.36 | | 80.36 | |
| | Clean | Ea. | 2.50 | 13.35 | | 15.85 | |
| | Minimum Charge | Job | | 181 | | 181 | |

# Finish Carpentry

## Bypass Sliding Door

| | Unit | Material | Labor | Equip. | Total | Specification |
|---|---|---|---|---|---|---|
| **Casing Trim** | | | | | | |
| **Single Width** | | | | | | |
| Demolish | Ea. | | 6.40 | | 6.40 | Cost includes material and labor to |
| Install | Opng. | 23.50 | 61.50 | | 85 | install 11/16" x 2-1/2" pine ranch |
| Demolish and Install | Opng. | 23.50 | 67.90 | | 91.40 | style casing for one side of a standard |
| Reinstall | Opng. | | 49.03 | | 49.03 | door opening. |
| Clean | Opng. | .52 | 2.67 | | 3.19 | |
| Paint | Ea. | 3.65 | 6.30 | | 9.95 | |
| Minimum Charge | Job | | 181 | | 181 | |
| **Double Width** | | | | | | |
| Demolish | Ea. | | 7.60 | | 7.60 | Cost includes material and labor to |
| Install | Opng. | 27.50 | 72.50 | | 100 | install 11/16" x 2-1/2" pine ranch |
| Demolish and Install | Opng. | 27.50 | 80.10 | | 107.60 | style door casing for one side of a |
| Reinstall | Opng. | | 57.86 | | 57.86 | double door opening. |
| Clean | Opng. | .61 | 5.35 | | 5.96 | |
| Paint | Ea. | 3.65 | 7.15 | | 10.80 | |
| Minimum Charge | Job | | 181 | | 181 | |
| **Jamb** | | | | | | |
| Demolish | Ea. | | 25 | | 25 | Includes material and labor to install |
| Install | Ea. | 100 | 9.75 | | 109.75 | flat pine jamb with square cut heads |
| Demolish and Install | Ea. | 100 | 34.75 | | 134.75 | and rabbeted sides for 6' 8" high and |
| Clean | Ea. | .12 | 6.65 | | 6.77 | 3-9/16" door including trim sets for |
| Paint | Ea. | 6.05 | 21 | | 27.05 | both sides. |
| Minimum Charge | Job | | 90.50 | | 90.50 | |
| **Stain** | | | | | | |
| Install | Ea. | 4.81 | 26 | | 30.81 | Includes labor and material to stain |
| Minimum Charge | Job | | 157 | | 157 | single door and trim on both sides. |
| **Shave & Refit** | | | | | | |
| Install | Ea. | | 30 | | 30 | Includes labor to shave and rework |
| Minimum Charge | Job | | 90.50 | | 90.50 | door to fit opening at the job site. |

## Base Molding

| | Unit | Material | Labor | Equip. | Total | Specification |
|---|---|---|---|---|---|---|
| **One Piece** | | | | | | |
| **1-5/8"** | | | | | | |
| Demolish | L.F. | | .49 | | .49 | Includes material and labor to install |
| Install | L.F. | .39 | 1.07 | | 1.46 | pine or birch base molding. |
| Demolish and Install | L.F. | .39 | 1.56 | | 1.95 | |
| Reinstall | L.F. | | .86 | | .86 | |
| Clean | L.F. | .03 | .16 | | .19 | |
| Paint | L.F. | .03 | .34 | | .37 | |
| Minimum Charge | Job | | 181 | | 181 | |
| **2-1/2"** | | | | | | |
| Demolish | L.F. | | .49 | | .49 | Cost includes material and labor to |
| Install | L.F. | .57 | 1.11 | | 1.68 | install 1/2" x 2-1/2" pine or birch |
| Demolish and Install | L.F. | .57 | 1.60 | | 2.17 | base molding. |
| Reinstall | L.F. | | .89 | | .89 | |
| Clean | L.F. | .03 | .16 | | .19 | |
| Paint | L.F. | .03 | .34 | | .37 | |
| Minimum Charge | Job | | 181 | | 181 | |

# Finish Carpentry

## Base Molding

| | Unit | Material | Labor | Equip. | Total | Specification |
|---|---|---|---|---|---|---|
| **3-1/2″** | | | | | | |
| Demolish | L.F. | | .49 | | .49 | Cost includes material and labor to |
| Install | L.F. | 1.70 | 1.16 | | 2.86 | install 9/16″ x 3-1/2″ pine or birch |
| Demolish and Install | L.F. | 1.70 | 1.65 | | 3.35 | base molding. |
| Reinstall | L.F. | | .93 | | .93 | |
| Clean | L.F. | .03 | .16 | | .19 | |
| Paint | L.F. | .03 | .37 | | .40 | |
| Minimum Charge | Job | | 181 | | 181 | |
| **6″** | | | | | | |
| Demolish | L.F. | | .49 | | .49 | Cost includes material and labor to |
| Install | L.F. | .81 | 1.26 | | 2.07 | install 1″ x 6″ pine or birch base |
| Demolish and Install | L.F. | .81 | 1.75 | | 2.56 | molding. |
| Reinstall | L.F. | | 1.01 | | 1.01 | |
| Clean | L.F. | .03 | .22 | | .25 | |
| Paint | L.F. | .06 | .47 | | .53 | |
| Minimum Charge | Job | | 181 | | 181 | |
| **8″** | | | | | | |
| Demolish | L.F. | | .59 | | .59 | Cost includes material and labor to |
| Install | L.F. | 1.10 | 1.39 | | 2.49 | install 1″ x 8″ pine or birch base |
| Demolish and Install | L.F. | 1.10 | 1.98 | | 3.08 | molding. |
| Reinstall | L.F. | | 1.11 | | 1.11 | |
| Clean | L.F. | .04 | .27 | | .31 | |
| Paint | L.F. | .06 | .52 | | .58 | |
| Minimum Charge | Job | | 181 | | 181 | |
| **Premium / Custom Grade** | | | | | | |
| Demolish | L.F. | | .59 | | .59 | Includes material and labor to install |
| Install | L.F. | 4.20 | 3.48 | | 7.68 | custom 2 or 3 piece oak or other |
| Demolish and Install | L.F. | 4.20 | 4.07 | | 8.27 | hardwood, stain grade trim. |
| Reinstall | L.F. | | 2.78 | | 2.78 | |
| Clean | L.F. | .04 | .27 | | .31 | |
| Paint | L.F. | .07 | .52 | | .59 | |
| Minimum Charge | Job | | 181 | | 181 | |
| **One Piece Oak** | | | | | | |
| **1-5/8″** | | | | | | |
| Demolish | L.F. | | .49 | | .49 | Cost includes material and labor to |
| Install | L.F. | .70 | 1.07 | | 1.77 | install 1/2″ x 1-5/8″ oak base |
| Demolish and Install | L.F. | .70 | 1.56 | | 2.26 | molding. |
| Reinstall | L.F. | | .86 | | .86 | |
| Clean | L.F. | .03 | .16 | | .19 | |
| Paint | L.F. | .09 | .47 | | .56 | |
| Minimum Charge | Job | | 181 | | 181 | |
| **2-1/2″** | | | | | | |
| Demolish | L.F. | | .49 | | .49 | Cost includes material and labor to |
| Install | L.F. | 1.07 | 1.09 | | 2.16 | install 1/2″ x 2-1/2″ oak base |
| Demolish and Install | L.F. | 1.07 | 1.58 | | 2.65 | molding. |
| Reinstall | L.F. | | .87 | | .87 | |
| Clean | L.F. | .03 | .16 | | .19 | |
| Paint | L.F. | .09 | .48 | | .57 | |
| Minimum Charge | Job | | 181 | | 181 | |
| **3-1/2″** | | | | | | |
| Demolish | L.F. | | .49 | | .49 | Cost includes material and labor to |
| Install | L.F. | 2.62 | 1.11 | | 3.73 | install 1/2″ x 3-1/2″ oak base |
| Demolish and Install | L.F. | 2.62 | 1.60 | | 4.22 | molding. |
| Reinstall | L.F. | | .89 | | .89 | |
| Clean | L.F. | .03 | .16 | | .19 | |
| Paint | L.F. | .09 | .48 | | .57 | |
| Minimum Charge | Job | | 181 | | 181 | |

# Finish Carpentry

| Base Molding | | Unit | Material | Labor | Equip. | Total | Specification |
|---|---|---|---|---|---|---|---|
| **6"** | | | | | | | |
| | Demolish | L.F. | | .49 | | .49 | Cost includes material and labor to |
| | Install | L.F. | 5.55 | 1.26 | | 6.81 | install 1" x 6" oak base molding. |
| | Demolish and Install | L.F. | 5.55 | 1.75 | | 7.30 | |
| | Reinstall | L.F. | | 1.01 | | 1.01 | |
| | Clean | L.F. | .04 | .27 | | .31 | |
| | Paint | L.F. | .10 | .50 | | .60 | |
| | Minimum Charge | Job | | 181 | | 181 | |
| **8"** | | | | | | | |
| | Demolish | L.F. | | .59 | | .59 | Cost includes material and labor to |
| | Install | L.F. | 6.45 | 1.39 | | 7.84 | install 1" x 8" oak base molding. |
| | Demolish and Install | L.F. | 6.45 | 1.98 | | 8.43 | |
| | Reinstall | L.F. | | 1.11 | | 1.11 | |
| | Clean | L.F. | .04 | .27 | | .31 | |
| | Paint | L.F. | .10 | .52 | | .62 | |
| | Minimum Charge | Job | | 181 | | 181 | |
| **Vinyl Base Molding** | | | | | | | |
| **2-1/2"** | | | | | | | |
| | Demolish | L.F. | | .49 | | .49 | Cost includes material and labor to |
| | Install | L.F. | .77 | 1.06 | | 1.83 | install 2-1/2" vinyl or rubber cove |
| | Demolish and Install | L.F. | .77 | 1.55 | | 2.32 | base including adhesive. |
| | Reinstall | L.F. | | 1.06 | | 1.06 | |
| | Clean | L.F. | | .24 | | .24 | |
| | Minimum Charge | Job | | 166 | | 166 | |
| **4"** | | | | | | | |
| | Demolish | L.F. | | .49 | | .49 | Cost includes material and labor to |
| | Install | L.F. | .79 | 1.06 | | 1.85 | install 4" vinyl or rubber cove base |
| | Demolish and Install | L.F. | .79 | 1.55 | | 2.34 | including adhesive. |
| | Reinstall | L.F. | | 1.06 | | 1.06 | |
| | Clean | L.F. | | .24 | | .24 | |
| | Minimum Charge | Job | | 166 | | 166 | |
| **6"** | | | | | | | |
| | Demolish | L.F. | | .49 | | .49 | Cost includes material and labor to |
| | Install | L.F. | 1.27 | 1.06 | | 2.33 | install 6" vinyl or rubber cove base |
| | Demolish and Install | L.F. | 1.27 | 1.55 | | 2.82 | including adhesive. |
| | Reinstall | L.F. | | 1.06 | | 1.06 | |
| | Clean | L.F. | | .24 | | .24 | |
| | Minimum Charge | Job | | 166 | | 166 | |
| **Prefinished** | | | | | | | |
| | Demolish | L.F. | | .49 | | .49 | Cost includes material and labor to |
| | Install | L.F. | 1.69 | 1.16 | | 2.85 | install 9/16" x 3-5/16" prefinished |
| | Demolish and Install | L.F. | 1.69 | 1.65 | | 3.34 | base molding. |
| | Reinstall | L.F. | | .93 | | .93 | |
| | Clean | L.F. | .03 | .16 | | .19 | |
| | Paint | L.F. | .03 | .37 | | .40 | |
| | Minimum Charge | Job | | 181 | | 181 | |
| **Shoe** | | | | | | | |
| | Demolish | L.F. | | .49 | | .49 | Includes material and labor to install |
| | Install | L.F. | .39 | 1.07 | | 1.46 | pine or birch base molding. |
| | Demolish and Install | L.F. | .39 | 1.56 | | 1.95 | |
| | Reinstall | L.F. | | .86 | | .86 | |
| | Clean | L.F. | .03 | .16 | | .19 | |
| | Paint | L.F. | .13 | .50 | | .63 | |
| | Minimum Charge | Job | | 181 | | 181 | |

# Finish Carpentry

## Base Molding

| Base Molding | | Unit | Material | Labor | Equip. | Total | Specification |
|---|---|---|---|---|---|---|---|
| **Carpeted** | | | | | | | |
| | Demolish | L.F. | | .20 | | .20 | Includes material and labor to install |
| | Install | L.F. | 1.32 | 2.02 | | 3.34 | carpet baseboard with adhesive. |
| | Demolish and Install | L.F. | 1.32 | 2.22 | | 3.54 | |
| | Reinstall | L.F. | | 1.62 | | 1.62 | |
| | Clean | L.F. | | .10 | | .10 | |
| | Minimum Charge | Job | | 167 | | 167 | |
| **Ceramic Tile** | | | | | | | |
| | Demolish | L.F. | | 1.08 | | 1.08 | Includes material and labor to install |
| | Install | L.F. | 3.92 | 4.65 | | 8.57 | thin set ceramic tile cove base |
| | Demolish and Install | L.F. | 3.92 | 5.73 | | 9.65 | including grout. |
| | Clean | L.F. | | .51 | | .51 | |
| | Minimum Charge | Job | | 167 | | 167 | |
| **Quarry Tile** | | | | | | | |
| | Demolish | L.F. | | 1.08 | | 1.08 | Includes material and labor to install |
| | Install | L.F. | 5.25 | 5.40 | | 10.65 | quarry tile base including grout. |
| | Demolish and Install | L.F. | 5.25 | 6.48 | | 11.73 | |
| | Clean | L.F. | | .51 | | .51 | |
| | Minimum Charge | Job | | 167 | | 167 | |
| **Caulk and Renail** | | | | | | | |
| | Install | L.F. | .01 | .57 | | .58 | Includes labor and material to renail |
| | Minimum Charge | Job | | 181 | | 181 | base and caulk where necessary. |

## Molding

| Molding | | Unit | Material | Labor | Equip. | Total | Specification |
|---|---|---|---|---|---|---|---|
| **Oak Base** | | | | | | | |
| | Demolish | L.F. | | .49 | | .49 | Cost includes material and labor to |
| | Install | L.F. | 1.07 | 1.09 | | 2.16 | install 1/2" x 2-1/2" oak base |
| | Demolish and Install | L.F. | 1.07 | 1.58 | | 2.65 | molding. |
| | Reinstall | L.F. | | .87 | | .87 | |
| | Clean | L.F. | .03 | .16 | | .19 | |
| | Paint | L.F. | .09 | .48 | | .57 | |
| | Minimum Charge | Job | | 181 | | 181 | |
| **Shoe** | | | | | | | |
| | Demolish | L.F. | | .49 | | .49 | Includes material and labor to install |
| | Install | L.F. | .39 | 1.07 | | 1.46 | pine or birch base molding. |
| | Demolish and Install | L.F. | .39 | 1.56 | | 1.95 | |
| | Reinstall | L.F. | | .86 | | .86 | |
| | Clean | L.F. | .03 | .16 | | .19 | |
| | Paint | L.F. | .13 | .50 | | .63 | |
| | Minimum Charge | Job | | 181 | | 181 | |
| **Quarter Round** | | | | | | | |
| | Demolish | L.F. | | .49 | | .49 | Includes material and labor to install |
| | Install | L.F. | .65 | 1.42 | | 2.07 | pine base quarter round molding. |
| | Demolish and Install | L.F. | .65 | 1.91 | | 2.56 | |
| | Reinstall | L.F. | | 1.13 | | 1.13 | |
| | Clean | L.F. | .03 | .16 | | .19 | |
| | Paint | L.F. | .07 | .79 | | .86 | |
| | Minimum Charge | Job | | 181 | | 181 | |
| **Chair Rail** | | | | | | | |
| | Demolish | L.F. | | .49 | | .49 | Cost includes material and labor to |
| | Install | L.F. | 1.54 | 1.34 | | 2.88 | install 5/8" x 2-1/2" oak chair rail |
| | Demolish and Install | L.F. | 1.54 | 1.83 | | 3.37 | molding. |
| | Reinstall | L.F. | | 1.07 | | 1.07 | |
| | Clean | L.F. | .03 | .16 | | .19 | |
| | Paint | L.F. | .07 | .79 | | .86 | |
| | Minimum Charge | Job | | 181 | | 181 | |

# Finish Carpentry

| Molding | | Unit | Material | Labor | Equip. | Total | Specification |
|---|---|---|---|---|---|---|---|
| **Crown** | | | | | | | |
| | Demolish | L.F. | | .49 | | .49 | Includes material and labor to install |
| | Install | L.F. | 1.97 | 1.45 | | 3.42 | unfinished pine crown molding. |
| | Demolish and Install | L.F. | 1.97 | 1.94 | | 3.91 | |
| | Reinstall | L.F. | | 1.16 | | 1.16 | |
| | Clean | L.F. | .04 | .21 | | .25 | |
| | Paint | L.F. | .07 | .79 | | .86 | |
| | Minimum Charge | Job | | 181 | | 181 | |
| **Cove** | | | | | | | |
| | Demolish | L.F. | | .49 | | .49 | Cost includes material and labor to |
| | Install | L.F. | 1.43 | 1.42 | | 2.85 | install 1/2" x 2-3/4" pine cove |
| | Demolish and Install | L.F. | 1.43 | 1.91 | | 3.34 | molding. |
| | Reinstall | L.F. | | 1.13 | | 1.13 | |
| | Clean | L.F. | .03 | .16 | | .19 | |
| | Paint | L.F. | .07 | .79 | | .86 | |
| | Minimum Charge | Job | | 181 | | 181 | |
| **Corner** | | | | | | | |
| | Demolish | L.F. | | .49 | | .49 | Includes material and labor to install |
| | Install | L.F. | .61 | .57 | | 1.18 | inside or outside pine corner molding. |
| | Demolish and Install | L.F. | .61 | 1.06 | | 1.67 | |
| | Reinstall | L.F. | | .45 | | .45 | |
| | Clean | L.F. | .03 | .16 | | .19 | |
| | Paint | L.F. | .07 | .79 | | .86 | |
| | Minimum Charge | Job | | 181 | | 181 | |
| **Picture** | | | | | | | |
| | Demolish | L.F. | | .49 | | .49 | Cost includes material and labor to |
| | Install | L.F. | 1.39 | 1.51 | | 2.90 | install 9/16" x 2-1/2" pine casing. |
| | Demolish and Install | L.F. | 1.39 | 2 | | 3.39 | |
| | Reinstall | L.F. | | 1.21 | | 1.21 | |
| | Clean | L.F. | .03 | .16 | | .19 | |
| | Paint | L.F. | .07 | .79 | | .86 | |
| | Minimum Charge | Job | | 181 | | 181 | |
| **Single Cased Opening** | | | | | | | |
| | Demolish | Ea. | | 25 | | 25 | Includes material and labor to install |
| | Install | Ea. | 21.50 | 22.50 | | 44 | flat pine jamb with square cut heads |
| | Demolish and Install | Ea. | 21.50 | 47.50 | | 69 | and rabbeted sides for 6' 8" high |
| | Clean | Ea. | .25 | 5.55 | | 5.80 | opening including trim sets for both |
| | Paint | Ea. | 1.32 | 7.85 | | 9.17 | sides. |
| | Minimum Charge | Job | | 181 | | 181 | |
| **Double Cased Opening** | | | | | | | |
| | Demolish | Ea. | | 25 | | 25 | Includes material and labor to install |
| | Install | Ea. | 43 | 26 | | 69 | flat pine jamb with square cut heads |
| | Demolish and Install | Ea. | 43 | 51 | | 94 | and rabbeted sides for 6' 8" high |
| | Clean | Ea. | .30 | 6.50 | | 6.80 | opening including trim sets for both |
| | Paint | Ea. | 1.53 | 9.25 | | 10.78 | sides. |
| | Minimum Charge | Job | | 181 | | 181 | |

| Window Trim Set | | Unit | Material | Labor | Equip. | Total | Specification |
|---|---|---|---|---|---|---|---|
| **Single** | | | | | | | |
| | Demolish | Ea. | | 6.60 | | 6.60 | Cost includes material and labor to |
| | Install | Opng. | 38 | 36 | | 74 | install 11/16" x 2-1/2" pine ranch |
| | Demolish and Install | Opng. | 38 | 42.60 | | 80.60 | style window casing. |
| | Reinstall | Opng. | | 28.93 | | 28.93 | |
| | Clean | Ea. | .36 | 3.81 | | 4.17 | |
| | Paint | Ea. | 1.24 | 7.50 | | 8.74 | |
| | Minimum Charge | Job | | 181 | | 181 | |

# Finish Carpentry

## Window Trim Set

| | Unit | Material | Labor | Equip. | Total | Specification |
|---|---|---|---|---|---|---|
| **Double** | | | | | | |
| Demolish | Ea. | | 7.40 | | 7.40 | Cost includes material and labor to |
| Install | Ea. | 51.50 | 45 | | 96.50 | install 11/16" x 2-1/2" pine ranch |
| Demolish and Install | Ea. | 51.50 | 52.40 | | 103.90 | style trim for casing one side of a |
| Reinstall | Ea. | | 36.16 | | 36.16 | double window opening. |
| Clean | Ea. | .65 | 4.45 | | 5.10 | |
| Paint | Ea. | 2.08 | 12.60 | | 14.68 | |
| Minimum Charge | Job | | 181 | | 181 | |
| **Triple** | | | | | | |
| Demolish | Ea. | | 8.45 | | 8.45 | Cost includes material and labor to |
| Install | Opng. | 69 | 60.50 | | 129.50 | install 11/16" x 2-1/2" pine ranch |
| Demolish and Install | Opng. | 69 | 68.95 | | 137.95 | style trim for casing one side of a |
| Reinstall | Opng. | | 48.21 | | 48.21 | triple window opening. |
| Clean | Ea. | .91 | 5.35 | | 6.26 | |
| Paint | Ea. | 2.92 | 17.50 | | 20.42 | |
| Minimum Charge | Job | | 181 | | 181 | |
| **Window Casing Per L.F.** | | | | | | |
| Demolish | L.F. | | .49 | | .49 | Cost includes material and labor to |
| Install | L.F. | 1.39 | 1.51 | | 2.90 | install 11/16" x 2-1/2" pine ranch |
| Demolish and Install | L.F. | 1.39 | 2 | | 3.39 | style trim for casing. |
| Reinstall | L.F. | | 1.21 | | 1.21 | |
| Clean | L.F. | .03 | .16 | | .19 | |
| Paint | L.F. | .07 | .79 | | .86 | |
| Minimum Charge | Job | | 181 | | 181 | |

## Window Sill

| | Unit | Material | Labor | Equip. | Total | Specification |
|---|---|---|---|---|---|---|
| **Wood** | | | | | | |
| Demolish | L.F. | | .49 | | .49 | Includes material and labor to install |
| Install | L.F. | 2.35 | 1.81 | | 4.16 | flat, wood window stool. |
| Demolish and Install | L.F. | 2.35 | 2.30 | | 4.65 | |
| Reinstall | L.F. | | 1.45 | | 1.45 | |
| Clean | L.F. | .03 | .16 | | .19 | |
| Paint | L.F. | .07 | .79 | | .86 | |
| Minimum Charge | Job | | 181 | | 181 | |
| **Marble** | | | | | | |
| Demolish | L.F. | | .74 | | .74 | Includes material and labor to install |
| Install | L.F. | 8.15 | 7.65 | | 15.80 | marble window sills, 6" x 3/4" thick. |
| Demolish and Install | L.F. | 8.15 | 8.39 | | 16.54 | |
| Reinstall | L.F. | | 6.10 | | 6.10 | |
| Clean | L.F. | .03 | .16 | | .19 | |
| Minimum Charge | Job | | 167 | | 167 | |

## Shelving

| | Unit | Material | Labor | Equip. | Total | Specification |
|---|---|---|---|---|---|---|
| **Pine** | | | | | | |
| **18"** | | | | | | |
| Demolish | L.F. | | .85 | | .85 | Cost includes material and labor to |
| Install | L.F. | 4.44 | 3.81 | | 8.25 | install 1" thick custom shelving board |
| Demolish and Install | L.F. | 4.44 | 4.66 | | 9.10 | 18" wide. |
| Reinstall | L.F. | | 3.05 | | 3.05 | |
| Clean | L.F. | .06 | .44 | | .50 | |
| Paint | L.F. | .81 | .50 | | 1.31 | |
| Minimum Charge | Job | | 181 | | 181 | |

| Shelving | | Unit | Material | Labor | Equip. | Total | Specification |
|---|---|---|---|---|---|---|---|
| **24"** | | | | | | | |
| | Demolish | L.F. | | .85 | | .85 | Cost includes material and labor to |
| | Install | L.F. | 5.95 | 4.25 | | 10.20 | install 1" thick custom shelving board. |
| | Demolish and Install | L.F. | 5.95 | 5.10 | | 11.05 | |
| | Reinstall | L.F. | | 3.40 | | 3.40 | |
| | Clean | L.F. | .08 | .67 | | .75 | |
| | Paint | L.F. | 1.11 | .66 | | 1.77 | |
| | Minimum Charge | Job | | 181 | | 181 | |
| **Particle Board** | | | | | | | |
| | Demolish | L.F. | | .78 | | .78 | Cost includes material and labor to |
| | Install | L.F. | 1.27 | 1.90 | | 3.17 | install 3/4" thick particle shelving |
| | Demolish and Install | L.F. | 1.27 | 2.68 | | 3.95 | board 18" wide. |
| | Reinstall | L.F. | | 1.52 | | 1.52 | |
| | Clean | L.F. | .06 | .44 | | .50 | |
| | Paint | S.F. | .13 | .73 | | .86 | |
| | Minimum Charge | Job | | 181 | | 181 | |
| **Plywood** | | | | | | | |
| | Demolish | L.F. | | .78 | | .78 | Cost includes material and labor to |
| | Install | L.F. | .80 | 5.55 | | 6.35 | install 3/4" thick plywood shelving |
| | Demolish and Install | L.F. | .80 | 6.33 | | 7.13 | board. |
| | Reinstall | L.F. | | 4.45 | | 4.45 | |
| | Clean | L.F. | .06 | .44 | | .50 | |
| | Paint | S.F. | .13 | .73 | | .86 | |
| | Minimum Charge | Job | | 181 | | 181 | |
| **Hardwood (oak)** | | | | | | | |
| | Demolish | L.F. | | .78 | | .78 | Includes material and labor to install |
| | Install | L.F. | 4.83 | 2.49 | | 7.32 | oak shelving, 1" x 12", incl. cleats and |
| | Demolish and Install | L.F. | 4.83 | 3.27 | | 8.10 | bracing. |
| | Reinstall | L.F. | | 2 | | 2 | |
| | Clean | L.F. | .06 | .44 | | .50 | |
| | Paint | S.F. | .13 | .73 | | .86 | |
| | Minimum Charge | Job | | 181 | | 181 | |
| **Custom Bookcase** | | | | | | | |
| | Demolish | L.F. | | 9.90 | | 9.90 | Includes material and labor to install |
| | Install | L.F. | 25.50 | 36 | | 61.50 | custom modular bookcase unit with |
| | Demolish and Install | L.F. | 25.50 | 45.90 | | 71.40 | clear pine faced frames, shelves 12" |
| | Reinstall | L.F. | | 28.93 | | 28.93 | O.C., 7' high, 8" deep. |
| | Clean | L.F. | 1.45 | 9.55 | | 11 | |
| | Paint | L.F. | 1.12 | 24 | | 25.12 | |
| | Minimum Charge | Job | | 181 | | 181 | |
| **Glass** | | | | | | | |
| | Demolish | L.F. | | .78 | | .78 | Includes material and labor to install |
| | Install | L.F. | 26 | 2.49 | | 28.49 | glass shelving, 1" x 12", incl. cleats |
| | Demolish and Install | L.F. | 26 | 3.27 | | 29.27 | and bracing. |
| | Reinstall | L.F. | | 2 | | 2 | |
| | Clean | L.F. | .07 | .41 | | .48 | |
| | Minimum Charge | Job | | 175 | | 175 | |

| Closet Shelving | | Unit | Material | Labor | Equip. | Total | Specification |
|---|---|---|---|---|---|---|---|
| **Closet Shelf and Rod** | | | | | | | |
| | Demolish | L.F. | | .78 | | .78 | Cost includes material and labor to |
| | Install | L.F. | 2.35 | 6.05 | | 8.40 | install 1" thick custom shelving board |
| | Demolish and Install | L.F. | 2.35 | 6.83 | | 9.18 | 18" wide and 1" diameter clothes pole |
| | Reinstall | L.F. | | 4.82 | | 4.82 | with brackets 3' O.C. |
| | Clean | L.F. | .03 | .33 | | .36 | |
| | Paint | L.F. | .13 | .79 | | .92 | |
| | Minimum Charge | Job | | 181 | | 181 | |

205

# Finish Carpentry

## Closet Shelving

| | Unit | Material | Labor | Equip. | Total | Specification |
|---|---|---|---|---|---|---|
| **Clothing Rod** | | | | | | |
| Demolish | L.F. | | .52 | | .52 | Includes material and labor to install |
| Install | L.F. | 1.89 | 1.81 | | 3.70 | fir closet pole, 1-5/8" diameter. |
| Demolish and Install | L.F. | 1.89 | 2.33 | | 4.22 | |
| Reinstall | L.F. | | 1.45 | | 1.45 | |
| Clean | L.F. | .03 | .46 | | .49 | |
| Paint | L.F. | .12 | .86 | | .98 | |
| Minimum Charge | Job | | 181 | | 181 | |

## Stair Assemblies

| | Unit | Material | Labor | Equip. | Total | Specification |
|---|---|---|---|---|---|---|
| **Straight Hardwood** | | | | | | |
| Demolish | Ea. | | 350 | | 350 | Includes material and labor to install |
| Install | Flight | 1000 | 241 | | 1241 | factory cut and assembled straight |
| Demolish and Install | Flight | 1000 | 591 | | 1591 | closed box stairs with oak treads and |
| Clean | Flight | 3.63 | 23 | | 26.63 | prefinished stair rail with balusters. |
| Paint | Flight | 11.45 | 42 | | 53.45 | |
| Minimum Charge | Job | | 181 | | 181 | |
| **Clear Oak Tread** | | | | | | |
| Demolish | Ea. | | 9.15 | | 9.15 | Includes material and labor to install |
| Install | Ea. | 65 | 20 | | 85 | 1-1/4" thick clear oak treads per riser. |
| Demolish and Install | Ea. | 65 | 29.15 | | 94.15 | |
| Clean | Ea. | .11 | 2.29 | | 2.40 | |
| Paint | Ea. | .39 | 2.33 | | 2.72 | |
| Minimum Charge | Job | | 181 | | 181 | |
| **Landing** | | | | | | |
| Demolish | S.F. | | 3.09 | | 3.09 | Includes material and labor to install |
| Install | S.F. | 7.20 | 20 | | 27.20 | clear oak landing. |
| Demolish and Install | S.F. | 7.20 | 23.09 | | 30.29 | |
| Clean | S.F. | | .33 | | .33 | |
| Paint | S.F. | .31 | .78 | | 1.09 | |
| Minimum Charge | Job | | 181 | | 181 | |
| **Refinish / Stain** | | | | | | |
| Install | S.F. | 1.28 | 2.05 | | 3.33 | Includes labor and material to sand |
| Minimum Charge | Job | | 157 | | 157 | and finish (3 passes) with two coats of |
| | | | | | | urethane on a new floor. |
| **Spiral Hardwood** | | | | | | |
| Demolish | Ea. | | 350 | | 350 | Cost includes material and labor to |
| Install | Flight | 5150 | 480 | | 5630 | install 4' - 6' diameter spiral stairs with |
| Demolish and Install | Flight | 5150 | 830 | | 5980 | oak treads, factory cut and assembled |
| Clean | Flight | 3.63 | 23 | | 26.63 | with double handrails. |
| Paint | Flight | 11.45 | 42 | | 53.45 | |
| Minimum Charge | Job | | 181 | | 181 | |

## Stairs

| | Unit | Material | Labor | Equip. | Total | Specification |
|---|---|---|---|---|---|---|
| **Disappearing** | | | | | | |
| Demolish | Ea. | | 18.55 | | 18.55 | Includes material and labor to install a |
| Install | Ea. | 199 | 103 | | 302 | folding staircase. |
| Demolish and Install | Ea. | 199 | 121.55 | | 320.55 | |
| Reinstall | Ea. | | 82.65 | | 82.65 | |
| Clean | Ea. | .55 | 16.70 | | 17.25 | |
| Minimum Charge | Job | | 181 | | 181 | |

| Stair Components | Unit | Material | Labor | Equip. | Total | Specification |
|---|---|---|---|---|---|---|
| **Handrail w / Balusters** | | | | | | |
| Demolish | L.F. | | 2.47 | | 2.47 | Includes material and labor to install |
| Install | L.F. | 34.50 | 7.55 | | 42.05 | prefinished assembled stair rail with |
| Demolish and Install | L.F. | 34.50 | 10.02 | | 44.52 | brackets, turned balusters and newel. |
| Clean | L.F. | .73 | 1.84 | | 2.57 | |
| Paint | L.F. | 1.61 | 3.70 | | 5.31 | |
| Minimum Charge | Job | | 181 | | 181 | |
| **Bannister** | | | | | | |
| Demolish | L.F. | | 2.47 | | 2.47 | Includes material and labor to install |
| Install | L.F. | 36 | 6.05 | | 42.05 | built-up oak railings. |
| Demolish and Install | L.F. | 36 | 8.52 | | 44.52 | |
| Clean | L.F. | .73 | 1.67 | | 2.40 | |
| Paint | L.F. | 1.61 | 2.86 | | 4.47 | |
| Minimum Charge | Job | | 181 | | 181 | |

# Cabinets and Countertops

**Wall and Base Cabinets**

**Countertop**

| Wall Cabinets | Unit | Material | Labor | Equip. | Total | Specification |
|---|---|---|---|---|---|---|
| **Good Grade Laminated** | | | | | | |
| **12″ Wide, 1 Door** | | | | | | |
| Demolish | Ea. | | 7.40 | | 7.40 | Includes material and labor to install |
| Install | Ea. | 120 | 33 | | 153 | good modular unit with melamine |
| Demolish and Install | Ea. | 120 | 40.40 | | 160.40 | laminated to particle board, in |
| Reinstall | Ea. | | 26.30 | | 26.30 | textured colors or wood grain print |
| Clean | Ea. | .55 | 5.15 | | 5.70 | finish, hinges and pulls. |
| Paint | Ea. | .48 | 11.25 | | 11.73 | |
| Minimum Charge | Job | | 181 | | 181 | |
| **15″ Wide, 1 Door** | | | | | | |
| Demolish | Ea. | | 9.25 | | 9.25 | Includes material and labor to install |
| Install | Ea. | 135 | 34 | | 169 | good modular unit with melamine |
| Demolish and Install | Ea. | 135 | 43.25 | | 178.25 | laminated to particle board, in |
| Reinstall | Ea. | | 27.04 | | 27.04 | textured colors or wood grain print |
| Clean | Ea. | .68 | 6.35 | | 7.03 | finish, hinges and pulls. |
| Paint | Ea. | .61 | 14.30 | | 14.91 | |
| Minimum Charge | Job | | 181 | | 181 | |
| **18″ Wide, 1 Door** | | | | | | |
| Demolish | Ea. | | 11.20 | | 11.20 | Includes material and labor to install |
| Install | Ea. | 149 | 34.50 | | 183.50 | good modular unit with melamine |
| Demolish and Install | Ea. | 149 | 45.70 | | 194.70 | laminated to particle board, in |
| Reinstall | Ea. | | 27.68 | | 27.68 | textured colors or wood grain print |
| Clean | Ea. | .81 | 7.60 | | 8.41 | finish, hinges and pulls. |
| Paint | Ea. | .73 | 16.55 | | 17.28 | |
| Minimum Charge | Job | | 181 | | 181 | |
| **21″ Wide, 1 Door** | | | | | | |
| Demolish | Ea. | | 12.90 | | 12.90 | Includes material and labor to install |
| Install | Ea. | 167 | 35 | | 202 | good modular unit with melamine |
| Demolish and Install | Ea. | 167 | 47.90 | | 214.90 | laminated to particle board, in |
| Reinstall | Ea. | | 28.09 | | 28.09 | textured colors or wood grain print |
| Clean | Ea. | .96 | 8.90 | | 9.86 | finish, hinges and pulls. |
| Paint | Ea. | .85 | 19.70 | | 20.55 | |
| Minimum Charge | Job | | 181 | | 181 | |
| **24″ w / Blind Corner** | | | | | | |
| Demolish | Ea. | | 14.80 | | 14.80 | Includes material and labor to install |
| Install | Ea. | 167 | 35.50 | | 202.50 | good modular unit with melamine |
| Demolish and Install | Ea. | 167 | 50.30 | | 217.30 | laminated to particle board, in |
| Reinstall | Ea. | | 28.50 | | 28.50 | textured colors or wood grain print |
| Clean | Ea. | 1.09 | 10.25 | | 11.34 | finish, hinges and pulls. |
| Paint | Ea. | .97 | 22.50 | | 23.47 | |
| Minimum Charge | Job | | 181 | | 181 | |

# Cabinets and Countertops

| Wall Cabinets | Unit | Material | Labor | Equip. | Total | Specification |
|---|---|---|---|---|---|---|
| **27" Wide, 2 Door** | | | | | | |
| Demolish | Ea. | | 16.45 | | 16.45 | Includes material and labor to install |
| Install | Ea. | 187 | 36.50 | | 223.50 | good modular unit with melamine |
| Demolish and Install | Ea. | 187 | 52.95 | | 239.95 | laminated to particle board, in |
| Reinstall | Ea. | | 29.22 | | 29.22 | textured colors or wood grain print |
| Clean | Ea. | 1.22 | 11.60 | | 12.82 | finish, hinges and pulls. |
| Paint | Ea. | 1.09 | 26 | | 27.09 | |
| Minimum Charge | Job | | 181 | | 181 | |
| **30" Wide, 2 Door** | | | | | | |
| Demolish | Ea. | | 18.55 | | 18.55 | Includes material and labor to install |
| Install | Ea. | 200 | 37.50 | | 237.50 | good modular unit with melamine |
| Demolish and Install | Ea. | 200 | 56.05 | | 256.05 | laminated to particle board, in |
| Reinstall | Ea. | | 29.98 | | 29.98 | textured colors or wood grain print |
| Clean | Ea. | 1.36 | 12.70 | | 14.06 | finish, hinges and pulls. |
| Paint | Ea. | 1.21 | 28.50 | | 29.71 | |
| Minimum Charge | Job | | 181 | | 181 | |
| **36" Wide, 2 Door** | | | | | | |
| Demolish | Ea. | | 22 | | 22 | Includes material and labor to install |
| Install | Ea. | 230 | 38.50 | | 268.50 | good modular unit with melamine |
| Demolish and Install | Ea. | 230 | 60.50 | | 290.50 | laminated to particle board, in |
| Reinstall | Ea. | | 30.77 | | 30.77 | textured colors or wood grain print |
| Clean | Ea. | 1.64 | 15.70 | | 17.34 | finish, hinges and pulls. |
| Paint | Ea. | 1.46 | 35 | | 36.46 | |
| Minimum Charge | Job | | 181 | | 181 | |
| **48" Wide, 2 Door** | | | | | | |
| Demolish | Ea. | | 29.50 | | 29.50 | Includes material and labor to install |
| Install | Ea. | 282 | 39.50 | | 321.50 | good modular unit with melamine |
| Demolish and Install | Ea. | 282 | 69 | | 351 | laminated to particle board, in |
| Reinstall | Ea. | | 31.44 | | 31.44 | textured colors or wood grain print |
| Clean | Ea. | 2.18 | 20.50 | | 22.68 | finish, hinges and pulls. |
| Paint | Ea. | 1.94 | 45 | | 46.94 | |
| Minimum Charge | Job | | 181 | | 181 | |
| **Above-Appliance** | | | | | | |
| Demolish | Ea. | | 18.55 | | 18.55 | Includes material and labor to install |
| Install | Ea. | 134 | 29 | | 163 | good modular unit with melamine |
| Demolish and Install | Ea. | 134 | 47.55 | | 181.55 | laminated to particle board, in |
| Reinstall | Ea. | | 23.33 | | 23.33 | textured colors or wood grain print |
| Clean | Ea. | 1.36 | 12.70 | | 14.06 | finish, hinges and pulls. |
| Paint | Ea. | 1.21 | 28.50 | | 29.71 | |
| Minimum Charge | Job | | 181 | | 181 | |
| **Better Grade Wood** | | | | | | |
| **12" Wide, 1 Door** | | | | | | |
| Demolish | Ea. | | 7.40 | | 7.40 | Includes material and labor to install |
| Install | Ea. | 161 | 33 | | 194 | custom modular unit with solid |
| Demolish and Install | Ea. | 161 | 40.40 | | 201.40 | hardwood faced frames, hardwood |
| Reinstall | Ea. | | 26.30 | | 26.30 | door frames and drawer fronts, |
| Clean | Ea. | .55 | 5.15 | | 5.70 | hardwood veneer on raised door |
| Paint | Ea. | .48 | 12.10 | | 12.58 | panels, hinges and pulls. |
| Minimum Charge | Job | | 181 | | 181 | |
| **15" Wide, 1 Door** | | | | | | |
| Demolish | Ea. | | 9.25 | | 9.25 | Includes material and labor to install |
| Install | Ea. | 180 | 34 | | 214 | custom modular unit with solid |
| Demolish and Install | Ea. | 180 | 43.25 | | 223.25 | hardwood faced frames, hardwood |
| Reinstall | Ea. | | 27.04 | | 27.04 | door frames and drawer fronts, |
| Clean | Ea. | .68 | 6.35 | | 7.03 | hardwood veneer on raised door |
| Paint | Ea. | .61 | 15 | | 15.61 | panels, hinges and pulls. |
| Minimum Charge | Job | | 181 | | 181 | |

# Cabinets and Countertops

| Wall Cabinets | | Unit | Material | Labor | Equip. | Total | Specification |
|---|---|---|---|---|---|---|---|
| **18" Wide, 1 Door** | | | | | | | |
| | Demolish | Ea. | | 11.20 | | 11.20 | Includes material and labor to install |
| | Install | Ea. | 198 | 34.50 | | 232.50 | custom modular unit with solid |
| | Demolish and Install | Ea. | 198 | 45.70 | | 243.70 | hardwood faced frames, hardwood |
| | Reinstall | Ea. | | 27.68 | | 27.68 | door frames and drawer fronts, |
| | Clean | Ea. | .81 | 7.60 | | 8.41 | hardwood veneer on raised door |
| | Paint | Ea. | .73 | 18.50 | | 19.23 | panels, hinges and pulls. |
| | Minimum Charge | Job | | 181 | | 181 | |
| **21" Wide, 1 Door** | | | | | | | |
| | Demolish | Ea. | | 12.90 | | 12.90 | Includes material and labor to install |
| | Install | Ea. | 222 | 35 | | 257 | custom modular unit with solid |
| | Demolish and Install | Ea. | 222 | 47.90 | | 269.90 | hardwood faced frames, hardwood |
| | Reinstall | Ea. | | 28.09 | | 28.09 | door frames and drawer fronts, |
| | Clean | Ea. | .96 | 8.90 | | 9.86 | hardwood veneer on raised door |
| | Paint | Ea. | .85 | 21 | | 21.85 | panels, hinges and pulls. |
| | Minimum Charge | Job | | 181 | | 181 | |
| **24" w / Blind Corner** | | | | | | | |
| | Demolish | Ea. | | 14.80 | | 14.80 | Includes material and labor to install |
| | Install | Ea. | 223 | 35.50 | | 258.50 | custom modular unit with solid |
| | Demolish and Install | Ea. | 223 | 50.30 | | 273.30 | hardwood faced frames, hardwood |
| | Reinstall | Ea. | | 28.50 | | 28.50 | door frames and drawer fronts, |
| | Clean | Ea. | 1.09 | 10.25 | | 11.34 | hardwood veneer on raised door |
| | Paint | Ea. | .97 | 24 | | 24.97 | panels, hinges and pulls. |
| | Minimum Charge | Job | | 181 | | 181 | |
| **27" Wide, 2 Door** | | | | | | | |
| | Demolish | Ea. | | 16.45 | | 16.45 | Includes material and labor to install |
| | Install | Ea. | 250 | 36.50 | | 286.50 | custom modular unit with solid |
| | Demolish and Install | Ea. | 250 | 52.95 | | 302.95 | hardwood faced frames, hardwood |
| | Reinstall | Ea. | | 29.22 | | 29.22 | door frames and drawer fronts, |
| | Clean | Ea. | 1.22 | 11.60 | | 12.82 | hardwood veneer on raised door |
| | Paint | Ea. | 1.09 | 26 | | 27.09 | panels, hinges and pulls. |
| | Minimum Charge | Job | | 181 | | 181 | |
| **30" Wide, 2 Door** | | | | | | | |
| | Demolish | Ea. | | 18.55 | | 18.55 | Includes material and labor to install |
| | Install | Ea. | 267 | 37.50 | | 304.50 | custom modular unit with solid |
| | Demolish and Install | Ea. | 267 | 56.05 | | 323.05 | hardwood faced frames, hardwood |
| | Reinstall | Ea. | | 29.98 | | 29.98 | door frames and drawer fronts, |
| | Clean | Ea. | 1.36 | 12.70 | | 14.06 | hardwood veneer on raised door |
| | Paint | Ea. | 1.21 | 31.50 | | 32.71 | panels, hinges and pulls. |
| | Minimum Charge | Job | | 181 | | 181 | |
| **36" Wide, 2 Door** | | | | | | | |
| | Demolish | Ea. | | 22 | | 22 | Includes material and labor to install |
| | Install | Ea. | 305 | 38.50 | | 343.50 | custom modular unit with solid |
| | Demolish and Install | Ea. | 305 | 60.50 | | 365.50 | hardwood faced frames, hardwood |
| | Reinstall | Ea. | | 30.77 | | 30.77 | door frames and drawer fronts, |
| | Clean | Ea. | 1.64 | 15.70 | | 17.34 | hardwood veneer on raised door |
| | Paint | Ea. | 1.46 | 35 | | 36.46 | panels, hinges and pulls. |
| | Minimum Charge | Job | | 181 | | 181 | |
| **48" Wide, 2 Door** | | | | | | | |
| | Demolish | Ea. | | 29.50 | | 29.50 | Includes material and labor to install |
| | Install | Ea. | 375 | 39.50 | | 414.50 | custom modular unit with solid |
| | Demolish and Install | Ea. | 375 | 69 | | 444 | hardwood faced frames, hardwood |
| | Reinstall | Ea. | | 31.44 | | 31.44 | door frames and drawer fronts, |
| | Clean | Ea. | 2.18 | 20.50 | | 22.68 | hardwood veneer on raised door |
| | Paint | Ea. | 1.94 | 45 | | 46.94 | panels, hinges and pulls. |
| | Minimum Charge | Job | | 181 | | 181 | |

# Cabinets and Countertops

| Wall Cabinets | | Unit | Material | Labor | Equip. | Total | Specification |
|---|---|---|---|---|---|---|---|
| **Above-appliance** | | | | | | | |
| | Demolish | Ea. | | 18.55 | | 18.55 | Includes material and labor to install |
| | Install | Ea. | 179 | 29 | | 208 | custom modular unit with solid |
| | Demolish and Install | Ea. | 179 | 47.55 | | 226.55 | hardwood faced frames, hardwood |
| | Reinstall | Ea. | | 23.33 | | 23.33 | door frames and drawer fronts, |
| | Clean | Ea. | 1.36 | 12.70 | | 14.06 | hardwood veneer on raised door |
| | Paint | Ea. | 1.21 | 31.50 | | 32.71 | panels, hinges and pulls. |
| | Minimum Charge | Job | | 181 | | 181 | |
| **Premium Grade Wood** | | | | | | | |
| **12″ Wide, 1 Door** | | | | | | | |
| | Demolish | Ea. | | 7.40 | | 7.40 | Includes material and labor to install |
| | Install | Ea. | 193 | 33 | | 226 | premium modular unit with solid |
| | Demolish and Install | Ea. | 193 | 40.40 | | 233.40 | hardwood faced frames, hardwood |
| | Reinstall | Ea. | | 26.30 | | 26.30 | door frames and drawer fronts, |
| | Clean | Ea. | .55 | 5.15 | | 5.70 | hardwood veneer on raised door |
| | Paint | Ea. | .48 | 13.10 | | 13.58 | panels, hinges and pulls. |
| | Minimum Charge | Job | | 181 | | 181 | |
| **15″ Wide, 1 Door** | | | | | | | |
| | Demolish | Ea. | | 9.25 | | 9.25 | Includes material and labor to install |
| | Install | Ea. | 241 | 34 | | 275 | premium modular unit with solid |
| | Demolish and Install | Ea. | 241 | 43.25 | | 284.25 | hardwood faced frames, hardwood |
| | Reinstall | Ea. | | 27.04 | | 27.04 | door frames and drawer fronts, |
| | Clean | Ea. | .68 | 6.35 | | 7.03 | hardwood veneer on raised door |
| | Paint | Ea. | .61 | 16.55 | | 17.16 | panels, hinges and pulls. |
| | Minimum Charge | Job | | 181 | | 181 | |
| **18″ Wide, 1 Door** | | | | | | | |
| | Demolish | Ea. | | 11.20 | | 11.20 | Includes material and labor to install |
| | Install | Ea. | 238 | 34.50 | | 272.50 | premium modular unit with solid |
| | Demolish and Install | Ea. | 238 | 45.70 | | 283.70 | hardwood faced frames, hardwood |
| | Reinstall | Ea. | | 27.68 | | 27.68 | door frames and drawer fronts, |
| | Clean | Ea. | .81 | 7.60 | | 8.41 | hardwood veneer on raised door |
| | Paint | Ea. | .73 | 19.70 | | 20.43 | panels, hinges and pulls. |
| | Minimum Charge | Job | | 181 | | 181 | |
| **21″ Wide, 1 Door** | | | | | | | |
| | Demolish | Ea. | | 12.90 | | 12.90 | Includes material and labor to install |
| | Install | Ea. | 267 | 35 | | 302 | premium modular unit with solid |
| | Demolish and Install | Ea. | 267 | 47.90 | | 314.90 | hardwood faced frames, hardwood |
| | Reinstall | Ea. | | 28.09 | | 28.09 | door frames and drawer fronts, |
| | Clean | Ea. | .96 | 8.90 | | 9.86 | hardwood veneer on raised door |
| | Paint | Ea. | .85 | 22.50 | | 23.35 | panels, hinges and pulls. |
| | Minimum Charge | Job | | 181 | | 181 | |
| **24″ w / Blind Corner** | | | | | | | |
| | Demolish | Ea. | | 14.80 | | 14.80 | Includes material and labor to install |
| | Install | Ea. | 267 | 35.50 | | 302.50 | premium modular unit with solid |
| | Demolish and Install | Ea. | 267 | 50.30 | | 317.30 | hardwood faced frames, hardwood |
| | Reinstall | Ea. | | 28.50 | | 28.50 | door frames and drawer fronts, |
| | Clean | Ea. | 1.09 | 10.25 | | 11.34 | hardwood veneer on raised door |
| | Paint | Ea. | .97 | 26 | | 26.97 | panels, hinges and pulls. |
| | Minimum Charge | Job | | 181 | | 181 | |
| **27″ Wide, 2 Door** | | | | | | | |
| | Demolish | Ea. | | 16.45 | | 16.45 | Includes material and labor to install |
| | Install | Ea. | 267 | 36.50 | | 303.50 | premium modular unit with solid |
| | Demolish and Install | Ea. | 267 | 52.95 | | 319.95 | hardwood faced frames, hardwood |
| | Reinstall | Ea. | | 29.22 | | 29.22 | door frames and drawer fronts, |
| | Clean | Ea. | 1.22 | 11.60 | | 12.82 | hardwood veneer on raised door |
| | Paint | Ea. | 1.09 | 28.50 | | 29.59 | panels, hinges and pulls. |
| | Minimum Charge | Job | | 181 | | 181 | |

# Cabinets and Countertops

| Wall Cabinets | | Unit | Material | Labor | Equip. | Total | Specification |
|---|---|---|---|---|---|---|---|
| **30" Wide, 2 Door** | | | | | | | |
| | Demolish | Ea. | | 18.55 | | 18.55 | Includes material and labor to install |
| | Install | Ea. | 320 | 37.50 | | 357.50 | premium modular unit with solid |
| | Demolish and Install | Ea. | 320 | 56.05 | | 376.05 | hardwood faced frames, hardwood |
| | Reinstall | Ea. | | 29.98 | | 29.98 | door frames and drawer fronts, |
| | Clean | Ea. | 1.36 | 12.70 | | 14.06 | hardwood veneer on raised door |
| | Paint | Ea. | 1.21 | 31.50 | | 32.71 | panels, hinges and pulls. |
| | Minimum Charge | Job | | 181 | | 181 | |
| **36" Wide, 2 Door** | | | | | | | |
| | Demolish | Ea. | | 22 | | 22 | Includes material and labor to install |
| | Install | Ea. | 370 | 38.50 | | 408.50 | premium modular unit with solid |
| | Demolish and Install | Ea. | 370 | 60.50 | | 430.50 | hardwood faced frames, hardwood |
| | Reinstall | Ea. | | 30.77 | | 30.77 | door frames and drawer fronts, |
| | Clean | Ea. | 1.64 | 15.70 | | 17.34 | hardwood veneer on raised door |
| | Paint | Ea. | 1.46 | 39.50 | | 40.96 | panels, hinges and pulls. |
| | Minimum Charge | Job | | 181 | | 181 | |
| **48" Wide, 2 Door** | | | | | | | |
| | Demolish | Ea. | | 29.50 | | 29.50 | Includes material and labor to install |
| | Install | Ea. | 450 | 39.50 | | 489.50 | premium modular unit with solid |
| | Demolish and Install | Ea. | 450 | 69 | | 519 | hardwood faced frames, hardwood |
| | Reinstall | Ea. | | 31.44 | | 31.44 | door frames and drawer fronts, |
| | Clean | Ea. | 2.18 | 20.50 | | 22.68 | hardwood veneer on raised door |
| | Paint | Ea. | 1.94 | 52.50 | | 54.44 | panels, hinges and pulls. |
| | Minimum Charge | Job | | 181 | | 181 | |
| **Above-appliance** | | | | | | | |
| | Demolish | Ea. | | 18.55 | | 18.55 | Includes material and labor to install |
| | Install | Ea. | 216 | 29 | | 245 | premium modular unit with solid |
| | Demolish and Install | Ea. | 216 | 47.55 | | 263.55 | hardwood faced frames, hardwood |
| | Reinstall | Ea. | | 23.33 | | 23.33 | door frames and drawer fronts, |
| | Clean | Ea. | 1.36 | 12.70 | | 14.06 | hardwood veneer on raised door |
| | Paint | Ea. | 1.21 | 31.50 | | 32.71 | panels, hinges, pulls. |
| | Minimum Charge | Job | | 181 | | 181 | |
| **Premium Hardwood** | | | | | | | |
| **12" Wide, 1 Door** | | | | | | | |
| | Demolish | Ea. | | 7.40 | | 7.40 | Includes material and labor to install |
| | Install | Ea. | 210 | 33 | | 243 | premium hardwood modular unit with |
| | Demolish and Install | Ea. | 210 | 40.40 | | 250.40 | solid hardwood faced frames, drawer |
| | Reinstall | Ea. | | 26.30 | | 26.30 | fronts, and door panels, steel drawer |
| | Clean | Ea. | .55 | 5.15 | | 5.70 | guides, hinges, pulls, laminated |
| | Paint | Ea. | .48 | 14.30 | | 14.78 | interior. |
| | Minimum Charge | Job | | 181 | | 181 | |
| **15" Wide, 1 Door** | | | | | | | |
| | Demolish | Ea. | | 9.25 | | 9.25 | Includes material and labor to install |
| | Install | Ea. | 315 | 34 | | 349 | premium hardwood modular unit with |
| | Demolish and Install | Ea. | 315 | 43.25 | | 358.25 | solid hardwood faced frames, drawer |
| | Reinstall | Ea. | | 27.04 | | 27.04 | fronts, and door panels, steel drawer |
| | Clean | Ea. | .68 | 6.35 | | 7.03 | guides, hinges, pulls, laminated |
| | Paint | Ea. | .61 | 17.50 | | 18.11 | interior. |
| | Minimum Charge | Job | | 181 | | 181 | |
| **18" Wide, 1 Door** | | | | | | | |
| | Demolish | Ea. | | 11.20 | | 11.20 | Includes material and labor to install |
| | Install | Ea. | 260 | 34.50 | | 294.50 | premium hardwood modular unit with |
| | Demolish and Install | Ea. | 260 | 45.70 | | 305.70 | solid hardwood faced frames, drawer |
| | Reinstall | Ea. | | 27.68 | | 27.68 | fronts, and door panels, steel drawer |
| | Clean | Ea. | .81 | 7.60 | | 8.41 | guides, hinges, pulls, laminated |
| | Paint | Ea. | .73 | 21 | | 21.73 | interior. |
| | Minimum Charge | Job | | 181 | | 181 | |

# Cabinets and Countertops

| Wall Cabinets | Unit | Material | Labor | Equip. | Total | Specification |
|---|---|---|---|---|---|---|
| **21" Wide, 1 Door** | | | | | | |
| Demolish | Ea. | | 12.90 | | 12.90 | Includes material and labor to install |
| Install | Ea. | 292 | 35 | | 327 | premium hardwood modular unit with |
| Demolish and Install | Ea. | 292 | 47.90 | | 339.90 | solid hardwood faced frames, drawer |
| Reinstall | Ea. | | 28.09 | | 28.09 | fronts, and door panels, steel drawer |
| Clean | Ea. | .96 | 8.90 | | 9.86 | guides, hinges, pulls, laminated |
| Paint | Ea. | .85 | 24 | | 24.85 | interior. |
| Minimum Charge | Job | | 181 | | 181 | |
| **24" w / Blind Corner** | | | | | | |
| Demolish | Ea. | | 14.80 | | 14.80 | Includes material and labor to install |
| Install | Ea. | 293 | 35.50 | | 328.50 | premium hardwood modular unit with |
| Demolish and Install | Ea. | 293 | 50.30 | | 343.30 | solid hardwood faced frames, drawer |
| Reinstall | Ea. | | 28.50 | | 28.50 | fronts, and door panels, steel drawer |
| Clean | Ea. | 1.09 | 10.25 | | 11.34 | guides, hinges, pulls, laminated |
| Paint | Ea. | .97 | 28.50 | | 29.47 | interior. |
| Minimum Charge | Job | | 181 | | 181 | |
| **27" Wide, 2 Door** | | | | | | |
| Demolish | Ea. | | 16.45 | | 16.45 | Includes material and labor to install |
| Install | Ea. | 325 | 36.50 | | 361.50 | premium hardwood modular unit with |
| Demolish and Install | Ea. | 325 | 52.95 | | 377.95 | solid hardwood faced frames, drawer |
| Reinstall | Ea. | | 29.22 | | 29.22 | fronts, and door panels, steel drawer |
| Clean | Ea. | 1.22 | 11.60 | | 12.82 | guides, hinges, pulls, laminated |
| Paint | Ea. | 1.09 | 31.50 | | 32.59 | interior. |
| Minimum Charge | Job | | 181 | | 181 | |
| **30" Wide, 2 Door** | | | | | | |
| Demolish | Ea. | | 18.55 | | 18.55 | Includes material and labor to install |
| Install | Ea. | 350 | 37.50 | | 387.50 | premium hardwood modular unit with |
| Demolish and Install | Ea. | 350 | 56.05 | | 406.05 | solid hardwood faced frames, drawer |
| Reinstall | Ea. | | 29.98 | | 29.98 | fronts, and door panels, steel drawer |
| Clean | Ea. | 1.36 | 12.70 | | 14.06 | guides, hinges, pulls, laminated |
| Paint | Ea. | 1.21 | 35 | | 36.21 | interior. |
| Minimum Charge | Job | | 181 | | 181 | |
| **36" Wide, 2 Door** | | | | | | |
| Demolish | Ea. | | 22 | | 22 | Includes material and labor to install |
| Install | Ea. | 400 | 38.50 | | 438.50 | premium hardwood modular unit with |
| Demolish and Install | Ea. | 400 | 60.50 | | 460.50 | solid hardwood faced frames, drawer |
| Reinstall | Ea. | | 30.77 | | 30.77 | fronts, and door panels, steel drawer |
| Clean | Ea. | 1.64 | 15.70 | | 17.34 | guides, hinges, pulls, laminated |
| Paint | Ea. | 1.46 | 45 | | 46.46 | interior. |
| Minimum Charge | Job | | 181 | | 181 | |
| **48" Wide, 2 Door** | | | | | | |
| Demolish | Ea. | | 29.50 | | 29.50 | Includes material and labor to install |
| Install | Ea. | 490 | 39.50 | | 529.50 | premium hardwood modular unit with |
| Demolish and Install | Ea. | 490 | 69 | | 559 | solid hardwood faced frames, drawer |
| Reinstall | Ea. | | 31.44 | | 31.44 | fronts, and door panels, steel drawer |
| Clean | Ea. | 2.18 | 20.50 | | 22.68 | guides, hinges, pulls, laminated |
| Paint | Ea. | 1.94 | 52.50 | | 54.44 | interior. |
| Minimum Charge | Job | | 181 | | 181 | |
| **Above-appliance** | | | | | | |
| Demolish | Ea. | | 18.55 | | 18.55 | Includes material and labor to install |
| Install | Ea. | 235 | 29 | | 264 | premium hardwood modular unit with |
| Demolish and Install | Ea. | 235 | 47.55 | | 282.55 | solid hardwood faced frames, drawer |
| Reinstall | Ea. | | 23.33 | | 23.33 | fronts, and door panels, steel drawer |
| Clean | Ea. | 1.36 | 12.70 | | 14.06 | guides, hinges, pulls, laminated |
| Paint | Ea. | 1.21 | 35 | | 36.21 | interior. |
| Minimum Charge | Job | | 181 | | 181 | |

# Cabinets and Countertops

| Wall Cabinets | Unit | Material | Labor | Equip. | Total | Specification |
|---|---|---|---|---|---|---|
| **Medicine Cabinet** | | | | | | |
| **Good Grade** | | | | | | |
| Demolish | Ea. | | 12.35 | | 12.35 | Cost includes material and labor to |
| Install | Ea. | 138 | 26 | | 164 | install 14″ x 18″ recessed medicine |
| Demolish and Install | Ea. | 138 | 38.35 | | 176.35 | cabinet with stainless steel frame, |
| Reinstall | Ea. | | 20.66 | | 20.66 | mirror. Light not included. |
| Clean | Ea. | .02 | 12 | | 12.02 | |
| Paint | Ea. | 1.11 | 19.70 | | 20.81 | |
| Minimum Charge | Job | | 181 | | 181 | |
| **Good Grade Lighted** | | | | | | |
| Demolish | Ea. | | 12.35 | | 12.35 | Cost includes material and labor to |
| Install | Ea. | 365 | 30 | | 395 | install 14″ x 18″ recessed medicine |
| Demolish and Install | Ea. | 365 | 42.35 | | 407.35 | cabinet with stainless steel frame, |
| Reinstall | Ea. | | 24.11 | | 24.11 | mirror and light. |
| Clean | Ea. | .02 | 12 | | 12.02 | |
| Paint | Ea. | 1.11 | 19.70 | | 20.81 | |
| Minimum Charge | Job | | 181 | | 181 | |
| **Better Grade** | | | | | | |
| Demolish | Ea. | | 12.35 | | 12.35 | Includes material and labor to install |
| Install | Ea. | 117 | 26 | | 143 | recessed medicine cabinet with |
| Demolish and Install | Ea. | 117 | 38.35 | | 155.35 | polished chrome frame and mirror. |
| Reinstall | Ea. | | 20.66 | | 20.66 | Light not included. |
| Clean | Ea. | .02 | 12 | | 12.02 | |
| Paint | Ea. | 1.11 | 19.70 | | 20.81 | |
| Minimum Charge | Job | | 181 | | 181 | |
| **Better Grade Lighted** | | | | | | |
| Demolish | Ea. | | 12.35 | | 12.35 | Includes material and labor to install |
| Install | Ea. | 340 | 30 | | 370 | recessed medicine cabinet with |
| Demolish and Install | Ea. | 340 | 42.35 | | 382.35 | polished chrome frame, mirror and |
| Reinstall | Ea. | | 24.11 | | 24.11 | light. |
| Clean | Ea. | .02 | 12 | | 12.02 | |
| Paint | Ea. | 1.11 | 19.70 | | 20.81 | |
| Minimum Charge | Job | | 181 | | 181 | |
| **Premium Grade** | | | | | | |
| Demolish | Ea. | | 12.35 | | 12.35 | Cost includes material and labor to |
| Install | Ea. | 272 | 26 | | 298 | install 14″ x 24″ recessed medicine |
| Demolish and Install | Ea. | 272 | 38.35 | | 310.35 | cabinet with beveled mirror, frameless |
| Reinstall | Ea. | | 20.66 | | 20.66 | swing door. Light not included. |
| Clean | Ea. | .02 | 12 | | 12.02 | |
| Paint | Ea. | 1.11 | 19.70 | | 20.81 | |
| Minimum Charge | Job | | 181 | | 181 | |
| **Premium Grade Light** | | | | | | |
| Demolish | Ea. | | 12.35 | | 12.35 | Cost includes material and labor to |
| Install | Ea. | 495 | 30 | | 525 | install 36″ x 30″ surface mounted |
| Demolish and Install | Ea. | 495 | 42.35 | | 537.35 | medicine cabinet with beveled tri-view |
| Reinstall | Ea. | | 24.11 | | 24.11 | mirror, frameless swing door and light. |
| Clean | Ea. | .02 | 12 | | 12.02 | |
| Paint | Ea. | 1.11 | 19.70 | | 20.81 | |
| Minimum Charge | Job | | 181 | | 181 | |
| **Bath Mirror** | | | | | | |
| Demolish | Ea. | | 9.25 | | 9.25 | Cost includes material and labor to |
| Install | Ea. | 51.50 | 18.10 | | 69.60 | install 18″ x 24″ surface mount mirror |
| Demolish and Install | Ea. | 51.50 | 27.35 | | 78.85 | with stainless steel frame. |
| Reinstall | Ea. | | 14.46 | | 14.46 | |
| Clean | Ea. | .02 | .80 | | .82 | |
| Minimum Charge | Job | | 181 | | 181 | |

# Cabinets and Countertops

| Wall Cabinets | | Unit | Material | Labor | Equip. | Total | Specification |
|---|---|---|---|---|---|---|---|
| **Garage** | | | | | | | |
| | Demolish | L.F. | | 7.40 | | 7.40 | Includes material and labor to install |
| | Install | L.F. | 59 | 18.10 | | 77.10 | good modular unit with melamine |
| | Demolish and Install | L.F. | 59 | 25.50 | | 84.50 | laminated to particle board, in |
| | Reinstall | L.F. | | 14.46 | | 14.46 | textured colors or wood grain print |
| | Clean | L.F. | .55 | 5.15 | | 5.70 | finish, hinges and pulls. |
| | Paint | L.F. | .48 | 11.25 | | 11.73 | |
| | Minimum Charge | Job | | 181 | | 181 | |
| **Strip and Refinish** | | | | | | | |
| | Install | L.F. | 1.11 | 5.70 | | 6.81 | Includes labor and material to strip, |
| | Minimum Charge | Job | | 157 | | 157 | prep and refinish exterior of cabinets. |

| Tall Cabinets | | Unit | Material | Labor | Equip. | Total | Specification |
|---|---|---|---|---|---|---|---|
| **Good Grade Laminated** | | | | | | | |
| | Demolish | L.F. | | 13.20 | | 13.20 | Includes material and labor to install |
| | Install | L.F. | 241 | 204 | | 445 | custom modular unit with solid |
| | Demolish and Install | L.F. | 241 | 217.20 | | 458.20 | hardwood faced frames, hardwood |
| | Reinstall | L.F. | | 162.97 | | 162.97 | door frames and drawer fronts, |
| | Clean | L.F. | 1.45 | 9.55 | | 11 | hardwood veneer on raised door |
| | Paint | L.F. | 1.12 | 22.50 | | 23.62 | panels, hinges and pulls. |
| | Minimum Charge | Job | | 181 | | 181 | |
| **Better Grade Wood** | | | | | | | |
| | Demolish | L.F. | | 13.20 | | 13.20 | Includes material and labor to install |
| | Install | L.F. | 320 | 204 | | 524 | custom modular unit with solid |
| | Demolish and Install | L.F. | 320 | 217.20 | | 537.20 | hardwood faced frames, hardwood |
| | Reinstall | L.F. | | 162.97 | | 162.97 | door frames and drawer fronts, |
| | Clean | L.F. | 1.45 | 9.55 | | 11 | hardwood veneer on raised door |
| | Paint | L.F. | 1.12 | 24 | | 25.12 | panels, hinges and pulls. |
| | Minimum Charge | Job | | 181 | | 181 | |
| **Premium Grade Wood** | | | | | | | |
| | Demolish | L.F. | | 13.20 | | 13.20 | Includes material and labor to install |
| | Install | L.F. | 430 | 204 | | 634 | premium modular unit with solid |
| | Demolish and Install | L.F. | 430 | 217.20 | | 647.20 | hardwood faced frames, hardwood |
| | Reinstall | L.F. | | 162.97 | | 162.97 | door frames and drawer fronts, |
| | Clean | L.F. | 1.45 | 9.55 | | 11 | hardwood veneer on raised door |
| | Paint | L.F. | 1.12 | 26 | | 27.12 | panels, hinges and pulls. |
| | Minimum Charge | Job | | 181 | | 181 | |
| **Premium Hardwood** | | | | | | | |
| | Demolish | L.F. | | 13.20 | | 13.20 | Includes material and labor to install |
| | Install | L.F. | 560 | 204 | | 764 | premium hardwood modular unit with |
| | Demolish and Install | L.F. | 560 | 217.20 | | 777.20 | solid hardwood faced frames, drawer |
| | Reinstall | L.F. | | 162.97 | | 162.97 | fronts, and door panels, steel drawer |
| | Clean | L.F. | 1.45 | 9.55 | | 11 | guides, hinges and pulls, laminated |
| | Paint | L.F. | 1.12 | 28.50 | | 29.62 | interior. |
| | Minimum Charge | Job | | 181 | | 181 | |

# Cabinets and Countertops

| Tall Cabinets | Unit | Material | Labor | Equip. | Total | Specification |
|---|---|---|---|---|---|---|
| **Single Oven, 27" Wide** | | | | | | |
| **Good Grade Laminated** | | | | | | |
| Demolish | Ea. | | 29.50 | | 29.50 | Includes material and labor to install |
| Install | Ea. | 540 | 90.50 | | 630.50 | good modular unit with melamine |
| Demolish and Install | Ea. | 540 | 120 | | 660 | laminated to particle board, in |
| Reinstall | Ea. | | 72.32 | | 72.32 | textured colors or wood grain print |
| Clean | Ea. | 4.54 | 16.70 | | 21.24 | finish, hinges and pulls. |
| Paint | Ea. | 1.89 | 50.50 | | 52.39 | |
| Minimum Charge | Job | | 181 | | 181 | |
| **Better Grade Veneer** | | | | | | |
| Demolish | Ea. | | 29.50 | | 29.50 | Includes material and labor to install |
| Install | Ea. | 955 | 90.50 | | 1045.50 | custom modular unit with solid |
| Demolish and Install | Ea. | 955 | 120 | | 1075 | hardwood faced frames, hardwood |
| Reinstall | Ea. | | 72.32 | | 72.32 | door frames and drawer fronts, |
| Clean | Ea. | 4.54 | 16.70 | | 21.24 | hardwood veneer on raised door |
| Paint | Ea. | 1.89 | 54.50 | | 56.39 | panels, hinges and pulls. |
| Minimum Charge | Job | | 181 | | 181 | |
| **Premium Grade Veneer** | | | | | | |
| Demolish | Ea. | | 29.50 | | 29.50 | Includes material and labor to install |
| Install | Ea. | 865 | 90.50 | | 955.50 | premium modular unit with solid |
| Demolish and Install | Ea. | 865 | 120 | | 985 | hardwood faced frames, hardwood |
| Reinstall | Ea. | | 72.32 | | 72.32 | door frames and drawer fronts, |
| Clean | Ea. | 4.54 | 16.70 | | 21.24 | hardwood veneer on raised door |
| Paint | Ea. | 1.89 | 59.50 | | 61.39 | panels, hinges and pulls. |
| Minimum Charge | Job | | 181 | | 181 | |
| **Premium Hardwood** | | | | | | |
| Demolish | Ea. | | 29.50 | | 29.50 | Includes material and labor to install |
| Install | Ea. | 945 | 90.50 | | 1035.50 | premium hardwood modular unit with |
| Demolish and Install | Ea. | 945 | 120 | | 1065 | solid hardwood faced frames, drawer |
| Reinstall | Ea. | | 72.32 | | 72.32 | fronts, and door panels, steel drawer |
| Clean | Ea. | 4.54 | 16.70 | | 21.24 | guides, hinges and pulls, laminated |
| Paint | Ea. | 1.89 | 64 | | 65.89 | interior. |
| Minimum Charge | Job | | 181 | | 181 | |
| **Single Oven, 30" Wide** | | | | | | |
| **Good Grade Laminated** | | | | | | |
| Demolish | Ea. | | 29.50 | | 29.50 | Includes material and labor to install |
| Install | Ea. | 715 | 90.50 | | 805.50 | good modular unit with melamine |
| Demolish and Install | Ea. | 715 | 120 | | 835 | laminated to particle board, in |
| Reinstall | Ea. | | 72.32 | | 72.32 | textured colors or wood grain print |
| Clean | Ea. | 4.54 | 16.70 | | 21.24 | finish, hinges and pulls. |
| Paint | Ea. | 1.89 | 50.50 | | 52.39 | |
| Minimum Charge | Job | | 181 | | 181 | |
| **Better Grade Veneer** | | | | | | |
| Demolish | Ea. | | 29.50 | | 29.50 | Includes material and labor to install |
| Install | Ea. | 840 | 90.50 | | 930.50 | custom modular unit with solid |
| Demolish and Install | Ea. | 840 | 120 | | 960 | hardwood faced frames, hardwood |
| Reinstall | Ea. | | 72.32 | | 72.32 | door frames and drawer fronts, |
| Clean | Ea. | 4.54 | 16.70 | | 21.24 | hardwood veneer on raised door |
| Paint | Ea. | 1.89 | 50.50 | | 52.39 | panels, hinges and pulls. |
| Minimum Charge | Job | | 181 | | 181 | |

# Cabinets and Countertops

| Tall Cabinets | Unit | Material | Labor | Equip. | Total | Specification |
|---|---|---|---|---|---|---|
| **Premium Grade Veneer** | | | | | | |
| Demolish | Ea. | | 29.50 | | 29.50 | Includes material and labor to install |
| Install | Ea. | 925 | 90.50 | | 1015.50 | premium modular unit with solid |
| Demolish and Install | Ea. | 925 | 120 | | 1045 | hardwood faced frames, hardwood |
| Reinstall | Ea. | | 72.32 | | 72.32 | door frames and drawer fronts, |
| Clean | Ea. | 4.54 | 16.70 | | 21.24 | hardwood veneer on raised door |
| Paint | Ea. | 1.89 | 50.50 | | 52.39 | panels, hinges and pulls. |
| Minimum Charge | Job | | 181 | | 181 | |
| **Premium Hardwood** | | | | | | |
| Demolish | Ea. | | 29.50 | | 29.50 | Includes material and labor to install |
| Install | Ea. | 1125 | 90.50 | | 1215.50 | premium hardwood modular unit with |
| Demolish and Install | Ea. | 1125 | 120 | | 1245 | solid hardwood faced frames, drawer |
| Reinstall | Ea. | | 72.32 | | 72.32 | fronts, and door panels, steel drawer |
| Clean | Ea. | 4.54 | 16.70 | | 21.24 | guides, hinges and pulls, laminated |
| Paint | Ea. | 1.89 | 50.50 | | 52.39 | interior. |
| Minimum Charge | Job | | 181 | | 181 | |
| **Utility 18″ W x 12″ D** | | | | | | |
| **Good Grade Laminated** | | | | | | |
| Demolish | Ea. | | 29.50 | | 29.50 | Includes material and labor to install |
| Install | Ea. | 360 | 72.50 | | 432.50 | good modular unit with melamine |
| Demolish and Install | Ea. | 360 | 102 | | 462 | laminated to particle board, in |
| Reinstall | Ea. | | 57.86 | | 57.86 | textured colors or wood grain print |
| Clean | Ea. | 1.07 | 8.10 | | 9.17 | finish, hinges and pulls. |
| Paint | Ea. | .73 | 19.70 | | 20.43 | |
| Minimum Charge | Job | | 181 | | 181 | |
| **Better Grade Veneer** | | | | | | |
| Demolish | Ea. | | 29.50 | | 29.50 | Includes material and labor to install |
| Install | Ea. | 480 | 72.50 | | 552.50 | custom modular unit with solid |
| Demolish and Install | Ea. | 480 | 102 | | 582 | hardwood faced frames, hardwood |
| Reinstall | Ea. | | 57.86 | | 57.86 | door frames and drawer fronts, |
| Clean | Ea. | 1.07 | 8.10 | | 9.17 | hardwood veneer on raised door |
| Paint | Ea. | .73 | 21 | | 21.73 | panels, hinges and pulls. |
| Minimum Charge | Job | | 181 | | 181 | |
| **Premium Grade Veneer** | | | | | | |
| Demolish | Ea. | | 29.50 | | 29.50 | Includes material and labor to install |
| Install | Ea. | 570 | 72.50 | | 642.50 | premium modular unit with solid |
| Demolish and Install | Ea. | 570 | 102 | | 672 | hardwood faced frames, hardwood |
| Reinstall | Ea. | | 57.86 | | 57.86 | door frames and drawer fronts, |
| Clean | Ea. | 1.07 | 8.10 | | 9.17 | hardwood veneer on raised door |
| Paint | Ea. | .73 | 24 | | 24.73 | panels, hinges and pulls. |
| Minimum Charge | Job | | 181 | | 181 | |
| **Premium Hardwood** | | | | | | |
| Demolish | Ea. | | 29.50 | | 29.50 | Includes material and labor to install |
| Install | Ea. | 625 | 72.50 | | 697.50 | premium hardwood modular unit with |
| Demolish and Install | Ea. | 625 | 102 | | 727 | solid hardwood faced frames, drawer |
| Reinstall | Ea. | | 57.86 | | 57.86 | fronts, and door panels, steel drawer |
| Clean | Ea. | 1.07 | 8.10 | | 9.17 | guides, hinges and pulls, laminated |
| Paint | Ea. | .73 | 26 | | 26.73 | interior. |
| Minimum Charge | Job | | 181 | | 181 | |

| Tall Cabinets | Unit | Material | Labor | Equip. | Total | Specification |
|---|---|---|---|---|---|---|
| **Utility 24″ W x 24″ D** | | | | | | |
| **Good Grade Laminated** | | | | | | |
| Demolish | Ea. | | 29.50 | | 29.50 | Includes material and labor to install |
| Install | Ea. | 485 | 90.50 | | 575.50 | good modular unit with melamine |
| Demolish and Install | Ea. | 485 | 120 | | 605 | laminated to particle board, in |
| Reinstall | Ea. | | 72.32 | | 72.32 | textured colors or wood grain print |
| Clean | Ea. | 1.40 | 10.65 | | 12.05 | finish, hinges and pulls. |
| Paint | Ea. | .97 | 26 | | 26.97 | |
| Minimum Charge | Job | | 181 | | 181 | |
| **Better Grade Veneer** | | | | | | |
| Demolish | Ea. | | 29.50 | | 29.50 | Includes material and labor to install |
| Install | Ea. | 650 | 90.50 | | 740.50 | custom modular unit with solid |
| Demolish and Install | Ea. | 650 | 120 | | 770 | hardwood faced frames, hardwood |
| Reinstall | Ea. | | 72.32 | | 72.32 | door frames and drawer fronts, |
| Clean | Ea. | 1.40 | 10.65 | | 12.05 | hardwood veneer on raised door |
| Paint | Ea. | .97 | 28.50 | | 29.47 | panels, hinges and pulls. |
| Minimum Charge | Job | | 181 | | 181 | |
| **Premium Grade Veneer** | | | | | | |
| Demolish | Ea. | | 29.50 | | 29.50 | Includes material and labor to install |
| Install | Ea. | 775 | 90.50 | | 865.50 | premium modular unit with solid |
| Demolish and Install | Ea. | 775 | 120 | | 895 | hardwood faced frames, hardwood |
| Reinstall | Ea. | | 72.32 | | 72.32 | door frames and drawer fronts, |
| Clean | Ea. | 1.40 | 10.65 | | 12.05 | hardwood veneer on raised door |
| Paint | Ea. | .97 | 31.50 | | 32.47 | panels, hinges and pulls. |
| Minimum Charge | Job | | 181 | | 181 | |
| **Premium Hardwood** | | | | | | |
| Demolish | Ea. | | 29.50 | | 29.50 | Includes material and labor to install |
| Install | Ea. | 845 | 90.50 | | 935.50 | premium hardwood modular unit with |
| Demolish and Install | Ea. | 845 | 120 | | 965 | solid hardwood faced frames, drawer |
| Reinstall | Ea. | | 72.32 | | 72.32 | fronts, and door panels, steel drawer |
| Clean | Ea. | 1.40 | 10.65 | | 12.05 | guides, hinges and pulls, laminated |
| Paint | Ea. | .97 | 35 | | 35.97 | interior. |
| Minimum Charge | Job | | 181 | | 181 | |
| **Plain Shelves** | | | | | | |
| Install | Ea. | 25.50 | 22.50 | | 48 | Includes labor and material to install |
| **Rotating Shelves** | | | | | | tall cabinet shelving, per set. |
| Install | Ea. | 122 | 18.10 | | 140.10 | Includes labor and material to install |
| **Strip and Refinish** | | | | | | lazy susan shelving for wall cabinet. |
| Install | L.F. | 1.64 | 14.30 | | 15.94 | Includes labor and material to strip, |
| Minimum Charge | Job | | 157 | | 157 | prep and refinish exterior of cabinets. |
| **Stain** | | | | | | |
| Install | L.F. | .19 | 2.86 | | 3.05 | Includes labor and material to replace |
| Minimum Charge | Job | | 157 | | 157 | normal prep and stain on doors and |
| | | | | | | exterior cabinets. |

| Base Cabinets | Unit | Material | Labor | Equip. | Total | Specification |
|---|---|---|---|---|---|---|
| **Good Grade Laminated** | | | | | | |
| **12″ w, 1 Door, 1 Drawer** | | | | | | |
| Demolish | Ea. | | 7.40 | | 7.40 | Includes material and labor to install |
| Install | Ea. | 167 | 29 | | 196 | good modular unit with melamine |
| Demolish and Install | Ea. | 167 | 36.40 | | 203.40 | laminate, textured colors or wood |
| Reinstall | Ea. | | 23.33 | | 23.33 | grain print finish including hinges and |
| Clean | Ea. | .73 | 5.35 | | 6.08 | pulls. |
| Paint | Ea. | .48 | 13.10 | | 13.58 | |
| Minimum Charge | Job | | 181 | | 181 | |
| **15″ w, 1 Door, 1 Drawer** | | | | | | |
| Demolish | Ea. | | 9.25 | | 9.25 | Includes material and labor to install |
| Install | Ea. | 175 | 30 | | 205 | good modular unit with melamine |
| Demolish and Install | Ea. | 175 | 39.25 | | 214.25 | laminate, textured colors or wood |
| Reinstall | Ea. | | 24.11 | | 24.11 | grain print finish including hinges and |
| Clean | Ea. | .91 | 6.65 | | 7.56 | pulls. |
| Paint | Ea. | .61 | 16.55 | | 17.16 | |
| Minimum Charge | Job | | 181 | | 181 | |
| **18″ w, 1 Door, 1 Drawer** | | | | | | |
| Demolish | Ea. | | 11 | | 11 | Includes material and labor to install |
| Install | Ea. | 191 | 31 | | 222 | good modular unit with melamine |
| Demolish and Install | Ea. | 191 | 42 | | 233 | laminate, textured colors or wood |
| Reinstall | Ea. | | 24.83 | | 24.83 | grain print finish including hinges and |
| Clean | Ea. | 1.07 | 8.10 | | 9.17 | pulls. |
| Paint | Ea. | .73 | 19.70 | | 20.43 | |
| Minimum Charge | Job | | 181 | | 181 | |
| **21″ w, 1 Door, 1 Drawer** | | | | | | |
| Demolish | Ea. | | 12.90 | | 12.90 | Includes material and labor to install |
| Install | Ea. | 208 | 32 | | 240 | good modular unit with melamine |
| Demolish and Install | Ea. | 208 | 44.90 | | 252.90 | laminate, textured colors or wood |
| Reinstall | Ea. | | 25.49 | | 25.49 | grain print finish including hinges and |
| Clean | Ea. | 1.30 | 9.55 | | 10.85 | pulls. |
| Paint | Ea. | .85 | 22.50 | | 23.35 | |
| Minimum Charge | Job | | 181 | | 181 | |
| **24″ w, 1 Door, 1 Drawer** | | | | | | |
| Demolish | Ea. | | 14.80 | | 14.80 | Includes material and labor to install |
| Install | Ea. | 228 | 32.50 | | 260.50 | good modular unit with melamine |
| Demolish and Install | Ea. | 228 | 47.30 | | 275.30 | laminate, textured colors or wood |
| Reinstall | Ea. | | 25.94 | | 25.94 | grain print finish including hinges and |
| Clean | Ea. | 1.40 | 10.65 | | 12.05 | pulls. |
| Paint | Ea. | .97 | 26 | | 26.97 | |
| Minimum Charge | Job | | 181 | | 181 | |
| **30″ Wide Sink Base** | | | | | | |
| Demolish | Ea. | | 18.55 | | 18.55 | Includes material and labor to install |
| Install | Ea. | 248 | 34 | | 282 | good modular unit with melamine |
| Demolish and Install | Ea. | 248 | 52.55 | | 300.55 | laminate, textured colors or wood |
| Reinstall | Ea. | | 27.04 | | 27.04 | grain print finish including hinges and |
| Clean | Ea. | 1.82 | 13.35 | | 15.17 | pulls. |
| Paint | Ea. | 1.21 | 31.50 | | 32.71 | |
| Minimum Charge | Job | | 181 | | 181 | |
| **36″ Wide Sink Base** | | | | | | |
| Demolish | Ea. | | 23 | | 23 | Includes material and labor to install |
| Install | Ea. | 275 | 35.50 | | 310.50 | good modular unit with melamine |
| Demolish and Install | Ea. | 275 | 58.50 | | 333.50 | laminate, textured colors or wood |
| Reinstall | Ea. | | 28.50 | | 28.50 | grain print finish including hinges and |
| Clean | Ea. | 2.01 | 15.70 | | 17.71 | pulls. |
| Paint | Ea. | 1.46 | 39.50 | | 40.96 | |
| Minimum Charge | Job | | 181 | | 181 | |

# Cabinets and Countertops

| Base Cabinets | Unit | Material | Labor | Equip. | Total | Specification |
|---|---|---|---|---|---|---|
| **36" Blind Corner** | | | | | | Includes material and labor to install |
| Demolish | Ea. | | 23 | | 23 | good modular unit with melamine |
| Install | Ea. | 360 | 40 | | 400 | laminate, textured colors or wood |
| Demolish and Install | Ea. | 360 | 63 | | 423 | grain print finish including hinges and |
| Reinstall | Ea. | | 32.14 | | 32.14 | pulls. |
| Clean | Ea. | 2.01 | 15.70 | | 17.71 | |
| Paint | Ea. | 1.46 | 39.50 | | 40.96 | |
| Minimum Charge | Job | | 181 | | 181 | |
| **42" w, 2 Door, 2 Drawer** | | | | | | Includes material and labor to install |
| Demolish | Ea. | | 27 | | 27 | good modular unit with melamine |
| Install | Ea. | 335 | 36.50 | | 371.50 | laminate, textured colors or wood |
| Demolish and Install | Ea. | 335 | 63.50 | | 398.50 | grain print finish including hinges and |
| Reinstall | Ea. | | 29.22 | | 29.22 | pulls. |
| Clean | Ea. | 2.60 | 19.05 | | 21.65 | |
| Paint | Ea. | 1.67 | 45 | | 46.67 | |
| Minimum Charge | Job | | 181 | | 181 | |
| **Clean Interior** | | | | | | Includes labor and materials to clean |
| Clean | L.F. | .73 | 4.04 | | 4.77 | the interior of a 27" cabinet. |
| Minimum Charge | Job | | 133 | | 133 | |
| **Better Grade Wood** | | | | | | |
| **12" w, 1 Door, 1 Drawer** | | | | | | Includes material and labor to install |
| Demolish | Ea. | | 7.40 | | 7.40 | custom modular unit including solid |
| Install | Ea. | 222 | 29 | | 251 | hardwood faced frames, hardwood |
| Demolish and Install | Ea. | 222 | 36.40 | | 258.40 | door frames and drawer fronts, |
| Reinstall | Ea. | | 23.33 | | 23.33 | hardwood veneer on raised door |
| Clean | Ea. | .73 | 5.35 | | 6.08 | panels, hinges and pulls. |
| Paint | Ea. | .48 | 14.30 | | 14.78 | |
| Minimum Charge | Job | | 181 | | 181 | |
| **15" w, 1 Door, 1 Drawer** | | | | | | Includes material and labor to install |
| Demolish | Ea. | | 9.25 | | 9.25 | custom modular unit including solid |
| Install | Ea. | 233 | 30 | | 263 | hardwood faced frames, hardwood |
| Demolish and Install | Ea. | 233 | 39.25 | | 272.25 | door frames and drawer fronts, |
| Reinstall | Ea. | | 24.11 | | 24.11 | hardwood veneer on raised door |
| Clean | Ea. | .91 | 6.65 | | 7.56 | panels, hinges and pulls. |
| Paint | Ea. | .61 | 18.50 | | 19.11 | |
| Minimum Charge | Job | | 181 | | 181 | |
| **18" w, 1 Door, 1 Drawer** | | | | | | Includes material and labor to install |
| Demolish | Ea. | | 11 | | 11 | custom modular unit including solid |
| Install | Ea. | 255 | 31 | | 286 | hardwood faced frames, hardwood |
| Demolish and Install | Ea. | 255 | 42 | | 297 | door frames and drawer fronts, |
| Reinstall | Ea. | | 24.83 | | 24.83 | hardwood veneer on raised door |
| Clean | Ea. | 1.07 | 8.10 | | 9.17 | panels, hinges and pulls. |
| Paint | Ea. | .73 | 21 | | 21.73 | |
| Minimum Charge | Job | | 181 | | 181 | |
| **21" w, 1 Door, 1 Drawer** | | | | | | Includes material and labor to install |
| Demolish | Ea. | | 12.90 | | 12.90 | custom modular unit including solid |
| Install | Ea. | 277 | 32 | | 309 | hardwood faced frames, hardwood |
| Demolish and Install | Ea. | 277 | 44.90 | | 321.90 | door frames and drawer fronts, |
| Reinstall | Ea. | | 25.49 | | 25.49 | hardwood veneer on raised door |
| Clean | Ea. | 1.30 | 9.55 | | 10.85 | panels, hinges and pulls. |
| Paint | Ea. | .85 | 24 | | 24.85 | |
| Minimum Charge | Job | | 181 | | 181 | |

| Base Cabinets | Unit | Material | Labor | Equip. | Total | Specification |
|---|---|---|---|---|---|---|
| **24" w, 1 Door, 1 Drawer** | | | | | | |
| Demolish | Ea. | | 14.80 | | 14.80 | Includes material and labor to install |
| Install | Ea. | 305 | 32.50 | | 337.50 | custom modular unit including solid |
| Demolish and Install | Ea. | 305 | 47.30 | | 352.30 | hardwood faced frames, hardwood |
| Reinstall | Ea. | | 25.94 | | 25.94 | door frames and drawer fronts, |
| Clean | Ea. | 1.40 | 10.65 | | 12.05 | hardwood veneer on raised door |
| Paint | Ea. | .97 | 28.50 | | 29.47 | panels, hinges and pulls. |
| Minimum Charge | Job | | 181 | | 181 | |
| **30" Wide Sink Base** | | | | | | |
| Demolish | Ea. | | 18.55 | | 18.55 | Includes material and labor to install |
| Install | Ea. | 330 | 34 | | 364 | custom modular unit including solid |
| Demolish and Install | Ea. | 330 | 52.55 | | 382.55 | hardwood faced frames, hardwood |
| Reinstall | Ea. | | 27.04 | | 27.04 | door frames and drawer fronts, |
| Clean | Ea. | 1.82 | 13.35 | | 15.17 | hardwood veneer on raised door |
| Paint | Ea. | 1.21 | 35 | | 36.21 | panels, hinges and pulls. |
| Minimum Charge | Job | | 181 | | 181 | |
| **36" Wide Sink Base** | | | | | | |
| Demolish | Ea. | | 23 | | 23 | Includes material and labor to install |
| Install | Ea. | 370 | 35.50 | | 405.50 | custom modular unit including solid |
| Demolish and Install | Ea. | 370 | 58.50 | | 428.50 | hardwood faced frames, hardwood |
| Reinstall | Ea. | | 28.50 | | 28.50 | door frames and drawer fronts, |
| Clean | Ea. | 2.01 | 15.70 | | 17.71 | hardwood veneer on raised door |
| Paint | Ea. | 1.46 | 45 | | 46.46 | panels, hinges and pulls. |
| Minimum Charge | Job | | 181 | | 181 | |
| **36" Blind Corner** | | | | | | |
| Demolish | Ea. | | 23 | | 23 | Includes material and labor to install |
| Install | Ea. | 480 | 40 | | 520 | custom modular unit including solid |
| Demolish and Install | Ea. | 480 | 63 | | 543 | hardwood faced frames, hardwood |
| Reinstall | Ea. | | 32.14 | | 32.14 | door frames and drawer fronts, |
| Clean | Ea. | 2.01 | 15.70 | | 17.71 | hardwood veneer on raised door |
| Paint | Ea. | 1.46 | 45 | | 46.46 | panels, hinges and pulls. |
| Minimum Charge | Job | | 181 | | 181 | |
| **42" w, 2 Door, 2 Drawer** | | | | | | |
| Demolish | Ea. | | 27 | | 27 | Includes material and labor to install |
| Install | Ea. | 445 | 36.50 | | 481.50 | modular unit including solid hardwood |
| Demolish and Install | Ea. | 445 | 63.50 | | 508.50 | faced frames, hardwood door frames |
| Reinstall | Ea. | | 29.22 | | 29.22 | and drawer fronts, hardwood veneer |
| Clean | Ea. | 2.60 | 19.05 | | 21.65 | on raised door panels, hinges and |
| Paint | Ea. | 1.67 | 52.50 | | 54.17 | pulls. |
| Minimum Charge | Job | | 181 | | 181 | |
| **Clean Interior** | | | | | | |
| Clean | L.F. | .73 | 4.04 | | 4.77 | Includes labor and materials to clean |
| Minimum Charge | Job | | 133 | | 133 | the interior of a 27" cabinet. |
| **Premium Grade Wood** | | | | | | |
| **12" w, 1 Door, 1 Drawer** | | | | | | |
| Demolish | Ea. | | 7.40 | | 7.40 | Includes material and labor to install |
| Install | Ea. | 267 | 14.60 | | 281.60 | premium hardwood modular unit with |
| Demolish and Install | Ea. | 267 | 22 | | 289 | solid hardwood faced frames, drawer |
| Reinstall | Ea. | | 11.66 | | 11.66 | fronts, and door panels, steel drawer |
| Clean | Ea. | .73 | 5.35 | | 6.08 | guides, hinges, pulls and laminated |
| Paint | Ea. | .48 | 15.75 | | 16.23 | interior. |
| Minimum Charge | Job | | 181 | | 181 | |

# Cabinets and Countertops

| Base Cabinets | Unit | Material | Labor | Equip. | Total | Specification |
|---|---|---|---|---|---|---|
| **15″ w, 1 Door, 1 Drawer** | | | | | | |
| Demolish | Ea. | | 9.25 | | 9.25 | Includes material and labor to install |
| Install | Ea. | 281 | 30 | | 311 | premium modular unit including solid |
| Demolish and Install | Ea. | 281 | 39.25 | | 320.25 | hardwood faced frames, hardwood |
| Reinstall | Ea. | | 24.11 | | 24.11 | door frames and drawer fronts, |
| Clean | Ea. | .91 | 6.65 | | 7.56 | hardwood veneer on raised door |
| Paint | Ea. | .61 | 19.70 | | 20.31 | panels, hinges and pulls. |
| Minimum Charge | Job | | 181 | | 181 | |
| **18″ w, 1 Door, 1 Drawer** | | | | | | |
| Demolish | Ea. | | 11 | | 11 | Includes material and labor to install |
| Install | Ea. | 305 | 31 | | 336 | premium modular unit including solid |
| Demolish and Install | Ea. | 305 | 42 | | 347 | hardwood faced frames, hardwood |
| Reinstall | Ea. | | 24.83 | | 24.83 | door frames and drawer fronts, |
| Clean | Ea. | 1.07 | 8.10 | | 9.17 | hardwood veneer on raised door |
| Paint | Ea. | .73 | 24 | | 24.73 | panels, hinges and pulls. |
| Minimum Charge | Job | | 181 | | 181 | |
| **21″ w, 1 Door, 1 Drawer** | | | | | | |
| Demolish | Ea. | | 12.90 | | 12.90 | Includes material and labor to install |
| Install | Ea. | 335 | 32 | | 367 | premium modular unit including solid |
| Demolish and Install | Ea. | 335 | 44.90 | | 379.90 | hardwood faced frames, hardwood |
| Reinstall | Ea. | | 25.49 | | 25.49 | door frames and drawer fronts, |
| Clean | Ea. | 1.30 | 9.55 | | 10.85 | hardwood veneer on raised door |
| Paint | Ea. | .85 | 26 | | 26.85 | panels, hinges and pulls. |
| Minimum Charge | Job | | 181 | | 181 | |
| **24″ w, 1 Door, 1 Drawer** | | | | | | |
| Demolish | Ea. | | 14.80 | | 14.80 | Includes material and labor to install |
| Install | Ea. | 365 | 32.50 | | 397.50 | premium modular unit including solid |
| Demolish and Install | Ea. | 365 | 47.30 | | 412.30 | hardwood faced frames, hardwood |
| Reinstall | Ea. | | 25.94 | | 25.94 | door frames and drawer fronts, |
| Clean | Ea. | 1.40 | 10.65 | | 12.05 | hardwood veneer on raised door |
| Paint | Ea. | .97 | 31.50 | | 32.47 | panels, hinges and pulls. |
| Minimum Charge | Job | | 181 | | 181 | |
| **30″ Wide Sink Base** | | | | | | |
| Demolish | Ea. | | 18.55 | | 18.55 | Includes material and labor to install |
| Install | Ea. | 395 | 34 | | 429 | premium modular unit including solid |
| Demolish and Install | Ea. | 395 | 52.55 | | 447.55 | hardwood faced frames, hardwood |
| Reinstall | Ea. | | 27.04 | | 27.04 | door frames and drawer fronts, |
| Clean | Ea. | 1.82 | 13.35 | | 15.17 | hardwood veneer on raised door |
| Paint | Ea. | 1.21 | 39.50 | | 40.71 | panels, hinges and pulls. |
| Minimum Charge | Job | | 181 | | 181 | |
| **36″ Wide Sink Base** | | | | | | |
| Demolish | Ea. | | 23 | | 23 | Includes material and labor to install |
| Install | Ea. | 440 | 35.50 | | 475.50 | premium modular unit including solid |
| Demolish and Install | Ea. | 440 | 58.50 | | 498.50 | hardwood faced frames, hardwood |
| Reinstall | Ea. | | 28.50 | | 28.50 | door frames and drawer fronts, |
| Clean | Ea. | 2.01 | 15.70 | | 17.71 | hardwood veneer on raised door |
| Paint | Ea. | 1.46 | 45 | | 46.46 | panels, hinges and pulls. |
| Minimum Charge | Job | | 181 | | 181 | |
| **36″ Blind Corner** | | | | | | |
| Demolish | Ea. | | 23 | | 23 | Includes material and labor to install |
| Install | Ea. | 580 | 40 | | 620 | premium modular unit including solid |
| Demolish and Install | Ea. | 580 | 63 | | 643 | hardwood faced frames, hardwood |
| Reinstall | Ea. | | 32.14 | | 32.14 | door frames and drawer fronts, |
| Clean | Ea. | 2.01 | 15.70 | | 17.71 | hardwood veneer on raised door |
| Paint | Ea. | 1.46 | 45 | | 46.46 | panels, hinges and pulls. |
| Minimum Charge | Job | | 181 | | 181 | |

# Cabinets and Countertops

| Base Cabinets | Unit | Material | Labor | Equip. | Total | Specification |
|---|---|---|---|---|---|---|
| **42" w, 2 Door, 2 Drawer** | | | | | | |
| Demolish | Ea. | | 27 | | 27 | Includes material and labor to install |
| Install | Ea. | 595 | 36.50 | | 631.50 | premium modular unit including solid |
| Demolish and Install | Ea. | 595 | 63.50 | | 658.50 | hardwood faced frames, hardwood |
| Reinstall | Ea. | | 29.22 | | 29.22 | door frames and drawer fronts, |
| Clean | Ea. | 2.60 | 19.05 | | 21.65 | hardwood veneer on raised door |
| Paint | Ea. | 1.67 | 52.50 | | 54.17 | panels, hinges and pulls. |
| Minimum Charge | Job | | 181 | | 181 | |
| **Clean Interior** | | | | | | |
| Clean | L.F. | .73 | 4.04 | | 4.77 | Includes labor and materials to clean |
| Minimum Charge | Job | | 133 | | 133 | the interior of a 27" cabinet. |
| **Premium Hardwood** | | | | | | |
| **12" w, 1 Door, 1 Drawer** | | | | | | |
| Demolish | Ea. | | 7.40 | | 7.40 | Includes material and labor to install |
| Install | Ea. | 292 | 29 | | 321 | premium hardwood modular unit with |
| Demolish and Install | Ea. | 292 | 36.40 | | 328.40 | solid hardwood faced frames, drawer |
| Reinstall | Ea. | | 23.33 | | 23.33 | fronts, and door panels, steel drawer |
| Clean | Ea. | .73 | 5.35 | | 6.08 | guides, hinges, pulls and laminated |
| Paint | Ea. | .48 | 17.50 | | 17.98 | interior. |
| Minimum Charge | Job | | 181 | | 181 | |
| **15" w, 1 Door, 1 Drawer** | | | | | | |
| Demolish | Ea. | | 9.25 | | 9.25 | Includes material and labor to install |
| Install | Ea. | 305 | 30 | | 335 | premium hardwood modular unit with |
| Demolish and Install | Ea. | 305 | 39.25 | | 344.25 | solid hardwood faced frames, drawer |
| Reinstall | Ea. | | 24.11 | | 24.11 | fronts, and door panels, steel drawer |
| Clean | Ea. | .91 | 6.65 | | 7.56 | guides, hinges, pulls and laminated |
| Paint | Ea. | .61 | 22.50 | | 23.11 | interior. |
| Minimum Charge | Job | | 181 | | 181 | |
| **18" w, 1 Door, 1 Drawer** | | | | | | |
| Demolish | Ea. | | 11 | | 11 | Includes material and labor to install |
| Install | Ea. | 335 | 31 | | 366 | premium hardwood modular unit with |
| Demolish and Install | Ea. | 335 | 42 | | 377 | solid hardwood faced frames, drawer |
| Reinstall | Ea. | | 24.83 | | 24.83 | fronts, and door panels, steel drawer |
| Clean | Ea. | 1.07 | 8.10 | | 9.17 | guides, hinges, pulls and laminated |
| Paint | Ea. | .73 | 26 | | 26.73 | interior. |
| Minimum Charge | Job | | 181 | | 181 | |
| **21" w, 1 Door, 1 Drawer** | | | | | | |
| Demolish | Ea. | | 12.90 | | 12.90 | Includes material and labor to install |
| Install | Ea. | 365 | 32 | | 397 | premium hardwood modular unit with |
| Demolish and Install | Ea. | 365 | 44.90 | | 409.90 | solid hardwood faced frames, drawer |
| Reinstall | Ea. | | 25.49 | | 25.49 | fronts, and door panels, steel drawer |
| Clean | Ea. | 1.30 | 9.55 | | 10.85 | guides, hinges, pulls and laminated |
| Paint | Ea. | .85 | 28.50 | | 29.35 | interior. |
| Minimum Charge | Job | | 181 | | 181 | |
| **24" w, 1 Door, 1 Drawer** | | | | | | |
| Demolish | Ea. | | 14.80 | | 14.80 | Includes material and labor to install |
| Install | Ea. | 395 | 32.50 | | 427.50 | premium hardwood modular unit with |
| Demolish and Install | Ea. | 395 | 47.30 | | 442.30 | solid hardwood faced frames, drawer |
| Reinstall | Ea. | | 25.94 | | 25.94 | fronts, and door panels, steel drawer |
| Clean | Ea. | 1.40 | 10.65 | | 12.05 | guides, hinges and pulls, laminated |
| Paint | Ea. | .97 | 35 | | 35.97 | interior. |
| Minimum Charge | Job | | 181 | | 181 | |

# Cabinets and Countertops

| Base Cabinets | Unit | Material | Labor | Equip. | Total | Specification |
|---|---|---|---|---|---|---|
| **30″ Wide Sink Base** | | | | | | |
| Demolish | Ea. | | 18.55 | | 18.55 | Includes material and labor to install |
| Install | Ea. | 435 | 34 | | 469 | premium hardwood modular unit with |
| Demolish and Install | Ea. | 435 | 52.55 | | 487.55 | solid hardwood faced frames, drawer |
| Reinstall | Ea. | | 27.04 | | 27.04 | fronts, and door panels, steel drawer |
| Clean | Ea. | 1.82 | 13.35 | | 15.17 | guides, hinges, pulls and laminated |
| Paint | Ea. | 1.21 | 39.50 | | 40.71 | interior. |
| Minimum Charge | Job | | 181 | | 181 | |
| **36″ Wide Sink Base** | | | | | | |
| Demolish | Ea. | | 23 | | 23 | Includes material and labor to install |
| Install | Ea. | 480 | 35.50 | | 515.50 | premium hardwood modular unit with |
| Demolish and Install | Ea. | 480 | 58.50 | | 538.50 | solid hardwood faced frames, drawer |
| Reinstall | Ea. | | 28.50 | | 28.50 | fronts, and door panels, steel drawer |
| Clean | Ea. | 2.01 | 15.70 | | 17.71 | guides, hinges, pulls and laminated |
| Paint | Ea. | 1.46 | 52.50 | | 53.96 | interior. |
| Minimum Charge | Job | | 181 | | 181 | |
| **36″ Blind Corner** | | | | | | |
| Demolish | Ea. | | 23 | | 23 | Includes material and labor to install |
| Install | Ea. | 625 | 40 | | 665 | premium hardwood modular unit with |
| Demolish and Install | Ea. | 625 | 63 | | 688 | solid hardwood faced frames, drawer |
| Reinstall | Ea. | | 32.14 | | 32.14 | fronts, and door panels, steel drawer |
| Clean | Ea. | 2.01 | 15.70 | | 17.71 | guides, hinges, pulls and laminated |
| Paint | Ea. | 1.46 | 52.50 | | 53.96 | interior. |
| Minimum Charge | Job | | 181 | | 181 | |
| **42″ w, 2 Door, 2 Drawer** | | | | | | |
| Demolish | Ea. | | 27 | | 27 | Includes material and labor to install |
| Install | Ea. | 780 | 36.50 | | 816.50 | premium hardwood modular unit with |
| Demolish and Install | Ea. | 780 | 63.50 | | 843.50 | solid hardwood faced frames, drawer |
| Reinstall | Ea. | | 29.22 | | 29.22 | fronts, and door panels, steel drawer |
| Clean | Ea. | 2.60 | 19.05 | | 21.65 | guides, hinges, pulls and laminated |
| Paint | Ea. | 1.67 | 63 | | 64.67 | interior. |
| Minimum Charge | Job | | 181 | | 181 | |
| **Clean Interior** | | | | | | |
| Clean | L.F. | .73 | 4.04 | | 4.77 | Includes labor and materials to clean |
| Minimum Charge | Job | | 133 | | 133 | the interior of a 27″ cabinet. |
| **Island** | | | | | | |
| **24″ Wide** | | | | | | |
| Demolish | Ea. | | 14.80 | | 14.80 | Includes material and labor to install |
| Install | Ea. | 440 | 30 | | 470 | custom modular unit with solid |
| Demolish and Install | Ea. | 440 | 44.80 | | 484.80 | hardwood faced frames, hardwood |
| Reinstall | Ea. | | 24.11 | | 24.11 | door frames and drawer fronts, |
| Clean | Ea. | 2.01 | 15.70 | | 17.71 | hardwood veneer on raised door |
| Paint | Ea. | 1.44 | 45 | | 46.44 | panels, hinges and pulls. |
| Minimum Charge | Job | | 181 | | 181 | |
| **30″ Wide** | | | | | | |
| Demolish | Ea. | | 18.55 | | 18.55 | Includes material and labor to install |
| Install | Ea. | 540 | 37.50 | | 577.50 | custom modular unit with solid |
| Demolish and Install | Ea. | 540 | 56.05 | | 596.05 | hardwood faced frames, hardwood |
| Reinstall | Ea. | | 30.13 | | 30.13 | door frames and drawer fronts, |
| Clean | Ea. | 2.60 | 19.05 | | 21.65 | hardwood veneer on raised door |
| Paint | Ea. | 1.82 | 52.50 | | 54.32 | panels, hinges and pulls. |
| Minimum Charge | Job | | 181 | | 181 | |

# Cabinets and Countertops

| Base Cabinets | | Unit | Material | Labor | Equip. | Total | Specification |
|---|---|---|---|---|---|---|---|
| **36″ Wide** | | | | | | | |
| | Demolish | Ea. | | 23 | | 23 | Includes material and labor to install |
| | Install | Ea. | 610 | 45 | | 655 | custom modular unit with solid |
| | Demolish and Install | Ea. | 610 | 68 | | 678 | hardwood faced frames, hardwood |
| | Reinstall | Ea. | | 36.16 | | 36.16 | door frames and drawer fronts, |
| | Clean | Ea. | 3.03 | 24.50 | | 27.53 | hardwood veneer on raised door |
| | Paint | Ea. | 2.19 | 63 | | 65.19 | panels, hinges and pulls. |
| | Minimum Charge | Job | | 181 | | 181 | |
| **48″ Wide** | | | | | | | |
| | Demolish | Ea. | | 29.50 | | 29.50 | Includes material and labor to install |
| | Install | Ea. | 885 | 60.50 | | 945.50 | custom modular unit with solid |
| | Demolish and Install | Ea. | 885 | 90 | | 975 | hardwood faced frames, hardwood |
| | Reinstall | Ea. | | 48.21 | | 48.21 | door frames and drawer fronts, |
| | Clean | Ea. | 3.63 | 29.50 | | 33.13 | hardwood veneer on raised door |
| | Paint | Ea. | 2.51 | 78.50 | | 81.01 | panels, hinges and pulls. |
| | Minimum Charge | Job | | 181 | | 181 | |
| **60″ Wide** | | | | | | | |
| | Demolish | Ea. | | 33 | | 33 | Includes material and labor to install |
| | Install | Ea. | 1075 | 75.50 | | 1150.50 | custom modular unit with solid |
| | Demolish and Install | Ea. | 1075 | 108.50 | | 1183.50 | hardwood faced frames, hardwood |
| | Reinstall | Ea. | | 60.27 | | 60.27 | door frames and drawer fronts, |
| | Clean | Ea. | 4.54 | 38 | | 42.54 | hardwood veneer on raised door |
| | Paint | Ea. | 2.51 | 105 | | 107.51 | panels, hinges and pulls. |
| | Minimum Charge | Job | | 181 | | 181 | |
| **Clean Interior** | | | | | | | |
| | Clean | L.F. | .73 | 4.04 | | 4.77 | Includes labor and materials to clean |
| | Minimum Charge | Job | | 133 | | 133 | the interior of a 27″ cabinet. |
| **Liquor Bar** | | | | | | | |
| | Demolish | L.F. | | 7.40 | | 7.40 | Includes material and labor to install |
| | Install | L.F. | 168 | 36 | | 204 | custom modular unit with solid |
| | Demolish and Install | L.F. | 168 | 43.40 | | 211.40 | hardwood faced frames, hardwood |
| | Reinstall | L.F. | | 28.93 | | 28.93 | door frames and drawer fronts, |
| | Clean | L.F. | .73 | 5.55 | | 6.28 | hardwood veneer on raised door |
| | Paint | L.F. | .48 | 14.30 | | 14.78 | panels, hinges and pulls. |
| | Minimum Charge | Job | | 181 | | 181 | |
| **Clean Interior** | | | | | | | |
| | Clean | L.F. | .73 | 4.04 | | 4.77 | Includes labor and materials to clean |
| | Minimum Charge | Job | | 133 | | 133 | the interior of a 27″ cabinet. |
| **Seal Interior** | | | | | | | |
| | Install | L.F. | .43 | 5.15 | | 5.58 | Includes labor and materials to seal a |
| | Minimum Charge | Job | | 157 | | 157 | cabinet interior. |
| **Back Bar** | | | | | | | |
| | Demolish | L.F. | | 7.40 | | 7.40 | Includes material and labor to install |
| | Install | L.F. | 168 | 36 | | 204 | custom modular unit with solid |
| | Demolish and Install | L.F. | 168 | 43.40 | | 211.40 | hardwood faced frames, hardwood |
| | Reinstall | L.F. | | 28.93 | | 28.93 | door frames and drawer fronts, |
| | Clean | L.F. | .73 | 5.55 | | 6.28 | hardwood veneer on raised door |
| | Paint | L.F. | .48 | 14.30 | | 14.78 | panels, hinges and pulls. |
| | Minimum Charge | Job | | 181 | | 181 | |
| **Clean Interior** | | | | | | | |
| | Clean | L.F. | .73 | 4.04 | | 4.77 | Includes labor and materials to clean |
| | Minimum Charge | Job | | 133 | | 133 | the interior of a 27″ cabinet. |

# Cabinets and Countertops

| Base Cabinets | | Unit | Material | Labor | Equip. | Total | Specification |
|---|---|---|---|---|---|---|---|
| **Seal Interior** | | | | | | | |
| | Install | L.F. | .43 | 5.15 | | 5.58 | Includes labor and materials to seal a |
| | Minimum Charge | Job | | 157 | | 157 | cabinet interior. |
| **Storage (garage)** | | | | | | | |
| | Demolish | L.F. | | 7.40 | | 7.40 | Includes material and labor to install |
| | Install | L.F. | 127 | 36 | | 163 | good modular unit with melamine |
| | Demolish and Install | L.F. | 127 | 43.40 | | 170.40 | laminate, textured colors or wood |
| | Reinstall | L.F. | | 28.93 | | 28.93 | grain print finish including hinges and |
| | Clean | L.F. | .73 | 5.55 | | 6.28 | pulls. |
| | Paint | L.F. | .48 | 14.30 | | 14.78 | |
| | Minimum Charge | Job | | 181 | | 181 | |
| **Clean Interior** | | | | | | | |
| | Clean | L.F. | .73 | 4.04 | | 4.77 | Includes labor and materials to clean |
| | Minimum Charge | Job | | 133 | | 133 | the interior of a 27" cabinet. |
| **Seal Interior** | | | | | | | |
| | Install | L.F. | .43 | 5.15 | | 5.58 | Includes labor and materials to seal a |
| | Minimum Charge | Job | | 157 | | 157 | cabinet interior. |
| **Built-in Desk** | | | | | | | |
| | Demolish | L.F. | | 7.40 | | 7.40 | Includes material and labor to install |
| | Install | L.F. | 168 | 36 | | 204 | custom modular unit with solid |
| | Demolish and Install | L.F. | 168 | 43.40 | | 211.40 | hardwood faced frames, hardwood |
| | Reinstall | L.F. | | 28.93 | | 28.93 | door frames and drawer fronts, |
| | Clean | L.F. | .73 | 5.55 | | 6.28 | hardwood veneer on raised door |
| | Paint | L.F. | .48 | 14.30 | | 14.78 | panels, hinges and pulls. |
| | Minimum Charge | Job | | 181 | | 181 | |
| **Built-in Bookcase** | | | | | | | |
| | Demolish | L.F. | | 9.90 | | 9.90 | Includes material and labor to install |
| | Install | L.F. | 25.50 | 36 | | 61.50 | custom modular bookcase unit with |
| | Demolish and Install | L.F. | 25.50 | 45.90 | | 71.40 | clear pine faced frames, shelves 12" |
| | Reinstall | L.F. | | 28.93 | | 28.93 | O.C., 7' high, 8" deep. |
| | Clean | L.F. | 1.45 | 9.55 | | 11 | |
| | Paint | L.F. | 1.12 | 24 | | 25.12 | |
| | Minimum Charge | Job | | 181 | | 181 | |
| **Strip and Refinish** | | | | | | | |
| | Install | L.F. | 1.11 | 5.70 | | 6.81 | Includes labor and material to strip, |
| | Minimum Charge | Job | | 157 | | 157 | prep and refinish exterior of cabinets. |
| **Stain** | | | | | | | |
| | Install | L.F. | .42 | 1.46 | | 1.88 | Includes labor and material to stain |
| | Minimum Charge | Job | | 181 | | 181 | door and exterior of cabinets. |

| Countertop | | Unit | Material | Labor | Equip. | Total | Specification |
|---|---|---|---|---|---|---|---|
| **Laminated** | | | | | | | |
| **With Splash** | | | | | | | |
| | Demolish | L.F. | | 4.94 | | 4.94 | Includes material and labor to install |
| | Install | L.F. | 31 | 12.90 | | 43.90 | one piece laminated top with 4" |
| | Demolish and Install | L.F. | 31 | 17.84 | | 48.84 | backsplash. |
| | Reinstall | L.F. | | 10.33 | | 10.33 | |
| | Clean | L.F. | .09 | .67 | | .76 | |
| | Minimum Charge | Job | | 181 | | 181 | |

# Cabinets and Countertops

| Countertop | | Unit | Material | Labor | Equip. | Total | Specification |
|---|---|---|---|---|---|---|---|
| **Roll Top** | | | | | | | |
| | Demolish | L.F. | | 4.94 | | 4.94 | Includes material and labor to install |
| | Install | L.F. | 11.10 | 12.05 | | 23.15 | one piece laminated top with rolled |
| | Demolish and Install | L.F. | 11.10 | 16.99 | | 28.09 | drip edge (post formed) and |
| | Reinstall | L.F. | | 9.64 | | 9.64 | backsplash. |
| | Clean | L.F. | .13 | 1.01 | | 1.14 | |
| | Minimum Charge | Job | | 181 | | 181 | |
| **Ceramic Tile** | | | | | | | |
| | Demolish | S.F. | | 2.47 | | 2.47 | Cost includes material and labor to |
| | Install | S.F. | 16.05 | 7.25 | | 23.30 | install 4-1/4" x 4-1/4" to 6" x 6" |
| | Demolish and Install | S.F. | 16.05 | 9.72 | | 25.77 | glazed tile set in mortar bed and grout |
| | Clean | S.F. | .07 | .51 | | .58 | on particle board substrate. |
| | Minimum Charge | Job | | 167 | | 167 | |
| **Cultured Marble** | | | | | | | |
| | Demolish | L.F. | | 4.94 | | 4.94 | Includes material and labor to install |
| | Install | L.F. | 31.50 | 36.50 | | 68 | marble countertop, 24" wide, no |
| | Demolish and Install | L.F. | 31.50 | 41.44 | | 72.94 | backsplash. |
| | Reinstall | L.F. | | 29.12 | | 29.12 | |
| | Clean | L.F. | .13 | 1.01 | | 1.14 | |
| | Minimum Charge | Job | | 167 | | 167 | |
| **With Splash** | | | | | | | |
| | Demolish | L.F. | | 4.94 | | 4.94 | Includes material and labor to install |
| | Install | L.F. | 35 | 36.50 | | 71.50 | marble countertop, 24" wide, with |
| | Demolish and Install | L.F. | 35 | 41.44 | | 76.44 | backsplash. |
| | Reinstall | L.F. | | 29.12 | | 29.12 | |
| | Clean | L.F. | .13 | 1.01 | | 1.14 | |
| | Minimum Charge | Job | | 167 | | 167 | |
| **Quarry Tile** | | | | | | | |
| | Demolish | S.F. | | 2.47 | | 2.47 | Includes material and labor to install |
| | Install | S.F. | 8.30 | 7.25 | | 15.55 | quarry tile countertop with no |
| | Demolish and Install | S.F. | 8.30 | 9.72 | | 18.02 | backsplash. |
| | Clean | S.F. | .07 | .51 | | .58 | |
| | Minimum Charge | Job | | 167 | | 167 | |
| **With Splash** | | | | | | | |
| | Demolish | S.F. | | 2.47 | | 2.47 | Includes material and labor to install |
| | Install | S.F. | 10.95 | 8.05 | | 19 | quarry tile countertop with backsplash. |
| | Demolish and Install | S.F. | 10.95 | 10.52 | | 21.47 | |
| | Clean | S.F. | .07 | .51 | | .58 | |
| | Minimum Charge | Job | | 167 | | 167 | |
| **Butcher Block** | | | | | | | |
| | Demolish | S.F. | | 2.47 | | 2.47 | Includes material and labor to install |
| | Install | S.F. | 32.50 | 6.45 | | 38.95 | solid laminated maple countertop with |
| | Demolish and Install | S.F. | 32.50 | 8.92 | | 41.42 | no backsplash. |
| | Reinstall | S.F. | | 5.17 | | 5.17 | |
| | Clean | S.F. | .02 | .21 | | .23 | |
| | Minimum Charge | Job | | 181 | | 181 | |
| **Solid Surface** | | | | | | | |
| | Demolish | L.F. | | 4.94 | | 4.94 | Includes material and labor to install |
| | Install | L.F. | 49 | 26 | | 75 | solid surface counter top 22" deep. |
| | Demolish and Install | L.F. | 49 | 30.94 | | 79.94 | |
| | Reinstall | L.F. | | 20.66 | | 20.66 | |
| | Clean | L.F. | .13 | 1.01 | | 1.14 | |
| | Minimum Charge | Job | | 181 | | 181 | |

# Cabinets and Countertops

## Vanity Cabinets

| Vanity Cabinets | Unit | Material | Labor | Equip. | Total | Specification |
|---|---|---|---|---|---|---|
| **Good Grade Laminated** | | | | | | |
| **24″ Wide, 2 Door** | | | | | | |
| Demolish | Ea. | | 14.80 | | 14.80 | Includes material and labor to install |
| Install | Ea. | 168 | 36 | | 204 | modular unit with melamine laminated |
| Demolish and Install | Ea. | 168 | 50.80 | | 218.80 | to particle board, textured colors or |
| Reinstall | Ea. | | 28.93 | | 28.93 | wood grain print finish, hinges and |
| Clean | Ea. | 1.40 | 10.65 | | 12.05 | pulls. |
| Paint | Ea. | .97 | 26 | | 26.97 | |
| Minimum Charge | Job | | 181 | | 181 | |
| **30″ Wide, 2 Door** | | | | | | |
| Demolish | Ea. | | 18.55 | | 18.55 | Includes material and labor to install |
| Install | Ea. | 194 | 45 | | 239 | modular unit with melamine laminated |
| Demolish and Install | Ea. | 194 | 63.55 | | 257.55 | to particle board, textured colors or |
| Reinstall | Ea. | | 36.16 | | 36.16 | wood grain print finish, hinges and |
| Clean | Ea. | 1.82 | 13.35 | | 15.17 | pulls. |
| Paint | Ea. | 1.21 | 31.50 | | 32.71 | |
| Minimum Charge | Job | | 181 | | 181 | |
| **36″ Wide, 2 Door** | | | | | | |
| Demolish | Ea. | | 23 | | 23 | Includes material and labor to install |
| Install | Ea. | 259 | 54.50 | | 313.50 | modular unit with melamine laminated |
| Demolish and Install | Ea. | 259 | 77.50 | | 336.50 | to particle board, textured colors or |
| Reinstall | Ea. | | 43.40 | | 43.40 | wood grain print finish, hinges and |
| Clean | Ea. | 2.01 | 15.70 | | 17.71 | pulls. |
| Paint | Ea. | 1.46 | 39.50 | | 40.96 | |
| Minimum Charge | Job | | 181 | | 181 | |
| **42″ w, 3 Doors / Drawer** | | | | | | |
| Demolish | Ea. | | 27 | | 27 | Includes material and labor to install |
| Install | Ea. | 375 | 58.50 | | 433.50 | modular unit with melamine laminated |
| Demolish and Install | Ea. | 375 | 85.50 | | 460.50 | to particle board, textured colors or |
| Reinstall | Ea. | | 46.73 | | 46.73 | wood grain print finish, hinges and |
| Clean | Ea. | 2.60 | 19.05 | | 21.65 | pulls. |
| Paint | Ea. | 1.67 | 45 | | 46.67 | |
| Minimum Charge | Job | | 181 | | 181 | |
| **48″ w, 3 Doors / Drawer** | | | | | | |
| Demolish | Ea. | | 29.50 | | 29.50 | Includes material and labor to install |
| Install | Ea. | 310 | 63.50 | | 373.50 | modular unit with melamine laminated |
| Demolish and Install | Ea. | 310 | 93 | | 403 | to particle board, textured colors or |
| Reinstall | Ea. | | 50.62 | | 50.62 | wood grain print finish, hinges and |
| Clean | Ea. | 3.63 | 29.50 | | 33.13 | pulls. |
| Paint | Ea. | 2.51 | 78.50 | | 81.01 | |
| Minimum Charge | Job | | 181 | | 181 | |
| **Clean Interior** | | | | | | |
| Install | L.F. | .73 | 5.55 | | 6.28 | Includes labor and materials to clean |
| Minimum Charge | Job | | 133 | | 133 | base cabinetry. |
| **Better Grade Wood** | | | | | | |
| **24″ Wide, 2 Door** | | | | | | |
| Demolish | Ea. | | 14.80 | | 14.80 | Includes material and labor to install |
| Install | Ea. | 226 | 36 | | 262 | custom modular unit with solid |
| Demolish and Install | Ea. | 226 | 50.80 | | 276.80 | hardwood faced frames, hardwood |
| Reinstall | Ea. | | 28.93 | | 28.93 | door frames and drawer fronts, |
| Clean | Ea. | 1.40 | 10.65 | | 12.05 | hardwood veneer on raised door |
| Paint | Ea. | .97 | 28.50 | | 29.47 | panels, hinges and pulls. |
| Minimum Charge | Job | | 181 | | 181 | |

# Cabinets and Countertops

| Vanity Cabinets | | Unit | Material | Labor | Equip. | Total | Specification |
|---|---|---|---|---|---|---|---|
| **30" Wide, 2 Door** | | | | | | | |
| | Demolish | Ea. | | 18.55 | | 18.55 | Includes material and labor to install |
| | Install | Ea. | 259 | 45 | | 304 | custom modular unit with solid |
| | Demolish and Install | Ea. | 259 | 63.55 | | 322.55 | hardwood faced frames, hardwood |
| | Reinstall | Ea. | | 36.16 | | 36.16 | door frames and drawer fronts, |
| | Clean | Ea. | 1.82 | 13.35 | | 15.17 | hardwood veneer on raised door |
| | Paint | Ea. | 1.21 | 35 | | 36.21 | panels, hinges and pulls. |
| | Minimum Charge | Job | | 181 | | 181 | |
| **36" Wide, 2 Door** | | | | | | | |
| | Demolish | Ea. | | 23 | | 23 | Includes material and labor to install |
| | Install | Ea. | 345 | 54.50 | | 399.50 | custom modular unit with solid |
| | Demolish and Install | Ea. | 345 | 77.50 | | 422.50 | hardwood faced frames, hardwood |
| | Reinstall | Ea. | | 43.40 | | 43.40 | door frames and drawer fronts, |
| | Clean | Ea. | 2.01 | 15.70 | | 17.71 | hardwood veneer on raised door |
| | Paint | Ea. | 1.46 | 45 | | 46.46 | panels, hinges and pulls. |
| | Minimum Charge | Job | | 181 | | 181 | |
| **42" w, 3 Doors / Drawer** | | | | | | | |
| | Demolish | Ea. | | 27 | | 27 | Includes material and labor to install |
| | Install | Ea. | 375 | 58.50 | | 433.50 | custom modular unit with solid |
| | Demolish and Install | Ea. | 375 | 85.50 | | 460.50 | hardwood faced frames, hardwood |
| | Reinstall | Ea. | | 46.73 | | 46.73 | door frames and drawer fronts, |
| | Clean | Ea. | 2.60 | 19.05 | | 21.65 | hardwood veneer on raised door |
| | Paint | Ea. | 1.67 | 52.50 | | 54.17 | panels, hinges and pulls. |
| | Minimum Charge | Job | | 181 | | 181 | |
| **48" w, 3 Doors / Drawer** | | | | | | | |
| | Demolish | Ea. | | 29.50 | | 29.50 | Includes material and labor to install |
| | Install | Ea. | 415 | 63.50 | | 478.50 | custom modular unit with solid |
| | Demolish and Install | Ea. | 415 | 93 | | 508 | hardwood faced frames, hardwood |
| | Reinstall | Ea. | | 50.62 | | 50.62 | door frames and drawer fronts, |
| | Clean | Ea. | 3.63 | 29.50 | | 33.13 | hardwood veneer on raised door |
| | Paint | Ea. | 2.51 | 78.50 | | 81.01 | panels, hinges and pulls. |
| | Minimum Charge | Job | | 181 | | 181 | |
| **Clean Interior** | | | | | | | |
| | Install | L.F. | .73 | 5.55 | | 6.28 | Includes labor and materials to clean |
| | Minimum Charge | Job | | 133 | | 133 | base cabinetry. |
| **Premium Grade Wood** | | | | | | | |
| **24" Wide, 2 Door** | | | | | | | |
| | Demolish | Ea. | | 14.80 | | 14.80 | Includes material and labor to install |
| | Install | Ea. | 267 | 36 | | 303 | premium modular unit with solid |
| | Demolish and Install | Ea. | 267 | 50.80 | | 317.80 | hardwood faced frames, hardwood |
| | Reinstall | Ea. | | 28.93 | | 28.93 | door frames and drawer fronts, |
| | Clean | Ea. | 1.40 | 10.65 | | 12.05 | hardwood veneer on raised door |
| | Paint | Ea. | .97 | 31.50 | | 32.47 | panels, hinges and pulls. |
| | Minimum Charge | Job | | 181 | | 181 | |
| **30" Wide, 2 Door** | | | | | | | |
| | Demolish | Ea. | | 18.55 | | 18.55 | Includes material and labor to install |
| | Install | Ea. | 305 | 45 | | 350 | premium modular unit with solid |
| | Demolish and Install | Ea. | 305 | 63.55 | | 368.55 | hardwood faced frames, hardwood |
| | Reinstall | Ea. | | 36.16 | | 36.16 | door frames and drawer fronts, |
| | Clean | Ea. | 1.82 | 13.35 | | 15.17 | hardwood veneer on raised door |
| | Paint | Ea. | 1.21 | 39.50 | | 40.71 | panels, hinges and pulls. |
| | Minimum Charge | Job | | 181 | | 181 | |

| Vanity Cabinets | Unit | Material | Labor | Equip. | Total | Specification |
|---|---|---|---|---|---|---|
| **36″ Wide, 2 Door** | | | | | | |
| Demolish | Ea. | | 23 | | 23 | Includes material and labor to install |
| Install | Ea. | 480 | 54.50 | | 534.50 | premium modular unit with solid |
| Demolish and Install | Ea. | 480 | 77.50 | | 557.50 | hardwood faced frames, hardwood |
| Reinstall | Ea. | | 43.40 | | 43.40 | door frames and drawer fronts, |
| Clean | Ea. | 2.01 | 15.70 | | 17.71 | hardwood veneer on raised door |
| Paint | Ea. | 1.46 | 45 | | 46.46 | panels, hinges and pulls. |
| Minimum Charge | Job | | 181 | | 181 | |
| **42″ w, 3 Doors / Drawer** | | | | | | |
| Demolish | Ea. | | 27 | | 27 | Includes material and labor to install |
| Install | Ea. | 460 | 58.50 | | 518.50 | premium modular unit with solid |
| Demolish and Install | Ea. | 460 | 85.50 | | 545.50 | hardwood faced frames, hardwood |
| Reinstall | Ea. | | 46.73 | | 46.73 | door frames and drawer fronts, |
| Clean | Ea. | 2.60 | 19.05 | | 21.65 | hardwood veneer on raised door |
| Paint | Ea. | 1.67 | 52.50 | | 54.17 | panels, hinges and pulls. |
| Minimum Charge | Job | | 181 | | 181 | |
| **48″ w, 3 Doors / Drawer** | | | | | | |
| Demolish | Ea. | | 29.50 | | 29.50 | Includes material and labor to install |
| Install | Ea. | 560 | 63.50 | | 623.50 | premium modular unit with solid |
| Demolish and Install | Ea. | 560 | 93 | | 653 | hardwood faced frames, hardwood |
| Reinstall | Ea. | | 50.62 | | 50.62 | door frames and drawer fronts, |
| Clean | Ea. | 3.63 | 29.50 | | 33.13 | hardwood veneer on raised door |
| Paint | Ea. | 2.51 | 78.50 | | 81.01 | panels, hinges and pulls. |
| Minimum Charge | Job | | 181 | | 181 | |
| **Clean Interior** | | | | | | |
| Install | L.F. | .73 | 5.55 | | 6.28 | Includes labor and materials to clean |
| Minimum Charge | Job | | 133 | | 133 | base cabinetry. |
| **Premium Hardwood** | | | | | | |
| **24″ Wide, 2 Door** | | | | | | |
| Demolish | Ea. | | 14.80 | | 14.80 | Includes material and labor to install |
| Install | Ea. | 335 | 36 | | 371 | premium modular unit with solid |
| Demolish and Install | Ea. | 335 | 50.80 | | 385.80 | hardwood faced frames, hardwood |
| Reinstall | Ea. | | 28.93 | | 28.93 | door frames and drawer fronts, |
| Clean | Ea. | 1.40 | 10.65 | | 12.05 | hardwood veneer on raised door |
| Paint | Ea. | .97 | 35 | | 35.97 | panels, hinges and pulls. |
| Minimum Charge | Job | | 181 | | 181 | |
| **30″ Wide, 2 Door** | | | | | | |
| Demolish | Ea. | | 18.55 | | 18.55 | Includes material and labor to install |
| Install | Ea. | 375 | 45 | | 420 | premium modular unit with solid |
| Demolish and Install | Ea. | 375 | 63.55 | | 438.55 | hardwood faced frames, hardwood |
| Reinstall | Ea. | | 36.16 | | 36.16 | door frames and drawer fronts, |
| Clean | Ea. | 1.82 | 13.35 | | 15.17 | hardwood veneer on raised door |
| Paint | Ea. | 1.21 | 39.50 | | 40.71 | panels, hinges and pulls. |
| Minimum Charge | Job | | 181 | | 181 | |
| **36″ Wide, 2 Door** | | | | | | |
| Demolish | Ea. | | 23 | | 23 | Includes material and labor to install |
| Install | Ea. | 550 | 54.50 | | 604.50 | premium modular unit with solid |
| Demolish and Install | Ea. | 550 | 77.50 | | 627.50 | hardwood faced frames, hardwood |
| Reinstall | Ea. | | 43.40 | | 43.40 | door frames and drawer fronts, |
| Clean | Ea. | 2.01 | 15.70 | | 17.71 | hardwood veneer on raised door |
| Paint | Ea. | 1.46 | 52.50 | | 53.96 | panels, hinges and pulls. |
| Minimum Charge | Job | | 181 | | 181 | |

# Cabinets and Countertops

## Vanity Cabinets

| Vanity Cabinets | Unit | Material | Labor | Equip. | Total | Specification |
|---|---|---|---|---|---|---|
| **42" w, 3 Doors / Drawer** | | | | | | Includes material and labor to install |
| Demolish | Ea. | | 27 | | 27 | premium modular unit with solid |
| Install | Ea. | 510 | 58.50 | | 568.50 | hardwood faced frames, hardwood |
| Demolish and Install | Ea. | 510 | 85.50 | | 595.50 | door frames and drawer fronts, |
| Reinstall | Ea. | | 46.73 | | 46.73 | hardwood veneer on raised door |
| Clean | Ea. | 2.60 | 19.05 | | 21.65 | panels, hinges and pulls. |
| Paint | Ea. | 1.67 | 63 | | 64.67 | |
| Minimum Charge | Job | | 181 | | 181 | |
| **48" w, 3 Doors / Drawer** | | | | | | Includes material and labor to install |
| Demolish | Ea. | | 29.50 | | 29.50 | premium modular unit with solid |
| Install | Ea. | 625 | 63.50 | | 688.50 | hardwood faced frames, hardwood |
| Demolish and Install | Ea. | 625 | 93 | | 718 | door frames and drawer fronts, |
| Reinstall | Ea. | | 50.62 | | 50.62 | hardwood veneer on raised door |
| Clean | Ea. | 3.63 | 29.50 | | 33.13 | panels, hinges and pulls. |
| Paint | Ea. | 2.51 | 78.50 | | 81.01 | |
| Minimum Charge | Job | | 181 | | 181 | |
| **Clean Interior** | | | | | | Includes labor and materials to clean |
| Install | L.F. | .73 | 5.55 | | 6.28 | base cabinetry. |
| Minimum Charge | Job | | 133 | | 133 | |
| **Strip and Refinish** | | | | | | Includes labor and material to strip, |
| Install | L.F. | 1.11 | 5.70 | | 6.81 | prep and refinish exterior of cabinets. |
| Minimum Charge | Job | | 157 | | 157 | |

## Vanity Cabinet Tops

| Vanity Cabinet Tops | Unit | Material | Labor | Equip. | Total | Specification |
|---|---|---|---|---|---|---|
| **Cultured Marble Top** | | | | | | Includes material and labor to install |
| Demolish | L.F. | | 4.94 | | 4.94 | cultured marble vanity top with |
| Install | L.F. | 39.50 | 21.50 | | 61 | integral sink, 22" deep. |
| Demolish and Install | L.F. | 39.50 | 26.44 | | 65.94 | |
| Reinstall | L.F. | | 17.13 | | 17.13 | |
| Clean | L.F. | .13 | 1.01 | | 1.14 | |
| Minimum Charge | Job | | 167 | | 167 | |
| **Laminated Top** | | | | | | Includes material and labor to install |
| Demolish | L.F. | | 2.96 | | 2.96 | one piece laminated top with 4" |
| Install | L.F. | 31 | 12.90 | | 43.90 | backsplash. |
| Demolish and Install | L.F. | 31 | 15.86 | | 46.86 | |
| Reinstall | L.F. | | 10.33 | | 10.33 | |
| Clean | L.F. | .09 | .67 | | .76 | |
| Minimum Charge | Job | | 181 | | 181 | |
| **Solid Surface** | | | | | | Includes material and labor to install |
| Demolish | L.F. | | 4.94 | | 4.94 | solid surface vanity top with integral |
| Install | L.F. | 68 | 27 | | 95 | sink installed, 22" deep. |
| Demolish and Install | L.F. | 68 | 31.94 | | 99.94 | |
| Reinstall | L.F. | | 21.43 | | 21.43 | |
| Clean | L.F. | .13 | 1.01 | | 1.14 | |
| Minimum Charge | Job | | 181 | | 181 | |

# Painting

**Roller Handle**

**Paint Brush**

| Paint Preparation, Walls | | Unit | Material | Labor | Equip. | Total | Specification |
|---|---|---|---|---|---|---|---|
| **Cover / Protect Floors** | | | | | | | |
| | Install | S.F. | .51 | .12 | | .63 | Includes material and labor to install |
| | Minimum Charge | Job | | 157 | | 157 | plastic masking sheet on large uninterrupted areas. |
| **Cover / Protect Walls** | | | | | | | |
| | Install | S.F. | .51 | .12 | | .63 | Includes material and labor to install |
| | Minimum Charge | Job | | 157 | | 157 | plastic masking sheet on walls. |
| **Clean Walls** | | | | | | | |
| **Light** | | | | | | | |
| | Clean | S.F. | | .10 | | .10 | Includes labor to wash gypsum |
| | Minimum Charge | Job | | 157 | | 157 | drywall or plaster wall surfaces. |
| **Heavy** | | | | | | | |
| | Clean | S.F. | | .13 | | .13 | Includes labor and material for heavy |
| | Minimum Charge | Job | | 157 | | 157 | cleaning (multiple applications) with detergent and solvent. |
| **Prep Walls** | | | | | | | |
| | Paint | S.F. | .03 | .16 | | .19 | Includes labor and material to prepare |
| | Minimum Charge | Job | | 157 | | 157 | for painting including scraping, patching and puttying. |
| **Sand Walls** | | | | | | | |
| | Paint | S.F. | | .10 | | .10 | Includes labor to sand gypsum drywall |
| | Minimum Charge | Job | | 157 | | 157 | wall surfaces. |
| **Seal Walls** | | | | | | | |
| **Large Area** | | | | | | | |
| | Paint | S.F. | .06 | .23 | | .29 | Includes labor and material to paint |
| | Minimum Charge | Job | | 157 | | 157 | with primer / sealer by roller. |
| **Spot** | | | | | | | |
| | Paint | S.F. | .06 | .27 | | .33 | Includes labor and material to seal |
| | Minimum Charge | Job | | 157 | | 157 | existing drywall with shellac-based material. |

| Paint Preparation, Ceilings | | Unit | Material | Labor | Equip. | Total | Specification |
|---|---|---|---|---|---|---|---|
| **Cover / Protect Floors** | | | | | | | |
| | Install | S.F. | .51 | .12 | | .63 | Includes material and labor to install |
| | Minimum Charge | Job | | 157 | | 157 | plastic masking sheet on large uninterrupted areas. |

# Painting

## Paint Preparation, Ceilings

| Paint Preparation, Ceilings | | Unit | Material | Labor | Equip. | Total | Specification |
|---|---|---|---|---|---|---|---|
| **Cover / Protect Walls** | | | | | | | |
| | Install | S.F. | .51 | .12 | | .63 | Includes material and labor to install |
| | Minimum Charge | Job | | 157 | | 157 | plastic masking sheet on walls. |
| **Prep Ceiling** | | | | | | | |
| | Paint | S.F. | .06 | .59 | | .65 | Includes labor and material to fill in |
| | Minimum Charge | Job | | 157 | | 157 | hairline cracks up to 1/8" with filler, sand and prep for paint. |
| **Sand Ceiling** | | | | | | | |
| | Paint | S.F. | | .15 | | .15 | Includes labor to sand gypsum drywall |
| | Minimum Charge | Job | | 157 | | 157 | ceiling surfaces. |
| **Seal Ceiling** | | | | | | | |
| **Large Area** | | | | | | | |
| | Paint | S.F. | .07 | .24 | | .31 | Includes labor and material to paint |
| | Minimum Charge | Job | | 157 | | 157 | ceiling, one coat flat latex. |
| **Spot** | | | | | | | |
| | Paint | S.F. | .06 | .27 | | .33 | Includes labor and material to seal |
| | Minimum Charge | Job | | 157 | | 157 | existing drywall with shellac-based material. |

## Paint / Texture, Walls

| Paint / Texture, Walls | | Unit | Material | Labor | Equip. | Total | Specification |
|---|---|---|---|---|---|---|---|
| **Texture Walls** | | | | | | | |
| **Spray** | | | | | | | |
| | Install | S.F. | .06 | .40 | | .46 | Includes labor and material to install |
| | Minimum Charge | Job | | 157 | | 157 | by spray, texture finish. |
| **Trowel** | | | | | | | |
| | Install | S.F. | .01 | .21 | | .22 | Includes labor and material to apply |
| | Minimum Charge | Job | | 157 | | 157 | hand troweled texture. |
| **Paint Walls 1 Coat** | | | | | | | |
| | Paint | S.F. | .07 | .24 | | .31 | Includes labor and material to paint, |
| | Minimum Charge | Job | | 157 | | 157 | one coat flat latex. |
| **Paint Walls 2 Coats** | | | | | | | |
| | Paint | S.F. | .14 | .39 | | .53 | Includes labor and material to paint, |
| | Minimum Charge | Job | | 157 | | 157 | two coats flat latex. |
| **Paint Walls 3 Coats** | | | | | | | |
| | Paint | S.F. | .21 | .48 | | .69 | Includes labor and material to paint, |
| | Minimum Charge | Job | | 157 | | 157 | three coats flat latex. |
| **Clean and Seal** | | | | | | | |
| | Paint | S.F. | .29 | .84 | | 1.13 | Includes labor and material to do light |
| | Minimum Charge | Job | | 157 | | 157 | cleaning, sealing with 2 coats of latex paint. |

## Paint / Texture, Ceilings

| Paint / Texture, Ceilings | | Unit | Material | Labor | Equip. | Total | Specification |
|---|---|---|---|---|---|---|---|
| **Texture Ceiling** | | | | | | | |
| **Spray** | | | | | | | |
| | Install | S.F. | .06 | .40 | | .46 | Includes labor and material to install |
| | Minimum Charge | Job | | 157 | | 157 | by spray, texture finish. |
| **Trowel** | | | | | | | |
| | Install | S.F. | .01 | .21 | | .22 | Includes labor and material to apply |
| | Minimum Charge | Job | | 157 | | 157 | hand troweled texture. |

# Painting

| Paint / Texture, Ceilings | | Unit | Material | Labor | Equip. | Total | Specification |
|---|---|---|---|---|---|---|---|
| **Paint Ceiling, 1 Coat** | | | | | | | |
| | Paint | S.F. | .07 | .24 | | .31 | Includes labor and material to paint |
| | Minimum Charge | Job | | 157 | | 157 | ceiling, one coat flat latex. |
| **Paint Ceiling, 2 Coats** | | | | | | | |
| | Paint | S.F. | .14 | .39 | | .53 | Includes labor and material to paint |
| | Minimum Charge | Job | | 157 | | 157 | two coats flat latex paint. |
| **Paint Ceiling, 3 Coats** | | | | | | | |
| | Paint | S.F. | .21 | .46 | | .67 | Includes labor and material to paint |
| | Minimum Charge | Job | | 157 | | 157 | ceiling, three coats flat latex. |
| **Clean and Seal** | | | | | | | |
| | Paint | S.F. | .21 | .66 | | .87 | Includes labor and material for light |
| | Minimum Charge | Job | | 157 | | 157 | cleaning, sealing and paint 3 coats of flat latex paint. |

| Plank Flooring | | Wood Strip Flooring | | | Tile Flooring | |

| Wood Plank Flooring | Unit | Material | Labor | Equip. | Total | Specification |
|---|---|---|---|---|---|---|
| **Maple** | | | | | | |
| **2-1/4"** | | | | | | |
| Demolish | S.F. | | 1.19 | | 1.19 | Includes material and labor to install |
| Install | S.F. | 4.65 | 1.80 | | 6.45 | unfinished T&G maple flooring, |
| Demolish and Install | S.F. | 4.65 | 2.99 | | 7.64 | 25/32" thick, 2-1/4" wide, random |
| Reinstall | S.F. | | 1.44 | | 1.44 | 3' to 16' lengths including felt |
| Clean | S.F. | | .33 | | .33 | underlayment, nailed in place over |
| Paint | S.F. | 1.28 | 2.05 | | 3.33 | prepared subfloor. |
| Minimum Charge | Job | | 181 | | 181 | |
| **3-1/4"** | | | | | | |
| Demolish | S.F. | | 1.19 | | 1.19 | Includes material and labor to install |
| Install | S.F. | 3.67 | 1.80 | | 5.47 | unfinished T&G maple flooring, |
| Demolish and Install | S.F. | 3.67 | 2.99 | | 6.66 | 33/32" thick, 3-1/4" wide, random |
| Reinstall | S.F. | | 1.44 | | 1.44 | 3' to 16' lengths including felt |
| Clean | S.F. | | .33 | | .33 | underlayment, nailed in place over |
| Paint | S.F. | 1.28 | 2.05 | | 3.33 | prepared subfloor. |
| Minimum Charge | Job | | 181 | | 181 | |
| **Sand and Finish** | | | | | | |
| Install | S.F. | .86 | .67 | | 1.53 | Includes labor and material to sand (3 |
| Minimum Charge | Job | | 181 | | 181 | passes) and finish and two coats of |
| | | | | | | urethane existing floor. |
| **Oak** | | | | | | |
| **2-1/4"** | | | | | | |
| Demolish | S.F. | | 1.19 | | 1.19 | Includes material and labor to install |
| Install | S.F. | 4.18 | 1.80 | | 5.98 | unfinished T&G oak flooring, 25/32" |
| Demolish and Install | S.F. | 4.18 | 2.99 | | 7.17 | thick, 2-1/4" wide, random 3' to 16' |
| Reinstall | S.F. | | 1.44 | | 1.44 | lengths including felt underlayment, |
| Clean | S.F. | | .33 | | .33 | nailed in place over prepared |
| Paint | S.F. | 1.28 | 2.05 | | 3.33 | subfloor. |
| Minimum Charge | Job | | 181 | | 181 | |
| **3-1/4"** | | | | | | |
| Demolish | S.F. | | 1.19 | | 1.19 | Includes material and labor to install |
| Install | S.F. | 5.70 | 1.28 | | 6.98 | unfinished T&G oak flooring, 25/32" |
| Demolish and Install | S.F. | 5.70 | 2.47 | | 8.17 | thick, 3-1/4" wide, random 3' to 16' |
| Reinstall | S.F. | | 1.02 | | 1.02 | lengths including felt underlayment, |
| Clean | S.F. | | .33 | | .33 | nailed in place over prepared |
| Paint | S.F. | 1.28 | 2.05 | | 3.33 | subfloor. |
| Minimum Charge | Job | | 181 | | 181 | |

# Flooring

| Wood Plank Flooring | | Unit | Material | Labor | Equip. | Total | Specification |
|---|---|---|---|---|---|---|---|
| **Sand and Finish** | | | | | | | |
| | Install | S.F. | 1.28 | 2.05 | | 3.33 | Includes labor and material to sand |
| | Minimum Charge | Job | | 181 | | 181 | and finish (3 passes) with two coats of urethane on a new floor. |
| **Walnut** | | | | | | | |
| **3" to 7"** | | | | | | | |
| | Demolish | S.F. | | 1.19 | | 1.19 | Includes material and labor to install |
| | Install | S.F. | 9.05 | 1.28 | | 10.33 | unfinished T&G walnut flooring, |
| | Demolish and Install | S.F. | 9.05 | 2.47 | | 11.52 | 25/32" thick, random 3' to 16' |
| | Reinstall | S.F. | | 1.02 | | 1.02 | lengths including felt underlayment, |
| | Clean | S.F. | | .33 | | .33 | nailed in place over prepared |
| | Paint | S.F. | 1.28 | 2.05 | | 3.33 | subfloor. |
| | Minimum Charge | Job | | 181 | | 181 | |
| **Sand and Finish** | | | | | | | |
| | Install | S.F. | 1.28 | 2.05 | | 3.33 | Includes labor and material to sand |
| | Minimum Charge | Job | | 181 | | 181 | and finish (3 passes) with two coats of urethane on a new floor. |
| **Pine** | | | | | | | |
| **2-1/4"** | | | | | | | |
| | Demolish | S.F. | | 1.19 | | 1.19 | Includes material and labor to install |
| | Install | S.F. | 7.35 | 1.36 | | 8.71 | unfinished T&G pine flooring, 25/32" |
| | Demolish and Install | S.F. | 7.35 | 2.55 | | 9.90 | thick, 2-1/4" wide, random 3' to 16' |
| | Reinstall | S.F. | | 1.09 | | 1.09 | lengths including felt underlayment, |
| | Clean | S.F. | | .33 | | .33 | nailed in place over prepared |
| | Paint | S.F. | .86 | .67 | | 1.53 | subfloor. |
| | Minimum Charge | Job | | 181 | | 181 | |
| **Sand and Finish** | | | | | | | |
| | Install | S.F. | 1.28 | 2.05 | | 3.33 | Includes labor and material to sand |
| | Minimum Charge | Job | | 181 | | 181 | and finish (3 passes) with two coats of urethane on a new floor. |
| **Prefinished Oak** | | | | | | | |
| **2-1/4"** | | | | | | | |
| | Demolish | S.F. | | 1.19 | | 1.19 | Includes material and labor to install |
| | Install | S.F. | 5.75 | 1.80 | | 7.55 | prefinished T&G oak flooring, 2-1/4" |
| | Demolish and Install | S.F. | 5.75 | 2.99 | | 8.74 | wide, random 3' to 16' lengths |
| | Reinstall | S.F. | | 1.44 | | 1.44 | including felt underlayment, nailed in |
| | Clean | S.F. | | .33 | | .33 | place over prepared subfloor. |
| | Minimum Charge | Job | | 181 | | 181 | |
| **3-1/4"** | | | | | | | |
| | Demolish | S.F. | | 1.19 | | 1.19 | Includes material and labor to install |
| | Install | S.F. | 7.40 | 1.66 | | 9.06 | prefinished T&G oak flooring, 25/32" |
| | Demolish and Install | S.F. | 7.40 | 2.85 | | 10.25 | thick, 3" to 7" wide, random 3' to 16' |
| | Reinstall | S.F. | | 1.33 | | 1.33 | lengths including felt underlayment, |
| | Clean | S.F. | | .33 | | .33 | nailed in place over prepared |
| | Minimum Charge | Job | | 181 | | 181 | subfloor. |
| **Sand and Finish New** | | | | | | | |
| | Install | S.F. | .86 | .90 | | 1.76 | Includes labor and material to sand (3 |
| | Minimum Charge | Job | | 181 | | 181 | passes) and finish, two coats of urethane, new floor. |
| **Refinish Existing** | | | | | | | |
| | Install | S.F. | .86 | .67 | | 1.53 | Includes labor and material to sand (3 |
| | Minimum Charge | Job | | 181 | | 181 | passes) and finish and two coats of urethane existing floor. |

# Flooring

## Wood Plank Flooring

| Wood Plank Flooring | | Unit | Material | Labor | Equip. | Total | Specification |
|---|---|---|---|---|---|---|---|
| **Urethane Coat** | | | | | | | |
| | Install | S.F. | .15 | .17 | | .32 | Includes labor and material to install |
| | Minimum Charge | Job | | 181 | | 181 | two coats of urethane, on existing floor. |
| **Clean and Wax** | | | | | | | |
| | Clean | S.F. | .02 | .21 | | .23 | Includes labor and material to wash |
| | Minimum Charge | Job | | 181 | | 181 | and wax a hardwood floor. |
| **Underlayment Per S.F.** | | | | | | | |
| | Demolish | S.F. | | .53 | | .53 | Cost includes material and labor to |
| | Install | S.F. | .80 | .48 | | 1.28 | install 1/4" lauan subfloor, standard |
| | Demolish and Install | S.F. | .80 | 1.01 | | 1.81 | interior grade, nailed every 6". |
| | Clean | S.F. | | .26 | | .26 | |
| | Minimum Charge | Job | | 181 | | 181 | |

## Wood Parquet Tile Floor

| Wood Parquet Tile Floor | | Unit | Material | Labor | Equip. | Total | Specification |
|---|---|---|---|---|---|---|---|
| **Oak** | | | | | | | |
| **9" x 9"** | | | | | | | |
| | Demolish | S.F. | | .89 | | .89 | Includes material and labor to install |
| | Install | S.F. | 4.82 | 2.89 | | 7.71 | prefinished oak 9" x 9" parquet block |
| | Demolish and Install | S.F. | 4.82 | 3.78 | | 8.60 | flooring, 5/16" thick, installed in |
| | Reinstall | S.F. | | 2.31 | | 2.31 | mastic. |
| | Clean | S.F. | | .33 | | .33 | |
| | Paint | S.F. | 1.28 | 2.05 | | 3.33 | |
| | Minimum Charge | Job | | 181 | | 181 | |
| **13" x 13"** | | | | | | | |
| | Demolish | S.F. | | .89 | | .89 | Includes material and labor to install |
| | Install | S.F. | 9.10 | 2.26 | | 11.36 | prefinished oak 13" x 13" parquet |
| | Demolish and Install | S.F. | 9.10 | 3.15 | | 12.25 | block flooring, 5/16" thick, installed in |
| | Reinstall | S.F. | | 1.81 | | 1.81 | mastic. |
| | Clean | S.F. | | .33 | | .33 | |
| | Paint | S.F. | 1.28 | 2.05 | | 3.33 | |
| | Minimum Charge | Job | | 181 | | 181 | |
| **Cherry** | | | | | | | |
| **9" x 9"** | | | | | | | |
| | Demolish | S.F. | | .89 | | .89 | Includes material and labor to install |
| | Install | S.F. | 8.15 | 2.89 | | 11.04 | prefinished cherry 9" x 9" parquet |
| | Demolish and Install | S.F. | 8.15 | 3.78 | | 11.93 | block flooring, 5/16" thick, installed in |
| | Reinstall | S.F. | | 2.89 | | 2.89 | mastic. |
| | Clean | S.F. | | .33 | | .33 | |
| | Paint | S.F. | 1.28 | 2.05 | | 3.33 | |
| | Minimum Charge | Job | | 181 | | 181 | |
| **13" x 13"** | | | | | | | |
| | Demolish | S.F. | | .89 | | .89 | Includes material and labor to install |
| | Install | S.F. | 9.30 | 2.26 | | 11.56 | prefinished cherry 13" x 13" parquet |
| | Demolish and Install | S.F. | 9.30 | 3.15 | | 12.45 | block flooring, 5/16" thick, installed in |
| | Reinstall | S.F. | | 2.26 | | 2.26 | mastic. |
| | Clean | S.F. | | .33 | | .33 | |
| | Paint | S.F. | 1.28 | 2.05 | | 3.33 | |
| | Minimum Charge | Job | | 181 | | 181 | |

| Wood Parquet Tile Floor | | Unit | Material | Labor | Equip. | Total | Specification |
|---|---|---|---|---|---|---|---|
| **Walnut** | | | | | | | |
| **9" x 9"** | | | | | | | |
| | Demolish | S.F. | | .89 | | .89 | Includes material and labor to install |
| | Install | S.F. | 5.25 | 2.89 | | 8.14 | prefinished walnut 9" x 9" parquet |
| | Demolish and Install | S.F. | 5.25 | 3.78 | | 9.03 | flooring in mastic. |
| | Reinstall | S.F. | | 2.31 | | 2.31 | |
| | Clean | S.F. | | .33 | | .33 | |
| | Paint | S.F. | 1.28 | 2.05 | | 3.33 | |
| | Minimum Charge | Job | | 181 | | 181 | |
| **13" x 13"** | | | | | | | |
| | Demolish | S.F. | | .89 | | .89 | Includes material and labor to install |
| | Install | S.F. | 9.70 | 2.26 | | 11.96 | prefinished walnut 13" x 13" parquet |
| | Demolish and Install | S.F. | 9.70 | 3.15 | | 12.85 | block flooring, 5/16" thick, installed in |
| | Reinstall | S.F. | | 2.26 | | 2.26 | mastic. |
| | Clean | S.F. | | .33 | | .33 | |
| | Paint | S.F. | 1.28 | 2.05 | | 3.33 | |
| | Minimum Charge | Job | | 181 | | 181 | |
| **Acrylic Impregnated** | | | | | | | |
| **Oak 12" x 12"** | | | | | | | |
| | Demolish | S.F. | | .89 | | .89 | Includes material and labor to install |
| | Install | S.F. | 8.45 | 2.58 | | 11.03 | red oak 12" x 12" acrylic |
| | Demolish and Install | S.F. | 8.45 | 3.47 | | 11.92 | impregnated parquet block flooring, |
| | Reinstall | S.F. | | 2.58 | | 2.58 | 5/16" thick, installed in mastic. |
| | Clean | S.F. | | .33 | | .33 | |
| | Minimum Charge | Job | | 181 | | 181 | |
| **Cherry 12" x 12"** | | | | | | | |
| | Demolish | S.F. | | .89 | | .89 | Includes material and labor to install |
| | Install | S.F. | 11.40 | 2.58 | | 13.98 | prefinished cherry 12" x 12" acrylic |
| | Demolish and Install | S.F. | 11.40 | 3.47 | | 14.87 | impregnated parquet block flooring, |
| | Reinstall | S.F. | | 2.58 | | 2.58 | 5/16" thick, installed in mastic. |
| | Clean | S.F. | | .33 | | .33 | |
| | Minimum Charge | Job | | 181 | | 181 | |
| **Ash 12" x 12"** | | | | | | | |
| | Demolish | S.F. | | .89 | | .89 | Includes material and labor to install |
| | Install | S.F. | 10.25 | 2.58 | | 12.83 | ash 12" x 12" acrylic impregnated |
| | Demolish and Install | S.F. | 10.25 | 3.47 | | 13.72 | parquet block flooring, 5/16" thick in |
| | Reinstall | S.F. | | 2.58 | | 2.58 | mastic. |
| | Clean | S.F. | | .33 | | .33 | |
| | Minimum Charge | Job | | 181 | | 181 | |
| **Teak** | | | | | | | |
| | Demolish | S.F. | | .89 | | .89 | Includes material and labor to install |
| | Install | S.F. | 7.35 | 2.26 | | 9.61 | prefinished teak parquet block |
| | Demolish and Install | S.F. | 7.35 | 3.15 | | 10.50 | flooring, 5/16" thick, and installed in |
| | Reinstall | S.F. | | 2.26 | | 2.26 | mastic. |
| | Clean | S.F. | | .33 | | .33 | |
| | Paint | S.F. | 1.28 | 2.05 | | 3.33 | |
| | Minimum Charge | Job | | 181 | | 181 | |
| **Clean and Wax** | | | | | | | |
| | Clean | S.F. | .02 | .21 | | .23 | Includes labor and material to wash |
| | Minimum Charge | Job | | 181 | | 181 | and wax a hardwood floor. |

# Flooring

| Ceramic Tile Flooring | | Unit | Material | Labor | Equip. | Total | Specification |
|---|---|---|---|---|---|---|---|
| **Economy Grade** | | | | | | | |
| | Demolish | S.F. | | .88 | | .88 | Cost includes material and labor to |
| | Install | S.F. | 4.59 | 6.55 | | 11.14 | install 4-1/4" x 4-1/4" ceramic tile in |
| | Demolish and Install | S.F. | 4.59 | 7.43 | | 12.02 | mortar bed including grout. |
| | Clean | S.F. | | .51 | | .51 | |
| | Minimum Charge | Job | | 167 | | 167 | |
| **Average Grade** | | | | | | | |
| | Demolish | S.F. | | .88 | | .88 | Cost includes material and labor to |
| | Install | S.F. | 6.10 | 6.65 | | 12.75 | install 4-1/4" x 4-1/4" ceramic tile in |
| | Demolish and Install | S.F. | 6.10 | 7.53 | | 13.63 | mortar bed including grout. |
| | Clean | S.F. | | .51 | | .51 | |
| | Minimum Charge | Job | | 167 | | 167 | |
| **Premium Grade** | | | | | | | |
| | Demolish | S.F. | | .88 | | .88 | Cost includes material and labor to |
| | Install | S.F. | 9.65 | 6.65 | | 16.30 | install 4-1/4" x 4-1/4" ceramic tile in |
| | Demolish and Install | S.F. | 9.65 | 7.53 | | 17.18 | mortar bed including grout. |
| | Clean | S.F. | | .51 | | .51 | |
| | Minimum Charge | Job | | 167 | | 167 | |
| **Re-grout** | | | | | | | |
| | Install | S.F. | .15 | 2.67 | | 2.82 | Includes material and labor to regrout |
| | Minimum Charge | Job | | 167 | | 167 | tile floors. |

| Hard Tile Flooring | | Unit | Material | Labor | Equip. | Total | Specification |
|---|---|---|---|---|---|---|---|
| **Thick Set Paver** | | | | | | | |
| **Brick** | | | | | | | |
| | Demolish | S.F. | | 1.85 | | 1.85 | Cost includes material and labor to |
| | Install | S.F. | .92 | 15.45 | | 16.37 | install 6" x 12" adobe brick paver with |
| | Demolish and Install | S.F. | .92 | 17.30 | | 18.22 | 1/2" mortar joints. |
| | Clean | S.F. | | .51 | | .51 | |
| | Minimum Charge | Job | | 167 | | 167 | |
| **Mexican Red** | | | | | | | |
| | Demolish | S.F. | | 1.85 | | 1.85 | Cost includes material and labor to |
| | Install | S.F. | 1.65 | 6.95 | | 8.60 | install 12" x 12" red Mexican paver |
| | Demolish and Install | S.F. | 1.65 | 8.80 | | 10.45 | tile in mortar bed with grout. |
| | Clean | S.F. | | .51 | | .51 | |
| | Minimum Charge | Job | | 167 | | 167 | |
| **Saltillo** | | | | | | | |
| | Demolish | S.F. | | .88 | | .88 | Cost includes material and labor to |
| | Install | S.F. | 1.17 | 6.95 | | 8.12 | install 12" x 12"saltillo tile in mortar |
| | Demolish and Install | S.F. | 1.17 | 7.83 | | 9 | bed with grout. |
| | Clean | S.F. | | .51 | | .51 | |
| | Minimum Charge | Job | | 167 | | 167 | |
| **Marble** | | | | | | | |
| **Premium Grade** | | | | | | | |
| | Demolish | S.F. | | .88 | | .88 | Cost includes material and labor to |
| | Install | S.F. | 20 | 14.50 | | 34.50 | install 3/8" x 12" x 12" marble, in |
| | Demolish and Install | S.F. | 20 | 15.38 | | 35.38 | mortar bed with grout. |
| | Clean | S.F. | | .51 | | .51 | |
| | Minimum Charge | Job | | 167 | | 167 | |

# Flooring

| Hard Tile Flooring | | Unit | Material | Labor | Equip. | Total | Specification |
|---|---|---|---|---|---|---|---|
| **Terrazzo** | | | | | | | |
| **Gray Cement** | | | | | | | |
| | Demolish | S.F. | | 1.18 | | 1.18 | Cost includes material and labor to |
| | Install | S.F. | 3.08 | 4.64 | 2.10 | 9.82 | install 1-3/4" terrazzo , #1 and #2 |
| | Demolish and Install | S.F. | 3.08 | 5.82 | 2.10 | 11 | chips in gray Portland cement. |
| | Clean | S.F. | | .51 | | .51 | |
| | Minimum Charge | Job | | 300 | 136 | 436 | |
| **White Cement** | | | | | | | |
| | Demolish | S.F. | | 1.18 | | 1.18 | Cost includes material and labor to |
| | Install | S.F. | 3.51 | 4.64 | 2.10 | 10.25 | install 1-3/4" terrazzo, #1 and #2 |
| | Demolish and Install | S.F. | 3.51 | 5.82 | 2.10 | 11.43 | chips in white Portland cement. |
| | Clean | S.F. | | .51 | | .51 | |
| | Minimum Charge | Job | | 300 | 136 | 436 | |
| **Non-skid Gray** | | | | | | | |
| | Demolish | S.F. | | 1.18 | | 1.18 | Cost includes material and labor to |
| | Install | S.F. | 5.60 | 10.05 | 4.54 | 20.19 | install 1-3/4" terrazzo, #1 and #2 |
| | Demolish and Install | S.F. | 5.60 | 11.23 | 4.54 | 21.37 | chips in gray Portland cement with |
| | Clean | S.F. | | .51 | | .51 | light non-skid abrasive. |
| | Minimum Charge | Job | | 300 | 136 | 436 | |
| **Non-skid White** | | | | | | | |
| | Demolish | S.F. | | 1.18 | | 1.18 | Cost includes material and labor to |
| | Install | S.F. | 6.15 | 10.05 | 4.54 | 20.74 | install 1-3/4" terrazzo, #1 and #2 |
| | Demolish and Install | S.F. | 6.15 | 11.23 | 4.54 | 21.92 | chips in white Portland cement with |
| | Clean | S.F. | | .51 | | .51 | light non-skid abrasive. |
| | Minimum Charge | Job | | 300 | 136 | 436 | |
| **Gray w / Brass Divider** | | | | | | | |
| | Demolish | S.F. | | 1.19 | | 1.19 | Cost includes material and labor to |
| | Install | S.F. | 7.70 | 10.95 | 4.95 | 23.60 | install 1-3/4" terrazzo, #1 and #2 |
| | Demolish and Install | S.F. | 7.70 | 12.14 | 4.95 | 24.79 | chips in gray Portland cement with |
| | Clean | S.F. | | .51 | | .51 | brass strips 2' O.C. each way. |
| | Minimum Charge | Job | | 300 | 136 | 436 | |
| **Clean** | | | | | | | |
| | Clean | S.F. | .15 | .34 | | .49 | Includes labor and material to clean |
| | Minimum Charge | Job | | 300 | 136 | 436 | terrazzo flooring. |
| **Slate** | | | | | | | |
| | Demolish | S.F. | | 1.06 | | 1.06 | Includes material and labor to install |
| | Install | S.F. | 7.50 | 3.31 | | 10.81 | slate tile flooring in thin set with grout. |
| | Demolish and Install | S.F. | 7.50 | 4.37 | | 11.87 | |
| | Clean | S.F. | | .51 | | .51 | |
| | Minimum Charge | Job | | 167 | | 167 | |
| **Granite** | | | | | | | |
| | Demolish | S.F. | | .87 | | .87 | Includes material and labor to install |
| | Install | S.F. | 20 | 3.33 | | 23.33 | granite tile flooring in thin set with |
| | Demolish and Install | S.F. | 20 | 4.20 | | 24.20 | grout. |
| | Reinstall | S.F. | | 3.33 | | 3.33 | |
| | Clean | S.F. | | .51 | | .51 | |
| | Minimum Charge | Job | | 167 | | 167 | |
| **Re-grout** | | | | | | | |
| | Install | S.F. | .15 | 2.67 | | 2.82 | Includes material and labor to regrout |
| | Minimum Charge | Job | | 167 | | 167 | tile floors. |

# Flooring

## Sheet Vinyl Per S.F.

| Sheet Vinyl Per S.F. | Unit | Material | Labor | Equip. | Total | Specification |
|---|---|---|---|---|---|---|
| **Economy Grade** | | | | | | |
| Demolish | S.F. | | .42 | | .42 | Includes material and labor to install |
| Install | S.F. | 1.93 | 1.04 | | 2.97 | resilient sheet vinyl flooring. |
| Demolish and Install | S.F. | 1.93 | 1.46 | | 3.39 | |
| Clean | S.F. | | .33 | | .33 | |
| Minimum Charge | Job | | 167 | | 167 | |
| **Average Grade** | | | | | | |
| Demolish | S.F. | | .42 | | .42 | Includes material and labor to install |
| Install | S.F. | 3.04 | 1.04 | | 4.08 | resilient sheet vinyl flooring. |
| Demolish and Install | S.F. | 3.04 | 1.46 | | 4.50 | |
| Clean | S.F. | | .33 | | .33 | |
| Minimum Charge | Job | | 167 | | 167 | |
| **Premium Grade** | | | | | | |
| Demolish | S.F. | | .42 | | .42 | Includes material and labor to install |
| Install | S.F. | 5.20 | 1.04 | | 6.24 | resilient sheet vinyl flooring. |
| Demolish and Install | S.F. | 5.20 | 1.46 | | 6.66 | |
| Clean | S.F. | | .33 | | .33 | |
| Minimum Charge | Job | | 167 | | 167 | |
| **Clean and Wax** | | | | | | |
| Clean | S.F. | .02 | .17 | | .19 | Includes labor and material to wash |
| Minimum Charge | Job | | 167 | | 167 | and wax a vinyl tile floor. |

## Sheet Vinyl

| Sheet Vinyl | Unit | Material | Labor | Equip. | Total | Specification |
|---|---|---|---|---|---|---|
| **Economy Grade** | | | | | | |
| Demolish | S.Y. | | 3.83 | | 3.83 | Includes material and labor to install |
| Install | S.Y. | 17.35 | 9.40 | | 26.75 | no wax sheet vinyl flooring. |
| Demolish and Install | S.Y. | 17.35 | 13.23 | | 30.58 | |
| Clean | S.Y. | | 2.32 | | 2.32 | |
| Minimum Charge | Job | | 167 | | 167 | |
| **Average Grade** | | | | | | |
| Demolish | S.Y. | | 3.83 | | 3.83 | Includes material and labor to install |
| Install | S.Y. | 27.50 | 9.40 | | 36.90 | no wax sheet vinyl flooring. |
| Demolish and Install | S.Y. | 27.50 | 13.23 | | 40.73 | |
| Clean | S.Y. | | 2.32 | | 2.32 | |
| Minimum Charge | Job | | 167 | | 167 | |
| **Premium Grade** | | | | | | |
| Demolish | S.Y. | | 3.83 | | 3.83 | Includes material and labor to install |
| Install | S.Y. | 46.50 | 9.40 | | 55.90 | no wax sheet vinyl flooring. |
| Demolish and Install | S.Y. | 46.50 | 13.23 | | 59.73 | |
| Clean | S.Y. | | 2.32 | | 2.32 | |
| Minimum Charge | Job | | 167 | | 167 | |
| **Clean and Wax** | | | | | | |
| Clean | S.F. | .02 | .17 | | .19 | Includes labor and material to wash |
| Minimum Charge | Job | | 167 | | 167 | and wax a vinyl tile floor. |

## Vinyl Tile

| Vinyl Tile | Unit | Material | Labor | Equip. | Total | Specification |
|---|---|---|---|---|---|---|
| **Economy Grade** | | | | | | |
| Demolish | S.F. | | .59 | | .59 | Includes material and labor to install |
| Install | S.F. | 3.03 | .67 | | 3.70 | no wax 12" x 12" vinyl tile. |
| Demolish and Install | S.F. | 3.03 | 1.26 | | 4.29 | |
| Clean | S.F. | | .33 | | .33 | |
| Minimum Charge | Job | | 167 | | 167 | |

# Flooring

## Vinyl Tile

| Vinyl Tile | | Unit | Material | Labor | Equip. | Total | Specification |
|---|---|---|---|---|---|---|---|
| **Average Grade** | | | | | | | |
| | Demolish | S.F. | | .59 | | .59 | Includes material and labor to install |
| | Install | S.F. | 5.90 | .67 | | 6.57 | no wax 12″ x 12″ vinyl tile. |
| | Demolish and Install | S.F. | 5.90 | 1.26 | | 7.16 | |
| | Clean | S.F. | | .33 | | .33 | |
| | Minimum Charge | Job | | 167 | | 167 | |
| **Premium Grade** | | | | | | | |
| | Demolish | S.F. | | .59 | | .59 | Includes material and labor to install |
| | Install | S.F. | 12.65 | .67 | | 13.32 | no wax 12″ x 12″ vinyl tile. |
| | Demolish and Install | S.F. | 12.65 | 1.26 | | 13.91 | |
| | Clean | S.F. | | .33 | | .33 | |
| | Minimum Charge | Job | | 167 | | 167 | |
| **Clean and Wax** | | | | | | | |
| | Clean | S.F. | .02 | .17 | | .19 | Includes labor and material to wash |
| | Minimum Charge | Job | | 167 | | 167 | and wax a vinyl tile floor. |

## Carpeting Per S.F.

| Carpeting Per S.F. | | Unit | Material | Labor | Equip. | Total | Specification |
|---|---|---|---|---|---|---|---|
| **Economy Grade** | | | | | | | |
| | Demolish | S.F. | | .07 | | .07 | Includes material and labor to install |
| | Install | S.F. | 1.22 | .65 | | 1.87 | carpet including tack strips and hot |
| | Demolish and Install | S.F. | 1.22 | .72 | | 1.94 | melt tape on seams. |
| | Clean | S.F. | | .46 | | .46 | |
| | Minimum Charge | Job | | 167 | | 167 | |
| **Average Grade** | | | | | | | |
| | Demolish | S.F. | | .07 | | .07 | Includes material and labor to install |
| | Install | S.F. | 1.43 | .65 | | 2.08 | carpet including tack strips and hot |
| | Demolish and Install | S.F. | 1.43 | .72 | | 2.15 | melt tape on seams. |
| | Clean | S.F. | | .46 | | .46 | |
| | Minimum Charge | Job | | 167 | | 167 | |
| **Premium Grade** | | | | | | | |
| | Demolish | S.F. | | .07 | | .07 | Includes material and labor to install |
| | Install | S.F. | 2.51 | .65 | | 3.16 | carpet including tack strips and hot |
| | Demolish and Install | S.F. | 2.51 | .72 | | 3.23 | melt tape on seams. |
| | Clean | S.F. | | .46 | | .46 | |
| | Minimum Charge | Job | | 167 | | 167 | |
| **Indoor/Outdoor** | | | | | | | |
| | Demolish | S.F. | | .07 | | .07 | Includes material and labor to install |
| | Install | S.F. | .79 | .79 | | 1.58 | indoor-outdoor carpet. |
| | Demolish and Install | S.F. | .79 | .86 | | 1.65 | |
| | Clean | S.F. | | .46 | | .46 | |
| | Minimum Charge | Job | | 167 | | 167 | |
| **100% Wool** | | | | | | | |
| *Average Grade* | | | | | | | |
| | Demolish | S.F. | | .07 | | .07 | Includes material and labor to install |
| | Install | S.F. | 8.70 | .66 | | 9.36 | carpet including tack strips and hot |
| | Demolish and Install | S.F. | 8.70 | .73 | | 9.43 | melt tape on seams. |
| | Clean | S.F. | | .46 | | .46 | |
| | Minimum Charge | Job | | 167 | | 167 | |
| *Premium Grade* | | | | | | | |
| | Demolish | S.F. | | .07 | | .07 | Includes material and labor to install |
| | Install | S.F. | 9.80 | .66 | | 10.46 | carpet including tack strips and hot |
| | Demolish and Install | S.F. | 9.80 | .73 | | 10.53 | melt tape on seams. |
| | Clean | S.F. | | .46 | | .46 | |
| | Minimum Charge | Job | | 167 | | 167 | |

# Flooring

## Carpeting Per S.F.

| | Unit | Material | Labor | Equip. | Total | Specification |
|---|---|---|---|---|---|---|
| **Luxury Grade** | | | | | | |
| Demolish | S.F. | | .07 | | .07 | Includes material and labor to install |
| Install | S.F. | 13.40 | .66 | | 14.06 | carpet including tack strips and hot |
| Demolish and Install | S.F. | 13.40 | .73 | | 14.13 | melt tape on seams. |
| Clean | S.F. | | .46 | | .46 | |
| Minimum Charge | Job | | 167 | | 167 | |
| **Berber** | | | | | | |
| **Average Grade** | | | | | | |
| Demolish | S.F. | | .07 | | .07 | Includes material and labor to install |
| Install | S.F. | 3.45 | .79 | | 4.24 | carpet including tack strips and hot |
| Demolish and Install | S.F. | 3.45 | .86 | | 4.31 | melt tape on seams. |
| Clean | S.F. | | .46 | | .46 | |
| Minimum Charge | Job | | 167 | | 167 | |
| **Premium Grade** | | | | | | |
| Demolish | S.F. | | .07 | | .07 | Includes material and labor to install |
| Install | S.F. | 5.95 | .79 | | 6.74 | carpet including tack strips and hot |
| Demolish and Install | S.F. | 5.95 | .86 | | 6.81 | melt tape on seams. |
| Clean | S.F. | | .46 | | .46 | |
| Minimum Charge | Job | | 167 | | 167 | |

## Carpeting

| | Unit | Material | Labor | Equip. | Total | Specification |
|---|---|---|---|---|---|---|
| **Indoor/Outdoor** | | | | | | |
| Demolish | S.Y. | | .99 | | .99 | Includes material and labor to install |
| Install | S.Y. | 7.15 | 7.10 | | 14.25 | indoor-outdoor carpet. |
| Demolish and Install | S.Y. | 7.15 | 8.09 | | 15.24 | |
| Reinstall | S.Y. | | 5.67 | | 5.67 | |
| Clean | S.Y. | | 4.17 | | 4.17 | |
| Minimum Charge | Job | | 167 | | 167 | |
| **Economy Grade** | | | | | | |
| Demolish | S.Y. | | .99 | | .99 | Includes material and labor to install |
| Install | S.Y. | 11 | 5.85 | | 16.85 | carpet including tack strips and hot |
| Demolish and Install | S.Y. | 11 | 6.84 | | 17.84 | melt tape on seams. |
| Reinstall | S.Y. | | 4.68 | | 4.68 | |
| Clean | S.Y. | | 4.17 | | 4.17 | |
| Minimum Charge | Job | | 167 | | 167 | |
| **Average Grade** | | | | | | |
| Demolish | S.Y. | | .99 | | .99 | Includes material and labor to install |
| Install | S.Y. | 12.85 | 5.85 | | 18.70 | carpet including tack strips and hot |
| Demolish and Install | S.Y. | 12.85 | 6.84 | | 19.69 | melt tape on seams. |
| Reinstall | S.Y. | | 4.68 | | 4.68 | |
| Clean | S.Y. | | 4.17 | | 4.17 | |
| Minimum Charge | Job | | 167 | | 167 | |
| **Premium Grade** | | | | | | |
| Demolish | S.Y. | | .99 | | .99 | Includes material and labor to install |
| Install | S.Y. | 22.50 | 5.85 | | 28.35 | carpet including tack strips and hot |
| Demolish and Install | S.Y. | 22.50 | 6.84 | | 29.34 | melt tape on seams. |
| Reinstall | S.Y. | | 4.68 | | 4.68 | |
| Clean | S.Y. | | 4.17 | | 4.17 | |
| Minimum Charge | Job | | 167 | | 167 | |

# Flooring

| Carpeting | | Unit | Material | Labor | Equip. | Total | Specification |
|---|---|---|---|---|---|---|---|
| **100% Wool** | | | | | | | |
| **Average Grade** | | | | | | | |
| | Demolish | S.Y. | | .99 | | .99 | Includes material and labor to install |
| | Install | S.Y. | 78 | 5.95 | | 83.95 | wool carpet including tack strips and |
| | Demolish and Install | S.Y. | 78 | 6.94 | | 84.94 | hot melt tape on seams. |
| | Reinstall | S.Y. | | 4.76 | | 4.76 | |
| | Clean | S.Y. | | 4.17 | | 4.17 | |
| | Minimum Charge | Job | | 167 | | 167 | |
| **Premium Grade** | | | | | | | |
| | Demolish | S.Y. | | .99 | | .99 | Includes material and labor to install |
| | Install | S.Y. | 88 | 5.95 | | 93.95 | carpet including tack strips and hot |
| | Demolish and Install | S.Y. | 88 | 6.94 | | 94.94 | melt tape on seams. |
| | Reinstall | S.Y. | | 4.76 | | 4.76 | |
| | Clean | S.Y. | | 4.17 | | 4.17 | |
| | Minimum Charge | Job | | 167 | | 167 | |
| **Luxury Grade** | | | | | | | |
| | Demolish | S.Y. | | .99 | | .99 | Includes material and labor to install |
| | Install | S.Y. | 121 | 5.95 | | 126.95 | carpet including tack strips and hot |
| | Demolish and Install | S.Y. | 121 | 6.94 | | 127.94 | melt tape on seams. |
| | Reinstall | S.Y. | | 4.76 | | 4.76 | |
| | Clean | S.Y. | | 4.17 | | 4.17 | |
| | Minimum Charge | Job | | 167 | | 167 | |
| **Berber** | | | | | | | |
| **Average Grade** | | | | | | | |
| | Demolish | S.Y. | | .99 | | .99 | Includes material and labor to install |
| | Install | S.Y. | 31 | 7.10 | | 38.10 | berber carpet including tack strips and |
| | Demolish and Install | S.Y. | 31 | 8.09 | | 39.09 | hot melt tape on seams. |
| | Reinstall | S.Y. | | 5.67 | | 5.67 | |
| | Clean | S.Y. | | 4.17 | | 4.17 | |
| | Minimum Charge | Job | | 167 | | 167 | |
| **Premium Grade** | | | | | | | |
| | Demolish | S.Y. | | .99 | | .99 | Includes material and labor to install |
| | Install | S.Y. | 54 | 7.10 | | 61.10 | carpet including tack strips and hot |
| | Demolish and Install | S.Y. | 54 | 8.09 | | 62.09 | melt tape on seams. |
| | Reinstall | S.Y. | | 5.67 | | 5.67 | |
| | Clean | S.Y. | | 4.17 | | 4.17 | |
| | Minimum Charge | Job | | 167 | | 167 | |

| Carpet Pad Per S.F. | | Unit | Material | Labor | Equip. | Total | Specification |
|---|---|---|---|---|---|---|---|
| **Urethane** | | | | | | | |
| | Demolish | S.F. | | .02 | | .02 | Includes material and labor to install |
| | Install | S.F. | .43 | .25 | | .68 | urethane carpet pad. |
| | Demolish and Install | S.F. | .43 | .27 | | .70 | |
| | Minimum Charge | Job | | 167 | | 167 | |
| **Foam Rubber Slab** | | | | | | | |
| | Demolish | S.F. | | .02 | | .02 | Includes material and labor to install |
| | Install | S.F. | .61 | .25 | | .86 | carpet pad, 3/8" thick foam rubber. |
| | Demolish and Install | S.F. | .61 | .27 | | .88 | |
| | Minimum Charge | Job | | 167 | | 167 | |
| **Waffle** | | | | | | | |
| | Demolish | S.F. | | .02 | | .02 | Includes material and labor to install |
| | Install | S.F. | .37 | .03 | | .40 | rubber waffle carpet pad. |
| | Demolish and Install | S.F. | .37 | .05 | | .42 | |
| | Minimum Charge | Job | | 167 | | 167 | |

# Flooring

## Carpet Pad Per S.F.

| Carpet Pad Per S.F. | Unit | Material | Labor | Equip. | Total | Specification |
|---|---|---|---|---|---|---|
| **Jute** | | | | | | |
| Demolish | S.F. | | .02 | | .02 | Includes material and labor to install |
| Install | S.F. | .67 | .22 | | .89 | jute hair carpet pad. |
| Demolish and Install | S.F. | .67 | .24 | | .91 | |
| Minimum Charge | Job | | 167 | | 167 | |
| **Rebound** | | | | | | |
| Demolish | S.F. | | .02 | | .02 | Includes material and labor to install |
| Install | S.F. | .31 | .18 | | .49 | rebound carpet pad. |
| Demolish and Install | S.F. | .31 | .20 | | .51 | |
| Minimum Charge | Job | | 167 | | 167 | |

## Carpet Pad

| Carpet Pad | Unit | Material | Labor | Equip. | Total | Specification |
|---|---|---|---|---|---|---|
| **Urethane** | | | | | | |
| Demolish | S.Y. | | .17 | | .17 | Includes material and labor to install |
| Install | S.Y. | 3.85 | 2.22 | | 6.07 | urethane carpet pad. |
| Demolish and Install | S.Y. | 3.85 | 2.39 | | 6.24 | |
| Reinstall | S.Y. | | 1.78 | | 1.78 | |
| Minimum Charge | Job | | 167 | | 167 | |
| **Foam Rubber Slab** | | | | | | |
| Demolish | S.Y. | | .17 | | .17 | Includes material and labor to install |
| Install | S.Y. | 5.45 | 2.22 | | 7.67 | rubber slab carpet pad. |
| Demolish and Install | S.Y. | 5.45 | 2.39 | | 7.84 | |
| Reinstall | S.Y. | | 1.78 | | 1.78 | |
| Minimum Charge | Job | | 167 | | 167 | |
| **Waffle** | | | | | | |
| Demolish | S.Y. | | .17 | | .17 | Includes material and labor to install |
| Install | S.Y. | 3.32 | .25 | | 3.57 | rubber waffle carpet pad. |
| Demolish and Install | S.Y. | 3.32 | .42 | | 3.74 | |
| Reinstall | S.Y. | | .20 | | .20 | |
| Minimum Charge | Job | | 167 | | 167 | |
| **Jute** | | | | | | |
| Demolish | S.Y. | | .17 | | .17 | Includes material and labor to install |
| Install | S.Y. | 6.05 | 1.96 | | 8.01 | jute hair carpet pad. |
| Demolish and Install | S.Y. | 6.05 | 2.13 | | 8.18 | |
| Reinstall | S.Y. | | 1.57 | | 1.57 | |
| Minimum Charge | Job | | 167 | | 167 | |
| **Rebound** | | | | | | |
| Demolish | S.Y. | | .17 | | .17 | Includes material and labor to install |
| Install | S.Y. | 2.83 | 1.66 | | 4.49 | rebound carpet pad. |
| Demolish and Install | S.Y. | 2.83 | 1.83 | | 4.66 | |
| Reinstall | S.Y. | | 1.33 | | 1.33 | |
| Minimum Charge | Job | | 167 | | 167 | |

## Stair Components

| Stair Components | Unit | Material | Labor | Equip. | Total | Specification |
|---|---|---|---|---|---|---|
| **Carpeting** | | | | | | |
| Demolish | Ea. | | 1.80 | | 1.80 | Includes material and labor to install |
| Install | Riser | 43 | 8.75 | | 51.75 | carpet and pad on stairs. |
| Demolish and Install | Riser | 43 | 10.55 | | 53.55 | |
| Reinstall | Riser | | 7.01 | | 7.01 | |
| Clean | Ea. | | 4.17 | | 4.17 | |
| Minimum Charge | Job | | 167 | | 167 | |

# Finish Mechanical

**Tub/Shower**

**Stainless Steel Double Sink**

**Water Closet**

| Commode | Unit | Material | Labor | Equip. | Total | Specification |
|---|---|---|---|---|---|---|
| Demolish | Ea. | | 40.50 | | 40.50 | Includes material and labor to install a |
| Install | Ea. | 201 | 138 | | 339 | toilet with valve, seat and cover. |
| Demolish and Install | Ea. | 201 | 178.50 | | 379.50 | |
| Reinstall | Ea. | | 110.08 | | 110.08 | |
| Clean | Ea. | .36 | 13.35 | | 13.71 | |
| Minimum Charge | Job | | 203 | | 203 | |

**Wall w / Flush Valve**

| | Unit | Material | Labor | Equip. | Total | Specification |
|---|---|---|---|---|---|---|
| Demolish | Ea. | | 40.50 | | 40.50 | Includes material and labor to install a |
| Install | Ea. | 365 | 126 | | 491 | wall hung toilet with flush valve, seat |
| Demolish and Install | Ea. | 365 | 166.50 | | 531.50 | and cover. |
| Reinstall | Ea. | | 100.59 | | 100.59 | |
| Clean | Ea. | .36 | 13.35 | | 13.71 | |
| Minimum Charge | Job | | 203 | | 203 | |

**Designer Floor Mount**

| | Unit | Material | Labor | Equip. | Total | Specification |
|---|---|---|---|---|---|---|
| Demolish | Ea. | | 40.50 | | 40.50 | Includes material and labor to install a |
| Install | Ea. | 585 | 138 | | 723 | toilet with valve, seat and cover. |
| Demolish and Install | Ea. | 585 | 178.50 | | 763.50 | |
| Reinstall | Ea. | | 110.08 | | 110.08 | |
| Clean | Ea. | .36 | 13.35 | | 13.71 | |
| Minimum Charge | Job | | 203 | | 203 | |

**Urinal**

| | Unit | Material | Labor | Equip. | Total | Specification |
|---|---|---|---|---|---|---|
| Demolish | Ea. | | 40.50 | | 40.50 | Includes material and labor to install a |
| Install | Ea. | 375 | 243 | | 618 | wall hung urinal with flush valve. |
| Demolish and Install | Ea. | 375 | 283.50 | | 658.50 | |
| Reinstall | Ea. | | 194.47 | | 194.47 | |
| Clean | Ea. | .36 | 13.35 | | 13.71 | |
| Minimum Charge | Job | | 203 | | 203 | |

**Bidet**

**Vitreous China**

| | Unit | Material | Labor | Equip. | Total | Specification |
|---|---|---|---|---|---|---|
| Demolish | Ea. | | 40.50 | | 40.50 | Includes material and labor to install a |
| Install | Ea. | 695 | 146 | | 841 | vitreous china bidet complete with |
| Demolish and Install | Ea. | 695 | 186.50 | | 881.50 | trim. |
| Reinstall | Ea. | | 116.68 | | 116.68 | |
| Clean | Ea. | .36 | 13.35 | | 13.71 | |
| Minimum Charge | Job | | 203 | | 203 | |

# Finish Mechanical

| Commode | | Unit | Material | Labor | Equip. | Total | Specification |
|---|---|---|---|---|---|---|---|
| **Chrome Fittings** | | | | | | | |
| | Install | Ea. | 169 | 50.50 | | 219.50 | Includes labor and materials to install chrome fittings for a bidet. |
| **Brass Fittings** | | | | | | | |
| | Install | Ea. | 186 | 50.50 | | 236.50 | Includes labor and materials to install brass fittings for a bidet. |
| **Seat** | | | | | | | |
| | Demolish | Ea. | | 16.90 | | 16.90 | Includes material and labor to install a toilet seat and cover. |
| | Install | Ea. | 30.50 | 16.90 | | 47.40 | |
| | Demolish and Install | Ea. | 30.50 | 33.80 | | 64.30 | |
| | Reinstall | Ea. | | 13.51 | | 13.51 | |
| | Clean | Ea. | .19 | 5.55 | | 5.74 | |
| | Minimum Charge | Job | | 203 | | 203 | |
| **Rough-in** | | | | | | | |
| | Install | Ea. | 315 | 257 | | 572 | Includes labor and materials to install water supply pipe with valves and drain, waste and vent pipe with all couplings, hangers and fasteners necessary. |

| Sink (assembly) | | Unit | Material | Labor | Equip. | Total | Specification |
|---|---|---|---|---|---|---|---|
| **Single** | | | | | | | |
| **Porcelain** | | | | | | | |
| | Demolish | Ea. | | 25.50 | | 25.50 | Includes material and labor to install a single bowl enamel finished cast iron kitchen sink with faucet and drain. |
| | Install | Ea. | 305 | 130 | | 435 | |
| | Demolish and Install | Ea. | 305 | 155.50 | | 460.50 | |
| | Reinstall | Ea. | | 104.18 | | 104.18 | |
| | Clean | Ea. | .23 | 9.55 | | 9.78 | |
| | Minimum Charge | Job | | 203 | | 203 | |
| **Stainless Steel** | | | | | | | |
| | Demolish | Ea. | | 25.50 | | 25.50 | Includes material and labor to install a single bowl stainless steel kitchen sink with faucet and drain. |
| | Install | Ea. | 525 | 130 | | 655 | |
| | Demolish and Install | Ea. | 525 | 155.50 | | 680.50 | |
| | Reinstall | Ea. | | 104.18 | | 104.18 | |
| | Clean | Ea. | .23 | 9.55 | | 9.78 | |
| | Minimum Charge | Job | | 203 | | 203 | |
| **Double** | | | | | | | |
| **Porcelain** | | | | | | | |
| | Demolish | Ea. | | 29 | | 29 | Includes material and labor to install a double bowl enamel finished cast iron kitchen sink with faucet and drain. |
| | Install | Ea. | 550 | 152 | | 702 | |
| | Demolish and Install | Ea. | 550 | 181 | | 731 | |
| | Reinstall | Ea. | | 121.55 | | 121.55 | |
| | Clean | Ea. | .36 | 13.35 | | 13.71 | |
| | Minimum Charge | Job | | 203 | | 203 | |
| **Stainless Steel** | | | | | | | |
| | Demolish | Ea. | | 29 | | 29 | Includes material and labor to install a double bowl stainless steel kitchen sink with faucet and drain. |
| | Install | Ea. | 335 | 152 | | 487 | |
| | Demolish and Install | Ea. | 335 | 181 | | 516 | |
| | Reinstall | Ea. | | 121.55 | | 121.55 | |
| | Clean | Ea. | .36 | 13.35 | | 13.71 | |
| | Minimum Charge | Job | | 203 | | 203 | |
| **Bar** | | | | | | | |
| | Demolish | Ea. | | 25.50 | | 25.50 | Includes material and labor to install a small single bowl stainless steel bar / vegetable / kitchen sink with faucet and drain. |
| | Install | Ea. | 141 | 101 | | 242 | |
| | Demolish and Install | Ea. | 141 | 126.50 | | 267.50 | |
| | Reinstall | Ea. | | 81.04 | | 81.04 | |
| | Clean | Ea. | .23 | 9.55 | | 9.78 | |
| | Minimum Charge | Job | | 203 | | 203 | |

# Finish Mechanical

## Sink (assembly)

| | Unit | Material | Labor | Equip. | Total | Specification |
|---|---|---|---|---|---|---|
| **Floor** | | | | | | |
| Demolish | Ea. | | 81 | | 81 | Includes material and labor to install |
| Install | Ea. | 665 | 166 | | 831 | an enameled cast iron floor mounted |
| Demolish and Install | Ea. | 665 | 247 | | 912 | corner service sink with faucet and |
| Reinstall | Ea. | | 132.60 | | 132.60 | drain. |
| Clean | Ea. | .36 | 6.65 | | 7.01 | |
| Minimum Charge | Job | | 203 | | 203 | |
| **Pedestal** | | | | | | |
| Demolish | Ea. | | 25.50 | | 25.50 | Includes material and labor to install a |
| Install | Ea. | 370 | 114 | | 484 | vitreous china pedestal lavatory with |
| Demolish and Install | Ea. | 370 | 139.50 | | 509.50 | faucet set and pop-up drain. |
| Reinstall | Ea. | | 91.16 | | 91.16 | |
| Clean | Ea. | .23 | 9.55 | | 9.78 | |
| Minimum Charge | Job | | 203 | | 203 | |
| **Vanity Lavatory** | | | | | | |
| Demolish | Ea. | | 25.50 | | 25.50 | Includes material and labor to install a |
| Install | Ea. | 268 | 135 | | 403 | vitreous china lavatory with faucet set |
| Demolish and Install | Ea. | 268 | 160.50 | | 428.50 | and pop-up drain. |
| Reinstall | Ea. | | 108.04 | | 108.04 | |
| Clean | Ea. | .23 | 9.55 | | 9.78 | |
| Minimum Charge | Job | | 203 | | 203 | |
| **Rough-in** | | | | | | |
| Install | Ea. | 216 | 340 | | 556 | Includes labor and materials to install copper supply pipe with valves and drain, waste and vent pipe with all couplings, hangers and fasteners necessary. |
| **Laundry** | | | | | | |
| Demolish | Ea. | | 26.50 | | 26.50 | Includes material and labor to install a |
| Install | Ea. | 109 | 112 | | 221 | laundry sink (wall mounted or with |
| Demolish and Install | Ea. | 109 | 138.50 | | 247.50 | legs) including faucet and pop up |
| Clean | Ea. | .23 | 9.55 | | 9.78 | drain. |
| Minimum Charge | Job | | 203 | | 203 | |

## Sink Only

| | Unit | Material | Labor | Equip. | Total | Specification |
|---|---|---|---|---|---|---|
| **Single** | | | | | | |
| **Porcelain** | | | | | | |
| Demolish | Ea. | | 25.50 | | 25.50 | Includes material and labor to install a |
| Install | Ea. | 232 | 145 | | 377 | single bowl enamel finished cast iron |
| Demolish and Install | Ea. | 232 | 170.50 | | 402.50 | kitchen sink. |
| Reinstall | Ea. | | 115.77 | | 115.77 | |
| Clean | Ea. | .23 | 9.55 | | 9.78 | |
| Minimum Charge | Job | | 203 | | 203 | |
| **Stainless Steel** | | | | | | |
| Demolish | Ea. | | 25.50 | | 25.50 | Includes material and labor to install a |
| Install | Ea. | 450 | 101 | | 551 | single bowl stainless steel kitchen sink. |
| Demolish and Install | Ea. | 450 | 126.50 | | 576.50 | |
| Reinstall | Ea. | | 81.04 | | 81.04 | |
| Clean | Ea. | .23 | 9.55 | | 9.78 | |
| Minimum Charge | Job | | 203 | | 203 | |

# Finish Mechanical

| Sink Only | | Unit | Material | Labor | Equip. | Total | Specification |
|---|---|---|---|---|---|---|---|
| **Double** | | | | | | | |
| Porcelain | | | | | | | |
| | Demolish | Ea. | | 29 | | 29 | Includes material and labor to install a |
| | Install | Ea. | 271 | 169 | | 440 | double bowl enamel finished cast iron |
| | Demolish and Install | Ea. | 271 | 198 | | 469 | kitchen sink. |
| | Reinstall | Ea. | | 135.07 | | 135.07 | |
| | Clean | Ea. | .36 | 13.35 | | 13.71 | |
| | Minimum Charge | Job | | 203 | | 203 | |
| Stainless Steel | | | | | | | |
| | Demolish | Ea. | | 29 | | 29 | Includes material and labor to install a |
| | Install | Ea. | 670 | 131 | | 801 | double bowl stainless steel kitchen |
| | Demolish and Install | Ea. | 670 | 160 | | 830 | sink. |
| | Reinstall | Ea. | | 104.57 | | 104.57 | |
| | Clean | Ea. | .36 | 13.35 | | 13.71 | |
| | Minimum Charge | Job | | 203 | | 203 | |
| **Bar** | | | | | | | |
| | Demolish | Ea. | | 25.50 | | 25.50 | Includes material and labor to install a |
| | Install | Ea. | 50.50 | 101 | | 151.50 | small single bowl stainless steel bar / |
| | Demolish and Install | Ea. | 50.50 | 126.50 | | 177 | vegetable / kitchen sink. |
| | Reinstall | Ea. | | 81.04 | | 81.04 | |
| | Clean | Ea. | .23 | 9.55 | | 9.78 | |
| | Minimum Charge | Job | | 203 | | 203 | |
| **Floor** | | | | | | | |
| | Demolish | Ea. | | 81 | | 81 | Includes material and labor to install |
| | Install | Ea. | 565 | 184 | | 749 | an enameled cast iron floor mounted |
| | Demolish and Install | Ea. | 565 | 265 | | 830 | corner service sink. |
| | Reinstall | Ea. | | 147.35 | | 147.35 | |
| | Clean | Ea. | .36 | 6.65 | | 7.01 | |
| | Minimum Charge | Job | | 203 | | 203 | |
| **Pedestal** | | | | | | | |
| | Demolish | Ea. | | 25.50 | | 25.50 | Includes material and labor to install a |
| | Install | Ea. | 268 | 127 | | 395 | vitreous china pedestal lavatory. |
| | Demolish and Install | Ea. | 268 | 152.50 | | 420.50 | |
| | Reinstall | Ea. | | 101.30 | | 101.30 | |
| | Clean | Ea. | .23 | 9.55 | | 9.78 | |
| | Minimum Charge | Job | | 203 | | 203 | |
| **Vanity Lavatory** | | | | | | | |
| | Demolish | Ea. | | 25.50 | | 25.50 | Includes material and labor to install a |
| | Install | Ea. | 186 | 127 | | 313 | vitreous china lavatory. |
| | Demolish and Install | Ea. | 186 | 152.50 | | 338.50 | |
| | Reinstall | Ea. | | 101.30 | | 101.30 | |
| | Clean | Ea. | .23 | 9.55 | | 9.78 | |
| | Minimum Charge | Job | | 203 | | 203 | |
| **Rough-in** | | | | | | | |
| | Install | Ea. | 189 | 315 | | 504 | Includes labor and materials to install copper supply pipe with valves and drain, waste and vent pipe with all couplings, hangers and fasteners necessary. |
| **Faucet Sink** | | | | | | | |
| Good Grade | | | | | | | |
| | Demolish | Ea. | | 20.50 | | 20.50 | Includes material and labor to install a |
| | Install | Ea. | 60.50 | 28 | | 88.50 | sink faucet and fittings. |
| | Demolish and Install | Ea. | 60.50 | 48.50 | | 109 | |
| | Reinstall | Ea. | | 22.37 | | 22.37 | |
| | Clean | Ea. | .14 | 8.35 | | 8.49 | |
| | Minimum Charge | Job | | 203 | | 203 | |

# Finish Mechanical

| Sink Only | | Unit | Material | Labor | Equip. | Total | Specification |
|---|---|---|---|---|---|---|---|
| **Better Grade** | | | | | | | |
| | Demolish | Ea. | | 20.50 | | 20.50 | Includes material and labor to install a |
| | Install | Ea. | 102 | 28 | | 130 | sink faucet and fittings. |
| | Demolish and Install | Ea. | 102 | 48.50 | | 150.50 | |
| | Reinstall | Ea. | | 22.37 | | 22.37 | |
| | Clean | Ea. | .14 | 8.35 | | 8.49 | |
| | Minimum Charge | Job | | 203 | | 203 | |
| **Premium Grade** | | | | | | | |
| | Demolish | Ea. | | 20.50 | | 20.50 | Includes material and labor to install a |
| | Install | Ea. | 198 | 35 | | 233 | sink faucet and fittings. |
| | Demolish and Install | Ea. | 198 | 55.50 | | 253.50 | |
| | Reinstall | Ea. | | 27.90 | | 27.90 | |
| | Clean | Ea. | .14 | 8.35 | | 8.49 | |
| | Minimum Charge | Job | | 203 | | 203 | |
| **Drain & Basket** | | | | | | | |
| | Demolish | Ea. | | 12.65 | | 12.65 | Includes material and labor to install a |
| | Install | Ea. | 13.35 | 25.50 | | 38.85 | sink drain and basket. |
| | Demolish and Install | Ea. | 13.35 | 38.15 | | 51.50 | |
| | Reinstall | Ea. | | 20.26 | | 20.26 | |
| | Clean | Ea. | .14 | 8.35 | | 8.49 | |
| | Minimum Charge | Job | | 203 | | 203 | |

| Bathtub | | Unit | Material | Labor | Equip. | Total | Specification |
|---|---|---|---|---|---|---|---|
| **Enameled** | | | | | | | |
| **Steel** | | | | | | | |
| | Demolish | Ea. | | 73 | | 73 | Includes material and labor to install a |
| | Install | Ea. | 365 | 133 | | 498 | formed steel bathtub with spout, |
| | Demolish and Install | Ea. | 365 | 206 | | 571 | mixing valve, shower head and |
| | Reinstall | Ea. | | 106.08 | | 106.08 | pop-up drain. |
| | Clean | Ea. | .73 | 22 | | 22.73 | |
| | Minimum Charge | Job | | 203 | | 203 | |
| **Cast Iron** | | | | | | | |
| | Demolish | Ea. | | 73 | | 73 | Includes material and labor to install a |
| | Install | Ea. | 870 | 166 | | 1036 | cast iron bath tub with spout, mixing |
| | Demolish and Install | Ea. | 870 | 239 | | 1109 | valve, shower head and pop-up drain. |
| | Reinstall | Ea. | | 132.60 | | 132.60 | |
| | Clean | Ea. | .73 | 22 | | 22.73 | |
| | Minimum Charge | Job | | 203 | | 203 | |
| **Fiberglass** | | | | | | | |
| | Demolish | Ea. | | 73 | | 73 | Includes material and labor to install |
| | Install | Ea. | 940 | 133 | | 1073 | an acrylic soaking tub with spout, |
| | Demolish and Install | Ea. | 940 | 206 | | 1146 | mixing valve, shower head and |
| | Reinstall | Ea. | | 106.08 | | 106.08 | pop-up drain. |
| | Clean | Ea. | .73 | 22 | | 22.73 | |
| | Minimum Charge | Job | | 203 | | 203 | |
| **Institutional** | | | | | | | |
| | Demolish | Ea. | | 73 | | 73 | Includes material and labor to install a |
| | Install | Ea. | 1000 | 243 | | 1243 | hospital / institutional type bathtub |
| | Demolish and Install | Ea. | 1000 | 316 | | 1316 | with spout, mixing valve, shower head |
| | Reinstall | Ea. | | 194.47 | | 194.47 | and pop-up drain. |
| | Clean | Ea. | .73 | 22 | | 22.73 | |
| | Minimum Charge | Job | | 203 | | 203 | |

# Finish Mechanical

| Bathtub | | Unit | Material | Labor | Equip. | Total | Specification |
|---|---|---|---|---|---|---|---|
| **Whirlpool (Acrylic)** | | | | | | | |
| | Demolish | Ea. | | 225 | | 225 | Includes material and labor to install a |
| | Install | Ea. | 2750 | 730 | | 3480 | molded fiberglass whirlpool tub. |
| | Demolish and Install | Ea. | 2750 | 955 | | 3705 | |
| | Reinstall | Ea. | | 583.42 | | 583.42 | |
| | Clean | Ea. | .73 | 22 | | 22.73 | |
| | Minimum Charge | Job | | 203 | | 203 | |
| **Pump / Motor** | | | | | | | |
| | Demolish | Ea. | | 56.50 | | 56.50 | Includes material and labor to install a |
| | Install | Ea. | 208 | 122 | | 330 | whirlpool tub pump / motor. |
| | Demolish and Install | Ea. | 208 | 178.50 | | 386.50 | |
| | Reinstall | Ea. | | 97.35 | | 97.35 | |
| | Clean | Ea. | .19 | 16.70 | | 16.89 | |
| | Minimum Charge | Job | | 203 | | 203 | |
| **Heater / Motor** | | | | | | | |
| | Demolish | Ea. | | 56.50 | | 56.50 | Includes material and labor to install a |
| | Install | Ea. | 296 | 180 | | 476 | whirlpool tub heater. |
| | Demolish and Install | Ea. | 296 | 236.50 | | 532.50 | |
| | Reinstall | Ea. | | 144.07 | | 144.07 | |
| | Clean | Ea. | .19 | 16.70 | | 16.89 | |
| | Minimum Charge | Job | | 203 | | 203 | |
| **Thermal Cover** | | | | | | | |
| | Demolish | Ea. | | 9 | | 9 | Includes material and labor to install a |
| | Install | Ea. | 194 | 25.50 | | 219.50 | whirlpool tub thermal cover. |
| | Demolish and Install | Ea. | 194 | 34.50 | | 228.50 | |
| | Reinstall | Ea. | | 20.26 | | 20.26 | |
| | Clean | Ea. | 1.82 | 16.70 | | 18.52 | |
| | Minimum Charge | Job | | 203 | | 203 | |
| **Tub / Shower Combination** | | | | | | | |
| | Demolish | Ea. | | 45 | | 45 | Includes material and labor to install a |
| | Install | Ea. | 615 | 182 | | 797 | fiberglass module tub with shower |
| | Demolish and Install | Ea. | 615 | 227 | | 842 | surround with spout, mixing valve, |
| | Reinstall | Ea. | | 145.86 | | 145.86 | shower head and pop-up drain. |
| | Clean | Ea. | .91 | 33.50 | | 34.41 | |
| | Minimum Charge | Job | | 203 | | 203 | |
| **Accessories** | | | | | | | |
| **Sliding Door** | | | | | | | |
| | Demolish | Ea. | | 18.55 | | 18.55 | Includes material and labor to install a |
| | Install | Ea. | 440 | 84.50 | | 524.50 | 48" aluminum framed tempered glass |
| | Demolish and Install | Ea. | 440 | 103.05 | | 543.05 | shower door. |
| | Reinstall | Ea. | | 67.77 | | 67.77 | |
| | Clean | Ea. | 1.52 | 11.10 | | 12.62 | |
| | Minimum Charge | Job | | 203 | | 203 | |
| **Shower Head** | | | | | | | |
| | Demolish | Ea. | | 5.05 | | 5.05 | Includes material and labor to install a |
| | Install | Ea. | 54.50 | 16.90 | | 71.40 | water saving shower head. |
| | Demolish and Install | Ea. | 54.50 | 21.95 | | 76.45 | |
| | Reinstall | Ea. | | 13.51 | | 13.51 | |
| | Clean | Ea. | .02 | 3.34 | | 3.36 | |
| | Minimum Charge | Job | | 203 | | 203 | |
| **Faucet Set** | | | | | | | |
| | Demolish | Ea. | | 25.50 | | 25.50 | Includes material and labor to install a |
| | Install | Ea. | 114 | 50.50 | | 164.50 | combination spout / diverter for a |
| | Demolish and Install | Ea. | 114 | 76 | | 190 | bathtub. |
| | Reinstall | Ea. | | 40.52 | | 40.52 | |
| | Clean | Ea. | .14 | 8.35 | | 8.49 | |
| | Minimum Charge | Job | | 203 | | 203 | |

# Finish Mechanical

## Bathtub

| Bathtub | Unit | Material | Labor | Equip. | Total | Specification |
|---|---|---|---|---|---|---|
| **Shower Rod** | | | | | | Includes material and labor to install a chrome plated shower rod. |
| Demolish | Ea. | | 3.09 | | 3.09 | |
| Install | Ea. | 16 | 28 | | 44 | |
| Demolish and Install | Ea. | 16 | 31.09 | | 47.09 | |
| Reinstall | Ea. | | 22.25 | | 22.25 | |
| Clean | Ea. | | 3.34 | | 3.34 | |
| Minimum Charge | Job | | 203 | | 203 | |
| **Rough-in** | | | | | | Includes labor and materials to install copper supply pipe with valves and drain, waste and vent pipe with all couplings, hangers and fasteners necessary. |
| Install | Ea. | 284 | 350 | | 634 | |

## Shower

| Shower | Unit | Material | Labor | Equip. | Total | Specification |
|---|---|---|---|---|---|---|
| **Fiberglass** | | | | | | |
| **32" x 32"** | | | | | | Includes material and labor to install a fiberglass shower stall with door, mixing valve and shower head and drain fitting. |
| Demolish | Ea. | | 152 | | 152 | |
| Install | Ea. | 505 | 133 | | 638 | |
| Demolish and Install | Ea. | 505 | 285 | | 790 | |
| Reinstall | Ea. | | 106.08 | | 106.08 | |
| Clean | Ea. | .73 | 22 | | 22.73 | |
| Minimum Charge | Job | | 203 | | 203 | |
| **36" x 36"** | | | | | | Includes material and labor to install a fiberglass shower stall with door, mixing valve and shower head and drain fitting. |
| Demolish | Ea. | | 152 | | 152 | |
| Install | Ea. | 580 | 133 | | 713 | |
| Demolish and Install | Ea. | 580 | 285 | | 865 | |
| Reinstall | Ea. | | 106.08 | | 106.08 | |
| Clean | Ea. | .73 | 22 | | 22.73 | |
| Minimum Charge | Job | | 203 | | 203 | |
| **35" x 60"** | | | | | | Includes material and labor to install a handicap fiberglass shower stall with door & seat, mixing valve and shower head and drain fitting. |
| Demolish | Ea. | | 152 | | 152 | |
| Install | Ea. | 650 | 182 | | 832 | |
| Demolish and Install | Ea. | 650 | 334 | | 984 | |
| Reinstall | Ea. | | 145.86 | | 145.86 | |
| Clean | Ea. | .73 | 22 | | 22.73 | |
| Minimum Charge | Job | | 203 | | 203 | |
| **Accessories** | | | | | | |
| **Single Door** | | | | | | Includes material and labor to install a shower door. |
| Demolish | Ea. | | 18.55 | | 18.55 | |
| Install | Ea. | 136 | 44.50 | | 180.50 | |
| Demolish and Install | Ea. | 136 | 63.05 | | 199.05 | |
| Reinstall | Ea. | | 35.77 | | 35.77 | |
| Clean | Ea. | 1.52 | 11.10 | | 12.62 | |
| Minimum Charge | Job | | 203 | | 203 | |
| **Shower Head** | | | | | | Includes material and labor to install a water saving shower head. |
| Demolish | Ea. | | 5.05 | | 5.05 | |
| Install | Ea. | 54.50 | 16.90 | | 71.40 | |
| Demolish and Install | Ea. | 54.50 | 21.95 | | 76.45 | |
| Reinstall | Ea. | | 13.51 | | 13.51 | |
| Clean | Ea. | .02 | 3.34 | | 3.36 | |
| Minimum Charge | Job | | 203 | | 203 | |

# Finish Mechanical

## Shower

| Shower | | Unit | Material | Labor | Equip. | Total | Specification |
|---|---|---|---|---|---|---|---|
| **Faucet Set** | | | | | | | |
| | Demolish | Ea. | | 25.50 | | 25.50 | Includes material and labor to install a |
| | Install | Ea. | 114 | 50.50 | | 164.50 | combination spout / diverter for a |
| | Demolish and Install | Ea. | 114 | 76 | | 190 | bathtub. |
| | Reinstall | Ea. | | 40.52 | | 40.52 | |
| | Clean | Ea. | .14 | 8.35 | | 8.49 | |
| | Minimum Charge | Job | | 203 | | 203 | |
| **Shower Pan** | | | | | | | |
| | Demolish | Ea. | | 18.75 | | 18.75 | Includes material and labor to install |
| | Install | Ea. | 206 | 50.50 | | 256.50 | the base portion of a fiberglass |
| | Demolish and Install | Ea. | 206 | 69.25 | | 275.25 | shower unit. |
| | Reinstall | Ea. | | 40.52 | | 40.52 | |
| | Clean | Ea. | .73 | 22 | | 22.73 | |
| | Minimum Charge | Job | | 203 | | 203 | |
| **Rough-in** | | | | | | | |
| | Install | Ea. | 335 | 355 | | 690 | Includes labor and materials to install copper supply pipe with valves and drain, waste and vent pipe with all couplings, hangers and fasteners necessary. |

## Ductwork

| Ductwork | | Unit | Material | Labor | Equip. | Total | Specification |
|---|---|---|---|---|---|---|---|
| **Return Grill** | | | | | | | |
| **Under 10" Wide** | | | | | | | |
| | Demolish | Ea. | | 8.95 | | 8.95 | Includes material and labor to install a |
| | Install | Ea. | 31.50 | 22.50 | | 54 | 10" x 10" air return register. |
| | Demolish and Install | Ea. | 31.50 | 31.45 | | 62.95 | |
| | Reinstall | Ea. | | 17.88 | | 17.88 | |
| | Clean | Ea. | .19 | 7.40 | | 7.59 | |
| | Minimum Charge | Job | | 201 | | 201 | |
| **12" to 20" Wide** | | | | | | | |
| | Demolish | Ea. | | 8.95 | | 8.95 | Includes material and labor to install a |
| | Install | Ea. | 58 | 23.50 | | 81.50 | 16" x 16" air return register. |
| | Demolish and Install | Ea. | 58 | 32.45 | | 90.45 | |
| | Reinstall | Ea. | | 18.94 | | 18.94 | |
| | Clean | Ea. | .19 | 7.40 | | 7.59 | |
| | Minimum Charge | Job | | 201 | | 201 | |
| **Over 20" Wide** | | | | | | | |
| | Demolish | Ea. | | 13.55 | | 13.55 | Includes material and labor to install a |
| | Install | Ea. | 112 | 36.50 | | 148.50 | 24" x 24" air return register. |
| | Demolish and Install | Ea. | 112 | 50.05 | | 162.05 | |
| | Reinstall | Ea. | | 29.27 | | 29.27 | |
| | Clean | Ea. | .19 | 8.35 | | 8.54 | |
| | Minimum Charge | Job | | 201 | | 201 | |
| **Supply Grill** | | | | | | | |
| **Baseboard Type** | | | | | | | |
| | Demolish | Ea. | | 6.40 | | 6.40 | Includes material and labor to install a |
| | Install | Ea. | 19.95 | 20 | | 39.95 | 14" x 6" baseboard air supply |
| | Demolish and Install | Ea. | 19.95 | 26.40 | | 46.35 | register. |
| | Reinstall | Ea. | | 16.10 | | 16.10 | |
| | Clean | Ea. | .19 | 7.40 | | 7.59 | |
| | Minimum Charge | Job | | 201 | | 201 | |

| Ductwork | Unit | Material | Labor | Equip. | Total | Specification |
|---|---|---|---|---|---|---|
| **10″ Wide** | | | | | | |
| Demolish | Ea. | | 7.45 | | 7.45 | Includes material and labor to install a |
| Install | Ea. | 29.50 | 20 | | 49.50 | 10″ x 6″ air supply register. |
| Demolish and Install | Ea. | 29.50 | 27.45 | | 56.95 | |
| Reinstall | Ea. | | 16.10 | | 16.10 | |
| Clean | Ea. | .19 | 7.40 | | 7.59 | |
| Minimum Charge | Job | | 201 | | 201 | |
| **12″ to 15″ Wide** | | | | | | |
| Demolish | Ea. | | 7.45 | | 7.45 | Includes material and labor to install a |
| Install | Ea. | 41.50 | 23.50 | | 65 | 14″ x 8″ air supply register. |
| Demolish and Install | Ea. | 41.50 | 30.95 | | 72.45 | |
| Reinstall | Ea. | | 18.94 | | 18.94 | |
| Clean | Ea. | .19 | 7.40 | | 7.59 | |
| Minimum Charge | Job | | 201 | | 201 | |
| **18″ to 24″ Wide** | | | | | | |
| Demolish | Ea. | | 8.95 | | 8.95 | Includes material and labor to install a |
| Install | Ea. | 57 | 31 | | 88 | 24″ x 8″ air supply register. |
| Demolish and Install | Ea. | 57 | 39.95 | | 96.95 | |
| Reinstall | Ea. | | 24.76 | | 24.76 | |
| Clean | Ea. | .19 | 8.35 | | 8.54 | |
| Minimum Charge | Job | | 201 | | 201 | |
| **30″ to 36″ Wide** | | | | | | |
| Demolish | Ea. | | 11.20 | | 11.20 | Includes material and labor to install a |
| Install | Ea. | 75 | 28.50 | | 103.50 | 30″ x 8″ air supply register. |
| Demolish and Install | Ea. | 75 | 39.70 | | 114.70 | |
| Reinstall | Ea. | | 22.99 | | 22.99 | |
| Clean | Ea. | .19 | 16.70 | | 16.89 | |
| Minimum Charge | Job | | 201 | | 201 | |
| **Diffuser** | | | | | | |
| **12″ Louver** | | | | | | |
| Demolish | Ea. | | 8.95 | | 8.95 | Includes material and labor to install a |
| Install | Ea. | 40 | 28.50 | | 68.50 | 12″ aluminum louvered diffuser. |
| Demolish and Install | Ea. | 40 | 37.45 | | 77.45 | |
| Reinstall | Ea. | | 22.99 | | 22.99 | |
| Clean | Ea. | .19 | 7.40 | | 7.59 | |
| Minimum Charge | Job | | 201 | | 201 | |
| **14″ to 20″ Louver** | | | | | | |
| Demolish | Ea. | | 8.95 | | 8.95 | Includes material and labor to install a |
| Install | Ea. | 44.50 | 40 | | 84.50 | 14″ to 20″ aluminum louvered diffuser. |
| Demolish and Install | Ea. | 44.50 | 48.95 | | 93.45 | |
| Reinstall | Ea. | | 32.19 | | 32.19 | |
| Clean | Ea. | .19 | 8.35 | | 8.54 | |
| Minimum Charge | Job | | 201 | | 201 | |
| **25″ to 32″ Louver** | | | | | | |
| Demolish | Ea. | | 13.55 | | 13.55 | Includes material and labor to install a |
| Install | Ea. | 58.50 | 57.50 | | 116 | 25″ to 32″ aluminum louvered diffuser. |
| Demolish and Install | Ea. | 58.50 | 71.05 | | 129.55 | |
| Reinstall | Ea. | | 45.99 | | 45.99 | |
| Clean | Ea. | .19 | 11.10 | | 11.29 | |
| Minimum Charge | Job | | 201 | | 201 | |
| **12″ Round** | | | | | | |
| Demolish | Ea. | | 12.40 | | 12.40 | Includes material and labor to install a |
| Install | Ea. | 37.50 | 33.50 | | 71 | 12″ diameter aluminum diffuser with a |
| Demolish and Install | Ea. | 37.50 | 45.90 | | 83.40 | butterfly damper. |
| Reinstall | Ea. | | 26.83 | | 26.83 | |
| Clean | Ea. | .19 | 7.40 | | 7.59 | |
| Minimum Charge | Job | | 201 | | 201 | |

| Ductwork | Unit | Material | Labor | Equip. | Total | Specification |
|---|---|---|---|---|---|---|
| **14" to 20" Round** | | | | | | |
| Demolish | Ea. | | 16.55 | | 16.55 | Includes material and labor to install a |
| Install | Ea. | 135 | 44.50 | | 179.50 | 20" diameter aluminum diffuser with a |
| Demolish and Install | Ea. | 135 | 61.05 | | 196.05 | butterfly damper. |
| Reinstall | Ea. | | 35.77 | | 35.77 | |
| Clean | Ea. | .19 | 8.35 | | 8.54 | |
| Minimum Charge | Job | | 201 | | 201 | |
| **Flush-out / Sanitize** | | | | | | |
| Install | L.F. | .73 | 3.34 | | 4.07 | Includes labor and material costs to |
| Minimum Charge | Job | | 201 | | 201 | clean ductwork. |

Lighting Fixture

Duplex Receptacle

| Electrical Per S.F. | Unit | Material | Labor | Equip. | Total | Specification |
|---|---|---|---|---|---|---|
| **Residential** | | | | | | |
| **Light Fixtures** | | | | | | |
| Install | S.F. | .24 | .20 | | .44 | Includes labor and material to replace house light fixtures. Apply S.F. cost to floor area including garages but not basements. |

| Circuits | Unit | Material | Labor | Equip. | Total | Specification |
|---|---|---|---|---|---|---|
| **Outlet with Wiring** | | | | | | |
| Demolish | Ea. | | 22 | | 22 | Includes material and labor to install |
| Install | Ea. | 11.05 | 27.50 | | 38.55 | general purpose outlet with cover, up |
| Demolish and Install | Ea. | 11.05 | 49.50 | | 60.55 | to 20 feet of #12/2 wire. |
| Reinstall | Ea. | | 21.86 | | 21.86 | |
| Clean | Ea. | | 1.67 | | 1.67 | |
| Minimum Charge | Job | | 199 | | 199 | |
| **GFCI Outlet w / Wiring** | | | | | | |
| Demolish | Ea. | | 22 | | 22 | Cost includes material and labor to |
| Install | Ea. | 45.50 | 32.50 | | 78 | install 120V GFCI receptacle and wall |
| Demolish and Install | Ea. | 45.50 | 54.50 | | 100 | plate, with up to 20 feet of #12/2 |
| Reinstall | Ea. | | 25.84 | | 25.84 | wire. |
| Clean | Ea. | | 1.67 | | 1.67 | |
| Minimum Charge | Job | | 199 | | 199 | |
| **Exterior Outlet w / Wiring** | | | | | | |
| Demolish | Ea. | | 22 | | 22 | Cost includes material and labor to |
| Install | Ea. | 37 | 33 | | 70 | install 110V waterproof external |
| Demolish and Install | Ea. | 37 | 55 | | 92 | receptacle and cover plate with up to |
| Reinstall | Ea. | | 26.51 | | 26.51 | 20' of #12/2 wire. |
| Clean | Ea. | | 1.67 | | 1.67 | |
| Minimum Charge | Job | | 199 | | 199 | |
| **240V Outlet w / Wiring** | | | | | | |
| Demolish | Ea. | | 22 | | 22 | Cost includes material and labor to |
| Install | Ea. | 80.50 | 62 | | 142.50 | install 240V receptacle and cover |
| Demolish and Install | Ea. | 80.50 | 84 | | 164.50 | plate with up to 20' of #12/2 wire. |
| Reinstall | Ea. | | 49.62 | | 49.62 | |
| Clean | Ea. | | 1.67 | | 1.67 | |
| Minimum Charge | Job | | 199 | | 199 | |

# Finish Electrical

| Circuits | Unit | Material | Labor | Equip. | Total | Specification |
|---|---|---|---|---|---|---|
| **TV / Cable Jack w / Wiring** | | | | | | |
| Demolish | Ea. | | 22 | | 22 | Includes material and labor to install |
| Install | Ea. | 19.80 | 25 | | 44.80 | TV/cable outlet box and cover plate |
| Demolish and Install | Ea. | 19.80 | 47 | | 66.80 | including 20' of wiring. |
| Reinstall | Ea. | | 19.88 | | 19.88 | |
| Clean | Ea. | | 1.67 | | 1.67 | |
| Minimum Charge | Job | | 199 | | 199 | |
| **Phone Jack with Wiring** | | | | | | |
| Demolish | Ea. | | 22 | | 22 | Includes material and labor to install |
| Install | Ea. | 11 | 15.30 | | 26.30 | phone jack and cover plate including |
| Demolish and Install | Ea. | 11 | 37.30 | | 48.30 | up to 20' of telephone cable. |
| Reinstall | Ea. | | 12.23 | | 12.23 | |
| Clean | Ea. | | 1.04 | | 1.04 | |
| Minimum Charge | Job | | 199 | | 199 | |

| Light Switch | Unit | Material | Labor | Equip. | Total | Specification |
|---|---|---|---|---|---|---|
| **Single** | | | | | | |
| **Switch** | | | | | | |
| Demolish | Ea. | | 4.42 | | 4.42 | Includes material and labor to install |
| Install | Ea. | 5.65 | 18.95 | | 24.60 | single switch and wall plate. Wiring is |
| Demolish and Install | Ea. | 5.65 | 23.37 | | 29.02 | not included. |
| Reinstall | Ea. | | 15.15 | | 15.15 | |
| Clean | Ea. | | 1.67 | | 1.67 | |
| Minimum Charge | Job | | 199 | | 199 | |
| **Plate** | | | | | | |
| Demolish | Ea. | | 2.21 | | 2.21 | Includes material and labor to install a |
| Install | Ea. | .37 | 4.97 | | 5.34 | one gang brown wall switch plate. |
| Demolish and Install | Ea. | .37 | 7.18 | | 7.55 | |
| Reinstall | Ea. | | 3.98 | | 3.98 | |
| Clean | Ea. | .08 | .33 | | .41 | |
| Minimum Charge | Job | | 199 | | 199 | |
| **Double** | | | | | | |
| **Switch** | | | | | | |
| Demolish | Ea. | | 8.85 | | 8.85 | Includes material and labor to install |
| Install | Ea. | 8.35 | 28.50 | | 36.85 | double switch and wall plate. Wiring |
| Demolish and Install | Ea. | 8.35 | 37.35 | | 45.70 | is not included. |
| Reinstall | Ea. | | 22.72 | | 22.72 | |
| Clean | Ea. | .08 | 5.35 | | 5.43 | |
| Minimum Charge | Job | | 199 | | 199 | |
| **Plate** | | | | | | |
| Demolish | Ea. | | 2.21 | | 2.21 | Includes material and labor to install a |
| Install | Ea. | .91 | 7.50 | | 8.41 | two gang brown wall switch plate. |
| Demolish and Install | Ea. | .91 | 9.71 | | 10.62 | |
| Reinstall | Ea. | | 6 | | 6 | |
| Clean | Ea. | .08 | .33 | | .41 | |
| Minimum Charge | Job | | 199 | | 199 | |
| **Triple** | | | | | | |
| **Switch** | | | | | | |
| Demolish | Ea. | | 13.40 | | 13.40 | Includes material and labor to install |
| Install | Ea. | 26 | 33 | | 59 | triple switch and wall plate. Wiring is |
| Demolish and Install | Ea. | 26 | 46.40 | | 72.40 | not included. |
| Reinstall | Ea. | | 26.51 | | 26.51 | |
| Clean | Ea. | .08 | 8 | | 8.08 | |
| Minimum Charge | Job | | 199 | | 199 | |

# Finish Electrical

| Light Switch | | Unit | Material | Labor | Equip. | Total | Specification |
|---|---|---|---|---|---|---|---|
| **Plate** | | | | | | | |
| | Demolish | Ea. | | 2.21 | | 2.21 | Includes material and labor to install a |
| | Install | Ea. | 1.36 | 12.45 | | 13.81 | three gang brown wall switch plate. |
| | Demolish and Install | Ea. | 1.36 | 14.66 | | 16.02 | |
| | Reinstall | Ea. | | 9.94 | | 9.94 | |
| | Clean | Ea. | .08 | .33 | | .41 | |
| | Minimum Charge | Job | | 199 | | 199 | |
| **Dimmer** | | | | | | | |
| **Switch** | | | | | | | |
| | Demolish | Ea. | | 4.42 | | 4.42 | Includes material and labor to install |
| | Install | Ea. | 19.65 | 23.50 | | 43.15 | dimmer switch. Wiring is not included. |
| | Demolish and Install | Ea. | 19.65 | 27.92 | | 47.57 | |
| | Reinstall | Ea. | | 18.71 | | 18.71 | |
| | Clean | Ea. | | 1.67 | | 1.67 | |
| | Minimum Charge | Job | | 199 | | 199 | |
| **Plate** | | | | | | | |
| | Demolish | Ea. | | 2.21 | | 2.21 | Includes material and labor to install a |
| | Install | Ea. | .37 | 4.97 | | 5.34 | one gang brown wall switch plate. |
| | Demolish and Install | Ea. | .37 | 7.18 | | 7.55 | |
| | Reinstall | Ea. | | 3.98 | | 3.98 | |
| | Clean | Ea. | .08 | .33 | | .41 | |
| | Minimum Charge | Job | | 199 | | 199 | |
| **With Wiring** | | | | | | | |
| **Single** | | | | | | | |
| | Demolish | Ea. | | 22 | | 22 | Includes material and labor to install |
| | Install | Ea. | 12.75 | 23.50 | | 36.25 | single switch and plate including up to |
| | Demolish and Install | Ea. | 12.75 | 45.50 | | 58.25 | 20' of romex cable. |
| | Reinstall | Ea. | | 18.60 | | 18.60 | |
| | Clean | Ea. | | 1.67 | | 1.67 | |
| | Minimum Charge | Job | | 199 | | 199 | |
| **Double** | | | | | | | |
| | Demolish | Ea. | | 22 | | 22 | Includes material and labor to install |
| | Install | Ea. | 30.50 | 40 | | 70.50 | double switch and plate including up |
| | Demolish and Install | Ea. | 30.50 | 62 | | 92.50 | to 20' of romex cable. |
| | Reinstall | Ea. | | 31.81 | | 31.81 | |
| | Clean | Ea. | .08 | 5.35 | | 5.43 | |
| | Minimum Charge | Job | | 199 | | 199 | |
| **Triple** | | | | | | | |
| | Demolish | Ea. | | 33 | | 33 | Includes material and labor to install |
| | Install | Ea. | 36.50 | 44.50 | | 81 | triple switch and plate including up to |
| | Demolish and Install | Ea. | 36.50 | 77.50 | | 114 | 20' of romex cable. |
| | Reinstall | Ea. | | 35.78 | | 35.78 | |
| | Clean | Ea. | .08 | 8 | | 8.08 | |
| | Minimum Charge | Job | | 199 | | 199 | |
| **Dimmer** | | | | | | | |
| | Demolish | Ea. | | 22 | | 22 | Includes material and labor to install |
| | Install | Ea. | 27 | 27.50 | | 54.50 | dimmer switch and cover plate |
| | Demolish and Install | Ea. | 27 | 49.50 | | 76.50 | including up to 20' of romex cable. |
| | Reinstall | Ea. | | 21.86 | | 21.86 | |
| | Clean | Ea. | | 1.67 | | 1.67 | |
| | Minimum Charge | Job | | 199 | | 199 | |

# Finish Electrical

| Cover for Outlet / Switch | | Unit | Material | Labor | Equip. | Total | Specification |
|---|---|---|---|---|---|---|---|
| **High Grade** | | | | | | | |
| | Demolish | Ea. | | 2.21 | | 2.21 | Includes material and labor to install |
| | Install | Ea. | 2.49 | 4.97 | | 7.46 | wall plate, stainless steel, 1 gang. |
| | Demolish and Install | Ea. | 2.49 | 7.18 | | 9.67 | |
| | Reinstall | Ea. | | 3.98 | | 3.98 | |
| | Clean | Ea. | .08 | .33 | | .41 | |
| | Minimum Charge | Job | | 199 | | 199 | |
| **Deluxe Grade** | | | | | | | |
| | Demolish | Ea. | | 2.21 | | 2.21 | Includes material and labor to install |
| | Install | Ea. | 5.10 | 4.97 | | 10.07 | wall plate, brushed brass, 1 gang. |
| | Demolish and Install | Ea. | 5.10 | 7.18 | | 12.28 | |
| | Reinstall | Ea. | | 3.98 | | 3.98 | |
| | Clean | Ea. | .08 | .33 | | .41 | |
| | Minimum Charge | Job | | 199 | | 199 | |

| Residential Light Fixture | | Unit | Material | Labor | Equip. | Total | Specification |
|---|---|---|---|---|---|---|---|
| **Ceiling** | | | | | | | |
| **Good Quality** | | | | | | | |
| | Demolish | Ea. | | 9.20 | | 9.20 | Includes material and labor to install |
| | Install | Ea. | 31.50 | 9.95 | | 41.45 | standard quality incandescent ceiling |
| | Demolish and Install | Ea. | 31.50 | 19.15 | | 50.65 | light fixture. Wiring is not included. |
| | Reinstall | Ea. | | 7.95 | | 7.95 | |
| | Clean | Ea. | .19 | 11.10 | | 11.29 | |
| | Minimum Charge | Job | | 199 | | 199 | |
| **Better Quality** | | | | | | | |
| | Demolish | Ea. | | 9.20 | | 9.20 | Includes material and labor to install |
| | Install | Ea. | 89 | 21 | | 110 | custom quality incandescent ceiling |
| | Demolish and Install | Ea. | 89 | 30.20 | | 119.20 | light fixture. Wiring is not included. |
| | Reinstall | Ea. | | 16.74 | | 16.74 | |
| | Clean | Ea. | .19 | 11.10 | | 11.29 | |
| | Minimum Charge | Job | | 199 | | 199 | |
| **Premium Quality** | | | | | | | |
| | Demolish | Ea. | | 9.20 | | 9.20 | Includes material and labor to install |
| | Install | Ea. | 263 | 21 | | 284 | deluxe quality incandescent ceiling |
| | Demolish and Install | Ea. | 263 | 30.20 | | 293.20 | light fixture. Wiring is not included. |
| | Reinstall | Ea. | | 16.74 | | 16.74 | |
| | Clean | Ea. | .19 | 11.10 | | 11.29 | |
| | Minimum Charge | Job | | 199 | | 199 | |
| **Recessed Ceiling** | | | | | | | |
| | Demolish | Ea. | | 18.40 | | 18.40 | Includes material and labor to install |
| | Install | Ea. | 43.50 | 13.25 | | 56.75 | standard quality recessed eyeball |
| | Demolish and Install | Ea. | 43.50 | 31.65 | | 75.15 | spotlight with housing. Wiring is not |
| | Reinstall | Ea. | | 10.60 | | 10.60 | included. |
| | Clean | Ea. | .03 | 2.78 | | 2.81 | |
| | Minimum Charge | Job | | 199 | | 199 | |
| **Recessed Eyeball** | | | | | | | |
| | Demolish | Ea. | | 18.40 | | 18.40 | Includes material and labor to install |
| | Install | Ea. | 64.50 | 14.20 | | 78.70 | custom quality recessed eyeball |
| | Demolish and Install | Ea. | 64.50 | 32.60 | | 97.10 | spotlight with housing. Wiring is not |
| | Reinstall | Ea. | | 11.36 | | 11.36 | included. |
| | Clean | Ea. | .03 | 2.78 | | 2.81 | |
| | Minimum Charge | Job | | 199 | | 199 | |

# Finish Electrical

| Residential Light Fixture | Unit | Material | Labor | Equip. | Total | Specification |
|---|---|---|---|---|---|---|
| **Recessed Shower Type** | | | | | | |
| Demolish | Ea. | | 18.40 | | 18.40 | Includes material and labor to install |
| Install | Ea. | 54 | 13.25 | | 67.25 | deluxe quality recessed eyeball |
| Demolish and Install | Ea. | 54 | 31.65 | | 85.65 | spotlight with housing. Wiring is not |
| Reinstall | Ea. | | 10.60 | | 10.60 | included. |
| Clean | Ea. | .03 | 2.78 | | 2.81 | |
| Minimum Charge | Job | | 199 | | 199 | |
| **Run Wiring** | | | | | | |
| Install | Ea. | 18.50 | 15.90 | | 34.40 | Includes labor and material to install a |
| Minimum Charge | Job | | 199 | | 199 | electric fixture utility box with |
| | | | | | | non-metallic cable. |
| **Fluorescent** | | | | | | |
| **Good Quality** | | | | | | |
| Demolish | Ea. | | 20 | | 20 | Includes material and labor to install |
| Install | Ea. | 48.50 | 57 | | 105.50 | standard quality 12" wide by 48" long |
| Demolish and Install | Ea. | 48.50 | 77 | | 125.50 | decorative surface mounted fluorescent |
| Reinstall | Ea. | | 45.44 | | 45.44 | fixture w/acrylic diffuser. |
| Clean | Ea. | .03 | 2.78 | | 2.81 | |
| Minimum Charge | Job | | 199 | | 199 | |
| **Better Quality** | | | | | | |
| Demolish | Ea. | | 20 | | 20 | Includes material and labor to install |
| Install | Ea. | 99.50 | 64 | | 163.50 | an interior fluorescent lighting fixture. |
| Demolish and Install | Ea. | 99.50 | 84 | | 183.50 | |
| Reinstall | Ea. | | 51.30 | | 51.30 | |
| Clean | Ea. | .03 | 2.78 | | 2.81 | |
| Minimum Charge | Job | | 199 | | 199 | |
| **Premium Quality** | | | | | | |
| Demolish | Ea. | | 20 | | 20 | Includes material and labor to install |
| Install | Ea. | 103 | 75 | | 178 | deluxe quality 24" wide by 48" long |
| Demolish and Install | Ea. | 103 | 95 | | 198 | decorative surface mounted fluorescent |
| Reinstall | Ea. | | 60.02 | | 60.02 | fixture w/acrylic diffuser. |
| Clean | Ea. | .03 | 2.78 | | 2.81 | |
| Minimum Charge | Job | | 199 | | 199 | |
| **Run Wiring** | | | | | | |
| Install | Ea. | 18.50 | 15.90 | | 34.40 | Includes labor and material to install a |
| Minimum Charge | Job | | 199 | | 199 | electric fixture utility box with |
| | | | | | | non-metallic cable. |
| **Exterior** | | | | | | |
| **Good Quality** | | | | | | |
| Demolish | Ea. | | 17.65 | | 17.65 | Includes material and labor to install |
| Install | Ea. | 37 | 25 | | 62 | standard quality incandescent outdoor |
| Demolish and Install | Ea. | 37 | 42.65 | | 79.65 | light fixture. Wiring is not included. |
| Reinstall | Ea. | | 19.88 | | 19.88 | |
| Clean | Ea. | .19 | 11.10 | | 11.29 | |
| Minimum Charge | Job | | 199 | | 199 | |
| **Better Quality** | | | | | | |
| Demolish | Ea. | | 17.65 | | 17.65 | Includes material and labor to install |
| Install | Ea. | 105 | 25 | | 130 | custom quality incandescent outdoor |
| Demolish and Install | Ea. | 105 | 42.65 | | 147.65 | light fixture. Wiring is not included. |
| Reinstall | Ea. | | 19.88 | | 19.88 | |
| Clean | Ea. | .19 | 11.10 | | 11.29 | |
| Minimum Charge | Job | | 199 | | 199 | |
| **Premium Quality** | | | | | | |
| Demolish | Ea. | | 17.65 | | 17.65 | Includes material and labor to install |
| Install | Ea. | 175 | 99.50 | | 274.50 | deluxe quality incandescent outdoor |
| Demolish and Install | Ea. | 175 | 117.15 | | 292.15 | light fixture. Wiring is not included. |
| Reinstall | Ea. | | 79.52 | | 79.52 | |
| Clean | Ea. | .19 | 11.10 | | 11.29 | |
| Minimum Charge | Job | | 199 | | 199 | |

| Residential Light Fixture | | Unit | Material | Labor | Equip. | Total | Specification |
|---|---|---|---|---|---|---|---|
| **Outdoor w / Pole** | | | | | | | Includes material and labor to install |
| | Demolish | Ea. | | 17.65 | | 17.65 | post lantern type incandescent outdoor |
| | Install | Ea. | 129 | 99.50 | | 228.50 | light fixture. Wiring is not included. |
| | Demolish and Install | Ea. | 129 | 117.15 | | 246.15 | |
| | Reinstall | Ea. | | 79.52 | | 79.52 | |
| | Clean | Ea. | .19 | 11.10 | | 11.29 | |
| | Minimum Charge | Job | | 199 | | 199 | |
| **Run Wiring** | | | | | | | Includes labor and material to install a |
| | Install | Ea. | 18.50 | 15.90 | | 34.40 | electric fixture utility box with |
| | Minimum Charge | Job | | 199 | | 199 | non-metallic cable. |
| **Track Lighting** | | | | | | | Includes material and labor to install |
| | Demolish | L.F. | | 6.15 | | 6.15 | track lighting. |
| | Install | L.F. | 16.80 | 16.55 | | 33.35 | |
| | Demolish and Install | L.F. | 16.80 | 22.70 | | 39.50 | |
| | Reinstall | L.F. | | 13.25 | | 13.25 | |
| | Clean | L.F. | .19 | 5.35 | | 5.54 | |
| | Minimum Charge | Job | | 199 | | 199 | |

| Commercial Light Fixture | | Unit | Material | Labor | Equip. | Total | Specification |
|---|---|---|---|---|---|---|---|
| **Fluorescent** | | | | | | | |
| **2 Bulb, 2'** | | | | | | | Includes material and labor to install a |
| | Demolish | Ea. | | 17.65 | | 17.65 | 2' long surface mounted fluorescent |
| | Install | Ea. | 35 | 49.50 | | 84.50 | light fixture with two 40 watt bulbs. |
| | Demolish and Install | Ea. | 35 | 67.15 | | 102.15 | |
| | Reinstall | Ea. | | 39.76 | | 39.76 | |
| | Clean | Ea. | .91 | 19.05 | | 19.96 | |
| | Minimum Charge | Job | | 199 | | 199 | |
| **2 Bulb, 4'** | | | | | | | Includes material and labor to install a |
| | Demolish | Ea. | | 17.65 | | 17.65 | 4' long surface mounted fluorescent |
| | Install | Ea. | 67 | 57 | | 124 | light fixture with two 40 watt bulbs. |
| | Demolish and Install | Ea. | 67 | 74.65 | | 141.65 | |
| | Reinstall | Ea. | | 45.44 | | 45.44 | |
| | Clean | Ea. | .91 | 19.05 | | 19.96 | |
| | Minimum Charge | Job | | 199 | | 199 | |
| **3 Bulb, 4'** | | | | | | | Includes material and labor to install a |
| | Demolish | Ea. | | 17.65 | | 17.65 | 4' long pendant mounted fluorescent |
| | Install | Ea. | 103 | 57 | | 160 | light fixture with three 34 watt bulbs. |
| | Demolish and Install | Ea. | 103 | 74.65 | | 177.65 | |
| | Reinstall | Ea. | | 45.44 | | 45.44 | |
| | Clean | Ea. | .91 | 19.05 | | 19.96 | |
| | Minimum Charge | Job | | 199 | | 199 | |
| **4 Bulb, 4'** | | | | | | | Includes material and labor to install a |
| | Demolish | Ea. | | 17.65 | | 17.65 | 4' long pendant mounted fluorescent |
| | Install | Ea. | 93.50 | 61 | | 154.50 | light fixture with four 34 watt bulbs. |
| | Demolish and Install | Ea. | 93.50 | 78.65 | | 172.15 | |
| | Reinstall | Ea. | | 48.94 | | 48.94 | |
| | Clean | Ea. | .91 | 19.05 | | 19.96 | |
| | Minimum Charge | Job | | 199 | | 199 | |
| **2 Bulb, 8'** | | | | | | | Includes material and labor to install a |
| | Demolish | Ea. | | 22 | | 22 | 8' long surface mounted fluorescent |
| | Install | Ea. | 103 | 75 | | 178 | light fixture with two 110 watt bulbs. |
| | Demolish and Install | Ea. | 103 | 97 | | 200 | |
| | Reinstall | Ea. | | 60.02 | | 60.02 | |
| | Clean | Ea. | .91 | 19.05 | | 19.96 | |
| | Minimum Charge | Job | | 199 | | 199 | |

| Commercial Light Fixture | | Unit | Material | Labor | Equip. | Total | Specification |
|---|---|---|---|---|---|---|---|
| **Run Wiring** | | | | | | | |
| | Install | Ea. | 18.50 | 15.90 | | 34.40 | Includes labor and material to install a |
| | Minimum Charge | Job | | 199 | | 199 | electric fixture utility box with |
| | | | | | | | non-metallic cable. |
| **Ceiling, Recessed** | | | | | | | |
| **Eyeball Type** | | | | | | | |
| | Demolish | Ea. | | 18.40 | | 18.40 | Includes material and labor to install |
| | Install | Ea. | 64.50 | 14.20 | | 78.70 | custom quality recessed eyeball |
| | Demolish and Install | Ea. | 64.50 | 32.60 | | 97.10 | spotlight with housing. Wiring is not |
| | Reinstall | Ea. | | 11.36 | | 11.36 | included. |
| | Clean | Ea. | .03 | 2.78 | | 2.81 | |
| | Minimum Charge | Job | | 199 | | 199 | |
| **Shower Type** | | | | | | | |
| | Demolish | Ea. | | 18.40 | | 18.40 | Includes material and labor to install |
| | Install | Ea. | 54 | 13.25 | | 67.25 | deluxe quality recessed eyeball |
| | Demolish and Install | Ea. | 54 | 31.65 | | 85.65 | spotlight with housing. Wiring is not |
| | Reinstall | Ea. | | 10.60 | | 10.60 | included. |
| | Clean | Ea. | .03 | 2.78 | | 2.81 | |
| | Minimum Charge | Job | | 199 | | 199 | |
| **Run Wiring** | | | | | | | |
| | Install | Ea. | 18.50 | 15.90 | | 34.40 | Includes labor and material to install a |
| | Minimum Charge | Job | | 199 | | 199 | electric fixture utility box with |
| | | | | | | | non-metallic cable. |
| **Ceiling Grid Type** | | | | | | | |
| **2 Tube** | | | | | | | |
| | Demolish | Ea. | | 26 | | 26 | Cost includes material and labor to |
| | Install | Ea. | 61 | 75 | | 136 | install 2 lamp fluorescent light fixture |
| | Demolish and Install | Ea. | 61 | 101 | | 162 | in 2' x 4' ceiling grid system including |
| | Reinstall | Ea. | | 60.02 | | 60.02 | lens and tubes. |
| | Clean | Ea. | .91 | 19.05 | | 19.96 | |
| | Minimum Charge | Job | | 199 | | 199 | |
| **4 Tube** | | | | | | | |
| | Demolish | Ea. | | 29.50 | | 29.50 | Cost includes material and labor to |
| | Install | Ea. | 69.50 | 84.50 | | 154 | install 4 lamp fluorescent light fixture |
| | Demolish and Install | Ea. | 69.50 | 114 | | 183.50 | in 2' x 4' ceiling grid system including |
| | Reinstall | Ea. | | 67.68 | | 67.68 | lens and tubes. |
| | Clean | Ea. | .91 | 19.05 | | 19.96 | |
| | Minimum Charge | Job | | 199 | | 199 | |
| **Acrylic Diffuser** | | | | | | | |
| | Demolish | Ea. | | 4.60 | | 4.60 | Includes material and labor to install |
| | Install | Ea. | 49.50 | 12.05 | | 61.55 | fluorescent light fixture w/acrylic |
| | Demolish and Install | Ea. | 49.50 | 16.65 | | 66.15 | diffuser. |
| | Reinstall | Ea. | | 9.64 | | 9.64 | |
| | Clean | Ea. | .58 | 3.34 | | 3.92 | |
| | Minimum Charge | Job | | 199 | | 199 | |
| **Louver Diffuser** | | | | | | | |
| | Demolish | Ea. | | 5.50 | | 5.50 | Includes material and labor to install |
| | Install | Ea. | 55.50 | 12.05 | | 67.55 | fluorescent light fixture w/louver |
| | Demolish and Install | Ea. | 55.50 | 17.55 | | 73.05 | diffuser. |
| | Reinstall | Ea. | | 9.64 | | 9.64 | |
| | Clean | Ea. | .58 | 3.34 | | 3.92 | |
| | Minimum Charge | Job | | 199 | | 199 | |
| **Run Wiring** | | | | | | | |
| | Install | Ea. | 18.50 | 15.90 | | 34.40 | Includes labor and material to install a |
| | Minimum Charge | Job | | 199 | | 199 | electric fixture utility box with |
| | | | | | | | non-metallic cable. |

# Finish Electrical

| Commercial Light Fixture | | Unit | Material | Labor | Equip. | Total | Specification |
|---|---|---|---|---|---|---|---|
| **Track Lighting** | | | | | | | |
| | Demolish | L.F. | | 6.15 | | 6.15 | Includes material and labor to install |
| | Install | L.F. | 16.80 | 16.55 | | 33.35 | track lighting. |
| | Demolish and Install | L.F. | 16.80 | 22.70 | | 39.50 | |
| | Reinstall | L.F. | | 13.25 | | 13.25 | |
| | Clean | L.F. | .19 | 5.35 | | 5.54 | |
| | Minimum Charge | Job | | 199 | | 199 | |
| **Emergency** | | | | | | | |
| | Demolish | Ea. | | 31.50 | | 31.50 | Includes material and labor to install |
| | Install | Ea. | 142 | 99.50 | | 241.50 | battery-powered emergency lighting |
| | Demolish and Install | Ea. | 142 | 131 | | 273 | unit with two (2) lights, including |
| | Reinstall | Ea. | | 79.52 | | 79.52 | wiring. |
| | Clean | Ea. | .45 | 19.05 | | 19.50 | |
| | Minimum Charge | Job | | 199 | | 199 | |
| **Run Wiring** | | | | | | | |
| | Install | Ea. | 18.50 | 15.90 | | 34.40 | Includes labor and material to install a |
| | Minimum Charge | Job | | 199 | | 199 | electric fixture utility box with |
| | | | | | | | non-metallic cable. |

| Fan | | Unit | Material | Labor | Equip. | Total | Specification |
|---|---|---|---|---|---|---|---|
| **Ceiling Paddle** | | | | | | | |
| **Good Quality** | | | | | | | |
| | Demolish | Ea. | | 24.50 | | 24.50 | Includes material and labor to install |
| | Install | Ea. | 86.50 | 40 | | 126.50 | standard ceiling fan. |
| | Demolish and Install | Ea. | 86.50 | 64.50 | | 151 | |
| | Reinstall | Ea. | | 31.81 | | 31.81 | |
| | Clean | Ea. | .36 | 16.70 | | 17.06 | |
| | Minimum Charge | Job | | 199 | | 199 | |
| **Better Quality** | | | | | | | |
| | Demolish | Ea. | | 24.50 | | 24.50 | Includes material and labor to install |
| | Install | Ea. | 144 | 40 | | 184 | better ceiling fan. |
| | Demolish and Install | Ea. | 144 | 64.50 | | 208.50 | |
| | Reinstall | Ea. | | 31.81 | | 31.81 | |
| | Clean | Ea. | .36 | 16.70 | | 17.06 | |
| | Minimum Charge | Job | | 199 | | 199 | |
| **Premium Quality** | | | | | | | |
| | Demolish | Ea. | | 24.50 | | 24.50 | Includes material and labor to install |
| | Install | Ea. | 340 | 49.50 | | 389.50 | deluxe ceiling fan. |
| | Demolish and Install | Ea. | 340 | 74 | | 414 | |
| | Reinstall | Ea. | | 39.76 | | 39.76 | |
| | Clean | Ea. | .36 | 16.70 | | 17.06 | |
| | Minimum Charge | Job | | 199 | | 199 | |
| **Light Kit** | | | | | | | |
| | Install | Ea. | 32 | 49.50 | | 81.50 | Includes labor and material to install a |
| | Minimum Charge | Job | | 199 | | 199 | ceiling fan light kit. |
| **Bathroom Exhaust** | | | | | | | |
| **Ceiling Mounted** | | | | | | | |
| | Demolish | Ea. | | 20 | | 20 | Cost includes material and labor to |
| | Install | Ea. | 46 | 39.50 | | 85.50 | install 60 CFM ceiling mounted |
| | Demolish and Install | Ea. | 46 | 59.50 | | 105.50 | bathroom exhaust fan, up to 10' of |
| | Reinstall | Ea. | | 31.71 | | 31.71 | wiring with one wall switch. |
| | Clean | Ea. | .19 | 6.65 | | 6.84 | |
| | Minimum Charge | Job | | 199 | | 199 | |

# Finish Electrical

## Fan

| Fan | Unit | Material | Labor | Equip. | Total | Specification |
|---|---|---|---|---|---|---|
| **Wall Mounted** | | | | | | |
| Demolish | Ea. | | 20 | | 20 | Cost includes material and labor to |
| Install | Ea. | 61.50 | 39.50 | | 101 | install 110 CFM wall mounted |
| Demolish and Install | Ea. | 61.50 | 59.50 | | 121 | bathroom exhaust fan, up to 10' of |
| Reinstall | Ea. | | 31.71 | | 31.71 | wiring with one wall switch. |
| Clean | Ea. | .19 | 6.65 | | 6.84 | |
| Minimum Charge | Job | | 199 | | 199 | |
| **Lighted** | | | | | | |
| Demolish | Ea. | | 20 | | 20 | Cost includes material and labor to |
| Install | Ea. | 44.50 | 39.50 | | 84 | install 50 CFM ceiling mounted lighted |
| Demolish and Install | Ea. | 44.50 | 59.50 | | 104 | exhaust fan, up to 10' of wiring with |
| Reinstall | Ea. | | 31.71 | | 31.71 | one wall switch.. |
| Clean | Ea. | .19 | 6.65 | | 6.84 | |
| Minimum Charge | Job | | 199 | | 199 | |
| **Blower Heater w / Light** | | | | | | |
| Demolish | Ea. | | 20 | | 20 | Includes material and labor to install |
| Install | Ea. | 91 | 66 | | 157 | ceiling blower type ventilator with |
| Demolish and Install | Ea. | 91 | 86 | | 177 | switch, light and snap-on grill. Includes |
| Reinstall | Ea. | | 52.85 | | 52.85 | 1300 watt/120 volt heater. |
| Clean | Ea. | .19 | 6.65 | | 6.84 | |
| Minimum Charge | Job | | 199 | | 199 | |
| **Fan Heater w / Light** | | | | | | |
| Demolish | Ea. | | 20 | | 20 | Includes material and labor to install |
| Install | Ea. | 117 | 66 | | 183 | circular ceiling fan heater unit, 1500 |
| Demolish and Install | Ea. | 117 | 86 | | 203 | watt, surface mounted. |
| Reinstall | Ea. | | 52.85 | | 52.85 | |
| Clean | Ea. | .19 | 6.65 | | 6.84 | |
| Minimum Charge | Job | | 199 | | 199 | |

### Whole House Exhaust
#### 36" Ceiling Mounted

| | Unit | Material | Labor | Equip. | Total | Specification |
|---|---|---|---|---|---|---|
| Install | Ea. | 710 | 99 | | 809 | Includes material and labor to install a |
| Clean | Ea. | .06 | 4.79 | | 4.85 | whole house exhaust fan. |
| Minimum Charge | Job | | 199 | | 199 | |

### Kitchen Exhaust
#### Standard Model

| | Unit | Material | Labor | Equip. | Total | Specification |
|---|---|---|---|---|---|---|
| Install | Ea. | 66.50 | 26.50 | | 93 | Includes labor and materials to install |
| Clean | Ea. | .06 | 4.79 | | 4.85 | a bathroom or kitchen vent fan. |
| Minimum Charge | Job | | 199 | | 199 | |

#### Low Noise Model

| | Unit | Material | Labor | Equip. | Total | Specification |
|---|---|---|---|---|---|---|
| Install | Ea. | 87 | 26.50 | | 113.50 | Includes labor and materials to install |
| Clean | Ea. | .06 | 4.79 | | 4.85 | a bathroom or kitchen vent fan, low |
| Minimum Charge | Job | | 199 | | 199 | noise model. |

## Low Voltage Systems

### Smoke Detector
#### Pre-wired

| | Unit | Material | Labor | Equip. | Total | Specification |
|---|---|---|---|---|---|---|
| Demolish | Ea. | | 9.20 | | 9.20 | Includes material and labor to install |
| Install | Ea. | 19.65 | 74.50 | | 94.15 | AC type smoke detector including |
| Demolish and Install | Ea. | 19.65 | 83.70 | | 103.35 | wiring. |
| Reinstall | Ea. | | 59.68 | | 59.68 | |
| Clean | Ea. | .08 | 8.35 | | 8.43 | |
| Minimum Charge | Job | | 199 | | 199 | |

# Finish Electrical

| Low Voltage Systems | | Unit | Material | Labor | Equip. | Total | Specification |
|---|---|---|---|---|---|---|---|
| **Battery-powered** | | | | | | | |
| | Demolish | Ea. | | 9.20 | | 9.20 | Includes material and labor to install |
| | Install | Ea. | 24 | 25 | | 49 | battery-powered type smoke detector. |
| | Demolish and Install | Ea. | 24 | 34.20 | | 58.20 | |
| | Reinstall | Ea. | | 19.88 | | 19.88 | |
| | Clean | Ea. | .08 | 8.35 | | 8.43 | |
| | Minimum Charge | Job | | 199 | | 199 | |
| **Run Wiring** | | | | | | | |
| | Install | Ea. | 18.50 | 15.90 | | 34.40 | Includes labor and material to install a |
| | Minimum Charge | Job | | 199 | | 199 | electric fixture utility box with |
| | | | | | | | non-metallic cable. |
| **Door Bell / Chimes** | | | | | | | |
| **Good Quality** | | | | | | | |
| | Demolish | Ea. | | 27.50 | | 27.50 | Includes material and labor to install |
| | Install | Ea. | 53 | 99.50 | | 152.50 | surface mounted 2 note door bell. |
| | Demolish and Install | Ea. | 53 | 127 | | 180 | Wiring is not included. |
| | Reinstall | Ea. | | 79.52 | | 79.52 | |
| | Clean | Ea. | .19 | 8.35 | | 8.54 | |
| | Minimum Charge | Job | | 199 | | 199 | |
| **Better Quality** | | | | | | | |
| | Demolish | Ea. | | 27.50 | | 27.50 | Includes material and labor to install |
| | Install | Ea. | 69 | 99.50 | | 168.50 | standard quality surface mounted 2 |
| | Demolish and Install | Ea. | 69 | 127 | | 196 | note door bell. Wiring is not included. |
| | Reinstall | Ea. | | 79.52 | | 79.52 | |
| | Clean | Ea. | .19 | 8.35 | | 8.54 | |
| | Minimum Charge | Job | | 199 | | 199 | |
| **Premium Quality** | | | | | | | |
| | Demolish | Ea. | | 27.50 | | 27.50 | Includes material and labor to install |
| | Install | Ea. | 78 | 99.50 | | 177.50 | deluxe quality surface mounted 2 note |
| | Demolish and Install | Ea. | 78 | 127 | | 205 | door bell. Wiring is not included. |
| | Reinstall | Ea. | | 79.52 | | 79.52 | |
| | Clean | Ea. | .19 | 8.35 | | 8.54 | |
| | Minimum Charge | Job | | 199 | | 199 | |
| **Run Wiring** | | | | | | | |
| | Install | Ea. | 18.50 | 15.90 | | 34.40 | Includes labor and material to install a |
| | Minimum Charge | Job | | 199 | | 199 | electric fixture utility box with |
| | | | | | | | non-metallic cable. |
| **Intercom System** | | | | | | | |
| **Intercom (master)** | | | | | | | |
| | Demolish | Ea. | | 73.50 | | 73.50 | Includes material and labor to install |
| | Install | Ea. | 555 | 199 | | 754 | master intercom station with AM/FM |
| | Demolish and Install | Ea. | 555 | 272.50 | | 827.50 | music and room monitoring. Wiring is |
| | Reinstall | Ea. | | 159.04 | | 159.04 | not included. |
| | Clean | Ea. | .19 | 22 | | 22.19 | |
| | Minimum Charge | Job | | 199 | | 199 | |
| **Intercom (remote)** | | | | | | | |
| | Demolish | Ea. | | 44 | | 44 | Includes material and labor to install |
| | Install | Ea. | 50.50 | 49.50 | | 100 | remote station for master intercom |
| | Demolish and Install | Ea. | 50.50 | 93.50 | | 144 | system. Wiring is not included. |
| | Reinstall | Ea. | | 39.76 | | 39.76 | |
| | Clean | Ea. | .19 | 8.35 | | 8.54 | |
| | Minimum Charge | Job | | 199 | | 199 | |

# Finish Electrical

| Low Voltage Systems | | Unit | Material | Labor | Equip. | Total | Specification |
|---|---|---|---|---|---|---|---|
| **Security System** | | | | | | | |
| **Alarm Panel** | | | | | | | |
| | Demolish | Ea. | | 88.50 | | 88.50 | Includes material and labor to install a |
| | Install | Ea. | 127 | 199 | | 326 | 6 zone burglar alarm panel. |
| | Demolish and Install | Ea. | 127 | 287.50 | | 414.50 | |
| | Reinstall | Ea. | | 159.04 | | 159.04 | |
| | Clean | Ea. | .19 | 8.35 | | 8.54 | |
| | Minimum Charge | Job | | 199 | | 199 | |
| **Motion Detector** | | | | | | | |
| | Demolish | Ea. | | 63 | | 63 | Includes material and labor to install a |
| | Install | Ea. | 231 | 173 | | 404 | ultrasonic motion detector for a |
| | Demolish and Install | Ea. | 231 | 236 | | 467 | security system. |
| | Reinstall | Ea. | | 138.30 | | 138.30 | |
| | Clean | Ea. | .19 | 8.35 | | 8.54 | |
| | Minimum Charge | Job | | 199 | | 199 | |
| **Door Switch** | | | | | | | |
| | Demolish | Ea. | | 27.50 | | 27.50 | Includes material and labor to install a |
| | Install | Ea. | 35 | 75 | | 110 | door / window contact for a security |
| | Demolish and Install | Ea. | 35 | 102.50 | | 137.50 | system. |
| | Reinstall | Ea. | | 60.02 | | 60.02 | |
| | Clean | Ea. | .19 | 2.67 | | 2.86 | |
| | Minimum Charge | Job | | 199 | | 199 | |
| **Window Switch** | | | | | | | |
| | Demolish | Ea. | | 27.50 | | 27.50 | Includes material and labor to install a |
| | Install | Ea. | 35 | 75 | | 110 | door / window contact for a security |
| | Demolish and Install | Ea. | 35 | 102.50 | | 137.50 | system. |
| | Reinstall | Ea. | | 60.02 | | 60.02 | |
| | Clean | Ea. | .19 | 2.67 | | 2.86 | |
| | Minimum Charge | Job | | 199 | | 199 | |
| **Satellite System** | | | | | | | |
| **Dish** | | | | | | | |
| | Demolish | Ea. | | 123 | | 123 | Includes material, labor and |
| | Install | Ea. | 910 | 330 | | 1240 | equipment to install 10' mesh dish. |
| | Demolish and Install | Ea. | 910 | 453 | | 1363 | |
| | Reinstall | Ea. | | 265.07 | | 265.07 | |
| | Clean | Ea. | 3.63 | 33.50 | | 37.13 | |
| | Minimum Charge | Job | | 199 | | 199 | |
| **Motor** | | | | | | | |
| | Demolish | Ea. | | 61.50 | | 61.50 | Includes material and labor to install a |
| | Install | Ea. | 395 | 166 | | 561 | television satellite dish motor unit. |
| | Demolish and Install | Ea. | 395 | 227.50 | | 622.50 | |
| | Reinstall | Ea. | | 132.53 | | 132.53 | |
| | Clean | Ea. | .19 | 8.35 | | 8.54 | |
| | Minimum Charge | Job | | 199 | | 199 | |
| **Television Antenna** | | | | | | | |
| **40' Pole** | | | | | | | |
| | Demolish | Ea. | | 69 | | 69 | Includes material and labor to install |
| | Install | Ea. | 23 | 124 | | 147 | stand-alone 1"-2" metal pole, 10' long. |
| | Demolish and Install | Ea. | 23 | 193 | | 216 | Cost does not include antenna. |
| | Reinstall | Ea. | | 99.40 | | 99.40 | |
| | Clean | Ea. | .73 | 33.50 | | 34.23 | |
| | Paint | Ea. | 7.20 | 39.50 | | 46.70 | |
| | Minimum Charge | Job | | 199 | | 199 | |
| **Rotor Unit** | | | | | | | |
| | Demolish | Ea. | | 55 | | 55 | Includes material and labor to install a |
| | Install | Ea. | 107 | 49.50 | | 156.50 | television antenna rotor. |
| | Demolish and Install | Ea. | 107 | 104.50 | | 211.50 | |
| | Reinstall | Ea. | | 39.76 | | 39.76 | |
| | Clean | Ea. | .73 | 33.50 | | 34.23 | |
| | Minimum Charge | Job | | 199 | | 199 | |

# Finish Electrical

| Low Voltage Systems | Unit | Material | Labor | Equip. | Total | Specification |
|---|---|---|---|---|---|---|
| **Single Booster** | | | | | | |
| Demolish | Ea. | | 55 | | 55 | Includes material and labor to install |
| Install | Ea. | 43 | 49.50 | | 92.50 | standard grade VHF television signal |
| Demolish and Install | Ea. | 43 | 104.50 | | 147.50 | booster unit and all hardware required |
| Reinstall | Ea. | | 39.76 | | 39.76 | for connection to TV cable. |
| Clean | Ea. | .03 | 4.17 | | 4.20 | |
| Minimum Charge | Job | | 199 | | 199 | |

| Gazebo | Gutter | Shutter |

| Window Treatment | Unit | Material | Labor | Equip. | Total | Specification |
|---|---|---|---|---|---|---|
| **Drapery** | | | | | | |
| **Good Grade** | | | | | | |
| Install | L.F. | 42 | 5.35 | | 47.35 | Includes material and labor to install |
| Reinstall | L.F. | | 4.27 | | 4.27 | good quality drapery. |
| Clean | L.F. | 2.66 | .13 | | 2.79 | |
| Minimum Charge | Job | | 133 | | 133 | |
| **Premium Grade** | | | | | | |
| Install | L.F. | 73 | 5.35 | | 78.35 | Includes material and labor to install |
| Reinstall | L.F. | | 4.27 | | 4.27 | premium quality drapery. |
| Clean | L.F. | 2.66 | .15 | | 2.81 | |
| Minimum Charge | Job | | 133 | | 133 | |
| **Lining** | | | | | | |
| Install | L.F. | 18.20 | 5.35 | | 23.55 | Includes material and labor to install |
| Reinstall | L.F. | | 4.27 | | 4.27 | drapery lining. |
| Clean | L.F. | 1.33 | .08 | | 1.41 | |
| Minimum Charge | Job | | 133 | | 133 | |
| **Valance Board** | | | | | | |
| Demolish | L.F. | | 1.48 | | 1.48 | Includes material and labor to install a |
| Install | L.F. | 4.65 | 10.65 | | 15.30 | drapery valance board. |
| Demolish and Install | L.F. | 4.65 | 12.13 | | 16.78 | |
| Reinstall | L.F. | | 8.54 | | 8.54 | |
| Clean | L.F. | 1.33 | .27 | | 1.60 | |
| Minimum Charge | Job | | 133 | | 133 | |
| **Rod** | | | | | | |
| Demolish | L.F. | | 3.71 | | 3.71 | Includes material and labor to install |
| Install | L.F. | 3.78 | 6.15 | | 9.93 | standard traverse drapery hardware. |
| Demolish and Install | L.F. | 3.78 | 9.86 | | 13.64 | |
| Reinstall | L.F. | | 4.90 | | 4.90 | |
| Clean | L.F. | .07 | .24 | | .31 | |
| Paint | L.F. | .06 | .61 | | .67 | |
| Minimum Charge | Job | | 133 | | 133 | |
| **Blinds** | | | | | | |
| **Mini-type** | | | | | | |
| Demolish | S.F. | | .78 | | .78 | Includes material and labor to install |
| Install | S.F. | 3.38 | .61 | | 3.99 | horizontal 1″ slat blinds. |
| Demolish and Install | S.F. | 3.38 | 1.39 | | 4.77 | |
| Reinstall | S.F. | | .49 | | .49 | |
| Clean | S.F. | .51 | .03 | | .54 | |
| Minimum Charge | Job | | 133 | | 133 | |

| Window Treatment | | Unit | Material | Labor | Equip. | Total | Specification |
|---|---|---|---|---|---|---|---|
| **Vertical Type** | | | | | | | |
| | Demolish | S.F. | | .78 | | .78 | Includes material and labor to install |
| | Install | S.F. | 5.70 | .79 | | 6.49 | vertical 3" - 5" cloth or PVC blinds. |
| | Demolish and Install | S.F. | 5.70 | 1.57 | | 7.27 | |
| | Reinstall | S.F. | | .63 | | .63 | |
| | Clean | S.F. | .26 | .03 | | .29 | |
| | Minimum Charge | Job | | 133 | | 133 | |
| **Vertical Type per L.F.** | | | | | | | |
| | Demolish | L.F. | | 1.24 | | 1.24 | Includes material and labor to install |
| | Install | L.F. | 34 | 3.56 | | 37.56 | vertical 3" - 5" cloth or PVC blinds x |
| | Demolish and Install | L.F. | 34 | 4.80 | | 38.80 | 72" long. |
| | Reinstall | L.F. | | 2.85 | | 2.85 | |
| | Clean | L.F. | 1.88 | .19 | | 2.07 | |
| | Minimum Charge | Job | | 133 | | 133 | |
| **Venetian Type** | | | | | | | |
| | Demolish | S.F. | | .78 | | .78 | Includes material and labor to install |
| | Install | S.F. | 3.88 | .61 | | 4.49 | horizontal 2" slat blinds. |
| | Demolish and Install | S.F. | 3.88 | 1.39 | | 5.27 | |
| | Reinstall | S.F. | | .49 | | .49 | |
| | Clean | S.F. | .26 | .03 | | .29 | |
| | Minimum Charge | Job | | 133 | | 133 | |
| **Wood Shutter** | | | | | | | |
| **27" x 36", 4 Panel** | | | | | | | |
| | Demolish | Ea. | | 25 | | 25 | Includes material and labor to install |
| | Install | Pr. | 94 | 21.50 | | 115.50 | moveable louver, up to 33" x 36", 4 |
| | Demolish and Install | Pr. | 94 | 46.50 | | 140.50 | panel shutter. |
| | Reinstall | Pr. | | 17.02 | | 17.02 | |
| | Clean | Ea. | .07 | 8 | | 8.07 | |
| | Paint | Ea. | 1.16 | 22.50 | | 23.66 | |
| | Minimum Charge | Job | | 181 | | 181 | |
| **33" x 36", 4 Panel** | | | | | | | |
| | Demolish | Ea. | | 25 | | 25 | Includes material and labor to install |
| | Install | Pr. | 94 | 21.50 | | 115.50 | moveable louver, up to 33" x 36", 4 |
| | Demolish and Install | Pr. | 94 | 46.50 | | 140.50 | panel shutter. |
| | Reinstall | Pr. | | 17.02 | | 17.02 | |
| | Clean | Ea. | .07 | 8 | | 8.07 | |
| | Paint | Ea. | 1.20 | 24 | | 25.20 | |
| | Minimum Charge | Job | | 181 | | 181 | |
| **39" x 36", 4 Panel** | | | | | | | |
| | Demolish | Ea. | | 25 | | 25 | Includes material and labor to install |
| | Install | Pr. | 106 | 21.50 | | 127.50 | moveable louver, up to 47" x 36", 4 |
| | Demolish and Install | Pr. | 106 | 46.50 | | 152.50 | panel shutter. |
| | Reinstall | Pr. | | 17.02 | | 17.02 | |
| | Clean | Ea. | .07 | 8 | | 8.07 | |
| | Paint | Ea. | 1.20 | 24 | | 25.20 | |
| | Minimum Charge | Job | | 181 | | 181 | |
| **47" x 36", 4 Panel** | | | | | | | |
| | Demolish | Ea. | | 25 | | 25 | Includes material and labor to install |
| | Install | Pr. | 106 | 21.50 | | 127.50 | moveable louver, up to 47" x 36", 4 |
| | Demolish and Install | Pr. | 106 | 46.50 | | 152.50 | panel shutter. |
| | Reinstall | Pr. | | 17.02 | | 17.02 | |
| | Clean | Ea. | .07 | 8 | | 8.07 | |
| | Paint | Ea. | 1.25 | 26 | | 27.25 | |
| | Minimum Charge | Job | | 181 | | 181 | |

# Improvements / Appliances / Treatments

| Stairs | | Unit | Material | Labor | Equip. | Total | Specification |
|---|---|---|---|---|---|---|---|
| **Concrete Steps** | | | | | | | |
| Precast | | | | | | | |
| | Demolish | Ea. | | 50.50 | 34.50 | 85 | Includes material and labor to install |
| | Install | Flight | 335 | 124 | 49.50 | 508.50 | precast concrete front entrance stairs, |
| | Demolish and Install | Flight | 335 | 174.50 | 84 | 593.50 | 4' wide, with 48" platform and 2 |
| | Clean | Ea. | | 3.71 | | 3.71 | risers. |
| | Paint | Ea. | 3.55 | 39.50 | | 43.05 | |
| | Minimum Charge | Job | | 325 | | 325 | |
| **Metal** | | | | | | | |
| Concrete Filled | | | | | | | |
| | Demolish | Ea. | | 14.80 | | 14.80 | Includes material and labor to install |
| | Install | Riser | 510 | 61 | 4.84 | 575.84 | steel, cement filled metal pan stairs |
| | Demolish and Install | Riser | 510 | 75.80 | 4.84 | 590.64 | with picket rail. |
| | Clean | Ea. | .11 | 2.29 | | 2.40 | |
| | Paint | Ea. | .39 | 2.33 | | 2.72 | |
| | Minimum Charge | Job | | 224 | | 224 | |
| Landing | | | | | | | |
| | Demolish | S.F. | | 3.71 | | 3.71 | Includes material and labor to install |
| | Install | S.F. | 106 | 7.15 | .57 | 113.72 | pre-erected conventional steel pan |
| | Demolish and Install | S.F. | 106 | 10.86 | .57 | 117.43 | landing. |
| | Clean | S.F. | .11 | .48 | | .59 | |
| | Paint | S.F. | .13 | .67 | | .80 | |
| | Minimum Charge | Job | | 224 | | 224 | |
| Railing | | | | | | | |
| | Demolish | L.F. | | 2.04 | | 2.04 | Includes material and labor to install |
| | Install | L.F. | 14.05 | 10.35 | .83 | 25.23 | primed steel pipe. |
| | Demolish and Install | L.F. | 14.05 | 12.39 | .83 | 27.27 | |
| | Clean | L.F. | .73 | 1.67 | | 2.40 | |
| | Paint | L.F. | .69 | 5.25 | | 5.94 | |
| | Minimum Charge | Job | | 224 | | 224 | |

| Elevator | | Unit | Material | Labor | Equip. | Total | Specification |
|---|---|---|---|---|---|---|---|
| **2 Stop Residential** | | | | | | | |
| | Install | Ea. | 10100 | 4800 | | 14900 | Includes labor, material and |
| | Clean | Ea. | .81 | 16.70 | | 17.51 | equipment to install 2 stop elevator for |
| | Minimum Charge | Job | | 480 | | 480 | residential use. |
| **2 Stop Commercial** | | | | | | | |
| | Install | Ea. | 38400 | 9625 | | 48025 | Includes labor, material and |
| | Clean | Ea. | .81 | 16.70 | | 17.51 | equipment to install 2 stop elevator for |
| | Minimum Charge | Job | | 480 | | 480 | apartment or commercial building with |
| | | | | | | | 2,000 lb/13 passenger capacity. |
| **3 Stop Commercial** | | | | | | | |
| | Install | Ea. | 48200 | 14800 | | 63000 | Includes labor, material and |
| | Clean | Ea. | .81 | 16.70 | | 17.51 | equipment to install 3 stop elevator for |
| | Minimum Charge | Job | | 480 | | 480 | apartment or commercial building with |
| | | | | | | | 2,000 lb/13 passenger capacity. |
| **4 Stop Commercial** | | | | | | | |
| | Install | Ea. | 58000 | 20000 | | 78000 | Includes labor, material and |
| | Clean | Ea. | .81 | 16.70 | | 17.51 | equipment to install 4 stop elevator for |
| | Minimum Charge | Job | | 480 | | 480 | apartment or commercial building with |
| | | | | | | | 2,000 lb/13 passenger capacity. |

# Improvements / Appliances / Treatments

| Elevator | | Unit | Material | Labor | Equip. | Total | Specification |
|---|---|---|---|---|---|---|---|
| **5 Stop Commercial** | | | | | | | Includes labor, material and |
| | Install | Ea. | 67500 | 25300 | | 92800 | equipment to install 5 stop elevator for |
| | Clean | Ea. | .81 | 16.70 | | 17.51 | apartment or commercial building with |
| | Minimum Charge | Job | | 480 | | 480 | 2,000 lb/13 passenger capacity. |

| Rangetop | | Unit | Material | Labor | Equip. | Total | Specification |
|---|---|---|---|---|---|---|---|
| **4-burner** | | | | | | | Cost includes material and labor to |
| | Demolish | Ea. | | 27 | | 27 | install 4-burner electric surface unit. |
| | Install | Ea. | 241 | 66.50 | | 307.50 | |
| | Demolish and Install | Ea. | 241 | 93.50 | | 334.50 | |
| | Reinstall | Ea. | | 53.01 | | 53.01 | |
| | Clean | Ea. | .06 | 24 | | 24.06 | |
| | Minimum Charge | Job | | 66.50 | | 66.50 | |
| **6-burner** | | | | | | | Includes material and labor to install a |
| | Demolish | Ea. | | 27 | | 27 | 6-burner cooktop unit. |
| | Install | Ea. | 1550 | 79.50 | | 1629.50 | |
| | Demolish and Install | Ea. | 1550 | 106.50 | | 1656.50 | |
| | Reinstall | Ea. | | 63.62 | | 63.62 | |
| | Clean | Ea. | .06 | 24 | | 24.06 | |
| | Minimum Charge | Job | | 66.50 | | 66.50 | |
| **Premium Brand w / Grill** | | | | | | | Includes material and labor to install |
| | Demolish | Ea. | | 27 | | 27 | electric downdraft cooktop with grill. |
| | Install | Ea. | 840 | 79.50 | | 919.50 | |
| | Demolish and Install | Ea. | 840 | 106.50 | | 946.50 | |
| | Reinstall | Ea. | | 63.62 | | 63.62 | |
| | Clean | Ea. | .06 | 24 | | 24.06 | |
| | Minimum Charge | Job | | 66.50 | | 66.50 | |

| Rangehood | | Unit | Material | Labor | Equip. | Total | Specification |
|---|---|---|---|---|---|---|---|
| **Vented** | | | | | | | |
| **30"** | | | | | | | |
| | Demolish | Ea. | | 24.50 | | 24.50 | Includes material and labor to install a |
| | Install | Ea. | 54 | 79.50 | | 133.50 | vented range hood. |
| | Demolish and Install | Ea. | 54 | 104 | | 158 | |
| | Reinstall | Ea. | | 63.62 | | 63.62 | |
| | Clean | Ea. | .06 | 6.85 | | 6.91 | |
| | Minimum Charge | Job | | 66.50 | | 66.50 | |
| **36"** | | | | | | | |
| | Demolish | Ea. | | 24.50 | | 24.50 | Includes material and labor to install a |
| | Install | Ea. | 150 | 79.50 | | 229.50 | vented range hood. |
| | Demolish and Install | Ea. | 150 | 104 | | 254 | |
| | Reinstall | Ea. | | 63.62 | | 63.62 | |
| | Clean | Ea. | .06 | 6.85 | | 6.91 | |
| | Minimum Charge | Job | | 66.50 | | 66.50 | |
| **42"** | | | | | | | |
| | Demolish | Ea. | | 24.50 | | 24.50 | Includes material and labor to install a |
| | Install | Ea. | 275 | 92 | | 367 | vented range hood. |
| | Demolish and Install | Ea. | 275 | 116.50 | | 391.50 | |
| | Reinstall | Ea. | | 73.76 | | 73.76 | |
| | Clean | Ea. | .06 | 6.85 | | 6.91 | |
| | Minimum Charge | Job | | 66.50 | | 66.50 | |

| Rangehood | | Unit | Material | Labor | Equip. | Total | Specification |
|---|---|---|---|---|---|---|---|
| **Ventless** | | | | | | | |
| **30"** | | | | | | | |
| | Demolish | Ea. | | 24.50 | | 24.50 | Includes material and labor to install a |
| | Install | Ea. | 70 | 49.50 | | 119.50 | ventless range hood. |
| | Demolish and Install | Ea. | 70 | 74 | | 144 | |
| | Reinstall | Ea. | | 39.76 | | 39.76 | |
| | Clean | Ea. | .06 | 6.85 | | 6.91 | |
| | Minimum Charge | Job | | 66.50 | | 66.50 | |
| **36"** | | | | | | | |
| | Demolish | Ea. | | 24.50 | | 24.50 | Includes material and labor to install a |
| | Install | Ea. | 185 | 79.50 | | 264.50 | ventless range hood. |
| | Demolish and Install | Ea. | 185 | 104 | | 289 | |
| | Reinstall | Ea. | | 63.62 | | 63.62 | |
| | Clean | Ea. | .06 | 6.85 | | 6.91 | |
| | Minimum Charge | Job | | 66.50 | | 66.50 | |
| **42"** | | | | | | | |
| | Demolish | Ea. | | 24.50 | | 24.50 | Includes material and labor to install a |
| | Install | Ea. | 250 | 66.50 | | 316.50 | ventless range hood. |
| | Demolish and Install | Ea. | 250 | 91 | | 341 | |
| | Reinstall | Ea. | | 53.01 | | 53.01 | |
| | Clean | Ea. | .06 | 6.85 | | 6.91 | |
| | Minimum Charge | Job | | 66.50 | | 66.50 | |

| Oven | | Unit | Material | Labor | Equip. | Total | Specification |
|---|---|---|---|---|---|---|---|
| **Free Standing** | | | | | | | |
| | Demolish | Ea. | | 27 | | 27 | Cost includes material and labor to |
| | Install | Ea. | 470 | 53.50 | | 523.50 | install 30" free standing electric range |
| | Demolish and Install | Ea. | 470 | 80.50 | | 550.50 | with self-cleaning oven. |
| | Reinstall | Ea. | | 42.69 | | 42.69 | |
| | Clean | Ea. | .06 | 24 | | 24.06 | |
| | Minimum Charge | Job | | 66.50 | | 66.50 | |
| **Single Wall Oven** | | | | | | | |
| | Demolish | Ea. | | 27 | | 27 | Includes material and labor to install a |
| | Install | Ea. | 475 | 99.50 | | 574.50 | built-in oven. |
| | Demolish and Install | Ea. | 475 | 126.50 | | 601.50 | |
| | Reinstall | Ea. | | 79.52 | | 79.52 | |
| | Clean | Ea. | .06 | 24 | | 24.06 | |
| | Minimum Charge | Job | | 66.50 | | 66.50 | |
| **Double Wall Oven** | | | | | | | |
| | Demolish | Ea. | | 27 | | 27 | Includes material and labor to install a |
| | Install | Ea. | 1475 | 181 | | 1656 | conventional double oven. |
| | Demolish and Install | Ea. | 1475 | 208 | | 1683 | |
| | Reinstall | Ea. | | 144.64 | | 144.64 | |
| | Clean | Ea. | .06 | 24 | | 24.06 | |
| | Minimum Charge | Job | | 66.50 | | 66.50 | |
| **Drop-in Type w / Range** | | | | | | | |
| | Demolish | Ea. | | 27 | | 27 | Includes material and labor to install a |
| | Install | Ea. | 530 | 66.50 | | 596.50 | built-in cooking range with oven. |
| | Demolish and Install | Ea. | 530 | 93.50 | | 623.50 | |
| | Reinstall | Ea. | | 53.01 | | 53.01 | |
| | Clean | Ea. | .06 | 24 | | 24.06 | |
| | Minimum Charge | Job | | 66.50 | | 66.50 | |

# Improvements / Appliances / Treatments

## Oven

| Oven | Unit | Material | Labor | Equip. | Total | Specification |
|------|------|----------|-------|--------|-------|---------------|
| **Hi/Lo w / Range, Microwave** | | | | | | Includes material and labor to install a |
| Demolish | Ea. | | 27 | | 27 | double oven, one conventional, one |
| Install | Ea. | 1825 | 360 | | 2185 | microwave. |
| Demolish and Install | Ea. | 1825 | 387 | | 2212 | |
| Reinstall | Ea. | | 289.28 | | 289.28 | |
| Clean | Ea. | .06 | 24 | | 24.06 | |
| Minimum Charge | Job | | 66.50 | | 66.50 | |
| **Hi/Lo w/ Range / Double Oven** | | | | | | Includes material and labor to install a |
| Demolish | Ea. | | 27 | | 27 | conventional double oven. |
| Install | Ea. | 1475 | 181 | | 1656 | |
| Demolish and Install | Ea. | 1475 | 208 | | 1683 | |
| Reinstall | Ea. | | 144.64 | | 144.64 | |
| Clean | Ea. | .06 | 24 | | 24.06 | |
| Minimum Charge | Job | | 66.50 | | 66.50 | |
| **Countertop Microwave** | | | | | | Includes material and labor to install a |
| Demolish | Ea. | | 9.25 | | 9.25 | 1.0 cubic foot microwave oven. |
| Install | Ea. | 150 | 33.50 | | 183.50 | |
| Demolish and Install | Ea. | 150 | 42.75 | | 192.75 | |
| Reinstall | Ea. | | 26.68 | | 26.68 | |
| Clean | Ea. | .06 | 12 | | 12.06 | |
| Minimum Charge | Job | | 66.50 | | 66.50 | |
| **Cabinet / Wall Mounted Microwave** | | | | | | Includes material and labor to install a |
| Demolish | Ea. | | 18.55 | | 18.55 | space saver microwave oven. |
| Install | Ea. | 590 | 99.50 | | 689.50 | |
| Demolish and Install | Ea. | 590 | 118.05 | | 708.05 | |
| Reinstall | Ea. | | 79.52 | | 79.52 | |
| Clean | Ea. | .06 | 12 | | 12.06 | |
| Minimum Charge | Job | | 66.50 | | 66.50 | |

## Dryer

| Dryer | Unit | Material | Labor | Equip. | Total | Specification |
|-------|------|----------|-------|--------|-------|---------------|
| **Basic Grade** | | | | | | Includes material and labor to install |
| Demolish | Ea. | | 12.35 | | 12.35 | electric or gas dryer. Vent kit not |
| Install | Ea. | 330 | 211 | | 541 | included. |
| Demolish and Install | Ea. | 330 | 223.35 | | 553.35 | |
| Reinstall | Ea. | | 168.87 | | 168.87 | |
| Clean | Ea. | .06 | 24 | | 24.06 | |
| Minimum Charge | Job | | 66.50 | | 66.50 | |
| **Good Grade** | | | | | | Includes material and labor to install |
| Demolish | Ea. | | 12.35 | | 12.35 | electric or gas dryer. Vent kit not |
| Install | Ea. | 405 | 211 | | 616 | included. |
| Demolish and Install | Ea. | 405 | 223.35 | | 628.35 | |
| Reinstall | Ea. | | 168.87 | | 168.87 | |
| Clean | Ea. | .06 | 24 | | 24.06 | |
| Minimum Charge | Job | | 66.50 | | 66.50 | |
| **Premium Grade** | | | | | | Includes material and labor to install |
| Demolish | Ea. | | 12.35 | | 12.35 | electric or gas dryer. Vent kit not |
| Install | Ea. | 1350 | 315 | | 1665 | included. |
| Demolish and Install | Ea. | 1350 | 327.35 | | 1677.35 | |
| Reinstall | Ea. | | 253.31 | | 253.31 | |
| Clean | Ea. | .06 | 24 | | 24.06 | |
| Minimum Charge | Job | | 66.50 | | 66.50 | |

# Improvements / Appliances / Treatments

## Dryer

| | Unit | Material | Labor | Equip. | Total | Specification |
|---|---|---|---|---|---|---|
| **Washer / Dryer Combination Unit** | | | | | | Includes material and labor to install |
| Demolish | Ea. | | 12.35 | | 12.35 | electric washer/dryer combination |
| Install | Ea. | 985 | 53.50 | | 1038.50 | unit, 27" wide, stackable or unitized. |
| Demolish and Install | Ea. | 985 | 65.85 | | 1050.85 | |
| Reinstall | Ea. | | 42.69 | | 42.69 | |
| Clean | Ea. | .06 | 24 | | 24.06 | |
| Minimum Charge | Job | | 66.50 | | 66.50 | |

## Washer

| | Unit | Material | Labor | Equip. | Total | Specification |
|---|---|---|---|---|---|---|
| **Basic Grade** | | | | | | Includes material and labor to install |
| Demolish | Ea. | | 12.35 | | 12.35 | washing machine. New hoses not |
| Install | Ea. | 335 | 135 | | 470 | included. |
| Demolish and Install | Ea. | 335 | 147.35 | | 482.35 | |
| Reinstall | Ea. | | 108.05 | | 108.05 | |
| Clean | Ea. | .06 | 24 | | 24.06 | |
| Minimum Charge | Job | | 66.50 | | 66.50 | |
| **Good Grade** | | | | | | Includes material and labor to install |
| Demolish | Ea. | | 12.35 | | 12.35 | washing machine. New hoses not |
| Install | Ea. | 555 | 203 | | 758 | included. |
| Demolish and Install | Ea. | 555 | 215.35 | | 770.35 | |
| Reinstall | Ea. | | 162.08 | | 162.08 | |
| Clean | Ea. | .06 | 24 | | 24.06 | |
| Minimum Charge | Job | | 66.50 | | 66.50 | |
| **Premium Grade** | | | | | | Includes material and labor to install |
| Demolish | Ea. | | 12.35 | | 12.35 | washing machine with digital |
| Install | Ea. | 1275 | 405 | | 1680 | computer readouts and large capacity. |
| Demolish and Install | Ea. | 1275 | 417.35 | | 1692.35 | New hoses not included. |
| Reinstall | Ea. | | 324.16 | | 324.16 | |
| Clean | Ea. | .06 | 24 | | 24.06 | |
| Minimum Charge | Job | | 66.50 | | 66.50 | |
| **Washer / Dryer Combination Unit** | | | | | | Includes material and labor to install |
| Demolish | Ea. | | 12.35 | | 12.35 | electric washer/dryer combination |
| Install | Ea. | 985 | 53.50 | | 1038.50 | unit, 27" wide, stackable or unitized. |
| Demolish and Install | Ea. | 985 | 65.85 | | 1050.85 | |
| Reinstall | Ea. | | 42.69 | | 42.69 | |
| Clean | Ea. | .06 | 24 | | 24.06 | |
| Minimum Charge | Job | | 66.50 | | 66.50 | |

## Refrigerator

| | Unit | Material | Labor | Equip. | Total | Specification |
|---|---|---|---|---|---|---|
| **12 Cubic Foot** | | | | | | Includes material and labor to install a |
| Demolish | Ea. | | 37 | | 37 | refrigerator. |
| Install | Ea. | 535 | 53.50 | | 588.50 | |
| Demolish and Install | Ea. | 535 | 90.50 | | 625.50 | |
| Reinstall | Ea. | | 42.69 | | 42.69 | |
| Clean | Ea. | .06 | 24 | | 24.06 | |
| Minimum Charge | Job | | 66.50 | | 66.50 | |
| **16 Cubic Foot** | | | | | | Includes material and labor to install a |
| Demolish | Ea. | | 37 | | 37 | refrigerator. |
| Install | Ea. | 565 | 59.50 | | 624.50 | |
| Demolish and Install | Ea. | 565 | 96.50 | | 661.50 | |
| Reinstall | Ea. | | 47.43 | | 47.43 | |
| Clean | Ea. | .06 | 24 | | 24.06 | |
| Minimum Charge | Job | | 66.50 | | 66.50 | |

| Refrigerator | Unit | Material | Labor | Equip. | Total | Specification |
|---|---|---|---|---|---|---|
| **18 Cubic Foot** | | | | | | |
| Demolish | Ea. | | 37 | | 37 | Includes material and labor to install a |
| Install | Ea. | 660 | 66.50 | | 726.50 | refrigerator. |
| Demolish and Install | Ea. | 660 | 103.50 | | 763.50 | |
| Reinstall | Ea. | | 53.36 | | 53.36 | |
| Clean | Ea. | .06 | 24 | | 24.06 | |
| Minimum Charge | Job | | 66.50 | | 66.50 | |
| **21 Cubic Foot** | | | | | | |
| Demolish | Ea. | | 37 | | 37 | Includes material and labor to install a |
| Install | Ea. | 840 | 76 | | 916 | refrigerator. |
| Demolish and Install | Ea. | 840 | 113 | | 953 | |
| Reinstall | Ea. | | 60.98 | | 60.98 | |
| Clean | Ea. | .06 | 24 | | 24.06 | |
| Minimum Charge | Job | | 66.50 | | 66.50 | |
| **24 Cubic Foot** | | | | | | |
| Demolish | Ea. | | 37 | | 37 | Includes material and labor to install a |
| Install | Ea. | 1125 | 76 | | 1201 | refrigerator. |
| Demolish and Install | Ea. | 1125 | 113 | | 1238 | |
| Reinstall | Ea. | | 60.98 | | 60.98 | |
| Clean | Ea. | .06 | 24 | | 24.06 | |
| Minimum Charge | Job | | 66.50 | | 66.50 | |
| **27 Cubic Foot** | | | | | | |
| Demolish | Ea. | | 37 | | 37 | Includes material and labor to install a |
| Install | Ea. | 2075 | 53.50 | | 2128.50 | refrigerator. |
| Demolish and Install | Ea. | 2075 | 90.50 | | 2165.50 | |
| Reinstall | Ea. | | 42.69 | | 42.69 | |
| Clean | Ea. | .06 | 24 | | 24.06 | |
| Minimum Charge | Job | | 66.50 | | 66.50 | |
| **Ice Maker** | | | | | | |
| Install | Ea. | 60.50 | 50.50 | | 111 | Includes labor and material to install |
| Minimum Charge | Job | | 66.50 | | 66.50 | an automatic ice maker in a refrigerator. |

| Freezer | Unit | Material | Labor | Equip. | Total | Specification |
|---|---|---|---|---|---|---|
| **15 Cubic Foot** | | | | | | |
| Demolish | Ea. | | 37 | | 37 | Cost includes material and labor to |
| Install | Ea. | 550 | 53.50 | | 603.50 | install 15 cubic foot freezer. |
| Demolish and Install | Ea. | 550 | 90.50 | | 640.50 | |
| Reinstall | Ea. | | 42.69 | | 42.69 | |
| Clean | Ea. | .06 | 24 | | 24.06 | |
| Minimum Charge | Job | | 66.50 | | 66.50 | |
| **18 Cubic Foot** | | | | | | |
| Demolish | Ea. | | 37 | | 37 | Cost includes material and labor to |
| Install | Ea. | 735 | 53.50 | | 788.50 | install 18 cubic foot freezer. |
| Demolish and Install | Ea. | 735 | 90.50 | | 825.50 | |
| Reinstall | Ea. | | 42.69 | | 42.69 | |
| Clean | Ea. | .06 | 24 | | 24.06 | |
| Minimum Charge | Job | | 66.50 | | 66.50 | |
| **21 Cubic Foot** | | | | | | |
| Demolish | Ea. | | 37 | | 37 | Includes material and labor to install a |
| Install | Ea. | 570 | 53.50 | | 623.50 | 15 to 23 cubic foot deep freezer. |
| Demolish and Install | Ea. | 570 | 90.50 | | 660.50 | |
| Reinstall | Ea. | | 42.69 | | 42.69 | |
| Clean | Ea. | .06 | 24 | | 24.06 | |
| Minimum Charge | Job | | 66.50 | | 66.50 | |

# Improvements / Appliances / Treatments

| Freezer | | Unit | Material | Labor | Equip. | Total | Specification |
|---|---|---|---|---|---|---|---|
| **24 Cubic Foot** | | | | | | | |
| | Demolish | Ea. | | 37 | | 37 | Includes material and labor to install a |
| | Install | Ea. | 635 | 107 | | 742 | 24 cubic foot deep freezer. |
| | Demolish and Install | Ea. | 635 | 144 | | 779 | |
| | Reinstall | Ea. | | 85.38 | | 85.38 | |
| | Clean | Ea. | .06 | 24 | | 24.06 | |
| | Minimum Charge | Job | | 66.50 | | 66.50 | |
| **Chest-type** | | | | | | | |
| | Demolish | Ea. | | 37 | | 37 | Cost includes material and labor to |
| | Install | Ea. | 550 | 53.50 | | 603.50 | install 15 cubic foot freezer. |
| | Demolish and Install | Ea. | 550 | 90.50 | | 640.50 | |
| | Clean | Ea. | .06 | 24 | | 24.06 | |
| | Minimum Charge | Job | | 66.50 | | 66.50 | |

| Dishwasher | | Unit | Material | Labor | Equip. | Total | Specification |
|---|---|---|---|---|---|---|---|
| **4 Cycle** | | | | | | | |
| | Demolish | Ea. | | 29.50 | | 29.50 | Includes material and labor to install |
| | Install | Ea. | 325 | 126 | | 451 | good grade automatic dishwasher. |
| | Demolish and Install | Ea. | 325 | 155.50 | | 480.50 | |
| | Reinstall | Ea. | | 100.92 | | 100.92 | |
| | Clean | Ea. | .06 | 24 | | 24.06 | |
| | Minimum Charge | Job | | 66.50 | | 66.50 | |

| Garbage Disposal | | Unit | Material | Labor | Equip. | Total | Specification |
|---|---|---|---|---|---|---|---|
| **In Sink Unit** | | | | | | | |
| | Demolish | Ea. | | 28 | | 28 | Cost includes material and labor to |
| | Install | Ea. | 82.50 | 50.50 | | 133 | install 1/2 HP custom disposal unit. |
| | Demolish and Install | Ea. | 82.50 | 78.50 | | 161 | |
| | Reinstall | Ea. | | 40.37 | | 40.37 | |
| | Clean | Ea. | .02 | 6.85 | | 6.87 | |
| | Minimum Charge | Job | | 66.50 | | 66.50 | |

| Trash Compactor | | Unit | Material | Labor | Equip. | Total | Specification |
|---|---|---|---|---|---|---|---|
| **4 to 1 Compaction** | | | | | | | |
| | Demolish | Ea. | | 27.50 | | 27.50 | Includes material and labor to install a |
| | Install | Ea. | 695 | 72.50 | | 767.50 | trash compactor. |
| | Demolish and Install | Ea. | 695 | 100 | | 795 | |
| | Reinstall | Ea. | | 57.86 | | 57.86 | |
| | Clean | Ea. | .06 | 16.70 | | 16.76 | |
| | Minimum Charge | Job | | 66.50 | | 66.50 | |

| Kitchenette Unit | | Unit | Material | Labor | Equip. | Total | Specification |
|---|---|---|---|---|---|---|---|
| **Range, Refrigerator and Sink** | | | | | | | |
| | Demolish | Ea. | | 110 | | 110 | Includes material and labor to install |
| | Install | Ea. | 3525 | 420 | | 3945 | range/refrigerator/sink unit, 72" |
| | Demolish and Install | Ea. | 3525 | 530 | | 4055 | wide, base unit only. |
| | Reinstall | Ea. | | 336.40 | | 336.40 | |
| | Clean | Ea. | .91 | 12 | | 12.91 | |
| | Minimum Charge | Job | | 66.50 | | 66.50 | |

# Improvements / Appliances / Treatments

| Bath Accessories | | Unit | Material | Labor | Equip. | Total | Specification |
|---|---|---|---|---|---|---|---|
| **Towel Bar** | | | | | | | |
| | Demolish | Ea. | | 6.20 | | 6.20 | Includes material and labor to install |
| | Install | Ea. | 42 | 15.05 | | 57.05 | towel bar up to 24" long. |
| | Demolish and Install | Ea. | 42 | 21.25 | | 63.25 | |
| | Reinstall | Ea. | | 12.05 | | 12.05 | |
| | Clean | Ea. | | 3.34 | | 3.34 | |
| | Minimum Charge | Job | | 181 | | 181 | |
| **Toothbrush Holder** | | | | | | | |
| | Demolish | Ea. | | 6.20 | | 6.20 | Includes material and labor to install a |
| | Install | Ea. | 16.65 | 18.10 | | 34.75 | surface mounted tumbler and |
| | Demolish and Install | Ea. | 16.65 | 24.30 | | 40.95 | toothbrush holder. |
| | Reinstall | Ea. | | 14.46 | | 14.46 | |
| | Clean | Ea. | | 3.34 | | 3.34 | |
| | Minimum Charge | Job | | 181 | | 181 | |
| **Grab Rail** | | | | | | | |
| | Demolish | Ea. | | 9.25 | | 9.25 | Includes material and labor to install a |
| | Install | Ea. | 33 | 15.70 | | 48.70 | 24" long grab bar. Blocking is not |
| | Demolish and Install | Ea. | 33 | 24.95 | | 57.95 | included. |
| | Reinstall | Ea. | | 12.58 | | 12.58 | |
| | Clean | Ea. | .36 | 5.55 | | 5.91 | |
| | Minimum Charge | Job | | 181 | | 181 | |
| **Soap Dish** | | | | | | | |
| | Demolish | Ea. | | 6.20 | | 6.20 | Includes material and labor to install a |
| | Install | Ea. | 12 | 18.10 | | 30.10 | surface mounted soap dish. |
| | Demolish and Install | Ea. | 12 | 24.30 | | 36.30 | |
| | Reinstall | Ea. | | 14.46 | | 14.46 | |
| | Clean | Ea. | | 3.34 | | 3.34 | |
| | Minimum Charge | Job | | 181 | | 181 | |
| **Toilet Paper Roller** | | | | | | | |
| | Demolish | Ea. | | 6.20 | | 6.20 | Includes material and labor to install a |
| | Install | Ea. | 18.60 | 12.05 | | 30.65 | surface mounted toilet tissue dispenser. |
| | Demolish and Install | Ea. | 18.60 | 18.25 | | 36.85 | |
| | Reinstall | Ea. | | 9.64 | | 9.64 | |
| | Clean | Ea. | .36 | 8.35 | | 8.71 | |
| | Minimum Charge | Job | | 181 | | 181 | |
| **Dispenser** | | | | | | | |
| **Soap** | | | | | | | |
| | Demolish | Ea. | | 8.25 | | 8.25 | Includes material and labor to install a |
| | Install | Ea. | 51.50 | 18.10 | | 69.60 | surface mounted soap dispenser. |
| | Demolish and Install | Ea. | 51.50 | 26.35 | | 77.85 | |
| | Reinstall | Ea. | | 14.46 | | 14.46 | |
| | Clean | Ea. | .36 | 8.35 | | 8.71 | |
| | Minimum Charge | Job | | 181 | | 181 | |
| **Towel** | | | | | | | |
| | Demolish | Ea. | | 9.25 | | 9.25 | Includes material and labor to install a |
| | Install | Ea. | 45.50 | 22.50 | | 68 | surface mounted towel dispenser. |
| | Demolish and Install | Ea. | 45.50 | 31.75 | | 77.25 | |
| | Reinstall | Ea. | | 18.08 | | 18.08 | |
| | Clean | Ea. | .36 | 11.10 | | 11.46 | |
| | Minimum Charge | Job | | 181 | | 181 | |
| **Seat Cover** | | | | | | | |
| | Demolish | Ea. | | 6.20 | | 6.20 | Includes material and labor to install a |
| | Install | Ea. | 38 | 24 | | 62 | surface mounted toilet seat cover |
| | Demolish and Install | Ea. | 38 | 30.20 | | 68.20 | dispenser. |
| | Reinstall | Ea. | | 19.29 | | 19.29 | |
| | Clean | Ea. | .36 | 8.35 | | 8.71 | |
| | Minimum Charge | Job | | 181 | | 181 | |

# Improvements / Appliances / Treatments

| Bath Accessories | | Unit | Material | Labor | Equip. | Total | Specification |
|---|---|---|---|---|---|---|---|
| **Sanitary Napkin** | | | | | | | |
| | Demolish | Ea. | | 15.60 | | 15.60 | Includes material and labor to install a |
| | Install | Ea. | 37.50 | 38 | | 75.50 | surface mounted sanitary napkin |
| | Demolish and Install | Ea. | 37.50 | 53.60 | | 91.10 | dispenser. |
| | Reinstall | Ea. | | 30.45 | | 30.45 | |
| | Clean | Ea. | .19 | 11.10 | | 11.29 | |
| | Minimum Charge | Job | | 181 | | 181 | |
| **Partition** | | | | | | | |
| **Urinal** | | | | | | | |
| | Demolish | Ea. | | 18.55 | | 18.55 | Includes material and labor to install a |
| | Install | Ea. | 223 | 90.50 | | 313.50 | urinal screen. |
| | Demolish and Install | Ea. | 223 | 109.05 | | 332.05 | |
| | Reinstall | Ea. | | 72.32 | | 72.32 | |
| | Clean | Ea. | .55 | 7.40 | | 7.95 | |
| | Minimum Charge | Job | | 181 | | 181 | |
| **Toilet** | | | | | | | |
| | Demolish | Ea. | | 55 | | 55 | Includes material and labor to install |
| | Install | Ea. | 535 | 145 | | 680 | baked enamel standard size partition, |
| | Demolish and Install | Ea. | 535 | 200 | | 735 | floor or ceiling mounted with one wall |
| | Reinstall | Ea. | | 115.71 | | 115.71 | and one door. |
| | Clean | Ea. | 3.63 | 16.70 | | 20.33 | |
| | Minimum Charge | Job | | 181 | | 181 | |
| **Handicap** | | | | | | | |
| | Demolish | Ea. | | 55 | | 55 | Includes material and labor to install |
| | Install | Ea. | 810 | 145 | | 955 | baked enamel handicap partition, |
| | Demolish and Install | Ea. | 810 | 200 | | 1010 | floor or ceiling mounted with one wall |
| | Reinstall | Ea. | | 115.71 | | 115.71 | and one door. |
| | Clean | Ea. | 3.63 | 16.70 | | 20.33 | |
| | Minimum Charge | Job | | 181 | | 181 | |

| Fire Prevention / Protection | | Unit | Material | Labor | Equip. | Total | Specification |
|---|---|---|---|---|---|---|---|
| **Fire Extinguisher** | | | | | | | |
| **5# Carbon Dioxide** | | | | | | | |
| | Install | Ea. | 143 | | | 143 | Includes labor and material to install one wall mounted 5 lb. carbon dioxide factory charged unit, complete with hose, horn and wall mounting bracket. |
| **10# Carbon Dioxide** | | | | | | | |
| | Install | Ea. | 176 | | | 176 | Includes labor and material to install one wall mounted 10 lb. carbon dioxide factory charged unit, complete with hose, horn and wall mounting bracket. |
| **15# Carbon Dioxide** | | | | | | | |
| | Install | Ea. | 209 | | | 209 | Includes labor and material to install one wall mounted 15 lb. carbon dioxide factory charged unit, complete with hose, horn and wall mounting bracket. |

# Improvements / Appliances / Treatments

| Fire Prevention / Protection | Unit | Material | Labor | Equip. | Total | Specification |
|---|---|---|---|---|---|---|
| **5# Dry Chemical** | | | | | | |
| Install | Ea. | 66 | | | 66 | Includes labor and material to install one wall mounted 5 lb. dry chemical factory charged unit, complete with hose, horn and wall mounting bracket. |
| **20# Dry Chemical** | | | | | | |
| Install | Ea. | 121 | | | 121 | Includes labor and material to install one wall mounted 20 lb. dry chemical factory charged unit, complete with hose, horn and wall mounting bracket. |

| Gutters | Unit | Material | Labor | Equip. | Total | Specification |
|---|---|---|---|---|---|---|
| **Galvanized** | | | | | | |
| Demolish | L.F. | | 1.24 | | 1.24 | Cost includes material and labor to install 5" galvanized steel gutter with enamel finish, fittings, hangers, and corners. |
| Install | L.F. | 1.49 | 3.35 | | 4.84 | |
| Demolish and Install | L.F. | 1.49 | 4.59 | | 6.08 | |
| Reinstall | L.F. | | 2.68 | | 2.68 | |
| Clean | L.F. | | .36 | | .36 | |
| Paint | L.F. | .19 | .97 | | 1.16 | |
| Minimum Charge | Job | | 201 | | 201 | |
| **Aluminum** | | | | | | |
| Demolish | L.F. | | 1.24 | | 1.24 | Cost includes material and labor to install 5" aluminum gutter with enamel finish, fittings, hangers, and corners. |
| Install | L.F. | 2.19 | 3.35 | | 5.54 | |
| Demolish and Install | L.F. | 2.19 | 4.59 | | 6.78 | |
| Reinstall | L.F. | | 2.68 | | 2.68 | |
| Clean | L.F. | | .36 | | .36 | |
| Paint | L.F. | .19 | .97 | | 1.16 | |
| Minimum Charge | Job | | 201 | | 201 | |
| **Copper** | | | | | | |
| Demolish | L.F. | | 1.24 | | 1.24 | Cost includes material and labor to install 5" half-round copper gutter with fittings, hangers, and corners. |
| Install | L.F. | 7.15 | 3.35 | | 10.50 | |
| Demolish and Install | L.F. | 7.15 | 4.59 | | 11.74 | |
| Reinstall | L.F. | | 2.68 | | 2.68 | |
| Clean | L.F. | | .36 | | .36 | |
| Minimum Charge | Job | | 201 | | 201 | |
| **Plastic** | | | | | | |
| Demolish | L.F. | | 1.24 | | 1.24 | Cost includes material and labor to install 4" white vinyl gutter fittings, hangers, and corners. |
| Install | L.F. | 1.10 | 3.29 | | 4.39 | |
| Demolish and Install | L.F. | 1.10 | 4.53 | | 5.63 | |
| Reinstall | L.F. | | 2.63 | | 2.63 | |
| Clean | L.F. | | .36 | | .36 | |
| Paint | L.F. | .19 | .97 | | 1.16 | |
| Minimum Charge | Job | | 201 | | 201 | |

| Downspouts | Unit | Material | Labor | Equip. | Total | Specification |
|---|---|---|---|---|---|---|
| **Galvanized** | | | | | | |
| Demolish | L.F. | | .85 | | .85 | Cost includes material and labor to install 4" diameter downspout with enamel finish. |
| Install | L.F. | 2.43 | 2.78 | | 5.21 | |
| Demolish and Install | L.F. | 2.43 | 3.63 | | 6.06 | |
| Reinstall | L.F. | | 2.22 | | 2.22 | |
| Clean | L.F. | | .36 | | .36 | |
| Paint | L.F. | .19 | .97 | | 1.16 | |
| Minimum Charge | Job | | 201 | | 201 | |

# Improvements / Appliances / Treatments

| Downspouts | Unit | Material | Labor | Equip. | Total | Specification |
|---|---|---|---|---|---|---|
| **Aluminum** | | | | | | |
| Demolish | L.F. | | .85 | | .85 | Includes material and labor to install |
| Install | L.F. | 2.75 | 2.87 | | 5.62 | aluminum enameled downspout. |
| Demolish and Install | L.F. | 2.75 | 3.72 | | 6.47 | |
| Reinstall | L.F. | | 2.30 | | 2.30 | |
| Clean | L.F. | | .36 | | .36 | |
| Paint | L.F. | .19 | .97 | | 1.16 | |
| Minimum Charge | Job | | 201 | | 201 | |
| **Copper** | | | | | | |
| Demolish | L.F. | | .85 | | .85 | Includes material and labor to install |
| Install | L.F. | 8.65 | 2.12 | | 10.77 | round copper downspout. |
| Demolish and Install | L.F. | 8.65 | 2.97 | | 11.62 | |
| Reinstall | L.F. | | 1.69 | | 1.69 | |
| Clean | L.F. | | .36 | | .36 | |
| Paint | L.F. | .19 | .97 | | 1.16 | |
| Minimum Charge | Job | | 201 | | 201 | |
| **Plastic** | | | | | | |
| Demolish | L.F. | | .85 | | .85 | Cost includes material and labor to |
| Install | L.F. | .83 | 1.92 | | 2.75 | install 2" x 3" vinyl rectangular |
| Demolish and Install | L.F. | .83 | 2.77 | | 3.60 | downspouts. |
| Reinstall | L.F. | | 1.53 | | 1.53 | |
| Clean | L.F. | | .36 | | .36 | |
| Paint | L.F. | .19 | .97 | | 1.16 | |
| Minimum Charge | Job | | 201 | | 201 | |

| Shutters | Unit | Material | Labor | Equip. | Total | Specification |
|---|---|---|---|---|---|---|
| **Exterior** | | | | | | |
| **25″ High** | | | | | | |
| Demolish | Ea. | | 9.25 | | 9.25 | Includes material and labor to install |
| Install | Pr. | 103 | 36 | | 139 | pair of exterior shutters 25" x 16", |
| Demolish and Install | Pr. | 103 | 45.25 | | 148.25 | unpainted, installed as fixed shutters |
| Reinstall | Pr. | | 36.16 | | 36.16 | on concrete or wood frame. |
| Clean | Ea. | .07 | 8 | | 8.07 | |
| Paint | Ea. | 1.52 | 16.90 | | 18.42 | |
| Minimum Charge | Job | | 181 | | 181 | |
| **39″ High** | | | | | | |
| Demolish | Ea. | | 9.25 | | 9.25 | Includes material and labor to install |
| Install | Pr. | 111 | 36 | | 147 | pair of shutters 39" x 16", unpainted, |
| Demolish and Install | Pr. | 111 | 45.25 | | 156.25 | installed as fixed shutters on concrete |
| Reinstall | Pr. | | 36.16 | | 36.16 | or wood frame. |
| Clean | Ea. | .07 | 8 | | 8.07 | |
| Paint | Ea. | 2.37 | 23 | | 25.37 | |
| Minimum Charge | Job | | 181 | | 181 | |
| **51″ High** | | | | | | |
| Demolish | Ea. | | 9.25 | | 9.25 | Includes material and labor to install |
| Install | Pr. | 123 | 36 | | 159 | pair of shutters 51" x 16", unpainted, |
| Demolish and Install | Pr. | 123 | 45.25 | | 168.25 | installed as fixed shutters on concrete |
| Reinstall | Pr. | | 36.16 | | 36.16 | or wood frame. |
| Clean | Ea. | .07 | 8 | | 8.07 | |
| Paint | Ea. | 3.08 | 23.50 | | 26.58 | |
| Minimum Charge | Job | | 181 | | 181 | |

# Improvements / Appliances / Treatments

| Shutters | | Unit | Material | Labor | Equip. | Total | Specification |
|---|---|---|---|---|---|---|---|
| **59″ High** | | | | | | | |
| | Demolish | Ea. | | 9.25 | | 9.25 | Includes material and labor to install |
| | Install | Pr. | 174 | 36 | | 210 | pair of shutters 59″ x 16″, unpainted, |
| | Demolish and Install | Pr. | 174 | 45.25 | | 219.25 | installed as fixed shutters on concrete |
| | Reinstall | Pr. | | 36.16 | | 36.16 | or wood frame. |
| | Clean | Ea. | .07 | 8 | | 8.07 | |
| | Paint | Ea. | 3.55 | 26 | | 29.55 | |
| | Minimum Charge | Job | | 181 | | 181 | |
| **67″ High** | | | | | | | |
| | Demolish | Ea. | | 9.25 | | 9.25 | Includes material and labor to install |
| | Install | Pr. | 175 | 40 | | 215 | pair of shutters 67″ x 16″, unpainted, |
| | Demolish and Install | Pr. | 175 | 49.25 | | 224.25 | installed as fixed shutters on concrete |
| | Reinstall | Pr. | | 40.18 | | 40.18 | or wood frame. |
| | Clean | Ea. | .07 | 8 | | 8.07 | |
| | Paint | Ea. | 4.06 | 29 | | 33.06 | |
| | Minimum Charge | Job | | 181 | | 181 | |
| **Interior Wood** | | | | | | | |
| **23″ x 24″, 2 Panel** | | | | | | | |
| | Demolish | Ea. | | 9.25 | | 9.25 | Cost includes material and labor to |
| | Install | Ea. | 95 | 21.50 | | 116.50 | install 23″ x 24″, 4 panel interior |
| | Demolish and Install | Ea. | 95 | 30.75 | | 125.75 | moveable pine shutter, 1-1/4″ louver, |
| | Reinstall | Ea. | | 17.02 | | 17.02 | knobs and hooks and hinges. |
| | Clean | Ea. | .07 | 8 | | 8.07 | |
| | Paint | Ea. | 1.16 | 22.50 | | 23.66 | |
| | Minimum Charge | Job | | 181 | | 181 | |
| **27″ x 24″, 4 Panel** | | | | | | | |
| | Demolish | Ea. | | 9.25 | | 9.25 | Cost includes material and labor to |
| | Install | Ea. | 111 | 21.50 | | 132.50 | install 27″ x 24″, 4 panel interior |
| | Demolish and Install | Ea. | 111 | 30.75 | | 141.75 | moveable pine shutter, 1-1/4″ louver, |
| | Reinstall | Ea. | | 17.02 | | 17.02 | knobs and hooks and hinges. |
| | Clean | Ea. | .07 | 8 | | 8.07 | |
| | Paint | Ea. | 1.16 | 22.50 | | 23.66 | |
| | Minimum Charge | Job | | 181 | | 181 | |
| **31″ x 24″, 4 Panel** | | | | | | | |
| | Demolish | Ea. | | 9.25 | | 9.25 | Cost includes material and labor to |
| | Install | Ea. | 128 | 21.50 | | 149.50 | install 31″ x 24″, 4 panel interior |
| | Demolish and Install | Ea. | 128 | 30.75 | | 158.75 | moveable pine shutter, 1-1/4″ louver, |
| | Reinstall | Ea. | | 17.02 | | 17.02 | knobs and hooks and hinges. |
| | Clean | Ea. | .07 | 8 | | 8.07 | |
| | Paint | Ea. | 1.16 | 22.50 | | 23.66 | |
| | Minimum Charge | Job | | 181 | | 181 | |
| **35″ x 24″, 4 Panel** | | | | | | | |
| | Demolish | Ea. | | 9.25 | | 9.25 | Cost includes material and labor to |
| | Install | Ea. | 128 | 21.50 | | 149.50 | install 35″ x 24″, 4 panel interior |
| | Demolish and Install | Ea. | 128 | 30.75 | | 158.75 | moveable pine shutter, 1-1/4″ louver, |
| | Reinstall | Ea. | | 17.02 | | 17.02 | knobs and hooks and hinges. |
| | Clean | Ea. | .07 | 8 | | 8.07 | |
| | Paint | Ea. | 1.16 | 22.50 | | 23.66 | |
| | Minimum Charge | Job | | 181 | | 181 | |
| **39″ x 24″, 4 Panel** | | | | | | | |
| | Demolish | Ea. | | 9.25 | | 9.25 | Cost includes material and labor to |
| | Install | Ea. | 147 | 21.50 | | 168.50 | install 39″ x 24″, 4 panel interior |
| | Demolish and Install | Ea. | 147 | 30.75 | | 177.75 | moveable pine shutter, 1-1/4″ louver, |
| | Reinstall | Ea. | | 17.02 | | 17.02 | knobs and hooks and hinges. |
| | Clean | Ea. | .07 | 8 | | 8.07 | |
| | Paint | Ea. | 1.16 | 22.50 | | 23.66 | |
| | Minimum Charge | Job | | 181 | | 181 | |

# Improvements / Appliances / Treatments

| Shutters | Unit | Material | Labor | Equip. | Total | Specification |
|---|---|---|---|---|---|---|
| **47" x 24", 4 Panel** | | | | | | |
| Demolish | Ea. | | 9.25 | | 9.25 | Cost includes material and labor to |
| Install | Ea. | 162 | 21.50 | | 183.50 | install 47" x 24", 4 panel interior |
| Demolish and Install | Ea. | 162 | 30.75 | | 192.75 | moveable pine shutter, 1-1/4" louver, |
| Reinstall | Ea. | | 17.02 | | 17.02 | knobs and hooks and hinges. |
| Clean | Ea. | .07 | 8 | | 8.07 | |
| Paint | Ea. | 1.20 | 24 | | 25.20 | |
| Minimum Charge | Job | | 181 | | 181 | |

| Awning | Unit | Material | Labor | Equip. | Total | Specification |
|---|---|---|---|---|---|---|
| **Standard Aluminum** | | | | | | |
| **36" Wide x 30" Deep** | | | | | | |
| Demolish | Ea. | | 9.25 | | 9.25 | Includes material and labor to install |
| Install | Ea. | 243 | 30 | | 273 | one aluminum awning with |
| Demolish and Install | Ea. | 243 | 39.25 | | 282.25 | weather-resistant finish. |
| Reinstall | Ea. | | 24.11 | | 24.11 | |
| Clean | Ea. | | 11.10 | | 11.10 | |
| Minimum Charge | Job | | 181 | | 181 | |
| **48" Wide x 30" Deep** | | | | | | |
| Demolish | Ea. | | 9.25 | | 9.25 | Includes material and labor to install |
| Install | Ea. | 271 | 36 | | 307 | one aluminum awning with |
| Demolish and Install | Ea. | 271 | 45.25 | | 316.25 | weather-resistant finish. |
| Reinstall | Ea. | | 28.93 | | 28.93 | |
| Clean | Ea. | | 11.10 | | 11.10 | |
| Minimum Charge | Job | | 181 | | 181 | |
| **60" Wide x 30" Deep** | | | | | | |
| Demolish | Ea. | | 18.55 | | 18.55 | Includes material and labor to install |
| Install | Ea. | 298 | 40 | | 338 | one aluminum awning with |
| Demolish and Install | Ea. | 298 | 58.55 | | 356.55 | weather-resistant finish. |
| Reinstall | Ea. | | 32.14 | | 32.14 | |
| Clean | Ea. | | 11.10 | | 11.10 | |
| Minimum Charge | Job | | 181 | | 181 | |
| **72" Wide x 30" Deep** | | | | | | |
| Demolish | Ea. | | 18.55 | | 18.55 | Includes material and labor to install |
| Install | Ea. | 325 | 45 | | 370 | one aluminum awning with |
| Demolish and Install | Ea. | 325 | 63.55 | | 388.55 | weather-resistant finish. |
| Reinstall | Ea. | | 36.16 | | 36.16 | |
| Clean | Ea. | | 11.10 | | 11.10 | |
| Minimum Charge | Job | | 181 | | 181 | |
| **Roll-up Type** | | | | | | |
| Demolish | S.F. | | .67 | | .67 | Includes material and labor to install |
| Install | S.F. | 11 | 3.62 | | 14.62 | an aluminum roll-up awning. |
| Demolish and Install | S.F. | 11 | 4.29 | | 15.29 | |
| Reinstall | S.F. | | 2.89 | | 2.89 | |
| Clean | S.F. | .03 | .56 | | .59 | |
| Minimum Charge | Job | | 181 | | 181 | |
| **Canvas** | | | | | | |
| **30" Wide** | | | | | | |
| Demolish | Ea. | | 5.55 | | 5.55 | Includes material and labor to install a |
| Install | Ea. | 215 | 30 | | 245 | canvas window awning. |
| Demolish and Install | Ea. | 215 | 35.55 | | 250.55 | |
| Reinstall | Ea. | | 24.11 | | 24.11 | |
| Clean | Ea. | | 3.34 | | 3.34 | |
| Minimum Charge | Job | | 181 | | 181 | |

# Improvements / Appliances / Treatments

## Awning

| | Unit | Material | Labor | Equip. | Total | Specification |
|---|---|---|---|---|---|---|
| **36″ Wide** | | | | | | |
| Demolish | Ea. | | 5.55 | | 5.55 | Includes material and labor to install a |
| Install | Ea. | 226 | 36 | | 262 | canvas window awning. |
| Demolish and Install | Ea. | 226 | 41.55 | | 267.55 | |
| Reinstall | Ea. | | 28.93 | | 28.93 | |
| Clean | Ea. | | 3.65 | | 3.65 | |
| Minimum Charge | Job | | 181 | | 181 | |
| **42″ Wide** | | | | | | |
| Demolish | Ea. | | 5.55 | | 5.55 | Includes material and labor to install a |
| Install | Ea. | 242 | 45 | | 287 | canvas window awning. |
| Demolish and Install | Ea. | 242 | 50.55 | | 292.55 | |
| Reinstall | Ea. | | 36.16 | | 36.16 | |
| Clean | Ea. | | 4.34 | | 4.34 | |
| Minimum Charge | Job | | 181 | | 181 | |
| **48″ Wide** | | | | | | |
| Demolish | Ea. | | 5.55 | | 5.55 | Includes material and labor to install a |
| Install | Ea. | 259 | 51.50 | | 310.50 | canvas window awning. |
| Demolish and Install | Ea. | 259 | 57.05 | | 316.05 | |
| Reinstall | Ea. | | 41.33 | | 41.33 | |
| Clean | Ea. | | 5.05 | | 5.05 | |
| Minimum Charge | Job | | 181 | | 181 | |
| **Cloth Canopy Cover** | | | | | | |
| **8′ x 10′** | | | | | | |
| Demolish | Ea. | | 305 | | 305 | Includes material and labor to install |
| Install | Ea. | 415 | 181 | | 596 | one 8′ x 10′ cloth canopy patio cover |
| Demolish and Install | Ea. | 415 | 486 | | 901 | with front bar and tension support |
| Reinstall | Ea. | | 144.64 | | 144.64 | rafters and 9″ valance. |
| Clean | Ea. | 2.90 | 44.50 | | 47.40 | |
| Minimum Charge | Job | | 360 | | 360 | |
| **8′ x 15′** | | | | | | |
| Demolish | Ea. | | 305 | | 305 | Includes material and labor to install |
| Install | Ea. | 560 | 181 | | 741 | one 8′ x 15′ cloth canopy patio cover |
| Demolish and Install | Ea. | 560 | 486 | | 1046 | with front bar and tension support |
| Reinstall | Ea. | | 144.64 | | 144.64 | rafters and 9″ valance. |
| Clean | Ea. | 2.90 | 66.50 | | 69.40 | |
| Minimum Charge | Job | | 360 | | 360 | |

## Vent

| | Unit | Material | Labor | Equip. | Total | Specification |
|---|---|---|---|---|---|---|
| **Small Roof Turbine** | | | | | | |
| Demolish | Ea. | | 9.25 | | 9.25 | Includes material and labor to install |
| Install | Ea. | 52.50 | 36 | | 88.50 | spinner ventilator, wind driven, |
| Demolish and Install | Ea. | 52.50 | 45.25 | | 97.75 | galvanized, 4″ neck diam, 180 CFM. |
| Reinstall | Ea. | | 28.96 | | 28.96 | |
| Clean | Ea. | | 5.95 | | 5.95 | |
| Minimum Charge | Job | | 203 | | 203 | |
| **Large Roof Turbine** | | | | | | |
| Demolish | Ea. | | 7.40 | | 7.40 | Includes material and labor to install |
| Install | Ea. | 60.50 | 51.50 | | 112 | spinner ventilator, wind driven, |
| Demolish and Install | Ea. | 60.50 | 58.90 | | 119.40 | galvanized, 8″ neck diam, 360 CFM. |
| Reinstall | Ea. | | 41.37 | | 41.37 | |
| Clean | Ea. | | 6.65 | | 6.65 | |
| Minimum Charge | Job | | 203 | | 203 | |

# Improvements / Appliances / Treatments

| Vent | | Unit | Material | Labor | Equip. | Total | Specification |
|---|---|---|---|---|---|---|---|
| **Gable Louvered** | | | | | | | |
| | Demolish | Ea. | | 18.55 | | 18.55 | Includes material and labor to install a |
| | Install | Ea. | 39 | 12.05 | | 51.05 | vinyl gable end vent. |
| | Demolish and Install | Ea. | 39 | 30.60 | | 69.60 | |
| | Reinstall | Ea. | | 9.64 | | 9.64 | |
| | Clean | Ea. | | 3.56 | | 3.56 | |
| | Paint | Ea. | .96 | 4.84 | | 5.80 | |
| | Minimum Charge | Job | | 181 | | 181 | |
| **Ridge Vent** | | | | | | | |
| | Demolish | L.F. | | .96 | | .96 | Includes material and labor to install a |
| | Install | L.F. | 2.95 | 2.60 | | 5.55 | mill finish aluminum ridge vent strip. |
| | Demolish and Install | L.F. | 2.95 | 3.56 | | 6.51 | |
| | Minimum Charge | Job | | 181 | | 181 | |
| **Foundation** | | | | | | | |
| | Demolish | Ea. | | 6.60 | | 6.60 | Includes material and labor to install |
| | Install | Ea. | 27 | 12.15 | | 39.15 | galvanized foundation block vent. |
| | Demolish and Install | Ea. | 27 | 18.75 | | 45.75 | |
| | Reinstall | Ea. | | 9.71 | | 9.71 | |
| | Clean | Ea. | .19 | 6.65 | | 6.84 | |
| | Minimum Charge | Job | | 181 | | 181 | |
| **Frieze** | | | | | | | |
| | Demolish | L.F. | | .66 | | .66 | Includes material and labor to install |
| | Install | L.F. | 1.03 | .82 | | 1.85 | pine frieze board. |
| | Demolish and Install | L.F. | 1.03 | 1.48 | | 2.51 | |
| | Reinstall | L.F. | | .66 | | .66 | |
| | Clean | L.F. | .04 | .22 | | .26 | |
| | Minimum Charge | Job | | 181 | | 181 | |
| **Water Heater Cap** | | | | | | | |
| | Demolish | Ea. | | 14.05 | | 14.05 | Includes material and labor to install a |
| | Install | Ea. | 27 | 50.50 | | 77.50 | galvanized steel water heater cap. |
| | Demolish and Install | Ea. | 27 | 64.55 | | 91.55 | |
| | Reinstall | Ea. | | 40.24 | | 40.24 | |
| | Clean | Ea. | 1.28 | 16.70 | | 17.98 | |

| Cupolas | | Unit | Material | Labor | Equip. | Total | Specification |
|---|---|---|---|---|---|---|---|
| **22″ x 22″** | | | | | | | |
| | Demolish | Ea. | | 176 | | 176 | Includes material and labor to install a |
| | Install | Ea. | 292 | 90.50 | | 382.50 | cedar cupola with aluminum roof |
| | Demolish and Install | Ea. | 292 | 266.50 | | 558.50 | covering. |
| | Reinstall | Ea. | | 72.32 | | 72.32 | |
| | Minimum Charge | Job | | 181 | | 181 | |
| **29″ x 29″** | | | | | | | |
| | Demolish | Ea. | | 176 | | 176 | Includes material and labor to install a |
| | Install | Ea. | 395 | 90.50 | | 485.50 | cedar cupola with aluminum roof |
| | Demolish and Install | Ea. | 395 | 266.50 | | 661.50 | covering. |
| | Reinstall | Ea. | | 72.32 | | 72.32 | |
| | Minimum Charge | Job | | 181 | | 181 | |
| **35″ x 35″** | | | | | | | |
| | Demolish | Ea. | | 176 | | 176 | Includes material and labor to install a |
| | Install | Ea. | 705 | 121 | | 826 | cedar cupola with aluminum roof |
| | Demolish and Install | Ea. | 705 | 297 | | 1002 | covering. |
| | Reinstall | Ea. | | 96.43 | | 96.43 | |
| | Minimum Charge | Job | | 181 | | 181 | |

| Cupolas | Unit | Material | Labor | Equip. | Total | Specification |
|---|---|---|---|---|---|---|
| **47" x 47"** | | | | | | |
| Demolish | Ea. | | 176 | | 176 | Includes material and labor to install a |
| Install | Ea. | 1250 | 181 | | 1431 | cedar cupola with aluminum roof |
| Demolish and Install | Ea. | 1250 | 357 | | 1607 | covering. |
| Reinstall | Ea. | | 144.64 | | 144.64 | |
| Minimum Charge | Job | | 181 | | 181 | |
| **Weather Vane** | | | | | | |
| Install | Ea. | 196 | 45 | | 241 | Includes minimum labor and |
| Minimum Charge | Job | | 181 | | 181 | equipment to install residential type weathervane. |

| Aluminum Carport | Unit | Material | Labor | Equip. | Total | Specification |
|---|---|---|---|---|---|---|
| **Natural Finish** | | | | | | |
| Demolish | S.F. | | 1.85 | | 1.85 | Includes material, labor and |
| Install | S.F. | 26.50 | 6.05 | 1.23 | 33.78 | equipment to install an aluminum |
| Demolish and Install | S.F. | 26.50 | 7.90 | 1.23 | 35.63 | carport. Foundations are not included. |
| Reinstall | S.F. | | 4.84 | .99 | 5.83 | |
| Clean | S.F. | .03 | .20 | | .23 | |
| Minimum Charge | Job | | 360 | | 360 | |
| **Enamel Finish** | | | | | | |
| Demolish | S.F. | | 1.85 | | 1.85 | Includes material, labor and |
| Install | S.F. | 26.50 | 6.05 | 1.23 | 33.78 | equipment to install an aluminum |
| Demolish and Install | S.F. | 26.50 | 7.90 | 1.23 | 35.63 | carport. Foundations are not included. |
| Reinstall | S.F. | | 4.84 | .99 | 5.83 | |
| Clean | S.F. | .03 | .20 | | .23 | |
| Minimum Charge | Job | | 360 | | 360 | |
| **20' x 20' Complete** | | | | | | |
| Demolish | Ea. | | 185 | | 185 | Includes material, labor and |
| Install | Ea. | 8225 | 605 | 123 | 8953 | equipment to install an aluminum |
| Demolish and Install | Ea. | 8225 | 790 | 123 | 9138 | carport. Foundations are not included. |
| Reinstall | Ea. | | 483.55 | 98.59 | 582.14 | |
| Clean | Ea. | .19 | 66.50 | | 66.69 | |
| Minimum Charge | Job | | 360 | | 360 | |
| **24' x 24' Complete** | | | | | | |
| Demolish | Ea. | | 185 | | 185 | Includes material, labor and |
| Install | Ea. | 11200 | 805 | 164 | 12169 | equipment to install an aluminum |
| Demolish and Install | Ea. | 11200 | 990 | 164 | 12354 | carport. Foundations are not included. |
| Reinstall | Ea. | | 644.74 | 131.46 | 776.20 | |
| Clean | Ea. | .19 | 133 | | 133.19 | |
| Minimum Charge | Job | | 360 | | 360 | |
| **Metal Support Posts** | | | | | | |
| Demolish | Ea. | | 2.47 | | 2.47 | Includes material and labor to install |
| Install | Ea. | 18.25 | 45 | | 63.25 | metal support posts for a carport. |
| Demolish and Install | Ea. | 18.25 | 47.47 | | 65.72 | |
| Reinstall | Ea. | | 36.16 | | 36.16 | |
| Clean | Ea. | .19 | 2.78 | | 2.97 | |
| Paint | Ea. | .14 | 6.30 | | 6.44 | |
| Minimum Charge | Job | | 360 | | 360 | |

# Improvements / Appliances / Treatments

| Storage Shed | | Unit | Material | Labor | Equip. | Total | Specification |
|---|---|---|---|---|---|---|---|
| **Aluminum** | | | | | | | |
| Pre-fab (8' x 10') | | | | | | | |
| | Demolish | Ea. | | 54 | | 54 | Includes material and labor to install |
| | Install | Ea. | 1750 | 530 | | 2280 | an aluminum storage shed. |
| | Demolish and Install | Ea. | 1750 | 584 | | 2334 | |
| | Clean | Ea. | 1.21 | 33.50 | | 34.71 | |
| | Minimum Charge | Ea. | | 450 | | 450 | |
| Pre-fab (10' x 12') | | | | | | | |
| | Demolish | Ea. | | 102 | | 102 | Includes material and labor to install |
| | Install | Ea. | 2275 | 530 | | 2805 | an aluminum storage shed. |
| | Demolish and Install | Ea. | 2275 | 632 | | 2907 | |
| | Clean | Ea. | 1.21 | 37 | | 38.21 | |
| | Minimum Charge | Ea. | | 450 | | 450 | |
| **Wood** | | | | | | | |
| Pre-fab (8' x 10') | | | | | | | |
| | Demolish | Ea. | | 54 | | 54 | Includes material and labor to install a |
| | Install | Ea. | 1550 | 530 | | 2080 | pre-fabricated wood storage shed. |
| | Demolish and Install | Ea. | 1550 | 584 | | 2134 | |
| | Clean | Ea. | 1.21 | 33.50 | | 34.71 | |
| | Minimum Charge | Ea. | | 450 | | 450 | |
| Pre-fab (10' x 12') | | | | | | | |
| | Demolish | Ea. | | 102 | | 102 | Includes material and labor to install a |
| | Install | Ea. | 1975 | 530 | | 2505 | pre-fabricated wood storage shed. |
| | Demolish and Install | Ea. | 1975 | 632 | | 2607 | |
| | Clean | Ea. | 1.21 | 37 | | 38.21 | |
| | Minimum Charge | Ea. | | 450 | | 450 | |

| Gazebo | | Unit | Material | Labor | Equip. | Total | Specification |
|---|---|---|---|---|---|---|---|
| **Good Grade** | | | | | | | |
| | Demolish | S.F. | | 2.96 | | 2.96 | Includes material and labor to install a |
| | Install | S.F. | 31 | 27 | | 58 | gazebo. |
| | Demolish and Install | S.F. | 31 | 29.96 | | 60.96 | |
| | Reinstall | S.F. | | 21.70 | | 21.70 | |
| | Clean | S.F. | .14 | 1.78 | | 1.92 | |
| | Minimum Charge | Job | | 181 | | 181 | |
| **Custom Grade** | | | | | | | |
| | Demolish | S.F. | | 2.96 | | 2.96 | Includes material and labor to install a |
| | Install | S.F. | 40.50 | 27 | | 67.50 | gazebo. |
| | Demolish and Install | S.F. | 40.50 | 29.96 | | 70.46 | |
| | Reinstall | S.F. | | 21.70 | | 21.70 | |
| | Clean | S.F. | .14 | 1.78 | | 1.92 | |
| | Minimum Charge | Job | | 181 | | 181 | |
| **Bench Seating** | | | | | | | |
| | Demolish | L.F. | | 4.94 | | 4.94 | Includes material and labor to install |
| | Install | L.F. | 2.42 | 18.10 | | 20.52 | pressure treated bench seating. |
| | Demolish and Install | L.F. | 2.42 | 23.04 | | 25.46 | |
| | Reinstall | L.F. | | 14.46 | | 14.46 | |
| | Clean | L.F. | .14 | 1.33 | | 1.47 | |
| | Paint | L.F. | .57 | 2.52 | | 3.09 | |
| | Minimum Charge | Job | | 181 | | 181 | |
| **Re-screen** | | | | | | | |
| | Install | S.F. | 1.17 | 1.45 | | 2.62 | Includes labor and material to |
| | Minimum Charge | Job | | 181 | | 181 | re-screen wood frame. |

# Improvements / Appliances / Treatments

| Pool | | Unit | Material | Labor | Equip. | Total | Specification |
|---|---|---|---|---|---|---|---|
| **Screen Enclosure** | | | | | | | |
| **Re-screen** | | | | | | | |
| | Install | SF Wall | | 4.48 | | 4.48 | Includes material and labor to install a |
| | Minimum Charge | Job | | 181 | | 181 | screen enclosure for a pool. |
| **Screen Door** | | | | | | | |
| | Demolish | Ea. | | 7.15 | | 7.15 | Includes material and labor to install |
| | Install | Ea. | 146 | 60.50 | | 206.50 | wood screen door with aluminum cloth |
| | Demolish and Install | Ea. | 146 | 67.65 | | 213.65 | screen. Frame and hardware not |
| | Reinstall | Ea. | | 48.21 | | 48.21 | included. |
| | Clean | Ea. | .13 | 9.60 | | 9.73 | |
| | Paint | Ea. | 3.51 | 12.60 | | 16.11 | |
| | Minimum Charge | Job | | 181 | | 181 | |
| **Heater / Motor** | | | | | | | |
| | Demolish | Ea. | | 35.50 | | 35.50 | Includes material and labor to install |
| | Install | Ea. | 2450 | 455 | | 2905 | swimming pool heater, not incl. base |
| | Demolish and Install | Ea. | 2450 | 490.50 | | 2940.50 | or pad, elec., 12 kW, 4,800 gal |
| | Reinstall | Ea. | | 363.03 | | 363.03 | pool, incl. pump. |
| | Clean | Ea. | 3.63 | 33.50 | | 37.13 | |
| | Minimum Charge | Job | | 205 | | 205 | |
| **Filter System** | | | | | | | |
| | Demolish | Ea. | | 59.50 | | 59.50 | Includes material, labor and |
| | Install | Total | 1450 | 325 | | 1775 | equipment to install sand filter system |
| | Demolish and Install | Total | 1450 | 384.50 | | 1834.50 | tank including hook-up to existing |
| | Reinstall | Total | | 259.33 | | 259.33 | equipment. Pump and motor not |
| | Minimum Charge | Job | | 203 | | 203 | included. |
| **Pump / Motor** | | | | | | | |
| | Demolish | Ea. | | 35.50 | | 35.50 | Includes material and labor to install a |
| | Install | Ea. | 445 | 81 | | 526 | 22 GPM pump. |
| | Demolish and Install | Ea. | 445 | 116.50 | | 561.50 | |
| | Reinstall | Ea. | | 64.83 | | 64.83 | |
| | Clean | Ea. | 3.63 | 33.50 | | 37.13 | |
| | Minimum Charge | Job | | 205 | | 205 | |
| **Pump Water** | | | | | | | |
| | Install | Day | | 360 | 81.50 | 441.50 | Includes labor and equipment to pump |
| | Minimum Charge | Job | | 166 | | 166 | water from a swimming pool. |
| **Replaster** | | | | | | | |
| | Install | SF Surf | 1.17 | 8.65 | | 9.82 | Includes labor and material to |
| | Minimum Charge | Job | | 166 | | 166 | replaster gunite pool with a surface |
| | | | | | | | area of 500 to 600 S.F. |
| **Solar Panels** | | | | | | | |
| | Demolish | S.F. | | 1.50 | | 1.50 | Includes material and labor to install |
| | Install | S.F. | 23 | 2.67 | | 25.67 | solar panel. |
| | Demolish and Install | S.F. | 23 | 4.17 | | 27.17 | |
| | Reinstall | S.F. | | 2.13 | | 2.13 | |
| | Minimum Charge | Ea. | | 450 | | 450 | |

| Construction Clean-up | Unit | Material | Labor | Equip. | Total | Specification |
|---|---|---|---|---|---|---|
| **Final** | | | | | | |
| Clean | S.F. | | .23 | | .23 | Includes labor for final site/job |
| Minimum Charge | Job | | 133 | | 133 | clean-up including detail cleaning. |

# Location Factors

Costs shown in *RSMeans Residential Cost Data* are based on National Averages for materials and installation. To adjust these costs to a specific location, simply multiply the base cost by the factor for that city. The data is arranged alphabetically by state and postal zip code numbers. For a city not listed, use the factor for a nearby city with similar economic characteristics.

| STATE | CITY | Residential |
|---|---|---|
| **ALABAMA** | | |
| 350-352 | Birmingham | .88 |
| 354 | Tuscaloosa | .79 |
| 355 | Jasper | .73 |
| 356 | Decatur | .79 |
| 357-358 | Huntsville | .85 |
| 359 | Gadsden | .76 |
| 360-361 | Montgomery | .78 |
| 362 | Anniston | .74 |
| 363 | Dothan | .77 |
| 364 | Evergreen | .75 |
| 365-366 | Mobile | .83 |
| 367 | Selma | .75 |
| 368 | Phenix City | .76 |
| 369 | Butler | .76 |
| **ALASKA** | | |
| 995-996 | Anchorage | 1.27 |
| 997 | Fairbanks | 1.29 |
| 998 | Juneau | 1.26 |
| 999 | Ketchikan | 1.30 |
| **ARIZONA** | | |
| 850,853 | Phoenix | .86 |
| 852 | Mesa/Tempe | .83 |
| 855 | Globe | .79 |
| 856-857 | Tucson | .85 |
| 859 | Show Low | .81 |
| 860 | Flagstaff | .86 |
| 863 | Prescott | .80 |
| 864 | Kingman | .83 |
| 865 | Chambers | .80 |
| **ARKANSAS** | | |
| 716 | Pine Bluff | .81 |
| 717 | Camden | .69 |
| 718 | Texarkana | .74 |
| 719 | Hot Springs | .69 |
| 720-722 | Little Rock | .85 |
| 723 | West Memphis | .79 |
| 724 | Jonesboro | .78 |
| 725 | Batesville | .75 |
| 726 | Harrison | .76 |
| 727 | Fayetteville | .71 |
| 728 | Russellville | .76 |
| 729 | Fort Smith | .78 |
| **CALIFORNIA** | | |
| 900-902 | Los Angeles | 1.08 |
| 903-905 | Inglewood | 1.04 |
| 906-908 | Long Beach | 1.03 |
| 910-912 | Pasadena | 1.04 |
| 913-916 | Van Nuys | 1.07 |
| 917-918 | Alhambra | 1.08 |
| 919-921 | San Diego | 1.06 |
| 922 | Palm Springs | 1.04 |
| 923-924 | San Bernardino | 1.04 |
| 925 | Riverside | 1.08 |
| 926-927 | Santa Ana | 1.05 |
| 928 | Anaheim | 1.08 |
| 930 | Oxnard | 1.09 |
| 931 | Santa Barbara | 1.08 |
| 932-933 | Bakersfield | 1.06 |
| 934 | San Luis Obispo | 1.07 |
| 935 | Mojave | 1.05 |
| 936-938 | Fresno | 1.09 |
| 939 | Salinas | 1.10 |
| 940-941 | San Francisco | 1.25 |
| 942,956-958 | Sacramento | 1.11 |
| 943 | Palo Alto | 1.18 |
| 944 | San Mateo | 1.23 |
| 945 | Vallejo | 1.16 |
| 946 | Oakland | 1.22 |
| 947 | Berkeley | 1.24 |
| 948 | Richmond | 1.25 |
| 949 | San Rafael | 1.23 |
| 950 | Santa Cruz | 1.14 |
| 951 | San Jose | 1.21 |
| 952 | Stockton | 1.08 |
| 953 | Modesto | 1.08 |

| STATE | CITY | Residential |
|---|---|---|
| **CALIFORNIA (CONT'D)** | | |
| 954 | Santa Rosa | 1.17 |
| 955 | Eureka | 1.11 |
| 959 | Marysville | 1.09 |
| 960 | Redding | 1.09 |
| 961 | Susanville | 1.09 |
| **COLORADO** | | |
| 800-802 | Denver | .93 |
| 803 | Boulder | .93 |
| 804 | Golden | .91 |
| 805 | Fort Collins | .89 |
| 806 | Greeley | .79 |
| 807 | Fort Morgan | .92 |
| 808-809 | Colorado Springs | .90 |
| 810 | Pueblo | .91 |
| 811 | Alamosa | .88 |
| 812 | Salida | .90 |
| 813 | Durango | .91 |
| 814 | Montrose | .87 |
| 815 | Grand Junction | .91 |
| 816 | Glenwood Springs | .90 |
| **CONNECTICUT** | | |
| 060 | New Britain | 1.11 |
| 061 | Hartford | 1.11 |
| 062 | Willimantic | 1.11 |
| 063 | New London | 1.10 |
| 064 | Meriden | 1.11 |
| 065 | New Haven | 1.11 |
| 066 | Bridgeport | 1.12 |
| 067 | Waterbury | 1.11 |
| 068 | Norwalk | 1.11 |
| 069 | Stamford | 1.12 |
| **D.C.** | | |
| 200-205 | Washington | .96 |
| **DELAWARE** | | |
| 197 | Newark | 1.04 |
| 198 | Wilmington | 1.05 |
| 199 | Dover | 1.03 |
| **FLORIDA** | | |
| 320,322 | Jacksonville | .82 |
| 321 | Daytona Beach | .90 |
| 323 | Tallahassee | .78 |
| 324 | Panama City | .75 |
| 325 | Pensacola | .82 |
| 326,344 | Gainesville | .81 |
| 327-328,347 | Orlando | .90 |
| 329 | Melbourne | .91 |
| 330-332,340 | Miami | .87 |
| 333 | Fort Lauderdale | .85 |
| 334,349 | West Palm Beach | .85 |
| 335-336,346 | Tampa | .92 |
| 337 | St. Petersburg | .79 |
| 338 | Lakeland | .89 |
| 339,341 | Fort Myers | .87 |
| 342 | Sarasota | .90 |
| **GEORGIA** | | |
| 300-303,399 | Atlanta | .89 |
| 304 | Statesboro | .71 |
| 305 | Gainesville | .79 |
| 306 | Athens | .79 |
| 307 | Dalton | .75 |
| 308-309 | Augusta | .80 |
| 310-312 | Macon | .81 |
| 313-314 | Savannah | .82 |
| 315 | Waycross | .75 |
| 316 | Valdosta | .73 |
| 317,398 | Albany | .78 |
| 318-319 | Columbus | .83 |
| **HAWAII** | | |
| 967 | Hilo | 1.22 |
| 968 | Honolulu | 1.25 |

# Location Factors

| STATE | CITY | Residential |
|---|---|---|
| **STATES & POSS.** | | |
| 969 | Guam | .99 |
| | | |
| **IDAHO** | | |
| 832 | Pocatello | .86 |
| 833 | Twin Falls | .73 |
| 834 | Idaho Falls | .75 |
| 835 | Lewiston | .97 |
| 836-837 | Boise | .87 |
| 838 | Coeur d'Alene | .95 |
| | | |
| **ILLINOIS** | | |
| 600-603 | North Suburban | 1.10 |
| 604 | Joliet | 1.11 |
| 605 | South Suburban | 1.10 |
| 606-608 | Chicago | 1.19 |
| 609 | Kankakee | .99 |
| 610-611 | Rockford | 1.06 |
| 612 | Rock Island | .97 |
| 613 | La Salle | 1.06 |
| 614 | Galesburg | 1.00 |
| 615-616 | Peoria | .99 |
| 617 | Bloomington | .98 |
| 618-619 | Champaign | 1.00 |
| 620-622 | East St. Louis | .99 |
| 623 | Quincy | .99 |
| 624 | Effingham | .99 |
| 625 | Decatur | .97 |
| 626-627 | Springfield | .96 |
| 628 | Centralia | 1.00 |
| 629 | Carbondale | .96 |
| | | |
| **INDIANA** | | |
| 460 | Anderson | .91 |
| 461-462 | Indianapolis | .94 |
| 463-464 | Gary | 1.03 |
| 465-466 | South Bend | .91 |
| 467-468 | Fort Wayne | .90 |
| 469 | Kokomo | .92 |
| 470 | Lawrenceburg | .87 |
| 471 | New Albany | .87 |
| 472 | Columbus | .92 |
| 473 | Muncie | .91 |
| 474 | Bloomington | .94 |
| 475 | Washington | .91 |
| 476-477 | Evansville | .90 |
| 478 | Terre Haute | .90 |
| 479 | Lafayette | .92 |
| | | |
| **IOWA** | | |
| 500-503,509 | Des Moines | .89 |
| 504 | Mason City | .77 |
| 505 | Fort Dodge | .76 |
| 506-507 | Waterloo | .78 |
| 508 | Creston | .80 |
| 510-511 | Sioux City | .85 |
| 512 | Sibley | .72 |
| 513 | Spencer | .74 |
| 514 | Carroll | .74 |
| 515 | Council Bluffs | .82 |
| 516 | Shenandoah | .74 |
| 520 | Dubuque | .85 |
| 521 | Decorah | .75 |
| 522-524 | Cedar Rapids | .93 |
| 525 | Ottumwa | .83 |
| 526 | Burlington | .86 |
| 527-528 | Davenport | .97 |
| | | |
| **KANSAS** | | |
| 660-662 | Kansas City | .98 |
| 664-666 | Topeka | .79 |
| 667 | Fort Scott | .88 |
| 668 | Emporia | .74 |
| 669 | Belleville | .79 |
| 670-672 | Wichita | .79 |
| 673 | Independence | .84 |
| 674 | Salina | .77 |
| 675 | Hutchinson | .79 |
| 676 | Hays | .82 |
| 677 | Colby | .83 |
| 678 | Dodge City | .81 |
| 679 | Liberal | .80 |
| | | |
| **KENTUCKY** | | |
| 400-402 | Louisville | .90 |
| 403-405 | Lexington | .88 |

| STATE | CITY | Residential |
|---|---|---|
| **KENTUCKY (CONT'D)** | | |
| 406 | Frankfort | .86 |
| 407-409 | Corbin | .77 |
| 410 | Covington | .99 |
| 411-412 | Ashland | .92 |
| 413-414 | Campton | .78 |
| 415-416 | Pikeville | .84 |
| 417-418 | Hazard | .73 |
| 420 | Paducah | .89 |
| 421-422 | Bowling Green | .89 |
| 423 | Owensboro | .88 |
| 424 | Henderson | .90 |
| 425-426 | Somerset | .77 |
| 427 | Elizabethtown | .86 |
| | | |
| **LOUISIANA** | | |
| 700-701 | New Orleans | .87 |
| 703 | Thibodaux | .84 |
| 704 | Hammond | .79 |
| 705 | Lafayette | .82 |
| 706 | Lake Charles | .83 |
| 707-708 | Baton Rouge | .85 |
| 710-711 | Shreveport | .78 |
| 712 | Monroe | .74 |
| 713-714 | Alexandria | .74 |
| | | |
| **MAINE** | | |
| 039 | Kittery | .87 |
| 040-041 | Portland | .89 |
| 042 | Lewiston | .88 |
| 043 | Augusta | .89 |
| 044 | Bangor | .87 |
| 045 | Bath | .87 |
| 046 | Machias | .88 |
| 047 | Houlton | .89 |
| 048 | Rockland | .88 |
| 049 | Waterville | .87 |
| | | |
| **MARYLAND** | | |
| 206 | Waldorf | .85 |
| 207-208 | College Park | .88 |
| 209 | Silver Spring | .86 |
| 210-212 | Baltimore | .90 |
| 214 | Annapolis | .84 |
| 215 | Cumberland | .85 |
| 216 | Easton | .68 |
| 217 | Hagerstown | .85 |
| 218 | Salisbury | .74 |
| 219 | Elkton | .80 |
| | | |
| **MASSACHUSETTS** | | |
| 010-011 | Springfield | 1.04 |
| 012 | Pittsfield | 1.02 |
| 013 | Greenfield | 1.01 |
| 014 | Fitchburg | 1.12 |
| 015-016 | Worcester | 1.13 |
| 017 | Framingham | 1.13 |
| 018 | Lowell | 1.13 |
| 019 | Lawrence | 1.13 |
| 020-022, 024 | Boston | 1.21 |
| 023 | Brockton | 1.12 |
| 025 | Buzzards Bay | 1.10 |
| 026 | Hyannis | 1.10 |
| 027 | New Bedford | 1.12 |
| | | |
| **MICHIGAN** | | |
| 480,483 | Royal Oak | 1.02 |
| 481 | Ann Arbor | 1.03 |
| 482 | Detroit | 1.06 |
| 484-485 | Flint | .97 |
| 486 | Saginaw | .93 |
| 487 | Bay City | .94 |
| 488-489 | Lansing | .95 |
| 490 | Battle Creek | .92 |
| 491 | Kalamazoo | .91 |
| 492 | Jackson | .93 |
| 493,495 | Grand Rapids | .80 |
| 494 | Muskegon | .88 |
| 496 | Traverse City | .79 |
| 497 | Gaylord | .82 |
| 498-499 | Iron mountain | .89 |
| | | |
| **MINNESOTA** | | |
| 550-551 | Saint Paul | 1.12 |
| 553-555 | Minneapolis | 1.16 |
| 556-558 | Duluth | 1.08 |

# Location Factors

| STATE | CITY | Residential | | STATE | CITY | Residential |
|---|---|---|---|---|---|---|
| **MINNESOTA (CONT'd)** | | | | **NEW JERSEY** | | |
| 559 | Rochester | 1.05 | | 070-071 | Newark | 1.12 |
| 560 | Mankato | 1.02 | | 072 | Elizabeth | 1.15 |
| 561 | Windom | .83 | | 073 | Jersey City | 1.11 |
| 562 | Willmar | .84 | | 074-075 | Paterson | 1.12 |
| 563 | St. Cloud | 1.07 | | 076 | Hackensack | 1.11 |
| 564 | Brainerd | .98 | | 077 | Long Branch | 1.12 |
| 565 | Detroit Lakes | .96 | | 078 | Dover | 1.12 |
| 566 | Bemidji | .96 | | 079 | Summit | 1.12 |
| 567 | Thief River Falls | .95 | | 080,083 | Vineland | 1.09 |
| | | | | 081 | Camden | 1.10 |
| **MISSISSIPPI** | | | | 082,084 | Atlantic City | 1.13 |
| 386 | Clarksdale | .75 | | 085-086 | Trenton | 1.11 |
| 387 | Greenville | .82 | | 087 | Point Pleasant | 1.10 |
| 388 | Tupelo | .76 | | 088-089 | New Brunswick | 1.12 |
| 389 | Greenwood | .78 | | | | |
| 390-392 | Jackson | .83 | | **NEW MEXICO** | | |
| 393 | Meridian | .80 | | 870-872 | Albuquerque | .85 |
| 394 | Laurel | .77 | | 873 | Gallup | .85 |
| 395 | Biloxi | .83 | | 874 | Farmington | .85 |
| 396 | Mccomb | .78 | | 875 | Santa Fe | .86 |
| 397 | Columbus | .76 | | 877 | Las Vegas | .85 |
| | | | | 878 | Socorro | .85 |
| **MISSOURI** | | | | 879 | Truth/Consequences | .84 |
| 630-631 | St. Louis | 1.03 | | 880 | Las Cruces | .83 |
| 633 | Bowling Green | .95 | | 881 | Clovis | .85 |
| 634 | Hannibal | .86 | | 882 | Roswell | .85 |
| 635 | Kirksville | .80 | | 883 | Carrizozo | .85 |
| 636 | Flat River | .94 | | 884 | Tucumcari | .86 |
| 637 | Cape Girardeau | .88 | | | | |
| 638 | Sikeston | .83 | | **NEW YORK** | | |
| 639 | Poplar Bluff | .83 | | 100-102 | New York | 1.34 |
| 640-641 | Kansas City | 1.03 | | 103 | Staten Island | 1.27 |
| 644-645 | St. Joseph | .95 | | 104 | Bronx | 1.29 |
| 646 | Chillicothe | .88 | | 105 | Mount Vernon | 1.14 |
| 647 | Harrisonville | .98 | | 106 | White Plains | 1.17 |
| 648 | Joplin | .84 | | 107 | Yonkers | 1.18 |
| 650-651 | Jefferson City | .88 | | 108 | New Rochelle | 1.18 |
| 652 | Columbia | .88 | | 109 | Suffern | 1.11 |
| 653 | Sedalia | .86 | | 110 | Queens | 1.28 |
| 654-655 | Rolla | .88 | | 111 | Long Island City | 1.31 |
| 656-658 | Springfield | .87 | | 112 | Brooklyn | 1.32 |
| | | | | 113 | Flushing | 1.30 |
| **MONTANA** | | | | 114 | Jamaica | 1.29 |
| 590-591 | Billings | .87 | | 115,117,118 | Hicksville | 1.18 |
| 592 | Wolf Point | .83 | | 116 | Far Rockaway | 1.29 |
| 593 | Miles City | .85 | | 119 | Riverhead | 1.19 |
| 594 | Great Falls | .89 | | 120-122 | Albany | .94 |
| 595 | Havre | .80 | | 123 | Schenectady | .95 |
| 596 | Helena | .86 | | 124 | Kingston | 1.03 |
| 597 | Butte | .85 | | 125-126 | Poughkeepsie | 1.05 |
| 598 | Missoula | .82 | | 127 | Monticello | 1.05 |
| 599 | Kalispell | .81 | | 128 | Glens Falls | .88 |
| | | | | 129 | Plattsburgh | .92 |
| **NEBRASKA** | | | | 130-132 | Syracuse | .96 |
| 680-681 | Omaha | .91 | | 133-135 | Utica | .92 |
| 683-685 | Lincoln | .87 | | 136 | Watertown | .89 |
| 686 | Columbus | .85 | | 137-139 | Binghamton | .94 |
| 687 | Norfolk | .89 | | 140-142 | Buffalo | 1.03 |
| 688 | Grand Island | .89 | | 143 | Niagara Falls | 1.00 |
| 689 | Hastings | .91 | | 144-146 | Rochester | .97 |
| 690 | Mccook | .83 | | 147 | Jamestown | .88 |
| 691 | North Platte | .89 | | 148-149 | Elmira | .85 |
| 692 | Valentine | .83 | | | | |
| 693 | Alliance | .83 | | **NORTH CAROLINA** | | |
| | | | | 270,272-274 | Greensboro | .84 |
| **NEVADA** | | | | 271 | Winston-Salem | .84 |
| 889-891 | Las Vegas | 1.02 | | 275-276 | Raleigh | .85 |
| 893 | Ely | .87 | | 277 | Durham | .84 |
| 894-895 | Reno | .94 | | 278 | Rocky Mount | .74 |
| 897 | Carson City | .95 | | 279 | Elizabeth City | .75 |
| 898 | Elko | .92 | | 280 | Gastonia | .85 |
| | | | | 281-282 | Charlotte | .86 |
| **NEW HAMPSHIRE** | | | | 283 | Fayetteville | .83 |
| 030 | Nashua | .95 | | 284 | Wilmington | .82 |
| 031 | Manchester | .95 | | 285 | Kinston | .74 |
| 032-033 | Concord | .93 | | 286 | Hickory | .79 |
| 034 | Keene | .76 | | 287-288 | Asheville | .82 |
| 035 | Littleton | .82 | | 289 | Murphy | .73 |
| 036 | Charleston | .74 | | | | |
| 037 | Claremont | .75 | | **NORTH DAKOTA** | | |
| 038 | Portsmouth | .94 | | 580-581 | Fargo | .79 |
| | | | | 582 | Grand Forks | .75 |
| | | | | 583 | Devils Lake | .78 |
| | | | | 584 | Jamestown | .73 |
| | | | | 585 | Bismarck | .78 |

| STATE | CITY | Residential |
|---|---|---|
| **NORTH DAKOTA (CONT'D)** | | |
| 586 | Dickinson | .77 |
| 587 | Minot | .82 |
| 588 | Williston | .77 |
| | | |
| **OHIO** | | |
| 430-432 | Columbus | .94 |
| 433 | Marion | .90 |
| 434-436 | Toledo | 1.01 |
| 437-438 | Zanesville | .90 |
| 439 | Steubenville | .95 |
| 440 | Lorain | .99 |
| 441 | Cleveland | 1.01 |
| 442-443 | Akron | .98 |
| 444-445 | Youngstown | .96 |
| 446-447 | Canton | .94 |
| 448-449 | Mansfield | .94 |
| 450 | Hamilton | .93 |
| 451-452 | Cincinnati | .93 |
| 453-454 | Dayton | .93 |
| 455 | Springfield | .94 |
| 456 | Chillicothe | .97 |
| 457 | Athens | .89 |
| 458 | Lima | .91 |
| | | |
| **OKLAHOMA** | | |
| 730-731 | Oklahoma City | .79 |
| 734 | Ardmore | .78 |
| 735 | Lawton | .81 |
| 736 | Clinton | .77 |
| 737 | Enid | .77 |
| 738 | Woodward | .76 |
| 739 | Guymon | .67 |
| 740-741 | Tulsa | .78 |
| 743 | Miami | .82 |
| 744 | Muskogee | .72 |
| 745 | Mcalester | .74 |
| 746 | Ponca City | .77 |
| 747 | Durant | .77 |
| 748 | Shawnee | .75 |
| 749 | Poteau | .78 |
| | | |
| **OREGON** | | |
| 970-972 | Portland | 1.02 |
| 973 | Salem | 1.00 |
| 974 | Eugene | 1.01 |
| 975 | Medford | 1.00 |
| 976 | Klamath Falls | 1.01 |
| 977 | Bend | 1.02 |
| 978 | Pendleton | 1.00 |
| 979 | Vale | .99 |
| | | |
| **PENNSYLVANIA** | | |
| 150-152 | Pittsburgh | .97 |
| 153 | Washington | .93 |
| 154 | Uniontown | .89 |
| 155 | Bedford | .88 |
| 156 | Greensburg | .93 |
| 157 | Indiana | .90 |
| 158 | Dubois | .89 |
| 159 | Johnstown | .89 |
| 160 | Butler | .92 |
| 161 | New Castle | .91 |
| 162 | Kittanning | .93 |
| 163 | Oil City | .90 |
| 164-165 | Erie | .94 |
| 166 | Altoona | .87 |
| 167 | Bradford | .90 |
| 168 | State College | .90 |
| 169 | Wellsboro | .89 |
| 170-171 | Harrisburg | .94 |
| 172 | Chambersburg | .89 |
| 173-174 | York | .91 |
| 175-176 | Lancaster | .91 |
| 177 | Williamsport | .84 |
| 178 | Sunbury | .91 |
| 179 | Pottsville | .90 |
| 180 | Lehigh Valley | 1.01 |
| 181 | Allentown | 1.04 |
| 182 | Hazleton | .90 |
| 183 | Stroudsburg | .91 |
| 184-185 | Scranton | .96 |
| 186-187 | Wilkes-Barre | .92 |
| 188 | Montrose | .90 |
| 189 | Doylestown | 1.05 |

| STATE | CITY | Residential |
|---|---|---|
| **PENNSYLVANIA (CONT'D)** | | |
| 190-191 | Philadelphia | 1.18 |
| 193 | Westchester | 1.11 |
| 194 | Norristown | 1.10 |
| 195-196 | Reading | .97 |
| | | |
| **PUERTO RICO** | | |
| 009 | San Juan | .75 |
| | | |
| **RHODE ISLAND** | | |
| 028 | Newport | 1.07 |
| 029 | Providence | 1.07 |
| | | |
| **SOUTH CAROLINA** | | |
| 290-292 | Columbia | .85 |
| 293 | Spartanburg | .85 |
| 294 | Charleston | .88 |
| 295 | Florence | .80 |
| 296 | Greenville | .84 |
| 297 | Rock Hill | .83 |
| 298 | Aiken | .99 |
| 299 | Beaufort | .83 |
| | | |
| **SOUTH DAKOTA** | | |
| 570-571 | Sioux Falls | .78 |
| 572 | Watertown | .74 |
| 573 | Mitchell | .76 |
| 574 | Aberdeen | .78 |
| 575 | Pierre | .75 |
| 576 | Mobridge | .74 |
| 577 | Rapid City | .76 |
| | | |
| **TENNESSEE** | | |
| 370-372 | Nashville | .83 |
| 373-374 | Chattanooga | .76 |
| 375,380-381 | Memphis | .82 |
| 376 | Johnson City | .71 |
| 377-379 | Knoxville | .73 |
| 382 | Mckenzie | .72 |
| 383 | Jackson | .70 |
| 384 | Columbia | .72 |
| 385 | Cookeville | .71 |
| | | |
| **TEXAS** | | |
| 750 | Mckinney | .74 |
| 751 | Waxahackie | .75 |
| 752-753 | Dallas | .82 |
| 754 | Greenville | .68 |
| 755 | Texarkana | .72 |
| 756 | Longview | .67 |
| 757 | Tyler | .73 |
| 758 | Palestine | .66 |
| 759 | Lufkin | .70 |
| 760-761 | Fort Worth | .81 |
| 762 | Denton | .76 |
| 763 | Wichita Falls | .79 |
| 764 | Eastland | .72 |
| 765 | Temple | .74 |
| 766-767 | Waco | .77 |
| 768 | Brownwood | .68 |
| 769 | San Angelo | .71 |
| 770-772 | Houston | .84 |
| 773 | Huntsville | .68 |
| 774 | Wharton | .70 |
| 775 | Galveston | .83 |
| 776-777 | Beaumont | .81 |
| 778 | Bryan | .73 |
| 779 | Victoria | .73 |
| 780 | Laredo | .73 |
| 781-782 | San Antonio | .80 |
| 783-784 | Corpus Christi | .77 |
| 785 | Mc Allen | .75 |
| 786-787 | Austin | .79 |
| 788 | Del Rio | .66 |
| 789 | Giddings | .69 |
| 790-791 | Amarillo | .77 |
| 792 | Childress | .75 |
| 793-794 | Lubbock | .75 |
| 795-796 | Abilene | .74 |
| 797 | Midland | .75 |
| 798-799,885 | El Paso | .74 |
| | | |
| **UTAH** | | |
| 840-841 | Salt Lake City | .81 |
| 842,844 | Ogden | .79 |
| 843 | Logan | .79 |

# Location Factors

| STATE | CITY | Residential |
|---|---|---|
| **UTAH (CONT'D)** | | |
| 845 | Price | .71 |
| 846-847 | Provo | .81 |
| | | |
| **VERMONT** | | |
| 050 | White River Jct. | .76 |
| 051 | Bellows Falls | .79 |
| 052 | Bennington | .81 |
| 053 | Brattleboro | .81 |
| 054 | Burlington | .82 |
| 056 | Montpelier | .83 |
| 057 | Rutland | .82 |
| 058 | St. Johnsbury | .79 |
| 059 | Guildhall | .78 |
| | | |
| **VIRGINIA** | | |
| 220-221 | Fairfax | 1.02 |
| 222 | Arlington | 1.04 |
| 223 | Alexandria | 1.07 |
| 224-225 | Fredericksburg | .94 |
| 226 | Winchester | .92 |
| 227 | Culpeper | 1.00 |
| 228 | Harrisonburg | .90 |
| 229 | Charlottesville | .91 |
| 230-232 | Richmond | .99 |
| 233-235 | Norfolk | 1.00 |
| 236 | Newport News | 1.00 |
| 237 | Portsmouth | .92 |
| 238 | Petersburg | .98 |
| 239 | Farmville | .90 |
| 240-241 | Roanoke | .98 |
| 242 | Bristol | .85 |
| 243 | Pulaski | .84 |
| 244 | Staunton | .92 |
| 245 | Lynchburg | .97 |
| 246 | Grundy | .84 |
| | | |
| **WASHINGTON** | | |
| 980-981,987 | Seattle | 1.02 |
| 982 | Everett | 1.05 |
| 983-984 | Tacoma | 1.01 |
| 985 | Olympia | 1.00 |
| 986 | Vancouver | .99 |
| 988 | Wenatchee | .94 |
| 989 | Yakima | .97 |
| 990-992 | Spokane | 1.00 |
| 993 | Richland | .98 |
| 994 | Clarkston | .98 |
| | | |
| **WEST VIRGINIA** | | |
| 247-248 | Bluefield | .88 |
| 249 | Lewisburg | .89 |
| 250-253 | Charleston | .95 |
| 254 | Martinsburg | .86 |
| 255-257 | Huntington | .96 |
| 258-259 | Beckley | .90 |
| 260 | Wheeling | .93 |
| 261 | Parkersburg | .91 |
| 262 | Buckhannon | .92 |
| 263-264 | Clarksburg | .91 |
| 265 | Morgantown | .92 |
| 266 | Gassaway | .92 |
| 267 | Romney | .88 |
| 268 | Petersburg | .90 |
| | | |
| **WISCONSIN** | | |
| 530,532 | Milwaukee | 1.08 |
| 531 | Kenosha | 1.05 |
| 534 | Racine | 1.04 |
| 535 | Beloit | 1.00 |
| 537 | Madison | 1.00 |
| 538 | Lancaster | .98 |
| 539 | Portage | .98 |
| 540 | New Richmond | 1.00 |
| 541-543 | Green Bay | 1.01 |
| 544 | Wausau | .95 |
| 545 | Rhinelander | .96 |
| 546 | La Crosse | .95 |
| 547 | Eau Claire | .99 |
| 548 | Superior | .99 |
| 549 | Oshkosh | .96 |
| | | |
| **WYOMING** | | |
| 820 | Cheyenne | .83 |
| 821 | Yellowstone Nat. Pk. | .75 |
| 822 | Wheatland | .75 |

| STATE | CITY | Residential |
|---|---|---|
| **WYOMING (CONT'D)** | | |
| 823 | Rawlins | .75 |
| 824 | Worland | .74 |
| 825 | Riverton | .74 |
| 826 | Casper | .77 |
| 827 | Newcastle | .74 |
| 828 | Sheridan | .80 |
| 829-831 | Rock Springs | .79 |
| | | |
| **CANADIAN FACTORS (reflect Canadian currency)** | | |
| **ALBERTA** | | |
| | Calgary | 1.13 |
| | Edmonton | 1.13 |
| | Fort McMurray | 1.16 |
| | Lethbridge | 1.13 |
| | Lloydminster | 1.08 |
| | Medicine Hat | 1.08 |
| | Red Deer | 1.08 |
| | | |
| **BRITISH COLUMBIA** | | |
| | Kamloops | 1.06 |
| | Prince George | 1.06 |
| | Vancouver | 1.07 |
| | Victoria | 1.01 |
| | | |
| **MANITOBA** | | |
| | Brandon | 1.03 |
| | Portage la Prairie | 1.03 |
| | Winnipeg | 1.03 |
| | | |
| **NEW BRUNSWICK** | | |
| | Bathurst | .96 |
| | Dalhousie | .95 |
| | Fredericton | 1.03 |
| | Moncton | .96 |
| | Newcastle | .96 |
| | St. John | 1.03 |
| | | |
| **NEWFOUNDLAND** | | |
| | Corner Brook | .97 |
| | St Johns | .99 |
| | | |
| **NORTHWEST TERRITORIES** | | |
| | Yellowknife | 1.08 |
| | | |
| **NOVA SCOTIA** | | |
| | Bridgewater | .98 |
| | Dartmouth | .99 |
| | Halifax | 1.01 |
| | New Glasgow | .98 |
| | Sydney | .97 |
| | Truro | .98 |
| | Yarmouth | .98 |
| | | |
| **ONTARIO** | | |
| | Barrie | 1.14 |
| | Brantford | 1.16 |
| | Cornwall | 1.16 |
| | Hamilton | 1.18 |
| | Kingston | 1.16 |
| | Kitchener | 1.11 |
| | London | 1.15 |
| | North Bay | 1.12 |
| | Oshawa | 1.15 |
| | Ottawa | 1.17 |
| | Owen Sound | 1.13 |
| | Peterborough | 1.13 |
| | Sarnia | 1.16 |
| | Sault Ste Marie | 1.09 |
| | St. Catharines | 1.11 |
| | Sudbury | 1.09 |
| | Thunder Bay | 1.14 |
| | Timmins | 1.12 |
| | Toronto | 1.19 |
| | Windsor | 1.13 |
| | | |
| **PRINCE EDWARD ISLAND** | | |
| | Charlottetown | .93 |
| | Summerside | .93 |
| | | |
| **QUEBEC** | | |
| | Cap-de-la-Madeleine | 1.15 |
| | Charlesbourg | 1.15 |
| | Chicoutimi | 1.18 |
| | Gatineau | 1.14 |
| | Granby | 1.14 |

# Location Factors

| STATE | CITY | Residential |
|---|---|---|
| QUEBEC (CONT'D) | | |
| | Hull | 1.14 |
| | Joliette | 1.15 |
| | Laval | 1.14 |
| | Montreal | 1.18 |
| | Quebec | 1.20 |
| | Rimouski | 1.18 |
| | Rouyn-Noranda | 1.14 |
| | Saint Hyacinthe | 1.14 |
| | Sherbrooke | 1.14 |
| | Sorel | 1.15 |
| | St Jerome | 1.14 |
| | Trois Rivieres | 1.15 |
| **SASKATCHEWAN** | | |
| | Moose Jaw | .95 |
| | Prince Albert | .94 |
| | Regina | .97 |
| | Saskatoon | .96 |
| **YUKON** | | |
| | Whitehorse | .94 |

# Abbreviations

| | |
|---|---|
| A | Area |
| ASTM | American Society for Testing and Materials |
| B.F. | Board feet |
| Carp. | Carpenter |
| C.F. | Cubic feet |
| CWJ | Composite wood joist |
| C.Y. | Cubic yard |
| Ea. | Each |
| Equip. | Equipment |
| Exp. | Exposure |
| Ext. | Exterior |
| F | Fahrenheit |
| Ft. | Foot, feet |
| Gal. | Gallon |
| Hr. | Hour |
| in. | Inch, inches |
| Inst. | Installation |
| Int. | Interior |
| Lb. | Pound |
| L.F. | Linear feet |
| LVL | Laminated veneer lumber |
| Mat. | Material |
| Max. | Maximum |
| MBF | Thousand board feet |
| MBM | Thousand feet board measure |
| MSF | Thousand square feet |
| Min. | Minimum |
| O.C. | On center |
| O&P | Overhead and profit |
| OWJ | Open web wood joist |
| Oz. | Ounce |
| Pr. | Pair |
| Quan. | Quantity |
| S.F. | Square foot |
| Sq. | Square, 100 square feet |
| S.Y. | Square yard |
| V.L.F. | Vertical linear feet |
| ′ | Foot, feet |
| ″ | Inch, inches |
| ° | Degrees |

# Index

# Index

## *Contractor's Pricing Guide:* Residential Detailed Costs 2008

Every aspect of residential construction, from overhead costs to residential lighting and wiring, is in here. All the detail you need to accurately estimate the costs of your work with or without markups—labor-hours, typical crews, and equipment are included as well. When you need a detailed estimate, this publication has all the costs to help you come up with a complete, on the money, price you can rely on to win profitable work.

**Unit Prices Now Updated to MasterFormat 2004!**

$39.95 per copy
Available Nov. 2007
Catalog no. 60338

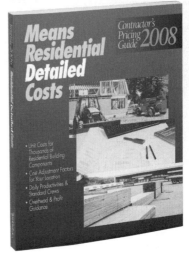

## *Contractor's Pricing Guide:* Residential Repair & Remodeling Costs 2008

This book provides total unit price costs for every aspect of the most common repair and remodeling projects. Organized in the order of construction by component and activity, it includes demolition and installation, cleaning, painting, and more. With simplified estimating methods, clear, concise descriptions, and technical specifications for each component, the book is a valuable tool for contractors who want to speed up their estimating time, while making sure their costs are on target.

$39.95 per copy
Available Nov. 2007
Catalog no. 60348

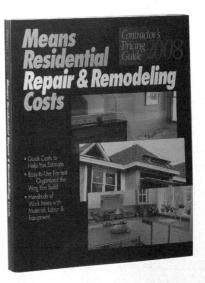

## *Contractor's Pricing Guide:* Residential Square Foot Costs 2008

Now available in one concise volume, all you need to know to plan and budget the cost of new homes. If you are looking for a quick reference, the model home section contains costs for over 250 different sizes and types of residences, with hundreds of easily applied modifications. If you need even more detail, the Assemblies Section lets you build your own costs or modify the model costs further. Hundreds of graphics are provided, along with forms and procedures to help you get it right.

$39.95 per copy
Available Nov. 2007
Catalog no. 60328

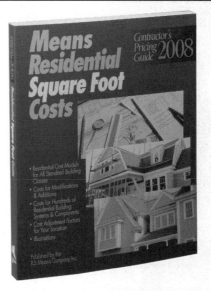

# RSMeans Building Construction Cost Data 2008

## Available in Softbound, Looseleaf, and Spanish Versions

Many customers enjoy the convenience and flexibility of the looseleaf binder, which increases the usefulness of *RSMeans Building Construction Cost Data 2008* by making it easy to add and remove pages. You can insert your own cost information pages, so everything is in one place. Copying pages for faxing is easier also. Whichever edition you prefer—softbound, looseleaf, or the new Spanish version—you'll be eligible to receive *RSMeans Quarterly Update Service* FREE. Current subscribers can receive *RSMeans Quarterly Update Service* via e-mail.

**Unit prices now updated to MasterFormat 2004!**

$149.95 per copy (English or Spanish)
Catalog no. 60018 (English) Available Oct. 2007
Catalog no. 60718 (Spanish) Available Dec. 2007

$187.95 per copy, looseleaf
Available Oct. 2007
Catalog no. 61018

---

# RSMeans Building Construction Cost Data 2008

### Now available in Spanish!

Offers you unchallenged unit price reliability in an easy-to-use arrangement. Whether used for complete, finished estimates or for periodic checks, it supplies more cost facts better and faster than any comparable source. Over 20,000 unit prices for 2008. The City Cost Indexes and Location Factors cover over 930 areas, for indexing to any project location in North America. Order and get *RSMeans Quarterly Update Service* FREE. You'll have year-long access to the RSMeans Estimating **HOTLINE** FREE with your subscription. Expert assistance when using RSMeans data is just a phone call away.

$149.95 per copy (English or Spanish)
Catalog no. 60018 (English) Available Oct. 2007
Catalog no. 60718 (Spanish) Available Dec. 2007

**Unit prices now updated to MasterFormat 2004!**

# RSMeans Metric Construction Cost Data 2008

A massive compendium of all the data from both the *RSMeans Building Construction Cost Data* AND *Heavy Construction Cost Data*, in **metric** format! Access all of this vital information from one complete source. It contains more than 600 pages of unit costs and 40 pages of assemblies costs. The Reference Section contains over 200 pages of tables, charts, and other estimating aids. A great way to stay in step with today's construction trends and rapidly changing costs.

$179.95 per copy
Available Dec. 2007
Catalog no. 63018

**For more information
visit the RSMeans Website
at www.rsmeans.com**

# Annual Cost Guides

## RSMeans Mechanical Cost Data 2008

- **HVAC**
- **Controls**

Total unit and systems price guidance for mechanical construction. . . materials, parts, fittings, and complete labor cost information. Includes prices for piping, heating, air conditioning, ventilation, and all related construction.

Plus new 2008 unit costs for:

- Over 2,500 installed HVAC/controls assemblies components
- "On-site" Location Factors for over 930 cities and towns in the U.S. and Canada
- Crews, labor, and equipment

**$149.95 per copy
Available Oct. 2007
Catalog no. 60028**

**Unit prices now updated to
MasterFormat 2004!**

## RSMeans Plumbing Cost Data 2008

Comprehensive unit prices and assemblies for plumbing, irrigation systems, commercial and residential fire protection, point-of-use water heaters, and the latest approved materials. This publication and its companion, *RSMeans Mechanical Cost Data*, provide full-range cost estimating coverage for all the mechanical trades.

Now contains more lines of no-hub CI soil pipe fittings, more flange-type escutcheons, fiberglass pipe insulation in a full range of sizes for 2-1/2" and 3" wall thicknesses, 220 lines of grease duct, and much more.

**$149.95 per copy
Available Oct. 2007
Catalog no. 60218**

## RSMeans Electrical Cost Data 2008

Pricing information for every part of electrical cost planning. More than 13,000 unit and systems costs with design tables; clear specifications and drawings; engineering guides; illustrated estimating procedures; complete labor-hour and materials costs for better scheduling and procurement; and the latest electrical products and construction methods.

- A variety of special electrical systems including cathodic protection
- Costs for maintenance, demolition, HVAC/ mechanical, specialties, equipment, and more

**$149.95 per copy
Available Oct. 2007
Catalog no. 60038**

**Unit prices now updated to
MasterFormat 2004!**

## RSMeans Electrical Change Order Cost Data 2008

*RSMeans Electrical Change Order Cost Data* provides you with electrical unit prices exclusively for pricing change orders—based on the recent, direct experience of contractors and suppliers. Analyze and check your own change order estimates against the experience others have had doing the same work. It also covers productivity analysis and change order cost justifications. With useful information for calculating the effects of change orders and dealing with their administration.

**$149.95 per copy
Available Nov. 2007
Catalog no. 60238**

## RSMeans Square Foot Costs 2008

*It's Accurate and Easy To Use!*

- **Updated price information** based on nationwide figures from suppliers, estimators, labor experts, and contractors
- "How-to-Use" sections, with **clear examples** of commercial, residential, industrial, and institutional structures
- Realistic graphics, offering true-to-life illustrations of building projects
- Extensive information on using square foot cost data, including sample estimates and alternate pricing methods

**$163.95 per copy
Available Nov. 2007
Catalog no. 60058**

## RSMeans Repair & Remodeling Cost Data 2008

**Commercial/Residential**

Use this valuable tool to estimate commercial and residential renovation and remodeling.

**Includes: New costs for hundreds of unique methods, materials, and conditions that only come up in repair and remodeling, PLUS:**

- Unit costs for over 15,000 construction components
- Installed costs for over 90 assemblies
- Over 930 "on-site" localization factors for the U.S. and Canada.

**Unit prices now updated to MasterFormat 2004!**

**$128.95 per copy
Available Nov. 2007
Catalog no. 60048**

# Annual Cost Guides

For more information
visit the RSMeans Website
at www.rsmeans.com

## RSMeans Facilities Construction Cost Data 2008

For the maintenance and construction of commercial, industrial, municipal, and institutional properties. Costs are shown for new and remodeling construction and are broken down into materials, labor, equipment, and overhead and profit. Special emphasis is given to sections on mechanical, electrical, furnishings, site work, building maintenance, finish work, and demolition.

More than 43,000 unit costs, plus assemblies costs and a comprehensive Reference Section are included.

**$357.95 per copy**
**Available Nov. 2007**
**Catalog no. 60208**

**Unit prices now updated to MasterFormat 2004!**

## RSMeans Light Commercial Cost Data 2008

Specifically addresses the light commercial market, which is a specialized niche in the construction industry. Aids you, the owner/designer/contractor, in preparing all types of estimates—from budgets to detailed bids. Includes new advances in methods and materials.

Assemblies Section allows you to evaluate alternatives in the early stages of design/planning.

Over 11,000 unit costs ensure that you have the prices you need. . . when you need them.

**$128.95 per copy**
**Available Nov. 2007**
**Catalog no. 60188**

## RSMeans Residential Cost Data 2008

Contains square foot costs for 30 basic home models with the look of today, plus hundreds of custom additions and modifications you can quote right off the page. With costs for the 100 residential systems you're most likely to use in the year ahead. Complete with blank estimating forms, sample estimates, and step-by-step instructions.

Now contains line items for cultured stone and brick, PVC trim lumber, and TPO roofing.

**$128.95 per copy**
**Available Oct. 2007**
**Catalog no. 60178**

**Unit prices now updated to MasterFormat 2004!**

## RSMeans Site Work & Landscape Cost Data 2008

Includes unit and assemblies costs for earthwork, sewerage, piped utilities, site improvements, drainage, paving, trees & shrubs, street openings/repairs, underground tanks, and more. Contains 57 tables of assemblies costs for accurate conceptual estimates.

Includes:
• Estimating for infrastructure improvements
• Environmentally-oriented construction
• ADA-mandated handicapped access
• Hazardous waste line items

**$149.95 per copy**
**Available Nov. 2007**
**Catalog no. 60288**

## RSMeans Assemblies Cost Data 2008

*RSMeans Assemblies Cost Data* takes the guesswork out of preliminary or conceptual estimates. Now you don't have to try to calculate the assembled cost by working up individual component costs. We've done all the work for you.

Presents detailed illustrations, descriptions, specifications, and costs for every conceivable building assembly—240 types in all—arranged in the easy-to-use UNIFORMAT II system. Each illustrated "assembled" cost includes a complete grouping of materials and associated installation costs, including the installing contractor's overhead and profit.

**$245.95 per copy**
**Available Oct. 2007**
**Catalog no. 60068**

**Unit prices now updated to MasterFormat 2004!**

## RSMeans Open Shop Building Construction Cost Data 2008

The latest costs for accurate budgeting and estimating of new commercial and residential construction. . . renovation work. . . change orders. . . cost engineering.

*RSMeans Open Shop "BCCD"* will assist you to:
• Develop benchmark prices for change orders
• Plug gaps in preliminary estimates and budgets
• Estimate complex projects
• Substantiate invoices on contracts
• Price ADA-related renovations

**$149.95 per copy**
**Available Dec. 2007**
**Catalog no. 60158**

**For more information
visit the RSMeans Website
at www.rsmeans.com**

# Annual Cost Guides

## RSMeans Building Construction Cost Data 2008
### Western Edition

This regional edition provides more precise cost information for western North America. Labor rates are based on union rates from 13 western states and western Canada. Included are western practices and materials not found in our national edition: tilt-up concrete walls, glu-lam structural systems, specialized timber construction, seismic restraints, and landscape and irrigation systems.

**$149.95 per copy
Available Dec. 2007
Catalog no. 60228**

**Unit prices now updated to
MasterFormat 2004!**

## RSMeans Heavy Construction Cost Data 2008

A comprehensive guide to heavy construction costs. Includes costs for highly specialized projects such as tunnels, dams, highways, airports, and waterways. Information on labor rates, equipment, and materials costs is included. Features unit price costs, systems costs, and numerous reference tables for costs and design.

**$149.95 per copy
Available Dec. 2007
Catalog no. 60168**

## RSMeans Construction Cost Indexes 2008

What materials and labor costs will change unexpectedly this year? By how much?

- Breakdowns for 316 major cities
- National averages for 30 key cities
- Expanded five major city indexes
- Historical construction cost indexes

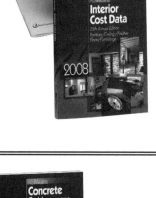

**$325.00 per year (subscription)
Catalog no. 50148**

**$81.25 individual quarters
Catalog no. 60148 A,B,C,D**

## RSMeans Interior Cost Data 2008

Provides you with prices and guidance needed to make accurate interior work estimates. Contains costs on materials, equipment, hardware, custom installations, furnishings, and labor costs. . . for new and remodel commercial and industrial interior construction, including updated information on office furnishings, and reference information.

**Unit prices now updated to MasterFormat 2004!**

**$149.95 per copy
Available Nov. 2007
Catalog no. 60098**

## RSMeans Concrete & Masonry Cost Data 2008

Provides you with cost facts for virtually all concrete/masonry estimating needs, from complicated formwork to various sizes and face finishes of brick and block—all in great detail. The comprehensive Unit Price Section contains more than 7,500 selected entries. Also contains an Assemblies [Cost] Section, and a detailed Reference Section that supplements the cost data.

**Unit prices now updated to MasterFormat 2004!**

**$136.95 per copy
Available Dec. 2007
Catalog no. 60118**

## RSMeans Labor Rates for the Construction Industry 2008

Complete information for estimating labor costs, making comparisons, and negotiating wage rates by trade for over 300 U.S. and Canadian cities. With 46 construction trades listed by local union number in each city, and historical wage rates included for comparison. Each city chart lists the county and is alphabetically arranged with handy visual flip tabs for quick reference.

**$326.95 per copy
Available Dec. 2007
Catalog no. 60128**

## RSMeans Facilities Maintenance & Repair Cost Data 2008

*RSMeans Facilities Maintenance & Repair Cost Data* gives you a complete system to manage and plan your facility repair and maintenance costs and budget efficiently. Guidelines for auditing a facility and developing an annual maintenance plan. Budgeting is included, along with reference tables on cost and management, and information on frequency and productivity of maintenance operations.

The only nationally recognized source of maintenance and repair costs. Developed in cooperation with the Civil Engineering Research Laboratory (CERL) of the Army Corps of Engineers.

**$326.95 per copy
Available Dec. 2007
Catalog no. 60308**

# Reference Books

**For more information
visit the RSMeans Website
at www.rsmeans.com**

## Value Engineering: Practical Applications

*For Design, Construction, Maintenance & Operations*

### by Alphonse Dell'Isola, PE

A tool for immediate application—for engineers, architects, facility managers, owners, and contractors. Includes making the case for VE—the management briefing; integrating VE into planning, budgeting, and design; conducting life cycle costing; using VE methodology in design review and consultant selection; case studies; VE workbook; and a life cycle costing program on disk.

$79.95 per copy
**Over 450 pages, illustrated, softcover**
**Catalog no. 67319A**

## Facilities Operations & Engineering Reference

### by the Association for Facilities Engineering and RSMeans

An all-in-one technical reference for planning and managing facility projects and solving day-to-day operations problems. Selected as the official certified plant engineer reference, this handbook covers financial analysis, maintenance, HVAC and energy efficiency, and more.

$54.98 per copy
**Over 700 pages, illustrated, hardcover**
**Catalog no. 67318**

## The Building Professional's Guide to Contract Documents

### 3rd Edition

### by Waller S. Poage, AIA, CSI, CVS

A comprehensive reference for owners, design professionals, contractors, and students

- Structure your documents for maximum efficiency.
- Effectively communicate construction requirements.
- Understand the roles and responsibilities of construction professionals.
- Improve methods of project delivery.

$32.48 per copy, 400 pages
**Diagrams and construction forms, hardcover**
**Catalog no. 67261A**

## Building Security: Strategies & Costs

### by David Owen

This comprehensive resource will help you evaluate your facility's security needs, and design and budget for the materials and devices needed to fulfill them.

Includes over 130 pages of RSMeans cost data for installation of security systems and materials, plus a review of more than 50 security devices and construction solutions.

$44.98 per copy
**350 pages, illustrated, hardcover**
**Catalog no. 67339**

## Cost Planning & Estimating for Facilities Maintenance

In this unique book, a team of facilities management authorities shares their expertise on:

- Evaluating and budgeting maintenance operations
- Maintaining and repairing key building components
- Applying *RSMeans Facilities Maintenance & Repair Cost Data* to your estimating

Covers special maintenance requirements of the ten major building types.

$89.95 per copy
**Over 475 pages, hardcover**
**Catalog no. 67314**

## Life Cycle Costing for Facilities

### by Alphonse Dell'Isola and Dr. Steven Kirk

Guidance for achieving higher quality design and construction projects at lower costs! Cost-cutting efforts often sacrifice quality to yield the cheapest product. Life cycle costing enables building designers and owners to achieve both. The authors of this book show how LCC can work for a variety of projects — from roads to HVAC upgrades to different types of buildings.

$99.95 per copy
**450 pages, hardcover**
**Catalog no. 67341**

## Planning & Managing Interior Projects 2nd Edition

### by Carol E. Farren, CFM

*Expert guidance on managing renovation & relocation projects.*

This book guides you through every step in relocating to a new space or renovating an old one. From initial meeting through design and construction, to post-project administration, it helps you get the most for your company or client. Includes sample forms, spec lists, agreements, drawings, and much more!

$34.98 per copy
**200 pages, softcover**
**Catalog no. 67245A**

## Builder's Essentials: Best Business Practices for Builders & Remodelers

*An Easy-to-Use Checklist System*

### by Thomas N. Frisby

A comprehensive guide covering all aspects of running a construction business, with more than 40 user-friendly checklists. Provides expert guidance on increasing your revenue and keeping more of your profit, planning for long-term growth, keeping good employees, and managing subcontractors.

$29.95 per copy
**Over 220 pages, softcover**
**Catalog no. 67329**

For more information
visit the RSMeans Website
at www.rsmeans.com

# Reference Books

## Interior Home Improvement
### Costs 9th Edition

Updated estimates for the most popular remodeling and repair projects—from small, do-it-yourself jobs to major renovations and new construction. Includes: kitchens & baths; new living space from your attic, basement, or garage; new floors, paint, and wallpaper; tearing out or building new walls; closets, stairs, and fireplaces; new energy-saving improvements, home theaters, and more!

**$24.95 per copy**
**250 pages, illustrated, softcover**
**Catalog no. 67308E**

## Exterior Home Improvement
### Costs 9th Edition

Updated estimates for the most popular remodeling and repair projects—from small, do-it-yourself jobs, to major renovations and new construction. Includes: curb appeal projects—landscaping, patios, porches, driveways, and walkways; new windows and doors; decks, greenhouses, and sunrooms; room additions and garages; roofing, siding, and painting; "green" improvements to save energy & water.

**$24.95 per copy**
**Over 275 pages, illustrated, softcover**
**Catalog no. 67309E**

## Builder's Essentials: Plan Reading & Material Takeoff

*For Residential and Light Commercial Construction*

### by Wayne J. DelPico

A valuable tool for understanding plans and specs, and accurately calculating material quantities. Step-by-step instructions and takeoff procedures based on a full set of working drawings.

**$35.95 per copy**
**Over 420 pages, softcover**
**Catalog no. 67307**

## Means Unit Price Estimating Methods
### New 4th Edition

This new edition includes up-to-date cost data and estimating examples, updated to reflect changes to the CSI numbering system and new features of RSMeans cost data. It describes the most productive, universally accepted ways to estimate, and uses checklists and forms to illustrate shortcuts and timesavers. A model estimate demonstrates procedures. A new chapter explores computer estimating alternatives.

**$59.95 per copy**
**Over 350 pages, illustrated, softcover**
**Catalog no. 67303B**

## Total Productive Facilities Management

### by Richard W. Sievert, Jr.

Today, facilities are viewed as strategic resources. . . elevating the facility manager to the role of asset manager supporting the organization's overall business goals. Now, Richard Sievert Jr., in this well-articulated guidebook, sets forth a new operational standard for the facility manager's emerging role. . . a comprehensive program for managing facilities as a true profit center.

**$29.98 per copy**
**275 pages, softcover**
**Catalog no. 67321**

## Means Environmental Remediation Estimating Methods 2nd Edition
### by Richard R. Rast

Guidelines for estimating 50 standard remediation technologies. Use it to prepare preliminary budgets, develop estimates, compare costs and solutions, estimate liability, review quotes, negotiate settlements.

**$49.98 per copy**
**Over 750 pages, illustrated, hardcover**
**Catalog no. 64777A**

## Concrete Repair and Maintenance Illustrated

### by Peter Emmons

Hundreds of illustrations show users how to analyze, repair, clean, and maintain concrete structures for optimal performance and cost effectiveness. From parking garages to roads and bridges to structural concrete, this comprehensive book describes the causes, effects, and remedies for concrete wear and failure. Invaluable for planning jobs, selecting materials, and training employees, this book is a must-have for concrete specialists, general contractors, facility managers, civil and structural engineers, and architects.

**$69.95 per copy**
**300 pages, illustrated, softcover**
**Catalog no. 67146**

# Reference Books

For more information
visit the RSMeans Website
at www.rsmeans.com

## Means Illustrated Construction
### Dictionary Condensed, 2nd Edition

The best portable dictionary for office or field use—an
essential tool for contractors, architects, insurance and
real estate personnel, facility managers, homeowners, and
anyone who needs quick, clear definitions for construction
terms. The second edition has been further enhanced with
updates and hundreds of new terms and illustrations . . .
in keeping with the most recent developments in the
construction industry.

Now with a quick-reference Spanish section. Includes tools
and equipment, materials, tasks, and more!

**$59.95 per copy**
**Over 500 pages, softcover**
**Catalog no. 67282A**

## Means Repair & Remodeling
### Estimating New 4th Edition
#### By Edward B. Wetherill and RSMeans

This important reference focuses on the unique problems
of estimating renovations of existing structures, and helps
you determine the true costs of remodeling through careful
evaluation of architectural details and a site visit.

*New section on disaster restoration costs.*

**$69.95 per copy**
**Over 450 pages, illustrated, hardcover**
**Catalog no. 67265B**

## Facilities Planning &
## Relocation
### by David D. Owen

A complete system for planning space needs and managing
relocations. Includes step-by-step manual, over 50 forms,
and extensive reference section on materials and
furnishings.

*New lower price and user-friendly format.*

**$89.95 per copy**
**Over 450 pages, softcover**
**Catalog no. 67301**

## Means Square Foot &
## UNIFORMAT Assemblies
## Estimating Methods 3rd Edition

Develop realistic square foot and assemblies costs for
budgeting and construction funding. The new edition
features updated guidance on square foot and assemblies
estimating using UNIFORMAT II. An essential reference for
anyone who performs conceptual estimates.

**$69.95 per copy**
**Over 300 pages, illustrated, softcover**
**Catalog no. 67145B**

## Means Electrical Estimating
## Methods 3rd Edition

Expanded edition includes sample estimates and cost
information in keeping with the latest version of the CSI
MasterFormat and UNIFORMAT II. Complete coverage
of fiber optic and uninterruptible power supply electrical
systems, broken down by components, and explained in
detail. Includes a new chapter on computerized estimating
methods. A practical companion to *RSMeans Electrical
Cost Data.*

**$64.95 per copy**
**Over 325 pages, hardcover**
**Catalog no. 67230B**

## Means Mechanical
## Estimating Methods 4th Edition

Completely updated, this guide assists you in making a
review of plans, specs, and bid packages, with suggestions
for takeoff procedures, listings, substitutions, and pre-bid
scheduling for all components of HVAC. Includes suggestions
for budgeting labor and equipment usage. Compares materials
and construction methods to allow you to select the best
option.

**$64.95 per copy**
**Over 350 pages, illustrated, softcover**
**Catalog no. 67294B**

## Means ADA Compliance Pricing
## Guide New 2nd Edition
### by Adaptive Environments and
### RSMeans

Completely updated and revised to the new 2004 *Americans
with Disabilities Act Accessibility Guidelines,*
this book features more than 70 of the most commonly
needed modifications for ADA compliance. Projects range
from installing ramps and walkways, widening
doorways and entryways, and installing and refitting
elevators, to relocating light switches and signage.

**$79.95 per copy**
**Over 350 pages, illustrated, softcover**
**Catalog no. 67310A**

## Project Scheduling &
## Management for Construction
### New 3rd Edition
#### by David R. Pierce, Jr.

A comprehensive yet easy-to-follow guide to construction
project scheduling and control—from vital project
management principles through the latest scheduling,
tracking, and controlling techniques. The author is a
leading authority on scheduling, with years of field and
teaching experience at leading academic institutions. Spend
a few hours with this book and come away with a solid
understanding of this essential management topic.

**$64.95 per copy**
**Over 300 pages, illustrated, hardcover**
**Catalog no. 67247B**

311

For more information
visit the RSMeans Website
at www.rsmeans.com

# Reference Books

## The Practice of Cost Segregation Analysis

**by Bruce A. Desrosiers and Wayne J. DelPico**

This expert guide walks you through the practice of cost segregation analysis, which enables property owners to defer taxes and benefit from "accelerated cost recovery" through depreciation deductions on assets that are properly identified and classified.

With a glossary of terms, sample cost segregation estimates for various building types, key information resources, and updates via a dedicated Web site, this book is a critical resource for anyone involved in cost segregation analysis.

$99.95 per copy
Over 225 pages
Catalog no. 67345

## Preventive Maintenance for Multi-Family Housing

**by John C. Maciha**

Prepared by one of the nation's leading experts on multi-family housing.

This complete PM system for apartment and condominium communities features expert guidance, checklists for buildings and grounds maintenance tasks and their frequencies, a reusable wall chart to track maintenance, and a dedicated Web site featuring customizable electronic forms. A must-have for anyone involved with multi-family housing maintenance and upkeep.

$89.95 per copy
225 pages
Catalog no. 67346

## How to Estimate with Means Data & CostWorks

**New 3rd Edition**

**by RSMeans and Saleh A. Mubarak, Ph.D.**

New 3rd Edition—fully updated with new chapters, plus new CD with updated *CostWorks* cost data and MasterFormat organization. Includes all major construction items—with more than 300 exercises and two sets of plans that show how to estimate for a broad range of construction items and systems—including general conditions and equipment costs.

$59.95 per copy
272 pages, softcover
Includes CostWorks CD
Catalog no. 67324B

## Job Order Contracting

*Expediting Construction Project Delivery*

**by Allen Henderson**

Expert guidance to help you implement JOC—fast becoming the preferred project delivery method for repair and renovation, minor new construction, and maintenance projects in the public sector and in many states and municipalities. The author, a leading JOC expert and practitioner, shows how to:

• Establish a JOC program

• Evaluate proposals and award contracts

• Handle general requirements and estimating

• Partner for maximum benefits

$89.95 per copy
192 pages, illustrated, hardcover
Catalog no. 67348

## Builder's Essentials: Estimating Building Costs

*For the Residential & Light Commercial Contractor*

**by Wayne J. DelPico**

Step-by-step estimating methods for residential and light commercial contractors. Includes a detailed look at every construction specialty—explaining all the components, takeoff units, and labor needed for well-organized, complete estimates. Covers correctly interpreting plans and specifications, and developing accurate and complete labor and material costs.

$29.95 per copy
Over 400 pages, illustrated, softcover
Catalog no. 67343

## Building & Renovating Schools

This all-inclusive guide covers every step of the school construction process—from initial planning, needs assessment, and design, right through moving into the new facility. A must-have resource for anyone concerned with new school construction or renovation. With square foot cost models for elementary, middle, and high school facilities, and real-life case studies of recently completed school projects.

The contributors to this book—architects, construction project managers, contractors, and estimators who specialize in school construction—provide start-to-finish, expert guidance on the process.

$99.95 per copy
Over 425 pages, hardcover
Catalog no. 67342

# Reference Books

For more information
visit the RSMeans Website
at www.rsmeans.com

## Residential & Light Commercial Construction Standards 2nd Edition

### by RSMeans and contributing authors

This book provides authoritative requirements and recommendations compiled from the nation's leading professional associations, industry publications, and building code organizations.

It's an all-in-one reference for establishing a standard for workmanship, quickly resolving disputes, and avoiding defect claims.

**$59.95 per copy**
**600 pages, illustrated, softcover**
**Catalog no. 67322A**

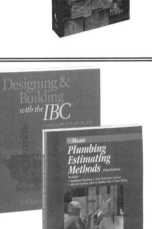

## Means Illustrated Construction Dictionary

### Unabridged 3rd Edition, with CD-ROM

Long regarded as the industry's finest, *Means Illustrated Construction Dictionary* is now even better. With the addition of over 1,000 new terms and hundreds of new illustrations, it is the clear choice for the most comprehensive and current information. The companion CD-ROM that comes with this new edition adds many extra features: larger graphics, expanded definitions, and links to both CSI MasterFormat numbers and product information.

**$99.95 per copy**
**Over 790 pages, illustrated, hardcover**
**Catalog no. 67292A**

## Designing & Building with the IBC 2nd Edition

### by Rolf Jensen & Associates, Inc.

This updated, comprehensive guide helps building professionals make the transition to the 2003 International Building Code®. Includes a side-by-side code comparison of the IBC 2003 to the IBC 2000 and the three primary model codes, a quick-find index, and professional code commentary. With illustrations, abbreviations key, and an extensive Resource section.

**$99.95 per copy**
**Over 875 pages, softcover**
**Catalog no. 67328A**

## Means Plumbing Estimating Methods 3rd Edition

### by Joseph Galeno and Sheldon Greene

Updated and revised! This practical guide walks you through a plumbing estimate, from basic materials and installation methods through change order analysis. *Plumbing Estimating Methods* covers residential, commercial, industrial, and medical systems, and features sample takeoff and estimate forms and detailed illustrations of systems and components.

**$29.98 per copy**
**330+ pages, softcover**
**Catalog no. 67283B**

## Understanding & Negotiating Construction Contracts

### by Kit Werremeyer

Take advantage of the author's 30 years' experience in small-to-large (including international) construction projects. Learn how to identify, understand, and evaluate high risk terms and conditions typically found in all construction contracts—then negotiate to lower or eliminate the risk, improve terms of payment, and reduce exposure to claims and disputes. The author avoids "legalese" and gives real-life examples from actual projects.

**$69.95 per copy**
**300 pages, softcover**
**Catalog no. 67350**

## Means Estimating Handbook

### 2nd Edition

Updated Second Edition answers virtually any estimating technical question—all organized by CSI MasterFormat. This comprehensive reference covers the full spectrum of technical data required to estimate construction costs. The book includes information on sizing, productivity, equipment requirements, code-mandated specifications, design standards, and engineering factors.

**$99.95 per copy**
**Over 900 pages, hardcover**
**Catalog no. 67276A**

## Means Spanish/English Construction Dictionary 2nd Edition

### by RSMeans and the International Code Council

This expanded edition features thousands of the most common words and useful phrases in the construction industry with easy-to-follow pronunciations in both Spanish and English. Over 800 new terms, phrases, and illustrations have been added. It also features a new stand-alone "Safety & Emergencies" section, with colored pages for quick access.

Unique to this dictionary are the systems illustrations showing the relationship of components in the most common building systems for all major trades.

**$23.95 per copy**
**Over 400 pages**
**Catalog no. 67327A**

For more information
visit the RSMeans Website
at www.rsmeans.com

# Seminars

## Means CostWorks® Training

This *one-day* seminar has been designed with the intention of assisting both new and existing users to become more familiar with the *Means CostWorks* program. The class is broken into two unique sections: (1) A one-half day presentation on the function of each icon; and each student will be shown how to use the software to develop a cost estimate. (2) Hands-on estimating exercises that will ensure that each student thoroughly understands how to use *CostWorks*. You must bring your own laptop computer to this course.

### Means CostWorks Benefits/Features:
- Estimate in your own spreadsheet format
- Power of RSMeans National Database
- Database automatically regionalized
- Save time with keyword searches
- Save time by establishing common estimate items in "Bookmark" files
- Customize your spreadsheet template
- Hot Key to Product Manufacturers' listings and specs
- Merge capability for networking environments
- View crews and assembly components
- AutoSave capability
- Enhanced sorting capability

## Unit Price Estimating

This interactive *two-day* seminar teaches attendees how to interpret project information and process it into final, detailed estimates with the greatest accuracy level.

The single most important credential an estimator can take to the job is the ability to visualize construction in the mind's eye, and thereby estimate accurately.

### Some of what you'll learn:
- Interpreting the design in terms of cost
- The most detailed, time-tested methodology for accurate "pricing"
- Key cost drivers—material, labor, equipment, staging, and subcontracts
- Understanding direct and indirect costs for accurate job cost accounting and change order management

**Who should attend:** Corporate and government estimators and purchasers, architects, engineers… and others needing to produce accurate project estimates.

## Square Foot and Assemblies Estimating

This *two-day* course teaches attendees how to quickly deliver accurate square foot estimates using limited budget and design information.

### Some of what you'll learn:
- How square foot costing gets the estimate done faster
- Taking advantage of a "systems" or "assemblies" format
- The RSMeans "building assemblies/square foot cost approach"
- How to create a very reliable preliminary and systems estimate using bare-bones design information

**Who should attend:** Facilities managers, facilities engineers, estimators, planners, developers, construction finance professionals… and others needing to make quick, accurate construction cost estimates at commercial, government, educational, and medical facilities.

## Repair and Remodeling Estimating

This *two-day* seminar emphasizes all the underlying considerations unique to repair/remodeling estimating and presents the correct methods for generating accurate, reliable R&R project costs using the unit price and assemblies methods.

### Some of what you'll learn:
- Estimating considerations—like labor-hours, building code compliance, working within existing structures, purchasing materials in smaller quantities, unforeseen deficiencies
- Identifying problems and providing solutions to estimating building alterations
- Rules for factoring in minimum labor costs, accurate productivity estimates, and allowances for project contingencies
- R&R estimating examples calculated using unit price and assemblies data

**Who should attend:** Facilities managers, plant engineers, architects, contractors, estimators, builders… and others who are concerned with the proper preparation and/or evaluation of repair and remodeling estimates.

## Mechanical and Electrical Estimating

This *two-day* course teaches attendees how to prepare more accurate and complete mechanical/electrical estimates, avoiding the pitfalls of omission and double-counting, while understanding the composition and rationale within the RSMeans Mechanical/Electrical database.

### Some of what you'll learn:
- The unique way mechanical and electrical systems are interrelated
- M&E estimates–conceptual, planning, budgeting, and bidding stages
- Order of magnitude, square foot, assemblies, and unit price estimating
- Comparative cost analysis of equipment and design alternatives

**Who should attend:** Architects, engineers, facilities managers, mechanical and electrical contractors… and others needing a highly reliable method for developing, understanding, and evaluating mechanical and electrical contracts.

## Green Building Planning & Construction

In this *two-day* course, learn about tailoring a building and its placement on the site to the local climate, site conditions, culture, and community. Includes information to reduce resource consumption and augment resource supply.

### Some of what you'll learn:
- Green technologies, materials, systems, and standards
- Energy efficiencies with energy modeling tools
- Cost vs. value of green products over their life cycle
- Low-cost strategies and economic incentives and funding
- Health, comfort, and productivity goals and techniques

**Who should attend:** Contractors, project managers, building owners, building officials, healthcare and insurance professionals.

## Facilities Maintenance and Repair Estimating

This *two-day* course teaches attendees how to plan, budget, and estimate the cost of ongoing and preventive maintenance and repair for existing buildings and grounds.

### Some of what you'll learn:
- The most financially favorable maintenance, repair, and replacement scheduling and estimating
- Auditing and value engineering facilities
- Preventive planning and facilities upgrading
- Determining both in-house and contract-out service costs
- Annual, asset-protecting M&R plan

**Who should attend:** Facility managers, maintenance supervisors, buildings and grounds superintendents, plant managers, planners, estimators… and others involved in facilities planning and budgeting.

## Practical Project Management for Construction Professionals

In this *two-day* course, acquire the essential knowledge and develop the skills to effectively and efficiently execute the day-to-day responsibilities of the construction project manager.

### Covers:
- General conditions of the construction contract
- Contract modifications: change orders and construction change directives
- Negotiations with subcontractors and vendors
- Effective writing: notification and communications
- Dispute resolution: claims and liens

**Who should attend:** Architects, engineers, owner's representatives, project managers.

## Life Cycle Costing for Facilities

This *two-day* course teaches attendees how to plan and conduct life cycle cost analysis studies.

### Some of what you'll learn:
- Initial project feasibility
- Developing guidelines for LCC studies and their accomplishment
- Selecting the best design
- Applying the latest economic models for energy conservation and greening of the environment

**Who should attend:** Professionals involved in planning, programming, real estate development, maintenance, operation, procurement, design, specifying, and construction.

# Seminars

**For more information
visit the RSMeans Website
at www.rsmeans.com**

## Scheduling and Project Management

This *two-day* course teaches attendees the most current and proven scheduling and management techniques needed to bring projects in on time and on budget.

**Some of what you'll learn:**
• Crucial phases of planning and scheduling
• How to establish project priorities and develop realistic schedules and management techniques
• Critical Path and Precedence Methods
• Special emphasis on cost control

**Who should attend:** Construction project managers, supervisors, engineers, estimators, contractors... and others who want to improve their project planning, scheduling, and management skills.

## Understanding & Negotiating Construction Contracts

In this *two-day* course, learn how to protect the assets of your company by justifying or eliminating commercial risk through negotiation of a contract's terms and conditions.

**Some of what you'll learn:**
• Myths and paradigms of contracts
• Scope of work, terms of payment and scheduling
• Dispute resolution
• Why clients love CLAIMS!
• Negotiating issues and much more

**Who should attend:** Contractors & subcontractors, material suppliers, project managers, risk & insurance managers, procurement managers, owners and facility managers, corporate executives.

## Site Work & Heavy Construction Estimating

This *two-day* course teaches attendees how to estimate earthwork, site utilities, foundations, and site improvements, using the assemblies and the unit price methods.

**Some of what you'll learn:**
• Basic site work and heavy construction estimating skills
• Estimating foundations, utilities, earthwork, and site improvements
• Correct equipment usage, quality control, and site investigation for estimating purposes

**Who should attend:** Project managers, design engineers, estimators, and contractors doing site work and heavy construction.

## Assessing Scope of Work for Facility Construction Estimating

This *two-day* course is a practical training program that addresses the vital importance of understanding the SCOPE of projects in order to produce accurate cost estimates in a facility repair and remodeling environment.

**Some of what you'll learn:**
• Discussions on site visits, plans/specs, record drawings of facilities, and site-specific lists
• Review of CSI divisions, including means, methods, materials, and the challenges of scoping each topic
• Exercises in SCOPE identification and SCOPE writing for accurate estimating of projects
• Hands-on exercises that require SCOPE, take-off, and pricing

**Who should attend:** Corporate and government estimators, planners, facility managers, and others who need to produce accurate project estimates.

# 2008 RSMeans Seminar Schedule

Note: Call for exact dates and details.

| Location | Dates |
|---|---|
| Las Vegas, NV | March |
| Washington, DC | April |
| Denver, CO | May |
| San Francisco, CA | June |
| Washington, DC | September |
| Dallas, TX | September |
| Las Vegas, NV | October |
| Orlando, FL | November |
| Atlantic City, NJ | October |
| San Diego, CA | December |

**1-800-334-3509, ext. 5115**

315

For more information
visit the RSMeans Website
at www.rsmeans.com

# Seminars

## Registration Information

**Register early... Save up to $100!** Register 30 days before the start date of a seminar and save $100 off your total fee. *Note: This discount can be applied only once per order. It cannot be applied to team discount registrations or any other special offer.*

**How to register** Register by phone today! The RSMeans toll-free number for making reservations is **1-800-334-3509, ext. 5115.**

**Individual seminar registration fee - $935.** *Means CostWorks®* **training registration fee - $375.** To register by mail, complete the registration form and return, with your full fee, to: Seminar Division, Reed Construction Data, RSMeans Seminars, 63 Smiths Lane, Kingston, MA 02364.

**Federal government pricing** All federal government employees save 25% off the regular seminar price. Other promotional discounts cannot be combined with the federal government discount.

**Team discount program** for two to four seminar registrations. Call for pricing: 1-800-334-3509, ext. 5115

**Multiple course discounts** When signing up for two or more courses, call for pricing.

**Refund policy** Cancellations will be accepted up to ten days prior to the seminar start. There are no refunds for cancellations received later than ten working days prior to the first day of the seminar. A $150 processing fee will be applied for all cancellations. Written notice of cancellation is required. Substitutions can be made at any time before the session starts. **No-shows are subject to the full seminar fee.**

**AACE approved courses** Many seminars described and offered here have been approved for 14 hours (1.4 recertification credits) of credit by the AACE International Certification Board toward meeting the continuing education requirements for recertification as a Certified Cost Engineer/Certified Cost Consultant.

**AIA Continuing Education** We are registered with the AIA Continuing Education System (AIA/CES) and are committed to developing quality learning activities in accordance with the CES criteria. Many seminars meet the AIA/CES criteria for Quality Level 2. AIA members may receive (14) learning units (LUs) for each two-day RSMeans course.

**NASBA CPE sponsor credits** We are part of the National Registry of CPE sponsors. Attendees may be eligible for (16) CPE credits.

**Daily course schedule** The first day of each seminar session begins at 8:30 a.m. and ends at 4:30 p.m. The second day begins at 8:00 a.m. and ends at 4:00 p.m. Participants are urged to bring a hand-held calculator, since many actual problems will be worked out in each session.

**Continental breakfast** Your registration includes the cost of a continental breakfast, a morning coffee break, and an afternoon break. These informal segments will allow you to discuss topics of mutual interest with other members of the seminar. (You are free to make your own lunch and dinner arrangements.)

**Hotel/transportation arrangements** RSMeans has arranged to hold a block of rooms at most host hotels. To take advantage of special group rates when making your reservation, be sure to mention that you are attending the RSMeans seminar. You are, of course, free to stay at the lodging place of your choice. (**Hotel reservations and transportation arrangements should be made directly by seminar attendees.**)

**Important** Class sizes are limited, so please register as soon as possible.

*Note: Pricing subject to change.*

## Registration Form

**Call 1-800-334-3509, ext. 5115 to register or FAX 1-800-632-6732. Visit our Web site: www.rsmeans.com**

Please register the following people for the RSMeans construction seminars as shown here. We understand that we must make our own hotel reservations if overnight stays are necessary.

☐ Full payment of $_____enclosed.

☐ Bill me

Name of registrant(s)

(To appear on certificate of completion)

_____

_____

_____

_____

P.O. #: _____
 GOVERNMENT AGENCIES MUST SUPPLY PURCHASE ORDER NUMBER OR
 TRAINING FORM.

Firm name_____

Address_____

City/State/Zip_____

Telephone no._____ Fax no._____

E-mail address_____

Charge our registration(s) to: ☐ MasterCard ☐ VISA ☐ American Express ☐ Discover

Account no._____ Exp. date_____

Cardholder's signature_____

Seminar name_____

City _____ Dates _____

**Please mail check to: Seminar Division, Reed Construction Data, RSMeans Seminars, 63 Smiths Lane, P.O. Box 800, Kingston, MA 02364 USA**

# MeansData™

## CONSTRUCTION COSTS FOR SOFTWARE APPLICATIONS
### Your construction estimating software is only as good as your cost data.

A proven construction cost database is a mandatory part of any estimating package. The following list of software providers can offer you MeansData™ as an added feature for their estimating systems. See the table below for what types of products and services they offer (match their numbers). Visit online at **www.rsmeans.com/demosource/** for more information and free demos. Or call their numbers listed below.

1. **3D International**
713-871-7000
venegas@3di.com

2. **4Clicks-Solutions, LLC**
719-574-7721
mbrown@4clicks-solutions.com

3. **ArenaSoft Estimating**
888-370-8806
info@arenasoft.com

4. **Beck Technology**
214-303-6293
stewartcarroll@beckgroup.com

5. **BSD - Building Systems Design, Inc.**
888-273-7638
bsd@bsdsoftlink.com

6. **Building Explorer LLC**
949-500-9773
info@buildingexplorer.com

7. **CMS - Computerized Micro Solutions**
800-255-7407
cms@proest.com

8. **Corecon Technologies, Inc.**
714-895-7222
sales@corecon.com

9. **CorVet Systems**
301-622-9069
sales@corvetsys.com

10. **Digital Alchemy**
206-779-6308
info@DigitalAlchemyPro.com

11. **Earth Tech**
303-771-3103
kyle.knudson@earthtech.com

12. **Estimating Systems, Inc.**
800-967-8572
esipulsar@adelphia.net

13. **MC² - Management Computer**
800-225-5622
vkeys@mc2-ice.com

14. **Maximus Asset Solutions**
800-659-9001
assetsolutions@maximus.com

15. **PrioSoft**
888-394-0252
sales@priosoft.com

16. **Sage Timberline Office**
800-628-6583
productinfo.timberline@sage.com

17. **SchoolDude.com**
877-868-3833
info@schooldude.com

18. **US Cost, Inc.**
800-372-4003
sales@uscost.com

19. **Vanderweil Facility Advisors**
617-451-5100
info@VFA.com

20. **WinEstimator, Inc.**
800-950-2374
sales@winest.com

| TYPE | 1 | 2 | 3 | 4 | 5 | 6 | 7 | 8 | 9 | 10 | 11 | 12 | 13 | 14 | 15 | 16 | 17 | 18 | 19 | 20 |
|---|---|---|---|---|---|---|---|---|---|---|---|---|---|---|---|---|---|---|---|---|
| BID | | | • | | • | | • | | • | | | | • | | | • | | | | • |
| Estimating | | • | • | • | | • | | • | • | | • | • | • | | • | • | | • | | • |
| DOC/JOC/SABER | | • | • | | • | | | | • | | | • | | • | | • | | | | • |
| ID/IQ | | • | | | | | | | • | | | | • | | | | | | | • |
| Asset Mgmt. | | | | | | | | | | | | | | • | | | • | | • | • |
| Facility Mgmt. | • | | | | | | | | | | | | | • | | | • | | • | |
| Project Mgmt. | • | • | | | | | | • | • | | | | | | • | • | | | | |
| TAKE-OFF | | | • | | | | • | • | • | | • | | • | | | | • | • | | |
| EARTHWORK | | | | | | | | • | | | • | | • | | | | | | | |
| Pipe Flow | | | | | | | | | | | | | | | | | | | | |
| HVAC/Plumbing | | | • | | | | • | | • | | | | | | | | | | | |
| Roofing | | | • | | | | • | | • | | | | | | | | | | | |
| Design | • | | • | • | | • | | | | • | | | | | | • | | | | • |
| **Other Offers/Links:** | | | | | | | | | | | | | | | | | | | | |
| Accounting/HR | | • | • | | | | | | | | | | • | | | • | | | | |
| Scheduling | | | • | | | | | | | | | | | | | • | | • | | • |
| CAD | | | | • | | • | | | | • | | | | | | • | | | | • |
| PDA | | | | | | | | | | | | | | | | • | | • | | • |
| Lt. Versions | | • | | | | | • | | | | | | | | | • | | • | | |
| Consulting | • | • | • | • | | | • | | • | | • | | | • | | • | • | • | • | • |
| Training | | • | • | • | • | • | • | • | • | • | • | • | • | • | • | • | • | • | • | • |

**Qualified re-seller applications now being accepted. Call Carol Polio, ext. 5107.**

## FOR MORE INFORMATION
## CALL 1-800-448-8182, EXT. 5107 OR FAX 1-800-632-6732

For more information
visit the RSMeans Website
at www.rsmeans.com

# New Titles

## How Your House Works
### by Charlie Wing

A must-have reference for every homeowner, handyman, and contractor—for repair, remodeling, and new construction. This book uncovers the mysteries behind just about every major appliance and building element in your house—from electrical, heating and AC, to plumbing, framing, foundations and appliances. Clear, "exploded" drawings show exactly how things should be put together and how they function—what to check if they don't work, and what you can do that might save you having to call in a professional.

$21.95 per copy
160 pages, softcover
Catalog no. 67351

## Green Building: Project Planning & Cost Estimating 2nd Edition

This new edition has been completely updated with the latest in green building technologies, design concepts, standards, and costs. Now includes a 2008 Green Building *CostWorks* CD with more than 300 green building assemblies and over 5,000 unit price line items for sustainable building. The new edition is also full-color with all new case studies—plus a new chapter on deconstruction, a key aspect of green building.

$129.95 per copy
350 pages, softcover
Catalog no. 67338A

## Complete Book of Framing
### by Scot Simpson

This straightforward, easy-to-learn method will help framers, carpenters, and handy homeowners build their skills in rough carpentry and framing. Shows how to frame all the parts of a house: floors, walls, roofs, door & window openings, and stairs—with hundreds of color photographs and drawings that show every detail. The book gives beginners all the basics they need to go from zero framing knowledge to a journeyman level. And it provides valuable tips and tables for the experienced carpenter—plus "framer-friendly" tips and a dedicated Website to access framing formulas.

$29.95 per copy
352 pages, softcover
Catalog no. 67353

## Means Landscape Estimating Methods
### New 5th Edition

Answers questions about preparing competitive landscape construction estimates, with up-to-date cost estimates and the new MasterFormat classification system. Expanded and revised to address the latest materials and methods, including new coverage on approaches to green building that save water, reduce maintenance costs, and provide other benefits. Includes:

- Step-by-step explanation of the estimating process and a sample estimate for a major project.
- Sample forms and worksheets that save time and prevent errors—now available on a new companion Website.

$64.95 per copy
Over 350 pages, softcover
Catalog no. 67295C

## Construction Business Management
### by Nick Ganaway

Only 43% of construction firms stay in business after four years. Make sure your company thrives with valuable guidance from a pro with 25 years of success as a commercial contractor. Find out what it takes to build all aspects of a business that is profitable, enjoyable, and enduring. With a bonus chapter on retail construction.

$49.95 per copy
200 pages, softcover
Catalog no. 67352

## The Homeowner's Guide to Mold By Michael Pugliese

Expert guidance to protect your health and your home.

Mold, whether caused by leaks, humidity or flooding, is a real health and financial issue—for homeowners and contractors. This full-color book explains:

- Construction and maintenance practices to prevent mold
- How to inspect for and remove mold
- Mold remediation procedures and costs
- What to do after a flood
- How to deal with insurance companies if you're thinking of submitting a mold damages claim

$21.95 per copy
144 pages, softcover
Catalog no. 67344

# 2008 Order Form

| Qty. | Book no. | COST ESTIMATING BOOKS | Unit Price | Total |
|---|---|---|---|---|
| | 60068 | Assemblies Cost Data 2008 | $245.95 | |
| | 60018 | Building Construction Cost Data 2008 | 149.95 | |
| | 61018 | Building Const. Cost Data–Looseleaf Ed. 2008 | 187.95 | |
| | 60718 | Building Const. Cost Data–Spanish 2008 | 149.95 | |
| | 60228 | Building Const. Cost Data–Western Ed. 2008 | 149.95 | |
| | 60118 | Concrete & Masonry Cost Data 2008 | 136.95 | |
| | 50148 | Construction Cost Indexes 2008 (subscription) | 325.00 | |
| | 60148A | Construction Cost Index–January 2008 | 81.25 | |
| | 60148B | Construction Cost Index–April 2008 | 81.25 | |
| | 60148C | Construction Cost Index–July 2008 | 81.25 | |
| | 60148D | Construction Cost Index–October 2008 | 81.25 | |
| | 60348 | Contr. Pricing Guide: Resid. R & R Costs 2008 | 39.95 | |
| | 60338 | Contr. Pricing Guide: Resid. Detailed 2008 | 39.95 | |
| | 60328 | Contr. Pricing Guide: Resid. Sq. Ft. 2008 | 39.95 | |
| | 60238 | Electrical Change Order Cost Data 2008 | 149.95 | |
| | 60038 | Electrical Cost Data 2008 | 149.95 | |
| | 60208 | Facilities Construction Cost Data 2008 | 357.95 | |
| | 60308 | Facilities Maintenance & Repair Cost Data 2008 | 326.95 | |
| | 60168 | Heavy Construction Cost Data 2008 | 149.95 | |
| | 60098 | Interior Cost Data 2008 | 149.95 | |
| | 60128 | Labor Rates for the Const. Industry 2008 | 326.95 | |
| | 60188 | Light Commercial Cost Data 2008 | 128.95 | |
| | 60028 | Mechanical Cost Data 2008 | 149.95 | |
| | 63018 | Metric Construction Cost Data 2008 | 179.95 | |
| | 60158 | Open Shop Building Const. Cost Data 2008 | 149.95 | |
| | 60218 | Plumbing Cost Data 2008 | 149.95 | |
| | 60048 | Repair and Remodeling Cost Data 2008 | 128.95 | |
| | 60178 | Residential Cost Data 2008 | 128.95 | |
| | 60288 | Site Work & Landscape Cost Data 2008 | 149.95 | |
| | 60058 | Square Foot Costs 2008 | 163.95 | |
| | 62018 | Yardsticks for Costing (2008) | 149.95 | |
| | 62017 | Yardsticks for Costing (2007) | 136.95 | |
| | | **REFERENCE BOOKS** | | |
| | 67310A | ADA Compliance Pricing Guide, 2nd Ed. | 79.95 | |
| | 67330 | Bldrs Essentials: Adv. Framing Methods | 12.98 | |
| | 67329 | Bldrs Essentials: Best Bus. Practices for Bldrs | 29.95 | |
| | 67298A | Bldrs Essentials: Framing/Carpentry 2nd Ed. | 24.95 | |
| | 67298AS | Bldrs Essentials: Framing/Carpentry Spanish | 24.95 | |
| | 67307 | Bldrs Essentials: Plan Reading & Takeoff | 35.95 | |
| | 67342 | Building & Renovating Schools | 99.95 | |
| | 67339 | Building Security: Strategies & Costs | 44.98 | |
| | 67353 | Complete Book of Framing | 29.95 | |
| | 67146 | Concrete Repair & Maintenance Illustrated | 69.95 | |
| | 67352 | Construction Business Management | 49.95 | |
| | 67314 | Cost Planning & Est. for Facil. Maint. | 89.95 | |
| | 67328A | Designing & Building with the IBC, 2nd Ed. | 99.95 | |
| | 67230B | Electrical Estimating Methods, 3rd Ed. | 64.95 | |
| | 64777A | Environmental Remediation Est. Methods, 2nd Ed. | 49.98 | |
| | 67343 | Estimating Bldg. Costs for Resi. & Lt. Comm. | 29.95 | |

| Qty. | Book no. | REFERENCE BOOKS (Cont.) | Unit Price | Total |
|---|---|---|---|---|
| | 67276A | Estimating Handbook, 2nd Ed. | $99.95 | |
| | 67318 | Facilities Operations & Engineering Reference | 54.98 | |
| | 67301 | Facilities Planning & Relocation | 89.95 | |
| | 67338A | Green Building: Proj. Planning & Cost Est., 2nd Ed. | 129.95 | |
| | 67349 | Home Addition & Renovation Project Costs | 29.95 | |
| | 67308E | Home Improvement Costs-Int. Projects, 9th Ed. | 24.95 | |
| | 67309E | Home Improvement Costs-Ext. Projects, 9th Ed. | 24.95 | |
| | 67344 | Homeowner's Guide to Mold | 21.95 | |
| | 67324B | How to Est.w/Means Data & CostWorks, 3rd Ed. | 59.95 | |
| | 67351 | How Your House Works | 21.95 | |
| | 67282A | Illustrated Const. Dictionary, Condensed, 2nd Ed. | 59.95 | |
| | 67292A | Illustrated Const. Dictionary, w/CD-ROM, 3rd Ed. | 99.95 | |
| | 67348 | Job Order Contracting | 89.95 | |
| | 67347 | Kitchen & Bath Project Costs | 29.95 | |
| | 67295C | Landscape Estimating Methods, 5th Ed. | 64.95 | |
| | 67341 | Life Cycle Costing for Facilities | 99.95 | |
| | 67294B | Mechanical Estimating Methods, 4th Ed. | 64.95 | |
| | 67245A | Planning & Managing Interior Projects, 2nd Ed. | 34.98 | |
| | 67283B | Plumbing Estimating Methods, 3rd Ed. | 29.98 | |
| | 67345 | Practice of Cost Segregation Analysis | 99.95 | |
| | 67337 | Preventive Maint. for Higher Education Facilities | 149.95 | |
| | 67346 | Preventive Maint. for Multi-Family Housing | 89.95 | |
| | 67326 | Preventive Maint. Guidelines for School Facil. | 149.95 | |
| | 67247B | Project Scheduling & Management for Constr. 3rd Ed. | 64.95 | |
| | 67265B | Repair & Remodeling Estimating Methods, 4th Ed. | 69.95 | |
| | 67322A | Resi. & Light Commercial Const. Stds., 2nd Ed. | 59.95 | |
| | 67327A | Spanish/English Construction Dictionary, 2nd Ed. | 23.95 | |
| | 67145B | Sq. Ft. & Assem. Estimating Methods, 3rd Ed. | 69.95 | |
| | 67321 | Total Productive Facilities Management | 29.98 | |
| | 67350 | Understanding and Negotiating Const. Contracts | 69.95 | |
| | 67303B | Unit Price Estimating Methods, 4th Ed. | 59.95 | |
| | 67319A | Value Engineering: Practical Applications | 79.95 | |

| | |
|---|---|
| MA residents add 5% state sales tax | |
| Shipping & Handling** | |
| Total (U.S. Funds)* | |

Prices are subject to change and are for U.S. delivery only. *Canadian customers may call for current prices. **Shipping & handling charges: Add 7% of total order for check and credit card payments. Add 9% of total order for invoiced orders.

**Send order to:**                                    **ADDV-1000**

Name (please print) _____

Company _____

☐ **Company**

☐ **Home Address** _____

_____

City/State/Zip _____

Phone # _____ P.O. # _____

(Must accompany all orders being billed)

Mail to: RSMeans, P.O. Box 800, Kingston, MA 02364-0800

# Reed Construction Data, Inc.

**Reed Construction Data, Inc.** is a leading worldwide provider of total construction information solutions. The company's portfolio of information products and services is designed specifically to help construction industry professionals advance their businesses with timely, accurate, and actionable project, product, and cost data. Reed Construction Data is a division of Reed Business Information, a member of the Reed Elsevier PLC group of companies.

## Cost Information

RSMeans, the undisputed market leader in construction costs, provides current cost and estimating information through its innovative MeansCostworks.com® web-based solution. In addition, RSMeans publishes annual cost books, estimating software, and a rich library of reference books. RSMeans also conducts a series of professional seminars and provides construction cost consulting for owners, manufacturers, designers, and contractors to sharpen personal skills and maximize the effective use of cost estimating and management tools.

## Project Data

Reed Construction Data assembles one of the largest databases of public and private project data for use by contractors, distributors, and building product manufacturers in the U.S. and Canadian markets. In addition, Reed Construction Data is the North American construction community's premier resource for project leads and bid documents. Reed Bulletin and Reed CONNECT™ provide project leads and project data through all stages of construction for many of the country's largest public sector, commercial, industrial, and multi-family residential projects.

## Building Product Information

Reed First Source™ in the U.S. and BuildCore in Canada are the only integrated building product information systems offered to the commercial construction industry for searching, selecting, and specifying building products. Written by industry professionals and organized using CSI MasterFormat™ 2004 criteria, the design and construction community uses this information to make better, more informed design decisions.

## Research and Analytics

Reed Construction Data's forecasting tools cover most aspects of the construction business in the U.S. and Canada. Our vast network of resources makes us uniquely qualified to give you the information you need to keep your business profitable.

## Associated Construction Publications (ACP)

Reed Construction Data's regional construction magazines cover the nation through a network of 14 regional magazines. Serving the construction market for more than 100 years, our magazines are a trusted source of news and information in the local and national construction communities.

For more information, please visit our website at www.reedconstructiondata.com

Reed Construction Data, Inc.
30 Technology Parkway South
Norcross, GA  30092-2912
(800) 322-6996
(800) 895-8661 (fax)
Email: info@reedbusiness.com